D1078011

Collins Student World Atlas

Collins
An imprint of HarperCollinsPublishers
77–85 Fulham Palace Road
London
W6 8JB

© HarperCollinsPublishers 2005
Maps © Bartholomew Ltd 2005

First published 2005, reprinted 2005
ISBN-10 0-00-719549-4 (Educational hardback)
ISBN-13 978-0-00-719549-4 (Educational hardback)
ISBN-10 0-00-719548-6 (Educational paperback)
ISBN-13 978-0-00-719548-6 (Educational paperback)
ISBN-10 0-00-719550-8 (Trade hardback)
ISBN-13 978-0-00-719550-8 (Trade hardback)
ISBN-10 0-00-719841-8 (Trade paperback)
ISBN-13 978-0-00-719841-8 (Trade paperback)

Imp 002

The contents of this edition of the Collins Student
World Atlas are believed correct at the time of
printing. Nevertheless the publishers can accept
no responsibility for errors or omissions, changes
in the detail given, or for any expense or loss
thereby caused.

Printed and bound in Thailand

British Library Cataloguing in Publication Data.
A catalogue record for this book is available from
the British Library.

All mapping in this atlas is generated from Collins
Bartholomew digital databases. Collins
Bartholomew, the UK's leading independent
geographical information supplier, can provide a
digital, custom, and premium mapping service to
a variety of markets.
For further information:
Tel: +44 (0) 141 306 3752
e-mail: collinsbartholomew@harpercollins.co.uk

visit our website at: www.collinsbartholomew.com

everything clicks at www.collins.co.uk

2 Contents

4 Map symbols and Map types
5 Map projections and Satellite images
6 Latitude and Longitude
7 Map scale

UNITED KINGDOM

8–9 **United Kingdom** Counties
10–11 **United Kingdom** Southeast England
12–13 **United Kingdom** Wales and Southwest England
14–15 **United Kingdom** Northern England
16–17 **United Kingdom** Northern Ireland and Southern Scotland
18–19 **United Kingdom** Northern Scotland
20–21 **United Kingdom** Climate
22 **United Kingdom** Relief
23 **United Kingdom** Rock types
24–25 **United Kingdom** Population and Migration
26–27 **United Kingdom** Economic activity
28 **United Kingdom** Energy
29 **United Kingdom** Tourism
30–31 **United Kingdom** Transport
32–33 **Greater Manchester**

EUROPE

34–35 **Europe** Relief
35 **Europe** Physical regions, Countries, European Union
36 **Europe** Climate
37 **Europe** Population
38 **Europe** Economic activity
39 **Europe** Tourism
40 **Scandinavia**
41 **Ireland**
42 **Netherlands, Belgium and Luxembourg**
43 **Rotterdam–Europoort**
44 **France**
45 **France** Regions, Population, Energy, Trade
46 **Poland**
47 **Poland** Regions, Population, Minerals and Energy, Conservation
48 **Spain and Portugal**
49 **Spain** Regions, Population, Tourism and Water management
50 **Italy**
51 **Italy** Regions, Earthquakes and Volcanoes
52–53 **Mediterranean Basin**
54–55 **Central Europe**
56–57 **Southeast Europe**
58–59 **Russian Federation**

NORTH AMERICA

60 **North America** Relief, Physical regions
61 **North America** Climate
62–63 **Canada**
63 **North America** Countries
64–65 **United States of America**
66 **United States** Population
67 **United States** Economic activity, Trade
68–69 **San Francisco**
70–71 **Mexico and the Caribbean**

SOUTH AMERICA

72–73 **South America**
72 **South America** Physical regions
73 **South America** Countries
74 **South America** Climate
75 **South America** Land cover
76–77 **Brazil**
76 São Paulo
78 **Brazil** Population
79 **Brazil** Economic activity, Trade
80–81 **Rondônia**

AFRICA

82 **Africa** Relief, Physical regions
83 **Africa** Climate
84–85 **Northern Africa**
84 **Africa** Countries
86 **Southern Africa**
87 **Kenya**
88 **Kenya** Population, Tourism
89 **Kenya** Economic activity,
Nairobi, Trade

ASIA

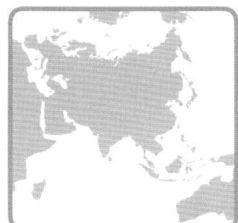

90–91 **Asia** Relief
91 **Asia** Physical regions, Countries
92 **Asia** Climate
93 **Asia** Monsoon
94–95 **Middle East**
94 **Middle East** Oil
96–97 **Pakistan, India, Bangladesh
and Myanmar**
97 Kolkata
98 **India** Population
99 **India** Tourism, Economic activity, Trade
100 **Bangladesh** Population, Economic
activity, Trade
101 **Bangladesh** Rainfall, Flood control
102–103 **China**
104–105 **Southeast Asia**
106 **Japan**
107 **Japan** Economic activity, Population,
Energy, Tectonics

WORLD

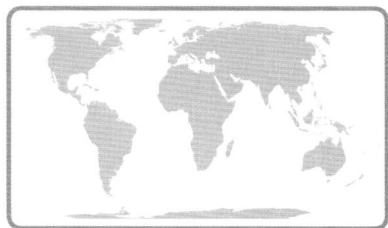

113 **World** Time zones,
International organizations
114–115 **World** Countries
116–117 **World** Relief
118–119 **World** Climate, Vegetation
120–121 **World** Tectonics
122–123 **World** Population
124 **World** Birth rates, Death rates
125 **World** Urban population,
Population change
126 **World** Literacy, Life expectancy
127 **World** Gross National Income,
Car ownership
128–129 **World** Environmental issues
130 **World** Energy production and
consumption
131 **World** Ore and Fuel production
132–133 **World** Tourism
134–135 **World** Communications
136–143 **World** Statistics

144–168 **Index**

OCEANIA

108–109 **Pacific Ocean**
110–111 **Australia and New Zealand**
111 **Australia and New Zealand** Climate
112 **The Arctic Ocean and Antarctica**

Map Symbols

Symbols are used, in the form of points, lines or areas, on maps to show the location of and information about specific features. The colour and size of a symbol can give an indication of the type of feature and its relative size.

The meaning of map symbols is explained in a key shown on each page. Symbols used on reference maps are shown below.

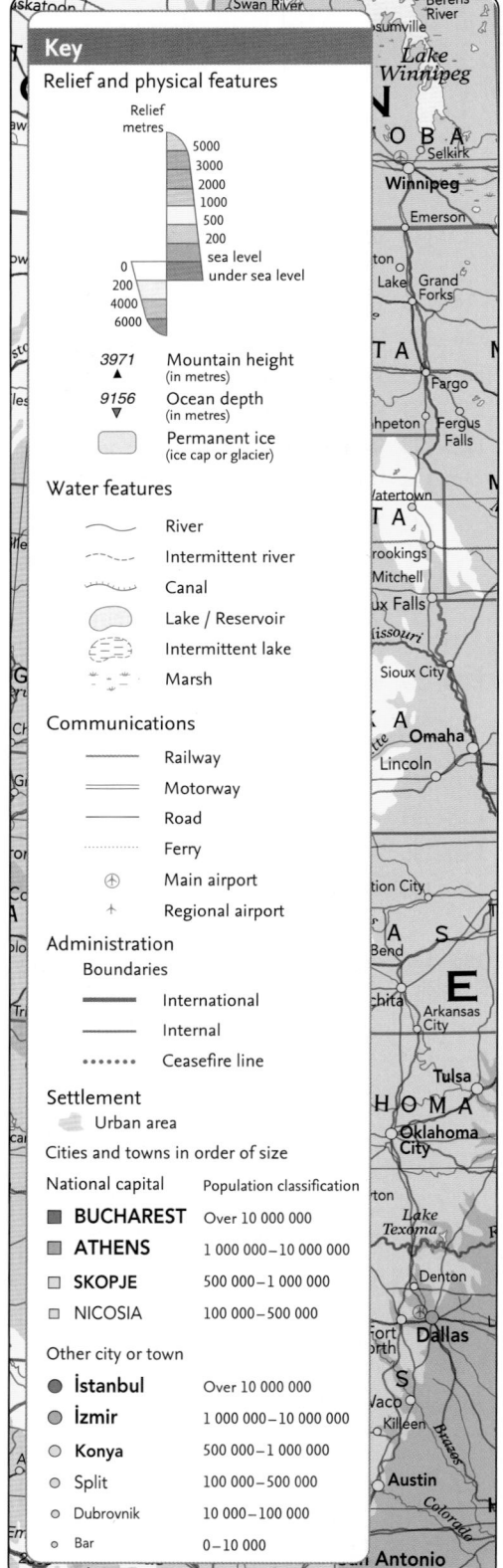

Map Types

Many types of map are included in the atlas to show different information. The type of map, its symbols and colours are carefully selected to show the theme of each map and to make them easy to understand. The main types of map used are explained below.

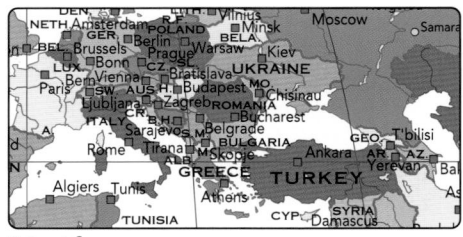

Extract from page 115

Political maps provide an overview of the size and location of countries in a specific area, such as a continent. Coloured squares indicate capital cities. Coloured circles represent other cities, with the size of the circle indicating the relative size of the city.

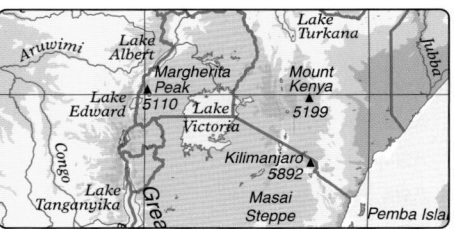

Extract from page 82

Physical or relief maps use colour to show oceans, seas, rivers, lakes, and the height of the land. The names and heights of major landforms are also indicated.

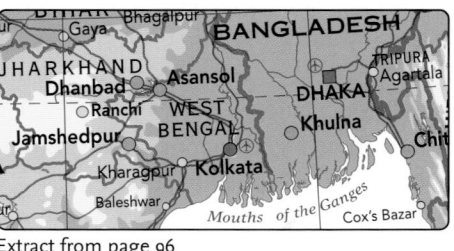

Extract from page 96

Physical/political maps bring together the information provided in the two types of map described above. They show relief and physical features as well as country borders, major cities and towns, roads, railways, and airports.

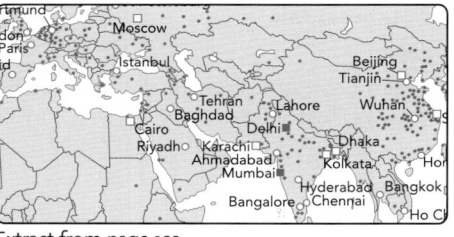

Extract from page 123

Distribution maps use different colours, symbols, or shading to show the location and distribution of natural or man-made features. In this map, symbols indicate the distribution of the world's largest cities.

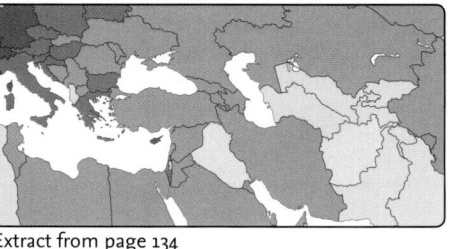

Extract from page 134

Graduated colour maps use dots, colours, or shading to show a feature's location and a measure of its intensity. Generally, the highest values are shaded with the darkest colours. In this map, colours are used to show the number of telephone lines per 100 people.

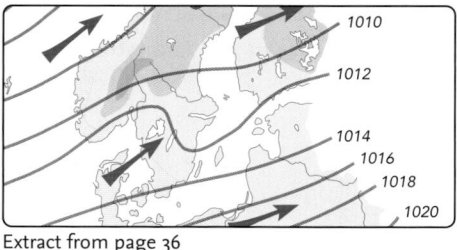

Extract from page 36

Isoline maps use thin lines to show the distribution of a feature. An isoline passes through places that have the same value or quantity. Isolines may show features such as temperature (isotherm), air pressure (isobar), or height of land (contour). The value of the line is usually written on it. On either side of the line the value will be higher or lower.

Because the Earth is a sphere and maps are flat, map makers (cartographers) have developed different ways of showing the Earth's surface on a flat piece of paper. These methods are called map projections, because they are based on the idea of the Earth's surface being 'projected' onto a piece of paper.

There are many types of map projection, but none of them show the Earth with perfect accuracy. Every map projection must stretch or distort the surface to make it fit onto a flat map. As a result, either shape, area, direction or distance will be distorted. The amount of distortion increases away from the point at which the globe touches the piece of paper onto which it is projected. Areas of increasing distortion are shown in red on the diagrams below. Map projections are carefully chosen in this atlas to show the area of the Earth's surface as accurately as possible. The three main types of map projection used are explained below.

Cylindrical Projections

 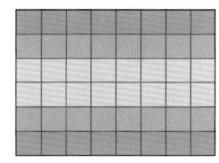

Cylindrical projections are constructed by projecting the surface of the globe or sphere (Earth) onto a cylinder that just touches the outside edges of that globe. Two examples of cylindrical projections are Mercator and Times.

Mercator Projection (see pages 104-105 for an example of this projection)

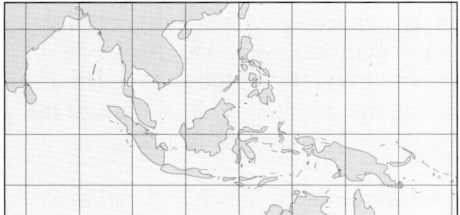

The Mercator cylindrical projection is a useful projection for areas near the equator and to about 15 degrees north or south of the equator, where distortion of shape is minimal. The projection is useful for navigation, since directions are plotted as straight lines.

Conic Projections

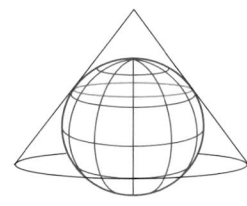 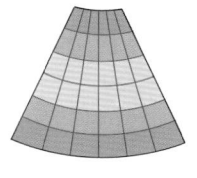

Conic projections are constructed by projecting the surface of a globe or sphere (Earth) onto a cone that just touches the outside edges of that globe. Examples of conic projections are Conic Equidistant and Albers Equal Area Conic.

Conic Equidistant Projection (see pages 58-59 for an example of this projection)

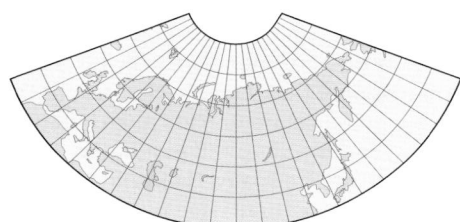

Conic projections are best suited for areas between 30° and 60° north and south of the equator when the east-west distance is greater than the north-south distance (such as Canada and Europe). The meridians are straight and spaced at equal intervals.

Azimuthal Projections

 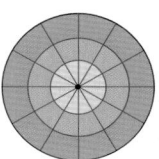

Azimuthal projections are constructed by projecting the surface of the globe or sphere (Earth) onto a flat surface that touches the globe at one point only. Some examples of azimuthal projections are Lambert Azimuthal Equal Area and Polar Stereographic.

Polar Stereographic Projection (see page 112 for an example of this projection)

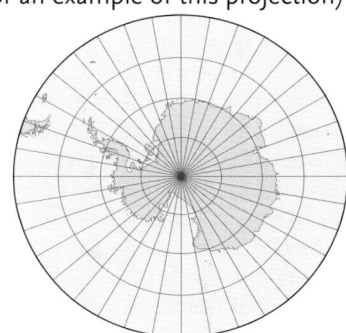

Azimuthal projections are useful for areas that have similar east-west and north-south dimensions such as Antarctica and Australia.

Satellite Images

Images captured by a large number of Earth-observing satellites provide unique views of the Earth. The science of gathering and interpreting such images is known as remote sensing. Geographers use images taken from high above the Earth to determine patterns, trends and basic characteristics of the Earth's surface. Satellites are fitted with different kinds of scanners or sensors to gather information about the Earth. The most well known satellites are Landsat and SPOT.

Satellite sensors detect electromagnetic radiation –X-rays, ultraviolet light, visible colours and microwave signals. This data can be processed to provide information on soils, land use, geology, pollution and weather patterns. Colours can be added to this data to help understand the images. In some cases (example shown here from page 43) this results in a 'false-colour' image where red areas represent vegetation and built-up areas show as blue/grey. Examples of satellite images are included in this atlas to illustrate geographical themes.

Latitude

Latitude is distance, measured in degrees, north and south of the equator. Lines of latitude circle the globe in an east-west direction. The distance between lines of latitude is always the same. They are also known as parallels of latitude. Because the circumference of Earth gets smaller toward the poles, the lines of latitude are shorter nearer the poles.

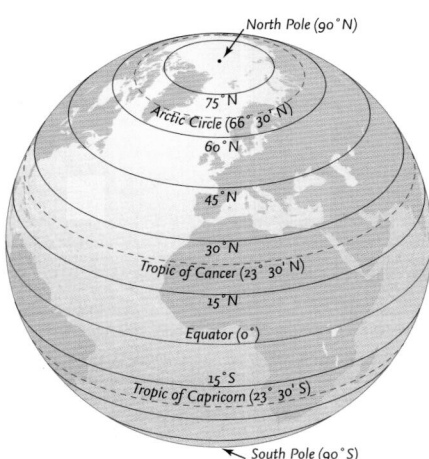

All lines of latitude have numbers between 0° and 90° and a direction, either north or south of the equator. The equator is at 0° latitude. The North Pole is at 90° north and the South Pole is at 90° south. The 'tilt' of Earth has given particular importance to some lines of latitude . They include:
- the Arctic Circle at 66° 30' north
- the Antarctic Circle at 66° 30' south
- the Tropic of Cancer at 23° 30' north
- the Tropic of Capricorn at 23° 30' south

The Equator also divides the Earth into two halves. The northern half, north of the Equator, is the **Northern Hemisphere.** The southern half, south of the Equator, is the **Southern Hemisphere.**

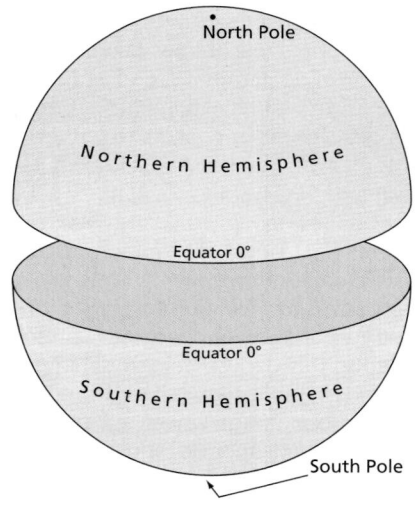

Longitude

Longitude is distance, measured in degrees, east and west of the Greenwich Meridian (prime meridian). Lines of longitude join the poles in a north-south direction. Because the lines join the poles, they are always the same length, but are farthest apart at the equator and closest together at the poles. These lines are also called meridians of longitude.

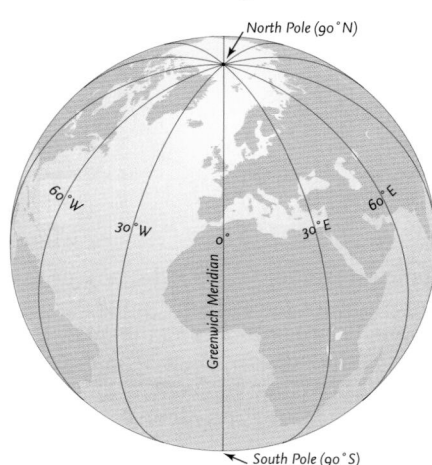

Longitude begins along the Greenwich Meridian (prime meridian), at 0°, in London, England. On the opposite side of Earth is the 180° meridian, which is the International Date Line. To the west of the prime meridian are Canada, the United States, and Brazil; to the east of the prime meridian are Germany, India and China. All lines of longitude have numbers between 0° and 180° and a direction, either east or west of the prime meridian.

The Greenwich Meridian and the International Date Line can also be used to divide the world into two halves. The half to the west of the Greenwich Meridian is the **Western Hemisphere.** The half to the east of the Greenwich Meridian is the **Eastern Hemisphere.**

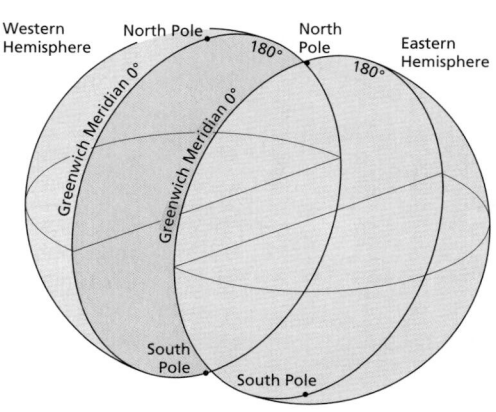

Finding Places

When lines of latitude and longitude are drawn on a map, they form a grid, which looks like a pattern of squares. This pattern is used to find places on a map. Latitude is always stated before longitude (e.g., 42°N 78°W).

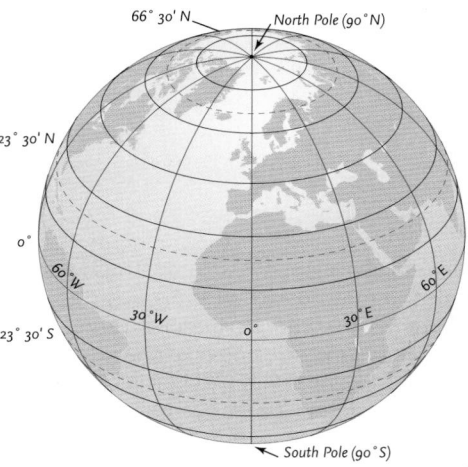

By stating latitude and then longitude of a place, it becomes much easier to find. On the map (below) point A is easy to find as it is exactly latitude 58° North of the Equator and longitude 4° West of the Greenwich Meridian (58°N 4°W).

To be even more accurate in locating a place, each degree of latitude and longitude can also be divided into smaller units called **minutes** ('). There are 60 minutes in each degree. On the map (below) Halkirk is one half (or 30/60ths) of the way past latitude 58°N, and one-half (or 30/60ths) of the way past longitude 3°W. Its latitude is therefore 58 degrees 30 minutes North and its longitude is 3 degrees 30 minutes West. This can be shortened to 58°30'N 3°30'W. Latitude and longitude for all the places and features named on the maps are included in the index.

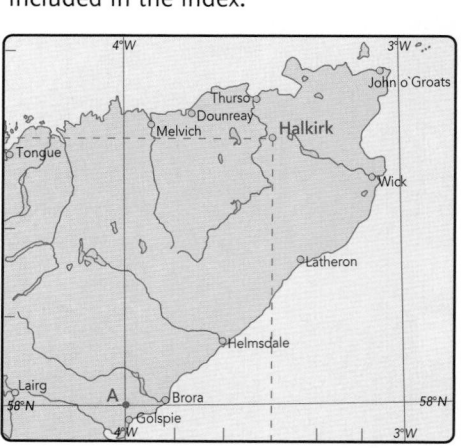

Scale

To draw a map of any part of the world, the area must be reduced, or 'scaled down,' to the size of a page in this atlas, a foldable road map, or a topographic map. The scale of the map indicates the amount by which an area has been reduced.

The scale of a map can also be used to determine the actual distance between two or more places or the actual size of an area on a map. The scale indicates the relationship between distances on the map and distances on the ground.

Scale can be shown
- **using words:** for example, 'one centimetre to one kilometre' (one centimetre on the map represents one kilometre on the ground), or 'one centimetre to 100 kilometres' (one centimetre on the map represents 100 kilometres on the ground).
- **using numbers:** for example, '1 : 100 000 or 1/100 000' (one centimetre on the map represents 100 000 centimetres on the ground), or '1 : 40 000 000 or 1/40 000 000' (one centimetre on the map represents 40 million centimetres on the ground). Normally, the large numbers with centimetres would be converted to metres or kilometres.
- **as a line scale:** for example,

Scale and Map Information

The scale of a map also determines how much information can be shown on it. As the area shown on a map becomes larger and larger, the amount of detail and the accuracy of the map becomes less and less.

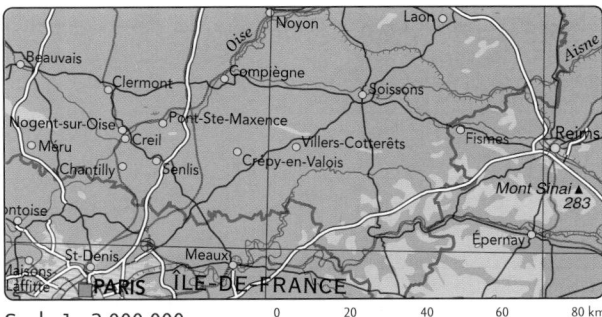

Scale 1 : 2 000 000

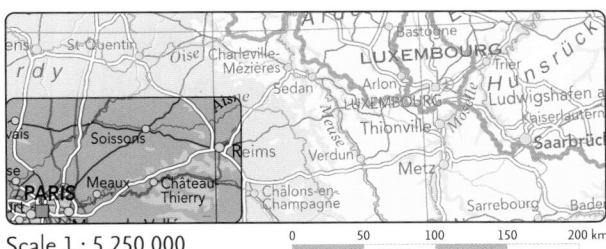

Scale 1 : 5 250 000

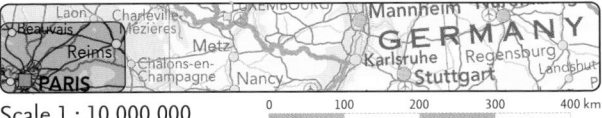

Scale 1 : 10 000 000

Measuring Distance

The instructions below show you how to determine how far apart places are on the map, then using the line scale, to determine the actual distance on the ground.

To use the line scale to measure the straight-line distance between two places on a map:
1. place the edge of a sheet of paper on the two places on a map,
2. on the paper, place a mark at each of the two places,
3. place the paper on the line scale,
4. measure the distance on the ground using the scale.

To find the distance between Calgary and Regina, line up the edge of a piece of paper between the two places and mark off the distance.

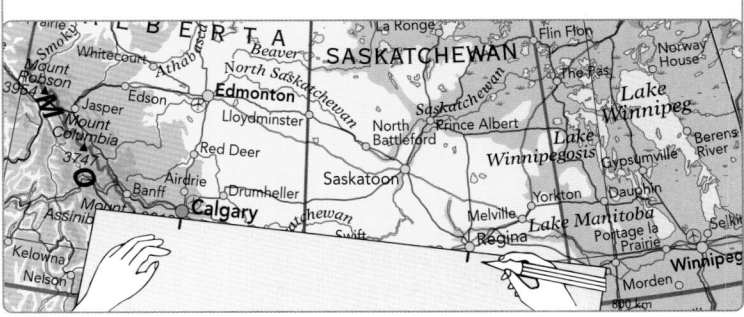

Compare this distance with the marks on the line scale. The straight-line distance between Calgary and Regina is about 650 kilometres.

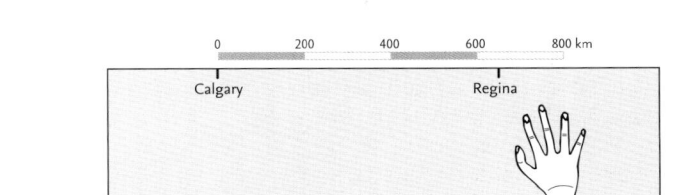

Often, the road or rail distance between two places is greater than the straight-line distance. To measure this distance:

1. place the edge of a sheet of paper on the map and mark off the start point on the paper,
2. move the paper so that its edge follows the bends and curves on the map (Hint: use the tip of your pencil to pin the edge of the paper to the curve as you pivot the paper around each curve),
3. mark off the end point on the sheet of paper,
4. place the paper on the line scale and read the actual distance following a road or railroad.

To find the distance by road between Calgary and Regina, mark off the start point, then twist the paper to follow the curve of the road through Medicine Hat, Swift Current, Moose Jaw, and then into Regina. The actual distance is about 750 kilometres.

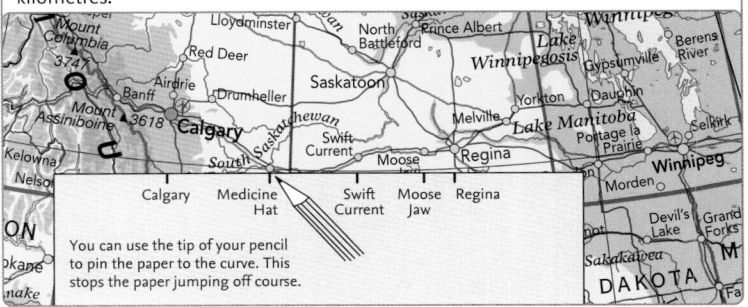

United Kingdom

ENGLAND
London
Cardiff
WALES
Edinburgh
SCOTLAND
Belfast
NORTHERN IRELAND
REPUBLIC OF IRELAND

West Central Scotland

NORTH LANARKSHIRE
Motherwell
Kirkintilloch
EAST DUNBARTON-SHIRE
GLASGOW CITY
Glasgow
Giffnock
Dumbarton
WEST DUNBARTON-SHIRE
RENFREWSHIRE
Paisley
EAST RENFREW SHIRE
Greenock
INVERCLYDE

East Central Scotland

Haddington
EAST LOTHIAN
Dalkeith
MIDLOTHIAN
Edinburgh
CITY OF EDINBURGH
CLACKMANNAN-SHIRE
Alloa
FALKIRK
Falkirk
Livingston
WEST LOTHIAN

SHETLAND
Lerwick

ORKNEY
Kirkwall

Stornoway
WESTERN ISLES

HIGHLAND
Inverness

ARGYLL AND BUTE
Lochgilphead

MORAY
Elgin

ABERDEEN-SHIRE
Aberdeen

PERTH & KINROSS
Perth

ANGUS
Forfar
Dundee
DUNDEE

STIRLING
Stirling
Alloa
8
Falkirk 7
Kirkintilloch
5
2
1 Dunbarton
Paisley
RENFREWSHIRE
3 4
Glasgow
6
Hamilton
Motherwell
SOUTH LANARKSHIRE

FIFE
Glenrothes

SCOTLAND

Edinburgh
10 Dalkeith
Livingston
9
MIDLOTHIAN
EAST LOTHIAN
Haddington

Kilmarnock
EAST AYRSHIRE
Irvine
NORTH AYRSHIRE
Ayr
SOUTH AYRSHIRE

SCOTTISH BORDERS
Newtown
St Boswells

Dumfries
DUMFRIES
AND

NORTHUMBERLAND
Morpeth

SCOTLAND
1. INVERCLYDE
2. WEST DUNBARTONSHIRE
3. EAST RENFREWSHIRE
4. GLASGOW CITY
5. EAST DUNBARTONSHIRE
6. NORTH LANARKSHIRE
7. FALKIRK
8. CLACKMANNANSHIRE
9. WEST LOTHIAN
10. EDINBURGH

NORTHERN IRELAND
1. NEWTOWNABBEY
2. CARRICKFERGUS
3. BELFAST
4. CASTLEREAGH
5. NORTH DOWN

Ballycastle
MOYLE
Ballymoney
BALLYMONEY
Coleraine
COLERAINE
Limavady
LIMAVADY
Londonderry

Scale 1 : 3 000 000

0   25   50   75   100 km

ENGLAND

1. MIDDLESBROUGH
2. READING
3. WOKINGHAM
4. BRACKNELL FOREST
5. WINDSOR & MAIDENHEAD
6. SLOUGH
7. THURROCK
8. MEDWAY TOWNS

WALES

1. BLAENAU GWENT
2. MERTHYR TYDFIL
3. TORFAEN
4. CAERPHILLY

Greater London

1. WESTMINSTER
2. KENSINGTON & CHELSEA
3. HAMMERSMITH & FULHAM

Greater London boroughs: HAVERING, BARKING & DAGENHAM, BEXLEY, GREENWICH, REDBRIDGE, BROMLEY, NEWHAM, WALTHAM FOREST, HACKNEY, TOWER HAMLETS, LEWISHAM, CITY, SOUTHWARK, CROYDON, ISLINGTON, CAMDEN, LAMBETH, ENFIELD, HARINGEY, SUTTON, BARNET, BRENT, WANDSWORTH, KINGSTON UPON THAMES, MERTON, HARROW, EALING, HOUNSLOW, RICHMOND UPON THAMES, HILLINGDON

ENGLAND counties: DURHAM, CUMBRIA, NORTH YORKSHIRE, EAST RIDING OF YORKSHIRE, LANCASHIRE, WEST YORKSHIRE, SOUTH YORKSHIRE, NORTH LINCOLNSHIRE, NORTH EAST LINCOLNSHIRE, LINCOLNSHIRE, MERSEYSIDE, GREATER MANCHESTER, CHESHIRE, DERBYSHIRE, NOTTINGHAMSHIRE, STAFFORDSHIRE, SHROPSHIRE, WEST MIDLANDS, WARWICKSHIRE, LEICESTERSHIRE, RUTLAND, NORFOLK, SUFFOLK, CAMBRIDGESHIRE, NORTHAMPTONSHIRE, HEREFORDSHIRE, WORCESTERSHIRE, BEDFORDSHIRE, HERTFORDSHIRE, ESSEX, GLOUCESTERSHIRE, OXFORDSHIRE, BUCKINGHAMSHIRE, GREATER LONDON, KENT, WILTSHIRE, BERKSHIRE, HAMPSHIRE, SURREY, WEST SUSSEX, EAST SUSSEX, SOMERSET, DORSET, DEVON, CORNWALL

Towns: Hartlepool, Stockton-on-Tees, Middlesbrough, Redcar & Cleveland, Darlington, Stockton-on-Tees, Northallerton, York, Beverley, Kingston upon Hull, Grimsby, Scunthorpe, Lincoln, Leeds, Preston, Blackburn with Darwen, Blackpool, Sheffield, Matlock, Nottingham, Derby, Stoke-on-Trent, Stafford, Telford and Wrekin, Shrewsbury, Chester, Mold, Ruthin, Wrexham, Leicester, Oakham, Peterborough, Cambridge, Norwich, Ipswich, Bedford, Luton, Milton Keynes, Northampton, Warwick, Birmingham, Worcester, Hereford, Gloucester, Aylesbury, Hertford, Chelmsford, Southend-on-Sea, Maidstone, Oxford, Reading, Slough, Windsor, Maidenhead, Wokingham, Bracknell, Grays, Swindon, Newbury, Winchester, Southampton, Portsmouth, Newport, Chichester, Brighton & Hove, Hove, Lewes, Bristol, Bath, Trowbridge, Thornbury, Weston-super-Mare, Taunton, Bournemouth, Poole, Dorchester, Exeter, Torquay, Torbay, Plymouth, Truro

CUMBRIA

WALES: POWYS, GWYNEDD, CONWY, DENBIGHSHIRE, FLINTSHIRE, CEREDIGION, CARMARTHENSHIRE, PEMBROKESHIRE, MONMOUTHSHIRE, NEWPORT, CARDIFF, VALE OF GLAMORGAN, BRIDGEND, NEATH PORT TALBOT, SWANSEA, RHONDDA CYNON TAFF

Welsh towns: Conwy, Caernarfon, Llangefni, Aberaeron, Haverfordwest, Carmarthen, Swansea, Bridgend, Barry, Cardiff, Newport, Pontypool, Ebbw Vale, Cwmbran, Llandrindod Wells

ISLE OF MAN — Douglas

ISLE OF ANGLESEY

ISLE OF WIGHT — Newport

NORTHERN IRELAND towns: Omagh, Cookstown, Strabane, Dungannon, Enniskillen, Armagh, Craigavon, Banbridge, Newry, Downpatrick, Belfast, Lisburn, Newtownards, Bangor, Castlereagh, Antrim

REPUBLIC OF IRELAND

FERMANAGH, OMAGH, DUNGANNON, ARMAGH, NEWRY & MOURNE, DOWN, ARDS, FRANCE, BELGIUM

ALDERNEY
GUERNSEY — St Peter Port
JERSEY — St Helier
CHANNEL ISLANDS (UK)

ISLES OF SCILLY — Hugh Town

National Statistics Online
www.statistics.gov.uk
The Scottish Parliament
www.scottish.parliament.uk
Northern Ireland Office
www.nio.gov.uk
The National Assembly for Wales
www.wales.gov.uk

Conic Equidistant projection

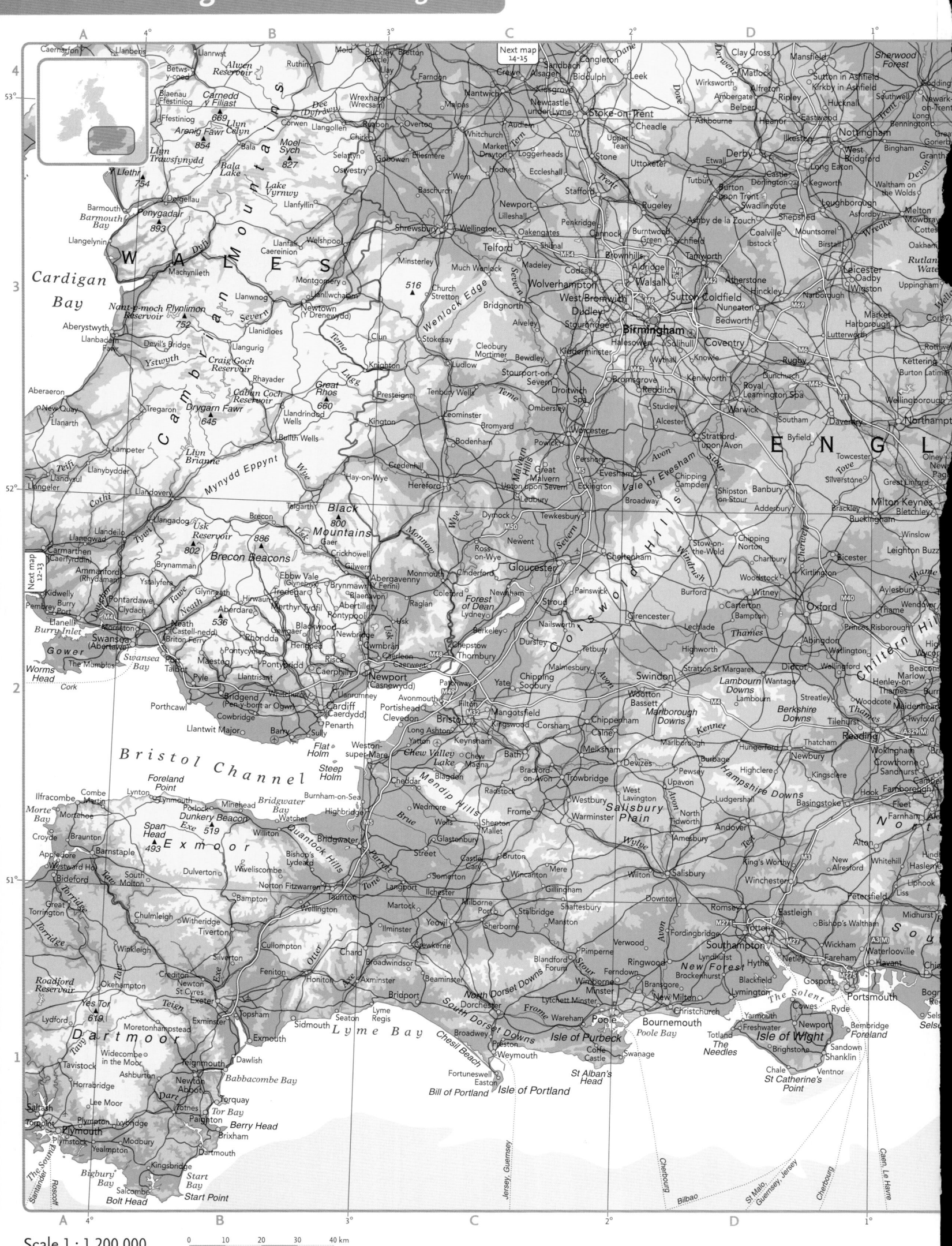

Scale 1 : 1 200 000

0   10   20   30   40 km

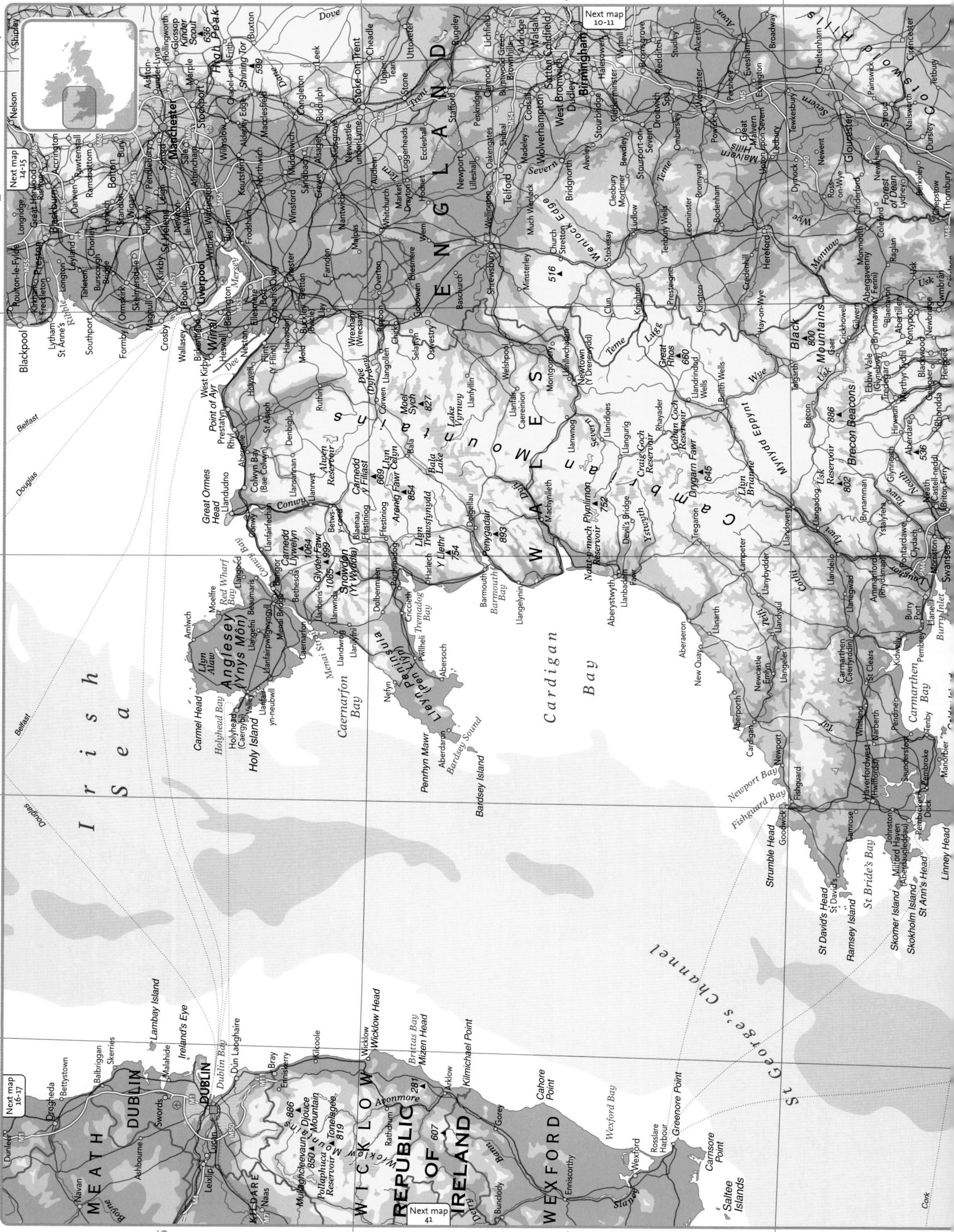

Scale 1 : 1 200 000

0   10   20   30   40 km

Next map 14-15
Next map 10-11
Next map 16-17
Next map 41

ENGLAND

WALES

REPUBLIC OF IRELAND

MEATH

DUBLIN

KILDARE

WICKLOW

WEXFORD

Irish Sea

Cardigan Bay

St George's Channel

Manchester
Liverpool
Birmingham
Gloucester
Shrewsbury
Wolverhampton
Hereford

Snowdon (Yr Wyddfa) 1085

Anglesey (Ynys Môn)

Holy Island

Bardsey Island

Dublin

Next map 10-11

Celtic Sea

Bristol Channel

English Channel

Lyme Bay

FRANCE

Channel Islands (UK)

Isles of Scilly

Conic Equidistant projection

Key

Relief and physical features

Relief metres

1000
500
200
100
50
0 sea level
under sea level

Mountain height (in metres)
▲ 1085

Water features

River
Canal
Lake / Reservoir

Communications

Railway
Motorway
Road
Car ferry
⊕ Main airport
+ Regional airport

Administration

Boundaries
— International
— Internal

Settlement

Urban area

Cities and towns in order of size

National capital
■ DUBLIN

● Birmingham
○ Liverpool
○ Bristol
○ Exeter
○ Llandeilo

Other city or town

0   10   20   30   40 km

Key

Relief and physical features

Relief metres
1000
500
200
100
0
sea level
under sea level
50
200

▲ 1085 Mountain height
(in metres)

Water features

River
Canal
Lake / Reservoir

Communications

Railway
Motorway
Road
Car ferry
⊕ Main airport
✈ Regional airport

Administration

Boundaries
International
Internal

Settlement

Urban area

Cities and towns in order of size

National capital   Other city or town

■ DUBLIN   ● Manchester
                       ◉ Liverpool
                       ◎ Belfast
                       ○ Carlisle
                       ∘ Keswick

Conic Equidistant projection

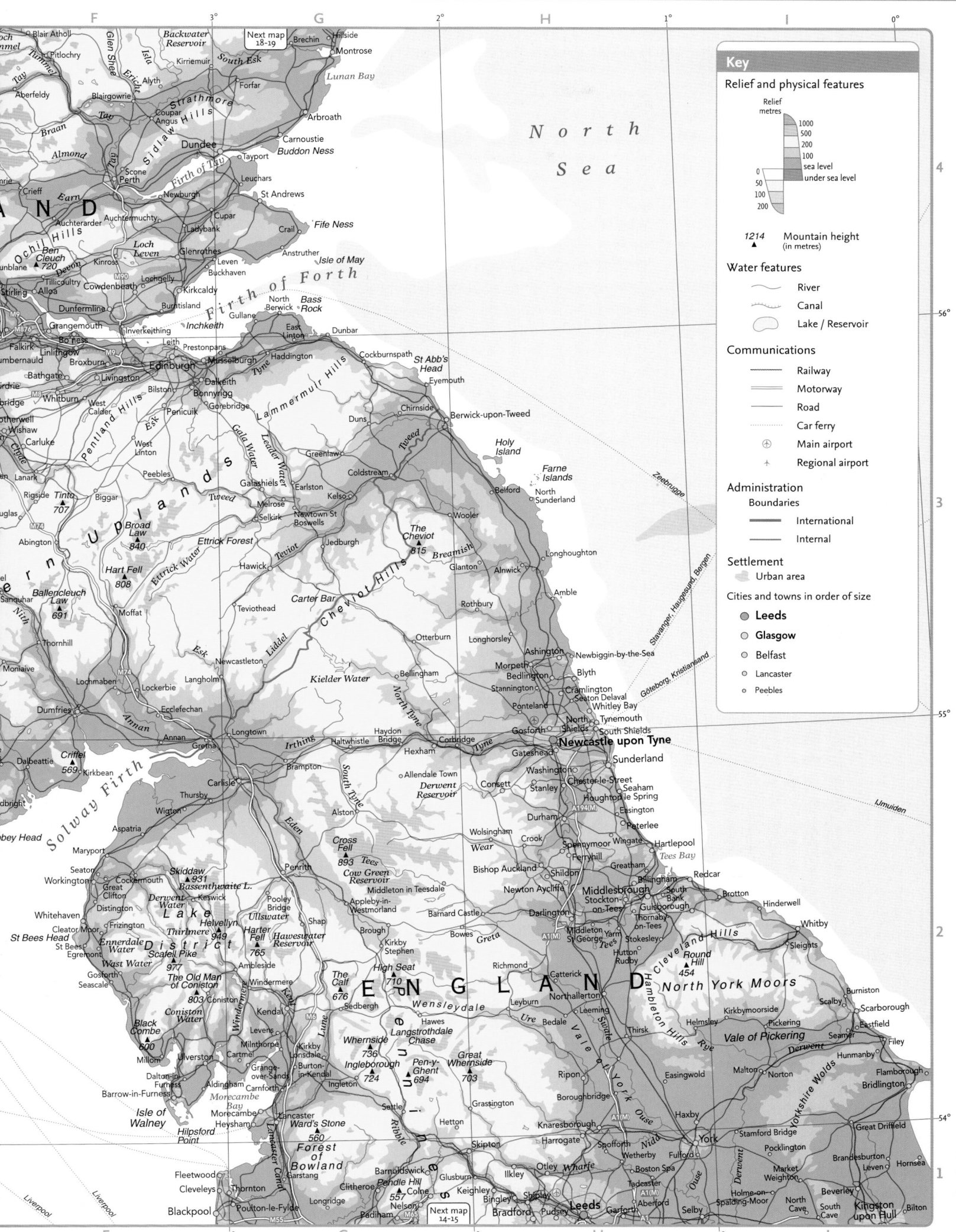

Key

Relief and physical features

Relief
metres
- 1000
- 500
- 200
- 100
- 0 sea level
- 50 under sea level
- 100
- 200

▲ 1214   Mountain height (in metres)

Water features
- River
- Canal
- Lake / Reservoir

Communications
- Railway
- Motorway
- Road
- Car ferry
- ⊕ Main airport
- ✈ Regional airport

Administration
Boundaries
- International
- Internal

Settlement
- Urban area

Cities and towns in order of size
- ● Leeds
- ◎ Glasgow
- ◉ Belfast
- ○ Lancaster
- ○ Peebles

Conic Equidistant projection

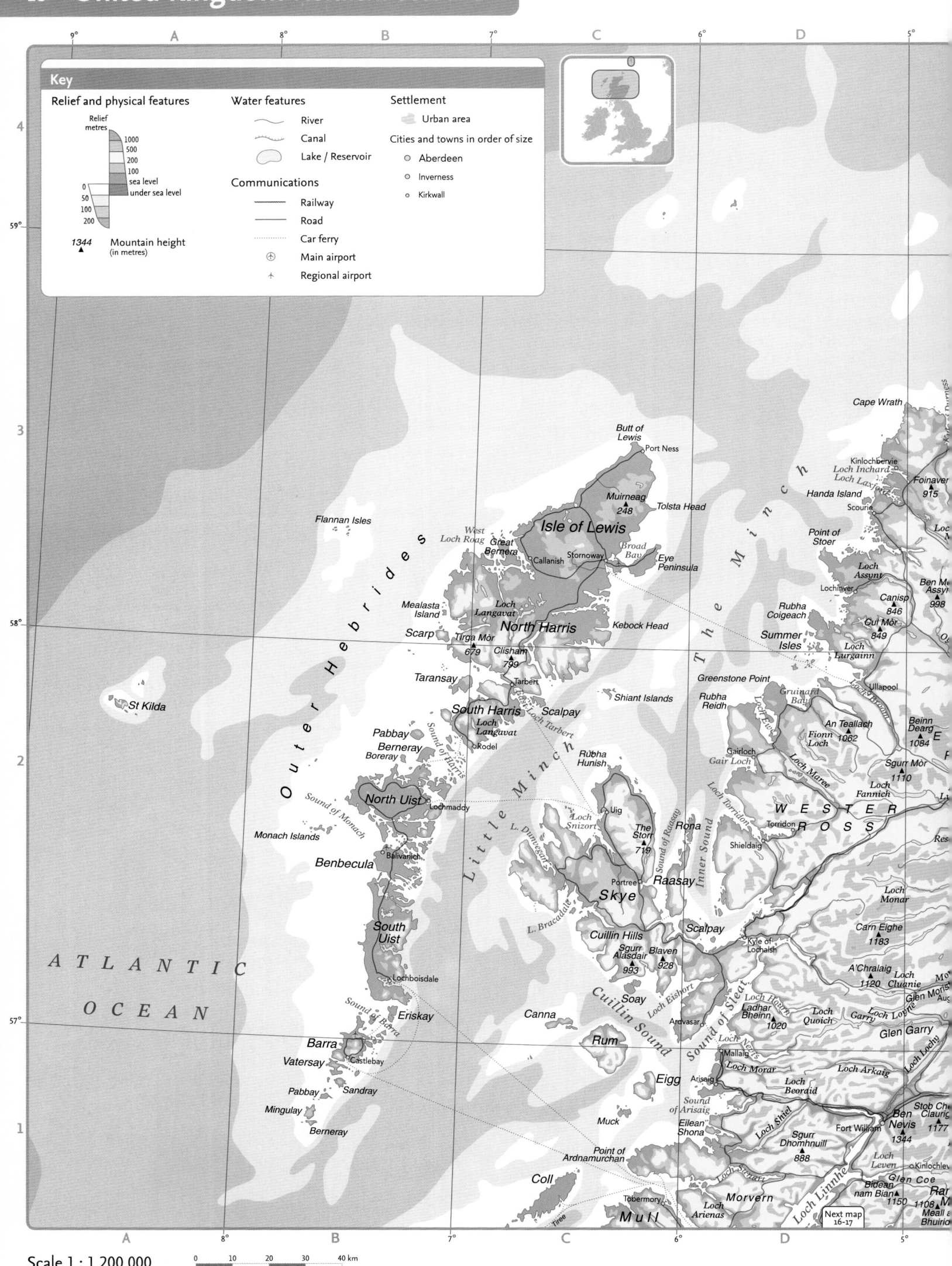

E · 4° · F · 3° · G · 2° · H · 1° · I

Mull Head
Papa Westray
Noup Head
The North Sound
Westray
Eday
Sanday
North Ronaldsay
North Ronaldsay Firth
Sanday Sound
Loth
Westray Firth
Rousay
Egilsay
Stronsay
Brough Head
Birsay
Stronsay Firth
Shapinsay
Auskerry
Orkney Islands
Loch of Harray
Finstown
Wide Firth
Kirkwall
Gritley
Loch of Stenness
Mainland
Stromness
Scapa Flow
Copinsay
Ward Hill
479
Burray
St Margaret's Hope
Hoy
Flotta
Burwick
South Walls
South Ronaldsay
Brough Ness
Pentland Skerries
Pentland Firth
Dunnet Head
Island of Stroma
Thurso Bay
Dunnet Bay
Duncansby Head
John o'Groats
Loch Heilen
Strathy Point
Dounreay
Thurso
Loch Watten
Wick
Sinclair's Bay
Melvich
Halkirk
CAITHNESS
Wick
Ben Loyal
764
Loch Loyal
Loch Naver
Thurso
Latheron
Klibreck
961
Loch Rimsdale
SUTHERLAND
Helmsdale
Helmsdale
Shin
Lairg
Brora
Bonar Bridge
Golspie
Dornoch
Dornoch Firth
Brora
Tarbat Ness
Tain
Balintore
Loch Glass
Nigg Bay
Cromarty
Invergordon
Moray Firth
Black Isle
Fortrose
Conon Bridge
Moray Firth
Beauly Firth
Inverness
Burghead
Lossiemouth
Portknockie
Portsoy
Troup Head
Fraserburgh
Buckie
Cullen
Banff
Macduff
Loch of Strathbeg
Elgin
Fochabers
Rattray Head
Crimond
Kinloss
Knock Hill
430
Aberchirder
North Ugie
Nairn
Forres
Isla
Keith
Turriff
New Pitsligo
Peterhead
Lossie
Rothes
Deveron
Mintlaw
Boddam
Findhorn
Dufftown
(Charlestown of Aberlour)
Huntly
Cruden Bay
Spey
STRATHBOGIE
Ythan
Grantown-on-Spey
Strathspey
Bogie
Insch
Urie
Ellon
Hills of Cromdale
Carn Mòr
804
Don
Oldmeldrum
Inverurie
Geal Charn
821
Avon
Kemnay
Kintore
Dyce
Cairn Gorm
Don
Westhill
Aberdeen
Carn Dearg
945
Ben Macdui
1309
Cairn Toul
1291
Braemar
Dee
Aboyne
Banchory
Dee
Portlethen
Newtonhill
Lochnagar
1155
Mount Keen
939
Ballater
Stonehaven
Grampian Mountains
Beinn Dearg
1008
Carn nan Gàbhar
Mayar
928
Water of Saughs
Inverbervie
Forest of Atholl 1121
Laurencekirk
Ben Alder
148
Loch Ericht
Loch Errochty
Blair Atholl
Backwater Reservoir
North Esk
South Esk
Hillside
Brechin
Montrose
Loch Garry
Loch Tummel
Pitlochry
Glen Shee
Isla
Kirriemuir
Forfar
Loch Rannoch
Schiehallion
1083
Tummel
Aberfeldy
Tay
Eriche
Alyth
Lunan Bay
Lyon
Blairgowrie
Strathmore
Arbroath

Next map 16-17

Adhliath Mountains
Kingussie
Aviemore
Newtonmore
Spey
Loch Ness
More
Ness

H 2° · H 1° · I
Herma Ness
Unst
Baltasound
Point of Fethaland
Isbister
Yell
Fetlar
Ronas Hill
450
Yell Sound
Out Skerries
Esha Ness
Hillswick
Toft
St Magnus Bay
Muckle Roe
Voe
Whalsay
Papa Stour
Melby
Walls
Scalloway
Lerwick
Bressay
Isle of Noss
Shetland Islands
Burra
Mainland
Mousa
Foula
Sumburgh
Bergen (& Hansholm)
(summer only)
Sumburgh Head
Torshavn
Fair Isle
Lerwick

G 2° · H 1° · I

North Sea

59°
60°
58°
57°

Conic Equidistant projection

1 Annual Rainfall and Winds

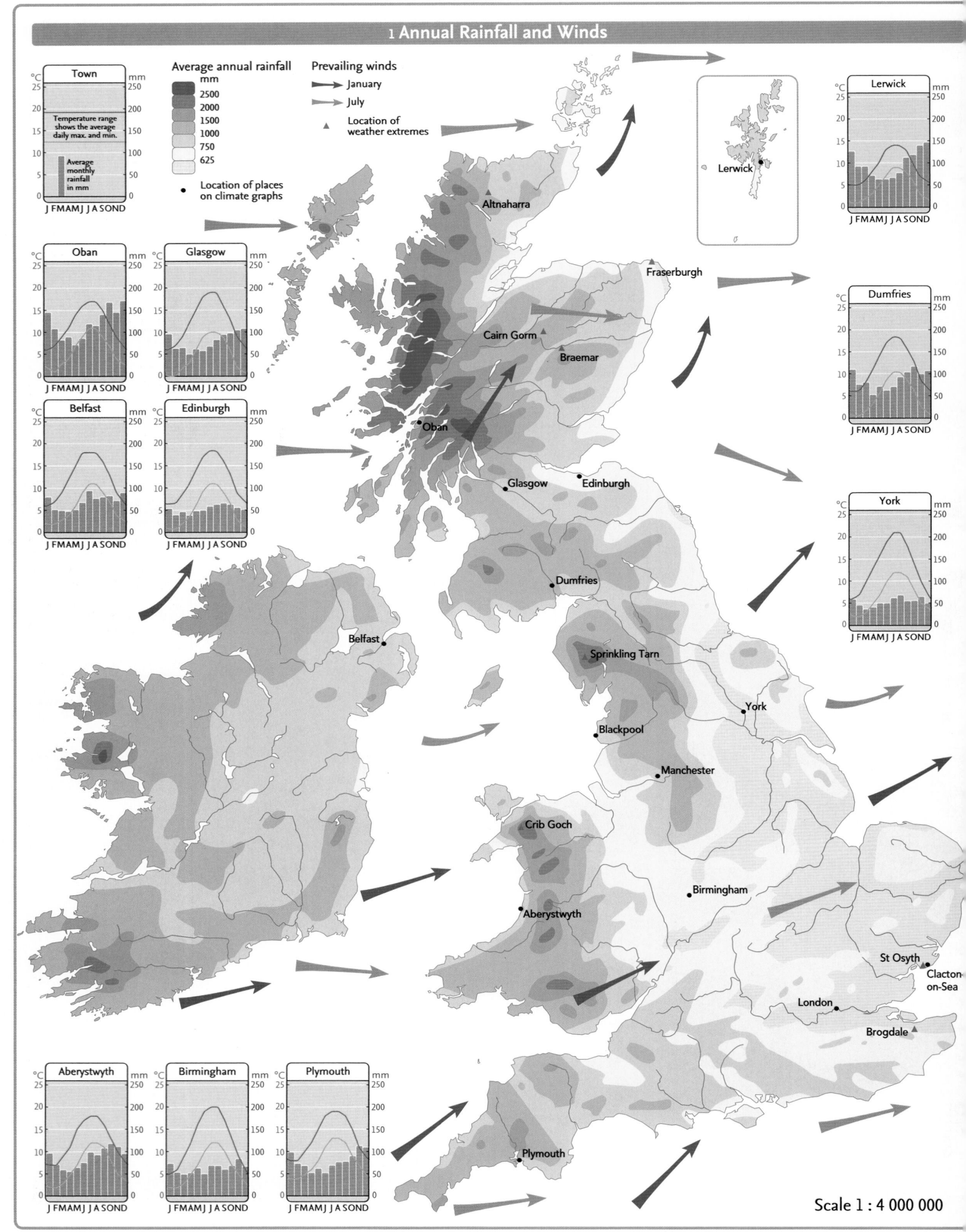

Town
°C / mm
Temperature range shows the average daily max. and min.
Average monthly rainfall in mm
J FMAMJ J A SOND

Average annual rainfall
mm
2500
2000
1500
1000
750
625

● Location of places on climate graphs

Prevailing winds
→ January
→ July
▲ Location of weather extremes

Oban
Glasgow
Belfast
Edinburgh
Lerwick
Dumfries
York
Aberystwyth
Birmingham
Plymouth

Altnaharra
Fraserburgh
Cairn Gorm
Braemar
Oban
Glasgow
Edinburgh
Dumfries
Sprinkling Tarn
York
Blackpool
Manchester
Belfast
Crib Goch
Birmingham
Aberystwyth
St Osyth
Clacton-on-Sea
London
Brogdale
Plymouth

Scale 1 : 4 000 000

2 Temperature and Currents

January

Temperature °C: 6, 4, 2, 0

Currents: → Warm   → Cold

July

Temperature °C: 16, 14, 12, 10

Currents: → Warm   → Cold

Scale 1 : 12 000 000

Met Office
www.metoffice.com
BBC Weather
www.bbc.co.uk/weather
UK Climate Impacts Programme
www.ukcip.org.uk

3 Weather Extremes

Temperature

	Value	Location	Date
Highest	38.5°	Brogdale, Kent	10th August 2003
Lowest	-27.2°	Braemar, Aberdeenshire	10th January 1982 & 11th February 1895
		Altnaharra, Highlands	30th December 1995

Rainfall

	Value	Location	Date
Highest in 1 year	6 528mm	Sprinkling Tarn, Cumbria	1954
Lowest annual average	513mm	St Osyth, Essex	
Highest annual average	4 000mm	Crib Goch, Gwynedd	

Winds

	Value	Location	Date
Strongest low-level gust	123 knots	Fraserburgh, Aberdeenshire	13th February 1989
Strongest high-level gust	150 knots	Cairn Gorm, Highland	20th March 1986

4 Climate Statistics

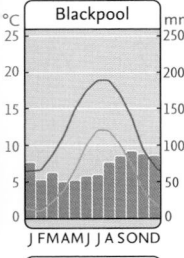

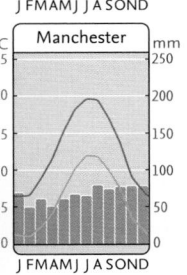

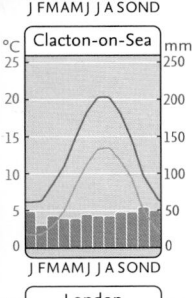

Aberystwyth

	Jan	Feb	Mar	Apr	May	Jun	Jul	Aug	Sep	Oct	Nov	Dec
Temperature - max. (°C)	7	7	9	11	15	17	18	18	16	13	10	8
Temperature - min. (°C)	2	2	3	5	7	10	12	12	11	8	5	4
Rainfall - (mm)	97	72	60	56	65	76	99	93	108	118	111	96

Belfast

	Jan	Feb	Mar	Apr	May	Jun	Jul	Aug	Sep	Oct	Nov	Dec
Temperature - max. (°C)	6	7	9	12	15	18	18	18	16	13	9	7
Temperature - min. (°C)	2	2	3	4	6	9	11	11	9	7	4	3
Rainfall - (mm)	80	52	50	48	52	68	94	77	80	83	72	90

Birmingham

	Jan	Feb	Mar	Apr	May	Jun	Jul	Aug	Sep	Oct	Nov	Dec
Temperature - max. (°C)	5	6	9	12	16	19	20	20	17	13	9	6
Temperature - min. (°C)	2	2	3	5	7	10	12	12	10	7	5	3
Rainfall - (mm)	74	54	50	53	64	50	69	69	61	69	84	67

Blackpool

	Jan	Feb	Mar	Apr	May	Jun	Jul	Aug	Sep	Oct	Nov	Dec
Temperature - max. (°C)	7	7	9	11	15	17	19	19	17	14	10	7
Temperature - min. (°C)	1	1	2	4	7	10	12	12	10	8	4	2
Rainfall - (mm)	78	54	64	51	53	59	61	78	86	93	89	87

Clacton-on-Sea

	Jan	Feb	Mar	Apr	May	Jun	Jul	Aug	Sep	Oct	Nov	Dec
Temperature - max. (°C)	6	6	9	11	15	18	20	20	18	15	10	7
Temperature - min. (°C)	2	2	3	5	8	11	13	14	12	9	5	3
Rainfall - (mm)	49	31	43	40	40	45	43	43	48	48	55	50

Dumfries

	Jan	Feb	Mar	Apr	May	Jun	Jul	Aug	Sep	Oct	Nov	Dec
Temperature - max. (°C)	6	6	8	11	14	17	19	18	16	13	9	7
Temperature - min. (°C)	1	1	2	3	6	9	11	10	9	6	3	1
Rainfall - (mm)	110	76	81	53	72	63	71	93	104	117	100	107

Edinburgh

	Jan	Feb	Mar	Apr	May	Jun	Jul	Aug	Sep	Oct	Nov	Dec
Temperature - max. (°C)	6	7	9	11	14	17	18	18	16	13	9	7
Temperature - min. (°C)	1	1	2	4	6	9	11	11	9	7	3	2
Rainfall - (mm)	54	40	47	39	49	50	59	63	66	63	56	52

Glasgow

	Jan	Feb	Mar	Apr	May	Jun	Jul	Aug	Sep	Oct	Nov	Dec
Temperature - max. (°C)	6	7	9	12	15	18	19	19	16	13	9	7
Temperature - min. (°C)	0	0	2	3	6	9	10	10	9	6	2	1
Rainfall - (mm)	96	63	65	50	62	58	68	83	95	98	105	108

Lerwick

	Jan	Feb	Mar	Apr	May	Jun	Jul	Aug	Sep	Oct	Nov	Dec
Temperature - max. (°C)	5	5	6	8	10	13	14	14	13	10	7	6
Temperature - min. (°C)	1	1	2	3	5	7	9	9	8	6	3	2
Rainfall - (mm)	127	93	93	72	64	64	67	78	113	119	140	147

London

	Jan	Feb	Mar	Apr	May	Jun	Jul	Aug	Sep	Oct	Nov	Dec
Temperature - max. (°C)	8	8	11	13	17	20	23	23	19	15	11	9
Temperature - min. (°C)	2	2	3	5	8	11	14	13	11	8	5	3
Rainfall - (mm)	52	34	42	45	47	53	38	47	57	62	52	54

Manchester

	Jan	Feb	Mar	Apr	May	Jun	Jul	Aug	Sep	Oct	Nov	Dec
Temperature - max. (°C)	6	7	9	12	15	18	20	20	17	14	9	7
Temperature - min. (°C)	1	1	3	4	7	10	12	12	10	8	4	2
Rainfall - (mm)	69	50	61	51	61	67	65	79	74	77	78	78

Oban

	Jan	Feb	Mar	Apr	May	Jun	Jul	Aug	Sep	Oct	Nov	Dec
Temperature - max. (°C)	6	7	9	11	14	16	17	17	15	12	9	7
Temperature - min. (°C)	2	1	3	4	7	9	11	11	9	7	4	3
Rainfall - (mm)	146	109	83	90	72	87	120	116	141	169	146	172

Plymouth

	Jan	Feb	Mar	Apr	May	Jun	Jul	Aug	Sep	Oct	Nov	Dec
Temperature - max. (°C)	8	8	10	12	15	18	19	19	18	15	11	9
Temperature - min. (°C)	4	4	5	6	8	11	13	13	12	9	7	5
Rainfall - (mm)	99	74	69	53	63	53	70	77	78	91	113	110

York

	Jan	Feb	Mar	Apr	May	Jun	Jul	Aug	Sep	Oct	Nov	Dec
Temperature - max. (°C)	6	7	10	13	16	19	21	21	18	14	10	7
Temperature - min. (°C)	2	2	3	5	7	10	12	12	10	8	5	4
Rainfall - (mm)	59	46	37	41	50	50	62	68	55	56	65	50

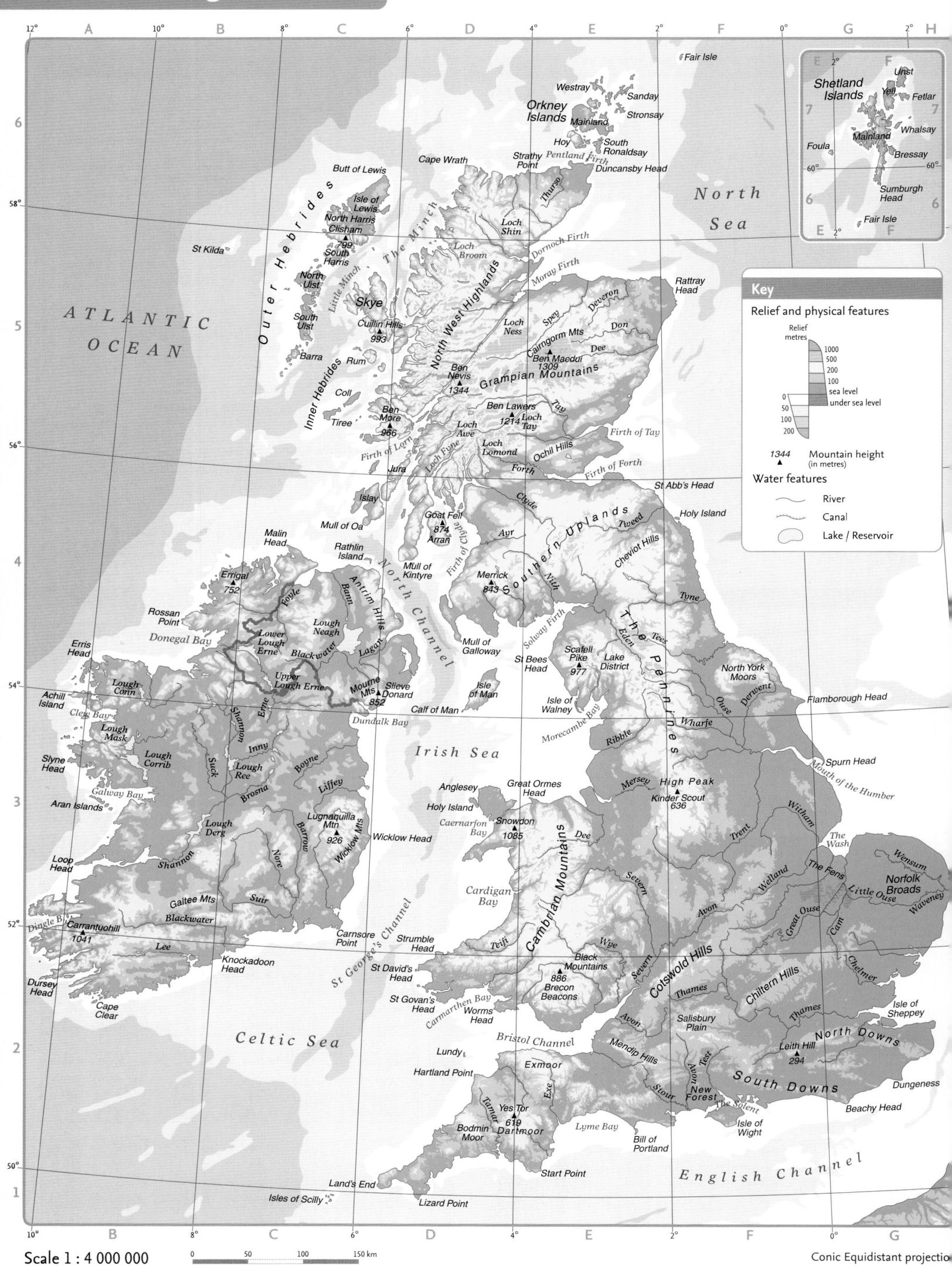

Scale 1 : 4 000 000

0   50   100   150 km

Conic Equidistant projection

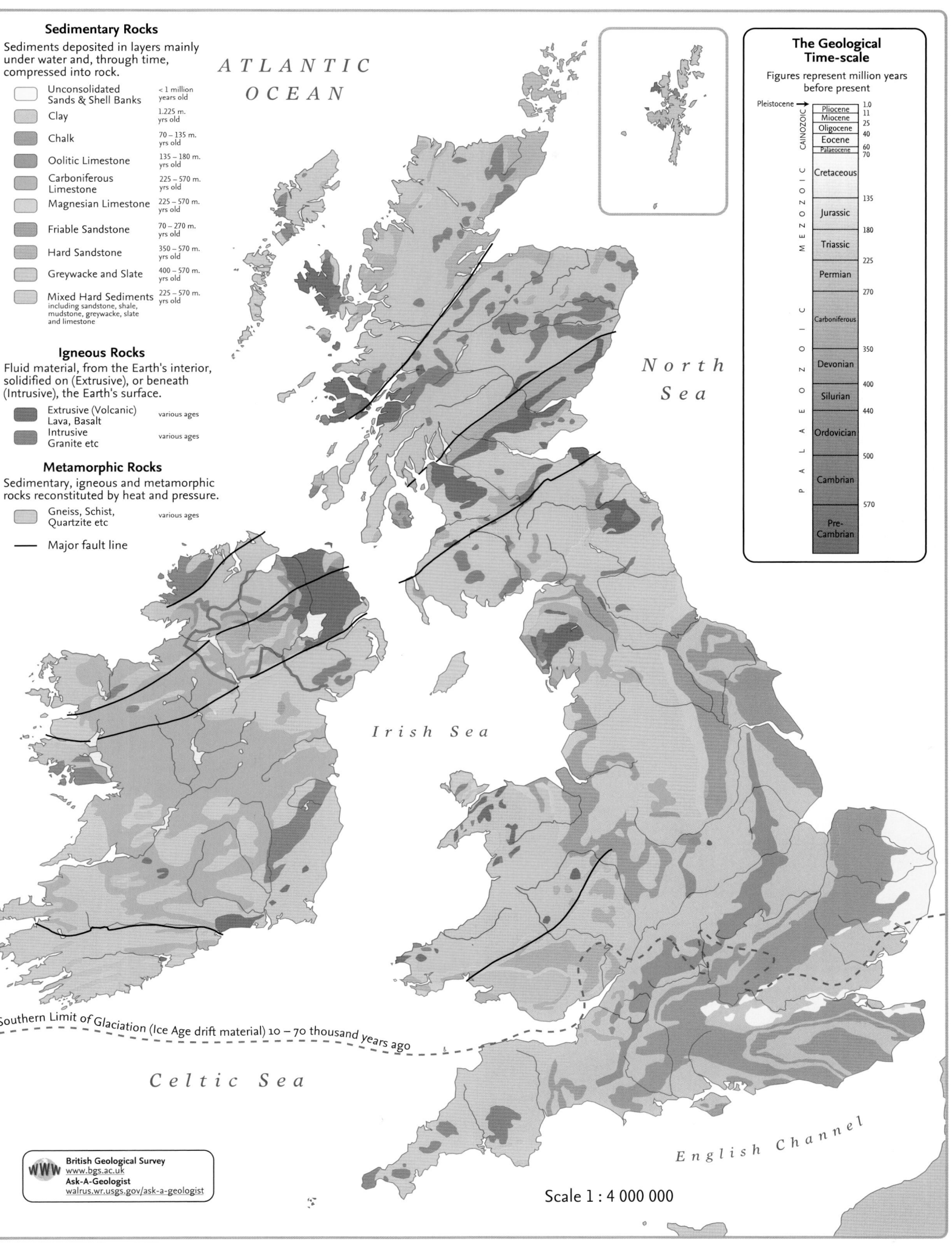

Sedimentary Rocks

Sediments deposited in layers mainly under water and, through time, compressed into rock.

	Unconsolidated Sands & Shell Banks	< 1 million years old
	Clay	1.225 m. yrs old
	Chalk	70 – 135 m. yrs old
	Oolitic Limestone	135 – 180 m. yrs old
	Carboniferous Limestone	225 – 570 m. yrs old
	Magnesian Limestone	225 – 570 m. yrs old
	Friable Sandstone	70 – 270 m. yrs old
	Hard Sandstone	350 – 570 m. yrs old
	Greywacke and Slate	400 – 570 m. yrs old
	Mixed Hard Sediments including sandstone, shale, mudstone, greywacke, slate and limestone	225 – 570 m. yrs old

Igneous Rocks

Fluid material, from the Earth's interior, solidified on (Extrusive), or beneath (Intrusive), the Earth's surface.

	Extrusive (Volcanic) Lava, Basalt	various ages
	Intrusive Granite etc	various ages

Metamorphic Rocks

Sedimentary, igneous and metamorphic rocks reconstituted by heat and pressure.

	Gneiss, Schist, Quartzite etc	various ages
——	Major fault line	

ATLANTIC OCEAN

North Sea

Irish Sea

Celtic Sea

English Channel

Southern Limit of Glaciation (Ice Age drift material) 10 – 70 thousand years ago

The Geological Time-scale

Figures represent million years before present

Pleistocene →

CAINOZOIC	Pliocene	1.0
	Miocene	11
	Oligocene	25
	Eocene	40
	Palaeocene	60 / 70
MESOZOIC	Cretaceous	
		135
	Jurassic	
		180
	Triassic	
		225
	Permian	
		270
PALAEOZOIC	Carboniferous	
		350
	Devonian	
		400
	Silurian	
		440
	Ordovician	
		500
	Cambrian	
		570
	Pre-Cambrian	

British Geological Survey
www.bgs.ac.uk
Ask-A-Geologist
walrus.wr.usgs.gov/ask-a-geologist

Scale 1 : 4 000 000

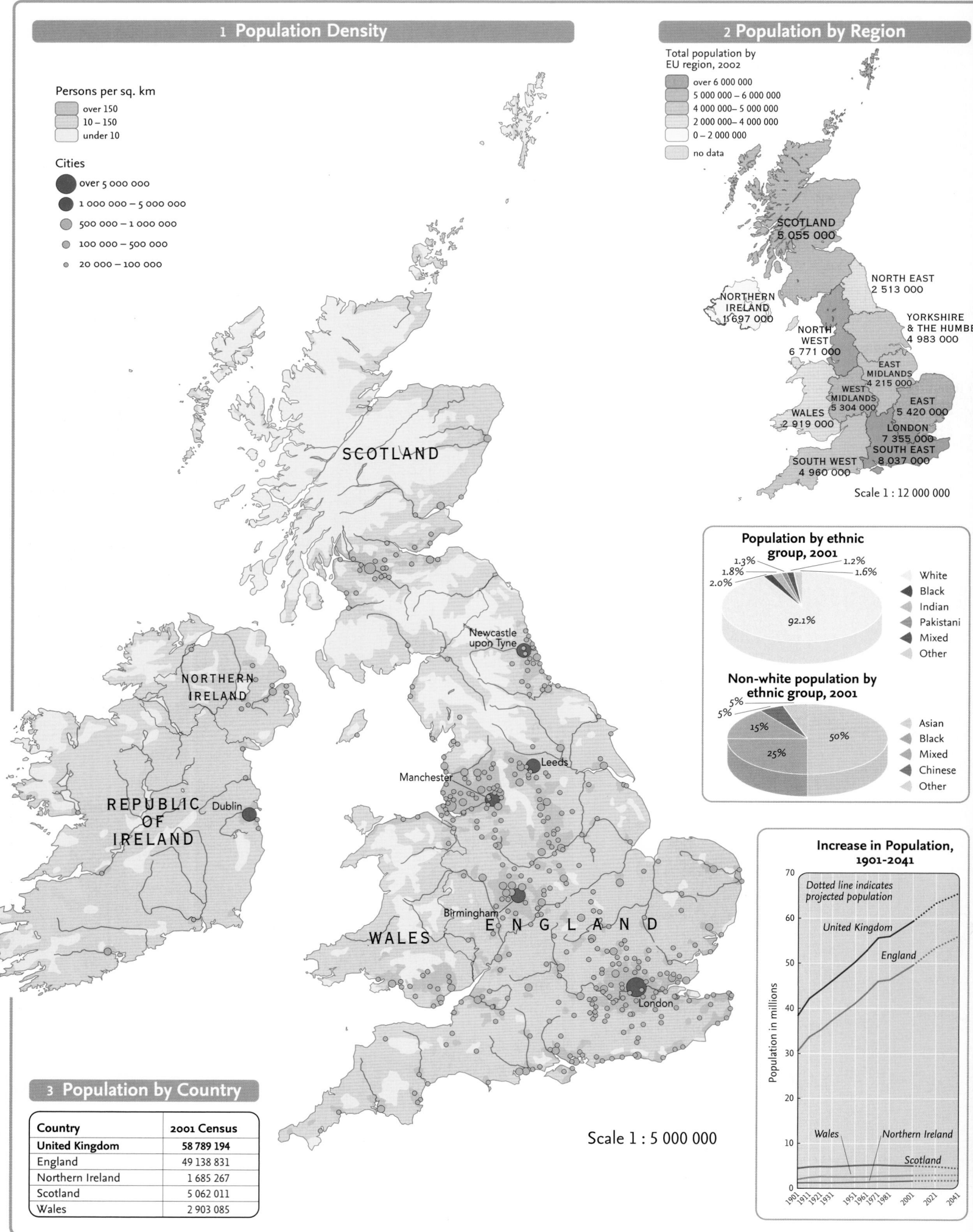

1 Population Density

Persons per sq. km
- over 150
- 10 – 150
- under 10

Cities
- over 5 000 000
- 1 000 000 – 5 000 000
- 500 000 – 1 000 000
- 100 000 – 500 000
- 20 000 – 100 000

SCOTLAND

NORTHERN IRELAND

REPUBLIC OF IRELAND

Dublin

Newcastle upon Tyne

Leeds

Manchester

Birmingham

WALES

ENGLAND

London

Scale 1 : 5 000 000

2 Population by Region

Total population by EU region, 2002
- over 6 000 000
- 5 000 000 – 6 000 000
- 4 000 000 – 5 000 000
- 2 000 000 – 4 000 000
- 0 – 2 000 000
- no data

SCOTLAND 5 055 000

NORTHERN IRELAND 1 697 000

NORTH EAST 2 513 000

YORKSHIRE & THE HUMBE 4 983 000

NORTH WEST 6 771 000

EAST MIDLANDS 4 215 000

WEST MIDLANDS 5 304 000

WALES 2 919 000

EAST 5 420 000

LONDON 7 355 000

SOUTH EAST 8 037 000

SOUTH WEST 4 960 000

Scale 1 : 12 000 000

Population by ethnic group, 2001

1.3% 1.2%
1.8% 1.6%
2.0%
92.1%

- White
- Black
- Indian
- Pakistani
- Mixed
- Other

Non-white population by ethnic group, 2001

5% 5%
15%
25%
50%

- Asian
- Black
- Mixed
- Chinese
- Other

Increase in Population, 1901-2041

Dotted line indicates projected population

United Kingdom

England

Wales   Northern Ireland

Scotland

Population in millions

3 Population by Country

Country	2001 Census
United Kingdom	**58 789 194**
England	49 138 831
Northern Ireland	1 685 267
Scotland	5 062 011
Wales	2 903 085

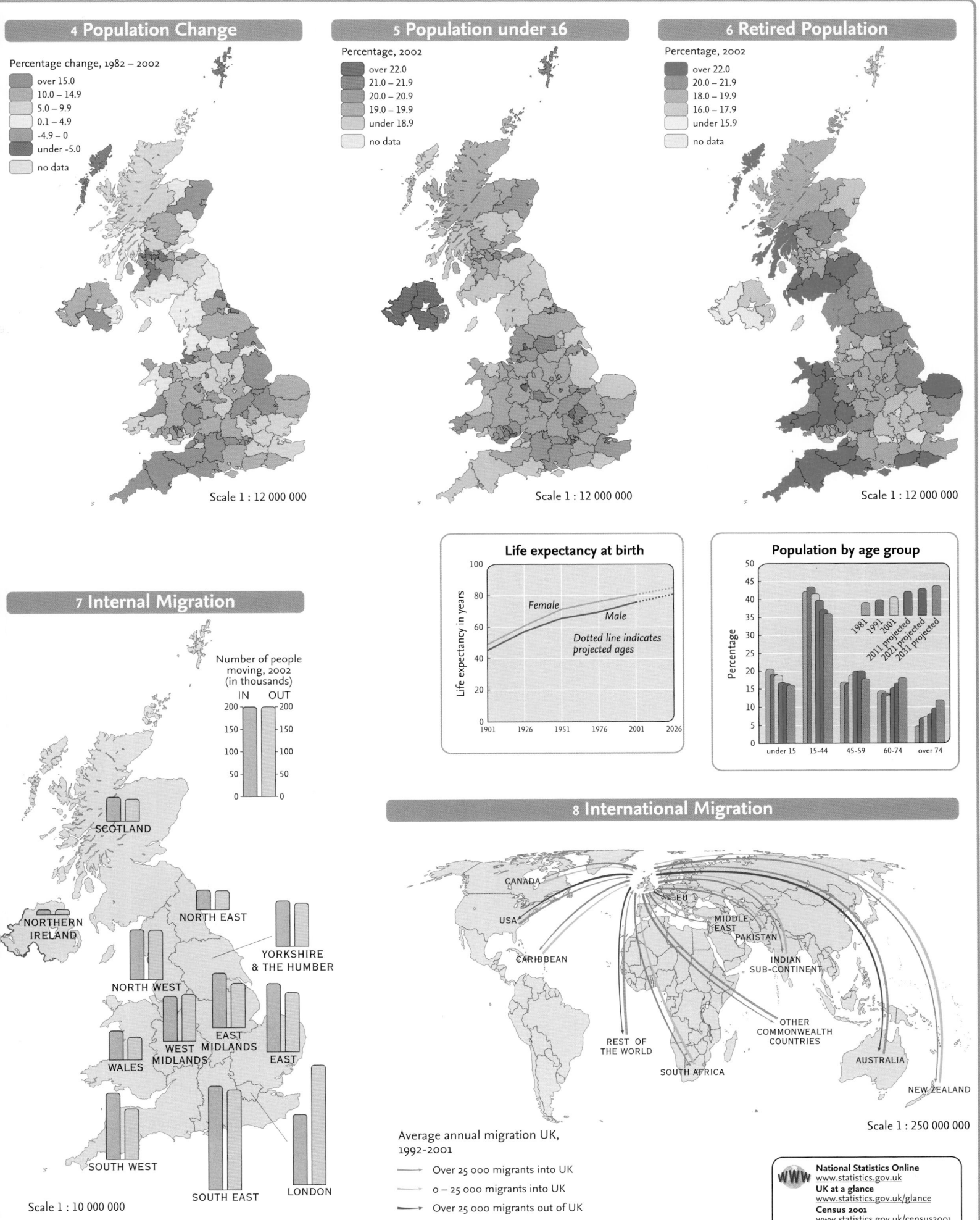

4 Population Change

Percentage change, 1982 – 2002

- over 15.0
- 10.0 – 14.9
- 5.0 – 9.9
- 0.1 – 4.9
- -4.9 – 0
- under -5.0
- no data

Scale 1 : 12 000 000

5 Population under 16

Percentage, 2002

- over 22.0
- 21.0 – 21.9
- 20.0 – 20.9
- 19.0 – 19.9
- under 18.9
- no data

Scale 1 : 12 000 000

6 Retired Population

Percentage, 2002

- over 22.0
- 20.0 – 21.9
- 18.0 – 19.9
- 16.0 – 17.9
- under 15.9
- no data

Scale 1 : 12 000 000

7 Internal Migration

Number of people moving, 2002 (in thousands)

IN OUT

SCOTLAND

NORTHERN IRELAND

NORTH EAST

YORKSHIRE & THE HUMBER

NORTH WEST

EAST MIDLANDS

WEST MIDLANDS

WALES

EAST

SOUTH WEST

SOUTH EAST

LONDON

Scale 1 : 10 000 000

Life expectancy at birth

Life expectancy in years

Female

Male

Dotted line indicates projected ages

1901 1926 1951 1976 2001 2026

Population by age group

Percentage

1981 1991 2001 2011 projected 2021 projected 2031 projected

under 15   15-44   45-59   60-74   over 74

8 International Migration

CANADA

EU

USA

MIDDLE EAST

PAKISTAN

CARIBBEAN

INDIAN SUB-CONTINENT

OTHER COMMONWEALTH COUNTRIES

REST OF THE WORLD

SOUTH AFRICA

AUSTRALIA

NEW ZEALAND

Scale 1 : 250 000 000

Average annual migration UK, 1992-2001

- Over 25 000 migrants into UK
- 0 – 25 000 migrants into UK
- Over 25 000 migrants out of UK
- 0 – 25 000 migrants out of UK

WWW **National Statistics Online**
www.statistics.gov.uk
UK at a glance
www.statistics.gov.uk/glance
Census 2001
www.statistics.gov.uk/census2001

1 Employment by Region

Agriculture

SCOTLAND

NORTHERN IRELAND

NORTH EAST

NORTH WEST

YORKSHIRE & THE HUMBER

EAST MIDLANDS

WEST MIDLANDS

EAST

WALES

LONDON

SOUTH EAST

SOUTH WEST

Percentage of total workforce employed in agriculture, 2001
- over 1.4
- 1.0 – 1.4
- 0.5 – 0.9
- 0 – 0.4

Scale 1 : 12 000 000

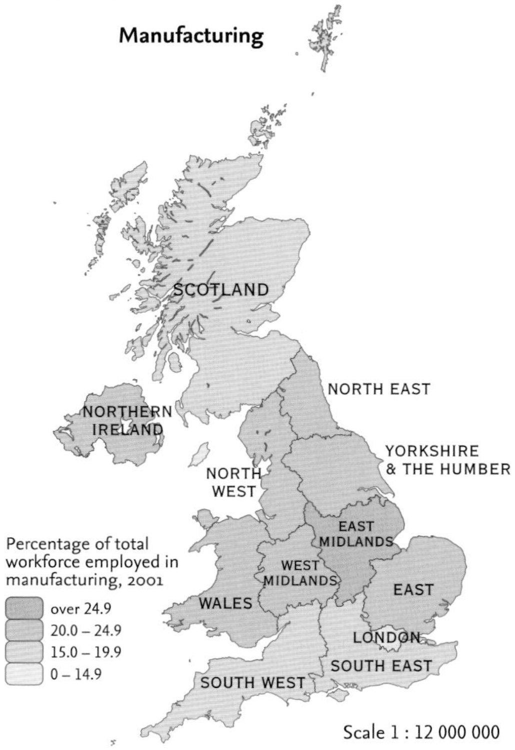

Manufacturing

SCOTLAND

NORTHERN IRELAND

NORTH EAST

NORTH WEST

YORKSHIRE & THE HUMBER

EAST MIDLANDS

WEST MIDLANDS

EAST

WALES

LONDON

SOUTH EAST

SOUTH WEST

Percentage of total workforce employed in manufacturing, 2001
- over 24.9
- 20.0 – 24.9
- 15.0 – 19.9
- 0 – 14.9

Scale 1 : 12 000 000

Services

SCOTLAND

NORTHERN IRELAND

NORTH EAST

NORTH WEST

YORKSHIRE & THE HUMBER

EAST MIDLANDS

WEST MIDLANDS

EAST

WALES

LONDON

SOUTH EAST

SOUTH WEST

Percentage of total workforce employed in services, 2001
- over 79.9
- 77.5 – 79.9
- 75.0 – 77.4
- 0 – 74.9

Scale 1 : 12 000 000

National Statistics Online
www.statistics.gov.uk
The Department of Trade and Industry
www.dti.gov.uk

2 Unemployment

SCOTLAND

NORTHERN IRELAND

NORTH EAST

NORTH WEST

YORKSHIRE & THE HUMBER

EAST MIDLANDS

WEST MIDLANDS

EAST

WALES

LONDON

SOUTH EAST

SOUTH WEST

Percentage of total workforce unemployed, 2003
- over 6.9
- 6.0 – 6.9
- 5.0 – 5.9
- 4.0 – 4.9
- 0 – 3.9

Scale 1 : 10 000 000

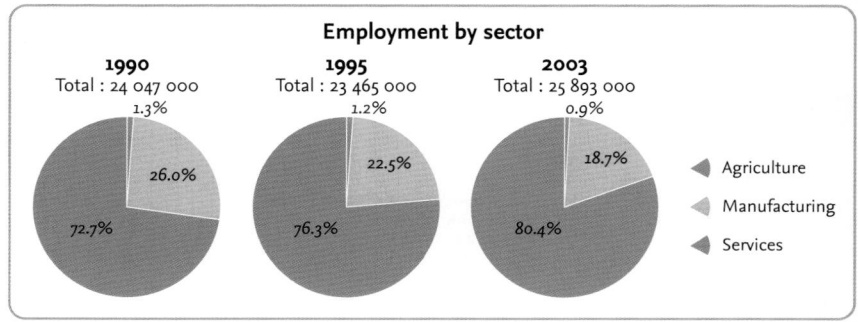

Employment by sector

1990	1995	2003
Total : 24 047 000	Total : 23 465 000	Total : 25 893 000
1.3%	1.2%	0.9%
26.0%	22.5%	18.7%
72.7%	76.3%	80.4%

- Agriculture
- Manufacturing
- Services

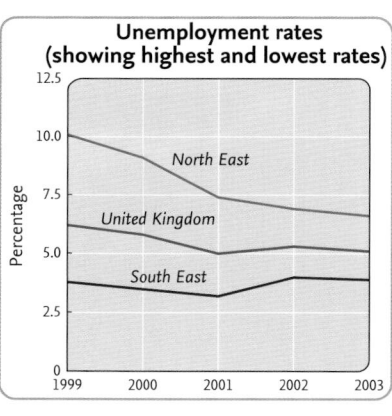

Unemployment rates (showing highest and lowest rates)

North East

United Kingdom

South East

Percentage

1999 2000 2001 2002 2003

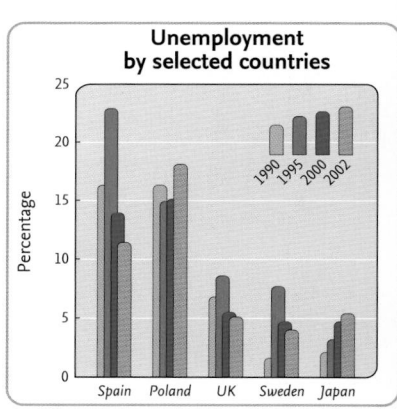

Unemployment by selected countries

Percentage

1990 1995 2000 2002

Spain Poland UK Sweden Japan

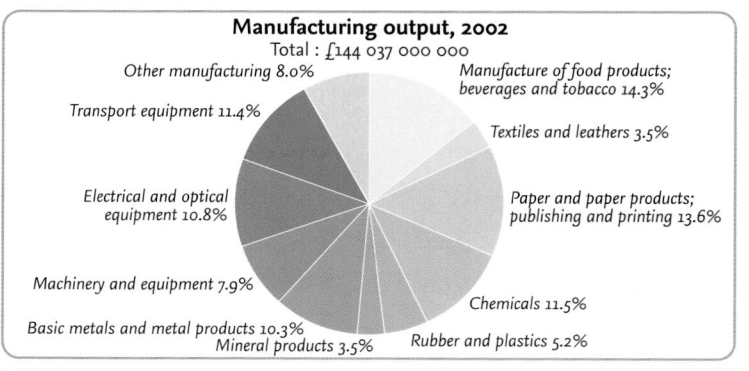

Manufacturing output, 2002
Total : £144 037 000 000

- Other manufacturing 8.0%
- Transport equipment 11.4%
- Electrical and optical equipment 10.8%
- Machinery and equipment 7.9%
- Basic metals and metal products 10.3%
- Mineral products 3.5%
- Rubber and plastics 5.2%
- Chemicals 11.5%
- Paper and paper products; publishing and printing 13.6%
- Textiles and leathers 3.5%
- Manufacture of food products; beverages and tobacco 14.3%

3 Land Use

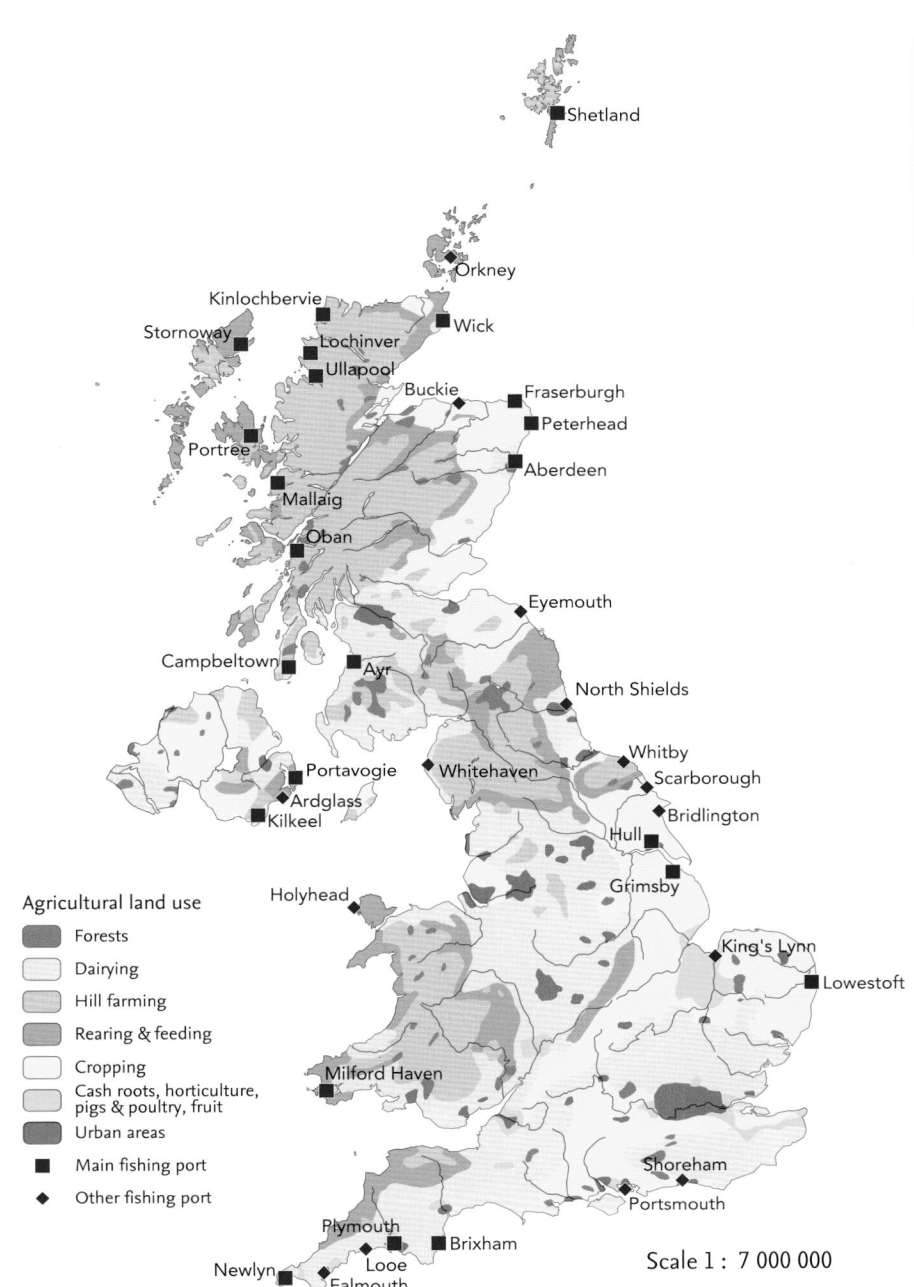

Agricultural land use
- Forests
- Dairying
- Hill farming
- Rearing & feeding
- Cropping
- Cash roots, horticulture, pigs & poultry, fruit
- Urban areas
- ■ Main fishing port
- ◆ Other fishing port

Scale 1 : 7 000 000

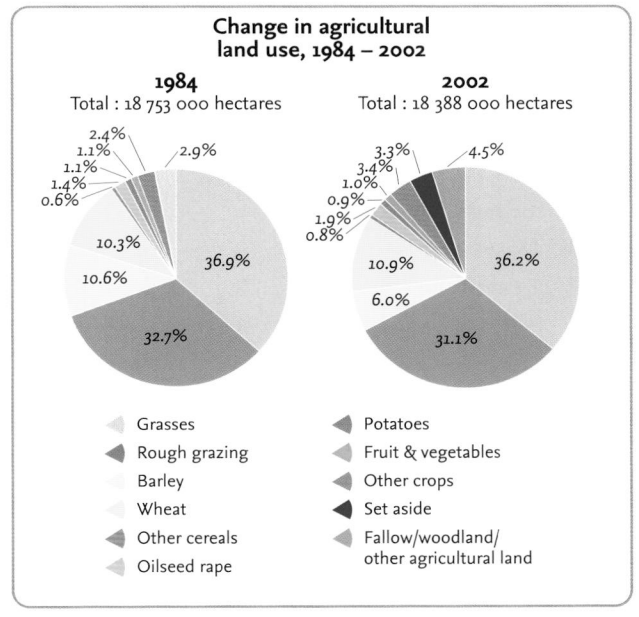

Change in agricultural land use, 1984 – 2002

1984
Total : 18 753 000 hectares

2.4%
1.1%
1.1%
1.4%
0.6%
2.9%
36.9%
10.3%
10.6%
32.7%

2002
Total : 18 388 000 hectares

3.3%
3.4%
1.0%
0.9%
1.9%
0.8%
4.5%
36.2%
10.9%
6.0%
31.1%

- Grasses
- Rough grazing
- Barley
- Wheat
- Other cereals
- Oilseed rape
- Potatoes
- Fruit & vegetables
- Other crops
- Set aside
- Fallow/woodland/ other agricultural land

4 International Trade

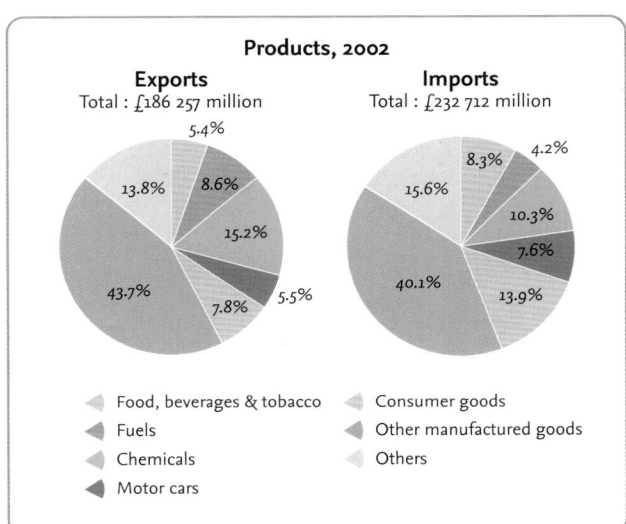

Products, 2002

Exports
Total : £186 257 million

5.4%
8.6%
13.8%
15.2%
43.7%
7.8%
5.5%

Imports
Total : £232 712 million

8.3%
4.2%
15.6%
10.3%
7.6%
40.1%
13.9%

- Food, beverages & tobacco
- Fuels
- Chemicals
- Motor cars
- Consumer goods
- Other manufactured goods
- Others

UK trade with European Union, 2002

Country	% of total UK exports	% of total UK imports
Germany	11.8	13.9
France	10.1	8.8
Rep. of Ireland	8.3	5.6
Netherlands	7.5	6.9
Belgium	5.7	5.6
Italy	4.6	4.6
Spain	4.6	3.9
Sweden	2.1	1.9
Denmark	1.5	1.5
Portugal	0.8	0.8
Finland	0.8	1.2
Austria	0.7	1.0
Greece	0.6	0.3

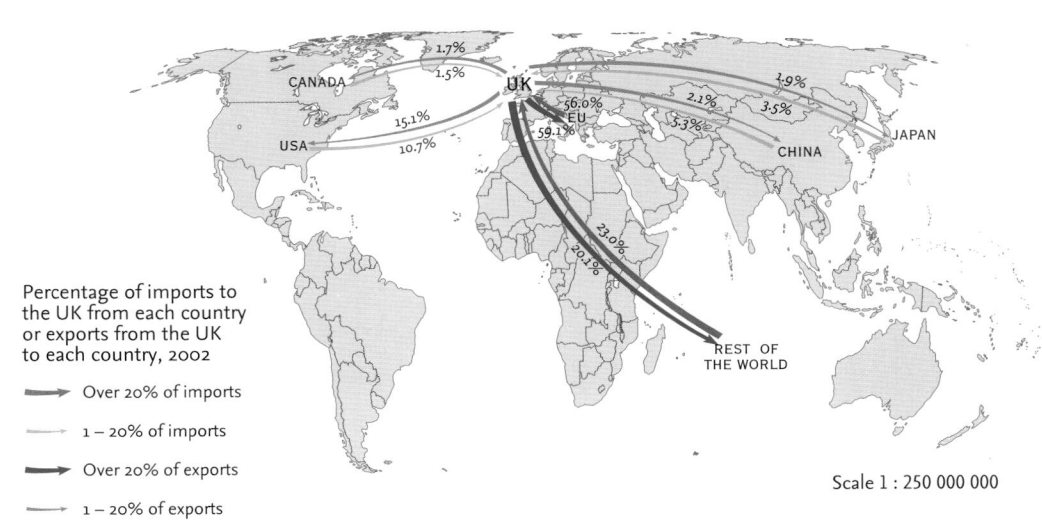

Percentage of imports to the UK from each country or exports from the UK to each country, 2002

→ Over 20% of imports
→ 1 – 20% of imports
→ Over 20% of exports
→ 1 – 20% of exports

Scale 1 : 250 000 000

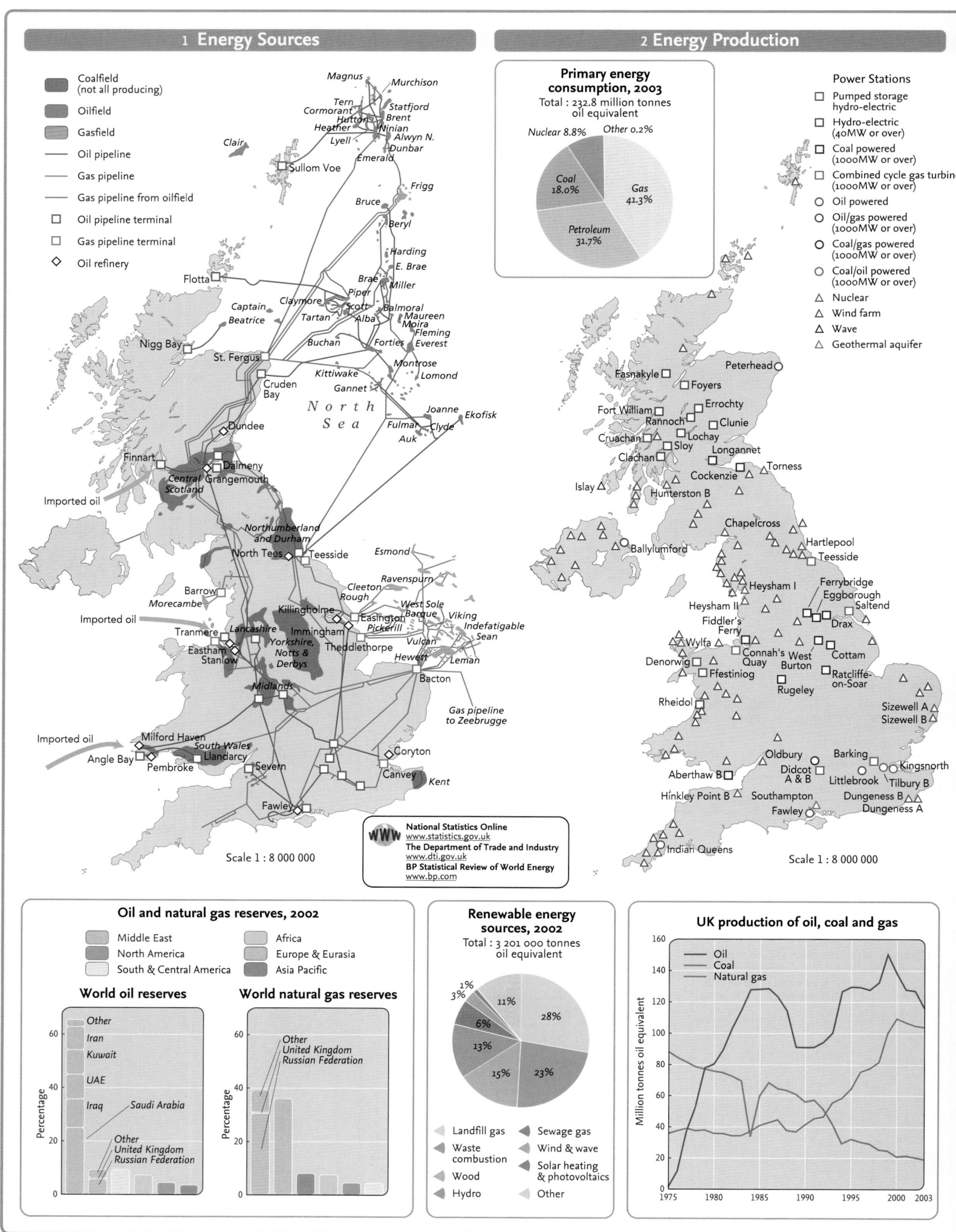

1 Energy Sources

Coalfield (not all producing)
Oilfield
Gasfield
Oil pipeline
Gas pipeline
Gas pipeline from oilfield
Oil pipeline terminal
Gas pipeline terminal
Oil refinery

Scale 1 : 8 000 000

National Statistics Online
www.statistics.gov.uk
The Department of Trade and Industry
www.dti.gov.uk
BP Statistical Review of World Energy
www.bp.com

2 Energy Production

Primary energy consumption, 2003
Total : 232.8 million tonnes oil equivalent

Nuclear 8.8%
Other 0.2%
Coal 18.0%
Gas 41.3%
Petroleum 31.7%

Power Stations
Pumped storage hydro-electric
Hydro-electric (40MW or over)
Coal powered (1000MW or over)
Combined cycle gas turbine (1000MW or over)
Oil powered
Oil/gas powered (1000MW or over)
Coal/gas powered (1000MW or over)
Coal/oil powered (1000MW or over)
Nuclear
Wind farm
Wave
Geothermal aquifer

Scale 1 : 8 000 000

Oil and natural gas reserves, 2002

Middle East
North America
South & Central America
Africa
Europe & Eurasia
Asia Pacific

World oil reserves
Other
Iran
Kuwait
UAE
Iraq
Saudi Arabia
Other
United Kingdom
Russian Federation

World natural gas reserves
Other
United Kingdom
Russian Federation

Renewable energy sources, 2002
Total : 3 201 000 tonnes oil equivalent

1%
3%
11%
28%
6%
13%
23%
15%

Landfill gas
Waste combustion
Wood
Hydro
Sewage gas
Wind & wave
Solar heating & photovoltaics
Other

UK production of oil, coal and gas

Oil
Coal
Natural gas

Million tonnes oil equivalent

160
140
120
100
80
60
40
20
0
1975 1980 1985 1990 1995 2000 2003

1 Tourist Attractions

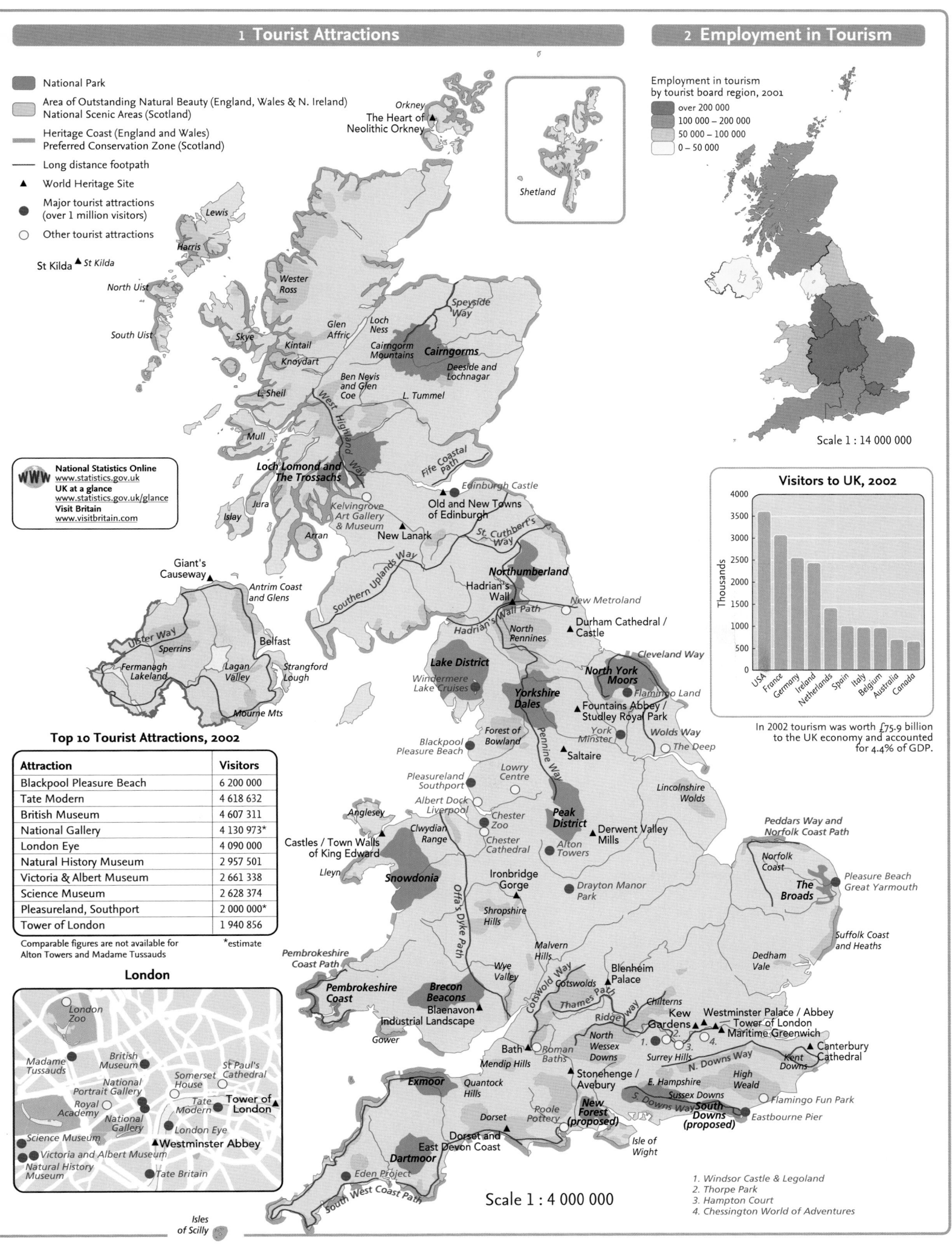

Legend:

- National Park
- Area of Outstanding Natural Beauty (England, Wales & N. Ireland) National Scenic Areas (Scotland)
- Heritage Coast (England and Wales) Preferred Conservation Zone (Scotland)
- Long distance footpath
- ▲ World Heritage Site
- ● Major tourist attractions (over 1 million visitors)
- ○ Other tourist attractions

WWW
National Statistics Online
www.statistics.gov.uk
UK at a glance
www.statistics.gov.uk/glance
Visit Britain
www.visitbritain.com

Top 10 Tourist Attractions, 2002

Attraction	Visitors
Blackpool Pleasure Beach	6 200 000
Tate Modern	4 618 632
British Museum	4 607 311
National Gallery	4 130 973*
London Eye	4 090 000
Natural History Museum	2 957 501
Victoria & Albert Museum	2 661 338
Science Museum	2 628 374
Pleasureland, Southport	2 000 000*
Tower of London	1 940 856

Comparable figures are not available for Alton Towers and Madame Tussauds   *estimate

London

Map labels: London Zoo, Madame Tussauds, British Museum, Somerset House, St Paul's Cathedral, National Portrait Gallery, Royal Academy, National Gallery, Tate Modern, Tower of London ▲, Science Museum, London Eye, Victoria and Albert Museum, Natural History Museum, Tate Britain, ▲ Westminster Abbey

2 Employment in Tourism

Employment in tourism by tourist board region, 2001
- over 200 000
- 100 000 – 200 000
- 50 000 – 100 000
- 0 – 50 000

Scale 1 : 14 000 000

Visitors to UK, 2002

Thousands (y-axis: 0 to 4000)

Countries (x-axis): USA, France, Germany, Ireland, Netherlands, Spain, Italy, Belgium, Australia, Canada

In 2002 tourism was worth £75.9 billion to the UK economy and accounted for 4.4% of GDP.

Map labels (main map):
Orkney, The Heart of Neolithic Orkney, Shetland, Lewis, Harris, North Uist, South Uist, St Kilda ▲ St Kilda, Wester Ross, Skye, Glen Affric, Loch Ness, Speyside Way, Kintail, Knoydart, Cairngorm Mountains, Cairngorms, Deeside and Lochnagar, Ben Nevis and Glen Coe, L. Tummel, L. Sheil, Mull, West Highland Way, Loch Lomond and The Trossachs, Jura, Islay, Arran, Kelvingrove Art Gallery & Museum, New Lanark, Fife Coastal Path, Edinburgh Castle, Old and New Towns of Edinburgh, St. Cuthbert's Way, Southern Uplands Way, Giant's Causeway ▲, Antrim Coast and Glens, Belfast, Ulster Way, Sperrins, Fermanagh Lakeland, Lagan Valley, Strangford Lough, Mourne Mts, Northumberland, Hadrian's Wall, Hadrian's Wall Path, New Metroland, North Pennines, Durham Cathedral / Castle ▲, Cleveland Way, Lake District, Windermere Lake Cruises, Yorkshire Dales, North York Moors, Flamingo Land, Fountains Abbey / Studley Royal Park ▲, Forest of Bowland, York Minster, Saltaire ▲, Wolds Way, The Deep, Blackpool Pleasure Beach, Lowry Centre, Pennine Way, Lincolnshire Wolds, Pleasureland Southport, Albert Dock Liverpool, Chester Zoo, Chester Cathedral, Peak District, Derwent Valley Mills, Alton Towers, Anglesey, Clwydian Range, Castles / Town Walls of King Edward, Lleyn, Snowdonia, Ironbridge Gorge, Drayton Manor Park, Offa's Dyke Path, Shropshire Hills, Peddars Way and Norfolk Coast Path, Norfolk Coast, The Broads, Pleasure Beach Great Yarmouth, Suffolk Coast and Heaths, Pembrokeshire Coast Path, Malvern Hills, Wye Valley, Brecon Beacons, Blaenavon Industrial Landscape, Gower, Pembrokeshire Coast, Cotswold Way, Cotswolds, Blenheim Palace, Thames Path, Dedham Vale, Chilterns, Kew Gardens ▲, Westminster Palace / Abbey ▲, Tower of London ▲, Maritime Greenwich ▲, Ridgeway, North Wessex Downs, Bath ▲, Roman Baths, Surrey Hills, N. Downs Way, Kent Downs, Canterbury Cathedral ▲, Mendip Hills, Stonehenge / Avebury ▲, E. Hampshire, High Weald, Exmoor, Quantock Hills, New Forest (proposed), Sussex Downs, S. Downs Way, South Downs (proposed), Flamingo Fun Park, Eastbourne Pier, Dorset, Poole Pottery, Isle of Wight, Dartmoor, Dorset and East Devon Coast, Eden Project, South West Coast Path, Isles of Scilly

1. Windsor Castle & Legoland
2. Thorpe Park
3. Hampton Court
4. Chessington World of Adventures

Scale 1 : 4 000 000

1 Road Network

M1 — Motorway and number

A1 — Linking primary road and number

WWW **UK at a glance**
www.statistics.gov.uk/glance
Department for Transport
www.dft.gov.uk
Highways Agency
www.highways.gov.uk

Thurso
A9
Inverness
Aberdeen
A82
A9
A90
A9
A9 M90
M80 M9
Edinburgh
Glasgow M8 A7
A74 A1
A75
Londonderry A26
A6 M2
A4 Belfast
M1 A1
Stranraer
A69 Newcastle upon Tyne
Carlisle A1(M)
A66 A66 A19
A6
M6 A1 A64 Scarborough
M55 A65
M58 M65 M62 M62
Liverpool M60 M180
Holyhead M56 Manchester A16
A55 A6
A5 A52 M1
M54 A1 A47
Birmingham A14 A11
M42 M6 A45 A12
Fishguard A40 M50 M1 A10(M)
A40 M40 M11 M25
M4 M4 London M2
M5 M3 M25 M20
A3 M23 Folkestone
A35 Brighton
A30 A38
Penzance

Scale 1 : 8 000 000

2 Rail Network

—— Inter-city and express routes

----- Channel Tunnel

Inverness
Aberdeen
Dundee
Glasgow Edinburgh
Londonderry
Larne
Belfast
Middlesbrough
Scarborough
York
Leeds Hull
Blackpool Doncaster
Liverpool Manchester Grimsby
Holyhead Crewe
King's Lynn
Birmingham Norwich
Peterborough
Fishguard Harwich
Newport
Bristol London
Dover
Portsmouth Brighton Hastings *Calais Paris Brusse*
Weymouth
Penzance

Scale 1 : 8 000 000

Transport to work, 2002

London

Percentage — Rail, Car, Bus, Foot, Bicycle, Motorcycle, Other

All of UK

Percentage — Rail, Car, Bus, Foot, Bicycle, Motorcycle, Other

Number of cars

Thousands — 1952, 1962, 1973, 1981, 1991, 1997, 2002

Mode of passenger transport

Billion passenger kilometres — Car, Bus, Rail
1955, 1960, 1965, 1970, 1975, 1980, 1985, 1990, 1995, 2000, 2002

3 Ports and Airports

Ports

- • Ports handling more than 1 million tonnes of cargo
- - - - Ferry routes with destinations
- • Ferry terminal

Airports
Passengers handled per year (thousands)

- Over 20 000
- 10 000 – 20 000
- 5000 – 10 000
- 2000 – 5000
- 1000 – 2000

- ◁ Domestic traffic
- ◁ International traffic
- • Other airports

Unst
Sullom Voe   Scatsta
Lerwick
Sumburgh
Bergen
Tórshavn
Seydisfjordur

Orkneys
Stromness   Kirkwall
Scrabster
Wick
Stornoway
Tarbert
Lochmaddy   Ullapool   Cromarty Firth
Benbecula   Uig   Inverness
Lochboisdale   Peterhead
Barra   Armadale   Aberdeen
Castlebay   Mallaig
Arinagour   Lochaline   Dundee
Tiree   Glensanda
Scarinish   Craignure   Oban
Glasgow
Scalasaig   Gourock   Rosyth
Dunoon   Clyde   Forth
Port Askaig   Rothesay   Edinburgh   *Zeebrugge*
Islay   Ardrossan
Kennacraig   Brodick   Troon
Campbeltown   Prestwick
Wemyss Bay   Newcastle   *Stavanger*
Bergen
Londonderry   Cairnryan   Tyne   *Gothenburg*
Larne   Stranraer   *Kristiansand*
Belfast   Tees/Hartlepool   *Amsterdam*
Belfast City   Teesside   *Haugesund*
Warrenpoint   Douglas
Isle of Man   Heysham   Leeds/   Hull/Humber
Fleetwood   Bradford   Hull
Dublin   Blackpool   Goole   Humberside   *Rotterdam*
Dublin   Liverpool   Manchester   Grimsby/Immingham   *Zeebrugge*
Dublin   Holyhead   River Trent
Dun Laoghaire   Mostyn
King's Lynn
East Midlands   Norwich
Rosslare   Birmingham   Cambridge
Rosslare   Fishguard   Stansted   Ipswich
Milford   Gloucestershire   Felixstowe   *Esbjerg*
Cork   Haven   Cardiff   Luton   London   Harwich   *Hamburg*
Pembroke   Swansea   Newport   Heathrow   Southend   *Hoek van Holland*
Port Talbot   London City
Bristol   Medway   Ramsgate
Gatwick   Dover   *Dunkirk*
Southampton   Newhaven   Lydd   *Calais*
Newquay   Bournemouth   Shoreham
Cornwall   Exeter   Poole   Cowes
Land's End   Weymouth   Portsmouth
St Marys   Fowey
Isles of Scilly   Penzance   *Dieppe*   Scale 1 : 8 000 000
Plymouth
Channel Is   *Caen*
Le Havre
Roscoff   *Cherbourg*
Santander   *Cherbourg*   *St Malo*
Channel Is   *Bilbao*
St Malo   *Channel Is*

4 Telecommunications

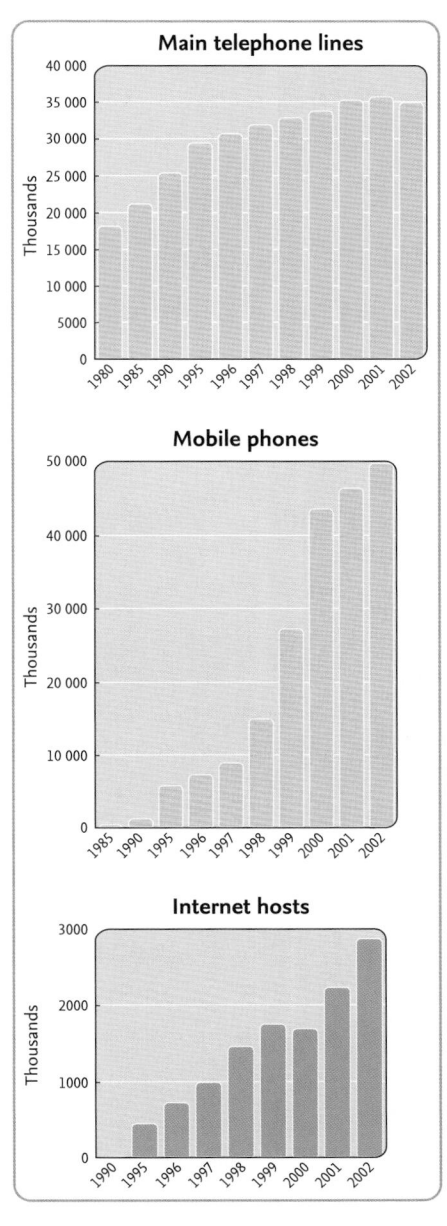

Main telephone lines

Mobile phones

Internet hosts

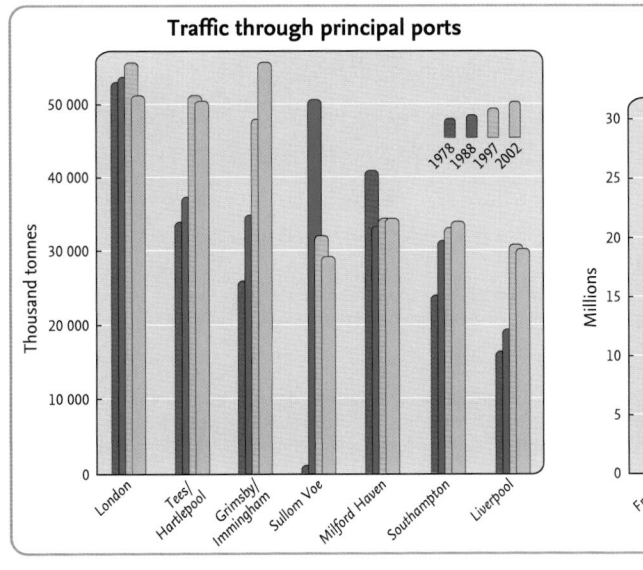

Traffic through principal ports

1978 1988 1997 2002

Thousand tonnes

London, Tees/Hartlepool, Grimsby/Immingham, Sullom Voe, Milford Haven, Southampton, Liverpool

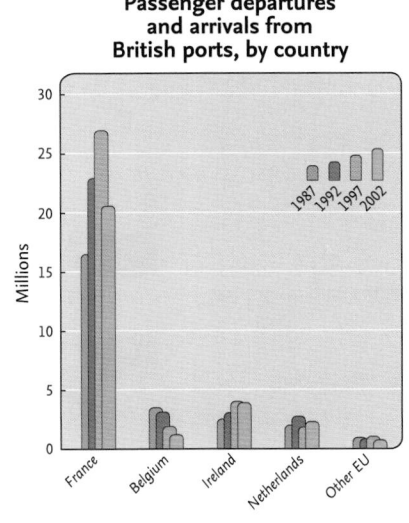

Passenger departures and arrivals from British ports, by country

1987 1992 1997 2002

Millions

France, Belgium, Ireland, Netherlands, Other EU

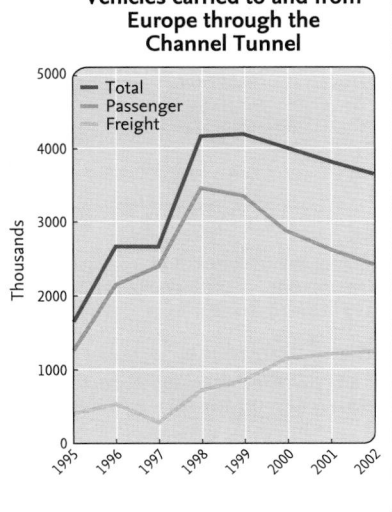

Vehicles carried to and from Europe through the Channel Tunnel

— Total
— Passenger
— Freight

Thousands

1995 1996 1997 1998 1999 2000 2001 2002

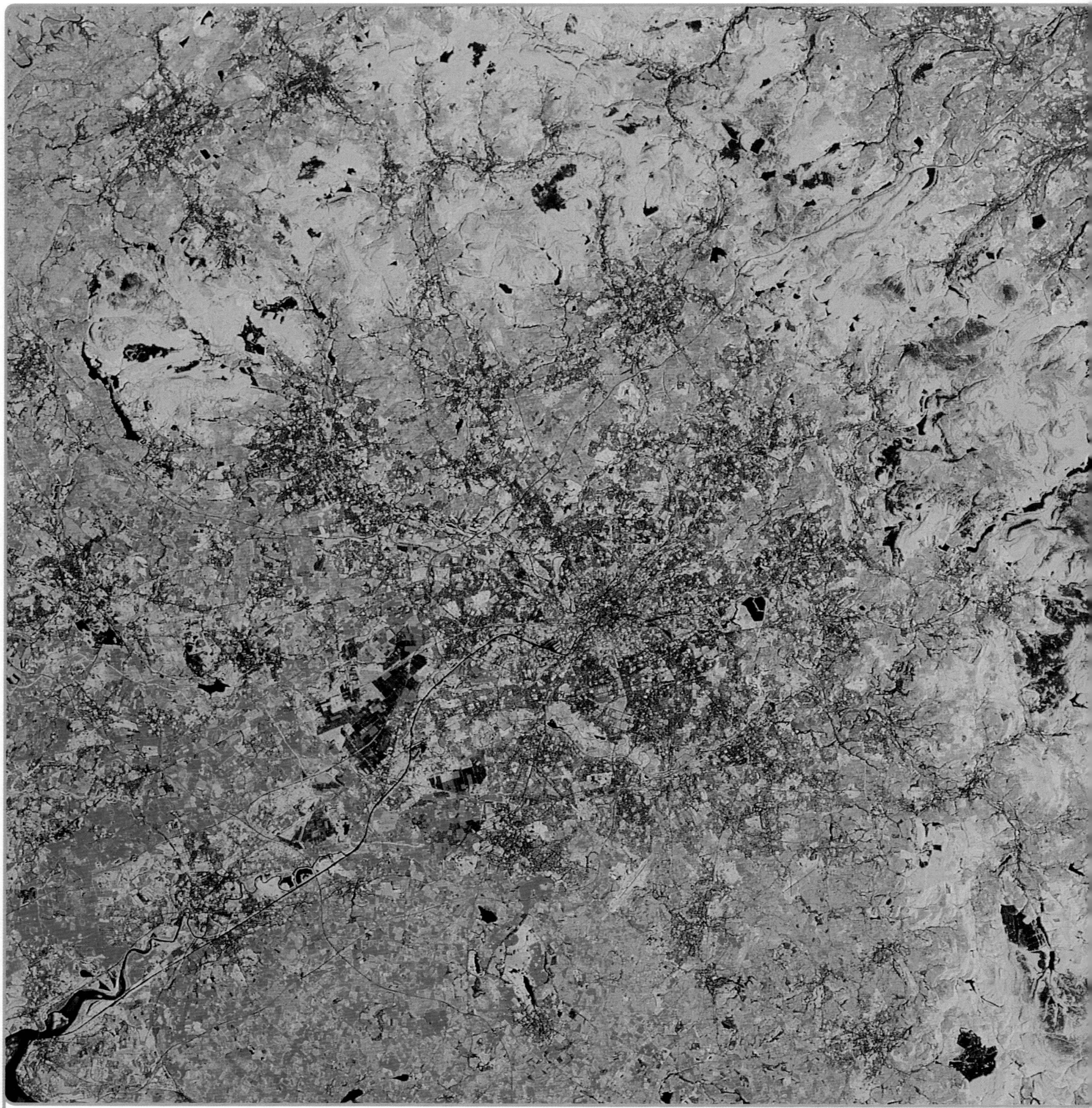

 Highland
The blue/green colour corresponds to grassland over 300 metres above sea level on the map opposite. In the higher areas of the Pennines the colour becomes greener as grassland changes to moorland, for example around Shining Tor.

 Lowland and arable land
The areas around Manchester appear as shades of orange and red. The cultivated areas near the river Mersey are redder.

 Built up area
These areas are dark blue on the satellite image. The largest area is the Manchester urban sprawl. In the top left of the image the built up areas of Blackburn and Accrington stand out from the surrounding farmland.

 Woodland
Some areas of woodland can be seen on the lower slopes of Shining Tor. The is also a small area near Alderley Edge.

 Reservoir
The small distinctive shape of these can be seen in the Pennines area. Examp are Watergrove Reservoir near Whitworth and Errwood Reservoir south of Whaley Bridge.

 Canal
The straight line of the Manchester Ship Canal can be seen running alongsid the winding course of the river Mersey.

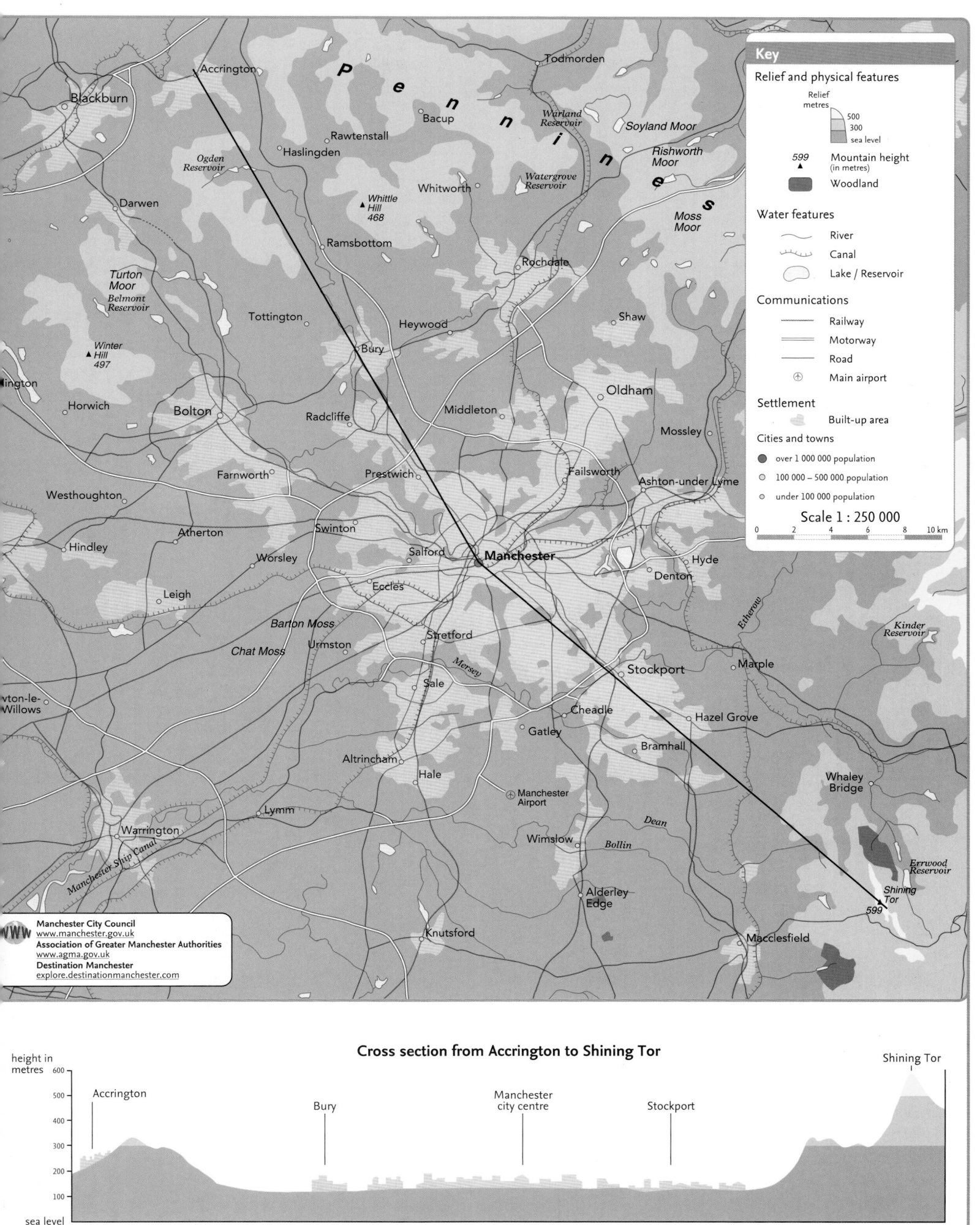

Key

Relief and physical features

Relief metres
500
300
sea level

599 ▲ Mountain height (in metres)

Woodland

Water features

River

Canal

Lake / Reservoir

Communications

Railway

Motorway

Road

⊕ Main airport

Settlement

Built-up area

Cities and towns

● over 1 000 000 population

○ 100 000 – 500 000 population

○ under 100 000 population

Scale 1 : 250 000

0   2   4   6   8   10 km

Manchester City Council
www.manchester.gov.uk
Association of Greater Manchester Authorities
www.agma.gov.uk
Destination Manchester
explore.destinationmanchester.com

Cross section from Accrington to Shining Tor

height in metres
600
500
400
300
200
100
sea level

Accrington   Bury   Manchester city centre   Stockport   Shining Tor

Scale 1 : 16 000 000

0   250   500   750   1000 km

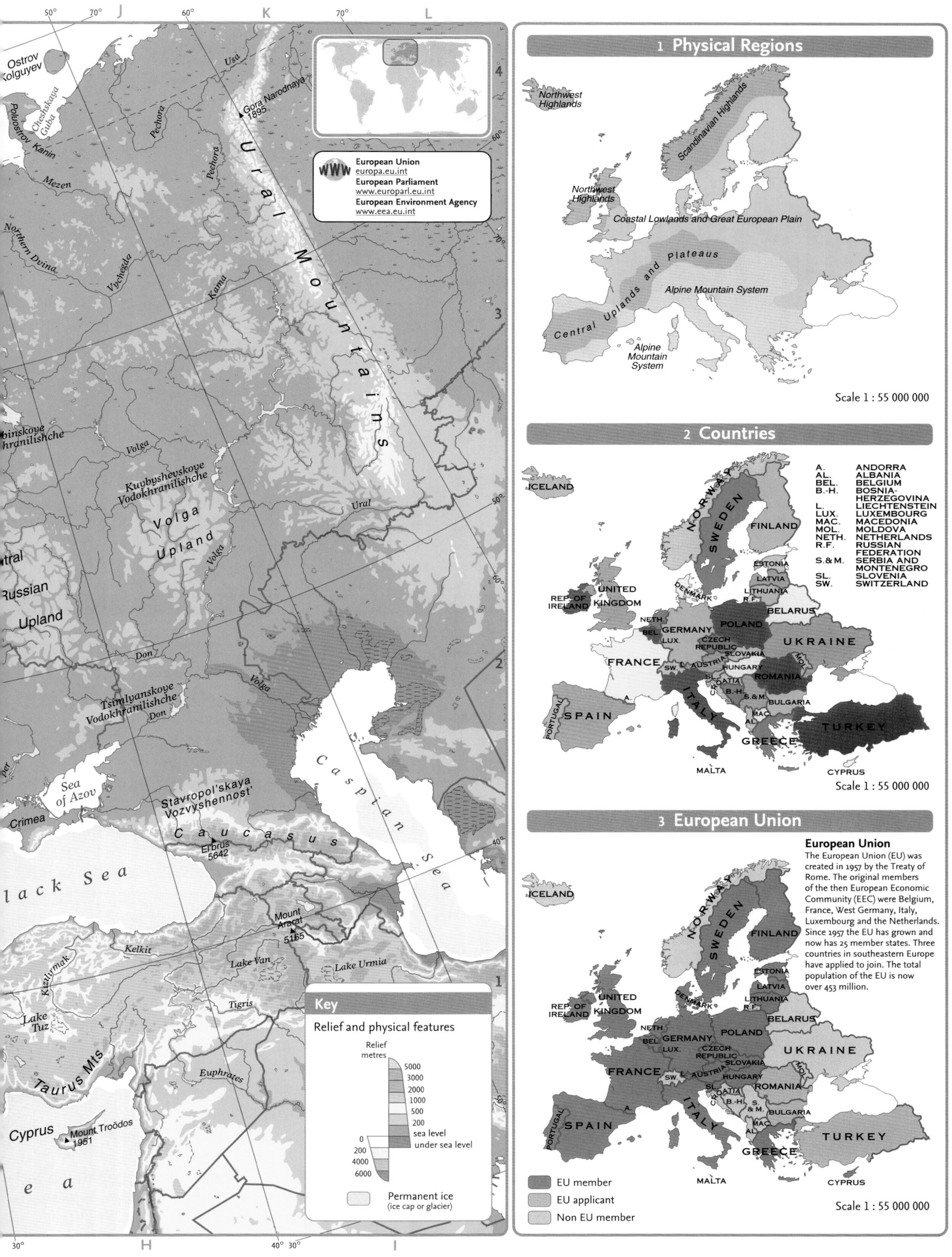

1 Physical Regions

Scale 1 : 55 000 000

2 Countries

Scale 1 : 55 000 000

3 European Union

European Union
The European Union (EU) was created in 1957 by the Treaty of Rome. The original members of the then European Economic Community (EEC) were Belgium, France, West Germany, Italy, Luxembourg and the Netherlands. Since 1957 the EU has grown and now has 25 member states. Three countries in southeastern Europe have applied to join. The total population of the EU is now over 453 million.

EU member
EU applicant
Non EU member

Scale 1 : 55 000 000

Conic Equidistant projection

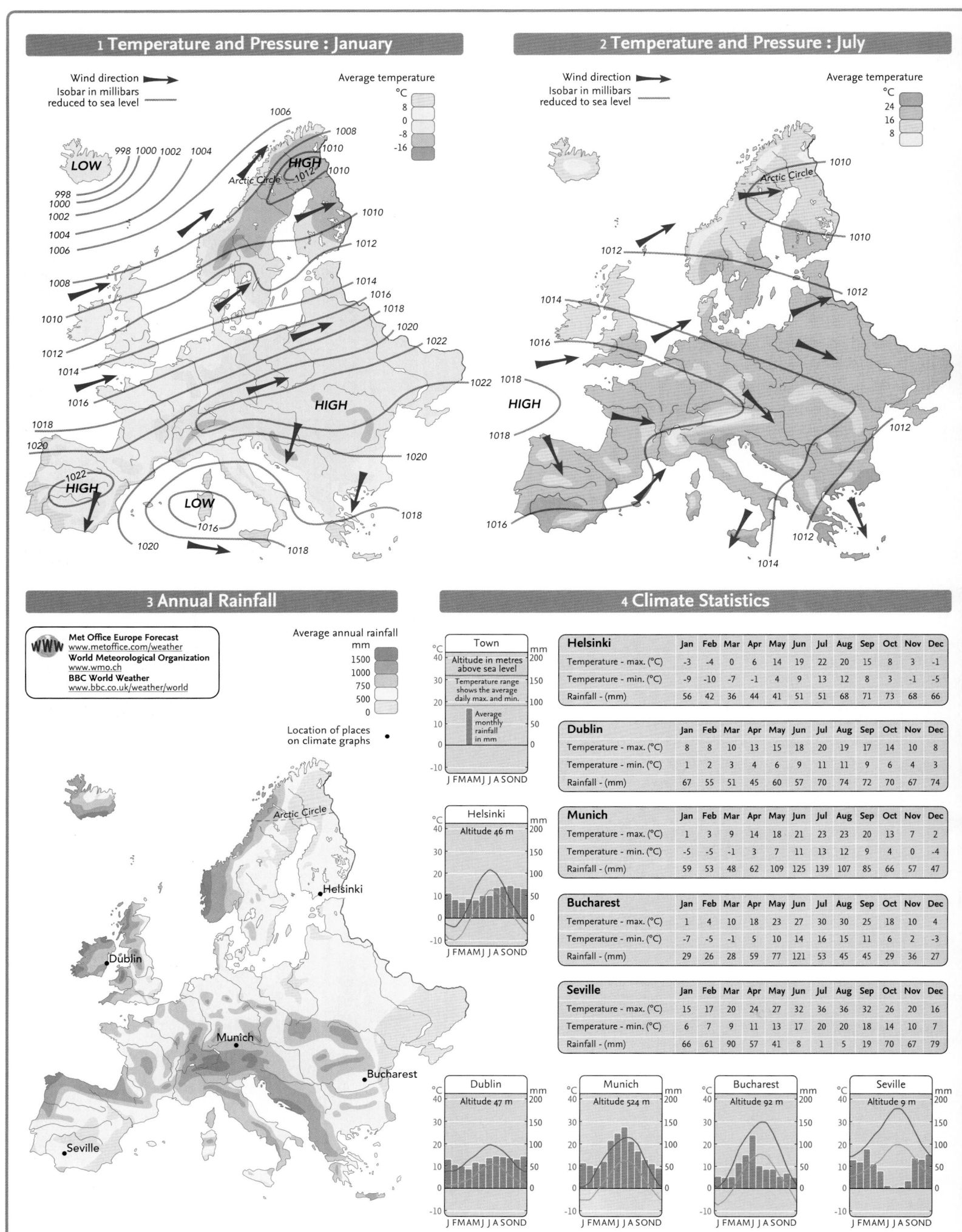

1 Temperature and Pressure : January

Wind direction ➤
Isobar in millibars reduced to sea level ——

Average temperature °C
8
0
-8
-16

2 Temperature and Pressure : July

Wind direction ➤
Isobar in millibars reduced to sea level ——

Average temperature °C
24
16
8

3 Annual Rainfall

Met Office Europe Forecast
www.metoffice.com/weather
World Meteorological Organization
www.wmo.ch
BBC World Weather
www.bbc.co.uk/weather/world

Average annual rainfall mm
1500
1000
750
500
0

Location of places on climate graphs ●

4 Climate Statistics

Helsinki	Jan	Feb	Mar	Apr	May	Jun	Jul	Aug	Sep	Oct	Nov	Dec
Temperature - max. (°C)	-3	-4	0	6	14	19	22	20	15	8	3	-1
Temperature - min. (°C)	-9	-10	-7	-1	4	9	13	12	8	3	-1	-5
Rainfall - (mm)	56	42	36	44	41	51	51	68	71	73	68	66

Dublin	Jan	Feb	Mar	Apr	May	Jun	Jul	Aug	Sep	Oct	Nov	Dec
Temperature - max. (°C)	8	8	10	13	15	18	20	19	17	14	10	8
Temperature - min. (°C)	1	2	3	4	6	9	11	11	9	6	4	3
Rainfall - (mm)	67	55	51	45	60	57	70	74	72	70	67	74

Munich	Jan	Feb	Mar	Apr	May	Jun	Jul	Aug	Sep	Oct	Nov	Dec
Temperature - max. (°C)	1	3	9	14	18	21	23	23	20	13	7	2
Temperature - min. (°C)	-5	-5	-1	3	7	11	13	12	9	4	0	-4
Rainfall - (mm)	59	53	48	62	109	125	139	107	85	66	57	47

Bucharest	Jan	Feb	Mar	Apr	May	Jun	Jul	Aug	Sep	Oct	Nov	Dec
Temperature - max. (°C)	1	4	10	18	23	27	30	30	25	18	10	4
Temperature - min. (°C)	-7	-5	-1	5	10	14	16	15	11	6	2	-3
Rainfall - (mm)	29	26	28	59	77	121	53	45	45	29	36	27

Seville	Jan	Feb	Mar	Apr	May	Jun	Jul	Aug	Sep	Oct	Nov	Dec
Temperature - max. (°C)	15	17	20	24	27	32	36	36	32	26	20	16
Temperature - min. (°C)	6	7	9	11	13	17	20	20	18	14	10	7
Rainfall - (mm)	66	61	90	57	41	8	1	5	19	70	67	79

Town
Altitude in metres above sea level
Temperature range shows the average daily max. and min.
Average monthly rainfall in mm

Helsinki — Altitude 46 m
Dublin — Altitude 47 m
Munich — Altitude 524 m
Bucharest — Altitude 92 m
Seville — Altitude 9 m

Scale 1 : 40 000 000

0 400 800 1200 1600 km

Conic projectio

1 Population Density

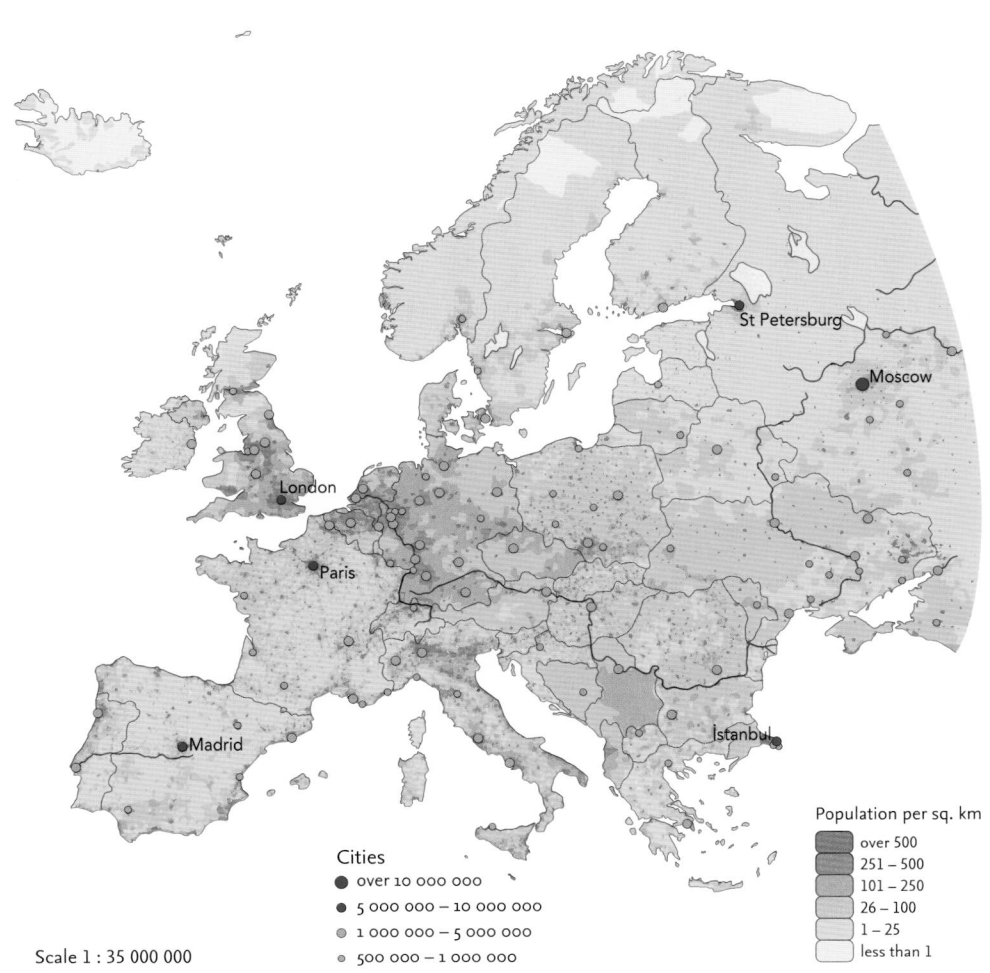

Cities
- ● over 10 000 000
- ● 5 000 000 – 10 000 000
- ○ 1 000 000 – 5 000 000
- ○ 500 000 – 1 000 000

Scale 1 : 35 000 000

Population per sq. km
- over 500
- 251 – 500
- 101 – 250
- 26 – 100
- 1 – 25
- less than 1

2 City Populations

City	Country	Population
Moscow	Russian Federation	10 672 000
Paris	France	9 854 000
İstanbul	Turkey	9 760 000
London	United Kingdom	7 615 000
Essen-Dortmund	Germany	6 566 000
St Petersburg	Russian Federation	5 315 000
Madrid	Spain	5 145 000
Barcelona	Spain	4 424 000
Milan	Italy	4 007 000
Frankfurt am Main	Germany	3 721 000
Berlin	Germany	3 328 000
Dusseldorf	Germany	3 325 000
Athens	Greece	3 238 000
Cologne	Germany	3 084 000
Katowice	Poland	2 914 000
Naples	Italy	2 905 000
Stuttgart	Germany	2 705 000
Hamburg	Germany	2 686 000
Rome	Italy	2 628 000
Kiev	Ukraine	2 623 000
Munich	Germany	2 318 000
Birmingham	United Kingdom	2 215 000
Warsaw	Poland	2 204 000
Manchester	United Kingdom	2 193 000
Vienna	Austria	2 190 000
Lisbon	Portugal	1 977 000
Bucharest	Romania	1 764 000
Stockholm	Sweden	1 729 000
Minsk	Belarus	1 709 000
Budapest	Hungary	1 670 000
Mannheim	Germany	1 625 000

www **EUROSTAT**
europa.eu.int/comm/eurostat
United Nations Population Information Network
www.un.org/popin

3 Population under 15

4 Population 60 and over

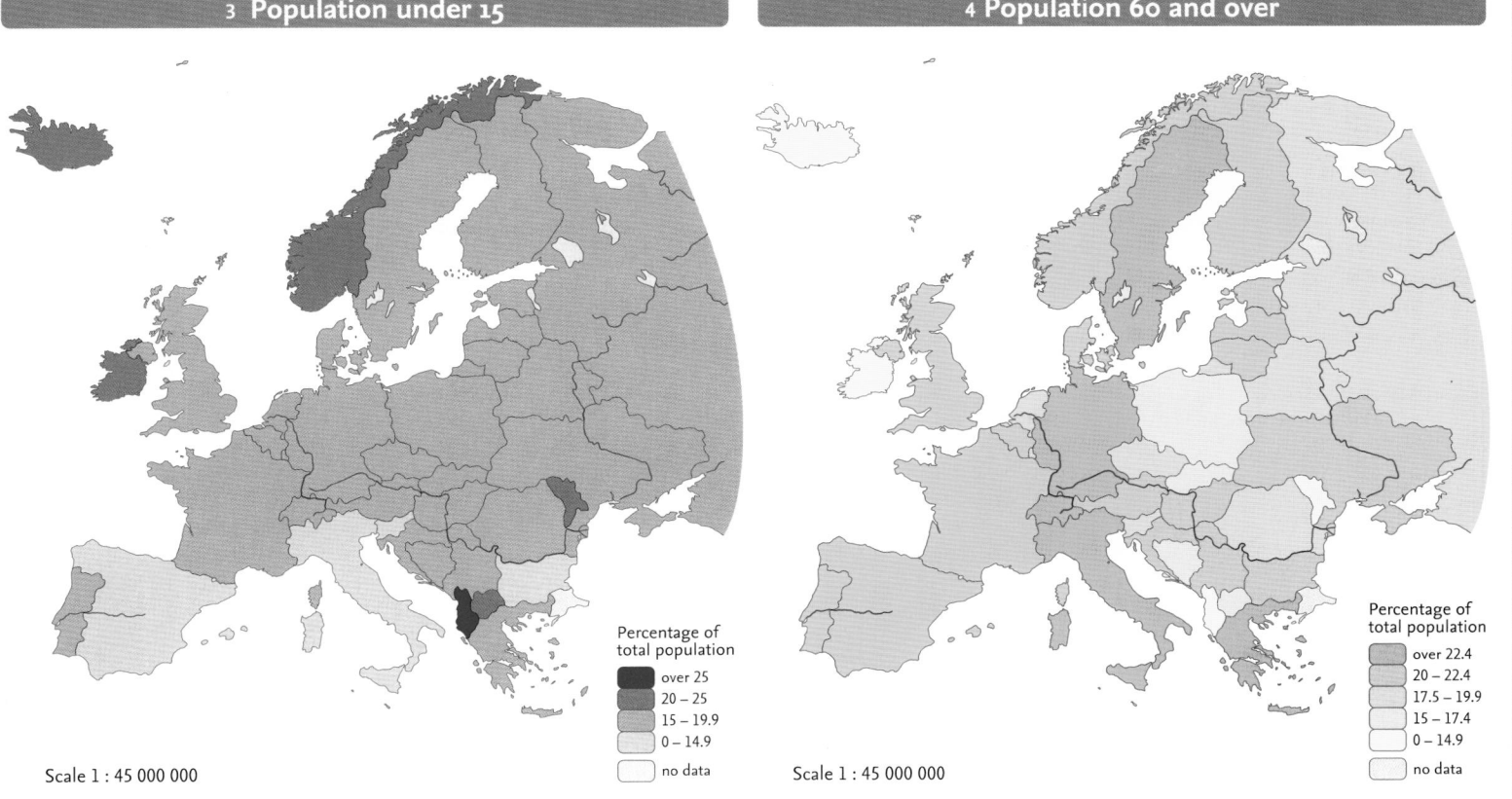

Percentage of total population
- over 25
- 20 – 25
- 15 – 19.9
- 0 – 14.9
- no data

Scale 1 : 45 000 000

Percentage of total population
- over 22.4
- 20 – 22.4
- 17.5 – 19.9
- 15 – 17.4
- 0 – 14.9
- no data

Scale 1 : 45 000 000

Economic Activity

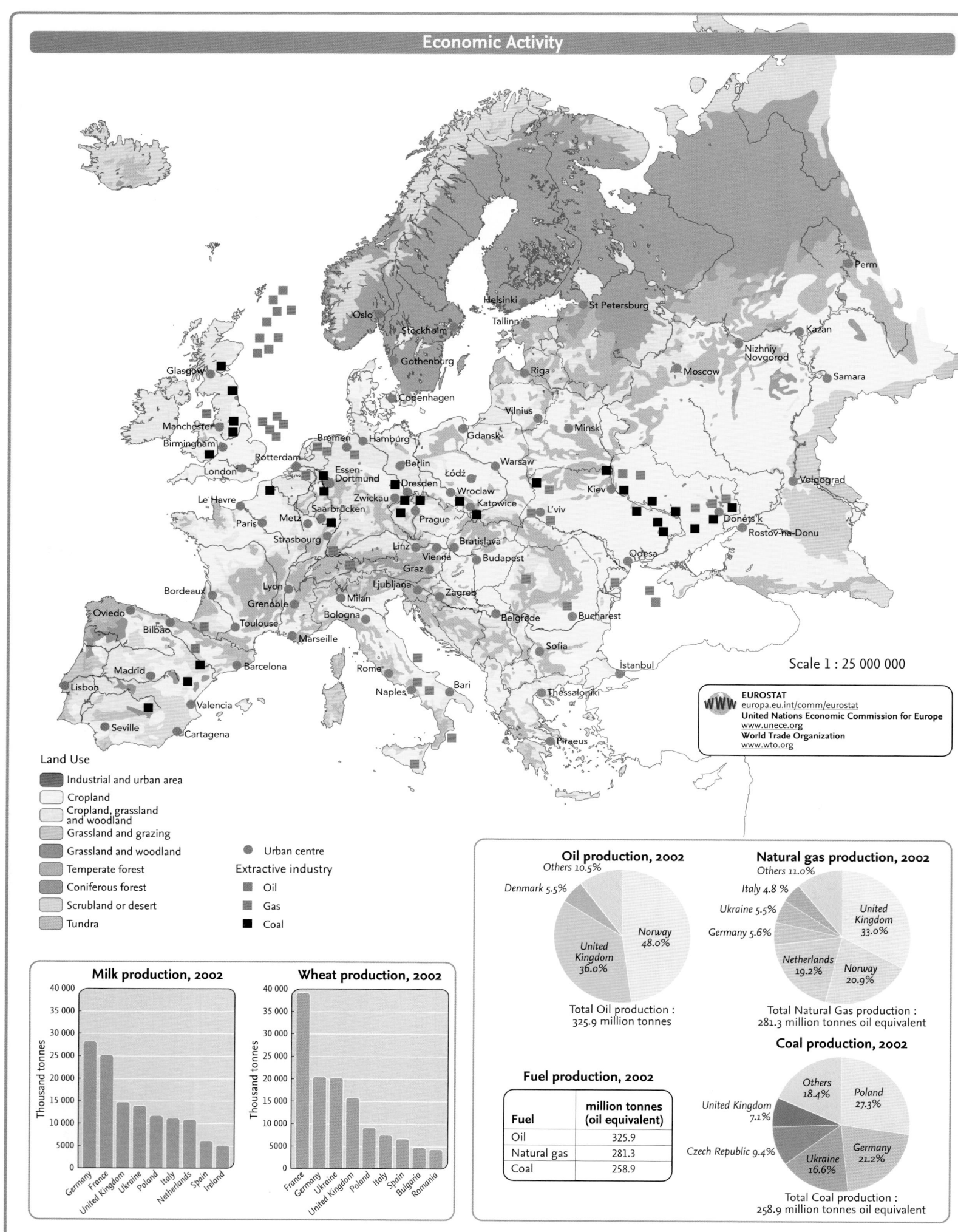

Scale 1 : 25 000 000

WWW EUROSTAT
europa.eu.int/comm/eurostat
United Nations Economic Commission for Europe
www.unece.org
World Trade Organization
www.wto.org

Land Use

- Industrial and urban area
- Cropland
- Cropland, grassland and woodland
- Grassland and grazing
- Grassland and woodland
- Temperate forest
- Coniferous forest
- Scrubland or desert
- Tundra

● Urban centre

Extractive industry
- Oil
- Gas
- Coal

Milk production, 2002

Thousand tonnes (y-axis 0 to 40 000)

Germany, France, United Kingdom, Ukraine, Poland, Italy, Netherlands, Spain, Ireland

Wheat production, 2002

Thousand tonnes (y-axis 0 to 40 000)

France, Germany, Ukraine, United Kingdom, Poland, Italy, Spain, Bulgaria, Romania

Oil production, 2002

- Others 10.5%
- Denmark 5.5%
- United Kingdom 36.0%
- Norway 48.0%

Total Oil production : 325.9 million tonnes

Natural gas production, 2002

- Others 11.0%
- Italy 4.8 %
- Ukraine 5.5%
- Germany 5.6%
- United Kingdom 33.0%
- Netherlands 19.2%
- Norway 20.9%

Total Natural Gas production : 281.3 million tonnes oil equivalent

Coal production, 2002

- Others 18.4%
- Poland 27.3%
- United Kingdom 7.1%
- Germany 21.2%
- Czech Republic 9.4%
- Ukraine 16.6%

Total Coal production : 258.9 million tonnes oil equivalent

Fuel production, 2002

Fuel	million tonnes (oil equivalent)
Oil	325.9
Natural gas	281.3
Coal	258.9

Tourism

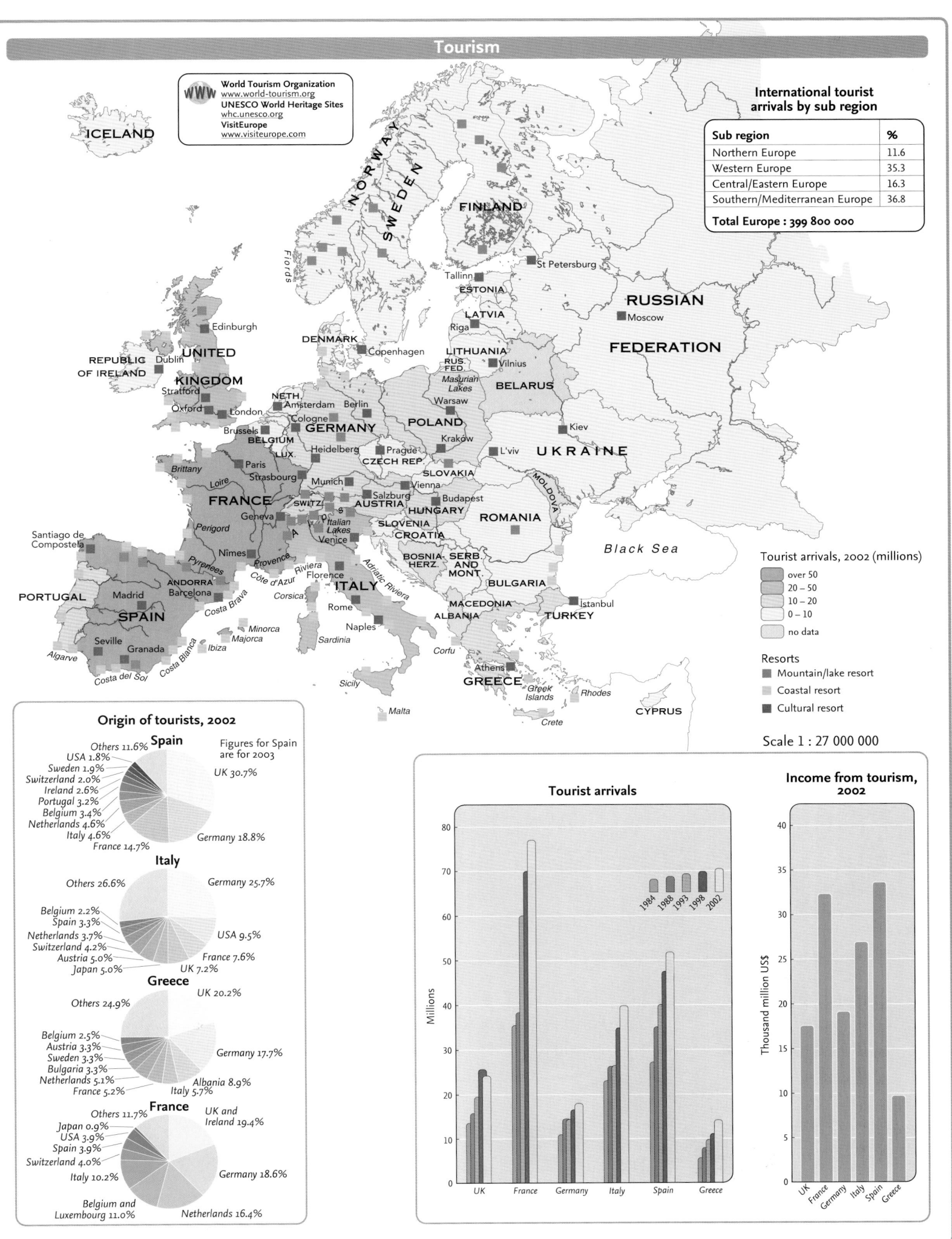

WWW World Tourism Organization
www.world-tourism.org
UNESCO World Heritage Sites
whc.unesco.org
VisitEurope
www.visiteurope.com

International tourist arrivals by sub region

Sub region	%
Northern Europe	11.6
Western Europe	35.3
Central/Eastern Europe	16.3
Southern/Mediterranean Europe	36.8
Total Europe : 399 800 000	

Tourist arrivals, 2002 (millions)
- over 50
- 20 – 50
- 10 – 20
- 0 – 10
- no data

Resorts
- Mountain/lake resort
- Coastal resort
- Cultural resort

Scale 1 : 27 000 000

Origin of tourists, 2002

Spain
Figures for Spain are for 2003
- Others 11.6%
- USA 1.8%
- Sweden 1.9%
- Switzerland 2.0%
- Ireland 2.6%
- Portugal 3.2%
- Belgium 3.4%
- Netherlands 4.6%
- Italy 4.6%
- France 14.7%
- UK 30.7%
- Germany 18.8%

Italy
- Others 26.6%
- Germany 25.7%
- Belgium 2.2%
- Spain 3.3%
- Netherlands 3.7%
- Switzerland 4.2%
- Austria 5.0%
- Japan 5.0%
- USA 9.5%
- France 7.6%
- UK 7.2%

Greece
- Others 24.9%
- UK 20.2%
- Belgium 2.5%
- Austria 3.3%
- Sweden 3.3%
- Bulgaria 3.3%
- Netherlands 5.1%
- France 5.2%
- Germany 17.7%
- Albania 8.9%
- Italy 5.7%

France
- Others 11.7%
- Japan 0.9%
- USA 3.9%
- Spain 3.9%
- Switzerland 4.0%
- Italy 10.2%
- Belgium and Luxembourg 11.0%
- Netherlands 16.4%
- UK and Ireland 19.4%
- Germany 18.6%

Tourist arrivals

(Legend: 1984, 1988, 1993, 1998, 2002)

Millions (axis: 0, 10, 20, 30, 40, 50, 60, 70, 80)
Countries: UK, France, Germany, Italy, Spain, Greece

Income from tourism, 2002

Thousand million US$ (axis: 0, 5, 10, 15, 20, 25, 30, 35, 40)
Countries: UK, France, Germany, Italy, Spain, Greece

ICELAND

Scale 1 : 7 500 000

0   100   200   300 km

Conic Equidistant projection

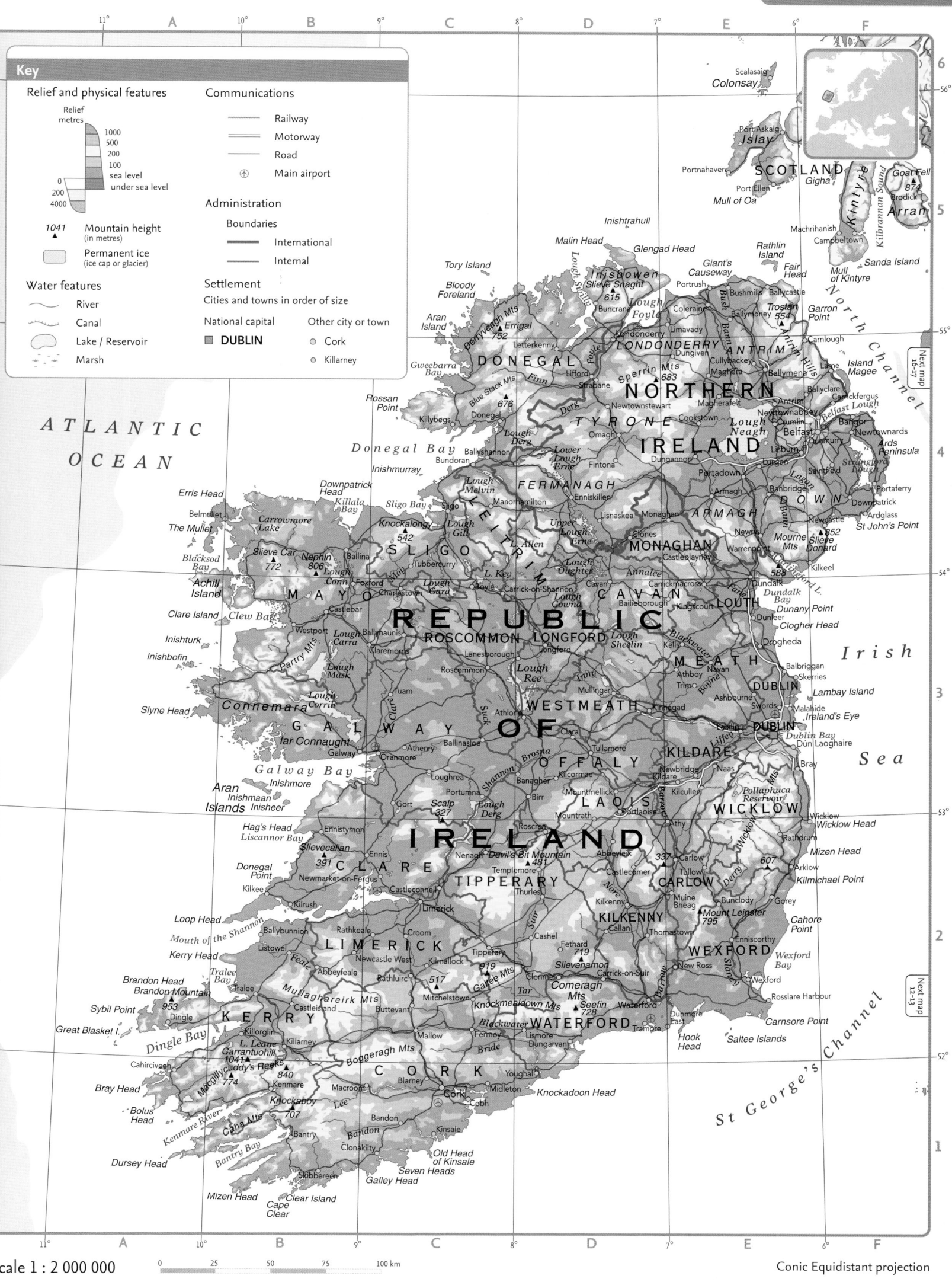

Key

Relief and physical features

Relief metres
1000
500
200
100
0 sea level
under sea level
200
4000

1041 ▲ Mountain height (in metres)

Permanent ice (ice cap or glacier)

Water features

~~~ River

~~~ Canal

Lake / Reservoir

Marsh

Communications

Railway

Motorway

Road

⊕ Main airport

Administration

Boundaries

International

Internal

Settlement

Cities and towns in order of size

National capital ■ DUBLIN

Other city or town
○ Cork
○ Killarney

ATLANTIC OCEAN

SCOTLAND

North Channel

Irish Sea

St George's Channel

REPUBLIC OF IRELAND

NORTHERN IRELAND

Scale 1 : 2 000 000

0 25 50 75 100 km

Conic Equidistant projection

Key

Relief and physical features

Relief metres
5000
3000
2000
1000
500
200
sea level
under sea level
0
200
4000
6000

▲ 818 Mountain height (in metres)

Water features

~ River
Canal
Lake / Reservoir
Marsh

Communications

Railway
Motorway
Road
⊕ Main airport

Administration

Boundaries
International
Internal

Settlement

Cities and towns in order of size

National capital
■ AMSTERDAM
□ THE HAGUE
□ LUXEMBOURG

Other city or town
● Rotterdam
○ Saarbrücken
○ Antwerp
○ Leuven

Scale 1 : 2 000 000

0   20   40   60   80 km

Conic Equidistant projection

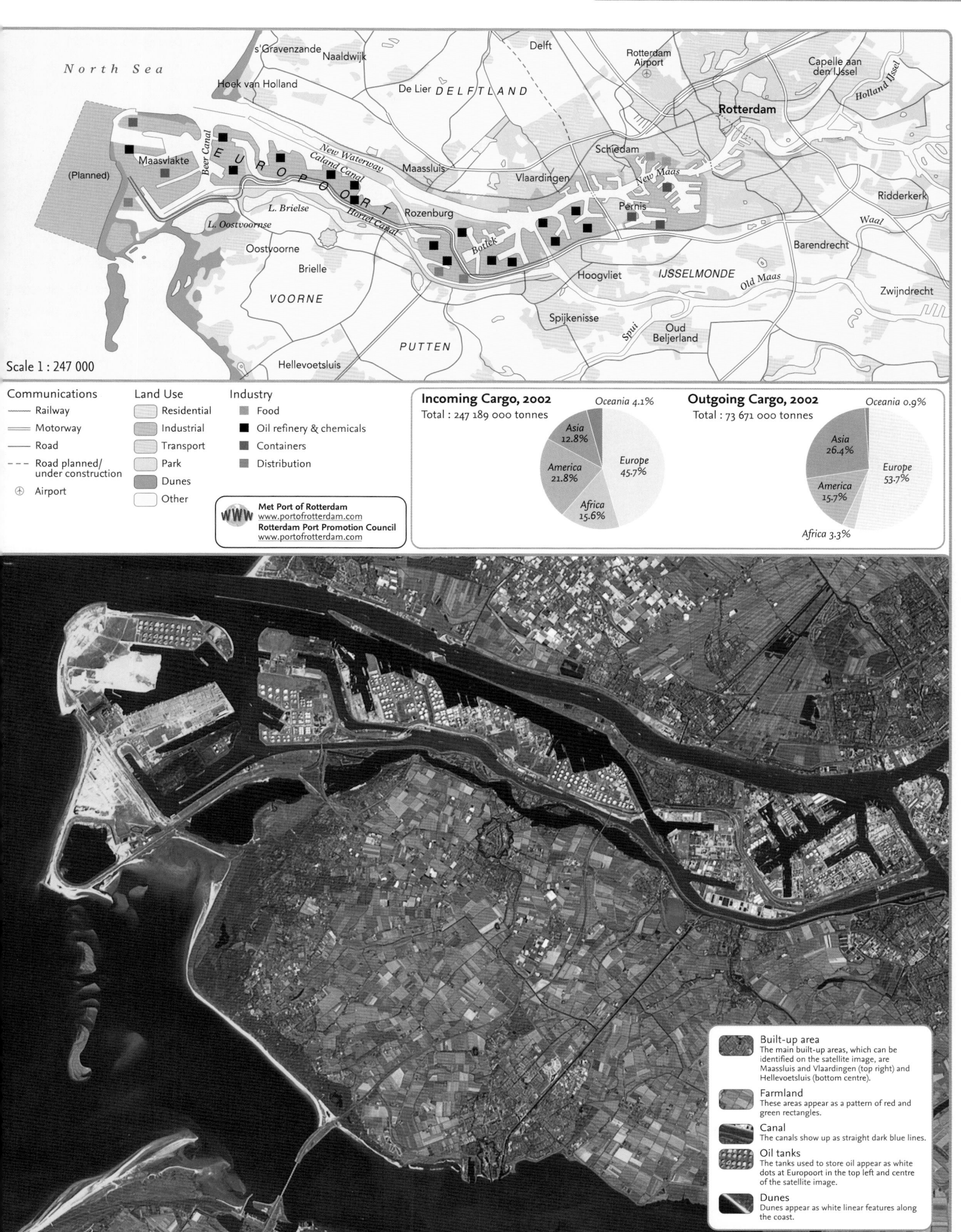

North Sea

s'Gravenzande
Naaldwijk
Delft
Rotterdam Airport
Capelle aan den IJssel
Hoek van Holland
De Lier DELFTLAND
Holland IJssel
Rotterdam
Maasvlakte
Beer Canal
E U R O P O O R T
New Waterway
Caland Canal
Maassluis
Schiedam
Vlaardingen
New Maas
Pernis
Ridderkerk
(Planned)
L. Brielse
Horrel Canal
Rozenburg
Botlek
Hoogvliet
IJSSELMONDE
Old Maas
Waal
Barendrecht
L. Oostvoornse
Oostvoorne
Brielle
VOORNE
Spijkenisse
Spui
Oud Beljerland
Zwijndrecht
PUTTEN
Hellevoetsluis

Scale 1 : 247 000

Communications
— Railway
═ Motorway
— Road
--- Road planned/ under construction
⊕ Airport

Land Use
Residential
Industrial
Transport
Park
Dunes
Other

Industry
Food
Oil refinery & chemicals
Containers
Distribution

Met Port of Rotterdam
www.portofrotterdam.com
Rotterdam Port Promotion Council
www.portofrotterdam.com

Incoming Cargo, 2002
Total : 247 189 000 tonnes

Oceania 4.1%
Asia 12.8%
America 21.8%
Europe 45.7%
Africa 15.6%

Outgoing Cargo, 2002
Total : 73 671 000 tonnes

Oceania 0.9%
Asia 26.4%
America 15.7%
Europe 53.7%
Africa 3.3%

Built-up area
The main built-up areas, which can be identified on the satellite image, are Maassluis and Vlaardingen (top right) and Hellevoetsluis (bottom centre).

Farmland
These areas appear as a pattern of red and green rectangles.

Canal
The canals show up as straight dark blue lines.

Oil tanks
The tanks used to store oil appear as white dots at Europoort in the top left and centre of the satellite image.

Dunes
Dunes appear as white linear features along the coast.

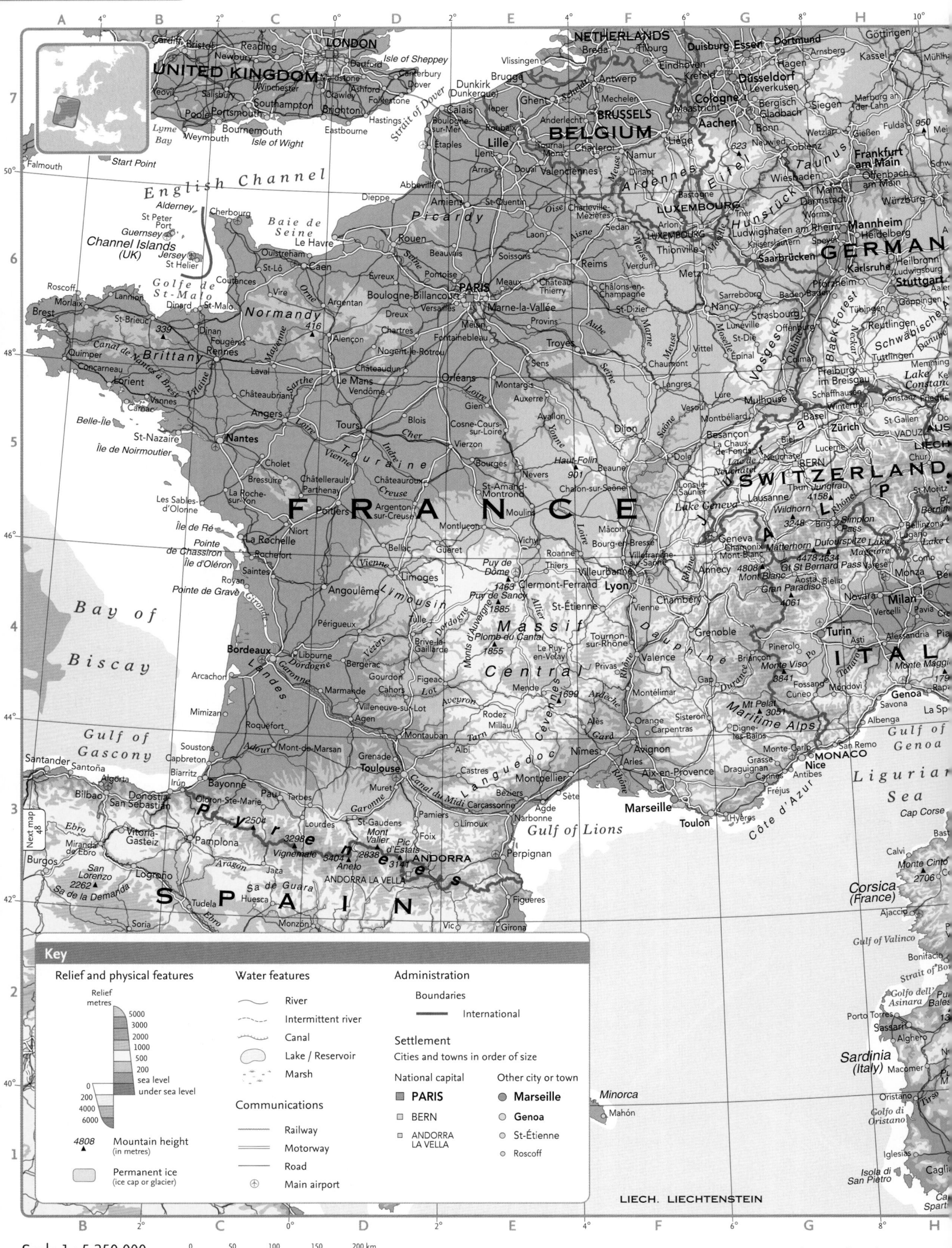

Key

Relief and physical features

Relief metres
5000
3000
2000
1000
500
200
sea level
under sea level
200
4000
6000

▲ 4808 Mountain height (in metres)

Permanent ice (ice cap or glacier)

Water features

∼ River
∼ Intermittent river
∼ Canal
Lake / Reservoir
Marsh

Communications

Railway
Motorway
Road
⊕ Main airport

Administration

Boundaries
—— International

Settlement

Cities and towns in order of size

National capital
■ PARIS
□ BERN
□ ANDORRA LA VELLA

Other city or town
● Marseille
○ Genoa
○ St-Étienne
○ Roscoff

LIECH. LIECHTENSTEIN

Scale 1 : 5 250 000

0   50   100   150   200 km

Lambert Conformal Conic project

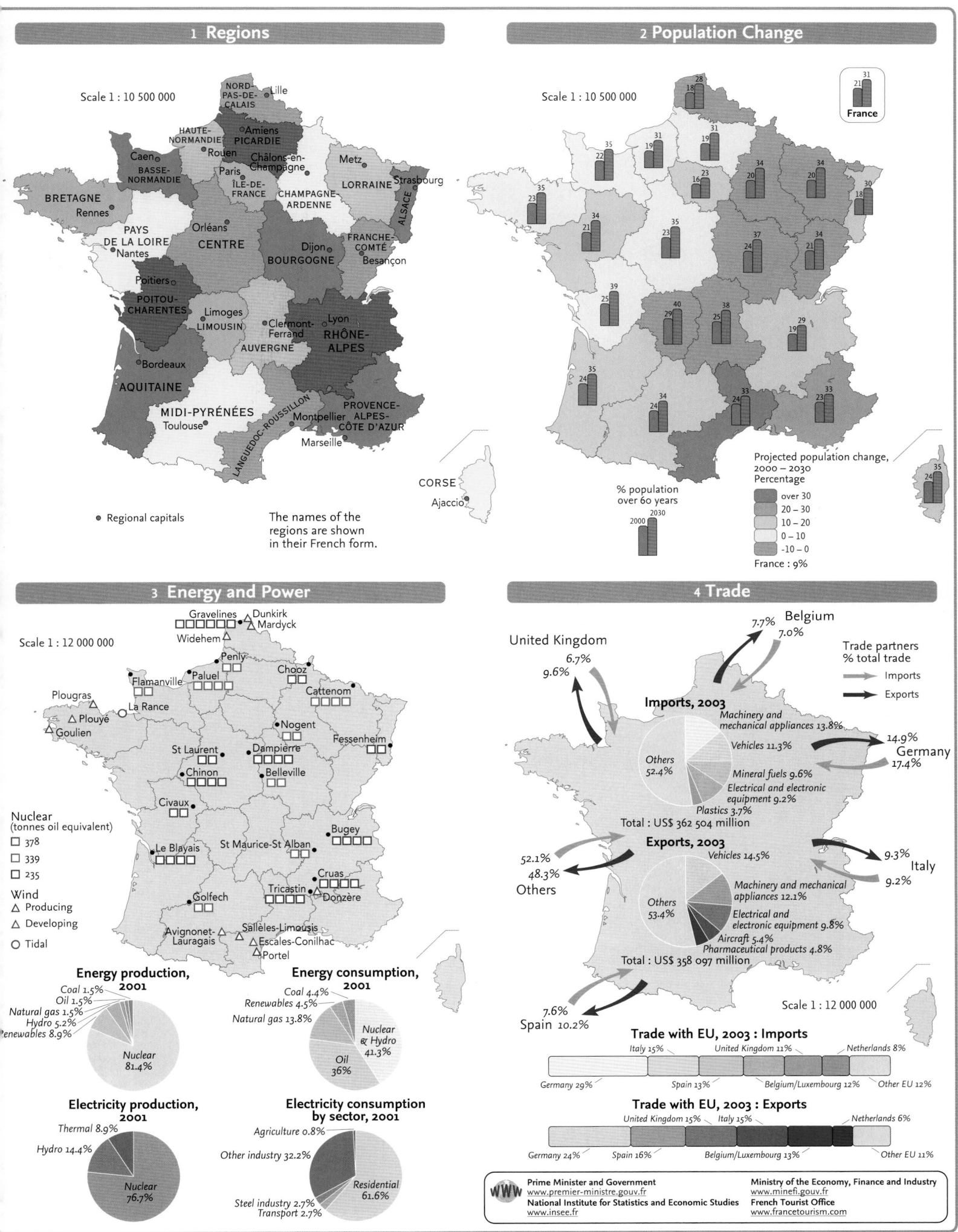

1 Regions

Scale 1 : 10 500 000

NORD-PAS-DE-CALAIS
Lille
HAUTE-NORMANDIE
PICARDIE
Amiens
Caen
Rouen
Châlons-en-Champagne
Metz
BASSE-NORMANDIE
Paris
ÎLE-DE-FRANCE
LORRAINE
Strasbourg
BRETAGNE
Rennes
CHAMPAGNE-ARDENNE
ALSACE
PAYS DE LA LOIRE
Orléans
CENTRE
Dijon
BOURGOGNE
FRANCHE-COMTÉ
Besançon
Nantes
Poitiers
POITOU-CHARENTES
Limoges
LIMOUSIN
Clermont-Ferrand
AUVERGNE
Lyon
RHÔNE-ALPES
Bordeaux
AQUITAINE
MIDI-PYRÉNÉES
Toulouse
LANGUEDOC-ROUSSILLON
Montpellier
PROVENCE-ALPES-CÔTE D'AZUR
Marseille
CORSE
Ajaccio

● Regional capitals

The names of the regions are shown in their French form.

2 Population Change

Scale 1 : 10 500 000

France: 31 / 21

% population over 60 years
2000 / 2030

Projected population change, 2000 – 2030
Percentage
- over 30
- 20 – 30
- 10 – 20
- 0 – 10
- -10 – 0

France : 9%

3 Energy and Power

Scale 1 : 12 000 000

Gravelines
Dunkirk
Mardyck
Widehem
Penly
Chooz
Flamanville
Paluel
Cattenom
Plougras
La Rance
Plouyé
Goulien
Nogent
Fessenheim
St Laurent
Dampierre
Chinon
Belleville
Civaux
Bugey
Le Blayais
St Maurice-St Alban
Cruas
Golfech
Tricastin
Donzère
Avignonet-Lauragais
Sallèles-Limousis
Escales-Conilhac
Portel

Nuclear
(tonnes oil equivalent)
□ 378
□ 339
□ 235

Wind
△ Producing
△ Developing
○ Tidal

Energy production, 2001
Coal 1.5%
Oil 1.5%
Natural gas 1.5%
Hydro 5.2%
Renewables 8.9%
Nuclear 81.4%

Energy consumption, 2001
Coal 4.4%
Renewables 4.5%
Natural gas 13.8%
Nuclear & Hydro 41.3%
Oil 36%

Electricity production, 2001
Thermal 8.9%
Hydro 14.4%
Nuclear 76.7%

Electricity consumption by sector, 2001
Agriculture 0.8%
Other industry 32.2%
Steel industry 2.7%
Transport 2.7%
Residential 61.6%

4 Trade

United Kingdom
6.7%
9.6%

Belgium
7.7%
7.0%

Germany
14.9%
17.4%

Trade partners % total trade
→ Imports
→ Exports

Imports, 2003
Machinery and mechanical appliances 13.8%
Vehicles 11.3%
Mineral fuels 9.6%
Electrical and electronic equipment 9.2%
Plastics 3.7%
Others 52.4%
Total : US$ 362 504 million

Exports, 2003
Vehicles 14.5%
Machinery and mechanical appliances 12.1%
Electrical and electronic equipment 9.8%
Aircraft 5.4%
Pharmaceutical products 4.8%
Others 53.4%
Total : US$ 358 097 million

Others
52.1%
48.3%

Italy
9.3%
9.2%

Spain
7.6%
10.2%

Scale 1 : 12 000 000

Trade with EU, 2003 : Imports
Italy 15%
United Kingdom 11%
Netherlands 8%
Germany 29%
Spain 13%
Belgium/Luxembourg 12%
Other EU 12%

Trade with EU, 2003 : Exports
United Kingdom 15%
Italy 15%
Netherlands 6%
Germany 24%
Spain 16%
Belgium/Luxembourg 13%
Other EU 11%

www
Prime Minister and Government
www.premier-ministre.gouv.fr
National Institute for Statistics and Economic Studies
www.insee.fr

Ministry of the Economy, Finance and Industry
www.minefi.gouv.fr
French Tourist Office
www.francetourism.com

SWEDEN

Hanöbukten

Karlshamn Karlskrona

Baltic Sea

Bornholm
(Denmark) Allinge-Sandvig
Rønne
Neksø

Kap Arkona

Rügen
Stralsund
Grimmen Sassnitz
Greifswald
Wolgast

Demmin

Neubrandenburg
Neustrelitz Pasewalk
Prenzlau Police
Schwedt Szczecin
an der Oder
BERLIN
Frankfurt
an der Oder
Eisenhüttenstadt

GERMANY

Spree

Cottbus
Senftenberg
Hoyerswerda
Bautzen Żary
Meißen
Görlitz
Dresden
Erzgebirge Děčín Liberec
Teplice
Most Ústí nad Labem
Chomutov
Louny Mladá
Boleslav
Kladno Hradec Králové
PRAGUE Pardubice
Beroun
Říčany
Benešov
Sedlčany

CZECH REPUBLIC

Písek
Strakonice
Prachatice Tábor
Jihlava
České
Budějovice
Gmünd Jindřichův Hradec
Horn
Znojmo

Ustka
Słupsk Lębork
Sławno
Koszalin
Trzebiatów
Kołobrzeg
Świnoujście
Wolin Białogard
Gryfice
Nowogard Płoty
Świdwin
Szczecinek
Stargard Szczeciński
Gryfino
Pyrzyce Choszczno
Myślibórz Wałcz
Piła
Gorzów
Wielkopolski Notéć
Kostrzyn Skwierzyna
Świebodzin Obniki
Gniezno
Poznań
Grodzisk
Wielkopolski
Mosina
Zielona
Góra Leszno
Głogów
Bóbr
Polkowice
Lubin
Legnica
Jelenia
Góra Jawor
Gryfów
Śląski Świdnica
Wałbrzych
Wielka Sowa
1015
Trutnov Kłodzko
Paczków
Nysa
Kędzierzyn-Koźle
Opole
Tarnowskie Góry
Bytom
Gliwice
Racibórz Zory
Rybnik Katowice
Bruntál
Opava Jastrzębie-Zdrój
Ostrava
Frýdek-Mistek
Nový
Jičín
Přerov
Blansko
Vyškov Cadca
Žilina
Považská
Bystrica
Martin
Brno Uherské
Hradiště
Břeclav Chřiby Trenčín
Prievidza

SLOVAKIA

Wejherowo
Lębork
Gdynia
Kościerzyna
Wieżyca
328
Starogard
Gdański
Czersk
Chojnice
Świecie
Grudziądz
Chełmno
Bydgoszcz
Toruń
Inowrocław
Oborniki
Września
Konin
Kościan
Jarocin
Krotoszyn
Kalisz
Ostrów
Wielkopolski
Sieradz
Rawicz
Ostrzeszów
Kępno
Kluczbork
Oława
Brzeg
Wrocław
Świdnica
Oleśnica
Wieluń
Radomsko
Częstochowa
Tarnowskie Góry
Zawiercie
Dąbrowa Górnicza
Sosnowiec
Kraków
Bochnia

Władysławowo
Gdańsk
Tczew
Malbork
Elbląg
Starogard
Gdański
Ostróda
Dylewska Góra
312
Brodnica
Działdowo
Mława
Ciechanów
Płock
Kutno
Łowicz
Zgierz
Łódź
Pabianice
Piotrków
Trybunalski
Bełchatów
Tomaszów
Mazowiecki
Radom
Pionki
Skarżysko-Kamienna
Starachowice
Ostrowiec
Świętokrzyski
Kielce
Sandomierz
Tarnobrzeg
Stalowa Wola
Mielec
Tarnów

*Gulf of
Gdańsk* Mys Taran

Zelenograd
Kaliningrad
Baltiysk Pregolya
RUSSIAN FED.
Braniewo
Bartoszyce
Korsze
Olecko
Olsztyn
Szczytno
Nidzica
Łomża

Courland Lagoon

Nica
Skuodas
Salantai
Telšiai
Kretinga
Plungė
Klaipėda Rietavas
Gargždai
Šilalė
Šilutė Tauragė
Sovetsk
Bol'shakovo
Neman
Chernyakhovsk
Gusev
Pravdinsk
Bagrationovsk
Goldap
Węgorzewo
Jeziorо
Dobskie
Ełk Jeziоrо
Śniardwy
Pisz

LITHUANIA

Mažeikiai
Venta Biržai
Radviliškis
Šiauliai Pasvalys
Kelmė
Kėdainiai
Šeduva
Plunge
Jurbarkas
Kybartai Prienai
Marijampolė
Kaunas
Vilkaviškis
Kaišiadorys Trakai
VILNIUS
Alytus
Varėna
Merkys
Druskininkai
Suwałki
Sejny

Kupiškis
Rokiškis
Vyžuona
Panevėžys
Ukmergė
Molėtai
Jonava
Širvintos
Jieznas
Elektrėnai
Šalčininkai
Radun'
Lida

Białystok Vawkavysk
Hrodna
Shchuchyn
Masty Slonim
Sokółka
Augustów

BELARUS

Ostrów Mazowiecka
Siedlce
Biała
Podlaska
Łuków
Lubartów
Lublin
Chełm

WARSAW
Legionowo
Mińsk
Mazowiecki
Pruszków
Skierniewice
Góra
Kalwaria
Warka

POLAND

Zhabinka
Kobryn
Brest
Drahichyn
Ivan
Pripet

Byaroza
Ratne

Marshes
Pripet

Włodawa
Tomaszów
Lubelski
Biłgoraj
Zamość
Lubaczów
Jarosław
Rzeszów
Przemyśl
Jasło
Krosno
Sanok
Nowy Sącz
Gorlice
Nowy Targ
Babia Góra
1722
Gerlachovský štít
2655
Dumbier
2043
Ružomberok Kežmarok
Poprad
Prešov
Košice
Trebišov
Michalovce
Humenné

Volodymyr-Volyn.
Novovolyns'k
Sokal'
Chervonohrad

Zhydachiv
Kalush
Dolyna

Lviv
Horodok
Peremyshlyany
Berezhany
Dniester
Sambir
Drohobych
Stryy
Tarnica
1346 Carpathian
Mountains

UKRAINE

Yavoriv
Kam"yanka-
Buz'ka
Turiys'k

Tokaj
Miskolc
Nyíregyháza
Debrecen
Satu Mare

HUNGARY

Kazincbarcika
Berehove
Mukacheve
Khust
Tisza
Mizhhir"ya
Uzhhorod
Rakhiv
Sighetu
Marmaţiei

Kisújszállás
Karcag
Mezőtúr
Tiszafüred
Törökszentmiklós
Körös
Békés
Gyula
Békéscsaba
Oradea
Aleşd
Körös
Şimleu
Silvaniei
Zalău
Dej
Gherla
Cluj-Napoca
Turda
Baia Mare
Valea
lui Mihai
Carei
Satu Mare

ROMANIA

Vârful
Vlădeasa
1836

Târgu
Mureş

Key

Relief and physical features

Relief
metres
5000
3000
2000
1000
500
200
0 sea level
under sea level
200
4000
6000

▲ 2655 Mountain height
(in metres)

Water features

River
Canal
Lake / Reservoir
Marsh

Communications

Railway
Motorway
Road
⊕ Main airport

Administration

Boundaries
International

Settlement

Cities and towns in order of size

National capital
■ BERLIN
□ VILNIUS

Other city or town
● Katowice
○ Gdańsk
○ Bydgoszcz
○ Leszno

Next map
54-55

Scale 1 : 4 000 000

0   50   100   150   200 km

Lambert Conformal Conic projection

1 Regions

ZACHODNIOPOMORSKIE
Szczecin

Gdańsk
POMORSKIE
WARMIŃSKO-MAZURSKIE
Olsztyn

PODLASKIE
Białystok

Gorzów Wielkopolski
Bydgoszcz
KUJAWSKO-POMORSKIE

LUBUSKIE
Poznań
WIELKOPOLSKIE
MAZOWIECKIE
Warsaw

Łódź
ŁÓDZKIE

DOLNOŚLĄSKIE
Wrocław
Lublin
LUBELSKIE

OPOLSKIE
Opole
ŚLĄSKIE
Kielce
ŚWIĘTOKRZYSKIE

Katowice
Kraków
PODKARPACKIE
Rzeszów
MAŁOPOLSKIE

• Regional capitals

The names of the
regions are shown
in their Polish form.

Scale 1 : 8 000 000

2 Population

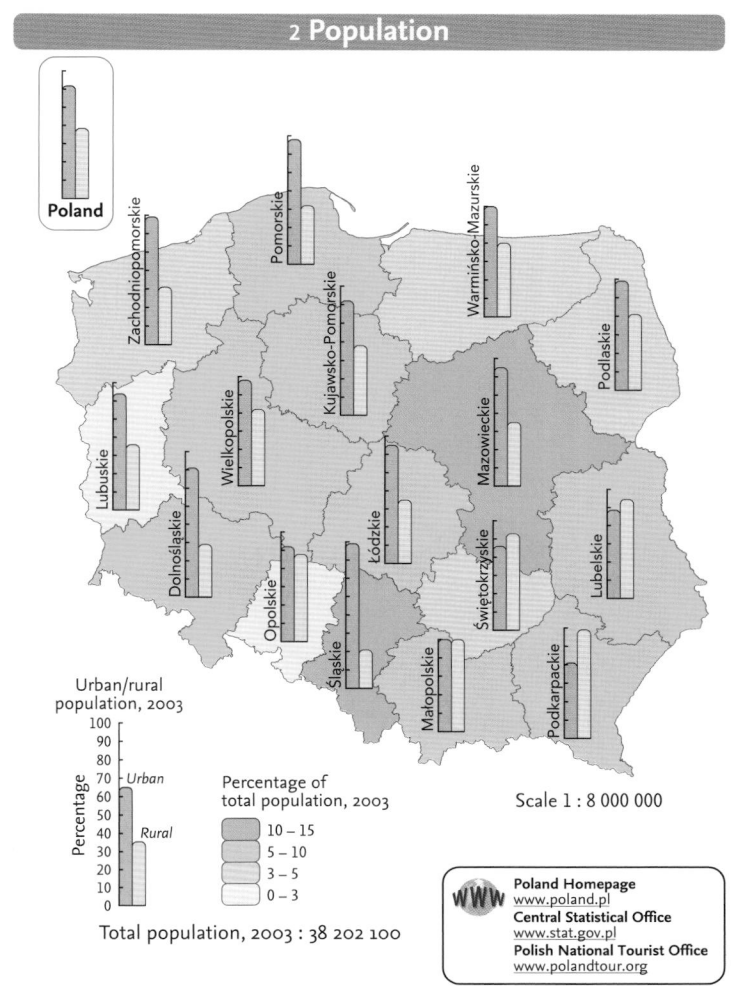

Poland

Zachodniopomorskie
Pomorskie
Warmińsko-Mazurskie
Lubuskie
Wielkopolskie
Kujawsko-Pomorskie
Podlaskie
Dolnośląskie
Łódzkie
Mazowieckie
Opolskie
Świętokrzyskie
Lubelskie
Śląskie
Małopolskie
Podkarpackie

Urban/rural
population, 2003

Urban
Rural

Percentage of
total population, 2003
■ 10 – 15
■ 5 – 10
■ 3 – 5
□ 0 – 3

Scale 1 : 8 000 000

Total population, 2003 : 38 202 100

WWW
Poland Homepage
www.poland.pl
Central Statistical Office
www.stat.gov.pl
Polish National Tourist Office
www.polandtour.org

3 Minerals and Energy

Gdańsk

Szczecin
Olsztyn
Białystok

Bydgoszcz

Gorzów Wielkopolski
Poznań
Warsaw

Łódź

Wrocław
Lublin

Kielce
Opole
Katowice
Kraków
Rzeszów

□ Iron and steel
□ Petroleum refinery products
□ Aluminium
□ Nickel
□ Iron ore
○ Coal
○ Crude petroleum
○ Cement
○ Lead
○ Copper
◇ Zinc
◇ Salt
◇ Phosphate
◇ Natural gas
◎ Processing plant or oil refinery

Scale 1 : 8 000 000

Mineral production, 2002

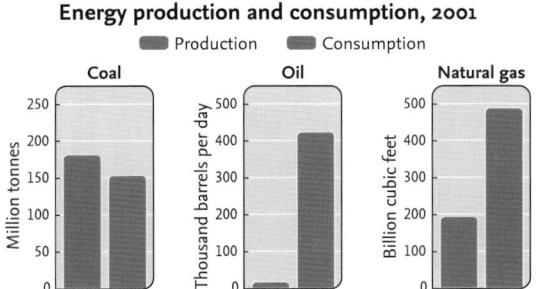

Copper
Zinc
Lead
Aluminium

0   100 200 300 400 500 600
Thousand tonnes

Energy production and consumption, 2001

■ Production   ■ Consumption

Coal
Million tonnes
250
200
150
100
50
0

Oil
Thousand barrels per day
500
400
300
200
100
0

Natural gas
Billion cubic feet
500
400
300
200
100
0

4 Conservation

Slowinski
Wigierski
Wolinski
⑧
Borow Tucholskich
Biebrzanski
Drawienski
Narwianski
④
Ujscie Warty
Bialowieski
Kampinoski ⑤
Wielkopolski
⑦
⑫
Poleski
⑩
⑩
Swietokrzyski
Karkonoski
Roztoczanski ⑥
Stolowe Mountains
Ojcowski
③ ②
⑨ ①
Babiogorski ⑪
Gorczanski
Magurski
Pieninski
Bieszczadzki
Tatrzanski

National parks
▲ Mountain
▲ Highland
▲ Lowland/forest/lake
▲ Coastal

Scale 1 : 8 000 000

World Heritage sites
① Wieliczka Salt Mine
② Cracow's Historic Centre
③ Auschwitz Concentration Camp
④ Belovezhskaya Pushcha / Bialowieza Forest
⑤ Historic Centre of Warsaw
⑥ Old City of Zamosc
⑦ Medieval Town of Torun
⑧ Castle of the Teutonic Order in Malbork
⑨ Kalwaria Zebrzydowska: the Mannerist Architectural and Park Landscape Complex and Pilgrimage Park
⑩ Churches of Peace in Jawor and Swidnica
⑪ Wooden Churches of Southern Little Poland
⑫ Muskauer Park / Park Muzakowski

Key

Relief and physical features

Relief
metres
5000
3000
2000
1000
500
200
sea level
0
under sea level
200
4000
6000

▲ 3482 Mountain height (in metres)

Water features

~ River
- - - Intermittent river
Canal
Lake / Reservoir
Marsh

Communications

Railway
Motorway
Road
⊕ Main airport

Administration

Boundaries
International

Settlement
Cities and towns in order of size

National capital
■ **MADRID**
□ ANDORRA LA VELLA

Other city or town
● **Barcelona**
○ **Seville**
○ Pamplona
○ Benidorm

Bay of Biscay

Gulf of Gascony

FRANCE

Mimizan Roquefort Montauban Tarn Albi
Soustons Mont-de-Marsan Grenade Toulouse Castres Montp
Capbreton Adour Muret Canal du Midi Béziers
Biarritz Bayonne Pau Tarbes Garonne Carcassonne Nar
Irún Oloron-Ste-Marie St-Gaudens Limoux Gul
Donostia San Sebastián Pamplona Lourdes Foix li Li
2504 Mont Valier Pic Pamiers
Vignemale d'Estats Perpignan
3298 3404 3141 **ANDORRA**
Jaca Aneto **ANDORRA LA VELLA**
Aragón Sa de Guara Figuer
Huesca Girona

A Coruña Ferrol Cervo
Cape Finisterre Betanzos Luarca Avilés Gijón-Xixón Llanes Santander Santoña Algorta Bilbao Vitoria-Gasteiz
Lugo Becerrea Oviedo Infiesto Picos de Europa 2081 2648 Reinosa Aguilar de Campóo Miranda de Ebro Logroño
Santiago de Compostela Sarria Cantabrian Mts Espigüete 2450 Ebro
Monforte de Lemos 2117 León San Lorenzo Sa de la Demanda
Vilagarcía de Arousa Ponferrada Astorga Esla Pisuerga Burgos 2262 Soria
Pontevedra Ourense Sa de la Cabrera Palencia Aranda de Duero Tudela
Vigo A Cañiza Sil Benavente Duero Calatayud
Tui 1415 Verín Bragança Zamora Valladolid Sigüenza Monzón
Viana do Castelo Braga Mirandela Macedo de Cavaleiros Tordesillas Segovia Calamocha Alcañiz 1201 Reus
Vila Real Douro Embalse de Almendra Medina del Campo Sa de Guadarrama Henares Serranía de Cuenca Tortosa
Oporto Lamego Salamanca Peñaranda de Bracamonte 2430 Peñalara 1920 Caimodorro Golf de Sant Jordi
Aveiro Viseu Guarda Ciudad Rodrigo Béjar Ávila **MADRID** Alcalá de Henares Guadalajara Cuenca 2020 Castelló de la Plana
Coimbra 1205 Sa da Estrela 1993 Fuenlabrada Arganda **SPAIN** Segorbe
Figueira da Foz Cáceres 1601 Sierra de Gredos Almanzor Navalmoral de la Mata Talavera de la Reina Tarancón Turia **Valencia**
Pombal Covilhã Plasencia 2592 Toledo Alcázar de San Juan Utiel Júcar Cullera
Caldas da Rainha Sierra de Guadalupe Corral de Cantos 1420 Villarrobledo Gandía Cabo de la Nao
Torres Vedras Santarém Valencia de Alcántara Las Villuercas Montes de Toledo Ciudad Real Tomelloso **Albacete** Almansa Alcoy-Alcoi
Portalegre Embalse de García Sola Guadiana Manzanares La Mancha Villena Benidorm
Amadora Elvas Mérida Don Benito Valdepeñas Hellín Elda Alicante
LISBON Badajoz Jabalón Puertollano Elche-Elx
C. da Roca Setúbal Zafra Pozoblanco Estrella 1300 Segura 1897 Caravaca de la Cruz Costa Blanca
Baía de Setúbal Sado Llerena Sierra Morena Linares Sierra de Segura La Sagra 2832 Murcia Torrevieja *Mediterranean Sea*
Sines Grândola Tentudia 1104 Córdoba Andújar Úbeda Lorca Cartagena
Beja Sa de Aracena Guadalquivir Jaén Cabo de Palos
Aljustrel Cortegana Guadajoz Alcalá la Real Baza Huércal-Overa
Castro Verde La Palma del Condado Écija Lucena Guadix Águilas Vera
Almodôvar Mértola Huelva **Seville** Puente Genil Osuna Granada Loja Sierra Nevada Almería
Lagos Algarve Las Marismas Utrera Morón de la Frontera Antequera Mulhacén 3482 Cabo de Gata
Sagres Portimão Tavira Sanlúcar de Barrameda Vélez-Málaga Motril Almuñécar
Cabo de São Vicente Faro *Golfo de Cádiz* Jerez de la Frontera Ronda Málaga Torremolinos
Cádiz El Puerto de Santa María Marbella Costa del Sol
San Fernando La Línea de la Concepción Gibraltar (UK)
Cabo Trafalgar Algeciras Strait of Gibraltar Punta Almina (Sp.) Ceuta I. de Alborán (Spain)
Tangier Cabo Negro
Asilah Tétouan **MOROCCO** Al Hoceima Melilla (Sp.)
Larache Tiztoutine
Souk el Arbaâ du Rharb Aknoul Saka Taourirt
Oued Beht Had Kourt Bab Termas 880 Next map 84-85 Taourirt

Canary Islands inset

Roque de los Muchachos 2426 Santa Cruz de la Palma
La Palma San Cristóbal de la Laguna *Tenerife* *Fuerteventura*
La Gomera Pico del Teide Santa Cruz de Tenerife Las Palmas de Gran Canaria Jandía 807
1487 3718 Pico de las Nieves Pta Pesebre
El Hierro 1500 San Sebastián de la Gomera Puerto del Rosario 724
Malpaso Puerto de la Estaca 1949 *Gran Canaria* Gran Tarajal
18° W 16° X Y 14° Z
Canary Islands Lanzarote 670 Arrieta
Playa Blanca Arreci
ALGIE Tipasa Cherchell Blid
Tipasa

Minorca inset

G 4° H
Minorca 40°
Ciutadella de Menorca Mahó

Balearic Islands

Balearic Islands Majorca 1445
Palma de Mallorca Man
Puig Major Ale
Ibiza Ibiza Formentera *Golfo de Valencia*

Scale 1 : 5 250 000

0 50 100 150 200 km

Lambert Conformal Conic projection

1 Regions

Santiago de Compostela
Oviedo
ASTURIAS
CANTABRIA
Santander
PAÍS VASCO
Pamplona
GALICIA
Vitoria-Gasteiz
NAVARRA
Logroño
LA RIOJA
CASTILLA Y LEÓN
Zaragoza
CATALUÑA
Valladolid
ARAGÓN
Barcelona
MADRID
ILLES BALEARS
Madrid
Toledo
CASTILLA-LA MANCHA
VALENCIA
Palma de Mallorca
EXTREMADURA
Valencia
Mérida
Murcia
MURCIA
ANDALUCÍA
Seville

Scale 1 : 12 000 000

ISLAS CANARIAS
Santa Cruz de Tenerife
Las Palmas de Gran Canaria

• Regional capitals

The names of the regions are shown in their Spanish form.

2 Population Change and Internal Migration

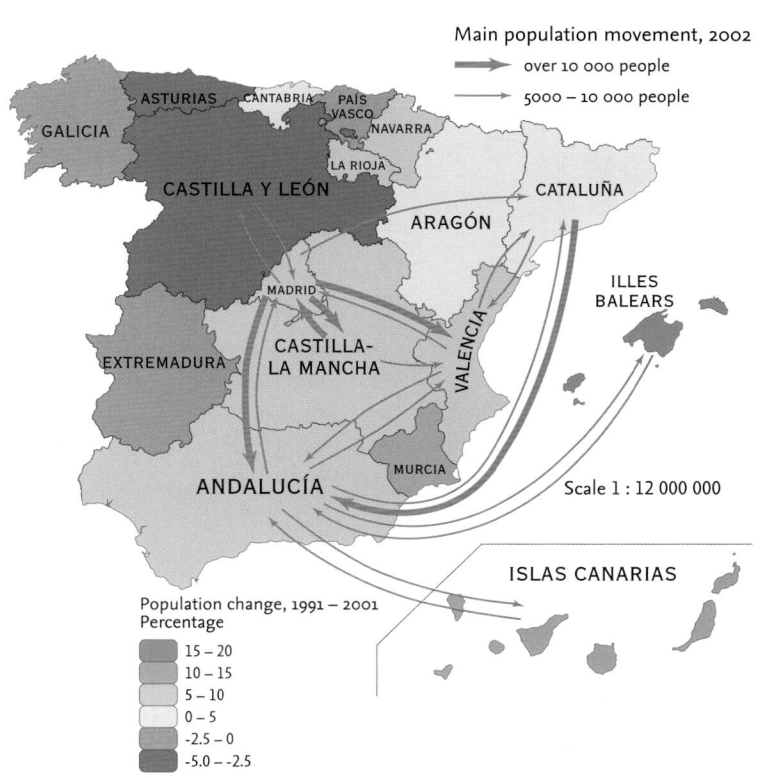

Main population movement, 2002
→ over 10 000 people
→ 5000 – 10 000 people

GALICIA
ASTURIAS
CANTABRIA
PAÍS VASCO
NAVARRA
LA RIOJA
CASTILLA Y LEÓN
CATALUÑA
ARAGÓN
MADRID
ILLES BALEARS
CASTILLA-LA MANCHA
VALENCIA
EXTREMADURA
MURCIA
ANDALUCÍA

Scale 1 : 12 000 000

ISLAS CANARIAS

Population change, 1991 – 2001
Percentage
15 – 20
10 – 15
5 – 10
0 – 5
-2.5 – 0
-5.0 – -2.5

3 Tourism

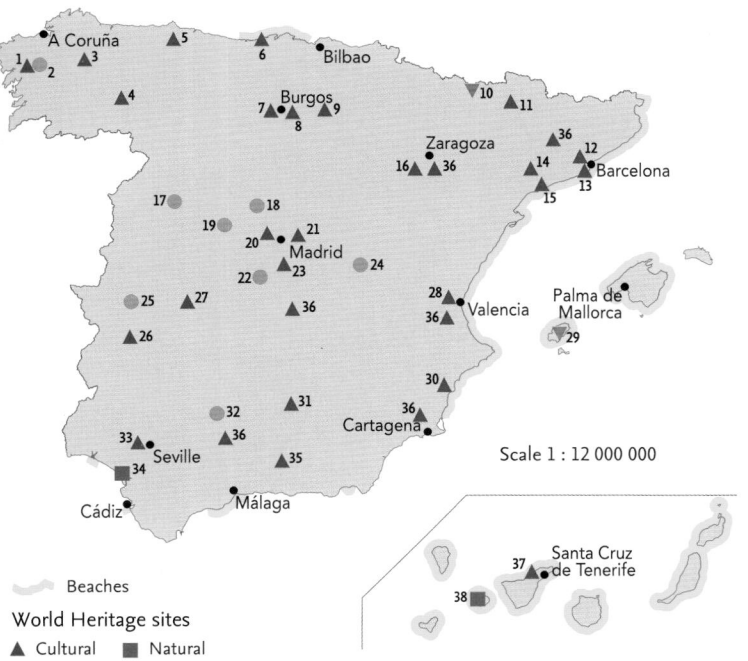

A Coruña
1 2 3 5
6 Bilbao
4
7 Burgos 9
8
10 11
Zaragoza
16 36 36 14 12
Barcelona
15 13
17 18
19
20 21
Madrid 24
22 23
25 27
28
36 Valencia
26
Palma de Mallorca
30 29
32 31
36 Cartagena
33 36
Seville 35
34
Cádiz Málaga

Scale 1 : 12 000 000

Santa Cruz de Tenerife
37
38

Beaches

World Heritage sites
▲ Cultural   ■ Natural
● City   ▽ Mixed

1   The Route of Santiago de Compostela
2   Santiago de Compostela (Old Town)
3   Roman Walls of Lugo
4   Las Médulas
5   Churches of the Kingdom of the Asturias
6   Altamira Cave
7   Burgos Cathedral
8   Archaeological Site of Atapuerca
9   San Millan Yuso and Suso Monasteries
10 Pyrenees - Mount Perdu
11 Catalan Romanesque Churches of the Vall de Boi
12 Parque Guell, Palacio Guell and Casa Mila, Barcelona
13 The Palau de la Musica Catalana and the Hospital de Sant Pau, Barcelona
14 Poblet Monastery
15 The archaeological ensemble of Tarraco
16 Mudejar Architecture of Aragón
17 Old City of Salamanca
18 Old Town of Segovia, including its aqueduct
19 Old Town of Ávila, including its Extra Muros churches

20 Monastery and Site of the Escorial, Madrid
21 University and Historic Precinct of Alcalá de Henares
22 Historic City of Toledo
23 Aranjuez Cultural Landscape
24 Historic Walled Town of Cuenca
25 Old Town of Cáceres
26 Archaeological Ensemble of Mérida
27 Royal Monastery of Santa Maria de Guadalupe
28 "La Lonja de la Seda" of Valencia
29 Ibiza, Biodiversity and Culture
30 The Palmeral of Elche
31 Renaissance Monumental Ensembles of Úbeda and Baeza
32 Mosque of Córdoba
33 Cathedral, the Alcazar and Archivo de Indias, Seville
34 Doñana National Park
35 Alhambra, Generalife and Albayzin, Granada
36 Rock-Art of the Mediterranean Basin on the Iberian Peninsula
37 San Cristóbal de la Laguna
38 Garajonay National Park

4 Water Management

Oviedo
Santander
I I
III
II Valladolid
Duero Ebro Zaragoza
Barcelona
Madrid
Tagus IV IX
Toledo Guadiana Júcar Valencia
V
Segura
VIII Murcia
Guadalquivir VI
Seville VII
Málaga
X
XI

Scale 1 : 12 000 000

▽ Dam
〜 River basin boundary

☐ River basins
I   Northern Basins
II   Duero Basin
III Ebro Basin
IV   Tagus Basin
V   Guadiana Basin
VI   Guadalquivir Basin

VII   Southern Basins
VIII Segura Basin
IX   Júcar Basin
X   La Palma
XI   Las Palmas

☐ Other areas

Government
www.la-moncloa.es
National Statistical Institute
www.ine.es
Tourism Studies Institute
www.iet.tourspain.es

Key

Administration

Boundaries

——— International

Settlement
Cities and towns in order of size

National capital		Other city or tow
ROME		Milan
SARAJEVO		Genoa
BERN		Venice
SAN MARINO		Ragusa

Key

Relief and physical features

Relief
metres

5000
3000
2000
1000
500
200
sea level
under sea level
200
4000
6000

▲ 4808 Mountain height
(in metres)

Permanent ice
(ice cap or glacier)

Water features

River

Canal

Lake / Reservoir

Communications

Railway

Motorway

Road

⊕ Main airport

Scale 1 : 5 250 000

0   50   100   150   200 km

Lambert Conformal Conic project

1 Regions

VALLE D'AOSTA
Aosta
Turin
PIEMONTE
LOMBARDIA
Milan
LIGURIA
Genoa
TRENTINO-ALTO ADIGE
Bolzano
VENETO
Venice
FRIULI-VENEZIA GIULIA
Trieste
EMILIA-ROMAGNA
Bologna
Florence
TOSCANA
Ancona
MARCHE
Perugia
UMBRIA
L'Aquila
ABRUZZO
LAZIO
Rome
MOLISE
Campobasso
CAMPANIA
Naples
PUGLIA
Bari
Potenza
BASILICATA
SARDEGNA
Cagliari
CALABRIA
Catanzaro
Palermo
SICILIA

• Regional capitals

The names of the regions are shown in their Italian form.

Scale 1 : 10 500 000

National Institute of Statistics
www.istat.it
Italian State Tourism Board
www.enit.it
USGS Volcano Hazards Program
volcanoes.usgs.gov
USGS National Earthquake Information Center
wwwneic.cr.usgs.gov

2 Regional Comparisons

Area
N S
Thousand sq. km
125
100
75
50
25
0

Land surface
North
35% Mountain
19% Hill
46% Plain
South
18% Mountain
53% Hill
29% Plain

Mountain
Hill
Plain

Population
N S
Millions
30
25
20
15
10
5
0

Population density
N S
People per sq. km
300
250
200
150
100
50
0

Natural population change
N S
Percentage
2.0
1.5
1.0
0.5
0
-0.5
-1.0
-1.5

VALLE D'AOSTA
PIEMONTE
LOMBARDIA
TRENTINO-ALTO ADIGE
FRIULI-VENEZIA GIULIA
VENETO
NORTH
EMILIA-ROMAGNA
LIGURIA
TOSCANA
MARCHE
UMBRIA
LAZIO
ABRUZZO
MOLISE
CAMPANIA
PUGLIA
SOUTH
BASILICATA
SARDEGNA
CALABRIA
SICILIA

Urban population
North
16.3%
83.7%
South
26.5%
73.5%

Urban
Rural

Scale 1 : 12 500 000

Birth rate
N S
Per 1000 people
12
10
8
6
4
2
0

Death rate
N S
Per 1000 people
12
10
8
6
4
2
0

Hospital beds
N S
Per 1000 people
5
4
3
2
1
0

Infant mortality rate
N S
Per 1000 people
8
6
4
2
0

Employment by sector
North
3.6%
59.1% 37.3%
South
9.2%
66.6% 24.2%

Agriculture
Industry
Services

Unemployment rate
N S
Percentage
20
15
10
5
0

GDP
N S
Billion Euros
700
600
500
400
300
200
100
0

3 Earthquakes and Volcanoes

Friuli 1976
Colli Euganei
Larderello
Monte Amiata
Monti Volsini
Avezzano 1915
Colli Albani
Roccamonfina
Campi Flegrei
Ischia
Monte Somma, Vesuvius
Campania & Basilicata 1980
Calabria 1905
Ustica
Stromboli
Lipari
Vulcano
Messina 1908
Mount Etna
Pantelleria

Volcanic rocks
Principal fault line

Volcanoes
△ Eruptive
◆ Sulphuric
▣ Fumaroles
▽ Submarine
● Major earthquake since 1900 greater than magnitude 6.5

Scale 1 : 10 500 000

4 Vesuvius Satellite Image

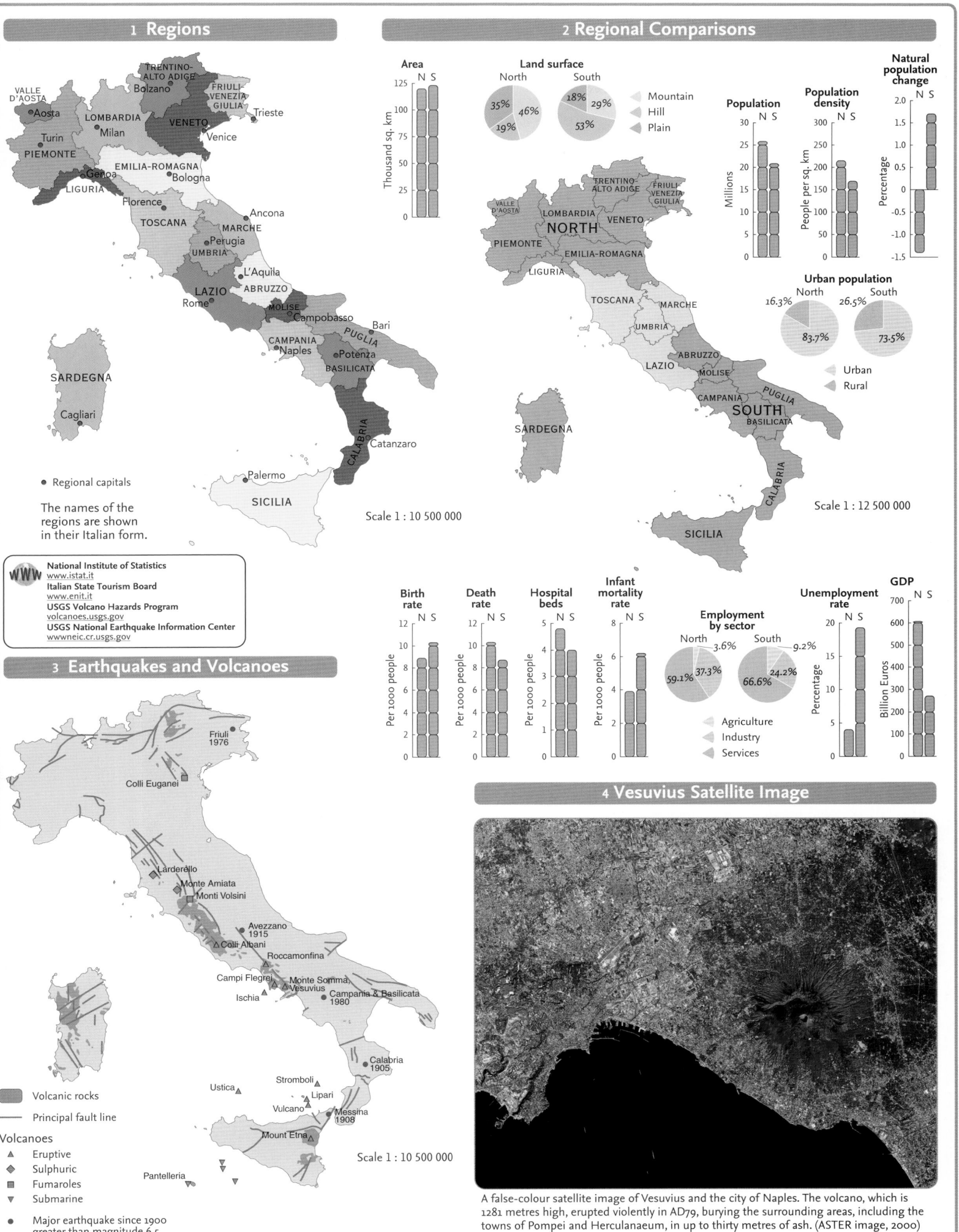

A false-colour satellite image of Vesuvius and the city of Naples. The volcano, which is 1281 metres high, erupted violently in AD79, burying the surrounding areas, including the towns of Pompei and Herculanaeum, in up to thirty metres of ash. (ASTER image, 2000)

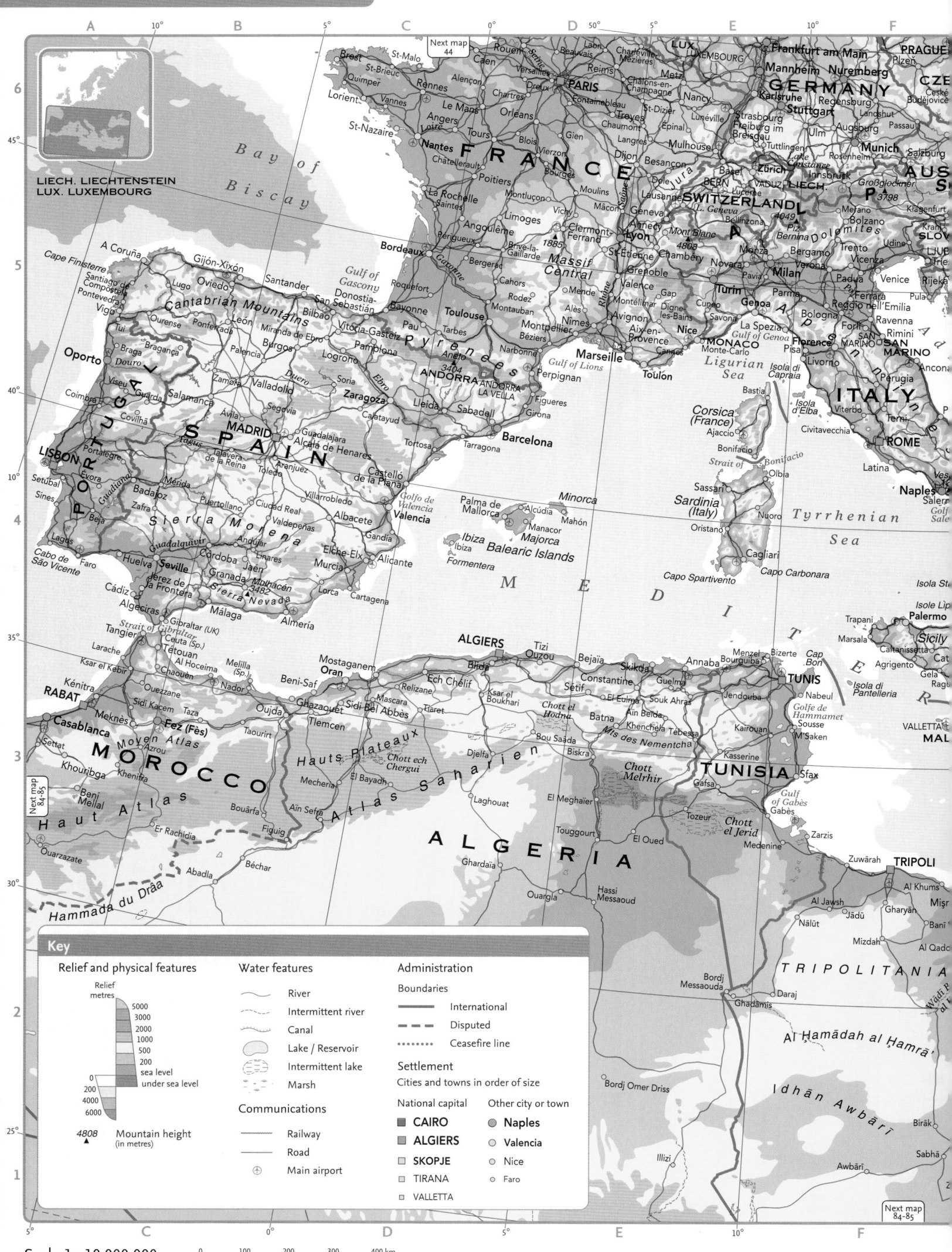

LIECH. LIECHTENSTEIN
LUX. LUXEMBOURG

Bay of Biscay

FRANCE

GERMANY

PORTUGAL

SPAIN

MADRID

LISBON

MOROCCO

ALGERIA

TUNISIA

TRIPOLITANIA

Next map 44

Next map 84-85

Next map 84-85

Key

Relief and physical features

Relief
metres

5000
3000
2000
1000
500
200
sea level
under sea level
0
200
4000
6000

▲ 4808   Mountain height
(in metres)

Water features

〰 River

〰 Intermittent river

Canal

Lake / Reservoir

Intermittent lake

Marsh

Communications

Railway

Road

⊕ Main airport

Administration

Boundaries

International

Disputed

Ceasefire line

Settlement

Cities and towns in order of size

National capital

■ **CAIRO**

■ **ALGIERS**

□ SKOPJE

□ TIRANA

□ VALLETTA

Other city or town

● Naples

◉ Valencia

○ Nice

○ Faro

Scale 1 : 10 000 000

0   100   200   300   400 km

Conic Equidistant projection

Scale 1 : 5 000 000

0   50   100   150   200 km

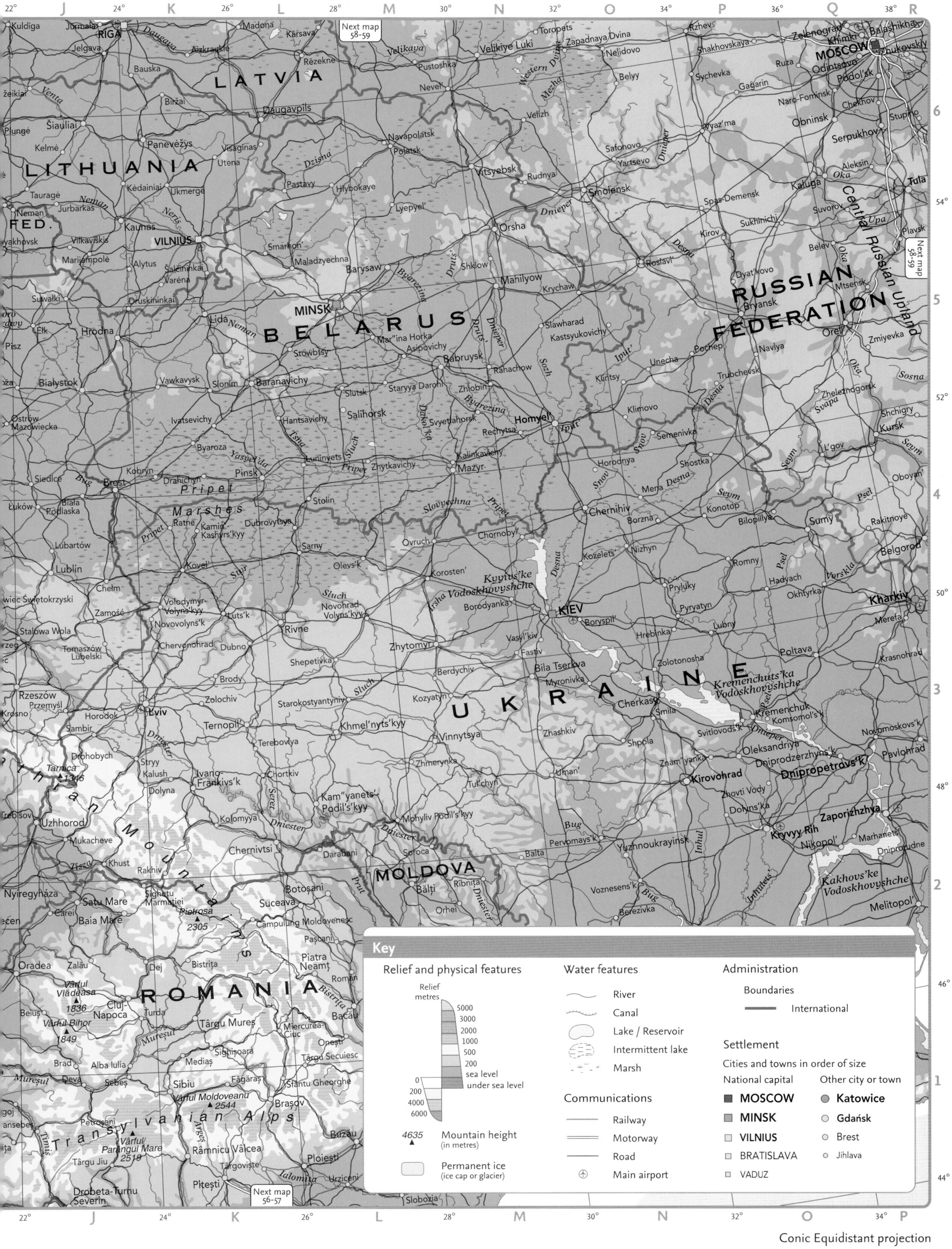

LATVIA

LITHUANIA

RUSSIAN FED.

BELARUS

MINSK

RUSSIAN FEDERATION

Central Russian Upland

UKRAINE

KIEV

Kharkiv

MOLDOVA

ROMANIA

Transylvanian Alps

Carpathian Mountains

Pripet Marshes

MOSCOW

Riga

Vilnius

Toropets

Velikiye Luki

Zapadnaya Dvina

Nelidovo

Belyy

Rzhev

Shakhovskaya

Zelenograd

Balashikha

Zhukovskiy

Odintsovo

Podol'sk

Khimki

Ruza

Gagarin

Naro-Fominsk

Chekhov

Stupino

Obninsk

Serpukhov

Aleksin

Tula

Plavsk

Jūrmala

Jelgava

Bauska

Aizkraukle

Madona

Kārsava

Rēzekne

Pustoshka

Nevel

Velizh

Vitsyebsk

Rudnya

Smolensk

Safonovo

Yartsevo

Vyaz'ma

Spas-Demensk

Sukhinichi

Kirov

Suvorov

Belev

Upa

Oka

Mtsensk

Orel

Zmiyevka

žeikiai

Plungė

Kelmė

Šiauliai

Panevėžys

Biržai

Visaginas

Utena

Daugavpils

Polatsk

Navapolatsk

Dzisna

Hlybokaye

Lyepyel'

Pastavy

Tauragė

Jurbarkas

Kaunas

Kėdainiai

Ukmergė

Vilnius

Smarhon'

Maladzyechna

Barysaw

Smilavichy

Mahilyow

Shklow

Orsha

Druts'

Dnieper

Desna

Bryansk

Navlya

Dyat'kovo

Trubchevsk

Pochep

Unecha

Klintsy

Klimovo

Semenivka

Shostka

Zhelznogorsk

Kursk

Svapa

Shchigry

L'gov

Oboyan'

Sosna

Marijampolė

Alytus

Varėna

Šalčininkai

Lida

Neman

Stowbtsy

Mar"ina Horka

Asipovichy

Babruysk

Rahachow

Slawharad

Kastsyukovichy

Krychaw

Zhlobin

Svyetlahorsk

Bydzhezina

Homyel

Iput'

Horodnya

Snov

Mena Desna

Konotop

Bilopillya

Romny

Sumy

Rakitnoye

Belgorod

Suwałki

Ełk

Pisz

Hrodna

Bialystok

Vawkavysk

Slonim

Baranavichy

Slutsk

Staryya Darohi

Salihorsk

Luninyets

Zhytkavichy

Mazyr

Rechytsa

Kalinkavichy

Chernihiv

Borzna

Nizhyn

Kozelets'

Pryluky

Lubny

Hadyach

Okhtyrka

Ostrów Mazowiecka

Siedlce

Biała Podlaska

Łuków

Lubartów

Lublin

Chełm

Zamość

Brest

Kobryn

Drahichyn

Pinsk

Ratne

Kamin'-Kashyrs'kyy

Dubrovytsya

Sarny

Ovruch

Korosten'

Olevs'k

Novohrad-Volyns'kyy

Zhytomyr

Berdychiv

Fastiv

Bila Tserkva

Vasyl'kiv

Boryspil'

Hrebinka

Pyryatyn

Poltava

Krasnohrad

Stalowa Wola

wiec Świętokrzyski

Tomaszów Lubelski

Volodymyr-Volyns'kyy

Novovolyns'k

Luts'k

Rivne

Dubno

Shepetivka

Kozyatyn

UKRAINE

Myronivka

Zolotonosha

Rzeszów

Przemyśl

Krosno

Lviv

Horodok

Sambir

Zolochiv

Ternopil'

Terebovlya

Starokostyantyniv

Khmel'nyts'kyy

Vinnytsya

Zhashkiv

Cherkasy

Smila

Svitlovods'k

Kremenchuk

Komsomol's'k

Novomoskovs'k

Pavlohrad

Tarnica 1346

Drohobych

Stryy

Kalush

Ivano-Frankivs'k

Dolyna

Chortkiv

Zhmerynka

Tul'chyn

Uman'

Znam"yanka

Kirovohrad

Oleksandriya

Dniprodzerzhyns'k

Dnipropetrovs'k

Uzhhorod

Mukacheve

Khust

Rakhiv

Kolomyya

Kam"yanets'-Podil's'kyy

Mohyliv Podil's'kyy

Chernivtsi

Darabani

Soroca

Balta

Pervomays'k

Zhovti Vody

Dolyns'ka

Kryvyy Rih

Nikopol'

Zaporizhzhya

Marhanets'

Dniprorudne

Nyiregyháza

Satu Mare

Sighetu Marmatiei

Pietrosa 2305

Botoşani

Campulung Moldovenesc

Suceava

Prut

Bălți

Ribnita

Dniester

Orhei

MOLDOVA

Voznesens'k

Berezivka

Kakhovs'ke Vodoskhovyshche

Melitopol'

Careii

Baia Mare

Piatra Neamţ

Roman

Paşcani

Yuzhnoukrayinsk

Oradea

Zalău

Dej

Bistriţa

Bacău

Vârful Vlădeasa 1836

Cluj-Napoca

Turda

Târgu Mureş

Miercurea Ciuc

Oneşti

Vârful Bihor 1849

Mureşul

Sighişoara

Medias

Sfântu Gheorghe

Brad

Deva

Sebeş

Alba Iulia

Sibiu

Făgăraş

Vârful Moldoveanu 2544

Braşov

Vârful Parângul Mare 2518

Râmnicu Vâlcea

Piteşti

Târgovişte

Ploieşti

Buzău

Drobeta-Turnu Severin

Târgu Jiu

Petroşani

Ialomiţa

Slobozia

Kyyivs'ke Vodoskhovyshche

Chornobyl'

Borodyanka

Irsha

Vodoskhovyshche

Kremenchuts'ka Vodoskhovyshche

Shpola

Oleksandriya

Next map 58-59
Next map 58-59
Next map 56-57

Key

Relief and physical features

Relief metres

5000
3000
2000
1000
500
200
0 sea level
under sea level
0
200
4000
6000

▲ 4635 Mountain height (in metres)

Permanent ice (ice cap or glacier)

Water features

River
Canal
Lake / Reservoir
Intermittent lake
Marsh

Communications

Railway
Motorway
Road
⊕ Main airport

Administration

Boundaries

International

Settlement

Cities and towns in order of size

National capital

■ MOSCOW
■ MINSK
□ VILNIUS
□ BRATISLAVA
□ VADUZ

Other city or town

● Katowice
○ Gdańsk
○ Brest
○ Jihlava

Conic Equidistant projection

Key

Relief and physical features

Relief metres

5000
3000
2000
1000
500
200
0 sea level
200
4000 under sea level
6000

▲ 3917 Mountain height (in metres)

Water features

~~~~ River

- - - - Intermittent river

==== Canal

Lake / Reservoir

Intermittent lake

Marsh

Communications

Railway

Motorway

Road

⊕ Main airport

Administration
Boundaries

International

••••••• Ceasefire line

Settlement
Cities and towns in order of size

National capital   Other city or town

■ **ATHENS**   ● **İstanbul**

□ SARAJEVO   ○ Konya

□ NICOSIA   ○ Split

○ Dubrovnik

Scale 1 : 5 000 000

0   50   100   150   200 km

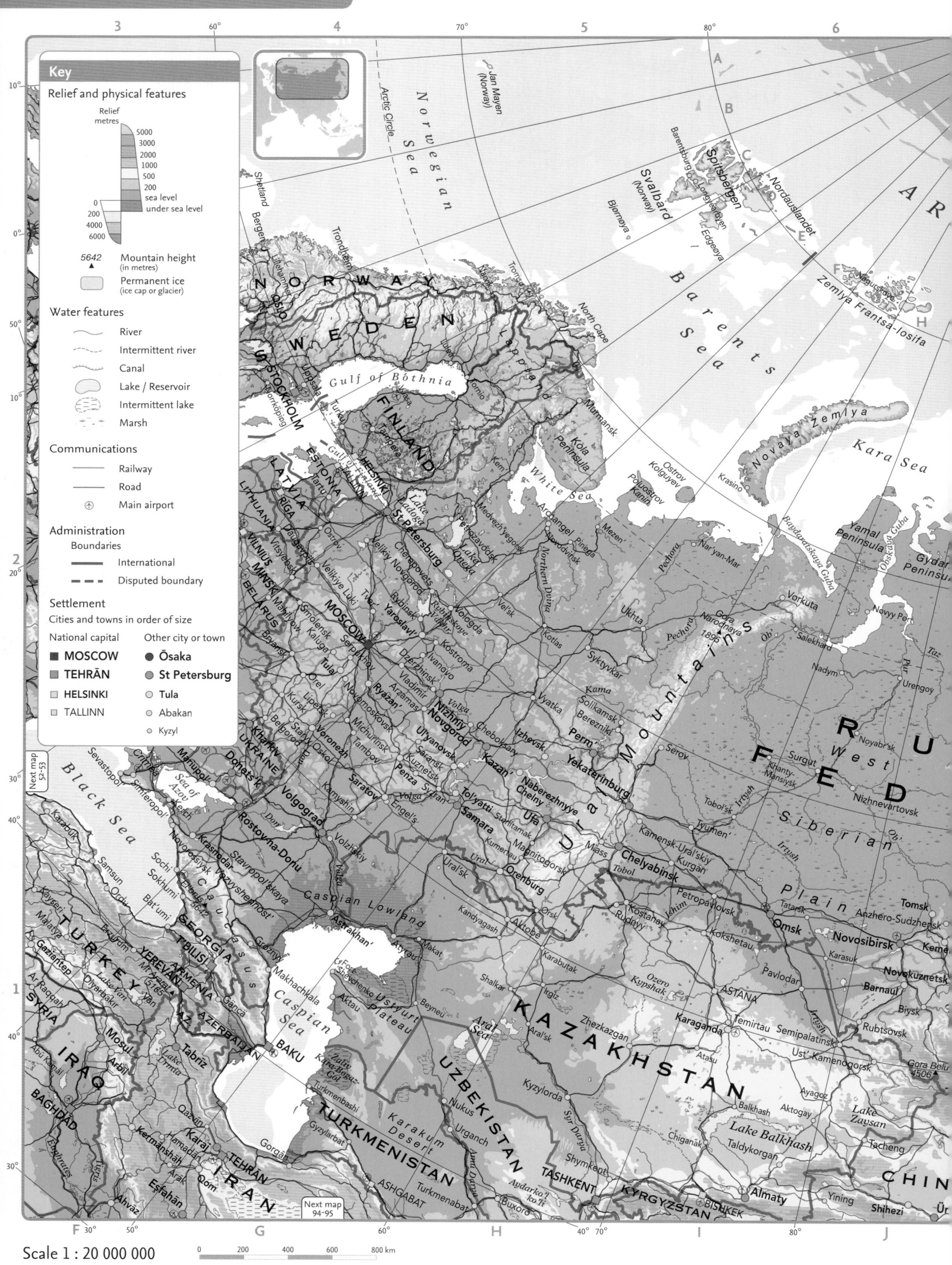

Key

Relief and physical features

Relief
metres
5000
3000
2000
1000
500
200
sea level
under sea level

5642 ▲ Mountain height
(in metres)

Permanent ice
(ice cap or glacier)

Water features

River
Intermittent river
Canal
Lake / Reservoir
Intermittent lake
Marsh

Communications

Railway
Road
⊕ Main airport

Administration

Boundaries
International
Disputed boundary

Settlement

Cities and towns in order of size

National capital   Other city or town

■ MOSCOW   ● Ōsaka
■ TEHRĀN   ● St Petersburg
□ HELSINKI   ○ Tula
□ TALLINN   ○ Abakan
                      ○ Kyzyl

Scale 1 : 20 000 000

0   200   400   600   800 km

Conic Equidistant projection

Key

Relief and physical features

Relief
metres
5000
3000
2000
1000
500
200
sea level
0
200
4000
6000
under sea level

Permanent ice
(ice cap or glacier)

Physical Regions

Pacific Ranges
Arctic Circle
Rocky Mountains
Canadian Shield
Interior Plains and Lowlands
Appalachian Highlands
Western Plateaus, Ranges and Basins
Coastal Lowlands
Tropic of Cancer
Central American Highlands
Caribbean Islands

Scale 1 : 100 000 000

Scale 1 : 40 000 000

0   500   1000   1500   2000 km

Lambert Azimuthal Equal Area projection

1 Temperature and Pressure : January

Average temperature
°C
24
16
8
0
-8
-16
-24
-32

Wind direction
Isobar in millibars
reduced to sea level

2 Temperature and Pressure : July

Average temperature
°C
32
24
16
8
0
-8

Wind direction
Isobar in millibars
reduced to sea level

3 Annual Rainfall

Average annual rainfall
mm
3000
2000
1000
500
250
0

Location of places on climate graphs ●

National Oceanic and Atmospheric Administration
www.noaa.gov
Met Office North America Forecast
www.metoffice.com/weather
World Meteorological Organization
www.wmo.ch
BBC World Weather
www.bbc.co.uk/weather/world

4 Climate Statistics

Town
Altitude in metres above sea level
Temperature range shows the average daily max. and min.
Average monthly rainfall in mm

Saskatoon	Jan	Feb	Mar	Apr	May	Jun	Jul	Aug	Sep	Oct	Nov	Dec
Temperature - max. (°C)	-13	-11	-3	9	18	22	25	24	17	11	-1	-9
Temperature - min. (°C)	-24	-22	-14	-3	3	9	11	9	3	-3	-11	-19
Rainfall - (mm)	23	13	18	18	36	66	61	48	38	23	13	15

Vancouver	Jan	Feb	Mar	Apr	May	Jun	Jul	Aug	Sep	Oct	Nov	Dec
Temperature - max. (°C)	5	7	10	14	18	21	23	23	18	14	9	6
Temperature - min. (°C)	0	1	3	4	8	11	12	12	9	7	4	2
Rainfall - (mm)	218	147	127	84	71	64	31	43	91	147	211	224

Detroit	Jan	Feb	Mar	Apr	May	Jun	Jul	Aug	Sep	Oct	Nov	Dec
Temperature - max. (°C)	-1	0	6	13	19	25	28	27	23	16	8	2
Temperature - min. (°C)	-7	-8	-3	3	9	14	17	17	13	7	1	-4
Rainfall - (mm)	53	53	64	64	84	91	84	69	71	61	61	58

Charleston	Jan	Feb	Mar	Apr	May	Jun	Jul	Aug	Sep	Oct	Nov	Dec
Temperature - max. (°C)	14	15	19	23	27	30	31	31	28	24	19	15
Temperature - min. (°C)	6	7	10	14	19	23	24	24	22	16	11	7
Rainfall - (mm)	74	84	86	71	81	119	185	168	130	81	58	71

Acapulco	Jan	Feb	Mar	Apr	May	Jun	Jul	Aug	Sep	Oct	Nov	Dec
Temperature - max. (°C)	31	31	31	32	32	33	32	33	32	32	32	31
Temperature - min. (°C)	22	22	22	23	25	25	25	25	24	24	23	22
Rainfall - (mm)	6	1	0	1	36	281	256	252	349	159	28	8

Scale 1 : 80 000 000

0   800   1600   2400   3200 km

Bonne projection

Key

Relief and physical features

Relief
metres
5000
3000
2000
1000
500
200
0 sea level
200
4000
6000 under sea level

6194 ▲ Mountain height (in metres)

Permanent ice (ice cap or glacier)

Water features

~ River

~ Canal

Lake / Reservoir

Intermittent lake

Marsh

Communications

Railway

Road

⊕ Main airport

Administration
Boundaries

International

Internal

Settlement
Cities and towns in order of size

National capital   Other city or town
■ OTTAWA   ● New York
□ NUUK   ● Montréal
                         ○ Winnipeg
                         ○ Saskatoon
                         ○ Churchill

0   200   400   600   800 km

North America Countries

B.	BELIZE
C.R.	COSTA RICA
D.R.	DOMINICAN REPUBLIC
E.S.	EL SALVADOR
G.	GUATEMALA
H.	HAITI
HO.	HONDURAS
J.	JAMAICA
N.	NICARAGUA
P.	PANAMA

Scale 1 : 95 000 000

GREENLAND

U.S.A.

CANADA

UNITED STATES OF AMERICA

Arctic Circle

Tropic of Cancer

MEXICO

THE BAHAMAS

CUBA   D.R.
H.
B.   HO.
G.   J.
E.S.   N.
C.R.   P.

CO.	CONNECTICUT
MASS.	MASSACHUSETTS
N.H.	NEW HAMPSHIRE
P.E.I.	PRINCE EDWARD ISLAND
PENN.	PENNSYLVANIA
R.I.	RHODE ISLAND
VER.	VERMONT

Next map 64-65

Lambert Conformal Conic projection

Scale 1 : 12 000 000

0   150   300   450   600 km

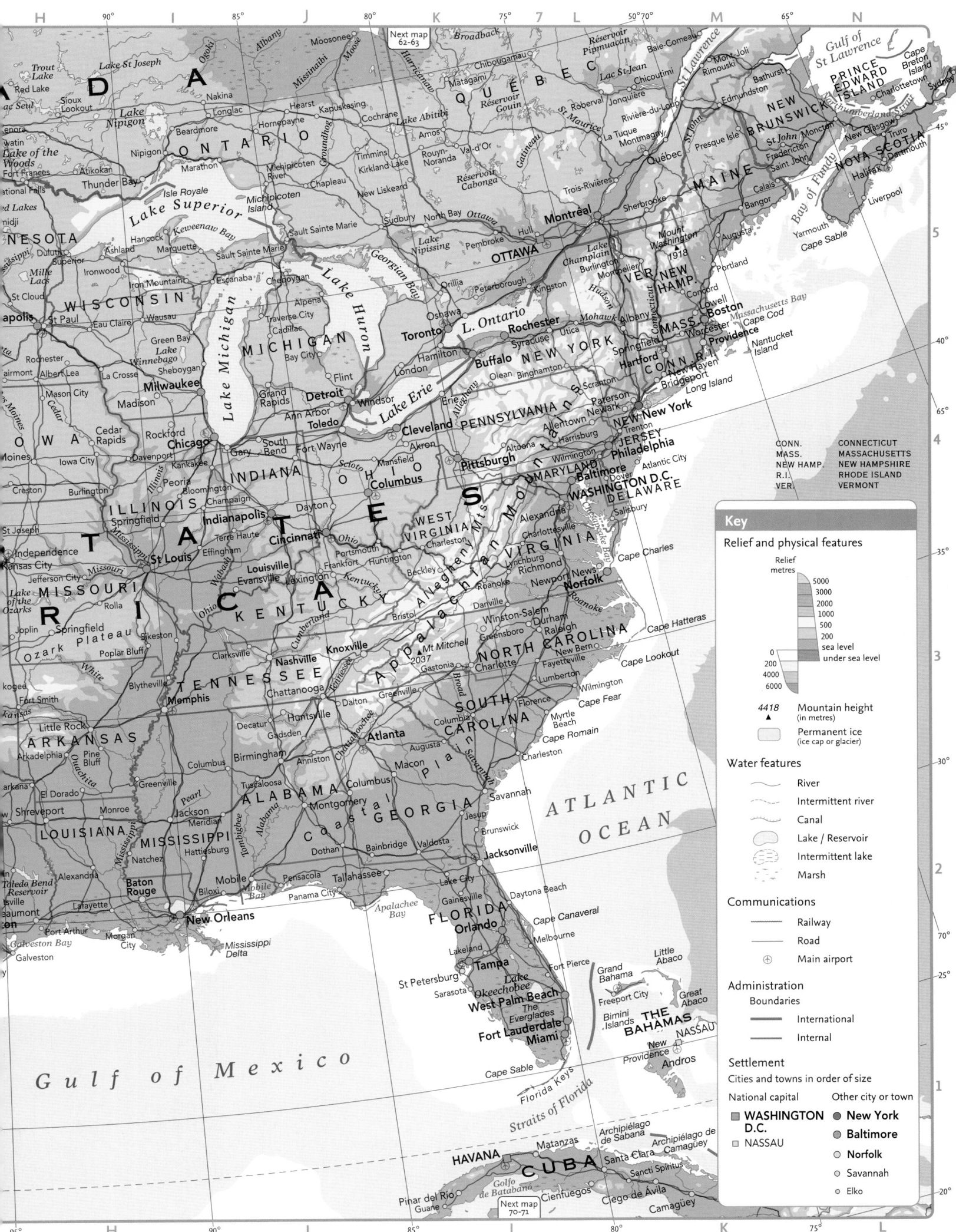

Key

Relief and physical features

Relief metres

5000
3000
2000
1000
500
200
sea level

0
200
4000
6000
under sea level

▲ 4418   Mountain height (in metres)

Permanent ice (ice cap or glacier)

Water features

River

Intermittent river

Canal

Lake / Reservoir

Intermittent lake

Marsh

Communications

Railway

Road

⊕   Main airport

Administration

Boundaries

International

Internal

Settlement

Cities and towns in order of size

National capital

■ **WASHINGTON D.C.**

□ NASSAU

Other city or town

● **New York**

● **Baltimore**

○ Norfolk

○ Savannah

○ Elko

CONN.   CONNECTICUT
MASS.   MASSACHUSETTS
NEW HAMP.   NEW HAMPSHIRE
R.I.   RHODE ISLAND
VER.   VERMONT

Lambert Conformal Conic projection

1 Population Density

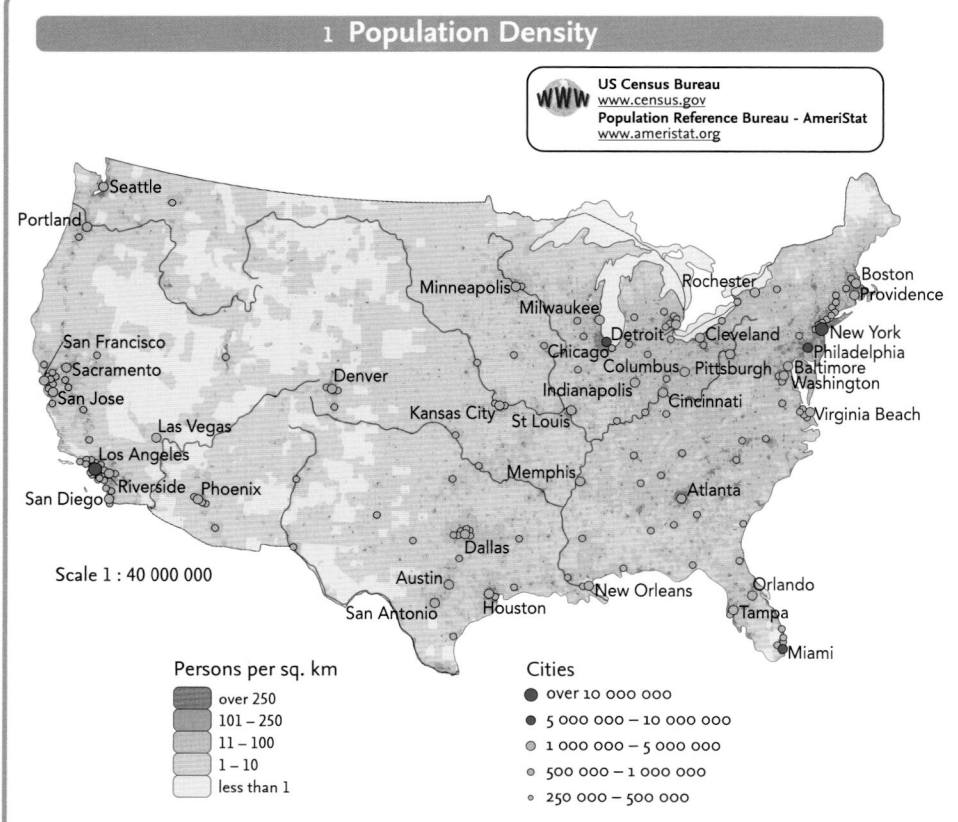

US Census Bureau
www.census.gov
Population Reference Bureau - AmeriStat
www.ameristat.org

Scale 1 : 40 000 000

Persons per sq. km
- over 250
- 101 – 250
- 11 – 100
- 1 – 10
- less than 1

Cities
- over 10 000 000
- 5 000 000 – 10 000 000
- 1 000 000 – 5 000 000
- 500 000 – 1 000 000
- 250 000 – 500 000

2 State Comparisons

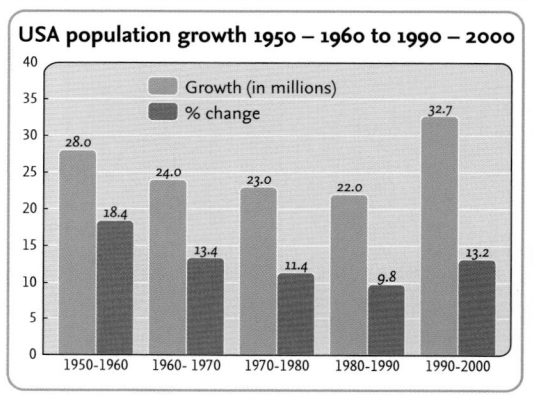

Unemployment rate, 2002 — CA WV — Percentage

Population, 2003 — CA WV — Millions

Population density, 2003 — CA WV — People per sq. mile

Violent crimes, 2002 — CA WV — Per 1000 population

Educated to college level, 2002 — CA WV — Percentage

Home ownership, 2002 — CA WV — Percentage

Average annual pay, 2002 — CA WV — US$ (thousands)

CALIFORNIA   WEST VIRGINIA

3 Main Urban Agglomerations

Urban agglomeration	1980	1990	2000	2005 (projected)
New York	15 601 150	16 086 000	17 846 000	18 498 000
Los Angeles	9 512 100	10 883 000	11 814 000	12 146 000
Chicago	7 216 000	7 374 000	8 333 000	8 711 000
Miami	3 122 000	3 969 000	4 946 000	5 380 000
Philadelphia	4 540 000	4 725 000	5 160 000	5 325 000
Dallas	2 468 000	3 219 000	4 172 000	4 612 000
Boston	3 281 000	3 428 000	4 049 000	4 313 000
Atlanta	1 625 000	2 184 000	3 542 000	4 284 000
Houston	2 424 000	2 922 000	3 849 000	4 283 000
Washington	2 777 000	3 376 000	3 949 000	4 190 000
Detroit	3 807 000	3 703 000	3 909 000	3 980 000
San Francisco	2 656 000	2 961 000	3 236 000	3 342 000
San Diego	1 718 000	2 356 000	2 683 000	2 818 000

4 Population Growth

USA population growth 1950 – 1960 to 1990 – 2000

- Growth (in millions)
- % change

	1950-1960	1960-1970	1970-1980	1980-1990	1990-2000
Growth (in millions)	28.0	24.0	23.0	22.0	32.7
% change	18.4	13.4	11.4	9.8	13.2

5 Population Change

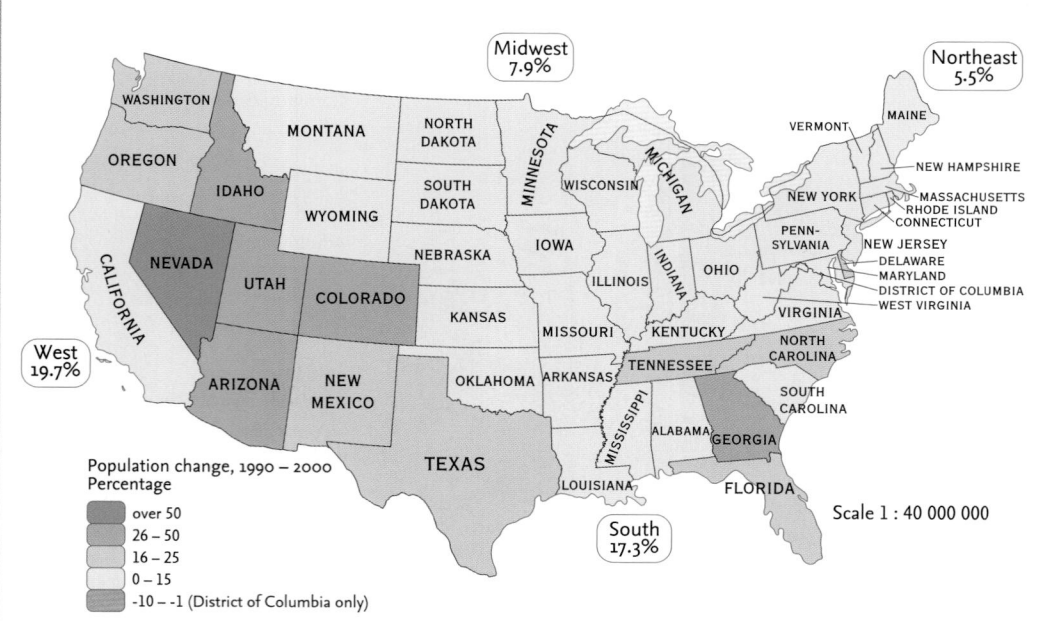

Midwest 7.9%

Northeast 5.5%

West 19.7%

South 17.3%

Population change, 1990 – 2000 Percentage
- over 50
- 26 – 50
- 16 – 25
- 0 – 15
- -10 – -1 (District of Columbia only)

Scale 1 : 40 000 000

6 Immigration

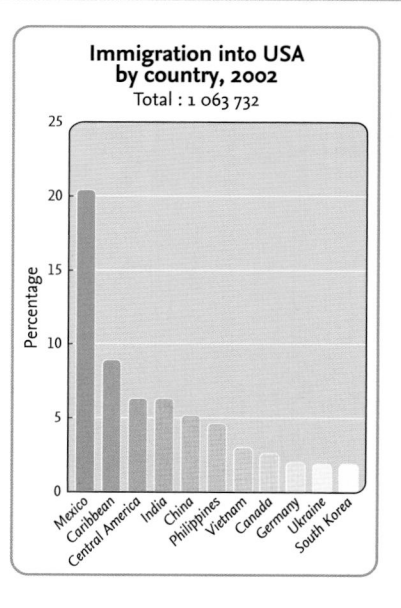

Immigration into USA by country, 2002
Total : 1 063 732

Percentage

Mexico, Caribbean, Central America, India, China, Philippines, Vietnam, Canada, Germany, Ukraine, South Korea

7 Economic Activity

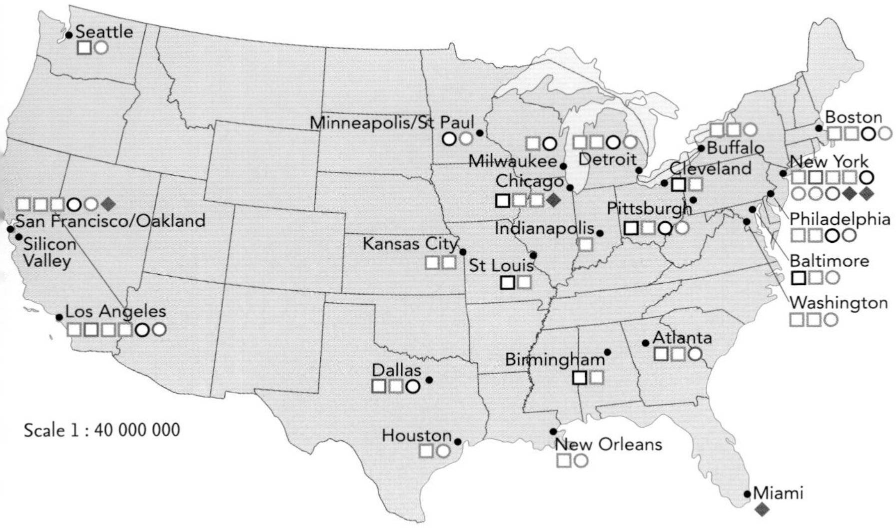

Seattle

Minneapolis/St Paul

Milwaukee
Chicago
Detroit
Buffalo
Cleveland

Boston

New York

San Francisco/Oakland
Silicon
Valley

Pittsburgh
Indianapolis
Kansas City
St Louis

Philadelphia

Baltimore

Washington

Los Angeles

Atlanta

Dallas

Birmingham

Houston

New Orleans

Miami

Scale 1 : 40 000 000

• Major industrial centre

Manufacturing industry

□ Metal working
□ Oil refinery
□ Shipbuilding
□ Aircraft manufacturing
□ Car manufacturing
□ Mechanical engineering

○ Electrical engineering
○ Publishing / Paper
○ Chemicals
○ Textiles
○ Food processing

Service industry

◆ Banking and finance
◆ Tourism

8 Silicon Valley

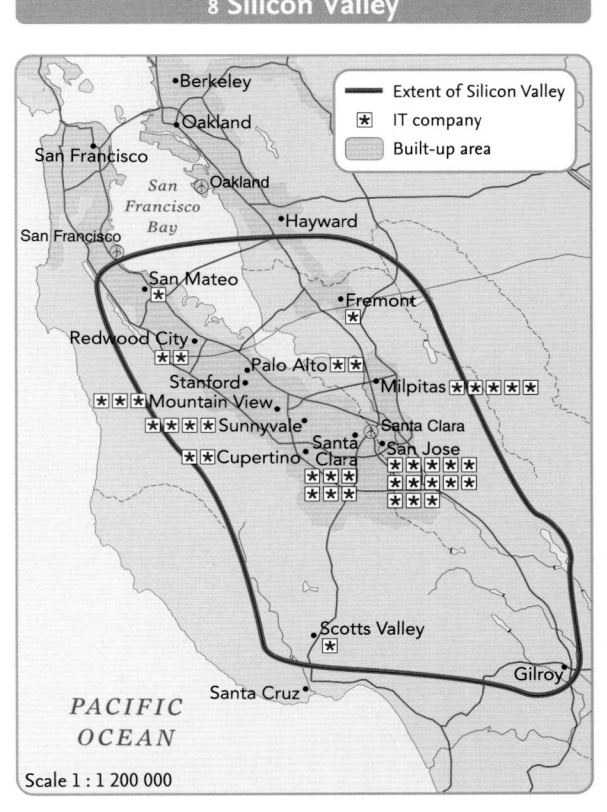

Berkeley
Oakland
San Francisco
Oakland
Hayward
San Francisco Bay
San Francisco
San Mateo
Fremont
Redwood City
Palo Alto
Stanford
Milpitas
Mountain View
Sunnyvale
Santa Clara
Cupertino
Santa Clara
San Jose
Scotts Valley
Gilroy
Santa Cruz

PACIFIC OCEAN

Scale 1 : 1 200 000

— Extent of Silicon Valley
✳ IT company
☐ Built-up area

Department of Commerce
www.commerce.gov
US Trade and Development Agency
www.tda.gov
UN Commodity Trade Statistics
unstats.un.org/unsd/comtrade

9 Trade

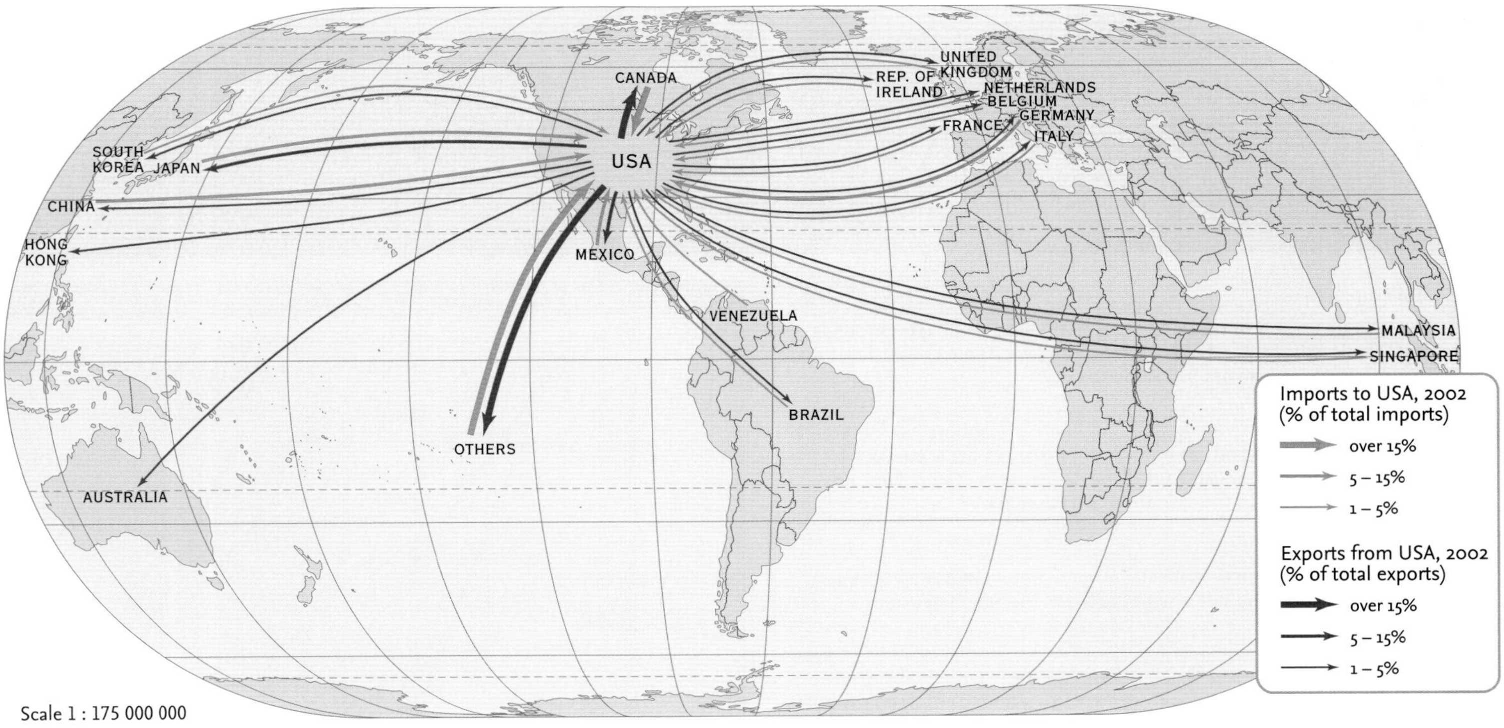

CANADA

UNITED KINGDOM
REP. OF IRELAND
NETHERLANDS
BELGIUM
FRANCE
GERMANY
ITALY

SOUTH KOREA JAPAN

CHINA

USA

HONG KONG

MEXICO

MALAYSIA

SINGAPORE

VENEZUELA

BRAZIL

OTHERS

AUSTRALIA

Scale 1 : 175 000 000

Imports to USA, 2002 (% of total imports)
→ over 15%
→ 5 – 15%
→ 1 – 5%

Exports from USA, 2002 (% of total exports)
→ over 15%
→ 5 – 15%
→ 1 – 5%

Import commodities, 2002

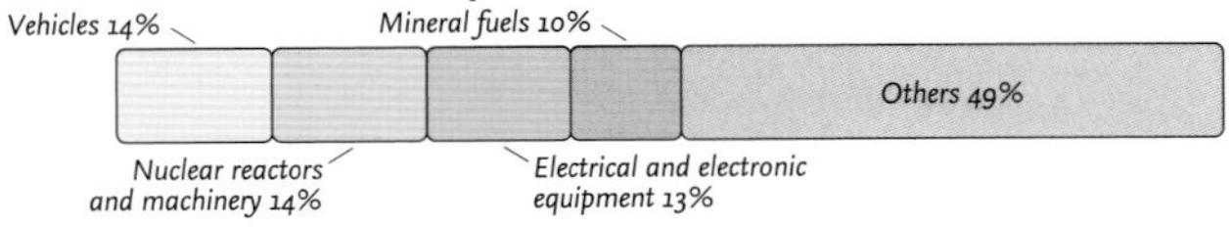

Vehicles 14%   Mineral fuels 10%   Others 49%

Nuclear reactors and machinery 14%   Electrical and electronic equipment 13%

Total : US$ 1 202 284 million

Export commodities, 2002

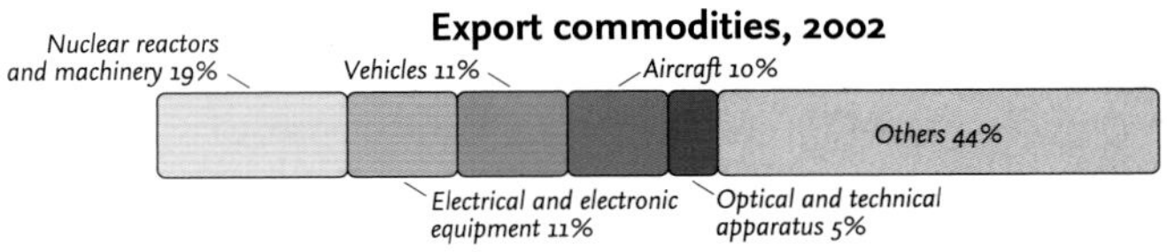

Nuclear reactors and machinery 19%   Vehicles 11%   Aircraft 10%   Others 44%

Electrical and electronic equipment 11%   Optical and technical apparatus 5%

Total : US$ 693 222 million

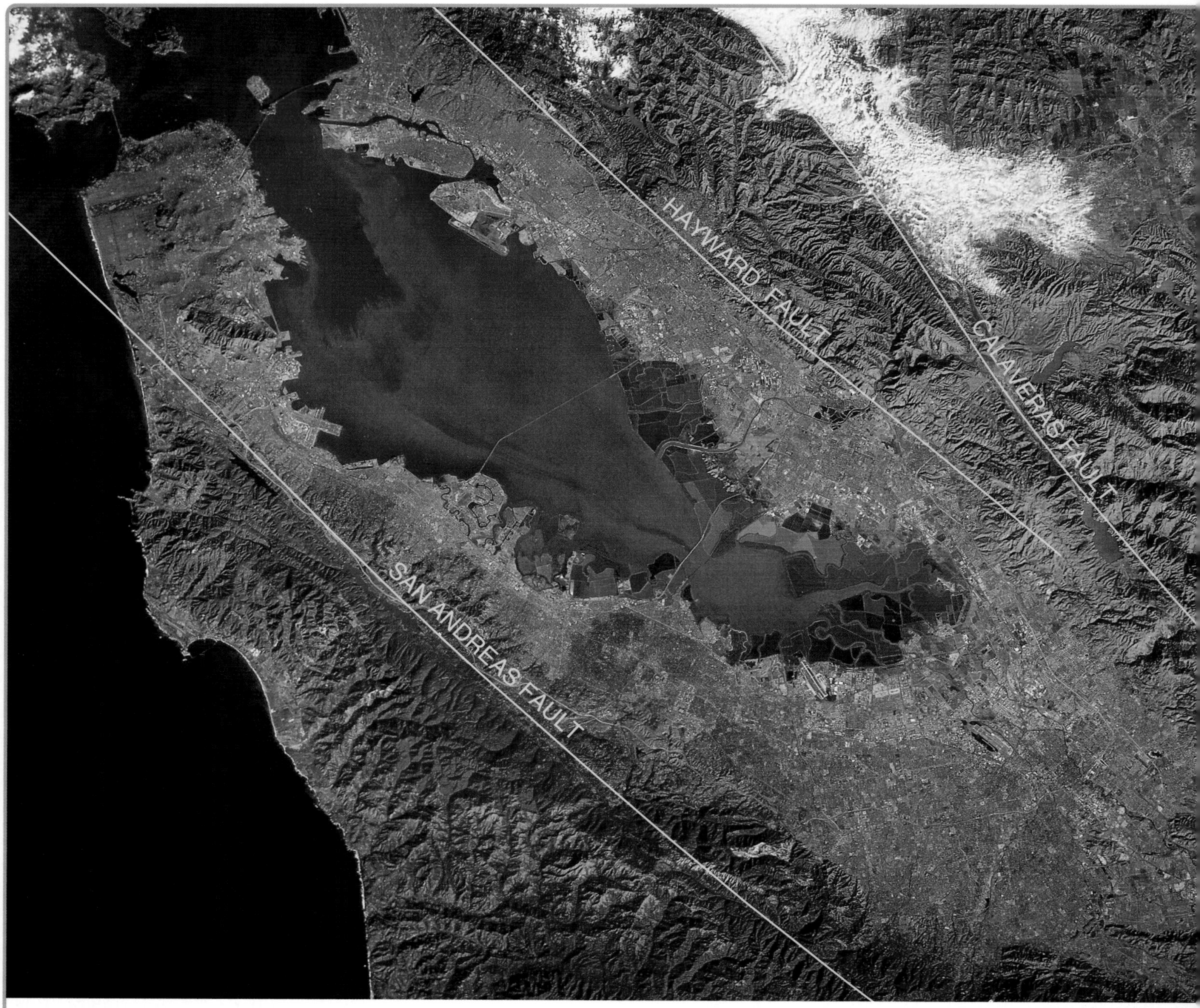

Built-up area

The built up area shown as blue/green on the satellite image surrounds San Francisco Bay and extends south to San Jose. Three bridges link the main built up areas across San Francisco Bay.

Woodland

Areas of dense woodland cover much of the Santa Cruz Mountains to the west of the San Andreas Fault Zone. Other areas of woodland are found on the ridges to the east of San Francisco Bay.

Marsh / Salt Marsh

Areas of dark green on the satellite image represent marshland in the Coyote Creek area and salt marshes between the San Mateo and Dumbarton Bridges.

Reservoir / lake

Lakes and reservoirs stand out from the surrounding land. Good examples are the Upper San Leandro Reservoir east of Piedmont and the San Andreas Lake which lies along the fault line.

Airport

A grey blue colour shows San Francisco International Airport as a flat rectangular strip of land jutting out into the bay.

Main fault line

Fault Lines in the San Francisco Bay Region

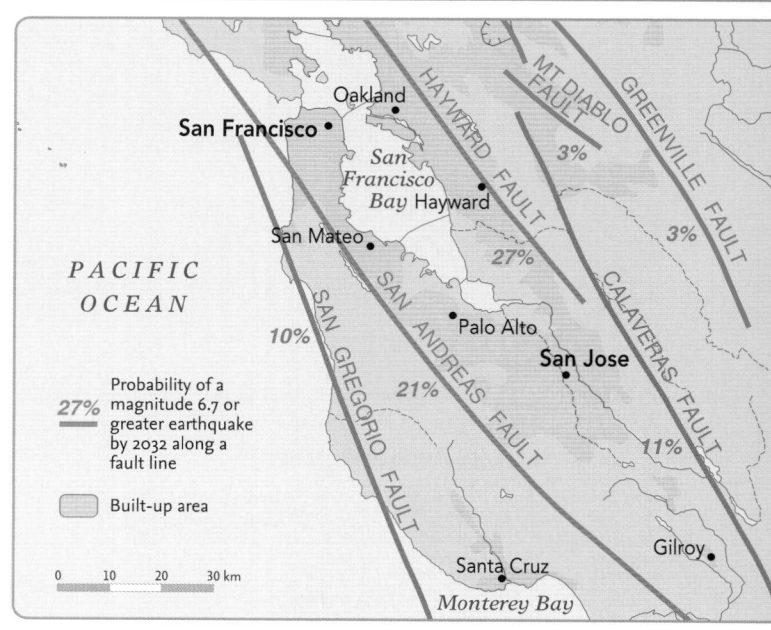

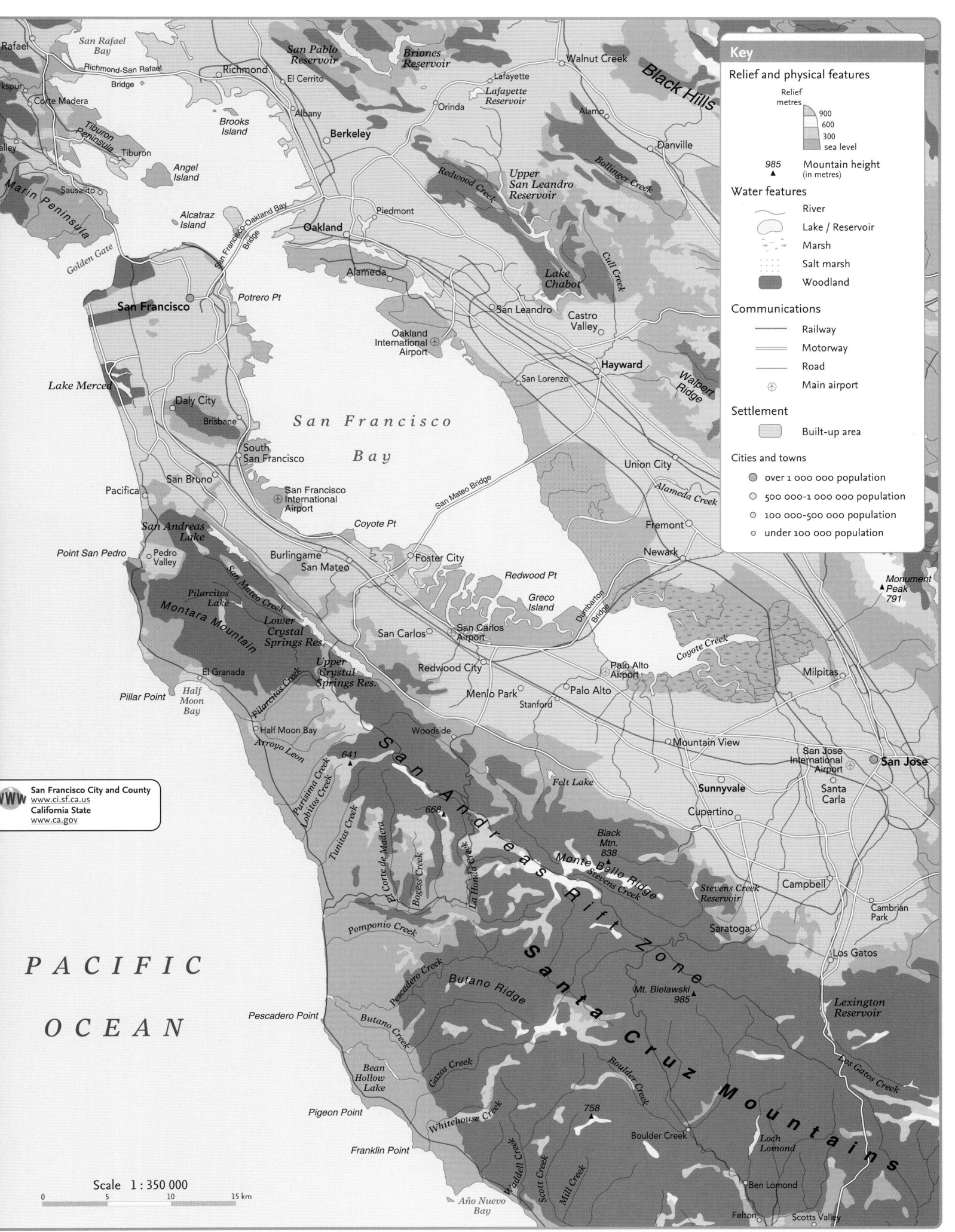

Key

Relief and physical features

Relief
metres
900
600
300
sea level

985 ▲ Mountain height (in metres)

Water features

River
Lake / Reservoir
Marsh
Salt marsh
Woodland

Communications

Railway
Motorway
Road
⊕ Main airport

Settlement

Built-up area

Cities and towns

● over 1 000 000 population
○ 500 000-1 000 000 population
○ 100 000-500 000 population
○ under 100 000 population

San Francisco City and County
www.ci.sf.ca.us
California State
www.ca.gov

Scale 1 : 350 000

0   5   10   15 km

PACIFIC OCEAN

United States • San Diego • Tijuana • Mexicali • Phoenix • Casa Grande • Tucson • Nogales • Douglas

ARIZONA • NEW MEXICO • Silver City • Deming • Las Cruces • El Paso • Ciudad Juárez • Roswell • Artesia • Lubbock • Big Spring • Midland • Odessa • San Angelo

UNITED STATES OF AMERICA • ARKANSAS • Little Rock • Wichita Falls • Lake Texoma • Arkadelphia • Pine Bluff • Greenville • MISSISSIPPI • Birmin...

Lawton • Denton • Dallas • Fort Worth • Abilene • Killeen • Waco • Austin • San Marcos • Houston • Texarkana • Longview • Shreveport • Monroe • Meridian • Jackson • Hattiesburg • Mobile • Biloxi • El Dorado • Ouachita • Natchez • Tuscalo...

TEXAS • Edwards Plateau • Pecos • Del Rio • San Antonio • Beeville • Victoria • Bay City • Galveston • Galveston Bay • Port Arthur • Beaumont • Lufkin • Toledo Bend Reservoir • Huntsville • LOUISIANA • Baton Rouge • Lafayette • Alexandria • New Orleans • Mississippi Delta

BAJA CALIFORNIA • Ensenada • Picacho del Diablo 3096 • San Felipe • Puerto Peñasco • Caborca • Lázaro Cárdenas • Gulf of California • Isla Ángel de la Guarda • Isla Tiburón • Isla Cedros • Bahía Sebastián Vizcaíno • Punta Eugenia • BAJA CALIFORNIA SUR • Santa Rosalía • Isla Carmen • Isla San José • Isla Santa Margarita • Villa Insurgentes • La Paz • Cabo Falso • San José del Cabo

SONORA • Hermosillo • Guaymas • Ciudad Obregón • Navojoa • Los Mochis • Guasave • Sierra Madre Occidental • CHIHUAHUA • Chihuahua • Cuauhtémoc • Ciudad Delicias • Hidalgo del Parral • Jiménez • Madera • Nuevo Casas Grandes • Ojinaga • Emory Peak 2385 • Serranías del Burro • Piedras Negras • Sabinas • COAHUILA • Monclova • Río Grande • Nuevo Laredo • Laredo • Falcon Lake • Reynosa • Matamoros

SINALOA • Culiacán • Mazatlán • DURANGO • Durango • MEXICO • ZACATECAS • Zacatecas • Gómez Palacio • Torreón • Saltillo • NUEVO LEÓN • Monterrey • Montemorelos • Cerro Peña Nevada 3664 • Ciudad Victoria • TAMAULIPAS • Padre Island • Laguna Madre

NAYARIT • Tepic • Acaponeta • Islas Marías • Puerto Vallarta • Cabo Corrientes • Guadalajara • JALISCO • Laguna de Chapala • AGUASCALIENTES • SAN LUIS POTOSÍ • San Luis Potosí • León • GUANAJUATO • Guanajuato • Irapuato • QUERÉTARO • Querétaro • HIDALGO • Pachuca • Ciudad de Valles • Ciudad Madero • Tampico • Laguna de Tamiahua • Tuxpan • Poza Rica

COLIMA • Nevado de Colima 4339 • MICHOACÁN • Morelia • Uruapan • Presa Infiernillo • Balsas • Lázaro Cárdenas • MÉXICO • Toluca • MÉXICO CITY • Cuernavaca • MORELOS • Popocatépetl 5452 • Tlaxcala • Puebla • PUEBLA • Córdoba • Orizaba • VERACRUZ • Veracruz • Coatzacoalcos • Minatitlán

GUERRERO • Chilpancingo • Acapulco • Sierra Madre del Sur • OAXACA • Oaxaca • Puerto Ángel • Gulf of Tehuantepec • Ciudad Ixtepec • Juchitán • Arriagá • Pijijiapan • TABASCO • Villahermosa • Ciudad del Carmen • Laguna de Términos • CAMPECHE • Campeche • Mérida • YUCATÁN • QUINTANA ROO • Escárcega • CHIAPAS • Tuxtla Gutiérrez • Tapachula • Quetzaltenango • Sipacate • Santa Ana • GUATEMALA • GUATEMALA CITY • San Salvador • EL SALVADOR • San Miguel • BELMOPAN • BELIZE • HONDURAS • TEGUCIGALPA • Golfo de Fonseca

Gulf of Mexico • Bahía de Campeche • Cabo Catoche

PACIFIC OCEAN

Mexican States numbered on map
1. AGUASCALIENTES
2. DISTRITO FEDERAL
3. TLAXCALA

Key

Relief and physical features

Relief metres
5000
3000
2000
1000
500
200
sea level
under sea level
0
200
4000
6000

▲ 5493 Mountain height (in metres)

Water features

~ River
~ Intermittent river
~ Canal
Lake / Reservoir
Intermittent lake
Marsh

Communications

Railway
Road
⊕ Main airport

Administration

Boundaries
International
Internal

Settlement
Cities and towns in order of size

National capital
■ MÉXICO CITY
■ BOGOTÁ
■ KINGSTON
□ NASSAU
□ CASTRIES

Other city or town
● Monterrey
○ Chihuahua
○ Oaxaca
○ Zacatecas

Scale 1 : 13 500 000

0   200   400   600   800 km

ATLANTIC OCEAN

Bermuda (UK) Hamilton

Tropic of Cancer

THE BAHAMAS

NASSAU

Grand Bahama
Little Abaco
Freeport City
Great Abaco
Bimini Islands
Eleuthera
New Providence
Cat Island
Andros
Exuma Cays
Exuma Sd.
San Salvador
Rum Cay
Long I.
Great Exuma
Crooked I. Pass.
Crooked Island
Mayaguana
Acklins Island
Caicos Islands
Turks and Caicos Islands (UK)
Little Inagua Island
Great Inagua
Turks Islands
Grand Turk

Atlanta
SOUTH CAROLINA
Greenville
Florence
Lumberton
Wilmington
Columbia
Myrtle Beach
Augusta
Macon
Cape Fear
Cape Romain
Charleston
GEORGIA
Savannah
Jesup
Bainbridge
Valdosta
Brunswick
Dalton
Gadsen
Columbus
Montgomery
Panama City
Tallahassee
Jacksonville
Lake City
FLORIDA
Gainesville
Daytona Beach
Orlando
Lakeland
Cape Canaveral
Tampa
Melbourne
St Petersburg
Sarasota
Fort Pierce
Lake Okeechobee
West Palm Beach
Fort Lauderdale
Miami
Cape Sable
Florida Keys
Straits of Florida
Apalachee Bay

HAVANA Matanzas
Pinar del Río
Guane
Archipiélago de Sabana
CUBA
Santa Clara
Cienfuegos
Sancti Spíritus
Ciego de Ávila
Archipiélago de Camagüey
Camagüey
Holguín
Las Tunas
Bayamo
Golfo de Batabanó
Archipiélago de los Canarreos
Archipiélago de los Jardines de la Reina
Golfo de Guacanayabo
Sa. Maestra
1994
Pico Turquino
Santiago de Cuba
Guantánamo
Baracoa
Cabo Antonio
Isla de la Juventud
Cabo Cruz
Little Cayman
Grand Cayman
Cayman Brac
Cayman Islands (UK)
Montego Bay
JAMAICA
KINGSTON
Jamaica Channel

Windward Passage
Port-de-Paix
Cap-Haïtien
Gonaïves
HAITI
PORT-AU-PRINCE
Jérémie
Les Cayes
Jacmel
Pico Duarte
3175
Santiago
SANTO DOMINGO
DOMINICAN REPUBLIC
Isla Beata
Cabo Beata
H i s p a n i o l a

Mona Passage
SAN JUAN
Mayagüez
Isla Mona
Ponce
PUERTO RICO (USA)
Virgin Is (UK)
Virgin Is (USA)

Leeward Islands
Anegada (UK)
Anguilla (UK)
St-Martin (Fr.)
St-Barthélemy (Fr.)
Sint Maarten (Neth.)
Barbuda
ANTIGUA AND BARBUDA
ST JOHN'S
Antigua
ST KITTS AND NEVIS
Montserrat (UK)
Guadeloupe (Fr.)
Basse-Terre
Marie-Galante (Fr.)
DOMINICA
ROSEAU
Martinique (Fr.)
Fort-de-France
ST LUCIA
CASTRIES
KINGSTOWN
ST VINCENT AND THE GRENADINES
BRIDGETOWN
BARBADOS
Windward Is.

L e s s e r   A n t i l l e s

GRENADA
ST GEORGE'S
Isla Blanquilla (Ven.)
Tobago
TRINIDAD & TOBAGO
PORT OF SPAIN
Trinidad

C a r i b b e a n   S e a

Laguna de Caratasca
Cayos Miskitos
Isla de Providencia (Colombia)
Isla de San Andrés (Colombia)
Islas del Maíz (Nic.)
Punta de Perlas
Cord. Isabella
Coco
Río Grande
MANAGUA
NICARAGUA
Lake Nicaragua
San Juan
COSTA RICA
SAN JOSÉ
Chirripó
3819
Península de Osa
Bahía de Coronado
Golfo de Nicoya
Península de Azuero
Golfo de Chiriquí
Isla de Coiba
David
Aguadulce
Punta Mala
PANAMA
PANAMA CITY
Colón
Panama Canal
Golfo de los Mosquitos
Golfo del Darién
La Palma
Gulf of Panama
Golfo de Cupica

Punta Gallinas
Península de la Guajira
Ríohacha
Maicao
Santa Marta
Barranquilla
Cartagena
Valledupar
Golfo de Venezuela
Punto Fijo
Coro
Maracaibo
Cabimas
Lake Maracaibo
Valera
Sierra de Perijá
Cúcuta
San Cristóbal
Cordillera Occidental
Turbo
Sincelejo
Montería
Quibdó
Medellín
Manizales
Pereira
Armenia
Palmira
Cali
Neiva
Ibagué
BOGOTÁ
Villavicencio
Buenaventura
Tumaco
Florencia
COLOMBIA
Cordillera Central
Cordillera Oriental
Magdalena
Cauca

CARACAS
Maiquetía
Barquisimeto
Valencia
Maracay
Acarigua
Guanare
Mérida
Pico Bolívar
5007
Barinas
San Fernando de Apure
Zaraza
El Tigre
VENEZUELA
Cumaná
Barcelona
Maturín
Tigre
Guárico
Orinoco Delta
Ciudad Bolívar
Orinoco
Ciudad Guayana
Embalse de Guri
El Callao
La Paragua
Cerro Yaví
2285
Guiana Highlands
La Gran Sabana
Pakaraima Mountains
Sierra Parima
Pico da Neblina
3014
BRAZIL
Tunja
Sierra Nevada del Cocuy
5493
Guaviare
Meta
Orinoco
Pen. de Paria
Güiria
Isla de Margarita
Netherlands Antilles
Aruba (Neth.)
Curaçao
Bonaire
Islas Los Roques (Ven.)
Isla Orchila (Ven.)
Isla La Tortuga (Ven.)

Next map 64-65
Next map 72-73
Next map 76-77

Lambert Conformal Conic projection

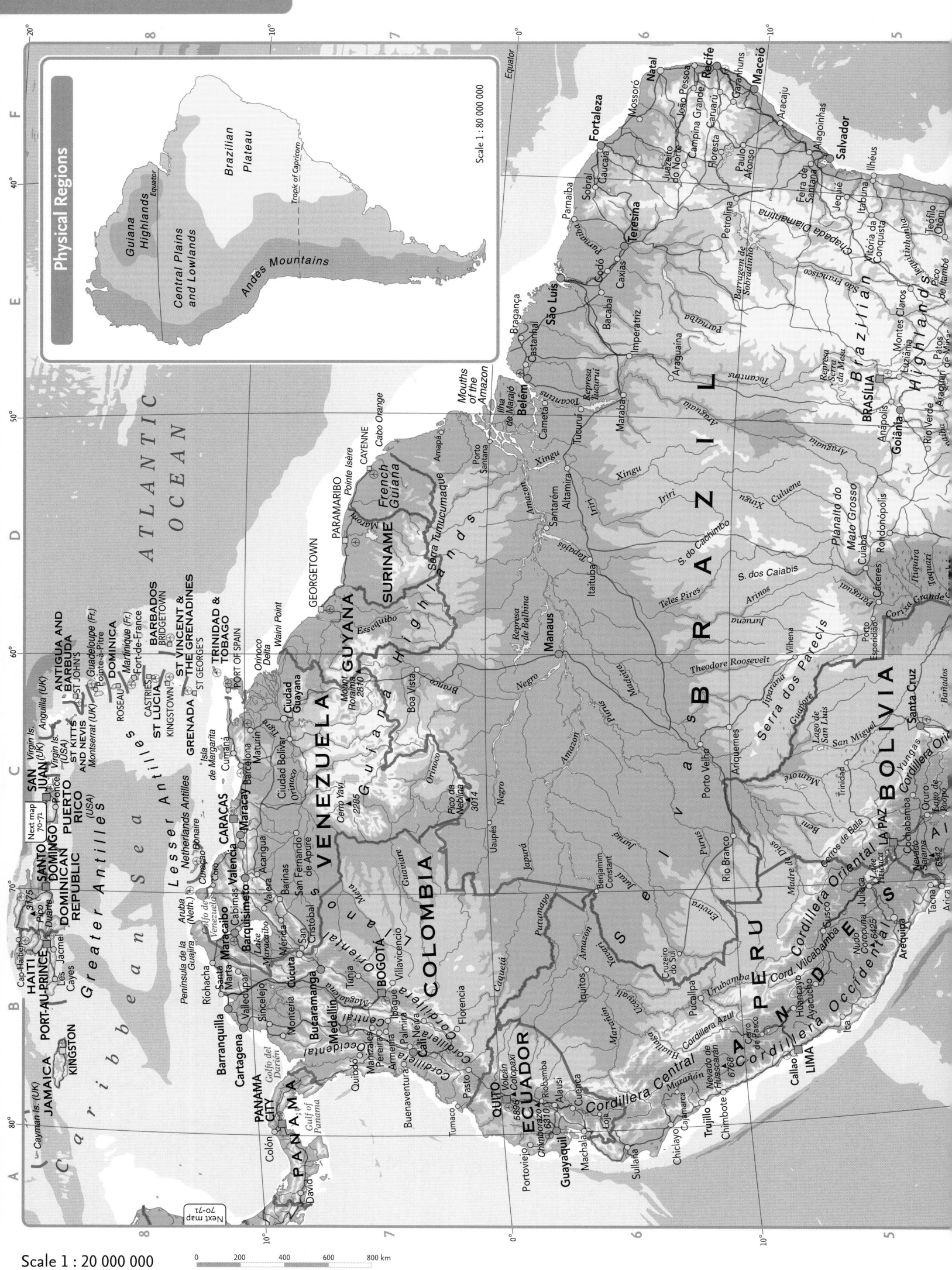

Physical Regions

Guiana Highlands

Brazilian Plateau

Central Plains and Lowlands

Andes Mountains

Equator

Tropic of Capricorn

Scale 1 : 80 000 000

ATLANTIC OCEAN

Caribbean Sea

Greater Antilles

Lesser Antilles

Netherlands Antilles

Cayman Is. (UK)

JAMAICA
KINGSTON

HAITI
PORT-AU-PRINCE
Cap-Haïtien
Les Cayes
Les Jacmel
Pico Duarte 3175

DOMINICAN REPUBLIC
SANTO DOMINGO

PUERTO RICO (USA)
SAN JUAN
Ponce

Virgin Is. (USA)
Virgin Is. (UK)
Anguilla (UK)

ANTIGUA AND BARBUDA
ST JOHN'S
ST KITTS AND NEVIS
Montserrat (UK)

Guadeloupe (Fr.)
Pointe-à-Pitre
DOMINICA
ROSEAU
Martinique (Fr.)
Fort-de-France
ST LUCIA
CASTRIES
BARBADOS
BRIDGETOWN
ST VINCENT & THE GRENADINES
KINGSTOWN
GRENADA
ST GEORGE'S
TRINIDAD & TOBAGO
PORT OF SPAIN

Aruba (Neth.)
Curaçao
Bonaire
Isla de Margarita

Next map 70-71

PANAMA
PANAMA CITY
Colón
David
Gulf of Panama
Golfo del Darién

COLOMBIA
BOGOTÁ
Barranquilla
Cartagena
Santa Marta
Riohacha
Valledupar
Sincelejo
Montería
Cúcuta
Bucaramanga
Medellín
Quibdó
Manizales
Pereira
Armenia
Ibagué
Palmira
Cali
Buenaventura
Neiva
Popayán
Pasto
Tumaco
Florencia
Villavicencio
Tunja

Cordillera Occidental
Cordillera Central
Cordillera Oriental

VENEZUELA
CARACAS
Maracaibo
Lake Maracaibo
Maracay
Valencia
Barquisimeto
Cabimas
Coro
Península de la Guajira
Golfo de Venezuela
Valera
Mérida
San Cristóbal
Barinas
Acarigua
San Fernando de Apure
Cumaná
Barcelona
Maturín
Ciudad Bolívar
Ciudad Guayana
Cerro Yaví 2286
Pico da Neblina 3014

Orinoco Delta
Orinoco

GUYANA
GEORGETOWN
Waini Point
Essequibo
Mount Roraima 2810
Boa Vista

SURINAME
PARAMARIBO
Maroni

French Guiana
CAYENNE
Pointe Isère
Cabo Orange

Guiana Highlands

ECUADOR
QUITO
Volcán Cotopaxi 5896
Chimborazo 6310
Portoviejo
Guayaquil
Machala
Riobamba
Alausi
Cuenca
Loja

Guayas

PERU
LIMA
Callao
Piura
Sullana
Chiclayo
Chimbote
Trujillo
Cajamarca
Chachapoyas
Iquitos
Pucallpa
Cerro de Pasco
Huánuco
Huancayo
Ayacucho
Nevado de Huascarán 6768
Coropuna 6425
Ica
Arequipa
Tacna

Cordillera Occidental
Cordillera Central
Cordillera Oriental
Cord. Vilcabamba
Nudo Ausangate 6425

BOLIVIA
LA PAZ
Santa Cruz
Cochabamba
Oruro
Sucre
Potosí
Trinidad
Riberalta
Yungas
Lago de San Luis
San Miguel
Cerros de Bala
Madre de Dios
Lake Titicaca
Juliaca
Cusco
Puno

Cordillera Oriental
Cordillera Occidental

B R A Z I L
BRASÍLIA
Goiânia
Anápolis
Goiás
Rio Verde

Natal
Recife
Maceió
Salvador
João Pessoa
Campina Grande
Caruaru
Garanhuns
Aracaju
Alagoinhas
Feira de Santana
Ilhéus
Itabuna
Vitória da Conquista
Jequié
Fortaleza
Mossoró
Sobral
Caucaia
Parnaíba
Teresina
Codó
Caxias
Bacabal
Imperatriz
São Luís
Bragança
Castanhal
Belém
Cametá
Tucuruí
Marabá
Santarém
Altamira
Itaituba

Araguaína
Petrolina
Juazeiro
Floresta
Paulo Afonso
Montes Claros
Teófilo Otoni
Governador Valadares
Pico da Bandeira 2890

Chapada Diamantina
Brazilian Highlands

Mouths of the Amazon
Ilha de Marajó
Amapá
Porto Santana

Amazon
Negro
Branco
Xingu
Iriri
Culuene
Tapajós
Teles Pires
Arinos
Juruena
Guaporé
Mamoré
Beni
Madeira
Purus
Juruá
Javari
Ucayali
Marañón
Napo
Putumayo
Caquetá
Japurá
Içá
Uaupés
Vaupés
Guaviare
Meta
Casiquiare
Ventuari
Apure
Caroní

Manaus
Represa de Balbina
Porto Velho
Ariquemes
Jiparaná
Vilhena
Theodore Roosevelt
Cruzeiro do Sul
Rio Branco
Benjamin Constant

Serra dos Parecis
Serra do Cachimbo
S. dos Caiabis
Planalto do Mato Grosso
Cuiabá
Cáceres
Rondonópolis
Corixa Grande
Paraguai

Serra Tumucumaque

Equator

Scale 1 : 20 000 000

0   200   400   600   800 km

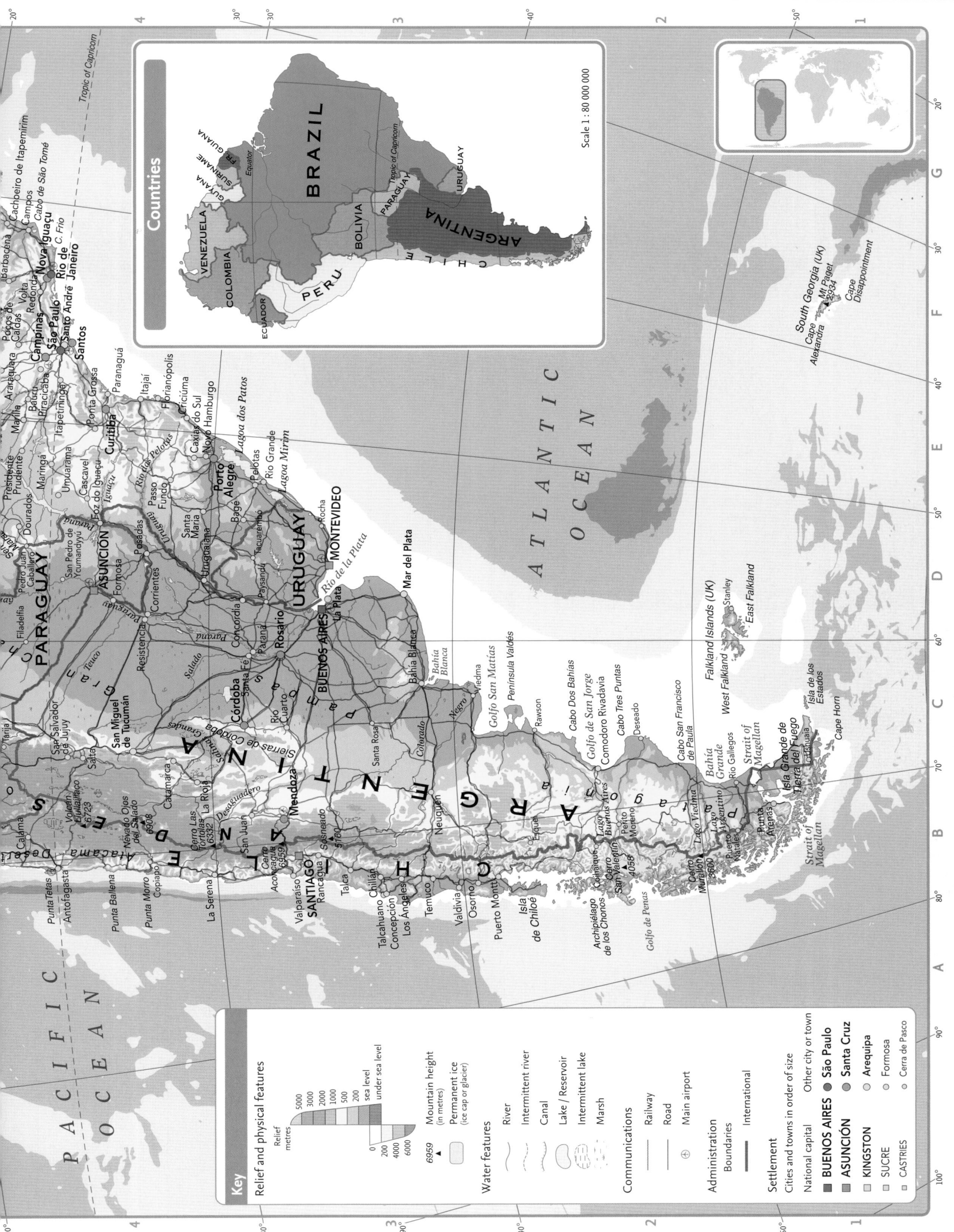

Countries

VENEZUELA
COLOMBIA
ECUADOR
PERU
BRAZIL
GUYANA
SURINAME
FR. GUIANA
BOLIVIA
PARAGUAY
CHILE
ARGENTINA
URUGUAY

Scale 1 : 80 000 000

ATLANTIC OCEAN

PACIFIC OCEAN

Tropic of Capricorn

Equator

Tropic of Capricorn

Key

Relief and physical features

Relief
metres
5000
3000
2000
1000
500
200
sea level
under sea level
0
200
4000
6000

6959 ▲ Mountain height
(in metres)

Permanent ice
(ice cap or glacier)

Water features

River
Intermittent river
Canal
Lake / Reservoir
Intermittent lake
Marsh

Communications

Railway
Road
⊕ Main airport

Administration

Boundaries
International

Settlement

Cities and towns in order of size

National capital | Other city or town
■ BUENOS AIRES | ● São Paulo
■ ASUNCIÓN | ● Santa Cruz
□ KINGSTON | ○ Arequipa
□ SUCRE | ○ Formosa
□ CASTRIES | ○ Cerro de Pasco

Lambert Azimuthal Equal Area projection

1 Temperature and Pressure : January

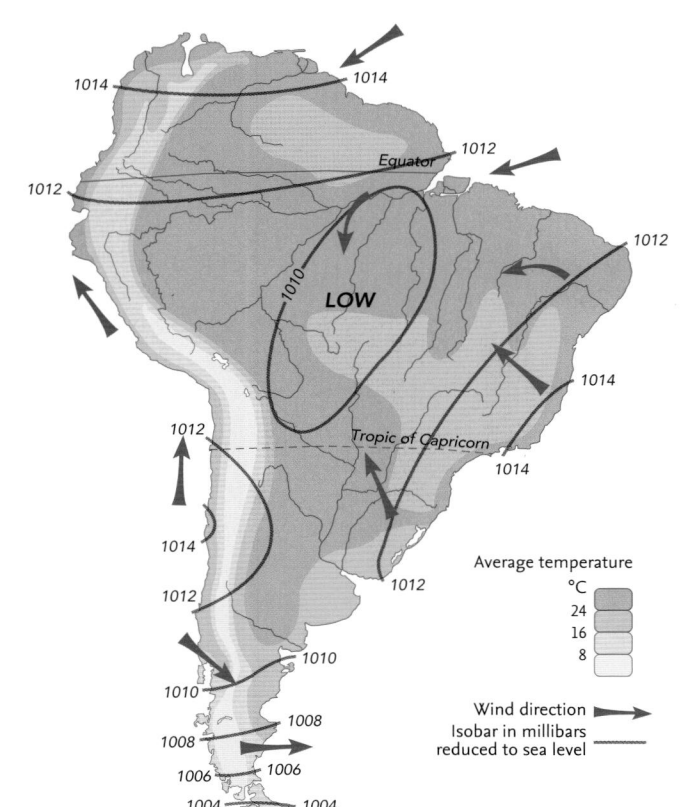

2 Temperature and Pressure : July

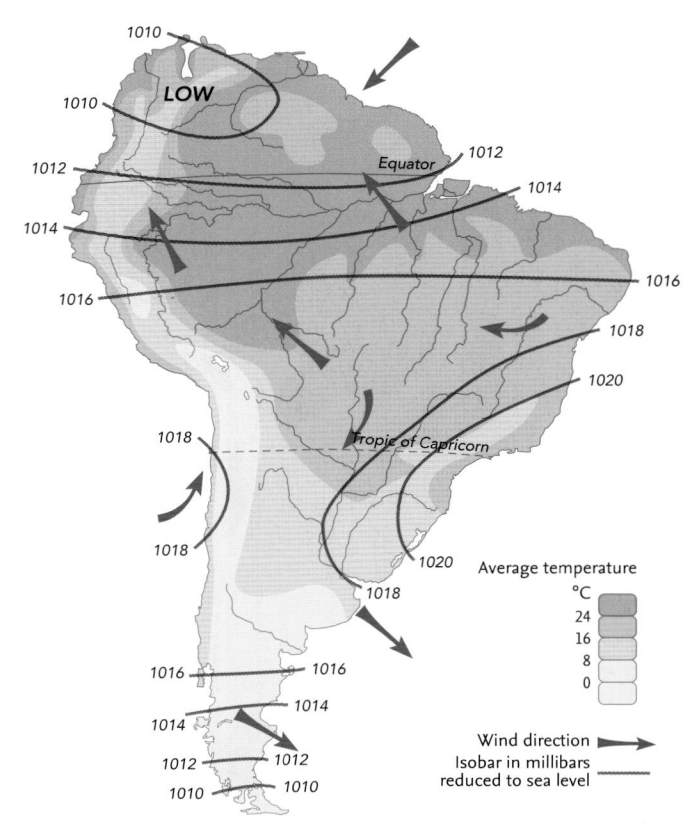

3 Annual Rainfall

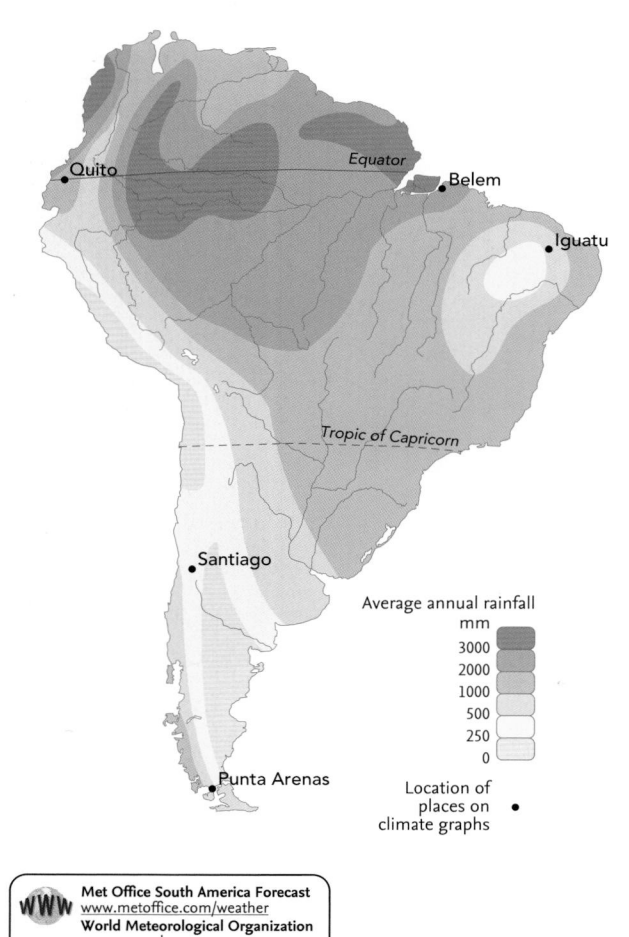

Average annual rainfall
mm
3000
2000
1000
500
250
0

Location of places on climate graphs •

Met Office South America Forecast
www.metoffice.com/weather
World Meteorological Organization
www.wmo.ch
BBC World Weather
www.bbc.co.uk/weather/world

4 Climate Statistics

Quito	Jan	Feb	Mar	Apr	May	Jun	Jul	Aug	Sep	Oct	Nov	Dec
Temperature - max. (°C)	22	22	22	21	21	22	22	23	23	22	22	22
Temperature - min. (°C)	8	8	8	8	8	7	7	7	7	8	7	8
Rainfall - (mm)	99	112	142	175	137	43	20	31	69	112	97	79

Belem	Jan	Feb	Mar	Apr	May	Jun	Jul	Aug	Sep	Oct	Nov	Dec
Temperature - max. (°C)	31	30	31	31	31	31	31	31	32	32	32	32
Temperature - min. (°C)	22	22	23	23	23	22	22	22	22	22	22	22
Rainfall - (mm)	318	358	358	320	259	170	150	112	89	84	66	155

Iguatu	Jan	Feb	Mar	Apr	May	Jun	Jul	Aug	Sep	Oct	Nov	Dec
Temperature - max. (°C)	34	33	32	31	31	31	32	32	35	36	36	36
Temperature - min. (°C)	23	23	23	23	22	22	21	21	22	23	23	23
Rainfall - (mm)	89	173	185	160	61	61	36	5	18	18	10	33

Santiago	Jan	Feb	Mar	Apr	May	Jun	Jul	Aug	Sep	Oct	Nov	Dec
Temperature - max. (°C)	29	29	27	23	18	14	15	17	19	22	26	28
Temperature - min. (°C)	12	11	9	7	5	3	3	4	6	7	9	11
Rainfall - (mm)	3	3	5	13	64	84	76	56	31	15	8	5

Punta Arenas	Jan	Feb	Mar	Apr	May	Jun	Jul	Aug	Sep	Oct	Nov	Dec
Temperature - max. (°C)	14	14	12	10	7	5	4	6	8	11	12	14
Temperature - min. (°C)	7	7	5	4	2	1	-1	1	2	3	4	6
Rainfall - (mm)	38	23	33	36	33	41	28	31	23	28	18	36

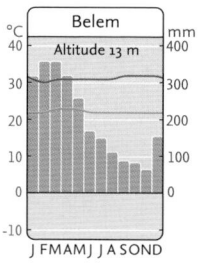
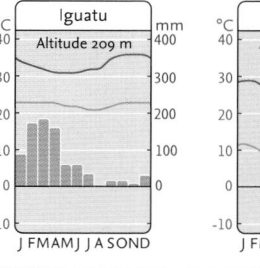
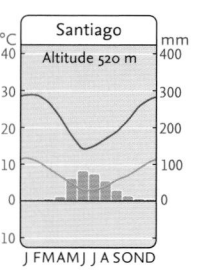
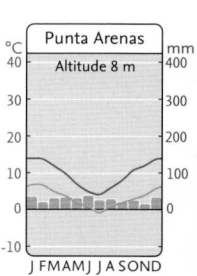

Scale 1 : 70 000 000

0   1000   2000   3000 km

Lambert Azimuthal Equal Area projection

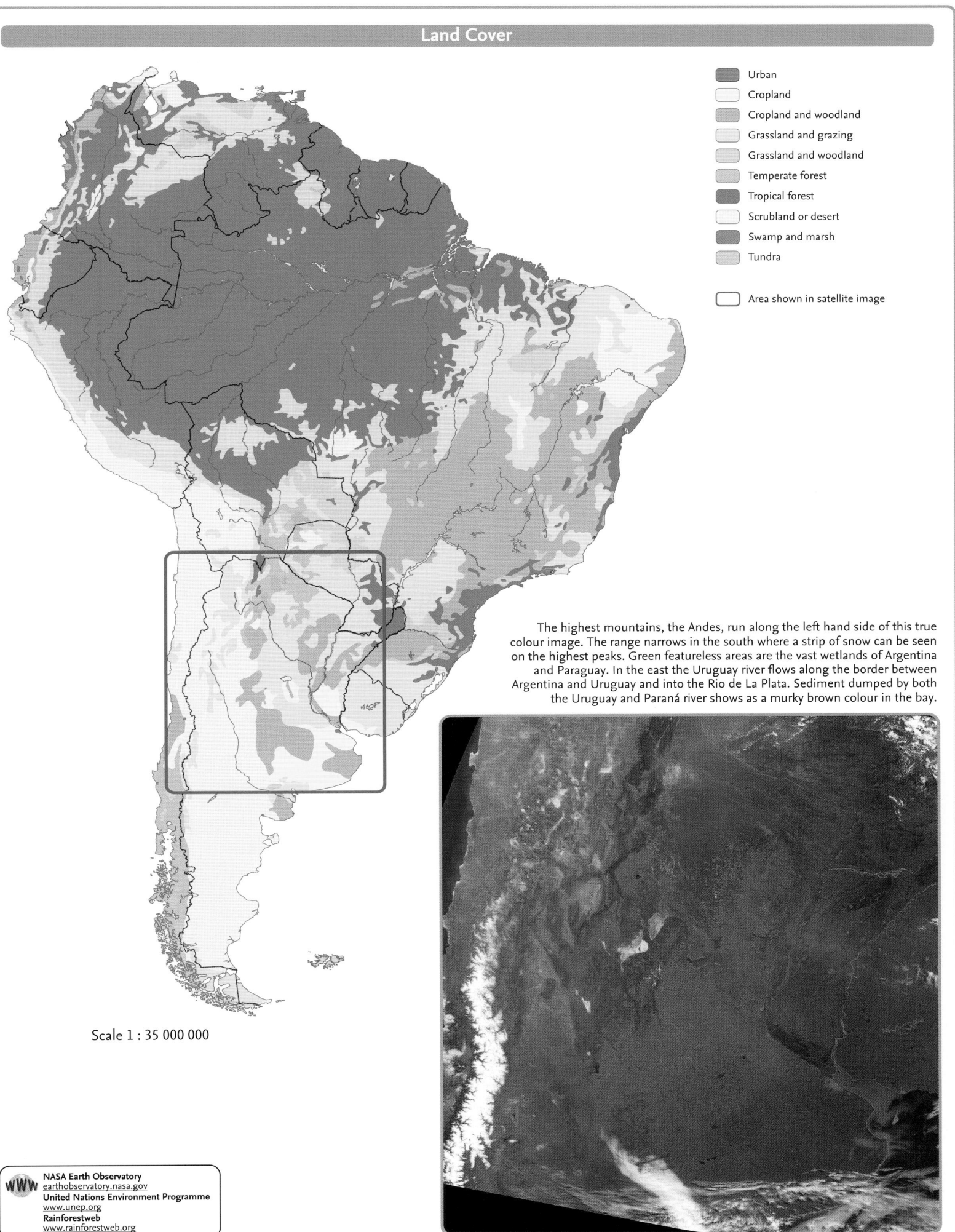

Land Cover

Legend:
- Urban
- Cropland
- Cropland and woodland
- Grassland and grazing
- Grassland and woodland
- Temperate forest
- Tropical forest
- Scrubland or desert
- Swamp and marsh
- Tundra

- Area shown in satellite image

The highest mountains, the Andes, run along the left hand side of this true colour image. The range narrows in the south where a strip of snow can be seen on the highest peaks. Green featureless areas are the vast wetlands of Argentina and Paraguay. In the east the Uruguay river flows along the border between Argentina and Uruguay and into the Rio de La Plata. Sediment dumped by both the Uruguay and Paraná river shows as a murky brown colour in the bay.

Scale 1 : 35 000 000

WWW
NASA Earth Observatory
earthobservatory.nasa.gov
United Nations Environment Programme
www.unep.org
Rainforestweb
www.rainforestweb.org

PACIFIC OCEAN

Galapagos Islands
(Ecuador)

Isla Santa Cruz
Isla San Cristóbal
Baquerizo
Moreno
Isla Isabela

COLOMBIA

Nevado de Huila
5750
Neiva
Popayán
Tumaco
Florencia
Pasto
Caquetá
Esmeraldas
Nevado de Cumbal
4764
Ibarra
Apaporis
Cabo de San Francisco
Uaupés
Negro
Pico da Neblina
3014
Orinoco
Cabo Pasado
Volcán Cotopaxi
5896
QUITO
Napo
Cabo Pantoja
Manta
Latacunga
Tena
Portoviejo
Chimborazo
6310
Ambato
Riobamba
Curaray
Japurá
Putumayo
Amazon
Bahía de Santa Elena
ECUADOR
Alausí
Macas
Tigre
Iquitos
Benjamim Constant
Jutaí
Tefé
Amazon
Guayaquil
Cuenca
Azogues
Pastaza
Marañón
Golfo de Guayaquil
Machala
A M A
Tumbes
Loja
Cord. del Condor
Talara
Macará
Cordillera Oriental
Yavari
Juruá
Coari
Sullana
Catacaos
Cordillera Central
Huallaga
Cordillera Azul
Tarapoto
Ucayali
Ituí
Purus
Bahía de Sechura
Olmos
Marañón
Cruzeiro do Sul
Envira
l i v a
Punta Negra
Chiclayo
Cajamarca
Pucallpa
Tarauacá
ACRE
Humaitá
Pacasmayo
Acre
Sena Madureira
Rio Branco
Abuná
Tarapuá
Trujillo
Nevado de Huascarán
6768
Huánuco
Urubamba
Cordillera Vilcabamba
Ucayali
Cobija
Madre de Dios
Riberalta
Abuná
RO
Ariquem
Chimbote
Cordillera Negra
Cerro de Pasco
Cordillera de Carabaya
Puerto Maldonado
Madidi
Huarmey
P E R U
Huancayo
Cusco
Apurimac
Inambari
Beni
Laguna Rogagua
Huacho
Cordillera Occidental
Huancavelica
Ayacucho
Cordillera Oriental
Cerros de Baía
Mamoré
Lago de San Luis
Callao
LIMA
Pisco
Ica
Abancay
Juliaca
San Borja
Llanos de Mojos
Trinidad
Nazca
Nudo Coropuna
6425
Lake Titicaca
6402
Yungas
Chala
Arequipa
LA PAZ
B O L
Moquegua
Cochabamba
Tacna
Nevado Sajama
6542
Oruro
San Cr
Arica
Altiplano
Cordillera Central
Sucre
Iquique
Salar de Coipasa
Lago de Poopó
Potosí
Uncia
Boy
Vi
Mont
Salar de Uyuni
Uyuni
Tocopilla
Tupiza
Tarija
Cordillera Occidental
Calama
Atacama
Punta Tetas
Salar de Atacama
San Salvador de Jujuy
Pichanal
Antofagasta
Volcán Llullaillaco
6723
Nevados de Cachi
6720
Salta
Taltal
D A R G E
Punta Ballena
Nevado Ojos del Salado
6908
San Miguel de Tucumán
Chañaral
Cerro Bonete
6872
Concepción
La Banda
Punta Morro
Copiapó
Sa Fe
Catamarca
La Rioja
Cord. de Oliva
Mejicana
6250
Cerro Champaquí 2880
La Serena
Cerro Las Tórtolas
6332
Patquía
Sierras de Córdoba
Cord
Coquimbo
C H I L E
Los Vilos
Cerro Aconcagua
6959
San Juan
Mendoza
Cord
Viña del Mar
Valparaíso
SANTIAGO
San Bernardo
Rancagua
Los Luis
R
Ne
72

São Paulo

Res. Juqueri
Juqueri
Caieiras
Res. Pirapora
Guarulhos
Tietê
Tietê
Osasco
Suzano
Cotia
Cotia
São Paulo
Pinheiros
São Caetano do Sul
Tamanduateí
Santo André
Res. Pedro Beicht
Billur-Mirim
Res. Guarapiranoa
Res. Billinos
Res. Rio das Pedras

Legend	
Residential	
Industrial	
Commercial	
Commercial/Residential	
Government	
Recreation	
Parks	
Other use	
Road	
Railway	

Scale 1 : 750 000
0   5   10   15 km

Key

Relief and physical features

Relief metres
5000
3000
2000
1000
500
200
0 sea level
200
4000
6000 under sea level

6959 ▲ Mountain height (in metres)

Water features

~~~ River
Intermittent river
Canal
Lake / Reservoir
Intermittent lake
Marsh

Communications

Railway
Road
⊕ Main airport

Administration

Boundaries
International
Internal
Disputed

Settlement

Cities and towns in order of size

National capital
■ BUENOS AIRES
■ BRASÍLIA
□ SUCRE

Other city or town
● São Paulo
● Recife
○ Teresina
○ Vitória
○ Salto

Scale 1 : 15 000 000
0   200   400   600   800 km

GUYANA

AMAPÁ

Mouths of the Amazon

Ilha de Marajó

Manaus

PARÁ

Belém

São Luís

Fortaleza

MARANHÃO

CEARÁ

Teresina

RIO GRANDE DO NORTE

Natal

PIAUÍ

PARAÍBA

João Pessoa

PERNAMBUCO

Recife

Olinda

ALAGOAS

Maceió

SERGIPE

Aracaju

B R A Z I L

M A T O   G R O S S O

Planalto do Mato Grosso

TOCANTINS

Brazilian Highlands

B A H I A

Salvador

PARAGUAY

MATO GROSSO DO SUL

Campo Grande

GOIÁS

BRASÍLIA

Goiânia

DISTRITO FEDERAL

MINAS   GERAIS

Pico de Itambé
2033

Pico de Bandeira
2890

Belo Horizonte

ESPÍRITO SANTO

Vitória

ASUNCIÓN

SÃO PAULO

São Paulo

Campinas

Santos

Nova Iguaçu

RIO DE JANEIRO

Rio de Janeiro

Niterói

PARANÁ

Curitiba

SANTA CATARINA

Florianópolis

URUGUAY

RIO GRANDE DO SUL

Porto Alegre

Tropic of Capricorn

A T L A N T I C

O C E A N

Lagoa dos Patos

Lagoa Mirim

BUENOS AIRES

Lambert Azimuthal Equal Area projection

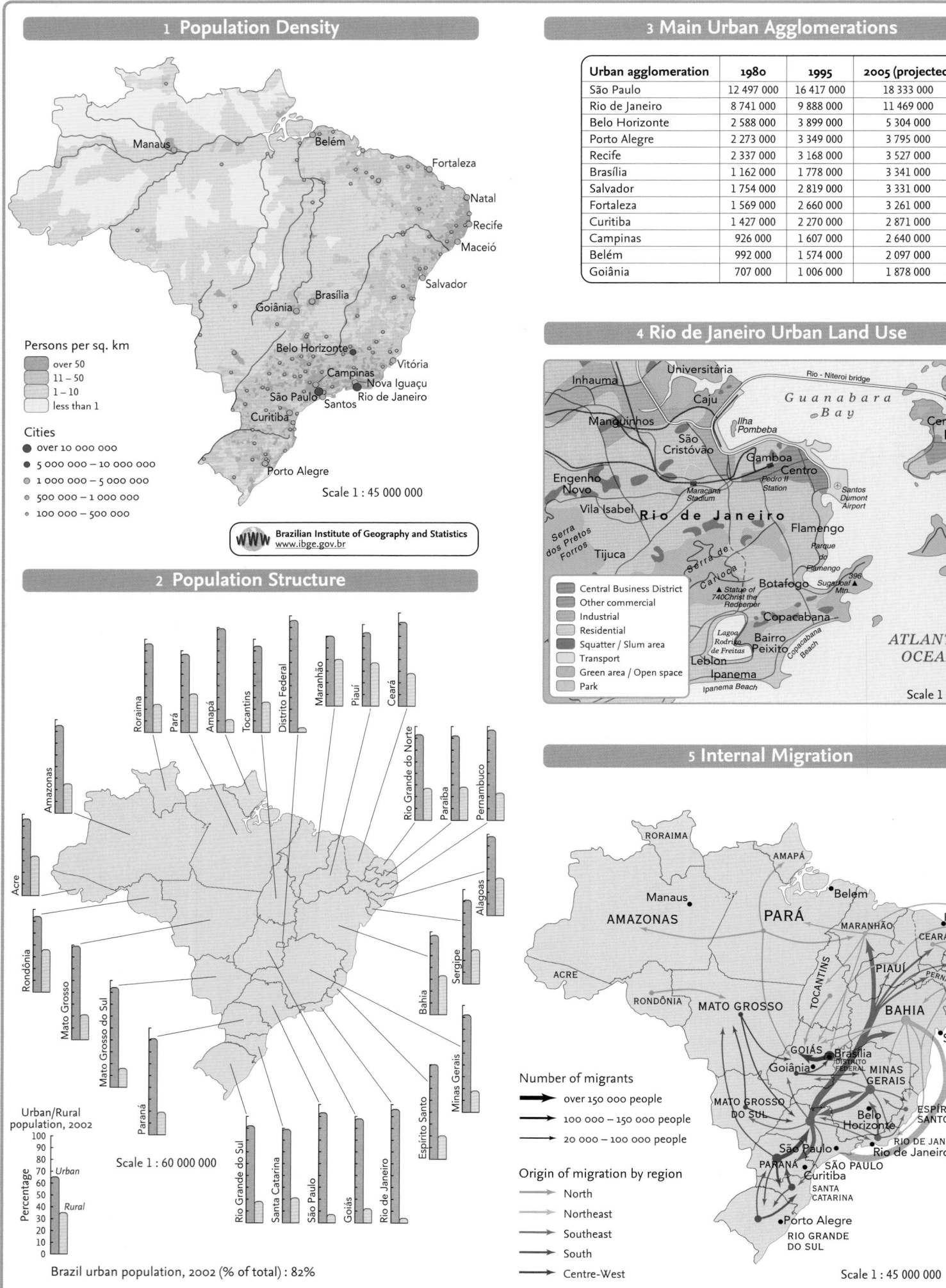

1 Population Density

Persons per sq. km
- over 50
- 11 – 50
- 1 – 10
- less than 1

Cities
- over 10 000 000
- 5 000 000 – 10 000 000
- 1 000 000 – 5 000 000
- 500 000 – 1 000 000
- 100 000 – 500 000

Scale 1 : 45 000 000

www Brazilian Institute of Geography and Statistics
www.ibge.gov.br

2 Population Structure

Urban/Rural
population, 2002

Urban
Rural

Scale 1 : 60 000 000

Brazil urban population, 2002 (% of total) : 82%

3 Main Urban Agglomerations

Urban agglomeration	1980	1995	2005 (projected)
São Paulo	12 497 000	16 417 000	18 333 000
Rio de Janeiro	8 741 000	9 888 000	11 469 000
Belo Horizonte	2 588 000	3 899 000	5 304 000
Porto Alegre	2 273 000	3 349 000	3 795 000
Recife	2 337 000	3 168 000	3 527 000
Brasília	1 162 000	1 778 000	3 341 000
Salvador	1 754 000	2 819 000	3 331 000
Fortaleza	1 569 000	2 660 000	3 261 000
Curitiba	1 427 000	2 270 000	2 871 000
Campinas	926 000	1 607 000	2 640 000
Belém	992 000	1 574 000	2 097 000
Goiânia	707 000	1 006 000	1 878 000

4 Rio de Janeiro Urban Land Use

- Central Business District
- Other commercial
- Industrial
- Residential
- Squatter / Slum area
- Transport
- Green area / Open space
- Park

Scale 1 : 200 000

5 Internal Migration

Number of migrants
- over 150 000 people
- 100 000 – 150 000 people
- 20 000 – 100 000 people

Origin of migration by region
- North
- Northeast
- Southeast
- South
- Centre-West

Scale 1 : 45 000 000

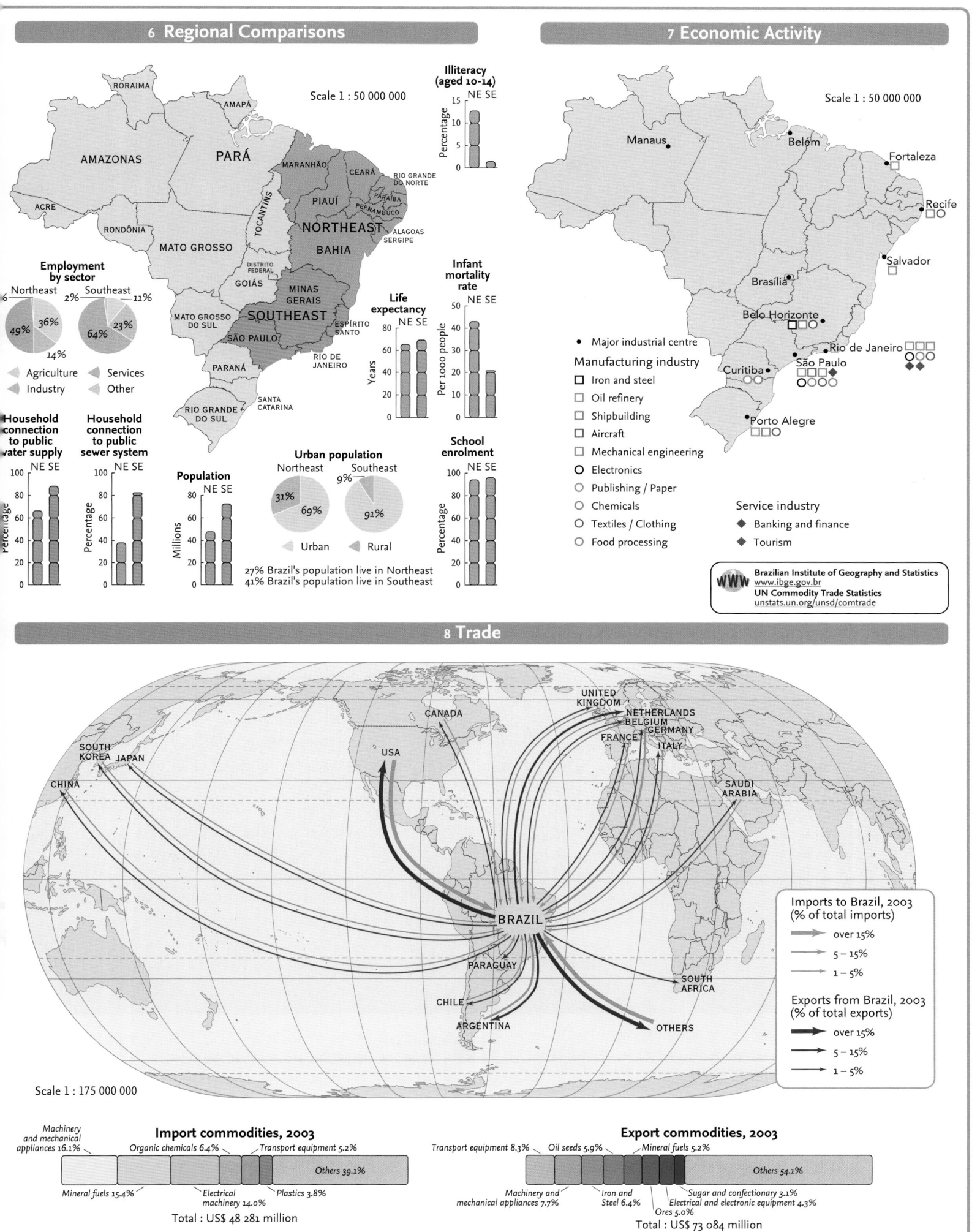

6 Regional Comparisons

Scale 1 : 50 000 000

RORAIMA
AMAPÁ
AMAZONAS
PARÁ
MARANHÃO
CEARÁ
RIO GRANDE DO NORTE
ACRE
RONDÔNIA
TOCANTINS
PIAUÍ
PARAÍBA
PERNAMBUCO
NORTHEAST
ALAGOAS
SERGIPE
MATO GROSSO
BAHIA
DISTRITO FEDERAL
GOIÁS
MINAS GERAIS
MATO GROSSO DO SUL
SOUTHEAST
ESPÍRITO SANTO
SÃO PAULO
RIO DE JANEIRO
PARANÁ
SANTA CATARINA
RIO GRANDE DO SUL

Illiteracy (aged 10-14)
NE SE
Percentage

Infant mortality rate
NE SE
Per 1000 people

Life expectancy
NE SE
Years

School enrolment
NE SE
Percentage

Employment by sector

Northeast
6% 2%
49% 36%
14%

Southeast
11%
64% 23%

◁ Agriculture   ◁ Services
◁ Industry   ◁ Other

Household connection to public water supply
NE SE
Percentage

Household connection to public sewer system
NE SE
Percentage

Population
NE SE
Millions

Urban population

Northeast
31% 69%

Southeast
9% 91%

◁ Urban   ◁ Rural

27% Brazil's population live in Northeast
41% Brazil's population live in Southeast

7 Economic Activity

Scale 1 : 50 000 000

Manaus
Belém
Fortaleza
Recife
Salvador
Brasília
Belo Horizonte
Rio de Janeiro
Curitiba
São Paulo
Porto Alegre

• Major industrial centre

Manufacturing industry
□ Iron and steel
□ Oil refinery
□ Shipbuilding
□ Aircraft
□ Mechanical engineering
○ Electronics
○ Publishing / Paper
○ Chemicals
○ Textiles / Clothing
○ Food processing

Service industry
◆ Banking and finance
◆ Tourism

WWW **Brazilian Institute of Geography and Statistics**
www.ibge.gov.br
UN Commodity Trade Statistics
unstats.un.org/unsd/comtrade

8 Trade

CANADA
UNITED KINGDOM
NETHERLANDS
BELGIUM
GERMANY
FRANCE
ITALY
SOUTH KOREA
JAPAN
CHINA
USA
SAUDI ARABIA
BRAZIL
PARAGUAY
SOUTH AFRICA
CHILE
ARGENTINA
OTHERS

Imports to Brazil, 2003 (% of total imports)
→ over 15%
→ 5 – 15%
→ 1 – 5%

Exports from Brazil, 2003 (% of total exports)
→ over 15%
→ 5 – 15%
→ 1 – 5%

Scale 1 : 175 000 000

Import commodities, 2003
Machinery and mechanical appliances 16.1%
Organic chemicals 6.4%
Transport equipment 5.2%
Others 39.1%
Mineral fuels 15.4%
Electrical machinery 14.0%
Plastics 3.8%
Total : US$ 48 281 million

Export commodities, 2003
Transport equipment 8.3%
Oil seeds 5.9%
Mineral fuels 5.2%
Others 54.1%
Machinery and mechanical appliances 7.7%
Iron and Steel 6.4%
Ores 5.0%
Sugar and confectionary 3.1%
Electrical and electronic equipment 4.3%
Total : US$ 73 084 million

Deforested areas
Yellowish green coloured lines mark land cleared of forest for commercial logging. Most of the deforestation has taken place in Rondônia state which covers most of the right hand side of the image.

Forest
Areas of forest appear deep green on the image. Left of centre the forests of the Pando region of Bolivia remain undisturbed.

Rivers
The course of the Madeira river is clearly visible where it flows through forest, top centre.

Highland
The highland areas of the Serra dos Parecis, in Rondônia state, appear dark brown.

Fires
Numerous smoke plumes from forest fires suggest the practice of slash and burn farming is still underway.

Water bodies
Deep reservoirs are almost black in the image, however the outlines of shallower lagoons on the Bolivian side of the border show clearly in pale green.

64° 60° 56°

São Luís de Cassianã
Pirapetinga
Três Casas
Natal
Canudos
Barra do São Manuel
Fortaleza de Ituxi
Lábrea
Majuriã
Sintra
Prainha
Cuiabá
Majuriã
Macimirim
Castanho
Santa Rita
São Bento
Humaitá
Boa Esperança
Recreio
Mamoriá
Papagaios
Calama
Jatuarana
Sumaúma

A M A Z O N A S

Boca do Curuquetê
Estrema
Mutum
Foz do Jamari
Lago Verde
Jamari
Jacaretinga
Bom Jardim
Porto Velho
São Antônio
Campo Grande
São Carlos
São Pedro
Preto
Tabajara
Barracão do Barreto
Caldeirão
Jaciparaná
Caritianas
Queimada
Panelas
Jirau
São Sebastião
Ariquemes
Espírito Santo
Manoa
Abunã
Mutumparaná
Jacaré
Oriente
Nova Vida
Conceição
Araras
Ribeirão
Seringal Sétena
Aripuanã
Villa Bella
Guajará Mirim
Antuerpia
Jaru
Juína
Guayaramerín
Cataqueamã
Ji-Paraná
Presidente Hermes
Riberalta
Ivón
Batallas
Boa Hora
Jiparaná
Riozinho
Pimenta Bueno

B R A Z I L

R O N D Ô N I A

M A T O   G R O S S O

P A R Á

B E N I

B O L I V I A

S A N T A   C R U Z

Concepción
Triunfo
Rolim de Moura
Barão de Melgaço
Puerto Alejandría
Santa Rosa
Santa Rosa de Vigo
Costa Marques
Maloca Salamaim
Porto do Massacas
Vilhena
Agua Clara
Puerto Génova
Puerto Siles
San Simão
Consuelo
Pedras Negras
Porto Triunfo
Porto Amarante
Los Cusis
San Joaquín
San Ramón
Orobayaya
Mategua
Cassara
Frutuoso
Magdalena
Huacaraje
Baures
Puerto Villazon
Piso Firme
Palacios
El Carmen
San Joaquín
Puerto Saucedo
San Cristóbal
Porvenir
Sta Isabel

Santa Ana de Yacuma
Marsella
Guayabal
Holanda
Huachi
Fonte do Pau d'Agua

Santa Rosa
San Pedro
San Javier
La Esperanza
Monte Cristo
Puerto Frey
Cachal
Perseverancia
San Martín
Sarare
Rapulo
San Andrés
Trinidad
San Ignacio

Causes of deforestation in the Amazon Basin

Key

Relief and physical features

Relief metres
1000
500
200
sea level

1095 ▲ Mountain height (in metres)

Water features

~~~ River
Lake / Reservoir
Marsh

Communications

—— Road

Administration

Boundaries
━━ International
—— Internal

Settlement

Other city or town
◎ Porto Velho
◦ Panelas

▢ Area shown in satellite image

Scale 1 : 6 000 000

0   50   100   150 km

www Center for Global Environmental Education. The Amazon River
cgee.hamline.edu/rivers/Resources
Educational Web Adventures Amazon Interactive
www.eduweb.com/amazon.html
NASA Earth Observatory Amazonia
earthobservatory.nasa.gov/Study/LBA

— Hydro-electric power dam
– Hydro-electric power dam (planned)
◆ Mining operations
— Extent of Amazonia in Brazil

Land Use

Cropland and woodland
Grassland and grazing
Grassland and woodland
Tropical forest
Temperate forest
Scrubland or desert
Swamp or marsh
Deforestation

Communications

—— Railway
---- Railway (planned)
—— Road
---- Road (planned)

Scale 1 : 30 000 000

Equator
Macapá
Belém
São Luís
Manaus
Santarém
Marabá
Rio Branco
Porto Velho
Cuiabá

Tropic of Capricorn

Causes of deforestation in the Amazon Basin
• Clearing for cattle grazing
• Colonisation and subsequent subsistence agriculture
• Infrastructure improvements
• Commercial agriculture
• Commercial logging

Brazil deforestation
1990 – 2003

Area (thousand sq. km)

30
25
20
15
10
5
0

1990 1991 1992 1993 1994 1995 1996 1997 1998 1999 2000 2001 2002 2003

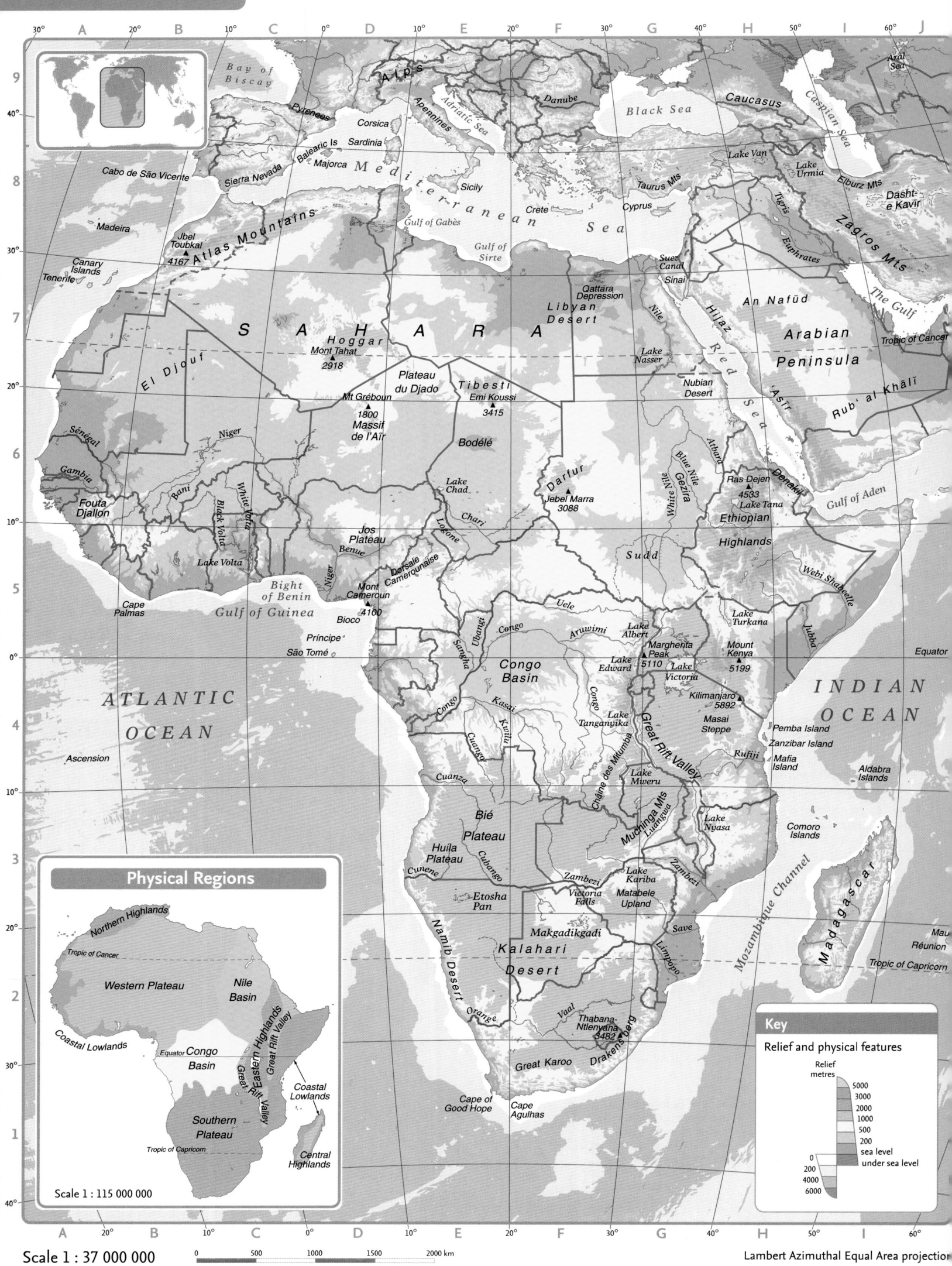

ALPS

Bay of
Biscay

Pyrenees

Corsica

Apennines

Adriatic Sea

Danube

Black Sea

Caucasus

Aral Sea

Caspian Sea

Cabo de São Vicente

Sierra Nevada

Balearic Is
Majorca

Sardinia

M e d i t e r r a n e a n

Sicily

Crete

Cyprus

Taurus Mts

Lake Van

Lake Urmia

Elburz Mts

Zagros Mts

Dasht-e Kavir

Madeira

Atlas Mountains

Jbel Toubkal
4167

Gulf of Gabès

S e a

Gulf of Sirte

Gulf of Sirte

Suez Canal

Sinai

Qattara Depression

Libyan Desert

Nile

Red Sea

Hijaz

'Asir

An Nafūd

Arabian Peninsula

Tropic of Cancer

The Gulf

Canary Islands
Tenerife

S A H A R A

Hoggar
Mont Tahat
2918

El Djouf

Plateau du Djado

Tibesti
Emi Koussi
3415

Lake Nasser

Nubian Desert

Rub' al Khālī

Sénégal

Niger

Mt Gréboun
1800
Massif de l'Aïr

Bodélé

Darfur
Jebel Marra
3088

Blue Nile

Atbara

Ras Dejen
4533
Lake Tana

Denakil

Gulf of Aden

Gambia

Bani

White Volta

Black Volta

Lake Chad

Chari

Logone

Gezira

White Nile

Ethiopian Highlands

Fouta Djallon

Jos Plateau

Benue

Niger

Dorsale Camerounaise

Sudd

Webi Shabeelle

Lake Volta

Bight of Benin

Mont Cameroun
4100

Uele

Cape Palmas

Gulf of Guinea

Bioco

Ubangi

Congo

Aruwimi

Lake Albert

Margherita Peak
5110

Lake Turkana

Jubba

Príncipe

São Tomé

Sangha

Congo Basin

Kasai

Lake Edward

Lake Victoria

Mount Kenya
5199

Equator

INDIAN OCEAN

ATLANTIC OCEAN

Congo

Kwilu

Lake Tanganyika

Congo

Lake Kivu

Kilimanjaro
5892

Masai Steppe

Pemba Island

Zanzibar Island

Mafia Island

Aldabra Islands

Ascension

Cuango

Cuanza

Chaîne des Mitumba

Great Rift Valley

Rufiji

Cape of Good Hope

Bié Plateau

Lake Mweru

Muchinga Mts

Luangwa

Lake Nyasa

Comoro Islands

Huíla Plateau

Cunene

Cubango

Zambezi

Lake Kariba

Zambezi

Madagascar

Mau

Réunion

Namib Desert

Etosha Pan

Victoria Falls

Matabele Upland

Mozambique Channel

Tropic of Capricorn

Makgadikgadi

Save

Limpopo

Kalahari Desert

Orange

Vaal

Thabana-Ntlenyana
3482

Drakensberg

Great Karoo

Cape Agulhas

Key

Relief and physical features

Relief metres

5000
3000
2000
1000
500
200
0
sea level
under sea level

200
4000
6000

Scale 1 : 37 000 000

0   500   1000   1500   2000 km

Lambert Azimuthal Equal Area projection

1 Temperature and Pressure : January

Average temperature
°C
32
24
16
8

Wind direction →
Isobar in millibars reduced to sea level

LOW

Tropic of Cancer
Equator
Tropic of Capricorn

2 Temperature and Pressure : July

Average temperature
°C
32
24
16
8

Wind direction →
Isobar in millibars reduced to sea level

Tropic of Cancer
Equator
Tropic of Capricorn

WWW Met Office Africa Forecast
www.metoffice.com/weather
World Meteorological Organization
www.wmo.ch
BBC World Weather
www.bbc.co.uk/weather/world

3 Annual Rainfall

Average annual rainfall
mm
3000
2000
1000
500
250
0

• Location of places on climate graphs

Algiers
Timbuktu
Conakry
Nairobi
Walvis Bay

Tropic of Cancer
Equator
Tropic of Capricorn

4 Climate Statistics

Algiers	Jan	Feb	Mar	Apr	May	Jun	Jul	Aug	Sep	Oct	Nov	Dec
Temperature - max. (°C)	15	16	17	20	23	26	28	29	27	23	19	16
Temperature - min. (°C)	9	9	11	13	15	18	21	22	21	17	13	11
Rainfall - (mm)	112	84	74	41	46	15	0	5	41	79	130	137

Timbuktu	Jan	Feb	Mar	Apr	May	Jun	Jul	Aug	Sep	Oct	Nov	Dec
Temperature - max. (°C)	27	31	34	38	41	40	37	35	37	37	33	28
Temperature - min. (°C)	14	17	21	24	27	29	27	27	26	24	19	15
Rainfall - (mm)	0	0	0	0	4	19	62	79	33	3	0	0

Conakry	Jan	Feb	Mar	Apr	May	Jun	Jul	Aug	Sep	Oct	Nov	Dec
Temperature - max. (°C)	31	31	32	32	32	30	28	28	29	31	31	31
Temperature - min. (°C)	22	23	23	23	24	23	22	22	23	23	24	23
Rainfall - (mm)	3	3	10	23	158	559	1298	1054	683	371	122	10

Nairobi	Jan	Feb	Mar	Apr	May	Jun	Jul	Aug	Sep	Oct	Nov	Dec
Temperature - max. (°C)	25	26	25	24	22	21	21	21	24	24	23	23
Temperature - min. (°C)	12	13	14	14	13	12	11	11	11	13	13	13
Rainfall - (mm)	38	64	125	211	158	46	15	23	31	53	109	86

Walvis Bay	Jan	Feb	Mar	Apr	May	Jun	Jul	Aug	Sep	Oct	Nov	Dec
Temperature - max. (°C)	23	23	23	24	23	23	21	20	19	19	22	22
Temperature - min. (°C)	15	16	15	13	11	9	8	9	11	12	14
Rainfall - (mm)	0	5	8	3	3	0	0	3	0	0	0	0

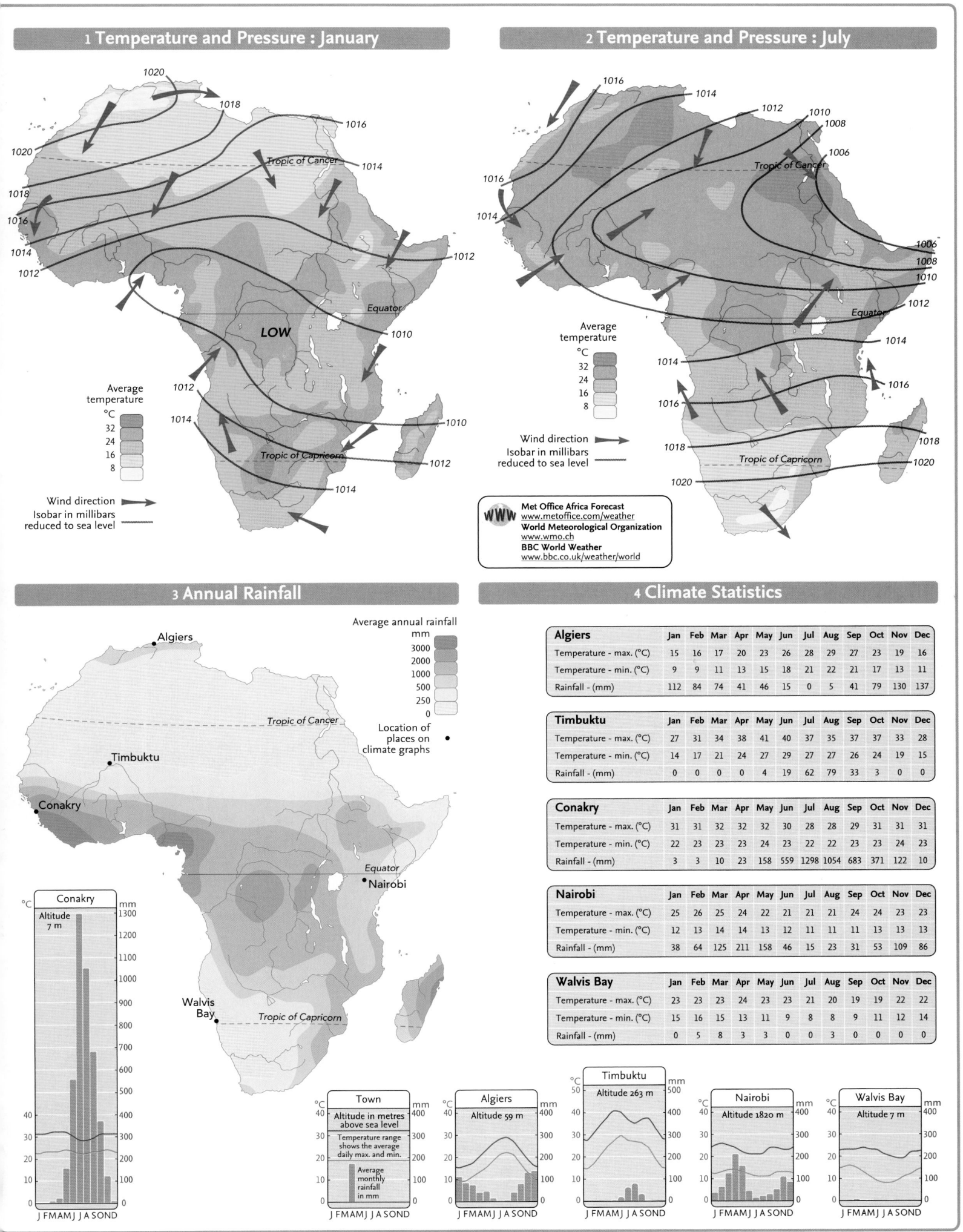

Conakry
°C Altitude 7 m mm
1300
...

Town
Altitude in metres above sea level
Temperature range shows the average daily max. and min.
Average monthly rainfall in mm
J FMAMJ J ASOND

Algiers
Altitude 59 m
J FMAMJ J ASOND

Timbuktu
°C Altitude 263 m mm
50 500
J FMAMJ J ASOND

Nairobi
Altitude 1820 m
J FMAMJ J ASOND

Walvis Bay
Altitude 7 m
J FMAMJ J ASOND

Scale 1 : 77 000 000

0   1000   2000   3000 km

Lambert Azimuthal Equal Area projection

PORTUGAL
LISBON
SPAIN
Mérida
Minorca
Sassari
Naples
ITA
Córdoba
Valencia
Ibiza
Palma de Mallorca
Majorca
Sardinia (Italy)
Cabo de São Vicente
Faro
Seville
Málaga
Murcia
Alicante
Balearic Islands
Cagliari
Palermo
Mo
Madeira (Portugal)
Tangier
Gibraltar (UK)
Ceuta (Sp.)
Melilla (Sp.)
Oran
ALGIERS
Bejaïa
Skikda
Annaba
TUNIS
Sicily (Italy)
Funchal
Tétouan
RABAT
Fez (Fès)
Oujda
Sidi Bel Abbès
Tlemcen
Blida
Sétif
Constantine
Bizerte
MALTA
VAL
Casablanca
Meknès
Djelfa
Batna
Kasserine
Sfax
Sousse
Kairouan
El Jadida
Settat
Beni Mellal
Bouârfa
Aïn Sefra
Laghouat
Biskra
Chott Melrhir
Gafsa
Gulf of Gabès
Safi
Marrakesh
Haut Atlas Mountains
Er Rachidia
Ghardaïa
Touggourt
TUNISIA
Medenine
Chott el Jerid
TRIPOLI
Jbel Toubkal ▲ 4167
MOROCCO
Ouarzazate
Béchar
Ouargla
Hassi Messaoud
Ghadāmis
Mişrātah
Agadir
Tiznit
Atlas
Abadla
El Goléa
Daraj
Nālūt
Canary Islands (Spain)
La Palma
Santa Cruz de Tenerife
Lanzarote
Guelmine
Ksabi
Bordj Omer Driss
Awbārī
L
Tenerife
Fuerteventura
Boujdour
Tindouf
In Salah
Murzūq
Ghāt
Las Palmas de Gran Canaria
Gran Canaria
LAÂYOUNE
ALGERIA
Sab
Tropic of Cancer
Ad Dakhla
Galtat Zemmour
Bir Mogrein
Aïn Ben Tili
Reggane
Arak
SAHARA
Hoggar
Mt Tahat ▲ 2918
Plateau du Djado
WESTERN SAHARA
Zouérat
Fdérik
Tamanrasset
Nouâdhibou
Râs Nouâdhibou
Choûm
Atâr
MAURITANIA
NIGER
Ponta do Sol
Santo Antão
Sal
Boa Vista
NOUAKCHOTT
Tidjikja
Anéfis
Arlit
Massif de l'Aïr
Mindelo
CAPE VERDE
Fogo
Santiago
PRAIA
St-Louis
Rosso
Sénégal
Timbuktu
Gao
Agadez
Tanout
Nguigmi
DAKAR
Cap Vert
Thiès
Kaolack
BANJUL
Matam
Nioro
MALI
Niger
Mopti
Tillabéri
NIAMEY
Birnin Konni
Maradi
Zinder
Lake Chad
SENEGAL
Kayes
Bani
San
Dosso
Sokoto
Katsina
Gashua
THE GAMBIA
Gambia
Tambacounda
BAMAKO
BURKINA
Kantchari
Gaya
Gusau
Kano
NDJAMENA
Maiduguri
GUINEA-BISSAU
BISSAU
Koundâra
Fouta Djallon
Labé
Siguiri
Sikasso
OUAGADOUGOU
Pô
Dapaong
Zaria
Potiskum
Fria
Bobo-Dioulasso
Wa
BENIN
Kaduna
Jos
Bauchi
Kumo
Maroua
CONAKRY
Kankan
Ferkessédougou
White Volta
Tamale
Parakou
Minna
ABUJA
NIGERIA
GUINEA
Beyla
CÔTE D'IVOIRE
Bouaké
Bondoukou
Wenchi
GHANA
TOGO
Ogbomosho
Ilorin
Lokoja
Benue
Garoua
FREETOWN
SIERRA LEONE
Bo
Zimmi
Guéckédou
Daloa
YAMOUSSOUKRO
Kumasi
Lake Volta
Abéokuta
Ibadan
Iwo
Benin City
Enugu
Makurdi
Mot
ATLANTIC OCEAN
MONROVIA
LIBERIA
Greenville
Sassandra
Abidjan
ACCRA
LOMÉ
Cotonou
PORTO-NOVO
Lagos
Warri
Onitsha
Calabar
CAMEROON
Bafoussam
Dorsale Camerounaise
Cape Palmas
Sekondi
Bight of Benin
Port Harcourt
Mont Cameroun ▲ 4100
Ngaoundéré
Tibati
Bertoua
Berbé
Gulf of Guinea
EQUATORIAL GUINEA
MALABO
Bioco
YAOUNDÉ
Douala
Nkongsamba
SÃO TOMÉ AND PRÍNCIPE
Príncipe
Bata
EQUATORIAL GUINEA
CO
São Tomé
SÃO TOMÉ
LIBREVILLE
Bifoun
GABON
Port-Gentil
Francevill
BRAZZAVILLE
Pointe-Noire
ANGOLA
Cabinda
KINSH
A
Matadi
Boma
M'ban
Congo
Uíge
LUANDA

Key

Relief and physical features

Relief metres
5000
3000
2000
1000
500
200
sea level
under sea level
0
200
4000
6000

5892 ▲ Mountain height (in metres)

Water features

~ River
~ Intermittent river
Canal
Lake / Reservoir
Intermittent lake
Marsh

Communications

Railway
Road
⊕ Main airport

Administration

Boundaries
—— International
---- Disputed

Settlement
Cities and towns in order of size

National capital
■ CAIRO
■ KINSHASA
□ JERUSALEM
□ DJIBOUTI
□ MALABO

Other city or town
● Lagos
● Abidjan
○ Kano
○ Luxor
○ Kankan

Scale 1 : 20 000 000

0   200   400   600   800 km

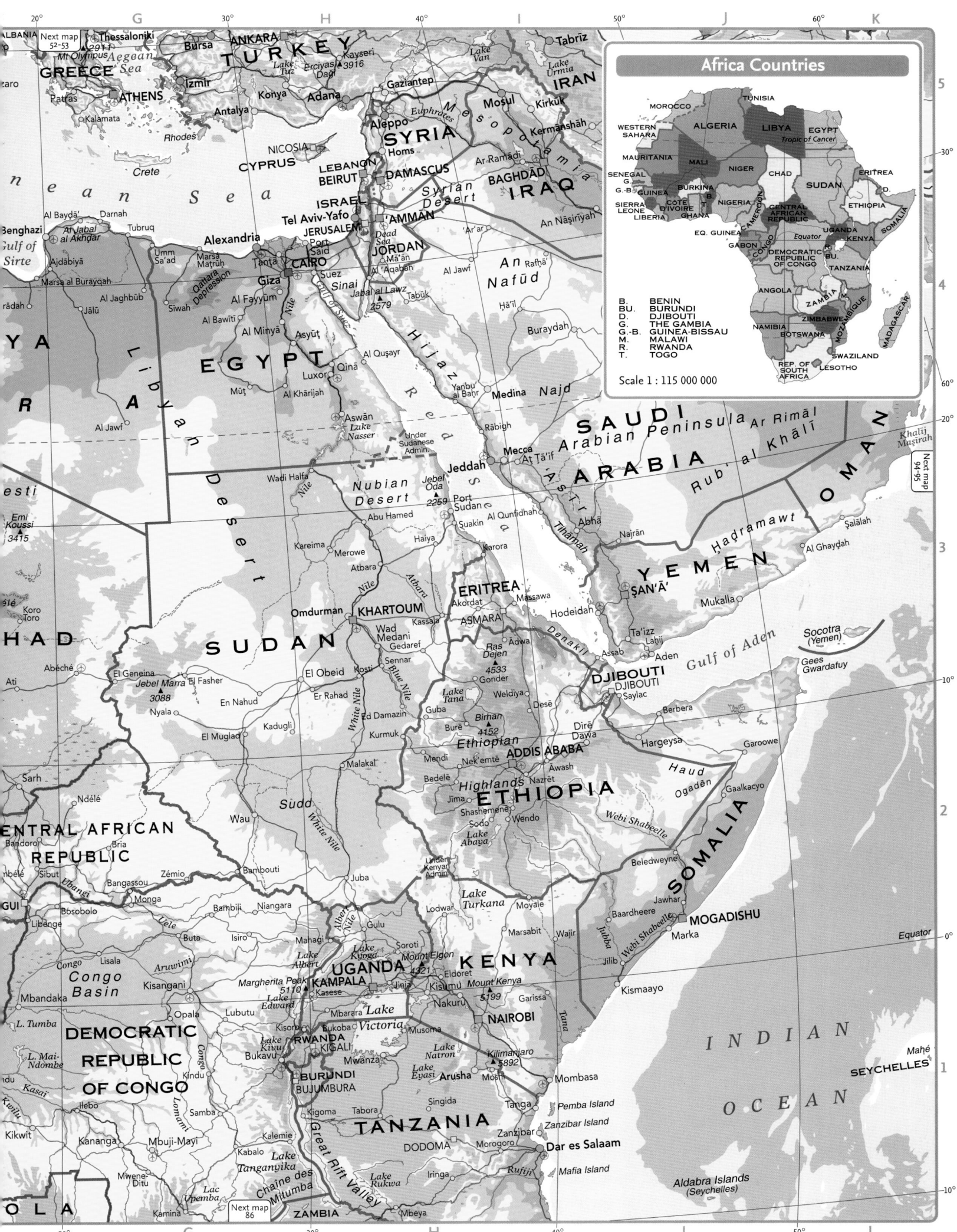

Africa Countries

MOROCCO
WESTERN SAHARA
TUNISIA
ALGERIA
LIBYA
EGYPT
MAURITANIA
MALI
NIGER
CHAD
SUDAN
ERITREA
SENEGAL
G.
G.-B.
GUINEA
BURKINA
NIGERIA
CENTRAL AFRICAN REPUBLIC
ETHIOPIA
D.
SIERRA LEONE
CÔTE D'IVOIRE
GHANA
BENIN
CAMEROON
UGANDA
KENYA
SOMALIA
LIBERIA
EQ. GUINEA
GABON
CONGO
DEMOCRATIC REPUBLIC OF CONGO
R.
BU.
TANZANIA
ANGOLA
ZAMBIA
M.
MALAWI
MOZAMBIQUE
MADAGASCAR
NAMIBIA
ZIMBABWE
BOTSWANA
REP. OF SOUTH AFRICA
SWAZILAND
LESOTHO
Tropic of Cancer
Equator

B. BENIN
BU. BURUNDI
D. DJIBOUTI
G. THE GAMBIA
G.-B. GUINEA-BISSAU
M. MALAWI
R. RWANDA
T. TOGO

Scale 1 : 115 000 000

Main map labels

GREECE — Thessaloniki, Mt Olympus 2911, Aegean Sea, ATHENS, Patras, Kalamata, Rhodes, Crete, Izmir, Antalya, Konya, Kayseri, Erciyas Dagi 3916

TURKEY — Bursa, ANKARA, Adana, Gaziantep, Mosul, Kirkuk, Tabriz, Lake Van, Lake Urmia, Kermanshah

IRAN

CYPRUS, NICOSIA

SYRIA — Aleppo, Homs, DAMASCUS, Mesopotamia, Euphrates, Ar Ramadi

IRAQ — BAGHDAD, An Nasiriyah

LEBANON, BEIRUT

ISRAEL — Tel Aviv-Yafo, JERUSALEM, Port Said

JORDAN — AMMAN, Ma'an, Al 'Aqabah, Ar'ar

Syrian Desert, An Nafud, Al Jawf, Rafha', Hā'īl, Buraydah

Benghazi, Al Baydā', Darnah, Tubruq, Gulf of Sirte, Ajdabiyā, Marsa al Burayqah, rādah, Al Jaghbūb, Jālū, Al Jawf

LIBYA — Al 'Azīzīyah

Alexandria, Umm Sa'ad, Marsa Matrūh, Tanta, CAIRO, Giza, Suez, Qattara Depression, Siwah, Al Fayyūm, Al Bawītī, Al Minyā, Asyūţ, Al Quşayr, Jabal al Lawz 2579, Tabūk

Sinai, Gulf of Suez, Hijaz

SAUDI ARABIA — Medina, Najd, Rābigh, Yanbu' al Baḥr, Mecca, At Tā'if, Jeddah, Al Qunfidhah, Abhā, Najrān, Arabian Peninsula, Ar Rimāl, Rub' al Khālī

EGYPT — Luxor, Qinā, Al Khārijah, Mūţ, Aswān, Lake Nasser, Under Sudanese Admin.

Red Sea, Wadi Halfa

OMAN — Khalīj Maşīrah, Şalālah, Al Ghaydah

YEMEN — ŞAN'Ā', Hodeidah, Ta'izz, Lahij, Aden, Mukalla, Hadramawt, Gulf of Aden, Socotra (Yemen), Gees Gwardafuy

Assab, Massawa, Denakil

ERITREA — Akordat, ASMARA, Karora, Haiya, Suakin, Port Sudan, Jebel Oda 2259, Nubian Desert, Abu Hamed, Kareima, Merowe, Atbara

SUDAN — Omdurman, KHARTOUM, Wad Medani, Gedaref, Kassala, Sennar, El Obeid, Kosti, Er Rahad, En Nahud, Kadugli, Ed Damazin, Kurmuk, El Muglad, Malakal, Wau, El Geneina, El Fasher, Jebel Marra 3088, Nyala, Blue Nile, White Nile, Nile, Athara

ETHIOPIA — Ras Dejen 4533, Gonder, 'Ādwa, Weldiya, Desē, Birhan 4152, Burē, Guba, Lake Tana, Mendi, Nek'emtē, ADDIS ABABA, Nazrēt, Āwash, Bedelē, Jima, Shashemenē, Sodo, Wendo, Lake Abaya, Ethiopian Highlands

DJIBOUTI — DJIBOUTI, Saylac, Berbera

SOMALIA — Hargeysa, Garoowe, Haud, Ogadēn, Gaalkacyo, Beledweyne, Baardheere, Jawhar, MOGADISHU, Marka, Webi Shabeelle, Jilib, Kismaayo, Jubba

CHAD — Emi Koussi 3415, Koro Toro, Abéché, Ati, Sarh, Ndélé, Bandoro

CENTRAL AFRICAN REPUBLIC — Bria, Zémio, Bambouti, Bangassou, BANGUI, Sibut, Monga, Bambili, Niangara, Uele, Ubangi, Bosobolo, Lisala, Buta, Isiro, Mahagi, Gulu, Aruwimi

DEMOCRATIC REPUBLIC OF CONGO — Mbandaka, L. Tumba, Opala, Lubutu, Kisangani, Congo Basin, Congo, Kindu, Kikwit, Ilebo, L. Mai-Ndombe, Kananga, Mbuji-Mayi, Kasai, Kutu, Samba, Lomami, Lac Upemba, Kamina, Kabalo, Lake Tanganyika, Chaîne des Mitumba, Kigoma

UGANDA — KAMPALA, Margherita Peak 5110, Mount Elgon 4321, Kasese, Jinja, Soroti, Lake Albert, Lake Edward, Lake Kyoga, Albert Nile, Mbarara, Kisoro, Bukoba

RWANDA — KIGALI, Lake Kivu, Bukavu

BURUNDI — BUJUMBURA

KENYA — Lodwar, Lake Turkana, Moyale, Marsabit, Wajir, Kisumu, Mount Kenya 5199, Eldoret, Nakuru, NAIROBI, Garissa, Musoma, Tana

Lake Victoria, Lake Natron, Lake Eyasi

TANZANIA — Mwanza, Arusha, Kilimanjaro 5892, Moshi, DODOMA, Singida, Tabora, Kalemie, Mbeya, Iringa, Morogoro, Dar es Salaam, Tanga, Zanzibar, Zanzibar Island, Pemba Island, Mafia Island, Rufiji, Great Rift Valley, Lake Rukwa

ZAMBIA

INDIAN OCEAN — Mahé, SEYCHELLES, Aldabra Islands (Seychelles)

Equator

Next map 52-53
Next map 94-95
Next map 86

Lambert Azimuthal Equal Area projection

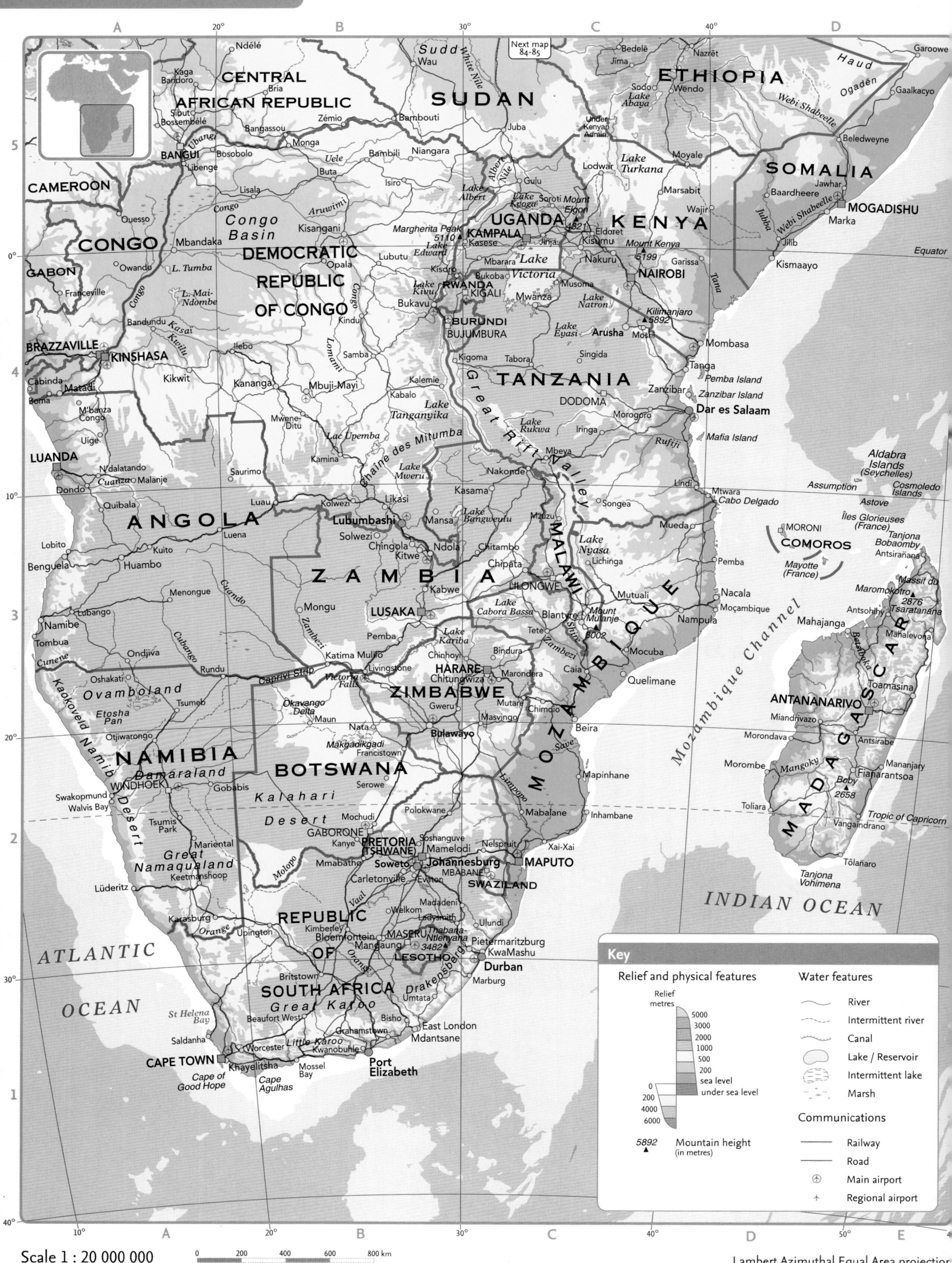

Scale 1 : 20 000 000

0   200   400   600   800 km

Lambert Azimuthal Equal Area projection

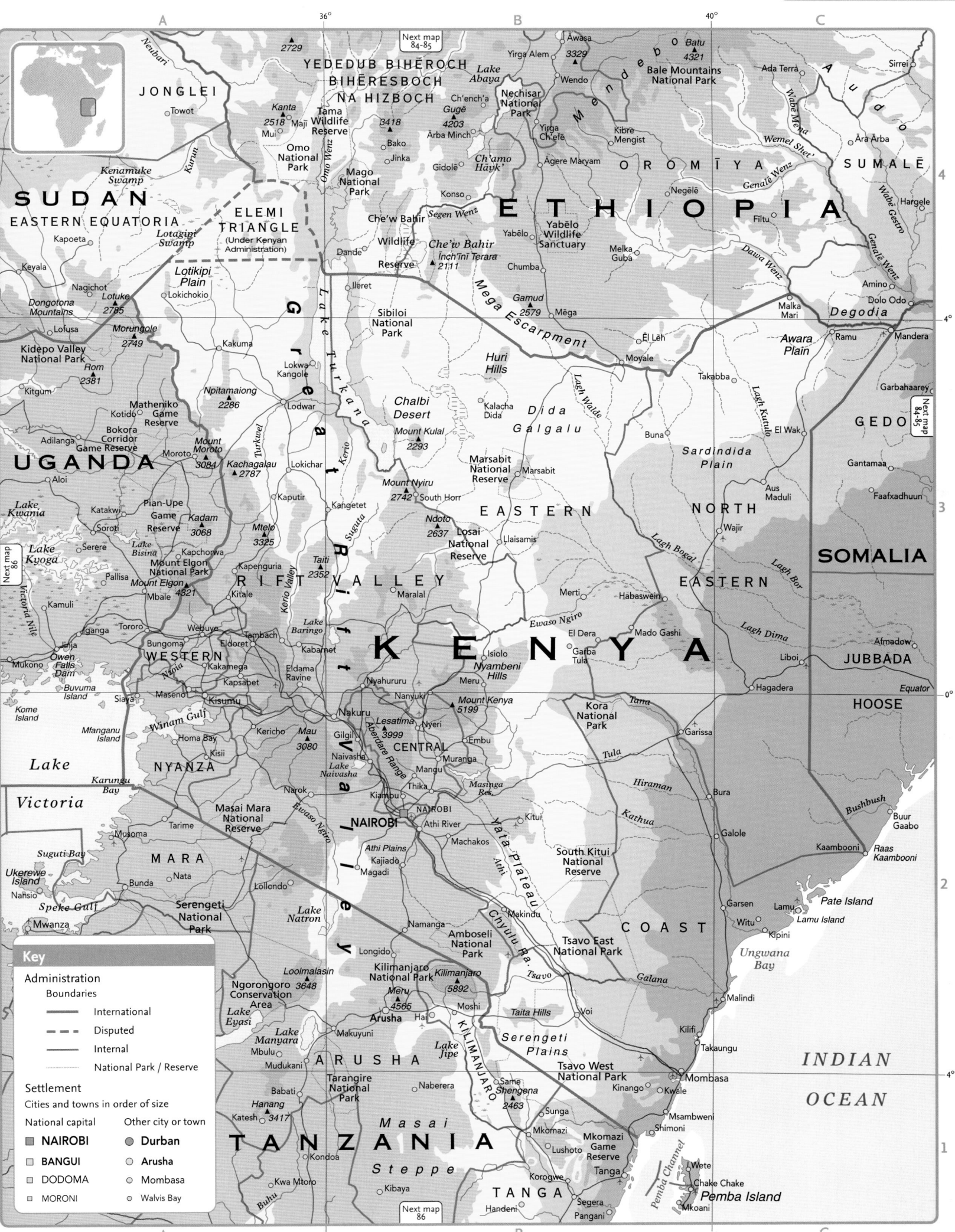

Key

Administration

Boundaries

— International

--- Disputed

— Internal

⋯ National Park / Reserve

Settlement

Cities and towns in order of size

National capital | Other city or town
■ **NAIROBI** | ● **Durban**
□ **BANGUI** | ○ **Arusha**
□ DODOMA | ○ Mombasa
□ MORONI | ○ Walvis Bay

Scale 1 : 5 000 000

0 50 100 150 200 km

Lambert Azimuthal Equal Area projection

1 Population Density

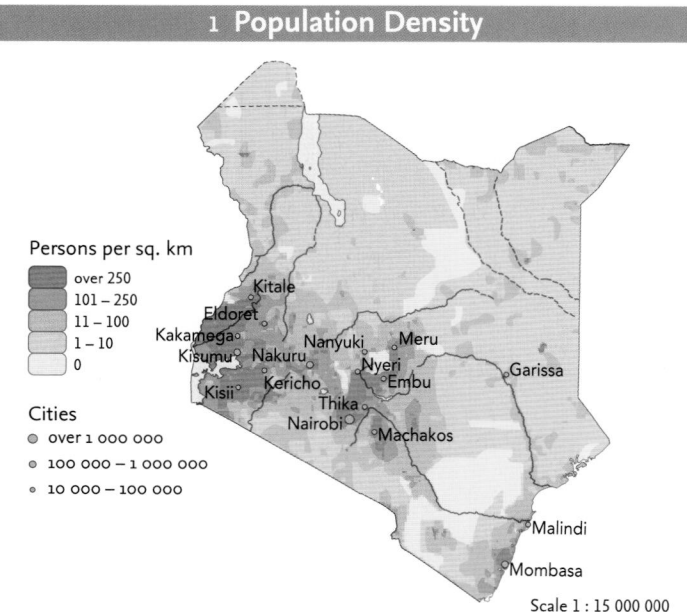

Persons per sq. km
- over 250
- 101 – 250
- 11 – 100
- 1 – 10
- 0

Cities
- ● over 1 000 000
- ● 100 000 – 1 000 000
- ● 10 000 – 100 000

Scale 1 : 15 000 000

2 Population Change

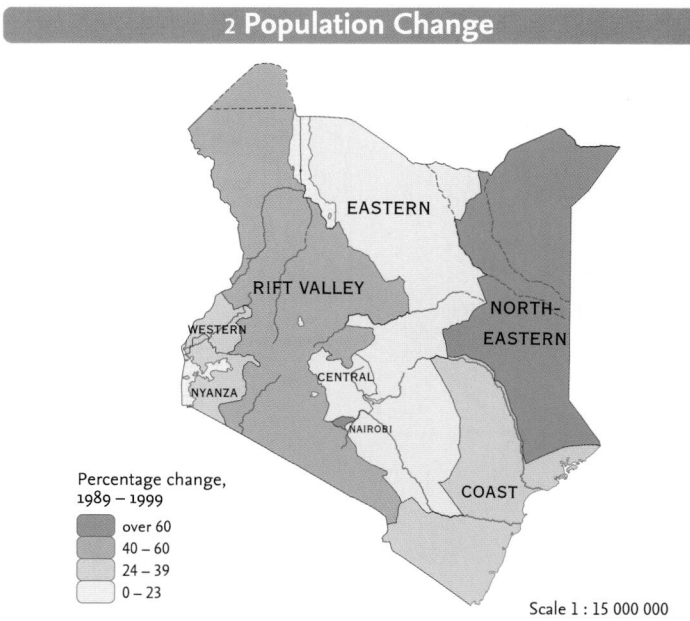

Percentage change, 1989 – 1999
- over 60
- 40 – 60
- 24 – 39
- 0 – 23

Scale 1 : 15 000 000

3 Urban Agglomerations

Urban agglomeration	1969 census	1989 census	1999 census
Nairobi	478 000	1 324 570	2 143 254
Mombasa	246 000	461 753	665 018
Kisumu	30 000	192 733	332 024
Nakuru	47 000	163 927	230 515
Eldoret	16 900	111 882	193 830

WWW **Government of Kenya**
http://www.kenya.go.ke/
Kenya Tourist Board
www.magicalkenya.com
Central Bureau of Statistics
www.cbs.go.ke

4 Population Growth

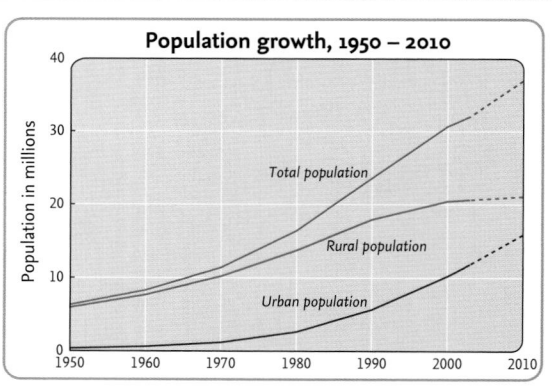

Population growth, 1950 – 2010

Total population
Rural population
Urban population

5 Tourism

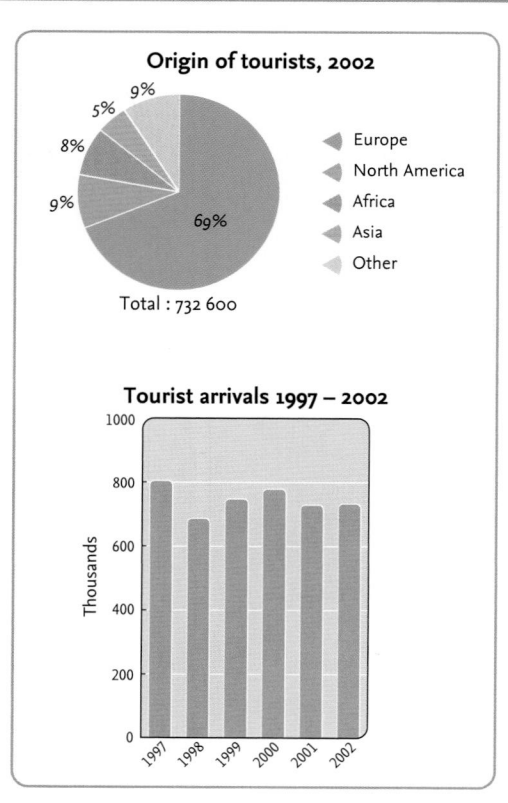

Origin of tourists, 2002
- Europe
- North America
- Africa
- Asia
- Other

Total : 732 600

Tourist arrivals 1997 – 2002

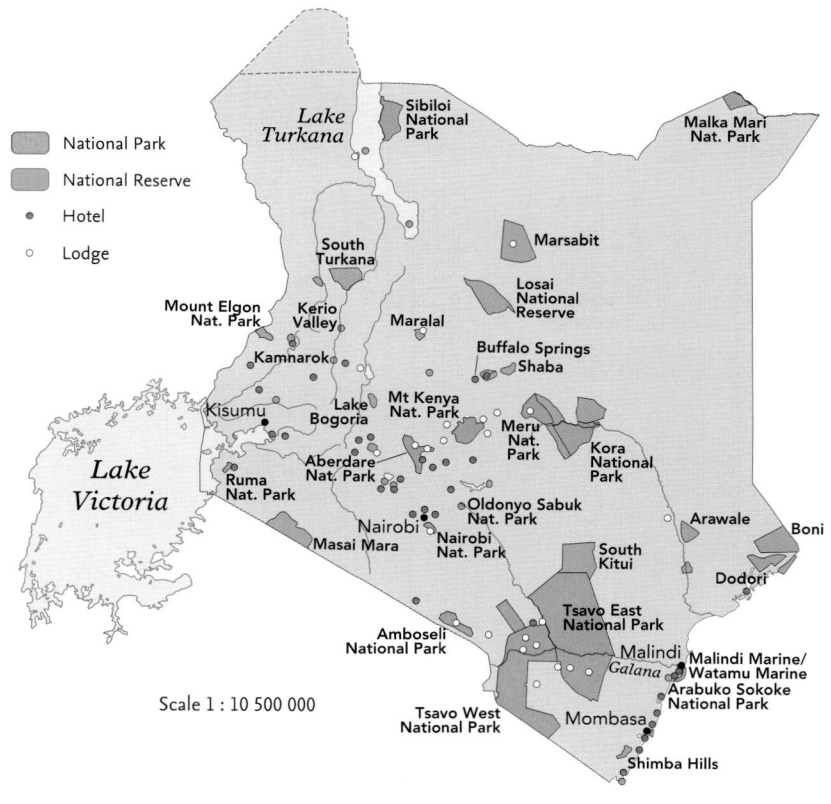

- National Park
- National Reserve
- ● Hotel
- ○ Lodge

Scale 1 : 10 500 000

6 Economic Activity

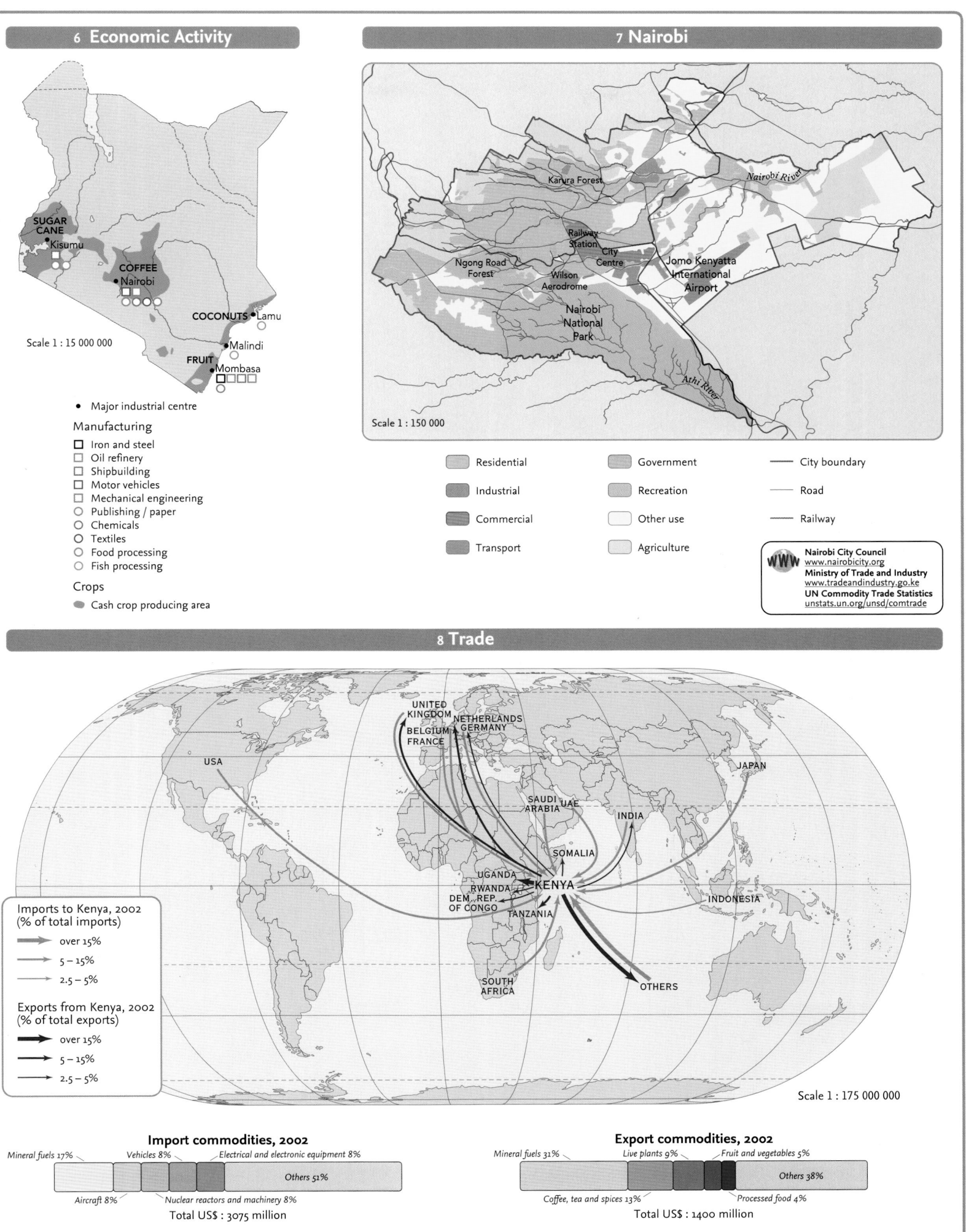

Scale 1 : 15 000 000

SUGAR CANE
● Kisumu

COFFEE
● Nairobi

COCONUTS ● Lamu

FRUIT
● Malindi
● Mombasa

- ● Major industrial centre

Manufacturing
- ☐ Iron and steel
- ☐ Oil refinery
- ☐ Shipbuilding
- ☐ Motor vehicles
- ☐ Mechanical engineering
- ○ Publishing / paper
- ○ Chemicals
- ○ Textiles
- ○ Food processing
- ○ Fish processing

Crops
- Cash crop producing area

7 Nairobi

Karura Forest
Nairobi River
Railway Station
City Centre
Ngong Road Forest
Wilson Aerodrome
Jomo Kenyatta International Airport
Nairobi National Park
Athi River

Scale 1 : 150 000

- Residential
- Industrial
- Commercial
- Transport
- Government
- Recreation
- Other use
- Agriculture
- ——— City boundary
- ——— Road
- ——— Railway

www Nairobi City Council
www.nairobicity.org
Ministry of Trade and Industry
www.tradeandindustry.go.ke
UN Commodity Trade Statistics
unstats.un.org/unsd/comtrade

8 Trade

UNITED KINGDOM
NETHERLANDS
GERMANY
BELGIUM
FRANCE
USA
SAUDI ARABIA UAE
INDIA
JAPAN
SOMALIA
UGANDA
RWANDA
DEM. REP. OF CONGO
KENYA
TANZANIA
INDONESIA
SOUTH AFRICA
OTHERS

Imports to Kenya, 2002 (% of total imports)
- → over 15%
- → 5 – 15%
- → 2.5 – 5%

Exports from Kenya, 2002 (% of total exports)
- → over 15%
- → 5 – 15%
- → 2.5 – 5%

Scale 1 : 175 000 000

Import commodities, 2002

Mineral fuels 17%   Vehicles 8%   Electrical and electronic equipment 8%
Others 51%
Aircraft 8%   Nuclear reactors and machinery 8%

Total US$: 3075 million

Export commodities, 2002

Mineral fuels 31%   Live plants 9%   Fruit and vegetables 5%
Others 38%
Coffee, tea and spices 13%   Processed food 4%

Total US$: 1400 million

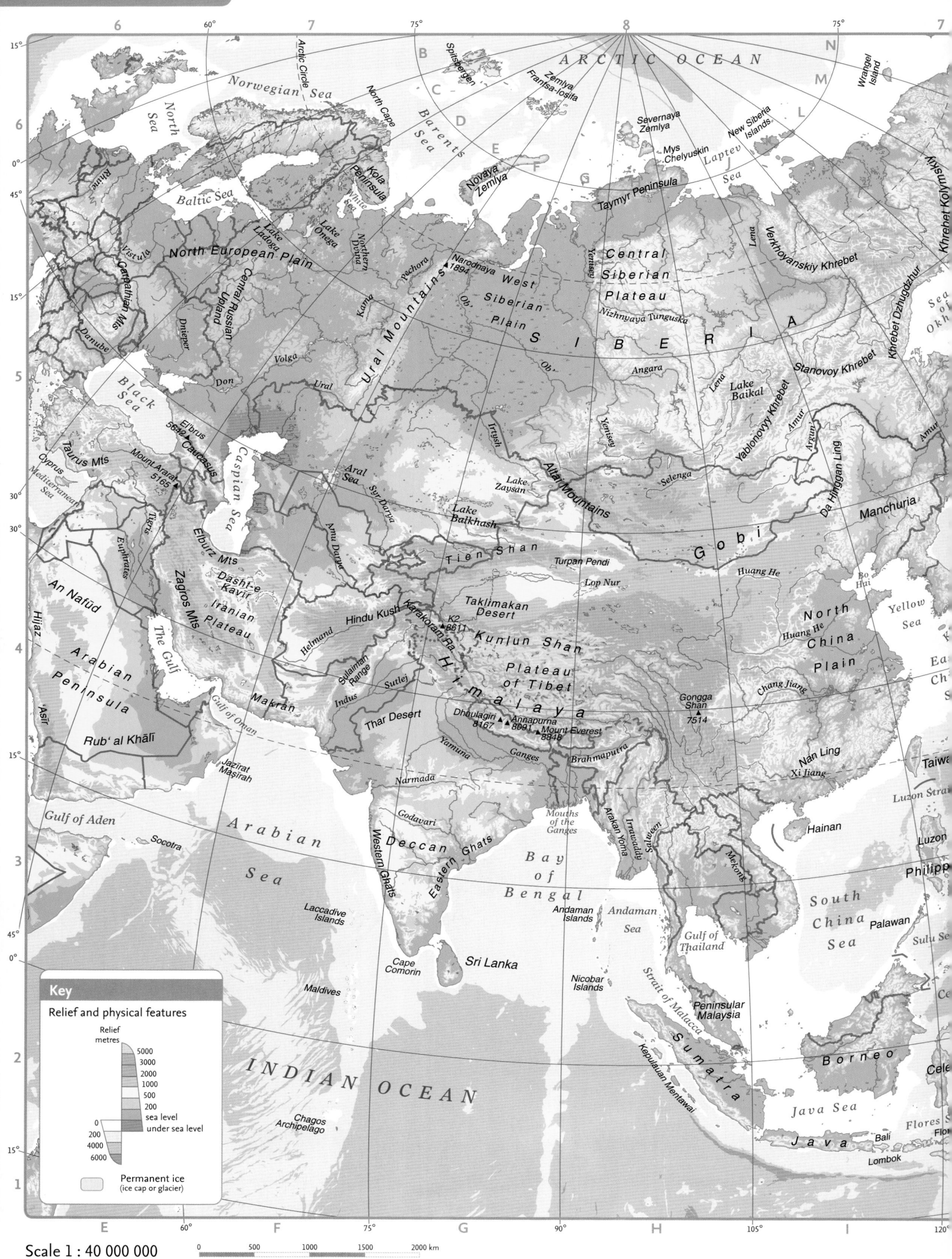

ARCTIC OCEAN

Norwegian Sea

North Sea

Baltic Sea

Rhine

Vistula

Carpathian Mts

Danube

Dnieper

North European Plain

Lake Ladoga

Lake Onega

Kola Peninsula

White Sea

Northern Dvina

Central Russian Upland

Kama

Volga

Don

Ural

Black Sea

El'brus 5642

Caucasus

Mount Ararat 5165

Caspian Sea

Taurus Mts

Cyprus

Mediterranean Sea

Elburz Mts

Dasht-e Kavir

Iranian Plateau

Zagros Mts

Tigris

Euphrates

The Gulf

An Nafūd

Hijaz

Asir

Arabian Peninsula

Rub' al Khālī

Gulf of Oman

Makran

Gulf of Aden

Socotra

Jazīrat Maşīrah

Arabian Sea

Laccadive Islands

Maldives

Chagos Archipelago

Cape Comorin

Sri Lanka

Spitsbergen

Arctic Circle

North Cape

Barents Sea

Novaya Zemlya

Zemlya Frantsa-Iosifa

Severnaya Zemlya

New Siberia Islands

Mys Chelyuskin

Taymyr Peninsula

Laptev Sea

Wrangel Island

Ural Mountains

Narodnaya 1894

Pechora

Ob'

West Siberian Plain

Central Siberian Plateau

Nizhnyaya Tunguska

SIBERIA

Yenisey

Ob'

Irtysh

Lena

Angara

Lena

Lake Baikal

Selenga

Verkhoyanskiy Khrebet

Stanovoy Khrebet

Yablonovyy Khrebet

Amur

Argun

Khrebet Dzhugdzhur

Sea of Okhotsk

Khrebet Kolymskiy

Aral Sea

Syr Darya

Amu Darya

Lake Balkhash

Lake Zaysan

Tien Shan

Altai Mountains

Turpan Pendi

Lop Nur

Taklimakan Desert

Kunlun Shan

Plateau of Tibet

Gobi

Da Hinggan Ling

Manchuria

Huang He

Bo Hai

North China Plain

Yellow Sea

Huang He

Chang Jiang

Hindu Kush

Karakoram Ra.

K2 8611

Himalaya

Dhaulagiri 8167

Annapurna 8091

Mount Everest 8848

Gongga Shan 7514

Sulaiman Range

Helmand

Indus

Sutlej

Thar Desert

Yamuna

Ganges

Brahmaputra

Narmada

Godavari

Deccan

Western Ghats

Eastern Ghats

Mouths of the Ganges

Arakan Yoma

Irrawaddy

Salween

Mekong

Nan Ling

Xi Jiang

Taiwan

Luzon Strait

Hainan

Luzon

Philippi

Bay of Bengal

Andaman Islands

Andaman Sea

Nicobar Islands

South China Sea

Palawan

Sulu Se

Gulf of Thailand

Strait of Malacca

Peninsular Malaysia

Kepulauan Mentawai

Sumatra

Borneo

Cele

Java Sea

Java

Bali

Lombok

Flores

Flo

INDIAN OCEAN

Scale 1 : 40 000 000

0   500   1000   1500   2000 km

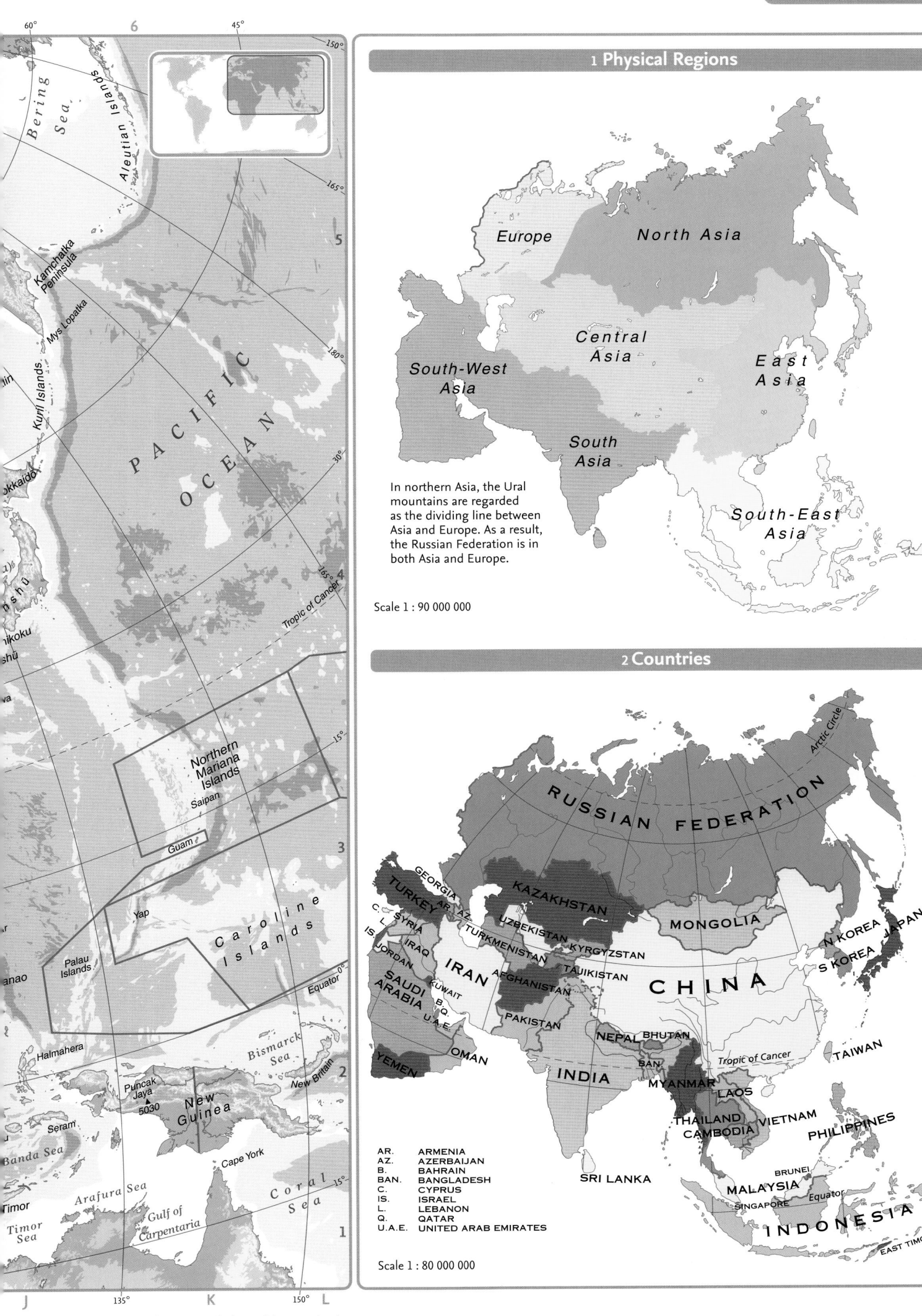

1 Physical Regions

Europe

North Asia

Central Asia

South-West Asia

East Asia

South Asia

South-East Asia

In northern Asia, the Ural mountains are regarded as the dividing line between Asia and Europe. As a result, the Russian Federation is in both Asia and Europe.

Scale 1 : 90 000 000

2 Countries

RUSSIAN FEDERATION

Arctic Circle

GEORGIA
TURKEY
AR.
AZ.
C.
SYRIA
IS.
IRAQ
JORDAN
SAUDI ARABIA
KUWAIT
B.
Q.
U.A.E.
OMAN
YEMEN

KAZAKHSTAN
UZBEKISTAN
TURKMENISTAN
KYRGYZSTAN
TAJIKISTAN
AFGHANISTAN
IRAN
PAKISTAN

MONGOLIA

CHINA

N.KOREA
S.KOREA
JAPAN

NEPAL BHUTAN
BAN.
INDIA
MYANMAR
LAOS
THAILAND
CAMBODIA
VIETNAM
Tropic of Cancer
TAIWAN

PHILIPPINES

SRI LANKA

MALAYSIA
BRUNEI
SINGAPORE
Equator

INDONESIA

EAST TIMOR

AR.   ARMENIA
AZ.   AZERBAIJAN
B.   BAHRAIN
BAN.   BANGLADESH
C.   CYPRUS
IS.   ISRAEL
L.   LEBANON
Q.   QATAR
U.A.E. UNITED ARAB EMIRATES

Scale 1 : 80 000 000

Bering Sea
Aleutian Islands
Kamchatka Peninsula
Mys Lopatka
Kuril Islands
Hokkaido
6
45°
60°
150°
165°
180°
5
4

PACIFIC OCEAN

Tropic of Cancer
30°
15°

Northern Mariana Islands
Saipan
Guam
Yap
Caroline Islands
Palau Islands
3
15°
Equator 0°

Halmahera
Bismarck Sea
New Britain
Seram
Puncak Jaya
5030
New Guinea
Banda Sea
Cape York
2
15°
Coral Sea
Timor Sea
Arafura Sea
Gulf of Carpentaria
1
J   135°   K   150°   L

Lambert Azimuthal Equal Area projection

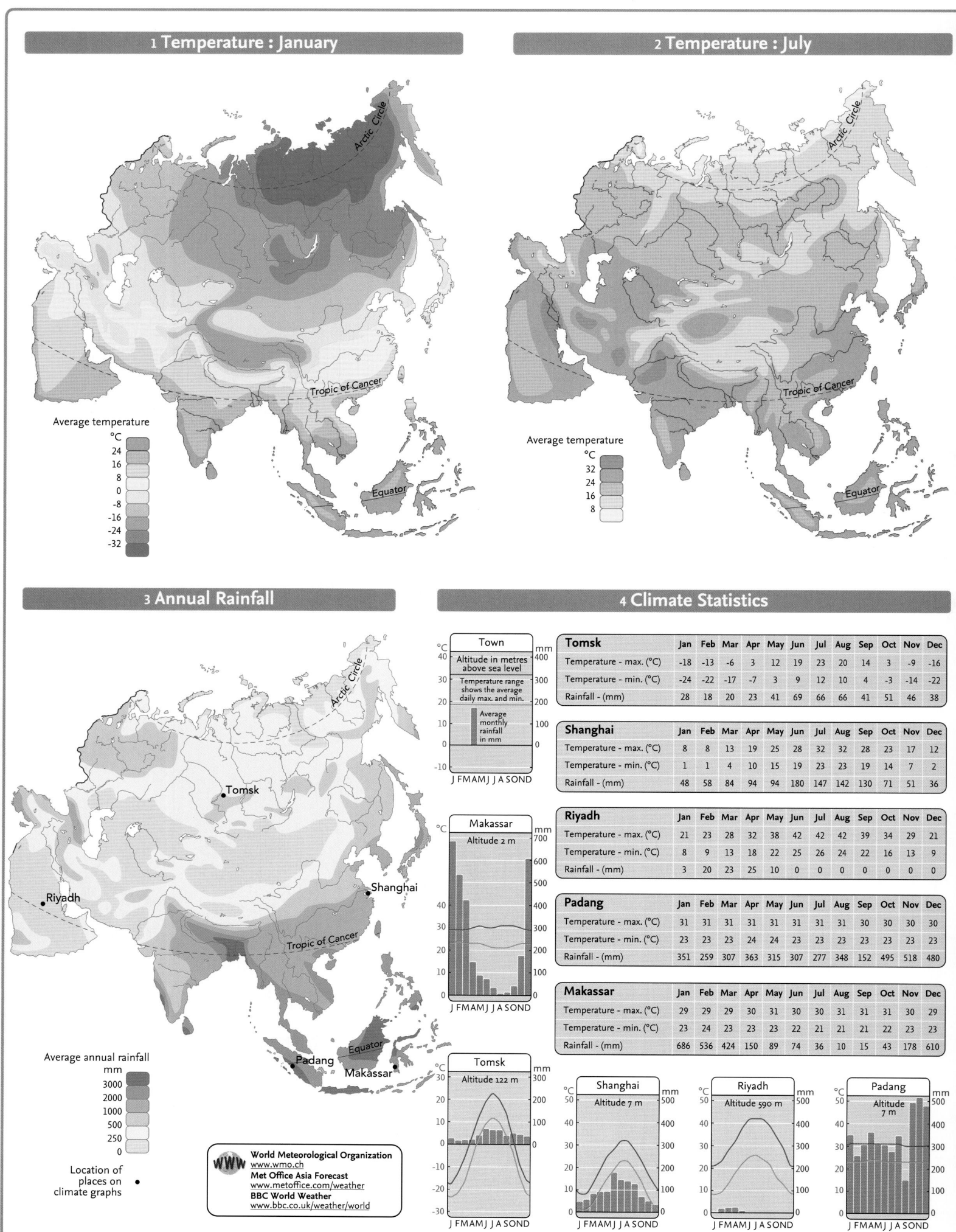

1 Temperature : January

Average temperature
°C
24
16
8
0
-8
-16
-24
-32

Arctic Circle
Tropic of Cancer
Equator

2 Temperature : July

Average temperature
°C
32
24
16
8

Arctic Circle
Tropic of Cancer
Equator

3 Annual Rainfall

Average annual rainfall
mm
3000
2000
1000
500
250
0

Location of places on climate graphs ●

Tomsk
Shanghai
Riyadh
Padang
Makassar

Arctic Circle
Tropic of Cancer
Equator

World Meteorological Organization
www.wmo.ch
Met Office Asia Forecast
www.metoffice.com/weather
BBC World Weather
www.bbc.co.uk/weather/world

4 Climate Statistics

Town
°C / mm
40 / 400
Altitude in metres above sea level
30 / 300
Temperature range shows the average daily max. and min.
20 / 200
Average monthly rainfall in mm
10 / 100
0
-10
J F M A M J J A S O N D

Tomsk	Jan	Feb	Mar	Apr	May	Jun	Jul	Aug	Sep	Oct	Nov	Dec
Temperature - max. (°C)	-18	-13	-6	3	12	19	23	20	14	3	-9	-16
Temperature - min. (°C)	-24	-22	-17	-7	3	9	12	10	4	-3	-14	-22
Rainfall - (mm)	28	18	20	23	41	69	66	66	41	51	46	38

Shanghai	Jan	Feb	Mar	Apr	May	Jun	Jul	Aug	Sep	Oct	Nov	Dec
Temperature - max. (°C)	8	8	13	19	25	28	32	32	28	23	17	12
Temperature - min. (°C)	1	1	4	10	15	19	23	23	19	14	7	2
Rainfall - (mm)	48	58	84	94	94	180	147	142	130	71	51	36

Riyadh	Jan	Feb	Mar	Apr	May	Jun	Jul	Aug	Sep	Oct	Nov	Dec
Temperature - max. (°C)	21	23	28	32	38	42	42	42	39	34	29	21
Temperature - min. (°C)	8	9	13	18	22	25	26	24	22	16	13	9
Rainfall - (mm)	3	20	23	25	10	0	0	0	0	0	0	0

Padang	Jan	Feb	Mar	Apr	May	Jun	Jul	Aug	Sep	Oct	Nov	Dec
Temperature - max. (°C)	31	31	31	31	31	31	31	31	30	30	30	30
Temperature - min. (°C)	23	23	23	24	24	23	23	23	23	23	23	23
Rainfall - (mm)	351	259	307	363	315	307	277	348	152	495	518	480

Makassar	Jan	Feb	Mar	Apr	May	Jun	Jul	Aug	Sep	Oct	Nov	Dec
Temperature - max. (°C)	29	29	29	30	31	30	30	31	31	31	30	29
Temperature - min. (°C)	23	24	23	23	23	22	21	21	21	22	23	23
Rainfall - (mm)	686	536	424	150	89	74	36	10	15	43	178	610

Makassar — Altitude 2 m
°C / mm
J F M A M J J A S O N D

Tomsk — Altitude 122 m
°C / mm
J F M A M J J A S O N D

Shanghai — Altitude 7 m
°C / mm
J F M A M J J A S O N D

Riyadh — Altitude 590 m
°C / mm
J F M A M J J A S O N D

Padang — Altitude 7 m
°C / mm
J F M A M J J A S O N D

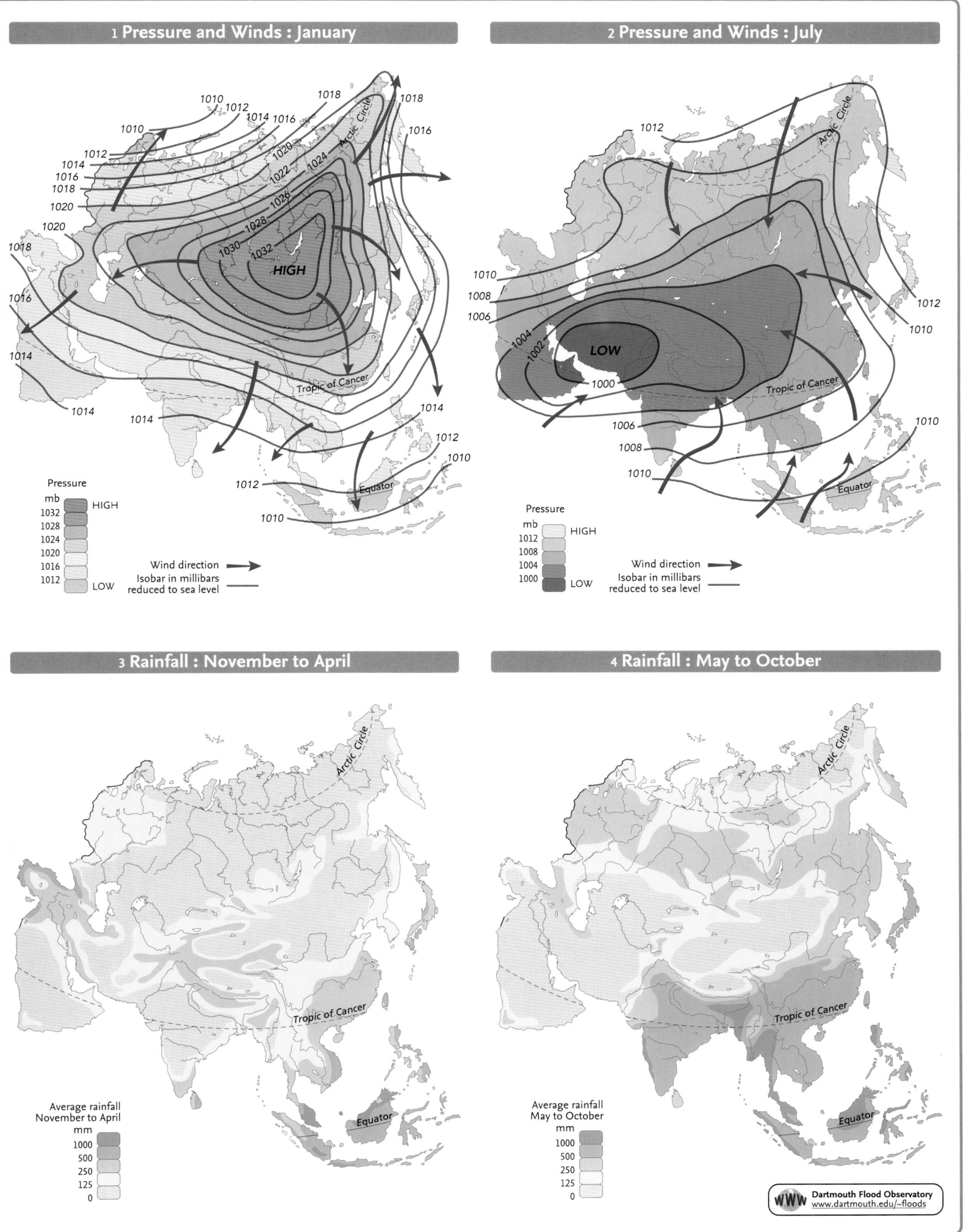

1 Pressure and Winds : January

Pressure
mb
1032 — HIGH
1028
1024
1020
1016
1012 — LOW

Wind direction →
Isobar in millibars
reduced to sea level

2 Pressure and Winds : July

Pressure
mb
1012 — HIGH
1008
1004
1000 — LOW

Wind direction →
Isobar in millibars
reduced to sea level

3 Rainfall : November to April

Average rainfall
November to April
mm
1000
500
250
125
0

4 Rainfall : May to October

Average rainfall
May to October
mm
1000
500
250
125
0

WWW Dartmouth Flood Observatory
www.dartmouth.edu/~floods

Scale 1 : 100 000 000

0 1000 2000 3000 4000 km

Lambert Azimuthal Equal Area projection

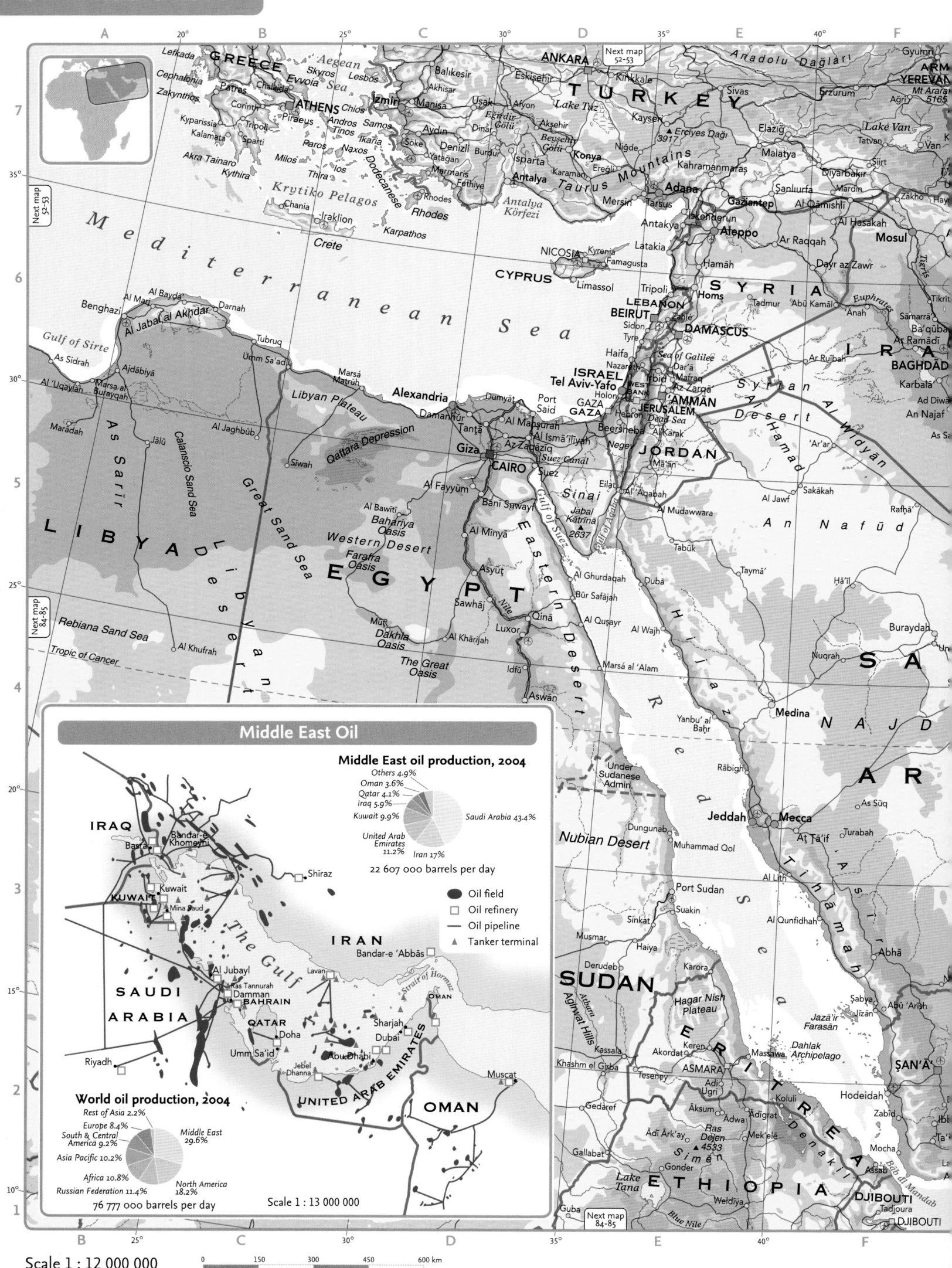

Next map 58–59

Next map 96–97

Countries and regions:
AZERBAIJAN
TURKMENISTAN
UZBEKISTAN
TAJIKISTAN
IRAN
AFGHANISTAN
PAKISTAN
INDIA
KUWAIT
BAHRAIN
QATAR
UNITED ARAB EMIRATES
OMAN
YEMEN

Seas and water bodies:
Caspian Sea
Karakum Desert
The Gulf
Gulf of Oman
Strait of Hormuz
Arabian Sea
Gulf of Aden

Capitals and cities (selection):
BAKU, Xankändi, Äli Bayramlı, Salyan, Länkäran, Ästärä, Ahar, Goris, Tabriz, Sahand, Sarab, Ardabil, Miäneh, Bandar-e Anzalī, Lāhījān, Rasht, Marägheh, andowäb, Zanjan, Zänjan, aymäniyah, Sanandaj, abja, Qazvin, Qom, TEHRĀN, Karaj, Qollen-ye Damāvand 5601, Chalus, Amol, Ghaem Shahr, Hamadān, Kangavar, Malāyer, Arāk, Borūjerd, Khorramābād, Nahāvand, Dezful, Shushtar, Masjed Soleymān, Ramhormoz, Ahvāz, An Nāsīrīyah, ash Shuyūkh, Basra, Abādān, Khorramshahr, KUWAIT, Al Jahrah, Farwāniyah, Al Ahmadi, Al Mish'ab, An Nu'ayrīyah, Al Jubayl, Ras Tannurah, Dammām, Dhahran, BAHRAIN, MANAMA, Abqaiq, Al Ghwaybiya, Al Hufūf, QATAR, Dukhan, DOHA, ABU DHABI, RIYADH, Al Biyādh, ulayyil, Al Qa'āmīyāt, DUSHANBE, Buxoro, Qarshi, ASHGABAT, Turkmenbashi, Nebitdag, Cheleken, Gumdag, Gyzylarbat, Bakharden, Gonbad-e Kavus, Bojnvrd, Quchan, Gorgan, Gorgān, Sari, Semnān, Damghan, Emāmrūd, Kāshmar, Sabzevār, Neyshābur, Mashhad, Torbat-e Jām, Torbat-e Heydarīyeh, Qāyen, Ferdows, Tabas, Bīrjand, Zābol, Kāshān, Ardestān, Nā'īn, Yazd, Esfahān, Shahr-e Kord, Shahrezā, Najafābād, Golpāyegān, Khunsar, Homayunshahr, Bāfq, Zarand, Kermān, Rafsanjān, Anār, Eqlīd, Abādeh, Ābarqū, Shahr Bābak, Sīrjān, Bāft, Bam, Zāhedān, Ladiz, Khāsh, Nok Kundi, Nushki, Dalbandin, Chaman, Quetta, Mastung, Kalat, Kandahār, Gereshk, Delārām, Farāh, Zaranj, Herāt, Gushgy, Bala Morghab, Chaghcharān, Gardēz, Khowst, Ghaznī, KĀBUL, Charikar, Bāmian, Jalālābād, Khyber Pass, Peshawar, ISLAMABAD, Rawalpindi, Nowshera, Mardan, Abbottabad, Mansehra, Gilgit, Chitral, Drosh, Barikot, Feyzābād, Khorugh, Mongora, Talagang, Kohat, Banmi, Daud Khel, Mianwali, Lakki, Dera Ismail Khan, Leiah, Khanewal, Multan, Muzaffargarh, Bahawalpur, Jhang, Faisalabad, Sargodha, Khanpur, Rahimyar Khan, Jacobabad, Shikarpur, Sukkur, Larkana, Sibi, Jampur, Rajanpur, Loralai, Dera Ghazi Khan, Mazar-e Sharif, Baghlān, Pol-e Khomri, Khanabad, Meymaneh, Sar-e Pol, Sheberghān, Andkhvoy, Khanabad, Termiz, Kerki, Sho'rchi, Tedzhen, Mayamey, Damghan

Deserts and physical features:
Elburz Mountains, Dasht-e Kavir, Dasht-e Lut, Zagros Mountains, Kūh-e Dīnār 4432, Kūh-e Dīnār, Daryācheh-ye Tashk, Daryācheh-ye Bakhtegan, Namakzār-e Shādād, Kavīr-i-Namak, Namakzār, Dasht-e Daryācheh-ye Sīstān, Dasht-e Mārgow, Dasht-e Arbu Lut, Gowd-e Zereh, Chagai Hills, Raskoh, Siahan Range, BALOCHISTAN, Hamun-i-Mashkel, Sulaiman Range, Hindu Kush, Kūh-e Bābā, Paropamisus, HAZARAJAT, Pamir, Kelifskiy Uzboy, Hari Rūd, Helmand, Makran, Hamūn-e Jaz Mūriān, Kermān Desert, Biaban, Thal Desert, Rub' al Khālī, Ar Rimal, Nu'aym, Al Hibāk, Jiddat al Harāsis, Jabal Akhdar, Jabal Mahrāt, Hadhramawt

Cities near coast:
Būshehr, Borāzjān, Kangān, Lamard, Bastak, Bandar-e Lengeh, Qeshm, Mināb, Jāsk, Chābahār, Gwadar, Pasni, Jiwani, Tump, Turbat, Panjgur, Saravan, Ladiz, Īrānshahr, Bandar-e 'Abbās, Al Khasab, OMAN, Sharjah, Dubai, Fujairah, MUSCAT, Matrah, Suhār, Al Khaburah, Al Buraymī, Nazwā, Ibrā, Sūr, Ra's al Hadd, Haymā, Dawqah, Salalah, Mirbāt, Ra's Fartak, Sayhūt, Ash Shihr, Mukalla, Al Ghaydah, Tarīm, Shibām, Habbān, Al Mukalla

Islands:
Jazīrat Masīrah, Khalīj Masīrah, Ra's Madrakah, Juzur al Halāniyāt, Socotra (Yemen)

Heights:
4074, 4420, 4432, 5601, 4425, 10

www
Organization of the Petroleum Exporting Countries
www.opec.org
World Energy Council
www.worldenergy.org
BP Statistical Review of World Energy
www.bp.com

Key

Relief and physical features

Relief metres

| 5000 |
| 3000 |
| 2000 |
| 1000 |
| 500 |
| 200 |
| sea level |
| 0 |
| under sea level |
| 200 |
| 4000 |
| 6000 |

▲ 5601   Mountain height (in metres)

Permanent ice (ice cap or glacier)

Water features

～ River

Intermittent river

Lake / Reservoir

Intermittent lake

Marsh

Communications

Railway

Road

⊕ Main airport

Administration
Boundaries

International

Disputed

Ceasefire line

Settlement
Cities and towns in order of size

National capital	Other city or town
■ CAIRO	● Adana
■ BAGHDĀD	○ Medina
□ KUWAIT	○ Port Sudan
□ ASMARA	○ Kerma

Albers Conic Equal Area projection

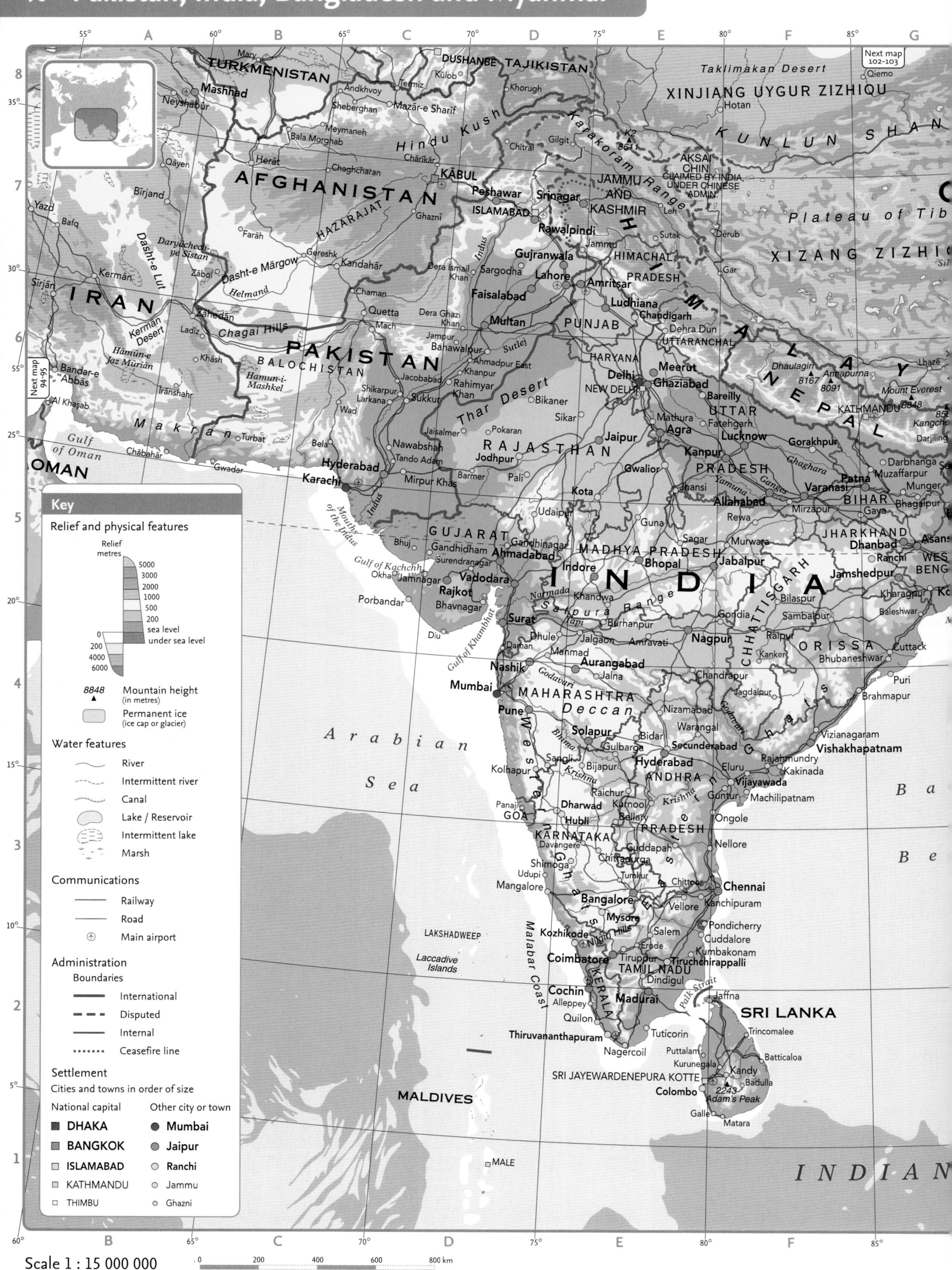

Key

Relief and physical features

Relief metres
5000
3000
2000
1000
500
200
0 sea level
under sea level
200
4000
6000

▲ 8848 Mountain height (in metres)

Permanent ice (ice cap or glacier)

Water features

~~~~ River

---- Intermittent river

Canal

Lake / Reservoir

Intermittent lake

Marsh

Communications

Railway

Road

⊕ Main airport

Administration

Boundaries

—— International

--- Disputed

—— Internal

······ Ceasefire line

Settlement

Cities and towns in order of size

National capital   Other city or town

■ DHAKA   ● Mumbai

■ BANGKOK   ● Jaipur

□ ISLAMABAD   ○ Ranchi

□ KATHMANDU   ○ Jammu

□ THIMBU   ○ Ghazni

Scale 1 : 15 000 000

0   200   400   600   800 km

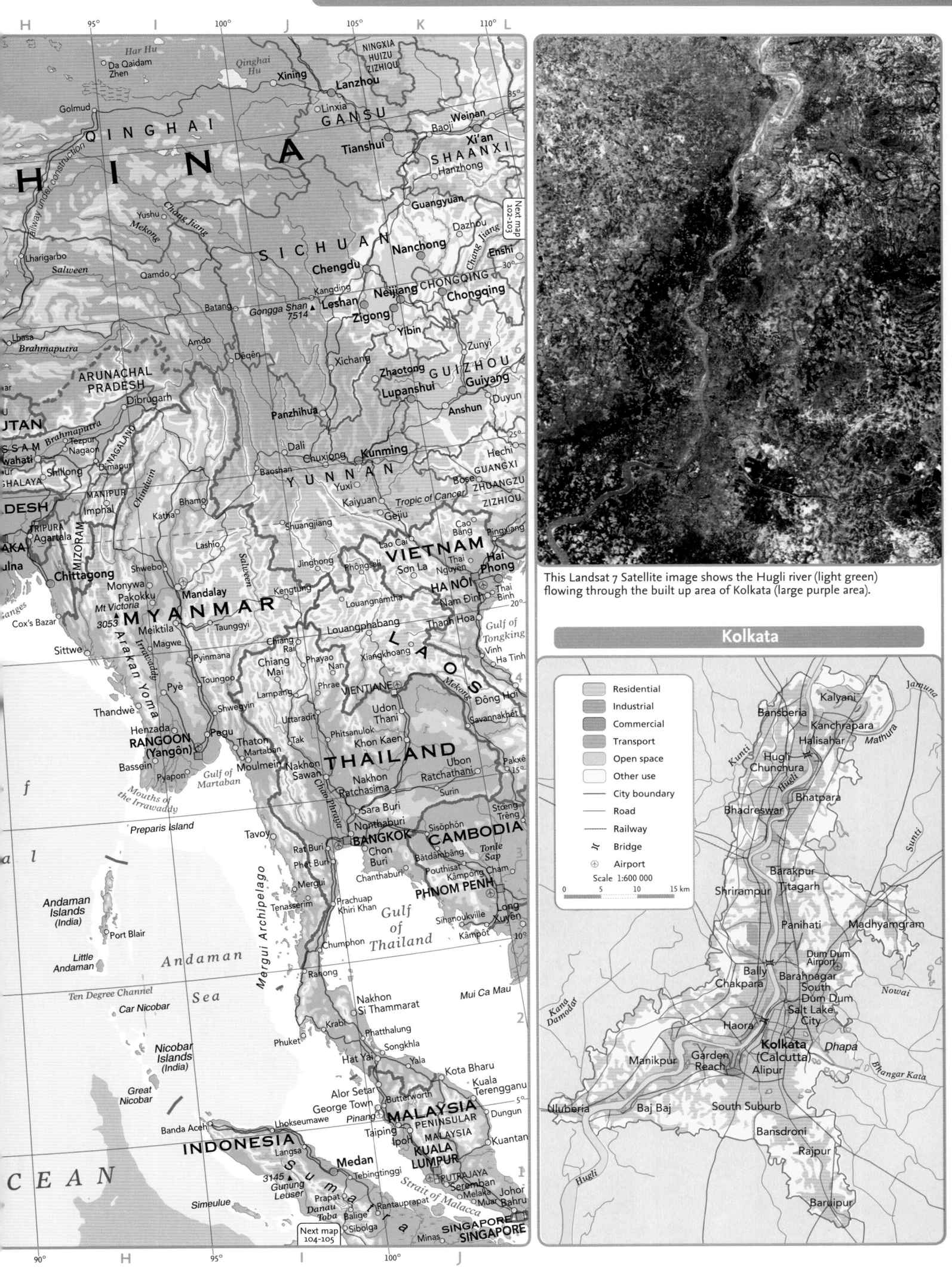

This Landsat 7 Satellite image shows the Hugli river (light green) flowing through the built up area of Kolkata (large purple area).

Kolkata

Legend:
- Residential
- Industrial
- Commercial
- Transport
- Open space
- Other use
- City boundary
- Road
- Railway
- Bridge
- Airport

Scale 1:600 000

0 5 10 15 km

1 Population Density

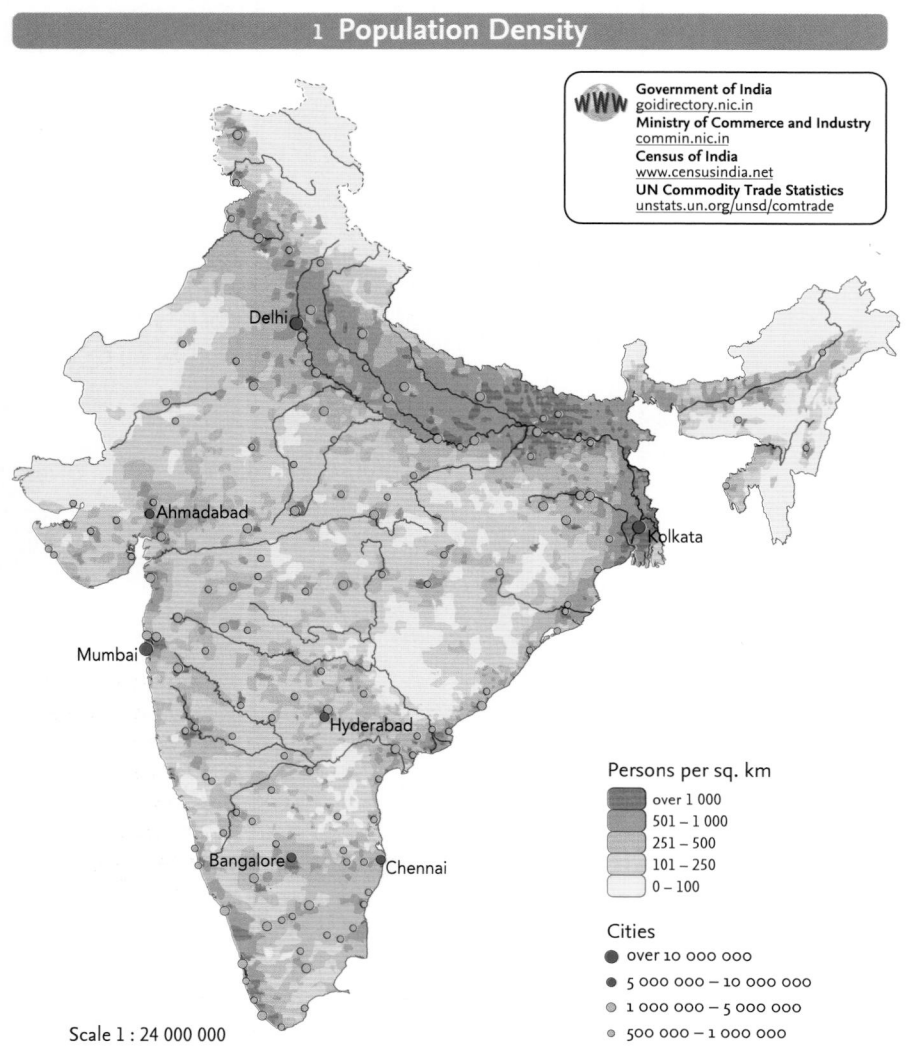

Persons per sq. km
- over 1 000
- 501 – 1 000
- 251 – 500
- 101 – 250
- 0 – 100

Cities
- over 10 000 000
- 5 000 000 – 10 000 000
- 1 000 000 – 5 000 000
- 500 000 – 1 000 000

Scale 1 : 24 000 000

2 Million Cities

Million city	2005 (projected)
Mumbai	18 337 000
Delhi	15 335 000
Kolkata	14 299 000
Chennai	6 915 000
Bangalore	6 533 000
Hyderabad	6 146 000
Ahmadabad	5 171 000
Pune	4 485 000
Surat	3 672 000
Kanpur	3 040 000
Jaipur	2 796 000
Lucknow	2 589 000
Nagpur	2 359 000
Patna	2 066 000
Indore	1 942 000
Vadodara	1 686 000
Bhopal	1 667 000
Coimbatore	1 628 000
Ludhiana	1 583 000
Visakhapatnam	1 468 000
Kochi	1 461 000
Nashik	1 408 000
Meerut	1 340 000
Faridabad	1 331 000
Varanasi	1 300 000
Ghaziabad	1 277 000
Asansol	1 272 000
Jamshedpur	1 246 000
Madurai	1 245 000
Jabalpur	1 234 000
Rajkot	1 205 000
Dhanbad	1 195 000
Allahabad	1 153 000
Amritsar	1 121 000
Srinagar	1 093 000
Vijayawada	1 093 000
Aurangabad	1 065 000
Durg-Bhilainagar	1 049 000
Solapur	1 012 000

3 Population Change

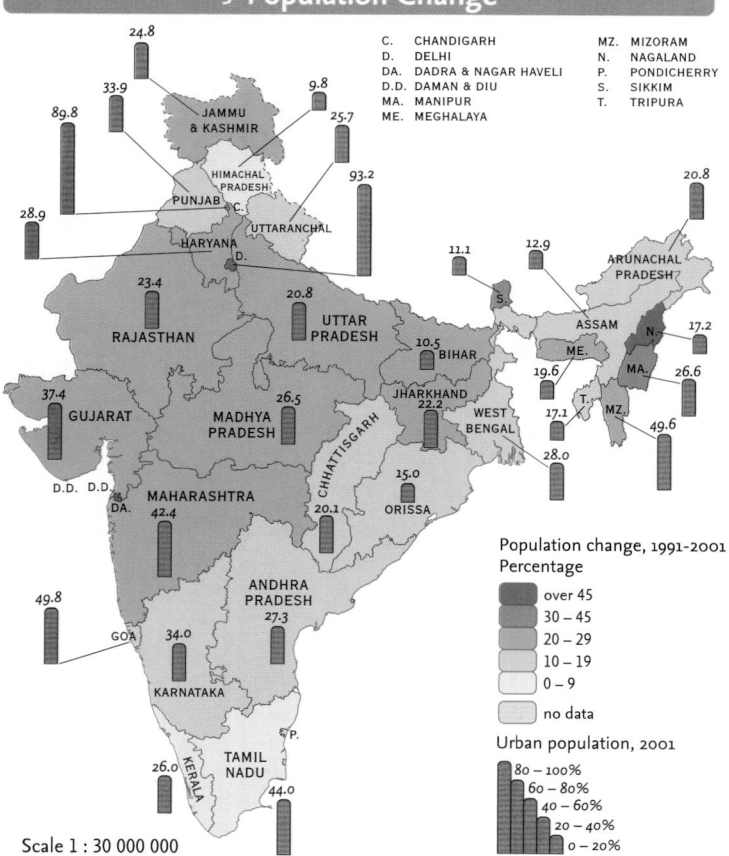

C.	CHANDIGARH	MZ.	MIZORAM
D.	DELHI	N.	NAGALAND
DA.	DADRA & NAGAR HAVELI	P.	PONDICHERRY
D.D.	DAMAN & DIU	S.	SIKKIM
MA.	MANIPUR	T.	TRIPURA
ME.	MEGHALAYA		

Population change, 1991-2001
Percentage
- over 45
- 30 – 45
- 20 – 29
- 10 – 19
- 0 – 9
- no data

Urban population, 2001
- 80 – 100%
- 60 – 80%
- 40 – 60%
- 20 – 40%
- 0 – 20%

Scale 1 : 30 000 000

4 Literacy

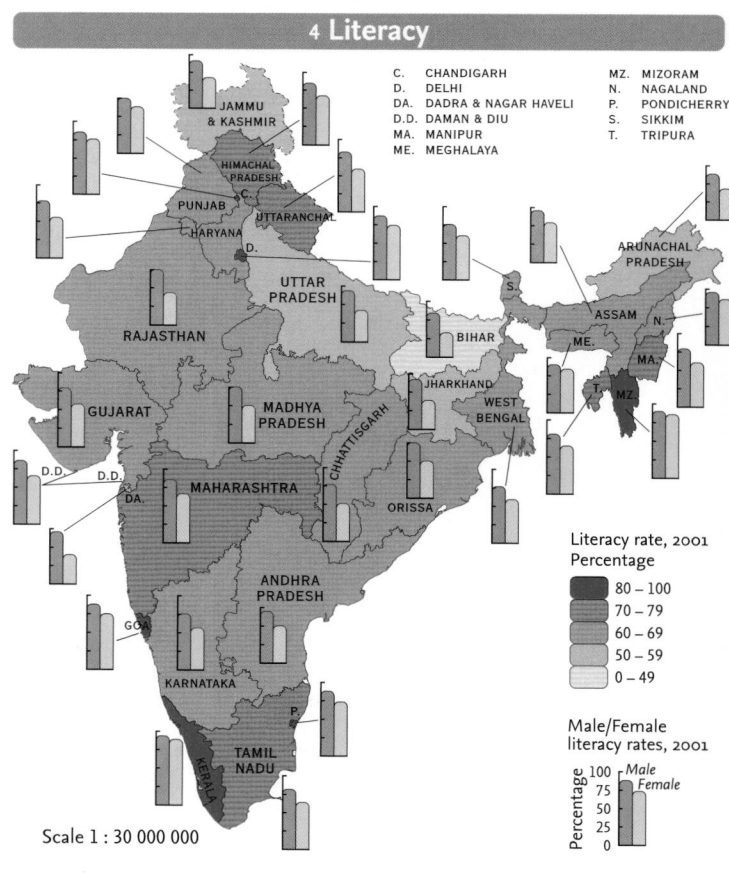

C.	CHANDIGARH	MZ.	MIZORAM
D.	DELHI	N.	NAGALAND
DA.	DADRA & NAGAR HAVELI	P.	PONDICHERRY
D.D.	DAMAN & DIU	S.	SIKKIM
MA.	MANIPUR	T.	TRIPURA
ME.	MEGHALAYA		

Literacy rate, 2001
Percentage
- 80 – 100
- 70 – 79
- 60 – 69
- 50 – 59
- 0 – 49

Male/Female
literacy rates, 2001

Male
Female

Scale 1 : 30 000 000

5 Tourism

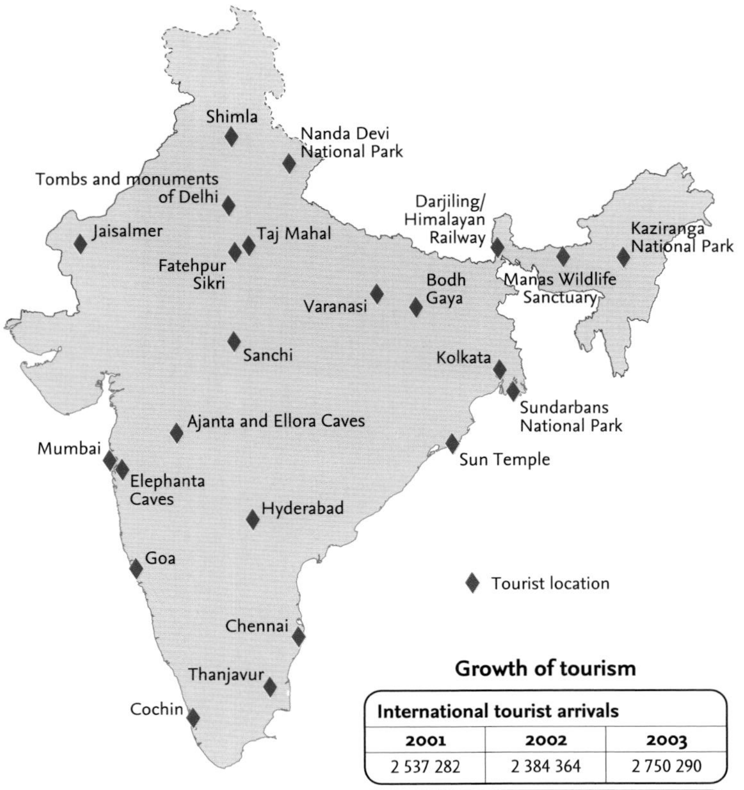

Shimla
Nanda Devi National Park
Tombs and monuments of Delhi
Jaisalmer
Taj Mahal
Darjiling/Himalayan Railway
Kaziranga National Park
Fatehpur Sikri
Varanasi
Bodh Gaya
Manas Wildlife Sanctuary
Sanchi
Kolkata
Ajanta and Ellora Caves
Sundarbans National Park
Mumbai
Sun Temple
Elephanta Caves
Hyderabad
Goa
Chennai
Thanjavur
Cochin

◆ Tourist location

Growth of tourism

International tourist arrivals		
2001	**2002**	**2003**
2 537 282	2 384 364	2 750 290

Tourist receipts US$		
2001	**2002**	**2003**
3 042 000 000	2 923 000 000	3 602 880 000

Scale 1 : 30 000 000

6 Economic Activity

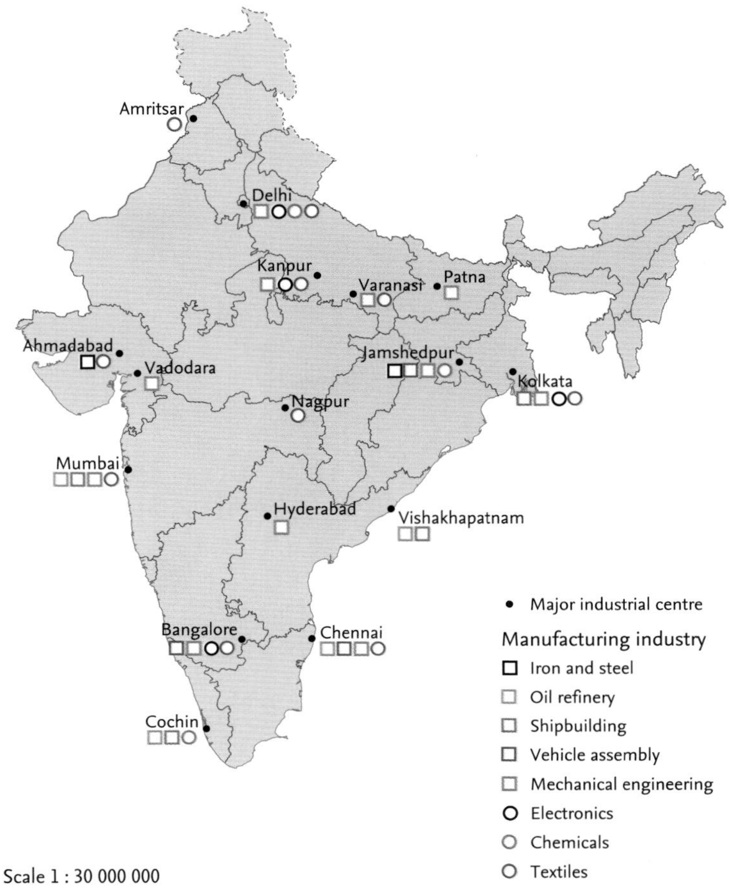

Amritsar
Delhi
Kanpur
Varanasi
Patna
Ahmadabad
Vadodara
Jamshedpur
Kolkata
Mumbai
Nagpur
Hyderabad
Vishakhapatnam
Bangalore
Chennai
Cochin

● Major industrial centre

Manufacturing industry
☐ Iron and steel
☐ Oil refinery
☐ Shipbuilding
☐ Vehicle assembly
☐ Mechanical engineering
○ Electronics
○ Chemicals
○ Textiles

Scale 1 : 30 000 000

7 Trade

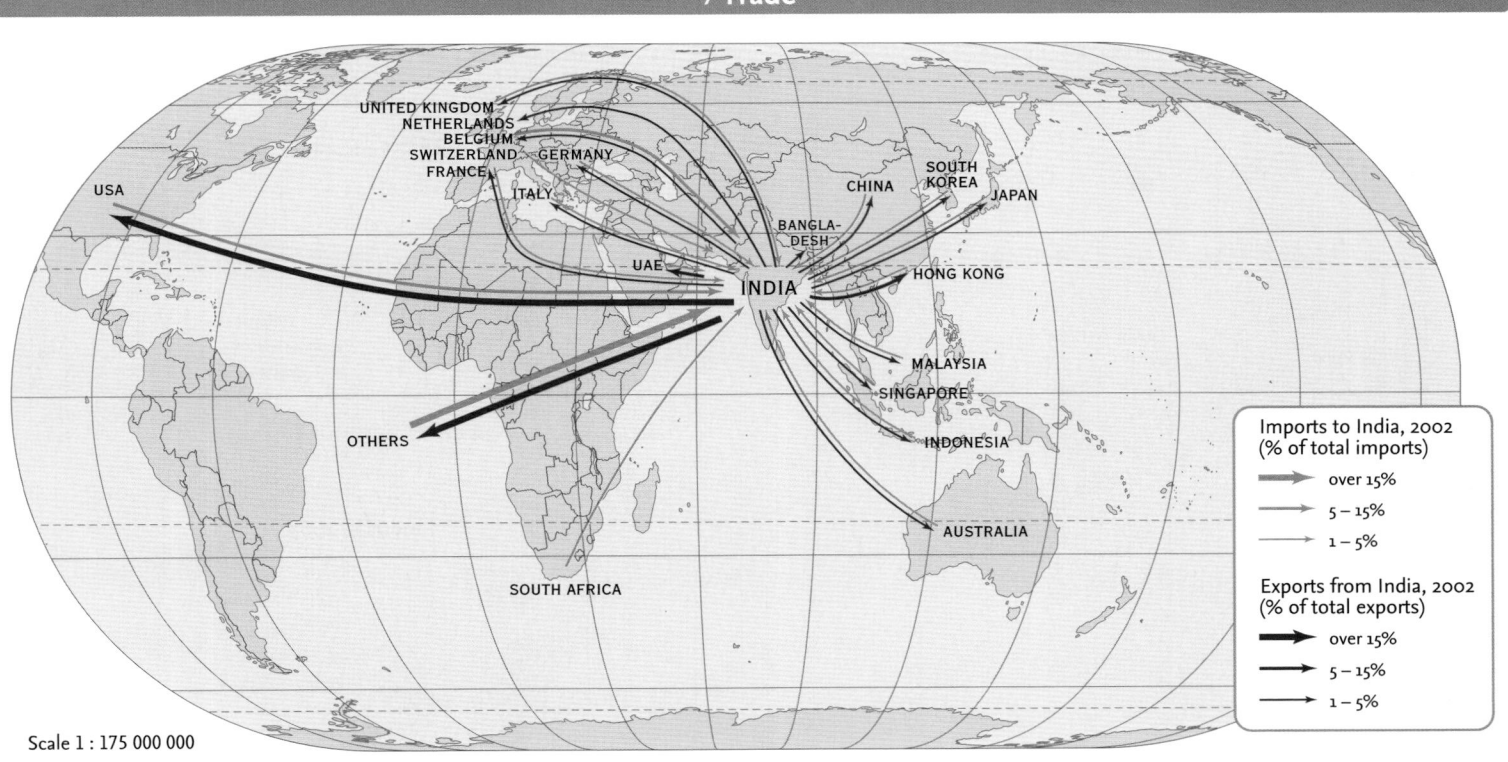

UNITED KINGDOM
NETHERLANDS
BELGIUM
SWITZERLAND
FRANCE
GERMANY
ITALY
USA
UAE
INDIA
BANGLA-DESH
CHINA
SOUTH KOREA
JAPAN
HONG KONG
MALAYSIA
SINGAPORE
INDONESIA
AUSTRALIA
SOUTH AFRICA
OTHERS

Imports to India, 2002
(% of total imports)
→ over 15%
→ 5 – 15%
→ 1 – 5%

Exports from India, 2002
(% of total exports)
→ over 15%
→ 5 – 15%
→ 1 – 5%

Scale 1 : 175 000 000

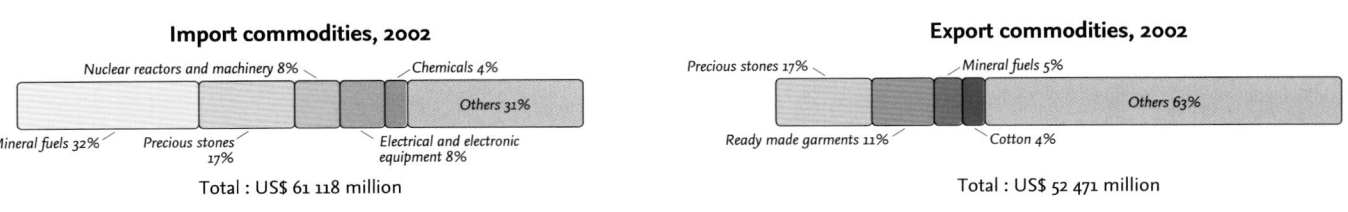

Import commodities, 2002

Nuclear reactors and machinery 8%
Chemicals 4%
Others 31%
Mineral fuels 32%
Precious stones 17%
Electrical and electronic equipment 8%

Total : US$ 61 118 million

Export commodities, 2002

Precious stones 17%
Mineral fuels 5%
Others 63%
Ready made garments 11%
Cotton 4%

Total : US$ 52 471 million

1 Population Density

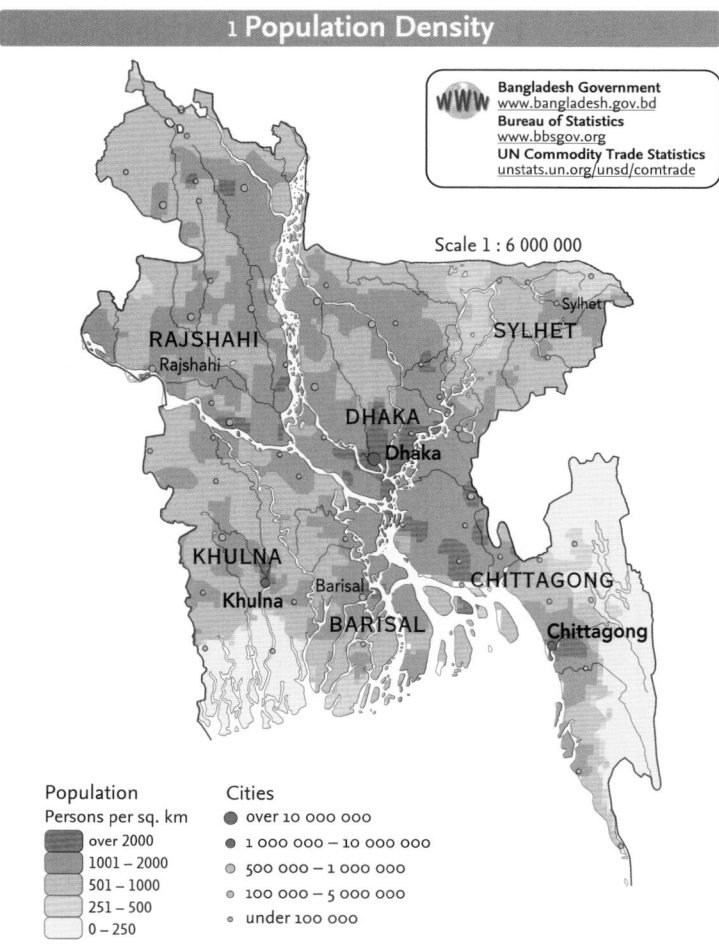

Scale 1 : 6 000 000

Bangladesh Government
www.bangladesh.gov.bd
Bureau of Statistics
www.bbsgov.org
UN Commodity Trade Statistics
unstats.un.org/unsd/comtrade

RAJSHAHI
Rajshahi

SYLHET
Sylhet

DHAKA
Dhaka

KHULNA
Khulna
Barisal
CHITTAGONG
BARISAL
Chittagong

Population
Persons per sq. km

	over 2000
	1001 – 2000
	501 – 1000
	251 – 500
	0 – 250

Cities

- over 10 000 000
- 1 000 000 – 10 000 000
- 500 000 – 1 000 000
- 100 000 – 5 000 000
- under 100 000

2 Population Growth

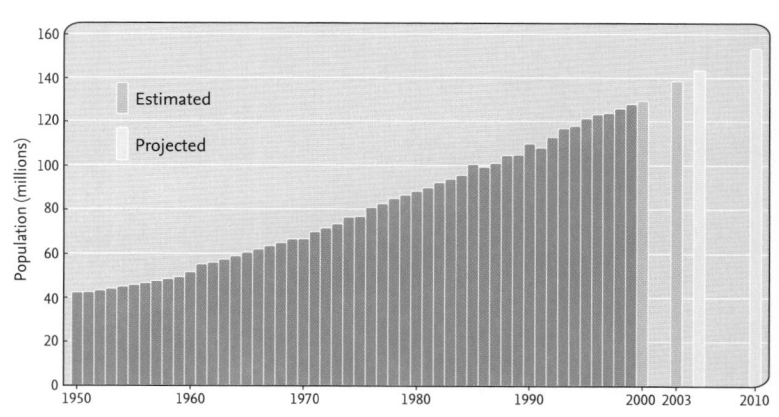

Estimated

Projected

Bangladesh Facts, 2002

Life expectancy at birth (years)	62
Adult literacy rate (percentage)	41
Infant mortality rate (per 1000 live births)	48
Population density (people per square kilometre)	1042
Urban population (percentage)	26

3 Main Urban Agglomerations

Urban agglomeration	1991 census	1998 estimate	2005 projection
Dhaka	6 105 160	10 979 000	15 921 000
Chittagong	2 040 663	2 906 000	4 468 000
Khulna	877 388	1 229 000	1 731 000

4 Economic Activity

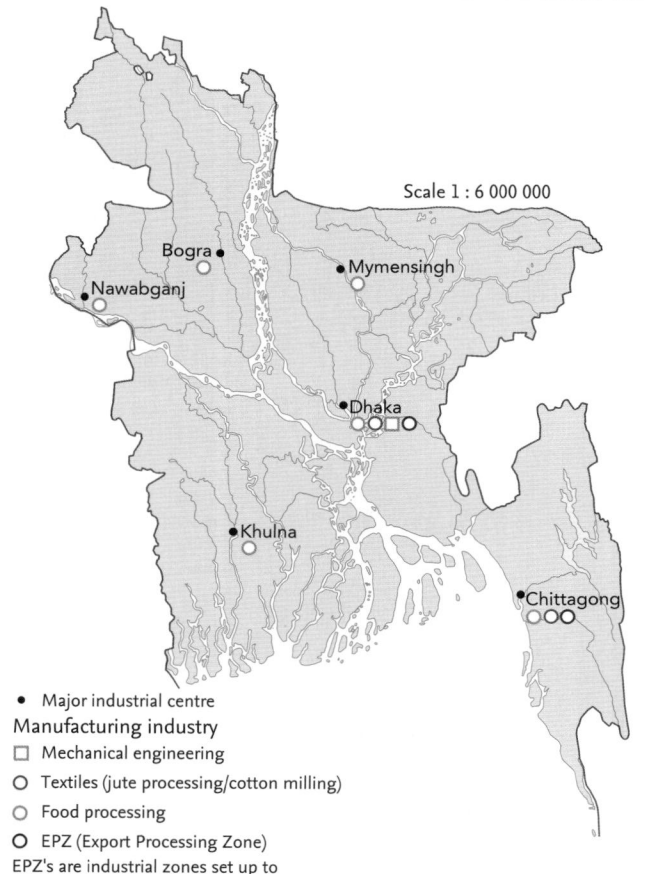

Scale 1 : 6 000 000

Bogra
Nawabganj
Mymensingh
Dhaka
Khulna
Chittagong

- Major industrial centre

Manufacturing industry

- ☐ Mechanical engineering
- ○ Textiles (jute processing/cotton milling)
- ○ Food processing
- ○ EPZ (Export Processing Zone)

EPZ's are industrial zones set up to
promote rapid economic growth.

5 Trade

Partners, 2003

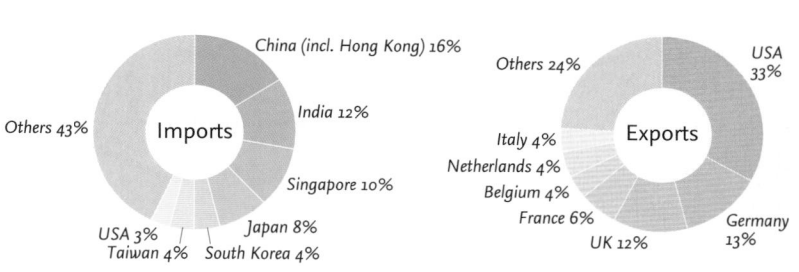

China (incl. Hong Kong) 16%
India 12%
Others 43%
Imports
Singapore 10%
USA 3%
Taiwan 4%
South Korea 4%
Japan 8%

Others 24%
USA 33%
Italy 4%
Netherlands 4%
Belgium 4%
Exports
France 6%
UK 12%
Germany 13%

Products, 2003

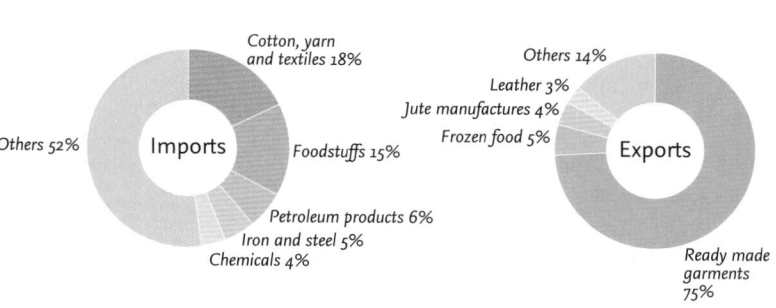

Cotton, yarn
and textiles 18%
Others 52%
Imports
Foodstuffs 15%
Petroleum products 6%
Iron and steel 5%
Chemicals 4%

Others 14%
Leather 3%
Jute manufactures 4%
Frozen food 5%
Exports
Ready made
garments
75%

Total : US$ 9648 million   Total : US$ 6548 million

6 Satellite Image

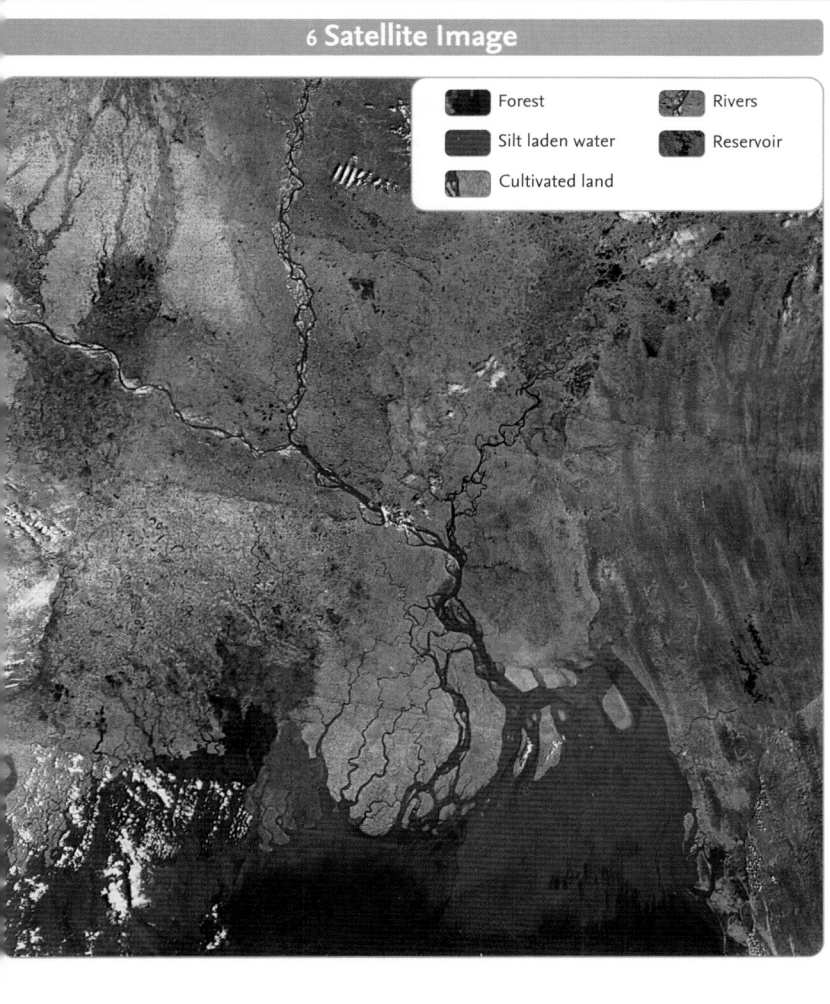

Forest		Rivers	
Silt laden water		Reservoir	
Cultivated land			

7 Bangladesh

Relief metres
3000
2000
1000
500
200
0 sea level
200

INDIA

BANGLADESH

DHAKA

Kolkata

Chittagong

Sundarbans

Mouths of the Ganges

Bay of Bengal

Tropic of Cancer

Scale 1 : 6 000 000

8 Annual Rainfall

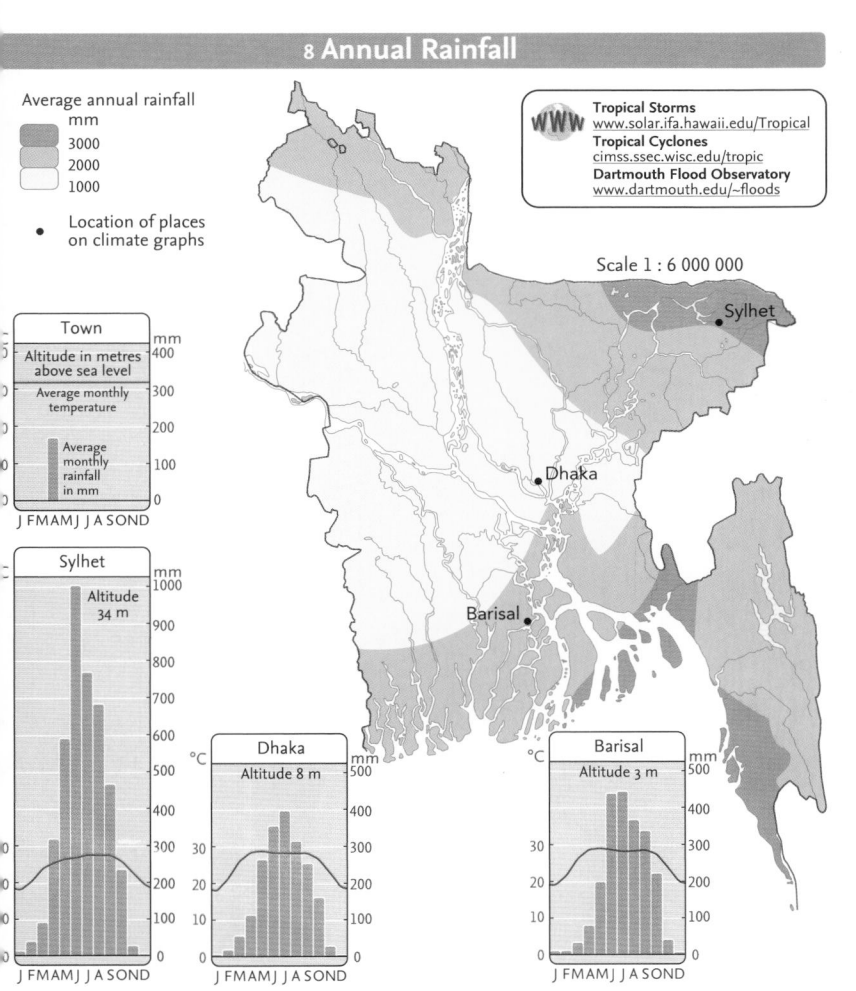

Average annual rainfall
mm
3000
2000
1000

• Location of places on climate graphs

Scale 1 : 6 000 000

Town
Altitude in metres above sea level
Average monthly temperature
Average monthly rainfall in mm
J F M A M J J A S O N D

Tropical Storms	www.solar.ifa.hawaii.edu/Tropical
Tropical Cyclones	cimss.ssec.wisc.edu/tropic
Dartmouth Flood Observatory	www.dartmouth.edu/~floods

Sylhet
Altitude 34 m

Dhaka
Altitude 8 m

Barisal
Altitude 3 m

9 Flood Control Projects

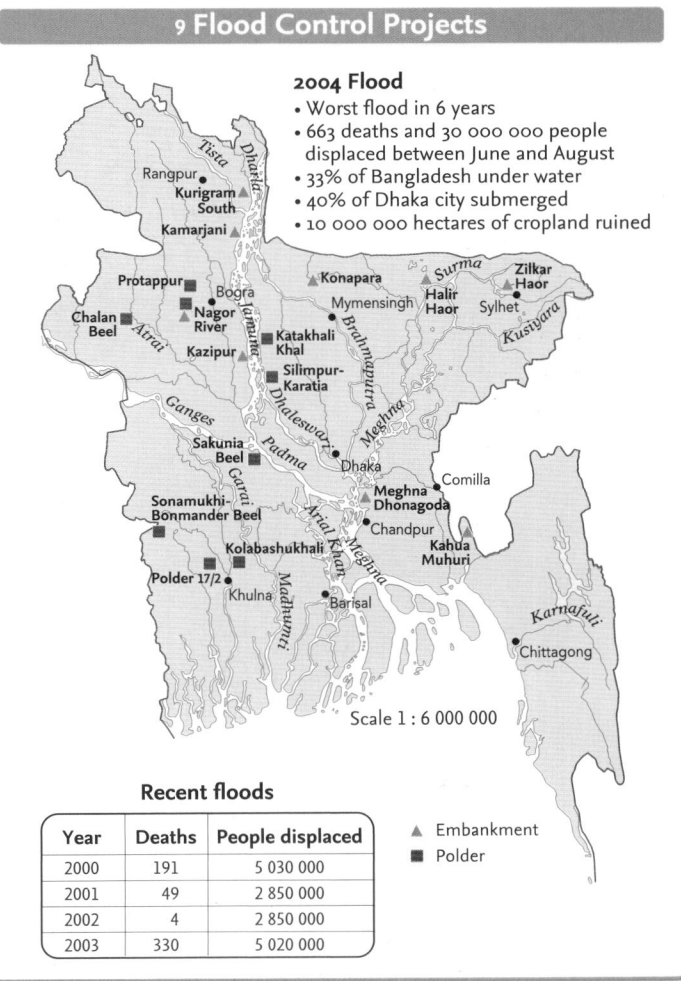

2004 Flood
• Worst flood in 6 years
• 663 deaths and 30 000 000 people displaced between June and August
• 33% of Bangladesh under water
• 40% of Dhaka city submerged
• 10 000 000 hectares of cropland ruined

Scale 1 : 6 000 000

Recent floods

Year	Deaths	People displaced
2000	191	5 030 000
2001	49	2 850 000
2002	4	2 850 000
2003	330	5 020 000

▲ Embankment
■ Polder

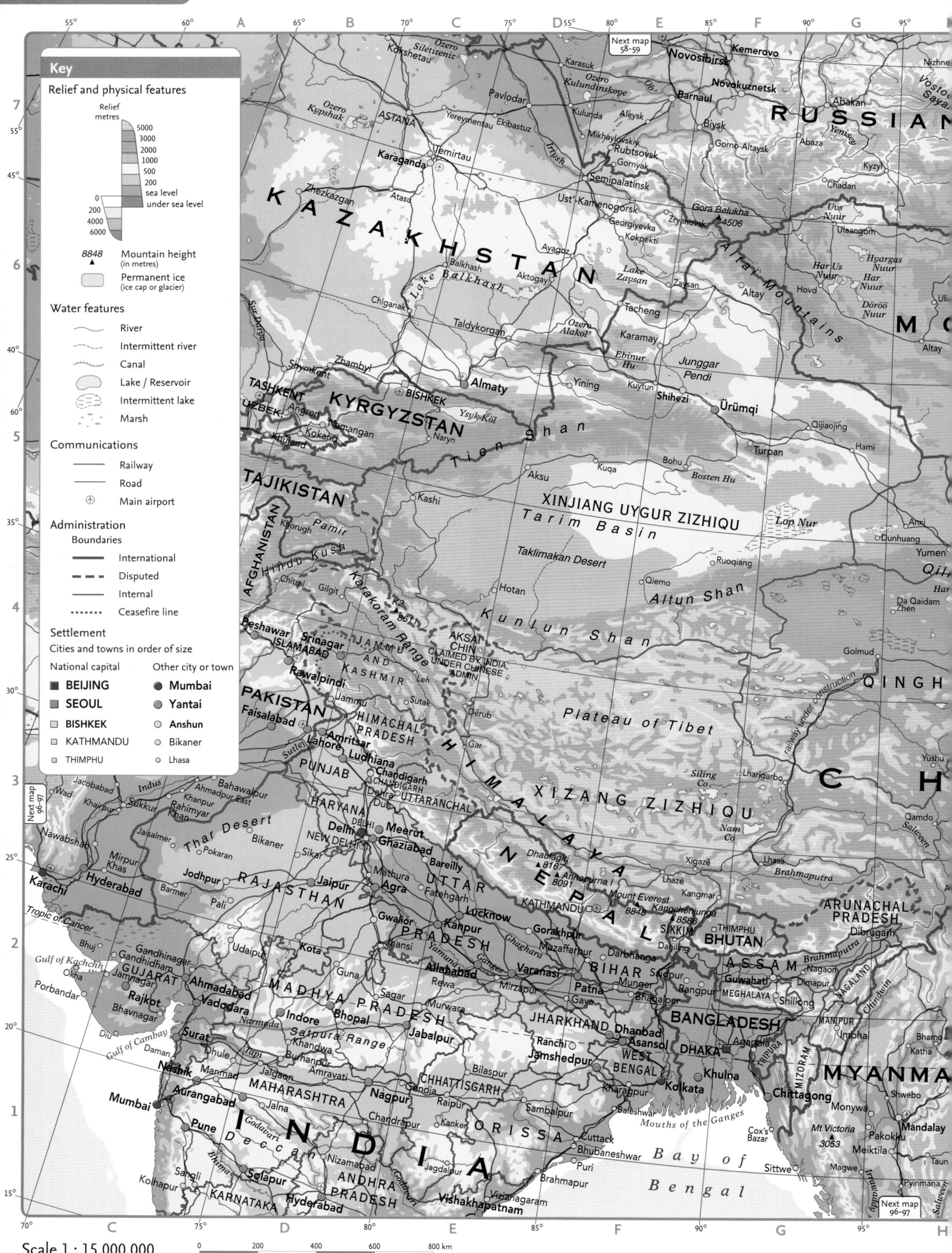

Key

Relief and physical features

Relief
metres
5000
3000
2000
1000
500
200
0 sea level
under sea level
200
4000
6000

8848 ▲ Mountain height
(in metres)
Permanent ice
(ice cap or glacier)

Water features

River
Intermittent river
Canal
Lake / Reservoir
Intermittent lake
Marsh

Communications

Railway
Road
⊕ Main airport

Administration

Boundaries
International
Disputed
Internal
Ceasefire line

Settlement

Cities and towns in order of size

National capital   Other city or town
■ BEIJING   ● Mumbai
▬ SEOUL   ● Yantai
□ BISHKEK   ○ Anshun
□ KATHMANDU   ○ Bikaner
□ THIMPHU   ○ Lhasa

Scale 1 : 15 000 000

0   200   400   600   800 km

Next map 106

Conic Equidistant projection

0   200   400   600   800 km

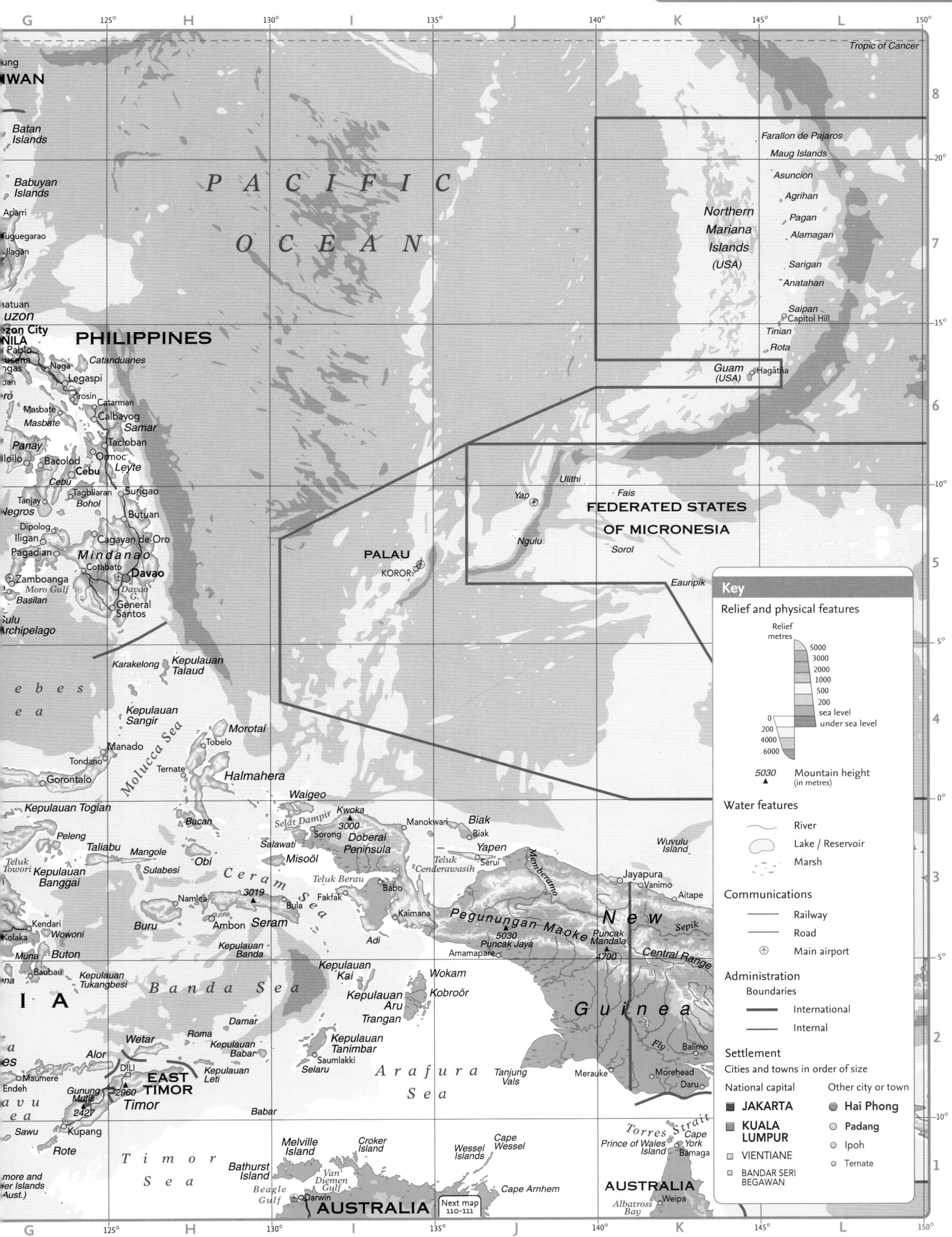

Tropic of Cancer

PACIFIC

OCEAN

Farallon de Pajaros
Maug Islands
Asuncion
Agrihan
Pagan
Alamagan
Northern
Mariana
Islands
(USA)
Sarigan
Anatahan

Saipan
Capitol Hill
Tinian
Rota

Guam
(USA)   Hagåtña

Batan
Islands

Babuyan
Islands

Aparri

Tuguegarao
Ilagan

uzon

uzon City
NILA
Pablo
gas
cema
Naga   Catanduanes
Legaspi
Irosin   Catarman
Calbayog   Samar
Masbate   Tacloban
Masbate   Ormoc   Leyte
Panay
Iloilo   Bacolod
Cebu   Cebu
Tagbilaran   Surigao
Tanjay   Bohol
Negros
Dipolog   Butuan
Iligan   Cagayan de Oro
Pagadian   Mindanao
Zamboanga   Cotabato   Davao
Moro Gulf   Davao
Basilan   General
Santos
Sulu
Archipelago

PHILIPPINES

**FEDERATED STATES
OF MICRONESIA**

Ulithi
Yap
Fais

Ngulu
Sorol

PALAU
KOROR
Eauripik

Karakelong
Kepulauan
Talaud

ebes
ea

Kepulauan
Sangir

Morotai
Manado   Tobelo
Tondano   Molucca Sea   Ternate
Gorontalo   Halmahera

Kepulauan Togian   Waigeo

Peleng   Bacan
Taliabu   Selat Dampir   Kwoka
Mangole   Salawati   3000   Manokwari
Teluk   Kepulauan   Obi   Sorong   Doberai   Biak
Towori   Banggai   Sulabesi   Misoöl   Peninsula   Biak
Kendari   Namlea   Teluk Berau   Yapen
Wowoni   3019   Bula   Fakfak   Yapen   Serui
Kolaka   Ambon   Babo
Muna   Buru   Seram   Kaimana   Adi
Buton   Kepulauan
Baubau   Banda   Amamapare
na   Kepulauan   Wokam
Tukangbesi   Kepulauan
Kai
Banda Sea   Kobroör
Kepulauan
Aru
Trangan
Damar   Kepulauan
Roma   Tanimbar
Wetar   Kepulauan   Saumlakki
Alor   Babar   Selaru
DILI   **EAST   Kepulauan   Arafura
TIMOR**   Leti
Gunung   Timor   Babar   **Sea**
Mutis
2960
2427

Jayapura
Vanimo
Wuvulu   Aitape
Island
Memberamo

Pegunungan Maoke   New
Puncak   Sepik
5030   Mandala
Puncak Jaya   4700
Central Range

Guinea
Fly   Balimo

Tanjung
Vals
Merauke
Morehead
Daru

AUSTRALIA

Torres Strait
Prince of Wales   Cape   Cape
Island   York
Bamaga

Melville   Croker
Island   Island   Wessel   Cape
Islands   Wessel

Maumere   Endeh   Bathurst   Van
avu   Island   Diemen
ea   2427   Gulf
Sawu   Kupang   Beagle
Rote   Gulf   Darwin
more and   **Timor**   **AUSTRALIA**
er Islands   **Sea**   Next map
Aust.)   110-111

Albatross   Weipa
Bay

Key

Relief and physical features

Relief
metres

5000
3000
2000
1000
500
200
sea level
0
under sea level
200
4000
6000

5030 ▲   Mountain height
(in metres)

Water features

~~~   River
Lake / Reservoir
Marsh

Communications

Railway
Road
⊕   Main airport

Administration
Boundaries
International
Internal

Settlement
Cities and towns in order of size
National capital   Other city or town
■ **JAKARTA**   ● Hai Phong
■ **KUALA   ○ Padang
LUMPUR**
□ VIENTIANE   ○ Ipoh
□ BANDAR SERI   ○ Ternate
BEGAWAN

Mercator projection

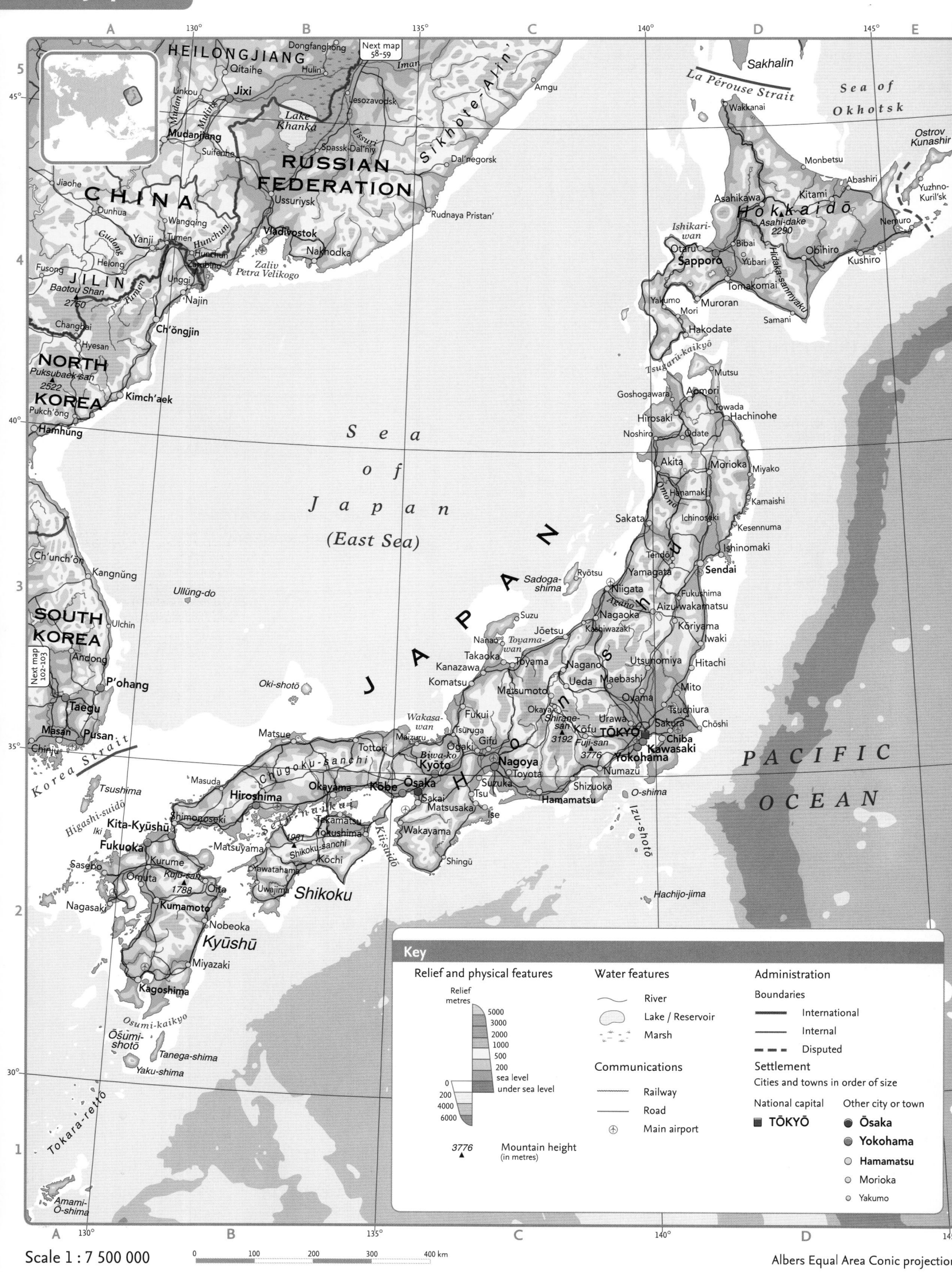

Scale 1 : 7 500 000

0   100   200   300   400 km

Albers Equal Area Conic projection

Key

Relief and physical features

Relief
metres

5000
3000
2000
1000
500
200
sea level
under sea level
0
200
4000
6000

3776 ▲   Mountain height
(in metres)

Water features

～～ River

⬭ Lake / Reservoir

❉ Marsh

Communications

── Railway

── Road

⊕ Main airport

Administration

Boundaries

── International

── Internal

┅┅ Disputed

Settlement

Cities and towns in order of size

National capital

◼ TŌKYŌ

Other city or town

● Ōsaka

● Yokohama

○ Hamamatsu

○ Morioka

○ Yakumo

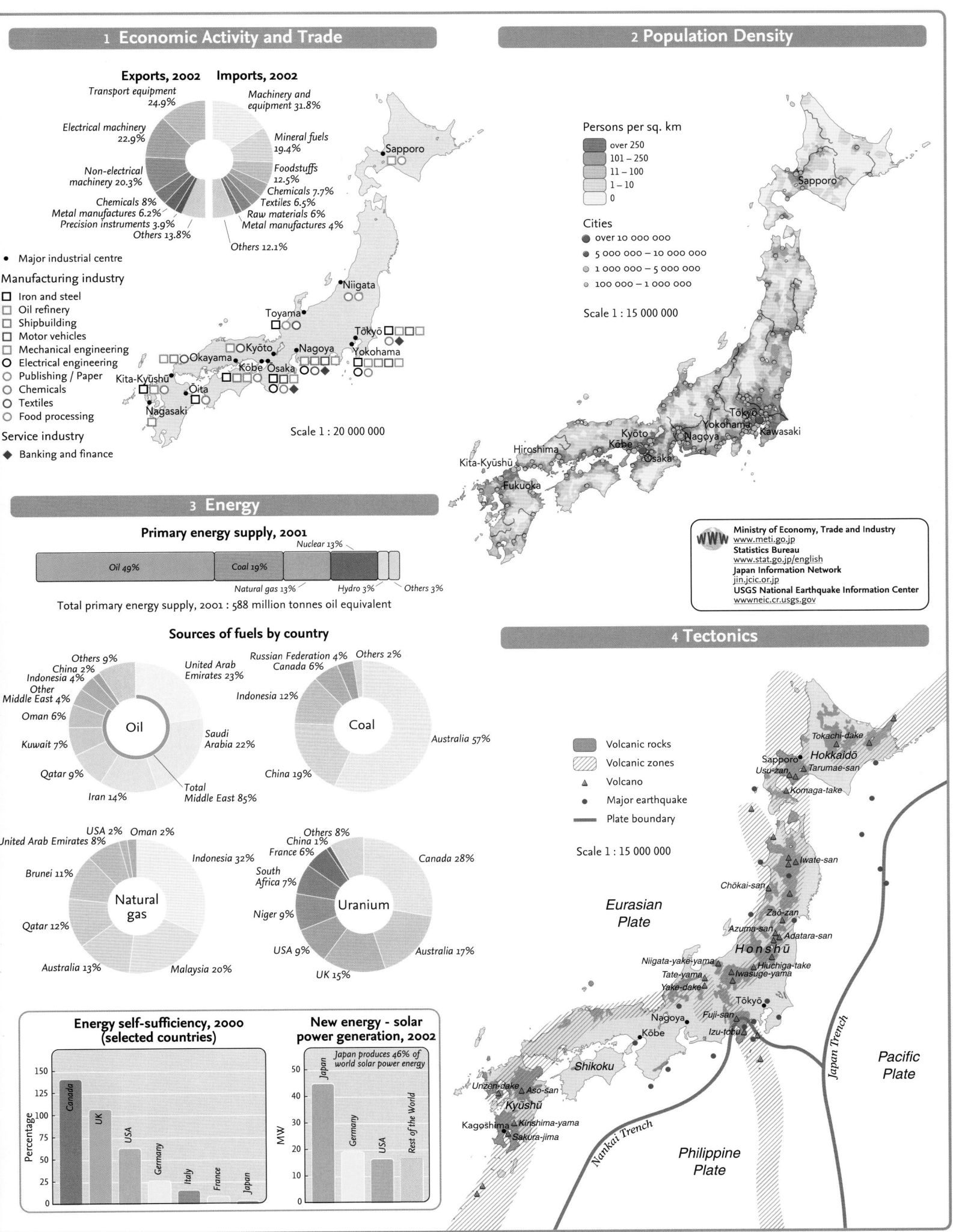

1 Economic Activity and Trade

Exports, 2002
Transport equipment 24.9%
Electrical machinery 22.9%
Non-electrical machinery 20.3%
Chemicals 8%
Metal manufactures 6.2%
Precision instruments 3.9%
Others 13.8%

Imports, 2002
Machinery and equipment 31.8%
Mineral fuels 19.4%
Foodstuffs 12.5%
Chemicals 7.7%
Textiles 6.5%
Raw materials 6%
Metal manufactures 4%
Others 12.1%

- Major industrial centre

Manufacturing industry
- Iron and steel
- Oil refinery
- Shipbuilding
- Motor vehicles
- Mechanical engineering
- Electrical engineering
- Publishing / Paper
- Chemicals
- Textiles
- Food processing

Service industry
- Banking and finance

Sapporo
Niigata
Toyama
Tōkyō
Kyōto
Nagoya
Yokohama
Okayama
Kōbe
Osaka
Kita-Kyūshū
Ōita
Nagasaki

Scale 1 : 20 000 000

2 Population Density

Persons per sq. km
- over 250
- 101 – 250
- 11 – 100
- 1 – 10
- 0

Cities
- over 10 000 000
- 5 000 000 – 10 000 000
- 1 000 000 – 5 000 000
- 100 000 – 1 000 000

Scale 1 : 15 000 000

Sapporo
Tōkyō
Yokohama
Kawasaki
Nagoya
Kyōto
Kōbe
Osaka
Hiroshima
Kita-Kyūshū
Fukuoka

WWW Ministry of Economy, Trade and Industry
www.meti.go.jp
Statistics Bureau
www.stat.go.jp/english
Japan Information Network
jin.jcic.or.jp
USGS National Earthquake Information Center
wwwneic.cr.usgs.gov

3 Energy

Primary energy supply, 2001
Oil 49%   Coal 19%   Natural gas 13%   Nuclear 13%   Hydro 3%   Others 3%

Total primary energy supply, 2001 : 588 million tonnes oil equivalent

Sources of fuels by country

Oil
Others 9%
China 2%
Indonesia 4%
Other Middle East 4%
Oman 6%
Kuwait 7%
Qatar 9%
Iran 14%
United Arab Emirates 23%
Saudi Arabia 22%
Total Middle East 85%

Coal
Russian Federation 4%
Canada 6%
Others 2%
Indonesia 12%
China 19%
Australia 57%

Natural gas
USA 2%
Oman 2%
United Arab Emirates 8%
Brunei 11%
Qatar 12%
Australia 13%
Malaysia 20%
Indonesia 32%

Uranium
Others 8%
China 1%
France 6%
South Africa 7%
Niger 9%
USA 9%
UK 15%
Australia 17%
Canada 28%

Energy self-sufficiency, 2000 (selected countries)
Percentage
Canada, UK, USA, Germany, Italy, France, Japan

New energy - solar power generation, 2002
MW
Japan produces 46% of world solar power energy
Japan, Germany, USA, Rest of the World

4 Tectonics

- Volcanic rocks
- Volcanic zones
- Volcano
- Major earthquake
- Plate boundary

Scale 1 : 15 000 000

Eurasian Plate
Pacific Plate
Philippine Plate

Japan Trench
Nankai Trench

Hokkaidō
Tokachi-dake
Sapporo
Usu-zan
Tarumae-san
Komaga-take

Honshū
Iwate-san
Chōkai-san
Zaō-zan
Azuma-san
Adatara-san
Niigata-yake-yama
Huchiga-take
Tate-yama
Iwasuge-yama
Yake-dake
Fuji-san
Izu-tobu
Tōkyō
Nagoya
Kōbe

Shikoku

Kyūshū
Unzen-dake
Aso-san
Kagoshima
Kirishima-yama
Sakura-jima

PAKISTAN
Karachi
Delhi
NEW DELHI
NEPAL
KATHMANDU
INDIA
Mumbai
Hyderabad
Bangalore
Chennai
SRI LANKA
Nicobar Islands (India)
4267
Andaman Islands (India)
Bay of Bengal
Ganges
Tropic of Cancer
Kolkata
DHAKA
BANG.
Thimphu
Plateau of Tibet
Kunlun Shan
Himalaya
CHINA
MONGOLIA
Gobi
Huang He
Shenyang
BEIJING
Tianjin
Xi'an
Nanjing
Wuhan
Nanchang
Chang Jiang
Kunming
Guangzhou
Fuzhou
Hangzhou
Shanghai
Yellow Sea
East China Sea
Chongqing
MYANMAR
RANGOON
HANOI
LAOS
VIENTIANE
THAILAND
BANGKOK
CAMBODIA
PHNOM PENH
VIETNAM
Ho Chi Minh City
Gulf of Thailand
MALAYSIA
KUALA LUMPUR
PUTRAJAYA
SINGAPORE
Medan
Sumatra
JAKARTA
Java
Borneo
Java Sea
Palembang
Makassar
Surabaya
Bali
Sumbawa
Sumba
Flores Sea
Celebes
Celebes Sea
INDONESIA
Molucas
Seram
Halmahera
5484
Bandar Seri Begawan
BRUNEI
Sulu Sea
Mindanao
Davao
KOROR
PALAU
8054
8967
Yap
Gaferut
Chuuk
PALIKIR
FED. STATES OF MICRONESIA
Pohnpei
Kosrae
DELAP-ULIGA-DJARRIT
MARSHALL ISLANDS
KIRIBATI
Gilbert Islands
BAIRIKI
YAREN
NAURU
Banaba
Beru
Baker I. (USA)
Howland I. (USA)
KIRIBATI
Phoenix Islands
Nikumaroro
Kanton
Rawaki
Manra
TUVALU
Nanumea
Nui
Vaitupu
Funafuti
VAIAKU
SOLOMON ISLANDS
HONIARA
Guadalcanal
Malaita
Santa Isabel
8322
Santa Cruz Islands
VANUATU
PORT VILA
Espiritu Santo
Tanna
New Caledonia (France)
Nouméa
Iles Loyauté
7633
New Hebrides Trench
FIJI
Vanua Levu
Viti Levu
SUVA
Wallis and Futuna (Fr)
Mata'utu
Vava'u Group
NUKU'ALOFA
TONGA
Ono-i-Lau
Tongatapu Group
Niue (NZ)
Tokelau (NZ)
Nukunonu
Fakaofo
Atafu
Swains Island (NZ)
Savai'i
APIA
Upolu
SAMOA
Fagatogo
Tutuila
American Samoa (USA)
Alofi
Horizon Deep
10800
South Fiji Basin
Kermadec Islands (NZ)
Raoul Island
Norfolk Island (Australia)
Lord Howe Island (Australia)
10047
Tasman Sea
Tasman Basin
5176
NEW ZEALAND
Auckland
North Island
WELLINGTON
Aoraki (Mt Cook)
3754
South Island
Chatham Rise
Chatham Islands (NZ)
Bounty Islands (NZ)
Antipodes Islands (NZ)
6096
Stewart Island
Snares Islands
Auckland Islands (NZ)
Campbell Plateau
Campbell Island (NZ)
Macquarie Island (Australia)
Macquarie Ridge

AUSTRALIA
Great Sandy Desert
Kimberley Plateau
North West Cape
Shark Bay
Great Victoria Desert
Great Sandy Desert
Simpson Desert
Nullarbor Plain
Great Australian Bight
Perth Basin
Perth
5746
C. Leeuwin
Adelaide
Kangaroo I.
Melbourne
5670
South Australian Basin
Hobart
Tasmania
King I.
Flinders I.
Bass Strait
Murray
Darling
CANBERRA
Sydney
Brisbane
Fraser I.
Great Dividing Range
Lord Howe Rise
Norfolk Island Ridge
Coral Sea Basin
Coral Sea
Great Barrier Reef
Arnhem Land
Darwin
Gulf of Carpentaria
Cape York Peninsula
PORT MORESBY
Torres Strait
Arafura Sea
Timor Sea
EAST TIMOR
DILI
Timor
Kepulauan Tanimbar
Weber
PAPUA NEW GUINEA
New Guinea
Puncak Jaya
5030
7288
Bismarck Sea
Admiralty Islands
New Ireland
New Britain
8940
Bougainville Island
New Britain Trench
North Australian Basin
West Australian Basin
6360
Mid-Indian Basin
INDIAN OCEAN
Investigator Ridge
Ninetyeast Ridge
East Indiaman Ridge
Java Trench (Sunda Trench)
7125
Cocos Basin
Kepulauan Mentawai
Java Ridge
Macassar Strait
Tropic of Capricorn
Rodrigues Island (Mauritius)
7102
Diamantina Deep
6602
Southeast Indian Ridge
Indian-Antarctic Ridge
Antarctic Circle
SOUTHERN

PHILIPPINES
MANILA
Luzon
Luzon Strait
Mindoro
Panay
Samar
Leyte
Negros
Palawan
5560
Cape Johnson Depth 10057
Philippine Trench
Philippine Basin
6745
West Mariana Basin
West Mariana Ridge
Pagan
Saipan
Capitol Hill
Tinian
Northern Mariana Islands (USA)
Hagåtña
Guam (USA)
Challenger Deep 10920
Mariana Trench
East Mariana Basin
Hall Islands
Yap Trench
West Caroline Basin
Kepulauan Talaud
Mortlock Islands
East Caroline Basin
7208
New Guinea Rise
Kapingamarangi Rise
Caroline Islands
MICRONESIA
MELANESIA
Melanesian Basin
Eauripik Rise
Gilbert Ridge
Central Pacific Basin
6957
Palmyra (USA)
Howland I. (USA)
Nauru

Hainan
South China Sea
T'AIPEI
7460
TAIWAN
Hong Kong
Okinawa
Ryukyu Islands (Japan)
9156
9780
Izu Trench
Ogasawara (Bonin) Trench
Bonin Islands (Japan)
Volcano Islands (Japan)
6345
Palau Ridge
Kyushu-Palau Ridge
South Honshu Ridge
Mariana Ridge
East China Sea
Kyūshū
Shikoku
Kōbe
Ōsaka
TŌKYŌ
Honshū
JAPAN
Hachijō-jima
Ramapo Deep 9695
NORTH KOREA
PYONGYANG
SEOUL
SOUTH KOREA
Sea of Japan (East Sea)
8412
Northwest Pacific Basin
Hokkaidō
Sakhalin
Sikhote-Alin
Amur
Manchuria
Harbin
Kuril Basin
Kuril Islands
Kuril Trench
9550
Japan Trench
Sea of Okhotsk
Kamchatka Peninsula
Kamchatka Basin
Bering Sea
Aleutian Basin
Nunivak Island
Aleutian Islands
Aleutian Trench
7822
6671
Emperor Seamount Chain
Emperor Trough
Chinook Trough
7900
Midway Islands (USA)
Kure Atoll
Laysan Island
Necker Island
Hawaiian Ridge
Hawaii
Mid Pacific Mountains
Mapmakers Seamounts
Wake Island (USA)
6530
PACIFIC OCEAN
Johnston Atoll (USA)
Howland I.

Scale 1 : 50 000 000

0 500 1000 1500 2000 km

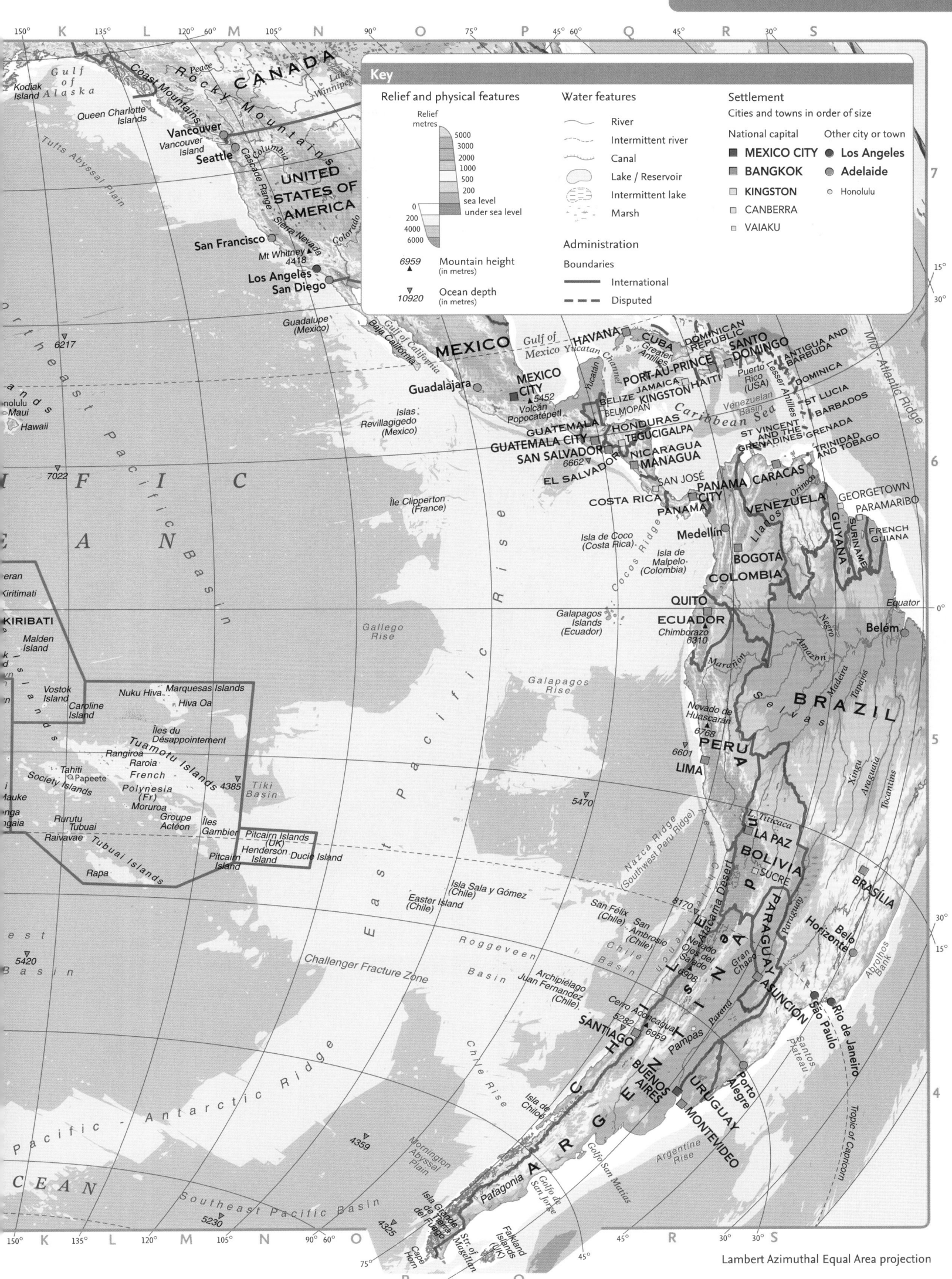

Lambert Azimuthal Equal Area projection

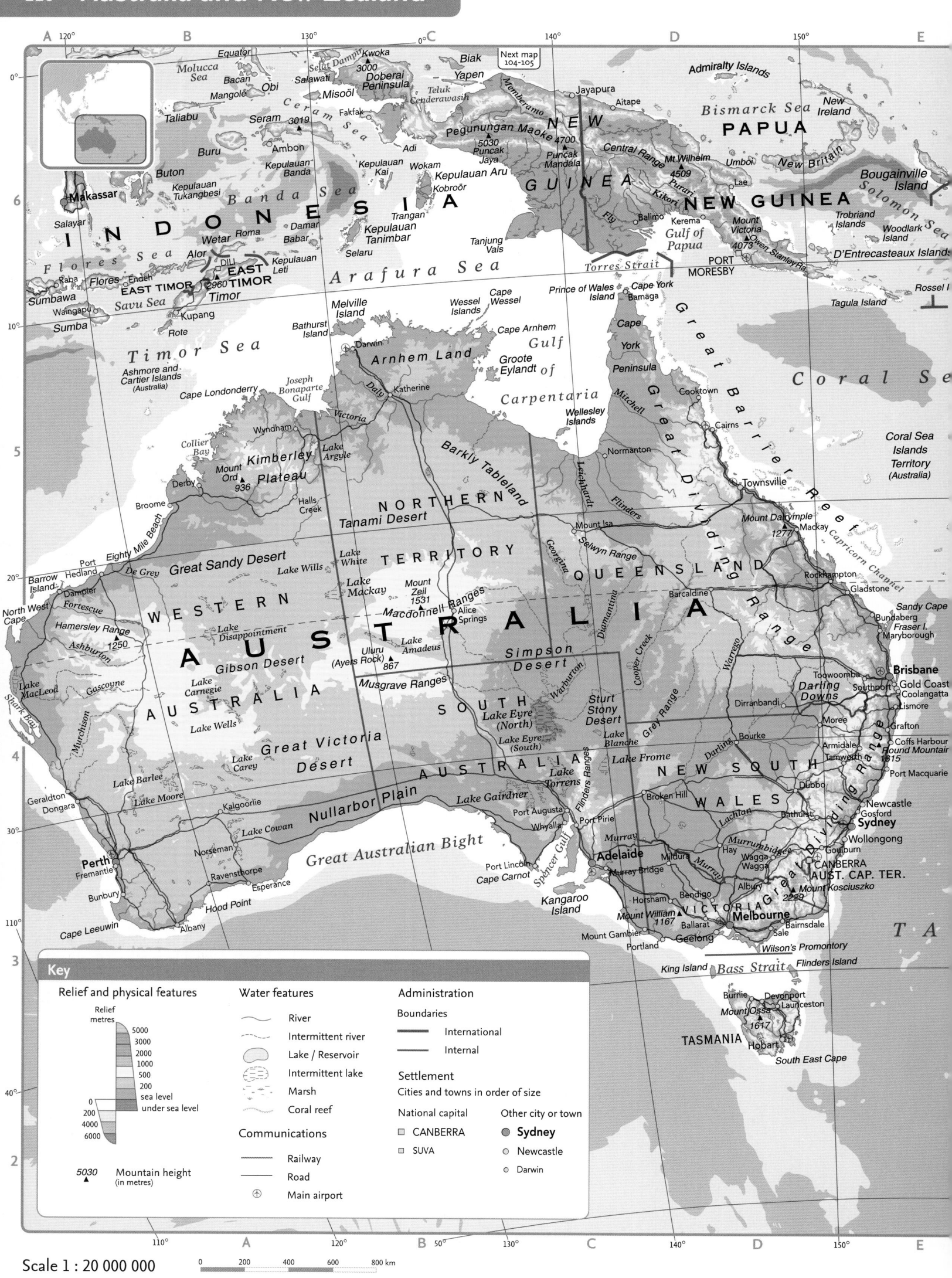

Next map
104–105

Key

Relief and physical features

Relief metres
5000
3000
2000
1000
500
200
sea level
under sea level
0
200
4000
6000

▲ 5030   Mountain height
(in metres)

Water features

～ River
～ Intermittent river
Lake / Reservoir
Intermittent lake
Marsh
Coral reef

Communications

Railway
Road
⊕ Main airport

Administration

Boundaries
International
Internal

Settlement
Cities and towns in order of size

National capital
□ CANBERRA
□ SUVA

Other city or town
● Sydney
○ Newcastle
○ Darwin

Scale 1 : 20 000 000

0   200   400   600   800 km

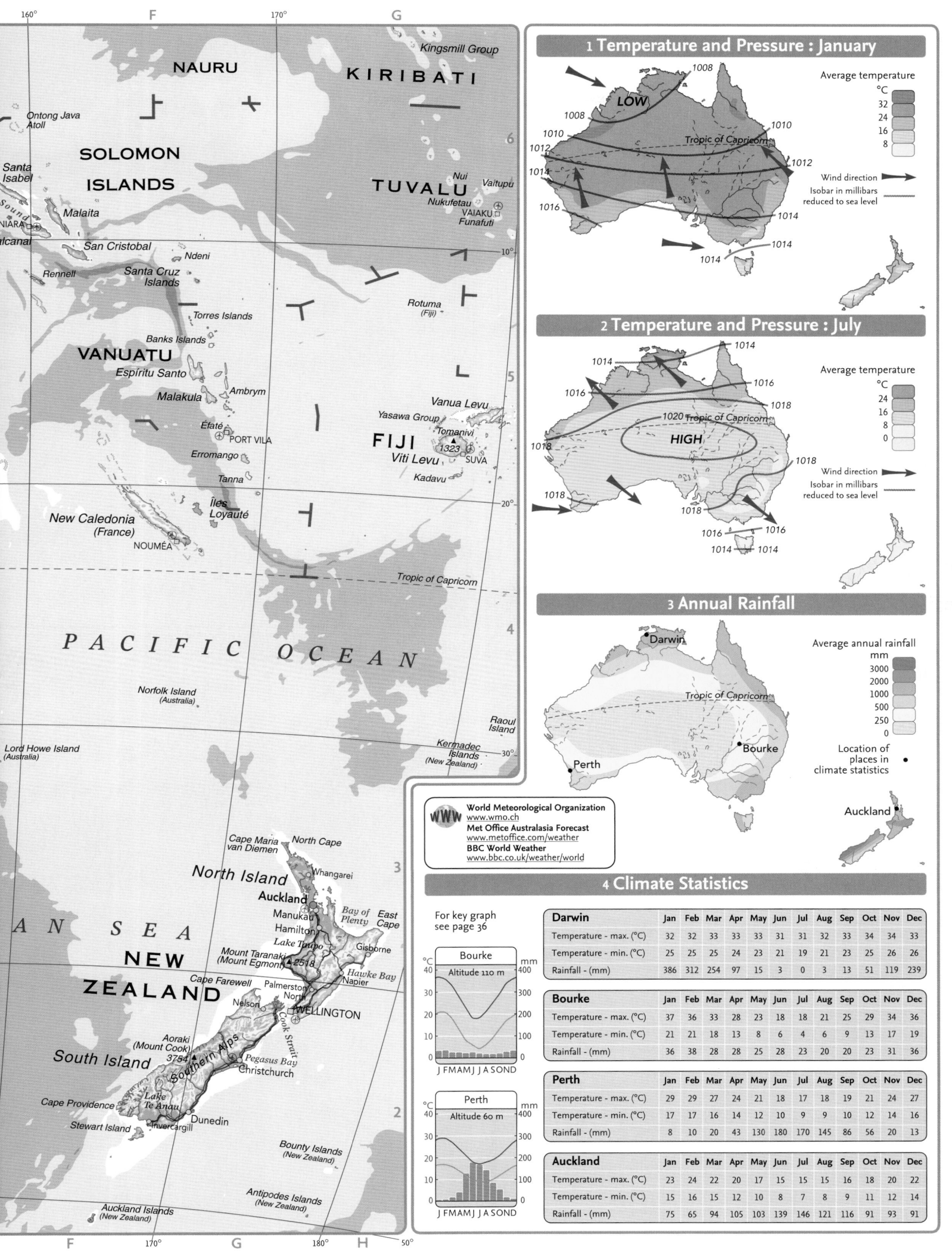

1 Temperature and Pressure : January

1008
LOW
1008
1010
1012
1014
1016
Tropic of Capricorn
1010
1012
1014
1014
1014

Average temperature
°C
32
24
16
8

Wind direction
Isobar in millibars
reduced to sea level

2 Temperature and Pressure : July

1014
1014
1016
1016
1018
1020 Tropic of Capricorn
HIGH
1018
1018
1018
1016
1018
1016
1014 1014

Average temperature
°C
24
16
8
0

Wind direction
Isobar in millibars
reduced to sea level

3 Annual Rainfall

Darwin

Tropic of Capricorn

Bourke

Perth

Average annual rainfall
mm
3000
2000
1000
500
250
0

Location of
places in
climate statistics

Auckland

World Meteorological Organization
www.wmo.ch
Met Office Australasia Forecast
www.metoffice.com/weather
BBC World Weather
www.bbc.co.uk/weather/world

4 Climate Statistics

For key graph
see page 36

Bourke
Altitude 110 m

Perth
Altitude 60 m

Darwin	Jan	Feb	Mar	Apr	May	Jun	Jul	Aug	Sep	Oct	Nov	Dec
Temperature - max. (°C)	32	32	33	33	33	31	31	32	33	34	34	33
Temperature - min. (°C)	25	25	25	24	23	21	19	21	23	25	26	26
Rainfall - (mm)	386	312	254	97	15	3	0	13	51	119	239

Bourke	Jan	Feb	Mar	Apr	May	Jun	Jul	Aug	Sep	Oct	Nov	Dec
Temperature - max. (°C)	37	36	33	28	23	18	18	21	25	29	34	36
Temperature - min. (°C)	21	21	18	13	8	6	4	6	9	13	17	19
Rainfall - (mm)	36	38	28	28	25	28	23	20	20	23	31	36

Perth	Jan	Feb	Mar	Apr	May	Jun	Jul	Aug	Sep	Oct	Nov	Dec
Temperature - max. (°C)	29	29	27	24	21	18	17	18	19	21	24	27
Temperature - min. (°C)	17	17	16	14	12	10	9	9	10	12	14	16
Rainfall - (mm)	8	10	20	43	130	180	170	145	86	56	20	13

Auckland	Jan	Feb	Mar	Apr	May	Jun	Jul	Aug	Sep	Oct	Nov	Dec
Temperature - max. (°C)	23	24	22	20	17	15	15	15	16	18	20	22
Temperature - min. (°C)	15	16	15	12	10	8	7	8	9	11	12	14
Rainfall - (mm)	75	65	94	105	103	139	146	121	116	91	93	91

Lambert Azimuthal Equal Area projection

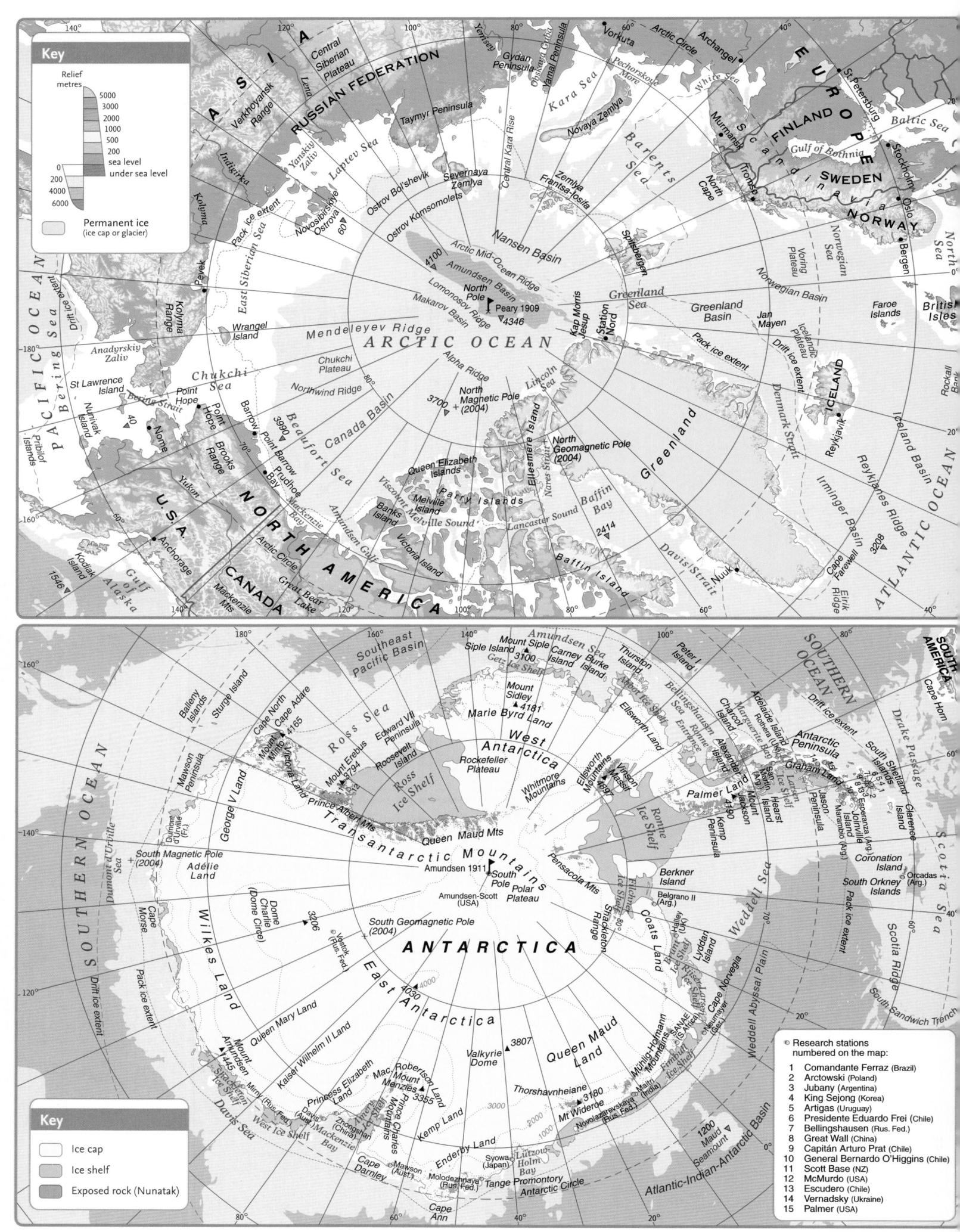

Key

Relief metres
- 5000
- 3000
- 2000
- 1000
- 500
- 200
- 0 sea level
- 0 under sea level
- 200
- 4000
- 6000

Permanent ice (ice cap or glacier)

Key
- Ice cap
- Ice shelf
- Exposed rock (Nunatak)

© Research stations numbered on the map:
1. Comandante Ferraz (Brazil)
2. Arctowski (Poland)
3. Jubany (Argentina)
4. King Sejong (Korea)
5. Artigas (Uruguay)
6. Presidente Eduardo Frei (Chile)
7. Bellingshausen (Rus. Fed.)
8. Great Wall (China)
9. Capitán Arturo Prat (Chile)
10. General Bernardo O'Higgins (Chile)
11. Scott Base (NZ)
12. McMurdo (USA)
13. Escudero (Chile)
14. Vernadsky (Ukraine)
15. Palmer (USA)

Scale 1 : 36 000 000

0   500   1000   1500 km

1 Time Zones

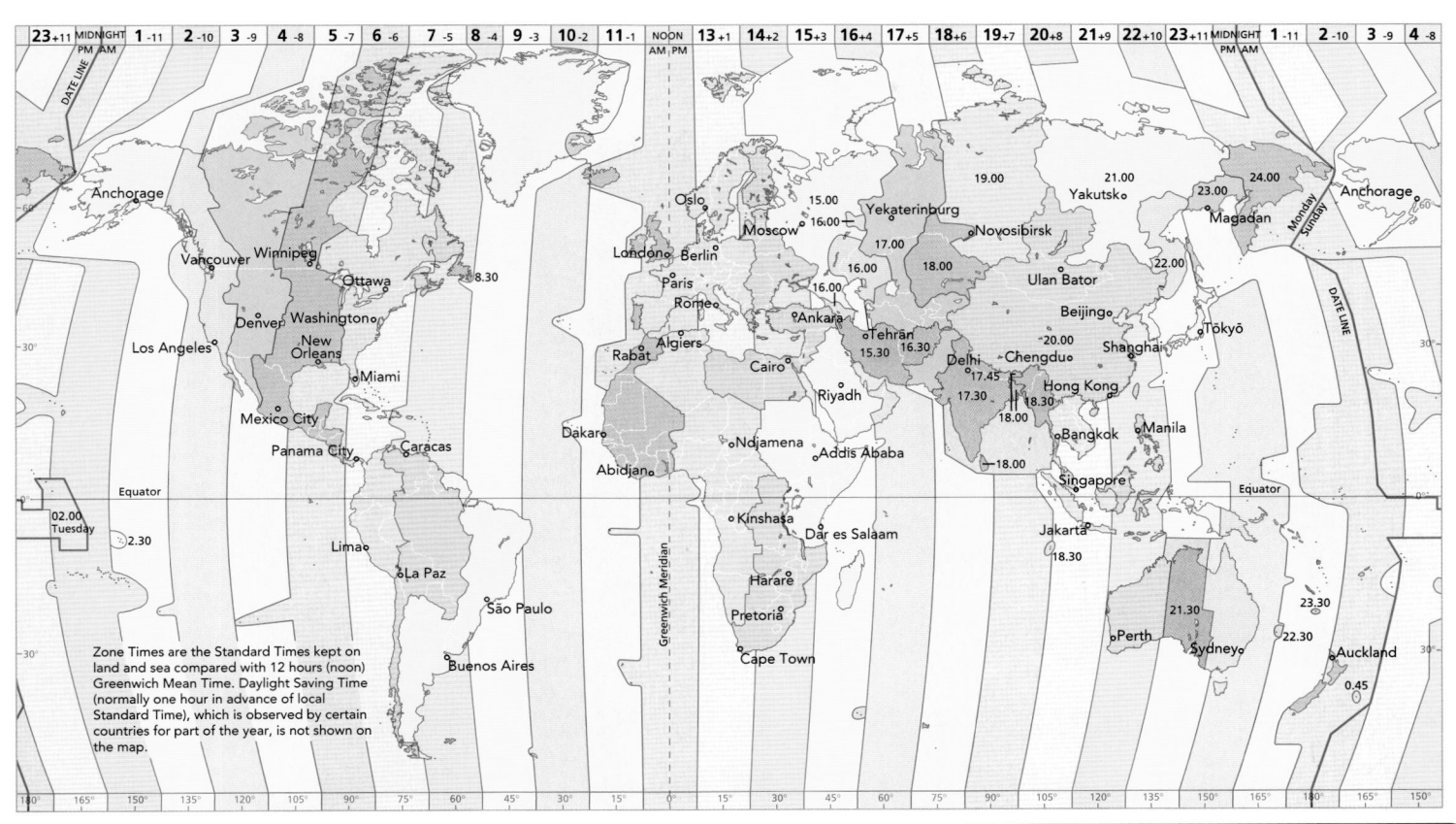

Zone Times are the Standard Times kept on land and sea compared with 12 hours (noon) Greenwich Mean Time. Daylight Saving Time (normally one hour in advance of local Standard Time), which is observed by certain countries for part of the year, is not shown on the map.

World Time
wwp.greenwichmeantime.com
The World Clock - Time Zones
www.timeanddate.com/worldclock

United Nations
www.un.org
Commonwealth
www.thecommonwealth.org

2 International Organizations

Andorra
Cyprus
Liechtenstein
Malta
San Marino

Antigua and Barbuda
Bahamas
Barbados
Dominica
Grenada
Jamaica
St Kitts and Nevis
St Vincent and the Grenadines
Trinidad and Tobago

Cape Verde
São Tomé and Príncipe

Bahrain
Qatar

Maldives

Fiji
Kiribati
Nauru
Samoa
Solomon Islands
Tonga
Tuvalu
Vanuatu

Comoros
Mauritius
Seychelles

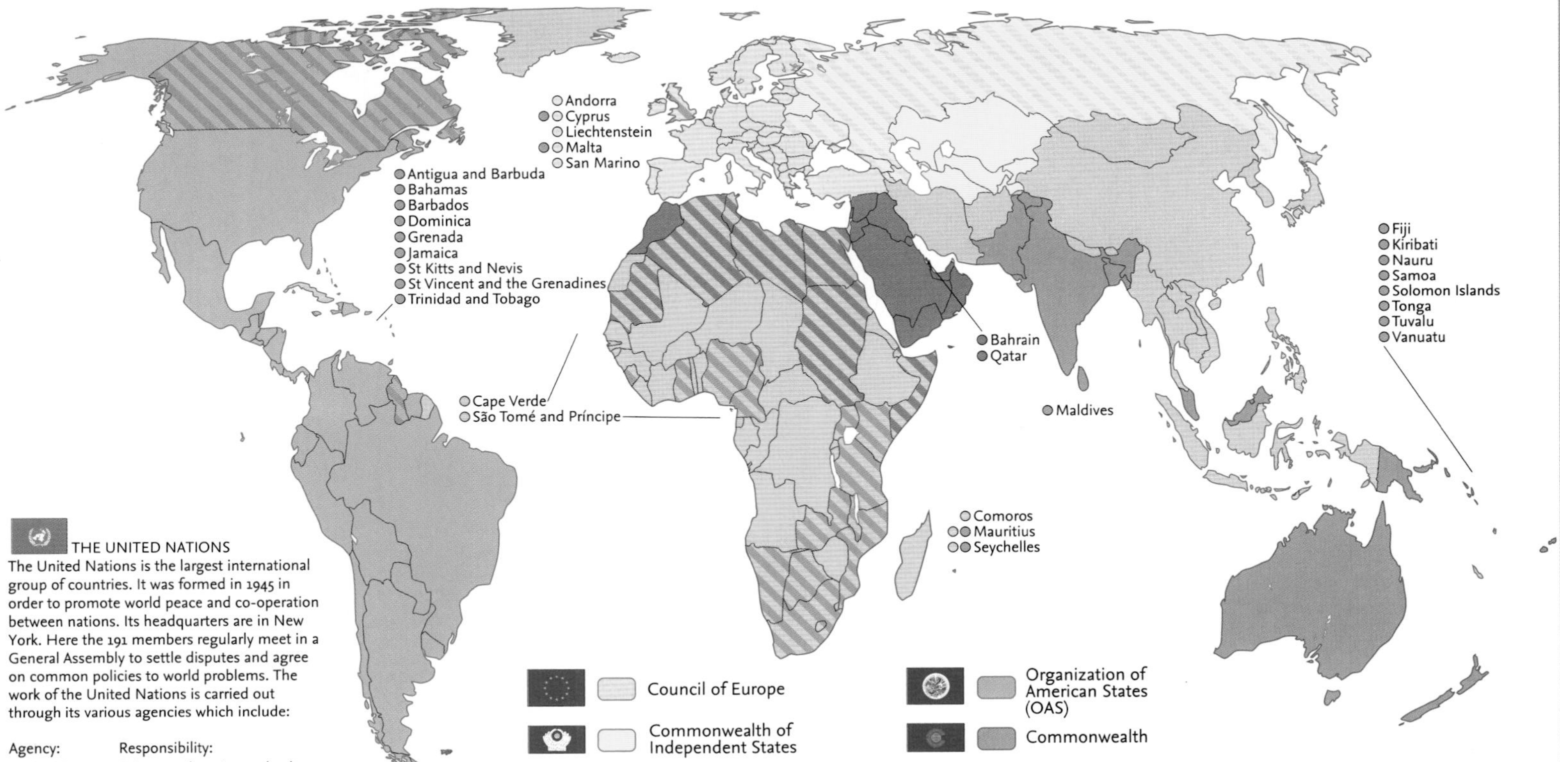

THE UNITED NATIONS

The United Nations is the largest international group of countries. It was formed in 1945 in order to promote world peace and co-operation between nations. Its headquarters are in New York. Here the 191 members regularly meet in a General Assembly to settle disputes and agree on common policies to world problems. The work of the United Nations is carried out through its various agencies which include:

Agency:	Responsibility:
UNESCO	Science, education and culture
UNICEF	Children's welfare
UNDRO	Disaster relief
UNHCR	Aid to refugees
WHO	Health
FAO	Food and agriculture
UNEP	Environment
UNDP	Development programme

Council of Europe

Commonwealth of Independent States

African Union (AU)

Arab League

Organization of American States (OAS)

Commonwealth

Not a member of any of the organizations shown on the map

Note:- Countries represented by colour stripes are those which are members of more than one of the International Organizations shown on the map.

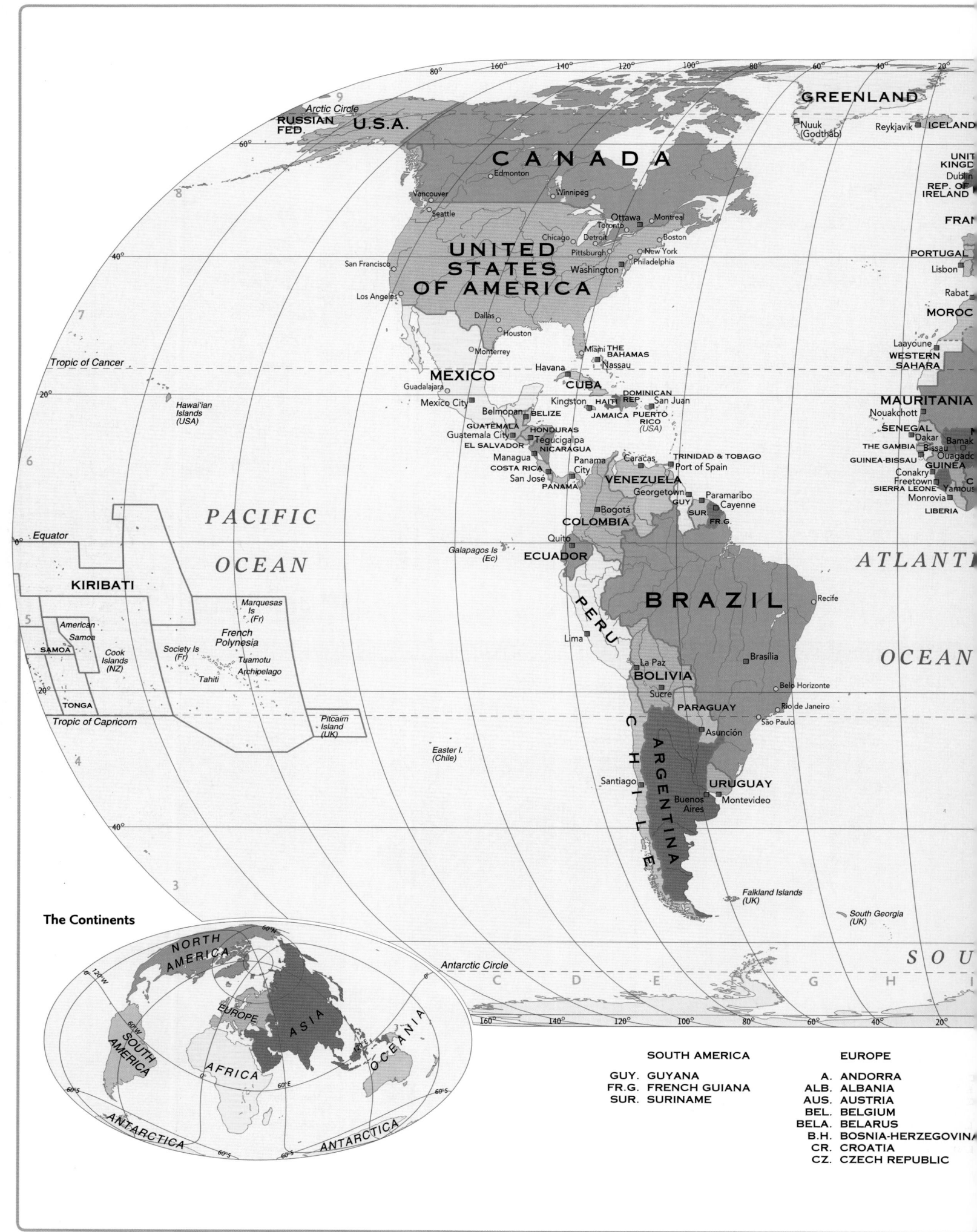

Arctic Circle
RUSSIAN FED.
U.S.A.
GREENLAND
60°
CANADA
Nuuk (Godthåb)
Reykjavik ICELAND
Edmonton
UNIT KINGD
Vancouver
Winnipeg
Dublin
REP. OF
Seattle
Ottawa Montreal
IRELAND
Toronto
FRAN
Chicago Detroit
Boston
40°
UNITED
Pittsburgh
New York
PORTUGAL
San Francisco
STATES
Washington
Philadelphia
Lisbon
OF AMERICA
Rabat
Los Angeles
MOROC
Dallas
Houston
Tropic of Cancer
Laayoune
Miami THE
20°
WESTERN
Monterrey
BAHAMAS
SAHARA
Havana
Nassau
MEXICO
CUBA
MAURITANIA
Guadalajara
Nouakchott
Kingston DOMINICAN San Juan
SENEGAL
Mexico City
Belmopan BELIZE
REP.
PUERTO
Dakar Bamak
Hawai'ian
HAITI
Bissau
Islands
GUATEMALA
JAMAICA
RICO
THE GAMBIA
(USA)
Guatemala City HONDURAS
(USA)
GUINEA-BISSAU GUINEA
EL SALVADOR Tegucigalpa
Conakry
Yamous
Managua NICARAGUA
TRINIDAD & TOBAGO
Freetown
COSTA RICA
Caracas Port of Spain
SIERRA LEONE Monrovia
San José
Panama
PACIFIC
PANAMA
City
Georgetown Paramaribo
LIBERIA
VENEZUELA
GUY. Cayenne
Bogotá
SUR.
OCEAN
FR. G.
COLOMBIA
Quito
ATLANTI
KIRIBATI
Galapagos Is
ECUADOR
Equator
(Ec)
Marquesas
Is
(Fr)
BRAZIL
Recife
American
French
PERU
Samoa
Polynesia
OCEAN
Lima
SAMOA
Society Is
Tuamotu
(Fr)
Cook
Archipelago
La Paz
Brasília
Islands
Tahiti
(NZ)
BOLIVIA
Belo Horizonte
TONGA
Sucre
Tropic of Capricorn
PARAGUAY
Rio de Janeiro
São Paulo
Easter I.
Asunción
(Chile)
Pitcairn
Island
(UK)
40°
Santiago
C
URUGUAY
H
ARGENTINA
Buenos
I
Montevideo
Aires
L
E
Falkland Islands
(UK)
South Georgia
(UK)
Antarctic Circle
S O U
C   D   E   G   H   I

160°   140°   120°   100°   80°   60°   40°   20°

The Continents

NORTH
AMERICA
EUROPE
ASIA
SOUTH
AMERICA
AFRICA
OCEANIA
ANTARCTICA
ANTARCTICA

SOUTH AMERICA	EUROPE
GUY. GUYANA	A. ANDORRA
FR.G. FRENCH GUIANA	ALB. ALBANIA
SUR. SURINAME	AUS. AUSTRIA
	BEL. BELGIUM
	BELA. BELARUS
	B.H. BOSNIA-HERZEGOVINA
	CR. CROATIA
	CZ. CZECH REPUBLIC

Scale 1 : 77 500 000

0   800   1600   2400   3200 km

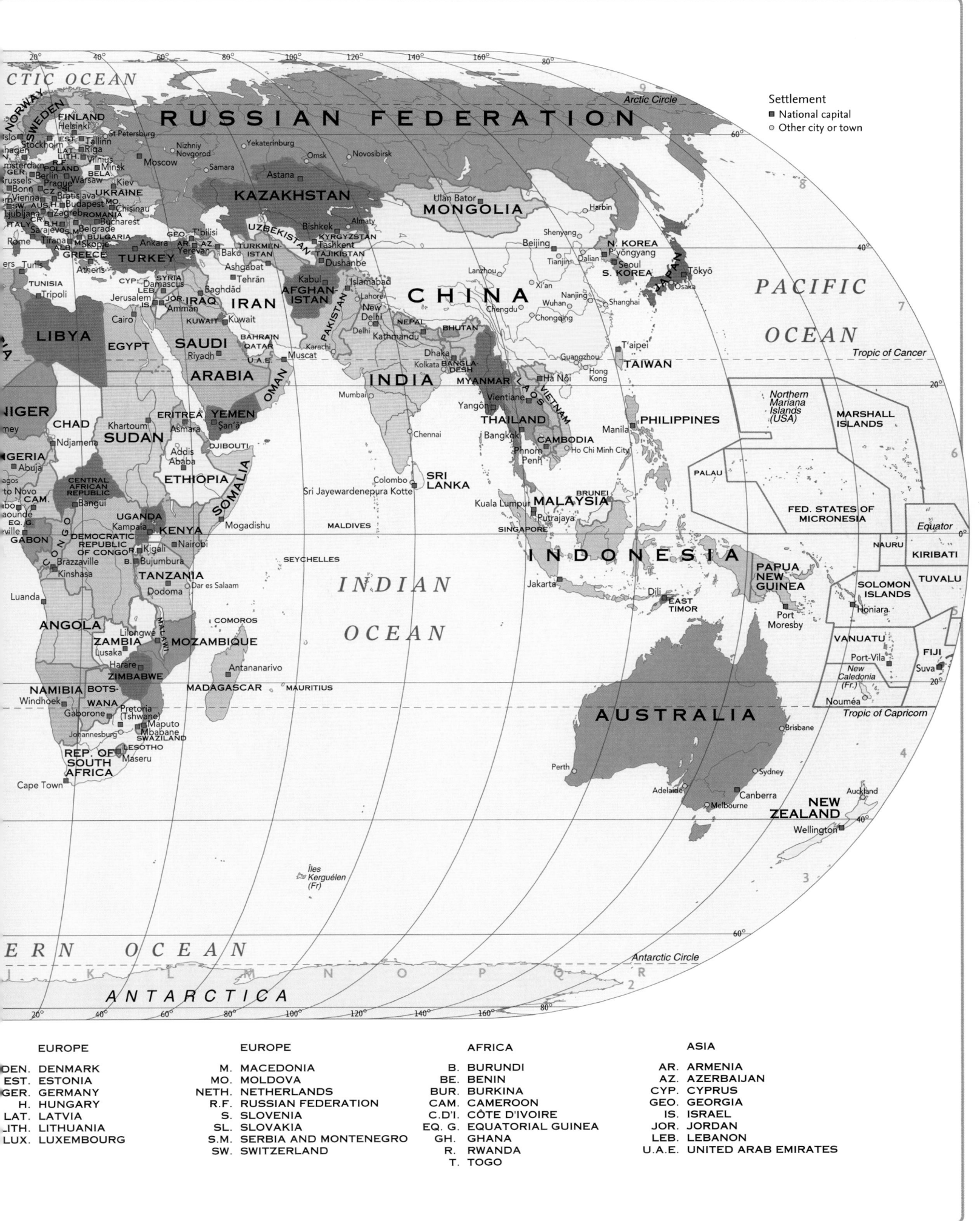

EUROPE		EUROPE		AFRICA		ASIA	
DEN.	DENMARK	M.	MACEDONIA	B.	BURUNDI	AR.	ARMENIA
EST.	ESTONIA	MO.	MOLDOVA	BE.	BENIN	AZ.	AZERBAIJAN
GER.	GERMANY	NETH.	NETHERLANDS	BUR.	BURKINA	CYP.	CYPRUS
H.	HUNGARY	R.F.	RUSSIAN FEDERATION	CAM.	CAMEROON	GEO.	GEORGIA
LAT.	LATVIA	S.	SLOVENIA	C.D'I.	CÔTE D'IVOIRE	IS.	ISRAEL
LITH.	LITHUANIA	SL.	SLOVAKIA	EQ. G.	EQUATORIAL GUINEA	JOR.	JORDAN
LUX.	LUXEMBOURG	S.M.	SERBIA AND MONTENEGRO	GH.	GHANA	LEB.	LEBANON
		SW.	SWITZERLAND	R.	RWANDA	U.A.E.	UNITED ARAB EMIRATES
				T.	TOGO		

Eckert IV projection

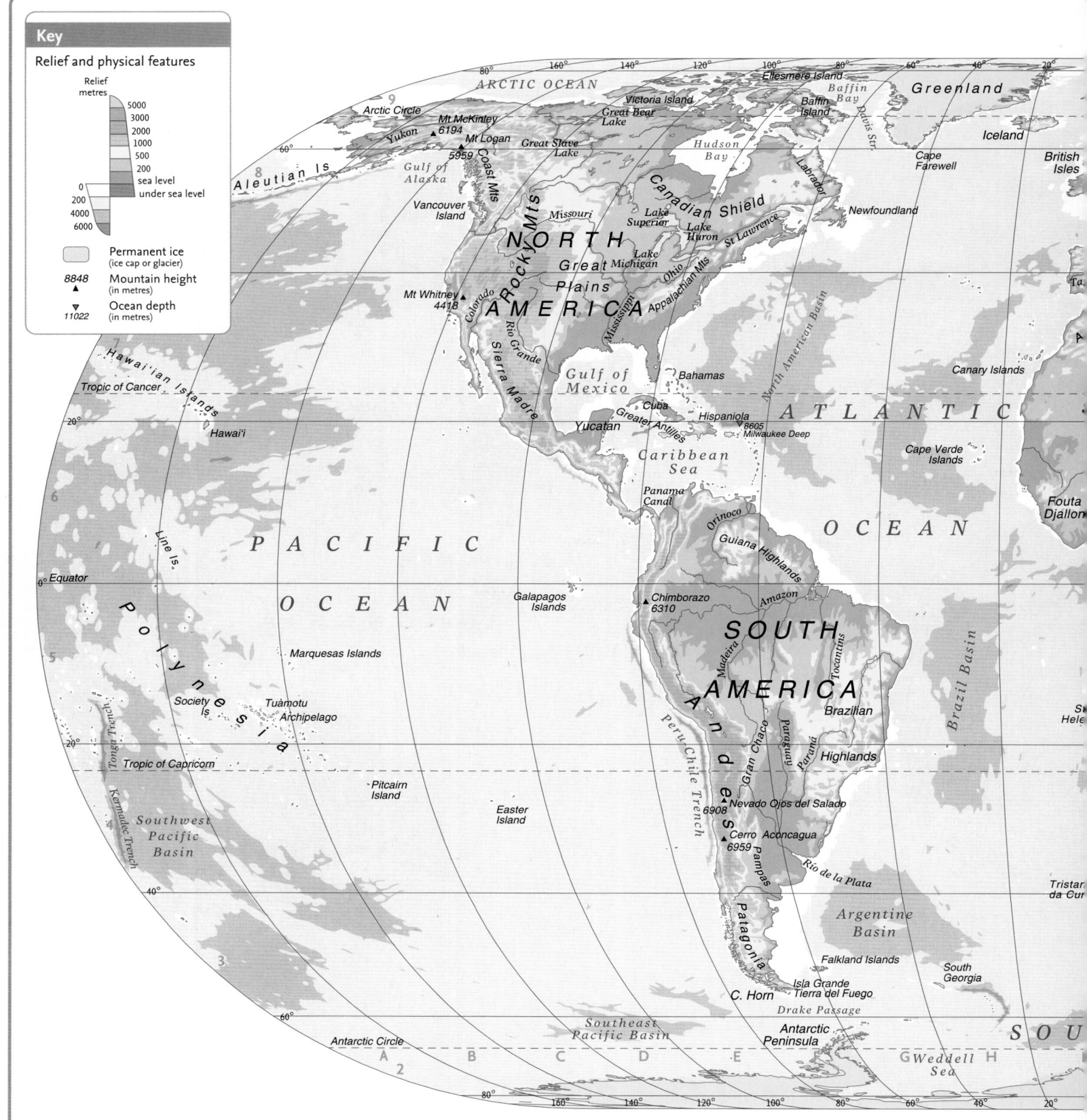

Key

Relief and physical features

Relief
metres

5000
3000
2000
1000
500
200
0   sea level
     under sea level
200
4000
6000

Permanent ice
(ice cap or glacier)

8848 ▲ Mountain height
(in metres)

11022 ▽ Ocean depth
(in metres)

Mountain heights	metres
Mt Everest (Nepal/China)	8848
K2 (Jammu & Kashmir/China)	8611
Kangchenjunga (Nepal/India)	8586
Dhaulagiri (Nepal)	8167
Annapurna (Nepal)	8091
Cerro Aconcagua (Argentina)	6959
Nevado Ojos del Salado (Arg./Chile)	6908
Chimborazo (Ecuador)	6310
Mt McKinley (USA)	6194
Mt Logan (Canada)	5959

Island areas	sq km
Greenland	2 175 600
New Guinea	808 510
Borneo	745 561
Madagascar	587 040
Baffin Island	507 451
Sumatra	473 606
Honshū	227 414
Great Britain	218 476
Victoria Island	217 291
Ellesmere Island	196 236

Continents	sq km
Asia	45 036 492
Africa	30 343 578
North America	24 680 331
South America	17 815 420
Antarctica	12 093 000
Europe	9 908 599
Oceania	8 923 000

Scale 1 : 80 000 000

0   800   1600   2400   3200 km

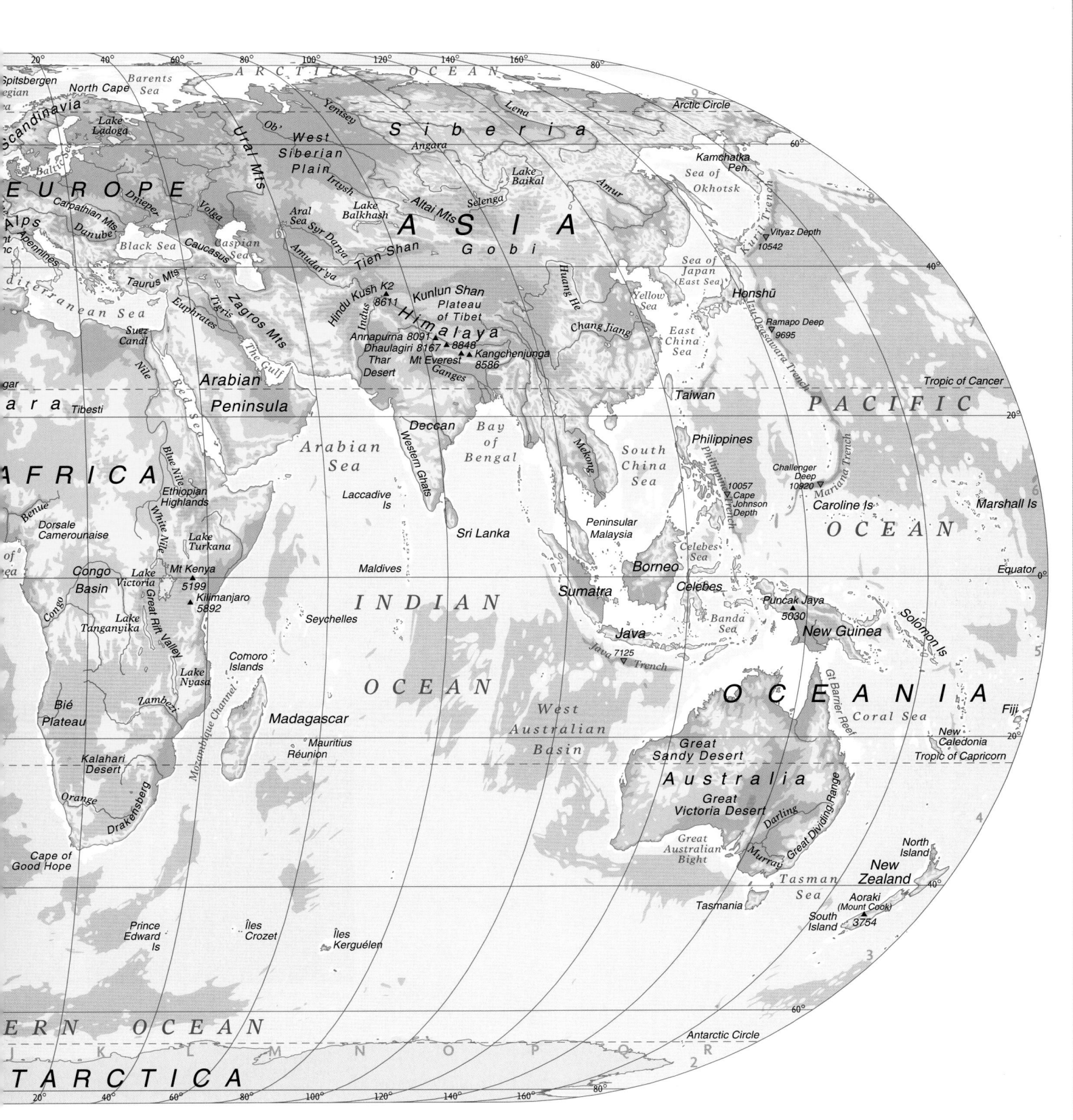

Oceans	sq km
Pacific Ocean	166 241 000
Atlantic Ocean	86 557 000
Indian Ocean	73 427 000
Arctic Ocean	9 485 000

Lake areas	sq km
Caspian Sea	371 000
Lake Superior	82 100
Lake Victoria	68 800
Lake Huron	59 600
Lake Michigan	57 800
Lake Tanganyika	32 900
Great Bear Lake	31 328
Lake Baikal	30 500
Lake Nyasa	30 044

River lengths	km
Nile (Africa)	6695
Amazon (S. America)	6516
Chang Jiang (Asia)	6380
Mississippi-Missouri (N. America)	5969
Ob'-Irtysh (Asia)	5568
Yenisey-Angara-Selenga (Asia)	5500
Huang He (Asia)	5464
Congo (Africa)	4667
Río de la Plata-Paraná (S. America)	4500
Mekong (Asia)	4425

Eckert IV projection

1 Climatic Regions and Ocean Currents

Climatic regions

- Ice cap
- Tundra climate, warmest month below 10°C
- Sub-arctic, rainy climate with severe cold winters and less than 4 months over 10°C
- Continental climate, rainy with warmest month below 22°C
- Continental climate, rainy with warmest month above 22°C
- Temperate, rainy climate with mild winter, coolest month above 0°C
- Wet subtropical, coolest month above 0°C, warmest month above 22°C
- Mediterranean, rainy with mild wet winter, dry summer
- Semi-arid, dry climate
- Desert climate
- Rainy tropical climate with no winter, coolest month above 18°C
- Rainy tropical climate, constantly wet throughout the year

Ocean currents
- → Cold
- → Warm
- → Seasonal

World Meteorological Organization
www.wmo.ch
Met Office
www.metoffice.com/weather
United Nations Environment Programme
www.unep.org
World Conservation Monitoring Centre
www.unep-wcmc.org
World Resources Institute Earthtrends
earthtrends.wri.org

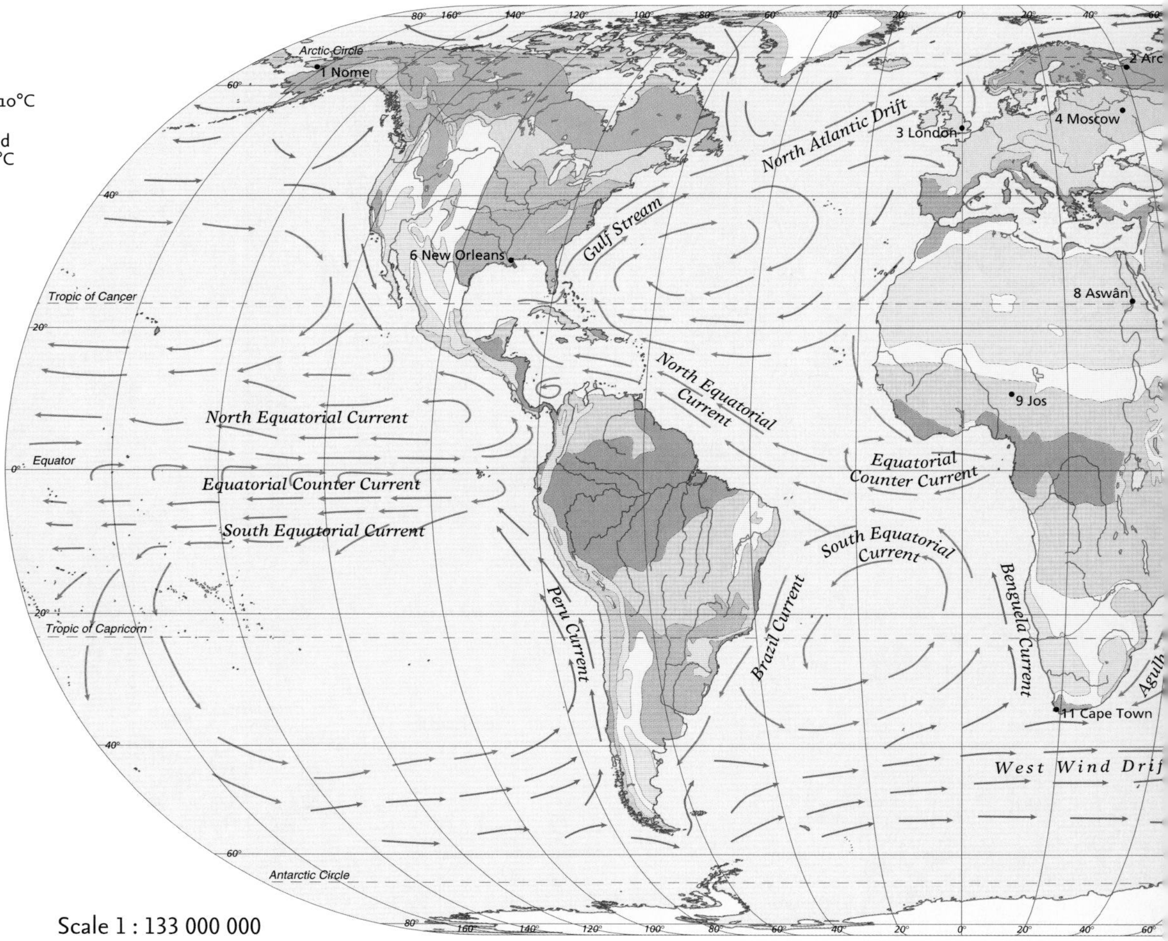

Scale 1 : 133 000 000

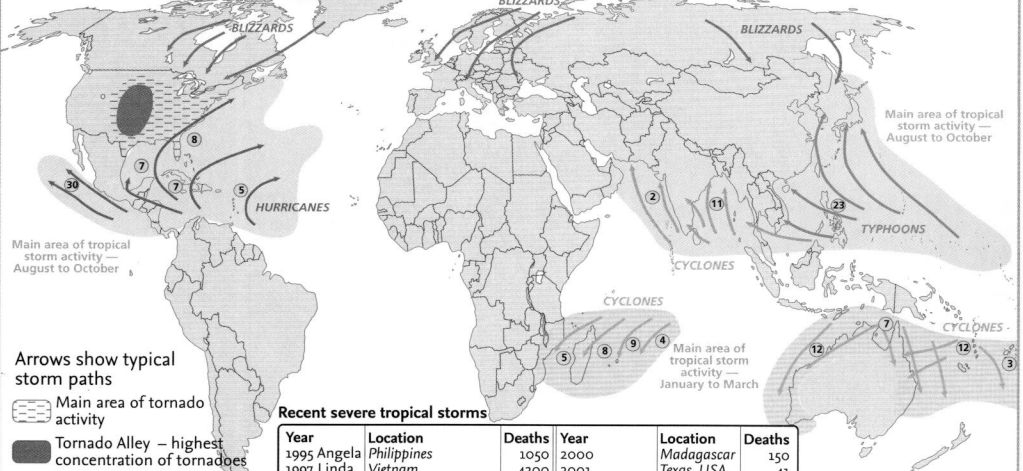

3 Tropical Storms

Arrows show typical storm paths
- Main area of tornado activity
- Tornado Alley – highest concentration of tornadoes
- 8 Likely number of severe tropical storms in 10 years

Recent severe tropical storms

Year	Location	Deaths	Year	Location	Deaths
1995 Angela	Philippines	1050	2000	Madagascar	150
1997 Linda	Vietnam	4300	2001	Texas, USA	41
1998 Mitch	Honduras, Nicaragua	12 000	2004 Rananim	China	131
1999	Orissa, India	2000	2004 Charley	Florida, USA	16

Scale 1 : 215 000 000

Hurricane Isabel, September 2003

World Weather Extremes

Hottest place - Annual mean	34.4°C Dalol, Ethiopia
Driest place - Annual mean	0.1 mm Atacama Desert, Chile
Most sunshine - Annual mean	90% Yuma, Arizona, USA (4000 hours)
Least sunshine	Nil for 182 days each year, South Pole
Coldest place - Annual mean	-56.6°C Plateau Station, Antarctica
Wettest place - Annual mean	11 873 mm Meghalaya, India
Most rainy days	Up to 350 per year Mount Waialeale, Hawaii, USA
Greatest snowfall	31 102 mm Mount Rainier, Washington, USA (19th February 1971 - 18th February 1972)
Windiest place	322 km per hour in gales, Commonwealth Bay, Antarctica

Tracks of major hurricanes 1980-2004
- → Allen 1980
- → Gilbert 1988
- → Andrew 1992
- → Gordon 1994
- → Fran 1996
- → Mitch 1998
- → Floyd 1999
- → Isabel 2003
- → Charley 2004

Scale 1: 60 000 000

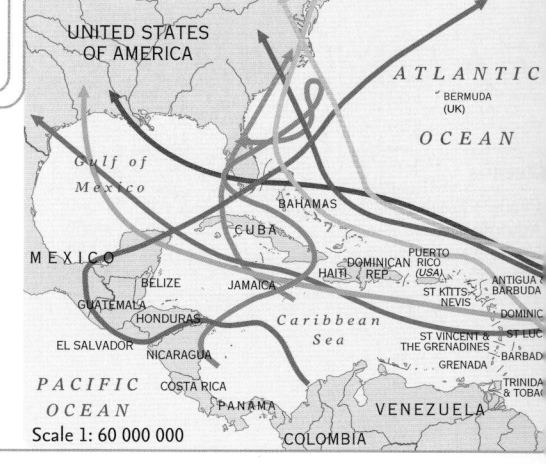

2 Climatic Graphs

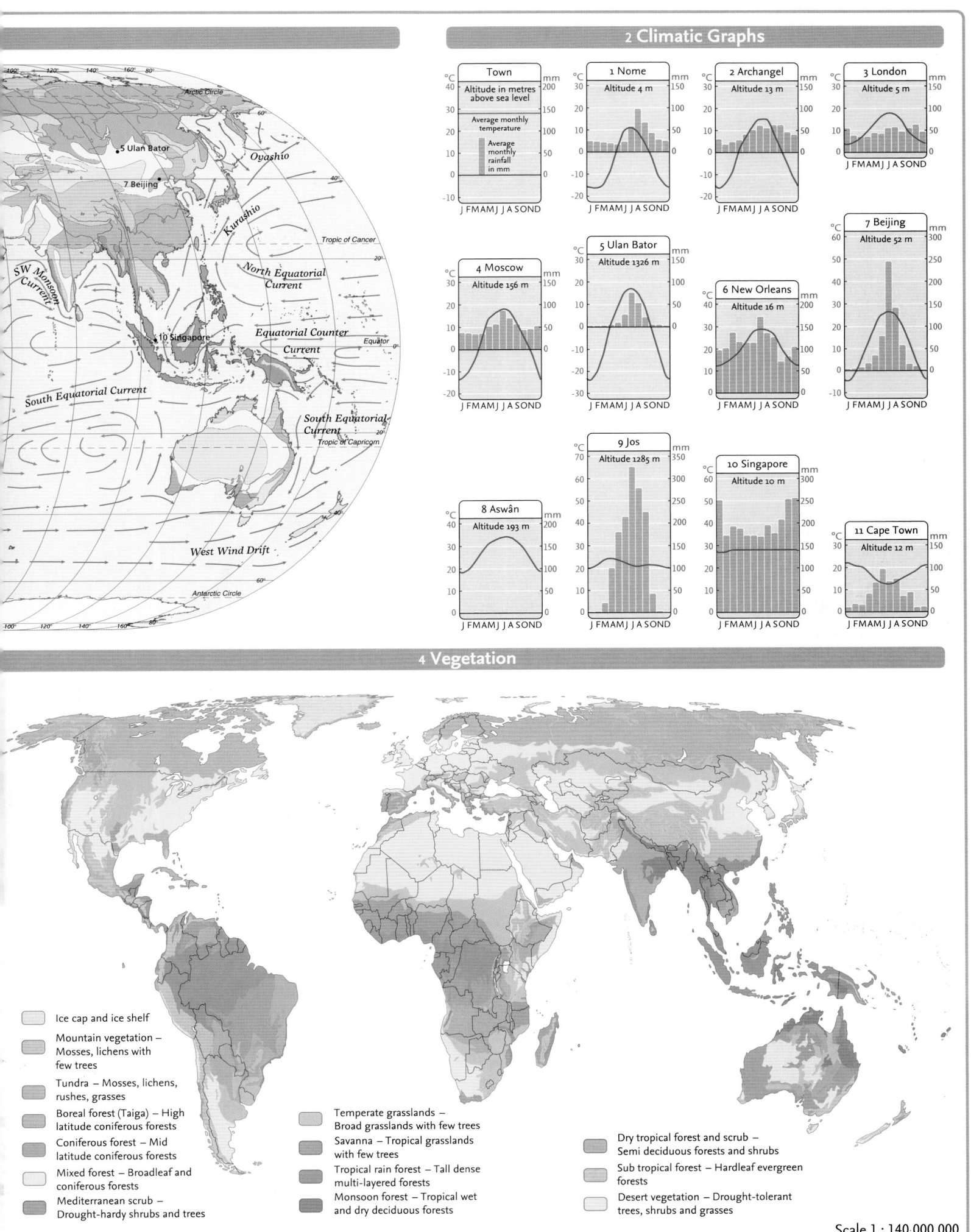

Town
Altitude in metres above sea level
Average monthly temperature
Average monthly rainfall in mm

1 Nome — Altitude 4 m

2 Archangel — Altitude 13 m

3 London — Altitude 5 m

4 Moscow — Altitude 156 m

5 Ulan Bator — Altitude 1326 m

6 New Orleans — Altitude 16 m

7 Beijing — Altitude 52 m

8 Aswân — Altitude 193 m

9 Jos — Altitude 1285 m

10 Singapore — Altitude 10 m

11 Cape Town — Altitude 12 m

Map labels: Arctic Circle, Ovashio, 5 Ulan Bator, 7 Beijing, Kurashio, Tropic of Cancer, North Equatorial Current, SW Monsoon Current, Equatorial Counter Current, 10 Singapore, Equator, South Equatorial Current, South Equatorial Current, Tropic of Capricorn, West Wind Drift, Antarctic Circle

4 Vegetation

Ice cap and ice shelf

Mountain vegetation – Mosses, lichens with few trees

Tundra – Mosses, lichens, rushes, grasses

Boreal forest (Taiga) – High latitude coniferous forests

Coniferous forest – Mid latitude coniferous forests

Mixed forest – Broadleaf and coniferous forests

Mediterranean scrub – Drought-hardy shrubs and trees

Temperate grasslands – Broad grasslands with few trees

Savanna – Tropical grasslands with few trees

Tropical rain forest – Tall dense multi-layered forests

Monsoon forest – Tropical wet and dry deciduous forests

Dry tropical forest and scrub – Semi deciduous forests and shrubs

Sub tropical forest – Hardleaf evergreen forests

Desert vegetation – Drought-tolerant trees, shrubs and grasses

Scale 1 : 140 000 000

1 Continental Drift

200 million
years ago

150 million
years ago

100 million
years ago

50 million
years ago

Major earthquakes

- ● 'Deadliest' earthquakes
- ● Magnitude over 7.5
- ○ Magnitude 5.5 – 7.5

Volcanic eruptions

- ▲ Major volcano
- ▲ Other volcano

EURASIAN PLATE

Gansu
Hebei
Liaoning
Ningxia
Qinghai
Unzen-dake
Sichuan
Tōkyō
Ō-yama
Yunnan/
Sichuan

PHILIPPINE
PLATE

Mt Pinatubo
Mayon

Kilauea

PACIFIC

PLATE

Rabaul

Gunung
Galunggung
Bali

INDO-AUSTRALIAN

PLATE

3 Plate Boundaries

――― Constructive boundary
▲▲▲ Destructive boundary
――― Conservative boundary

EURASIAN PLATE

NORTH
AMERICAN
PLATE

ARABIAN
PLATE

PHILIPPINE
PLATE

PACIFIC

PLATE

CARIBBEAN
PLATE

COCOS
PLATE

AFRICAN

PLATE

SOUTH
AMERICAN

INDO-AUSTRALIAN

SOUTH
AMERICAN

PLATE

PLATE

PLATE

NAZCA

PLATE

SCOTIA
PLATE

ANTARCTIC PLATE

SCOTIA
PLATE

→ Direction of
movement

Major earthquakes 1980 – 1987

Year	Location	*Force	Deaths
1980	Ech Chélif, Algeria	7.7	3500
1980	Southern Italy	6.9	3000
1981	Kerman, Iran	7.3	2500
1982	El Salvador	7.4	16
1982	Dhamar, Yemen	6.0	3000
1983	Eastern Turkey	7.1	1500
1985	Santiago, Chile	7.8	177
1985	Xinjiang Uygur, China	7.4	63
1985	Michoacán, Mexico	8.1	20 000
1986	El Salvador	7.5	1000
1987	Ecuador	7.0	2000

(Continental Drift globes labelled: PANGAEA, TETHYS, LAURASIA, GONDWANALAND, NORTH AMERICA, SOUTH AMERICA, EURASIA, AFRICA, ANTARCTICA, AUSTRALIA)

2 Earthquakes and Volcanoes

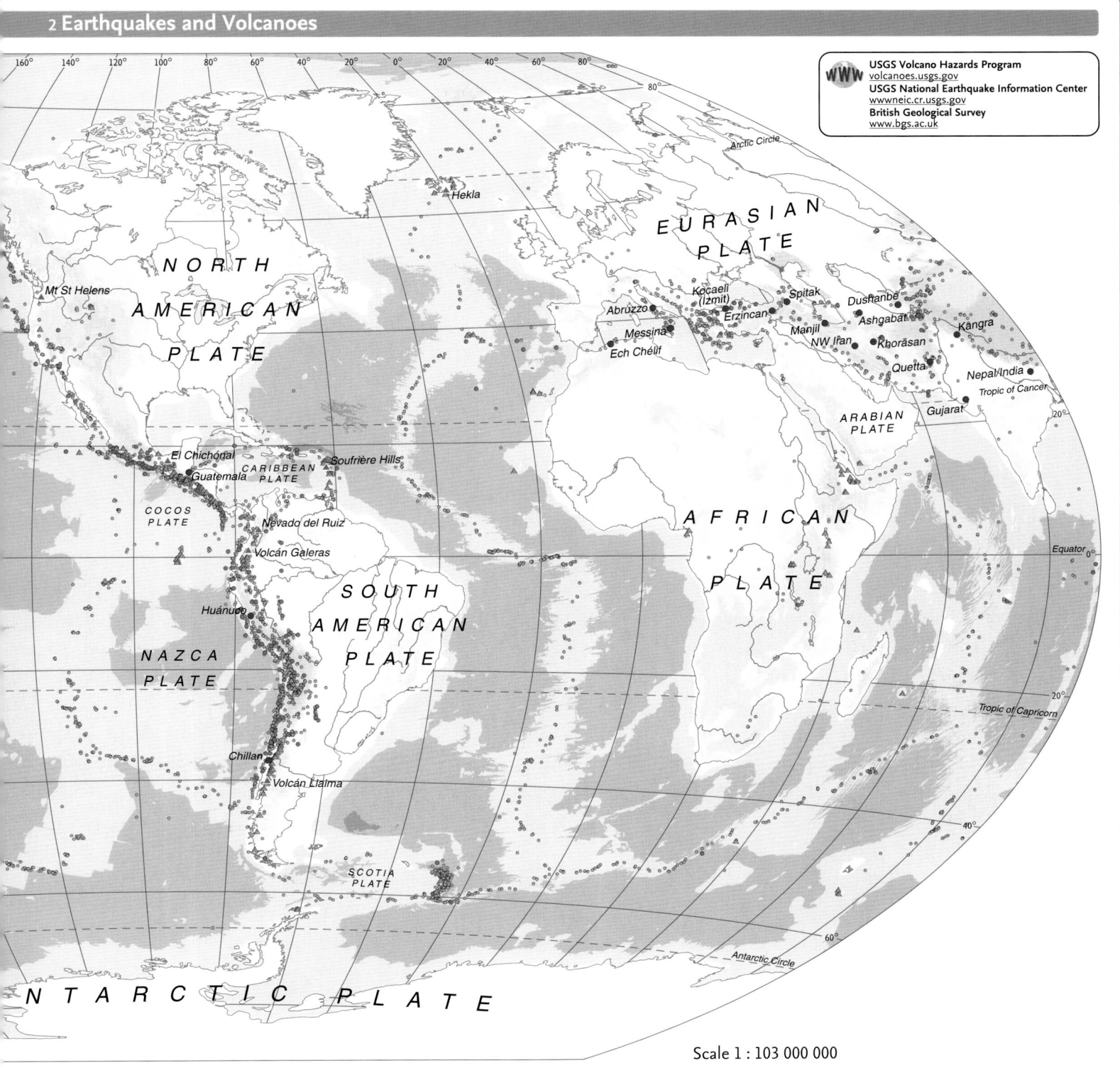

WWW **USGS Volcano Hazards Program**
volcanoes.usgs.gov
USGS National Earthquake Information Center
wwwneic.cr.usgs.gov
British Geological Survey
www.bgs.ac.uk

Scale 1 : 103 000 000

Major earthquakes 1988 – 1993

Year	Location	*Force	Deaths
1988	Yunnan, China	7.6	1000
1988	Spitak, Armenia	6.9	25 000
1988	Nepal / India	6.9	1000
1989	Loma Prieta, USA	7.1	63
1990	Manjil, Iran	7.7	50 000
1990	Luzon, Philippines	7.7	1600
1991	Georgia	7.1	114
1991	Uttar Pradesh, India	6.1	1600
1992	Flores, Indonesia	7.5	2500
1992	Erzincan, Turkey	6.8	500
1992	Cairo, Egypt	5.9	550
1993	Northern Japan	7.8	185
1993	Maharashtra, India	6.4	9748

Major earthquakes 1994 – 2003

Year	Location	*Force	Deaths
1994	Kuril Islands, Japan	8.3	10
1995	Kōbe, Japan	7.2	5502
1995	Sakhalin, Russian Fed.	7.6	2500
1996	Yunnan, China	7.0	251
1997	Quae'n, Iran	7.1	2400
1998	Papua New Guinea		2183
1999	İzmit, Turkey	7.4	17 118
1999	Chi-Chi, Taiwan		2400
2001	Gujarat, India	6.9	20 085
2002	Hindu Kush, Afghanistan	6.0	1000
2003	Boumerdes, Algeria	5.8	2266
2003	Bam, Iran	6.6	26 271

* Earthquake force measured on the Richter scale

Major volcanic eruptions since 1980

Year	Location
1980	Mount St Helens, USA
1982	El Chichónal, Mexico
1982	Gunung Galunggung, Indonesia
1983	Kilauea, Hawaii
1983	Ō-yama, Japan
1985	Nevado del Ruiz, Colombia
1986	Lake Nyos, Cameroon
1991	Hekla, Iceland
1991	Mount Pinatubo, Philippines
1991	Unzen-dake, Japan
1993	Mayon, Philippines
1993	Galeras, Colombia
1994	Volcán Llaima, Chile
1994	Rabaul, PNG
1997	Soufrière Hills, Montserrat

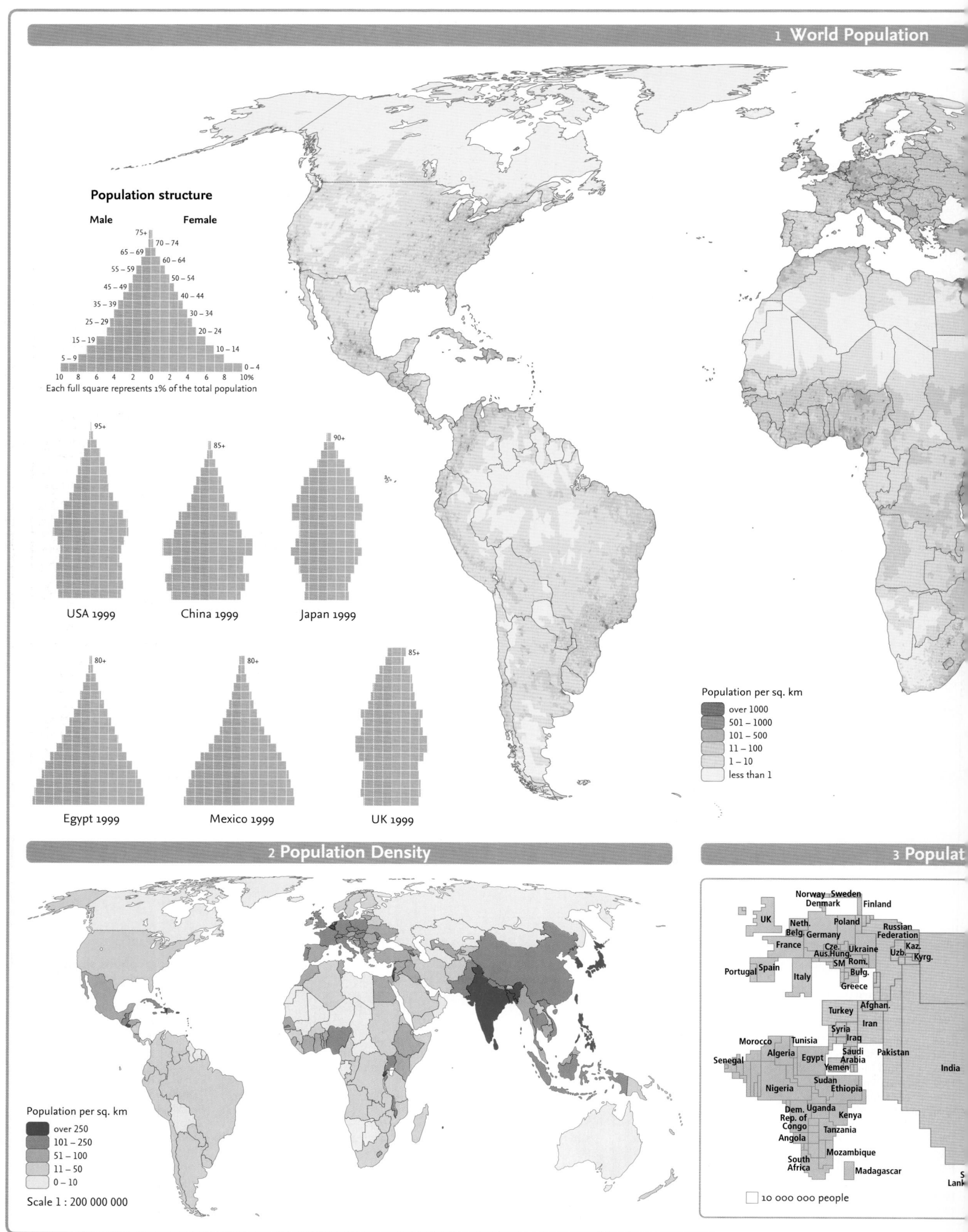

1 World Population

Population structure

Male   Female

75+
70 – 74
65 – 69
60 – 64
55 – 59
50 – 54
45 – 49
40 – 44
35 – 39
30 – 34
25 – 29
20 – 24
15 – 19
10 – 14
5 – 9
0 – 4

10 8 6 4 2 0 2 4 6 8 10%

Each full square represents 1% of the total population

95+
USA 1999

85+
China 1999

90+
Japan 1999

80+
Egypt 1999

80+
Mexico 1999

85+
UK 1999

Population per sq. km

	over 1000
	501 – 1000
	101 – 500
	11 – 100
	1 – 10
	less than 1

2 Population Density

Population per sq. km

	over 250
	101 – 250
	51 – 100
	11 – 50
	0 – 10

Scale 1 : 200 000 000

3 Populat

Norway Sweden
Denmark Finland
UK
Neth. Poland
Belg. Russian
Germany Federation
France Cze. Ukraine
Aus.Hung. Uzb. Kaz.
Portugal Spain SM Rom. Kyrg.
Italy Bulg.
Greece
Turkey Afghan.
Syria Iran
Morocco Tunisia Iraq
Algeria Egypt Saudi Pakistan
Senegal Arabia
Yemen India
Nigeria Sudan
Ethiopia
Dem. Uganda
Rep. of Kenya
Congo Tanzania
Angola
Mozambique
South Madagascar
Africa
S
Lank

☐ 10 000 000 people

Largest countries by population, 2003

Country and continent	Population
China Asia	1 289 161 000
India Asia	1 065 462 000
United States of America N America	294 043 000
Indonesia Asia	219 883 000
Brazil S America	178 470 000
Pakistan Asia	153 578 000
Bangladesh Asia	146 736 000
Russian Federation Europe/Asia	143 246 000
Japan Asia	127 654 000
Nigeria Africa	124 009 000
Mexico N America	103 457 000
Germany Europe	82 476 000
Vietnam Asia	81 377 000
Philippines Asia	79 999 000
Egypt Africa	71 931 000
Turkey Europe/Asia	71 325 000
Ethiopia Africa	70 678 000
Iran Asia	68 920 000
Thailand Asia	62 833 000
France Europe	60 144 000

Largest urban agglomerations, 2005

Urban agglomeration and country	Population (projected)
Tōkyō Japan	35 327 000
Mexico City Mexico	19 013 000
New York United States of America	18 498 000
Mumbai India	18 336 000
São Paulo Brazil	18 333 000
Delhi India	15 334 000
Kolkata India	14 299 000
Buenos Aires Argentina	13 349 000
Jakarta Indonesia	13 194 000
Shanghai China	12 665 000
Dhaka Bangladesh	12 560 000
Los Angeles United States of America	12 146 000
Karachi Pakistan	11 819 000
Rio de Janeiro Brazil	11 469 000
Ōsaka-Kōbe Japan	11 286 000
Cairo Egypt	11 146 000
Lagos Nigeria	11 135 000
Beijing China	10 849 000
Manila Philippines	10 677 000
Moscow Russian Federation	10 672 000

wWw United Nations Statistics Division
unstats.un.org
UN Population Information Network
www.un.org/popin
Population Reference Bureau
www.popnet.org
World Bank
www.worldbank.org

Scale 1 : 90 000 000

parisons

4 Urban Agglomerations

Scale 1 : 200 000 000

Million Cities, 2005
■ over 15 000 000
□ 10 000 000 – 15 000 000 people
○ 5 000 000 – 10 000 000 people
· 1 000 000 – 5 000 000 people

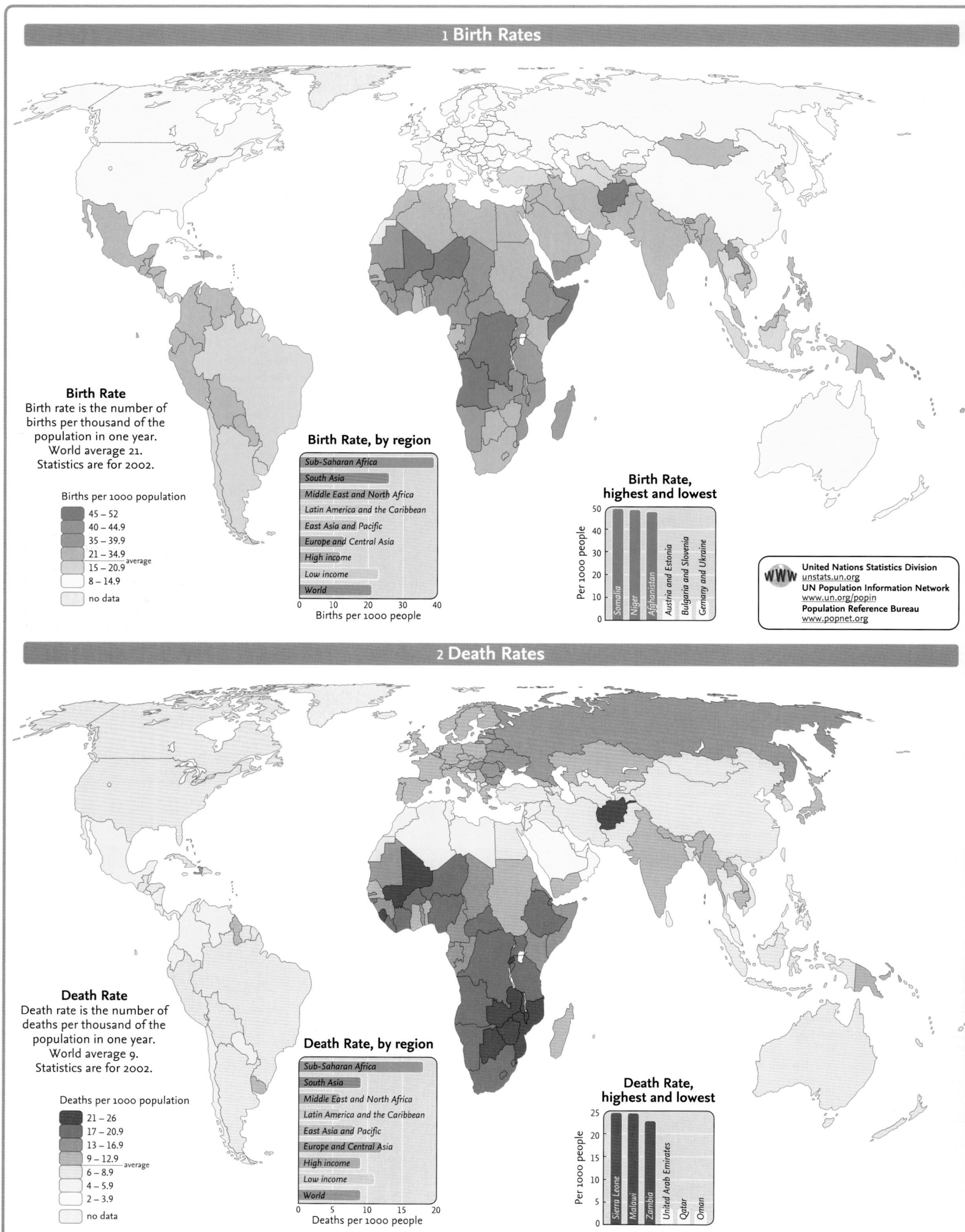

1 Birth Rates

Birth Rate

Birth rate is the number of births per thousand of the population in one year. World average 21. Statistics are for 2002.

Births per 1000 population

- 45 – 52
- 40 – 44.9
- 35 – 39.9
- 21 – 34.9 average
- 15 – 20.9
- 8 – 14.9
- no data

Birth Rate, by region

- Sub-Saharan Africa
- South Asia
- Middle East and North Africa
- Latin America and the Caribbean
- East Asia and Pacific
- Europe and Central Asia
- High income
- Low income
- World

0 10 20 30 40
Births per 1000 people

Birth Rate, highest and lowest

Per 1000 people

Somalia, Niger, Afghanistan, Austria and Estonia, Bulgaria and Slovenia, Germany and Ukraine

www United Nations Statistics Division
unstats.un.org
UN Population Information Network
www.un.org/popin
Population Reference Bureau
www.popnet.org

2 Death Rates

Death Rate

Death rate is the number of deaths per thousand of the population in one year. World average 9. Statistics are for 2002.

Deaths per 1000 population

- 21 – 26
- 17 – 20.9
- 13 – 16.9
- 9 – 12.9 average
- 6 – 8.9
- 4 – 5.9
- 2 – 3.9
- no data

Death Rate, by region

- Sub-Saharan Africa
- South Asia
- Middle East and North Africa
- Latin America and the Caribbean
- East Asia and Pacific
- Europe and Central Asia
- High income
- Low income
- World

0 5 10 15 20
Deaths per 1000 people

Death Rate, highest and lowest

Per 1000 people

Sierra Leone, Malawi, Zambia, United Arab Emirates, Qatar, Oman

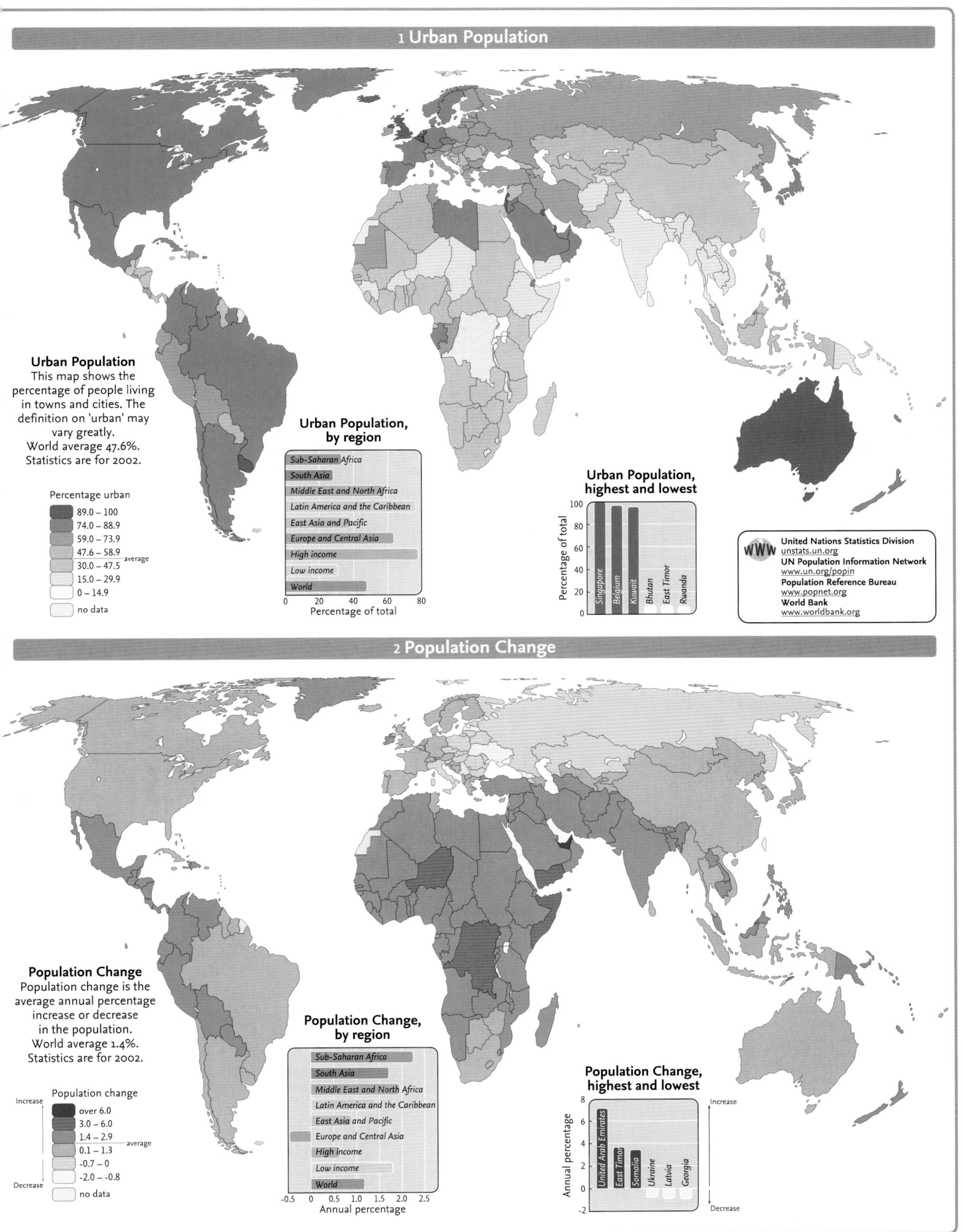

1 Urban Population

Urban Population
This map shows the percentage of people living in towns and cities. The definition on 'urban' may vary greatly. World average 47.6%. Statistics are for 2002.

Percentage urban
- 89.0 – 100
- 74.0 – 88.9
- 59.0 – 73.9
- 47.6 – 58.9 average
- 30.0 – 47.5
- 15.0 – 29.9
- 0 – 14.9
- no data

Urban Population, by region
- Sub-Saharan Africa
- South Asia
- Middle East and North Africa
- Latin America and the Caribbean
- East Asia and Pacific
- Europe and Central Asia
- High income
- Low income
- World

0   20   40   60   80
Percentage of total

Urban Population, highest and lowest
Percentage of total: Singapore, Belgium, Kuwait, Bhutan, East Timor, Rwanda

United Nations Statistics Division
unstats.un.org
UN Population Information Network
www.un.org/popin
Population Reference Bureau
www.popnet.org
World Bank
www.worldbank.org

2 Population Change

Population Change
Population change is the average annual percentage increase or decrease in the population. World average 1.4%. Statistics are for 2002.

Population change
Increase
- over 6.0
- 3.0 – 6.0
- 1.4 – 2.9 average
- 0.1 – 1.3
- -0.7 – 0
- -2.0 – -0.8
Decrease
- no data

Population Change, by region
- Sub-Saharan Africa
- South Asia
- Middle East and North Africa
- Latin America and the Caribbean
- East Asia and Pacific
- Europe and Central Asia
- High income
- Low income
- World

-0.5   0   0.5   1.0   1.5   2.0   2.5
Annual percentage

Population Change, highest and lowest
Annual percentage: United Arab Emirates, East Timor, Somalia, Ukraine, Latvia, Georgia
Increase / Decrease

Scale 1 : 140 000 000

Eckert IV projection

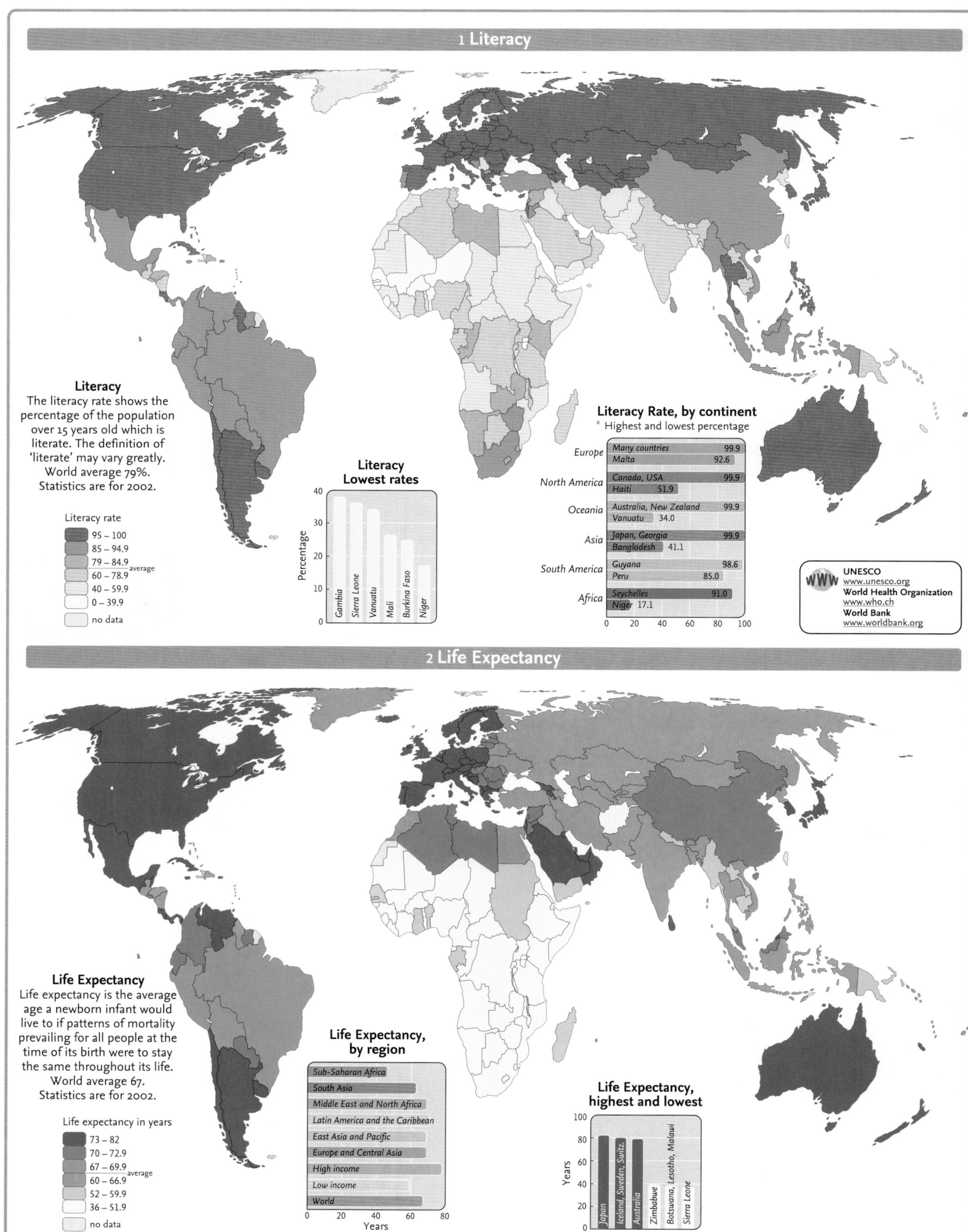

1 Literacy

Literacy
The literacy rate shows the percentage of the population over 15 years old which is literate. The definition of 'literate' may vary greatly. World average 79%. Statistics are for 2002.

Literacy rate
- 95 – 100
- 85 – 94.9
- 79 – 84.9 *average*
- 60 – 78.9
- 40 – 59.9
- 0 – 39.9
- no data

Literacy Lowest rates
Percentage (y-axis 0 to 40)
- Gambia
- Sierra Leone
- Vanuatu
- Mali
- Burkina Faso
- Niger

Literacy Rate, by continent
Highest and lowest percentage

Continent	Country	Percentage
Europe	Many countries	99.9
	Malta	92.6
North America	Canada, USA	99.9
	Haiti	51.9
Oceania	Australia, New Zealand	99.9
	Vanuatu	34.0
Asia	Japan, Georgia	99.9
	Bangladesh	41.1
South America	Guyana	98.6
	Peru	85.0
Africa	Seychelles	91.0
	Niger	17.1

(scale 0 to 100)

WWW UNESCO
www.unesco.org
World Health Organization
www.who.ch
World Bank
www.worldbank.org

2 Life Expectancy

Life Expectancy
Life expectancy is the average age a newborn infant would live to if patterns of mortality prevailing for all people at the time of its birth were to stay the same throughout its life. World average 67. Statistics are for 2002.

Life expectancy in years
- 73 – 82
- 70 – 72.9
- 67 – 69.9 *average*
- 60 – 66.9
- 52 – 59.9
- 36 – 51.9
- no data

Life Expectancy, by region
(Years, 0 to 80)
- Sub-Saharan Africa
- South Asia
- Middle East and North Africa
- Latin America and the Caribbean
- East Asia and Pacific
- Europe and Central Asia
- High income
- Low income
- World

Life Expectancy, highest and lowest
Years (0 to 100)
- Japan
- Iceland, Sweden, Switz.
- Australia
- Zimbabwe
- Botswana, Lesotho, Malawi
- Sierra Leone

1 Gross National Income

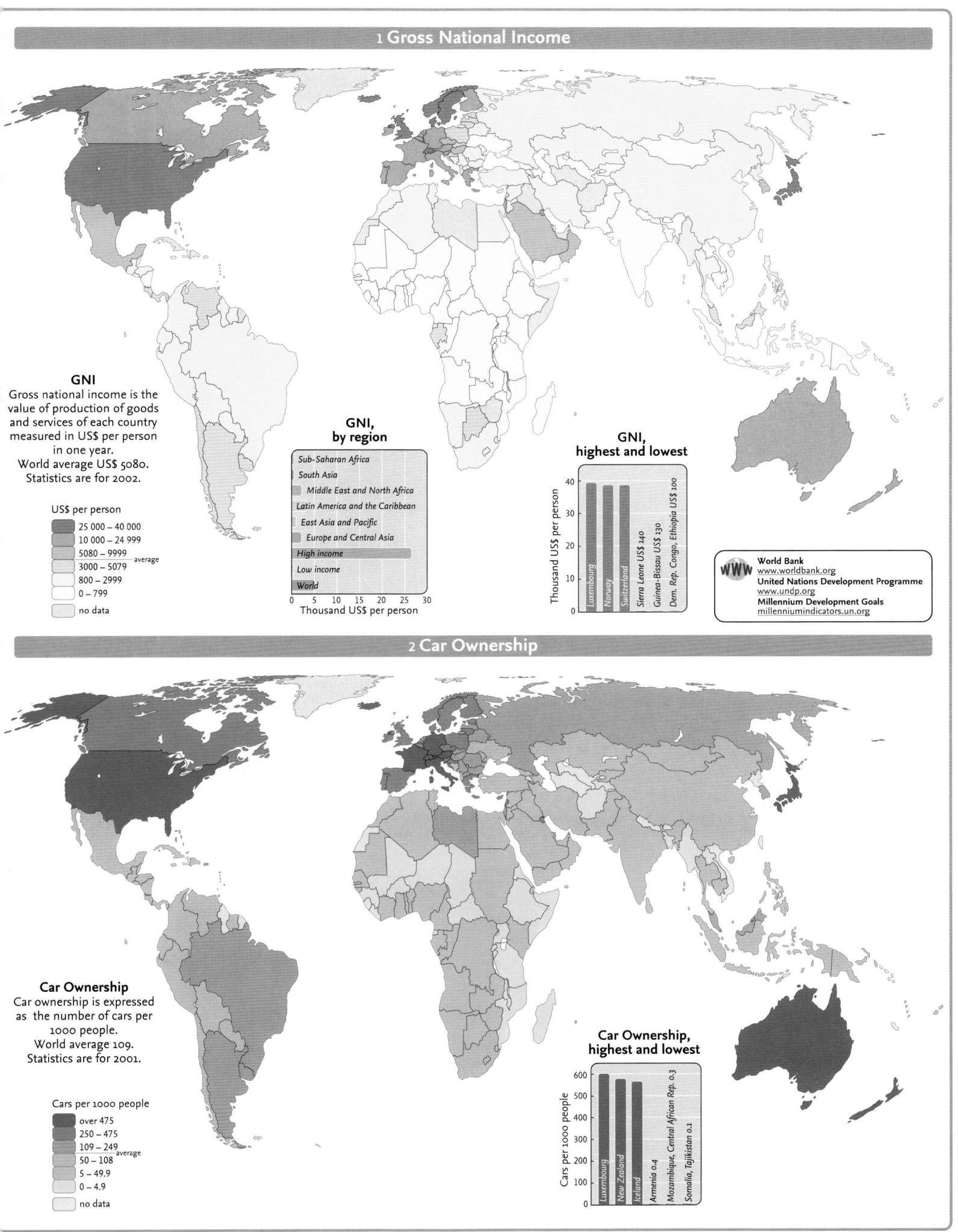

GNI

Gross national income is the value of production of goods and services of each country measured in US$ per person in one year.
World average US$ 5080.
Statistics are for 2002.

US$ per person

- 25 000 – 40 000
- 10 000 – 24 999
- 5080 – 9999 average
- 3000 – 5079
- 800 – 2999
- 0 – 799
- no data

GNI, by region

- Sub-Saharan Africa
- South Asia
- Middle East and North Africa
- Latin America and the Caribbean
- East Asia and Pacific
- Europe and Central Asia
- High income
- Low income
- World

0   5   10   15   20   25   30
Thousand US$ per person

GNI, highest and lowest

Thousand US$ per person

40 – 30 – 20 – 10 – 0

Luxembourg / Norway / Switzerland / Sierra Leone US$ 140 / Guinea-Bissau US$ 130 / Dem. Rep. Congo, Ethiopia US$ 100

WWW World Bank
www.worldbank.org
United Nations Development Programme
www.undp.org
Millennium Development Goals
millenniumindicators.un.org

2 Car Ownership

Car Ownership

Car ownership is expressed as the number of cars per 1000 people.
World average 109.
Statistics are for 2001.

Cars per 1000 people

- over 475
- 250 – 475
- 109 – 249 average
- 50 – 108
- 5 – 49.9
- 0 – 4.9
- no data

Car Ownership, highest and lowest

Cars per 1000 people

600 – 500 – 400 – 300 – 200 – 100 – 0

Luxembourg / New Zealand / Iceland / Armenia 0.4 / Mozambique, Central African Rep. 0.3 / Somalia, Tajikistan 0.1

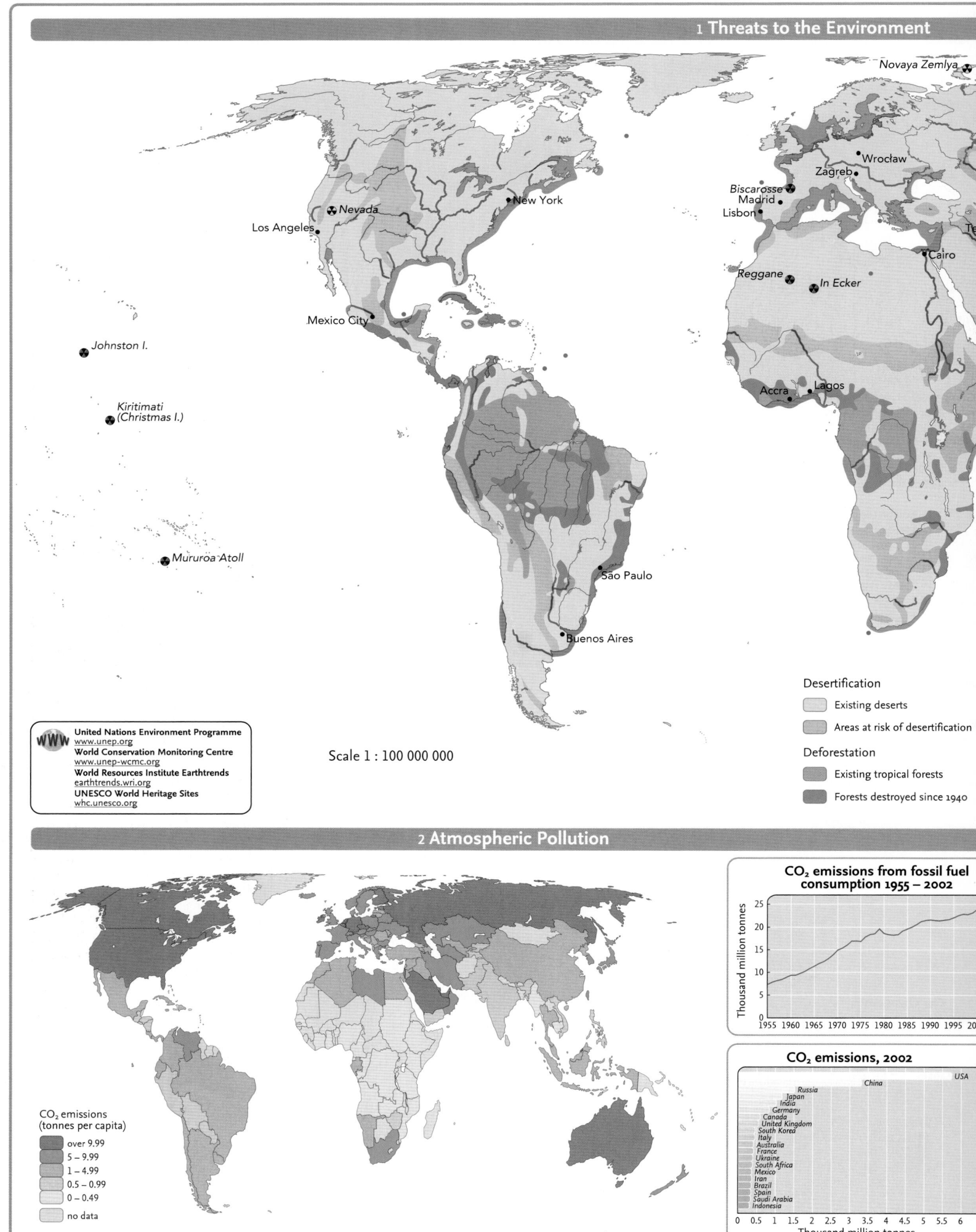

1 Threats to the Environment

Novaya Zemlya

Wrocław

Zagreb

Biscarosse
Madrid

Lisbon

Cairo

Reggane   In Ecker

Accra   Lagos

New York

Nevada

Los Angeles

Mexico City

Johnston I.

Kiritimati
(Christmas I.)

Mururoa Atoll

Sao Paulo

Buenos Aires

Tel

Scale 1 : 100 000 000

WWW
United Nations Environment Programme
www.unep.org
World Conservation Monitoring Centre
www.unep-wcmc.org
World Resources Institute Earthtrends
earthtrends.wri.org
UNESCO World Heritage Sites
whc.unesco.org

Desertification

Existing deserts

Areas at risk of desertification

Deforestation

Existing tropical forests

Forests destroyed since 1940

2 Atmospheric Pollution

CO₂ emissions from fossil fuel consumption 1955 – 2002

Thousand million tonnes

25
20
15
10
5

1955 1960 1965 1970 1975 1980 1985 1990 1995 200

CO₂ emissions, 2002

China   USA

Russia
Japan
India
Germany
Canada
United Kingdom
South Korea
Italy
Australia
France
Ukraine
South Africa
Mexico
Iran
Brazil
Spain
Saudi Arabia
Indonesia

0 0.5 1 1.5 2 2.5 3 3.5 4 4.5 5 5.5 6
Thousand million tonnes

CO₂ emissions
(tonnes per capita)

over 9.99

5 – 9.99

1 – 4.99

0.5 – 0.99

0 – 0.49

no data

Scale 1 : 200 000 000

ter pollution

	Severe coastal pollution	☢	Current nuclear test site
	Persistent coastal pollution	☢	Former nuclear test site
	Significant oil spill	●	Major city with air pollution. Problem due to industry and vehicle exhaust
	River pollution		

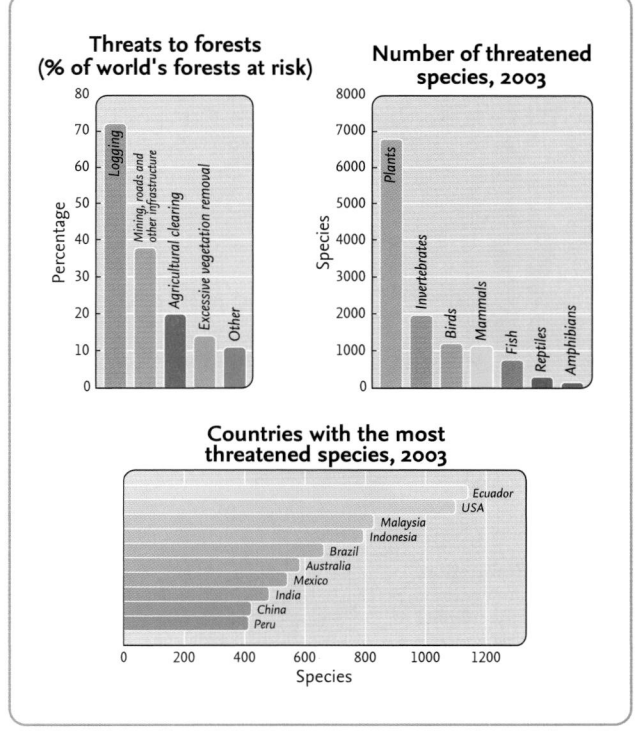

Threats to forests
(% of world's forests at risk)

Number of threatened species, 2003

Countries with the most threatened species, 2003

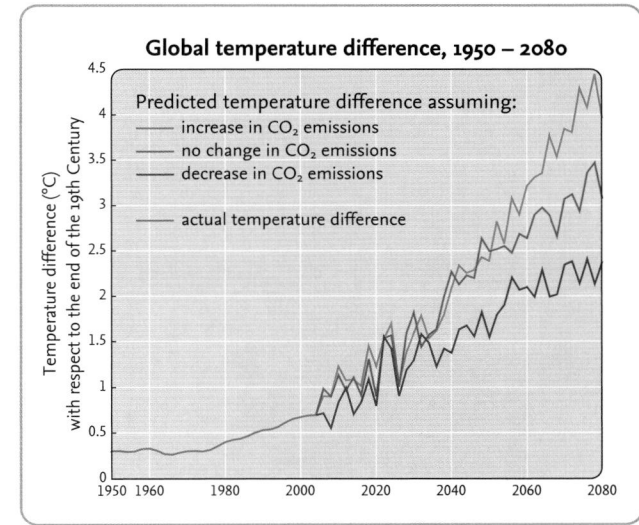

Global temperature difference, 1950 – 2080

Predicted temperature difference assuming:
- increase in CO_2 emissions
- no change in CO_2 emissions
- decrease in CO_2 emissions
- actual temperature difference

3 Forest and Coral Reefs at Risk

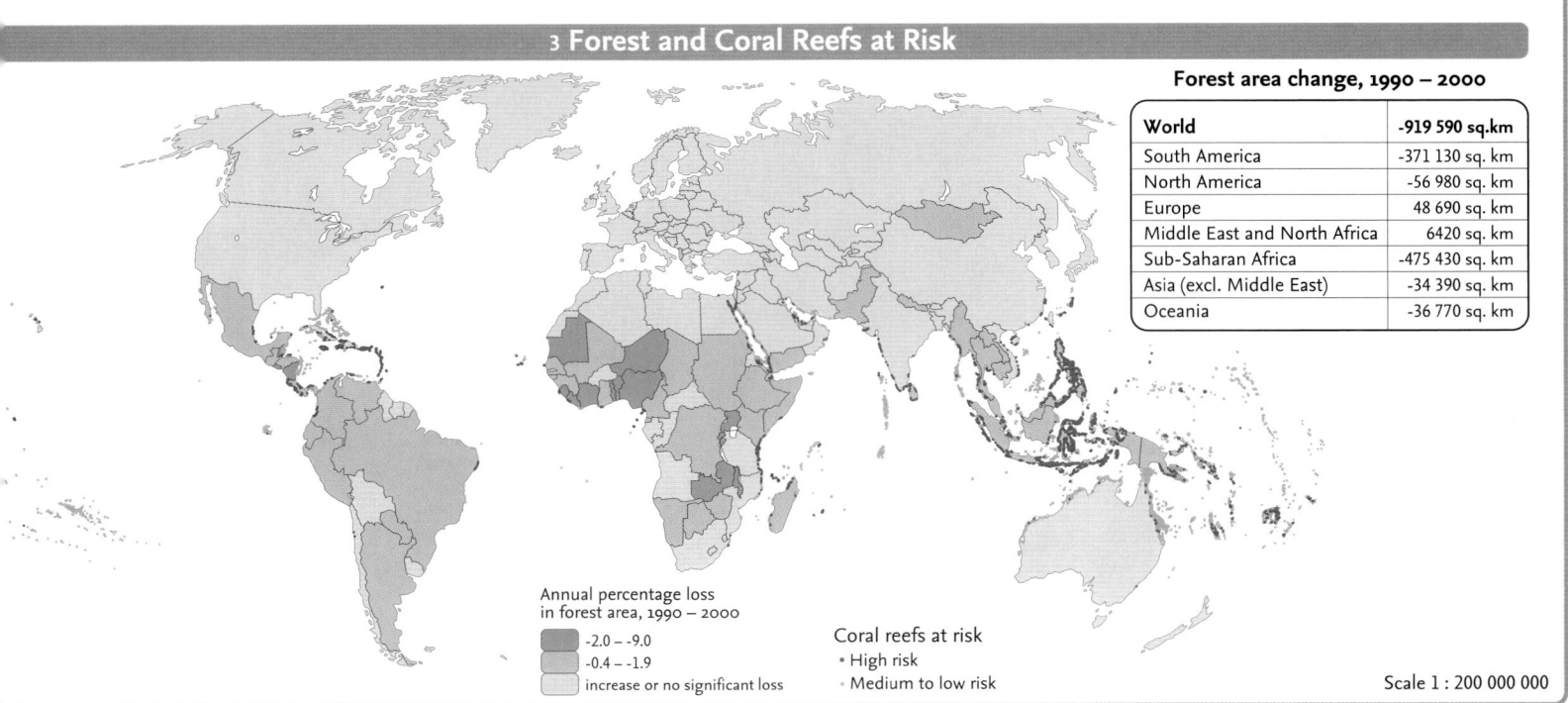

Forest area change, 1990 – 2000

World	-919 590 sq.km
South America	-371 130 sq. km
North America	-56 980 sq. km
Europe	48 690 sq. km
Middle East and North Africa	6420 sq. km
Sub-Saharan Africa	-475 430 sq. km
Asia (excl. Middle East)	-34 390 sq. km
Oceania	-36 770 sq. km

Annual percentage loss
in forest area, 1990 – 2000

- -2.0 – -9.0
- -0.4 – -1.9
- increase or no significant loss

Coral reefs at risk
- High risk
- Medium to low risk

Scale 1 : 200 000 000

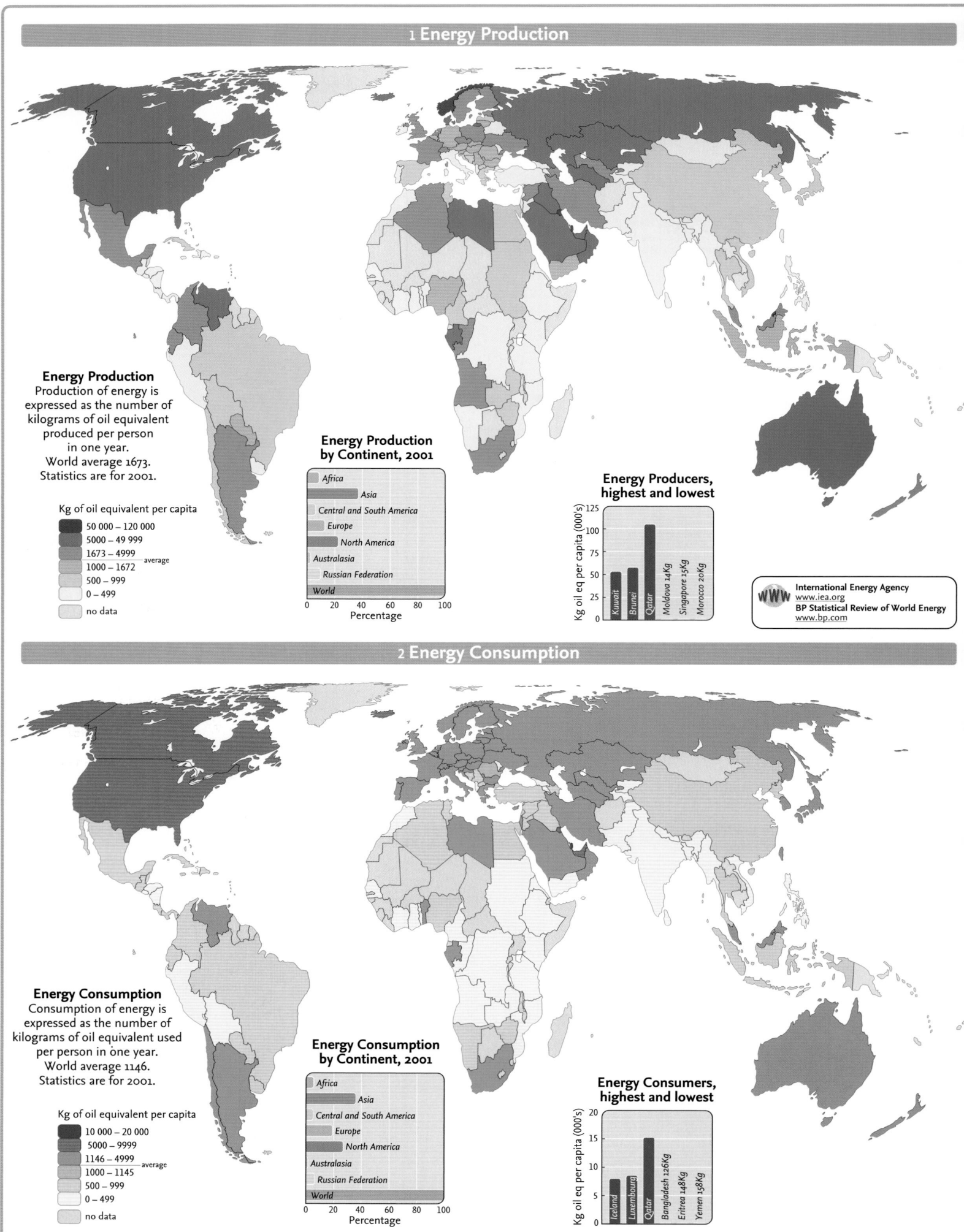

1 Energy Production

Energy Production

Production of energy is expressed as the number of kilograms of oil equivalent produced per person in one year.
World average 1673.
Statistics are for 2001.

Kg of oil equivalent per capita

- 50 000 – 120 000
- 5000 – 49 999
- 1673 – 4999 — average
- 1000 – 1672
- 500 – 999
- 0 – 499
- no data

Energy Production by Continent, 2001

- Africa
- Asia
- Central and South America
- Europe
- North America
- Australasia
- Russian Federation
- World

Percentage
0   20   40   60   80   100

Energy Producers, highest and lowest

Kg oil eq per capita (000's)
125
100
75
50
25
0

Kuwait | Brunei | Qatar | Moldova 14Kg | Singapore 15Kg | Morocco 20Kg

WWW **International Energy Agency**
www.iea.org
BP Statistical Review of World Energy
www.bp.com

2 Energy Consumption

Energy Consumption

Consumption of energy is expressed as the number of kilograms of oil equivalent used per person in one year.
World average 1146.
Statistics are for 2001.

Kg of oil equivalent per capita

- 10 000 – 20 000
- 5000 – 9999
- 1146 – 4999 — average
- 1000 – 1145
- 500 – 999
- 0 – 499
- no data

Energy Consumption by Continent, 2001

- Africa
- Asia
- Central and South America
- Europe
- North America
- Australasia
- Russian Federation
- World

Percentage
0   20   40   60   80   100

Energy Consumers, highest and lowest

Kg oil eq per capita (000's)
20
15
10
5
0

Iceland | Luxembourg | Qatar | Bangladesh 126Kg | Eritrea 148Kg | Yemen 158Kg

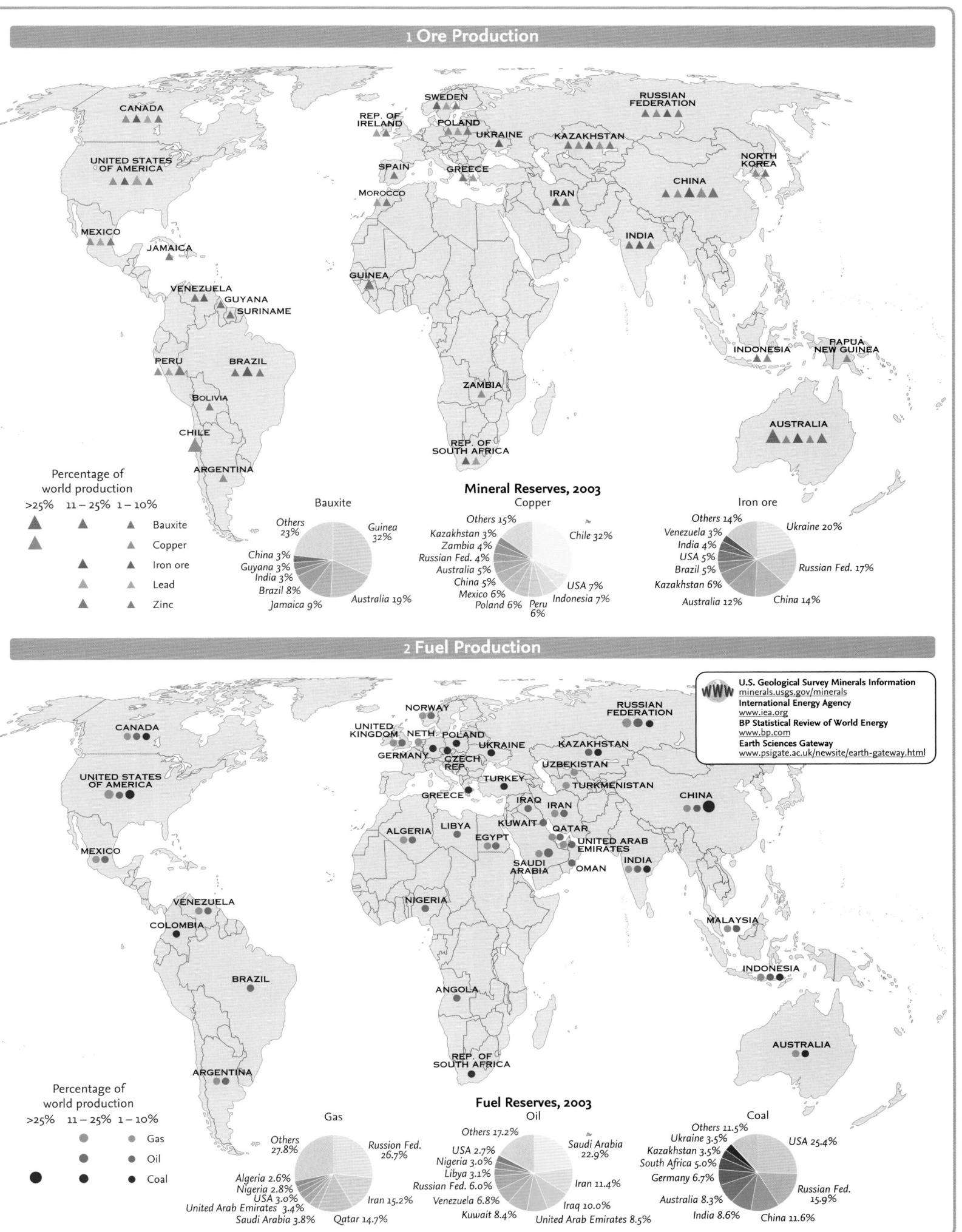

1 Ore Production

CANADA
UNITED STATES OF AMERICA
MEXICO
JAMAICA
VENEZUELA
GUYANA
SURINAME
PERU
BRAZIL
BOLIVIA
CHILE
ARGENTINA
REP. OF IRELAND
SPAIN
MOROCCO
GUINEA
SWEDEN
POLAND
UKRAINE
GREECE
ZAMBIA
REP. OF SOUTH AFRICA
RUSSIAN FEDERATION
KAZAKHSTAN
IRAN
INDIA
CHINA
NORTH KOREA
INDONESIA
PAPUA NEW GUINEA
AUSTRALIA

Percentage of world production

>25%   11 – 25%   1 – 10%

Bauxite
Copper
Iron ore
Lead
Zinc

Mineral Reserves, 2003

Bauxite
Others 23%
Guinea 32%
China 3%
Guyana 3%
India 3%
Brazil 8%
Jamaica 9%
Australia 19%

Copper
Others 15%
Kazakhstan 3%
Zambia 4%
Russian Fed. 4%
Australia 5%
China 5%
Mexico 6%
Poland 6%
Peru 6%
Indonesia 7%
USA 7%
Chile 32%

Iron ore
Others 14%
Venezuela 3%
India 4%
USA 5%
Brazil 5%
Kazakhstan 6%
Australia 12%
China 14%
Russian Fed. 17%
Ukraine 20%

2 Fuel Production

CANADA
UNITED STATES OF AMERICA
MEXICO
VENEZUELA
COLOMBIA
BRAZIL
ARGENTINA
NORWAY
UNITED KINGDOM
NETH.
GERMANY
POLAND
CZECH REP.
UKRAINE
GREECE
ALGERIA
LIBYA
EGYPT
NIGERIA
ANGOLA
REP. OF SOUTH AFRICA
RUSSIAN FEDERATION
KAZAKHSTAN
UZBEKISTAN
TURKEY
TURKMENISTAN
IRAQ
IRAN
KUWAIT
QATAR
UNITED ARAB EMIRATES
SAUDI ARABIA
OMAN
INDIA
CHINA
MALAYSIA
INDONESIA
AUSTRALIA

U.S. Geological Survey Minerals Information
minerals.usgs.gov/minerals
International Energy Agency
www.iea.org
BP Statistical Review of World Energy
www.bp.com
Earth Sciences Gateway
www.psigate.ac.uk/newsite/earth-gateway.html

Percentage of world production

>25%   11 – 25%   1 – 10%

Gas
Oil
Coal

Fuel Reserves, 2003

Gas
Others 27.8%
Russion Fed. 26.7%
Algeria 2.6%
Nigeria 2.8%
USA 3.0%
United Arab Emirates 3.4%
Saudi Arabia 3.8%
Qatar 14.7%
Iran 15.2%

Oil
Others 17.2%
USA 2.7%
Nigeria 3.0%
Libya 3.1%
Russian Fed. 6.0%
Venezuela 6.8%
Kuwait 8.4%
United Arab Emirates 8.5%
Iraq 10.0%
Iran 11.4%
Saudi Arabia 22.9%

Coal
Others 11.5%
Ukraine 3.5%
Kazakhstan 3.5%
South Africa 5.0%
Germany 6.7%
Australia 8.3%
India 8.6%
China 11.6%
Russian Fed. 15.9%
USA 25.4%

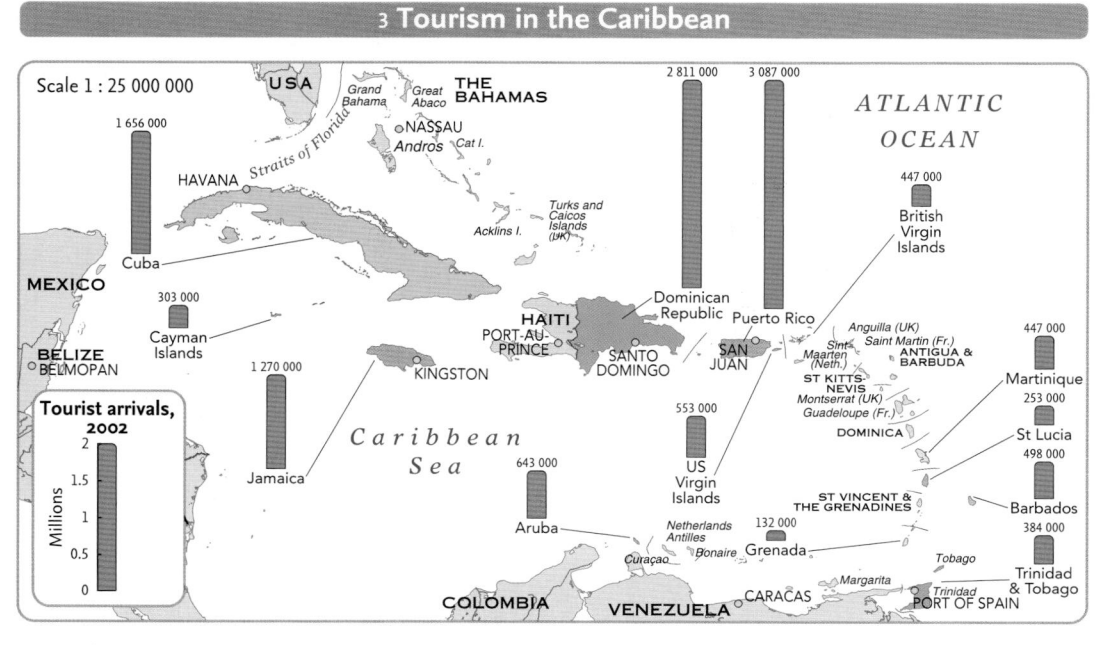

WWW World Tourism Organization
www.world-tourism.org
UNESCO World Heritage Sites
whc.unesco.org

GREENLAND

ARCTIC

U.S.A.

C A N A D A

Banff National Park

Yellowstone National Park
Rocky Mountains National Park
Yosemite National Park

UNITED STATES OF AMERICA

Boston
New York
Washington

San Francisco

Los Angeles
Las Vegas
Grand Canyon

Atlanta

Charleston

New Orleans

Orlando

Tampa

Miami

Bermuda

MEXICO

Chichen Itza

Cancun

The Bahamas

CUBA

DOMINICAN REP.

HAITI

JAMAICA

PUERTO RICO (USA)

The Caribbean

TRINIDAD & TOBAGO

Tikal

BELIZE

Acapulco

GUATEMALA

HONDURAS

EL SALVADOR

NICARAGUA

COSTA RICA

PANAMA

VENEZUELA

COLOMBIA

GUY

SUR

FR.G

Galapagos Is (Ec)

ECUADOR

Amazonia

PERU

B R A Z I L

Cuzco

BOLIVIA

PARAGUAY

Rio de Janeiro

Iguaçu Falls

URUGUAY

Buenos Aires

A R G E N T I N A

C H I L E

Hawaiian Islands

PACIFIC

OCEAN

KIRIBATI

W. SAMOA

Marquesas Is (Fr.)

Cook Islands (NZ)

Society Is (Fr.)

French Polynesia

Tahiti

Tuamoto Is

TONGA

Pitcairn Island (UK)

Easter I. (Chile)

Falkland Islands (UK)

South Georgia (UK)

Azores

TUNISIA

Madeira

MOROCCO

Canary Islands

WESTERN SAHARA

ALGERIA

LIB

MAURITANIA

MALI

NIGER

CH

SENEGAL

The Gambia

GUINEA-BISSAU

GUINEA

SIERRA LEONE

C. D'I.

BUR.

BE.

LIBERIA

NIGERIA

CAM.

EQ. G.

GABON

ATLANTIC

OCEAN

ANG

National NAMIB

R S A

Cape Town

South National

SEE PAGE 3
EUROPE TOU

■ Safari / Wilderness / Trekking area
■ Beach / Leisure resort
■ City resort
■ Cultural / Historical resort

Scale 1 : 90 000 000

Scale 1 : 25 000 000

USA

Grand Bahama

Great Abaco

THE BAHAMAS

NASSAU

Andros

Cat I.

2 811 000

3 087 000

ATLANTIC OCEAN

447 000

British Virgin Islands

HAVANA

1 656 000

Straits of Florida

Turks and Caicos Islands (UK)

Acklins I.

MEXICO

Cuba

Cayman Islands

303 000

1 270 000

Jamaica

KINGSTON

HAITI

PORT-AU-PRINCE

Dominican Republic

SANTO DOMINGO

Puerto Rico

SAN JUAN

US Virgin Islands

553 000

Anguilla (UK)

Saint Martin (Fr.)

Sint Maarten (Neth.)

ANTIGUA & BARBUDA

ST KITTS NEVIS

Montserrat (UK)

Guadeloupe (Fr.)

DOMINICA

447 000

Martinique

253 000

St Lucia

498 000

ST VINCENT & THE GRENADINES

Barbados

384 000

BELIZE

BELMOPAN

Tourist arrivals, 2002

Millions

2
1.5
1
0.5
0

Caribbean Sea

643 000

Aruba

Netherlands Antilles

Bonaire

Curaçao

Grenada

132 000

Margarita

Tobago

Trinidad

Trinidad & Tobago

PORT OF SPAIN

COLOMBIA

VENEZUELA

CARACAS

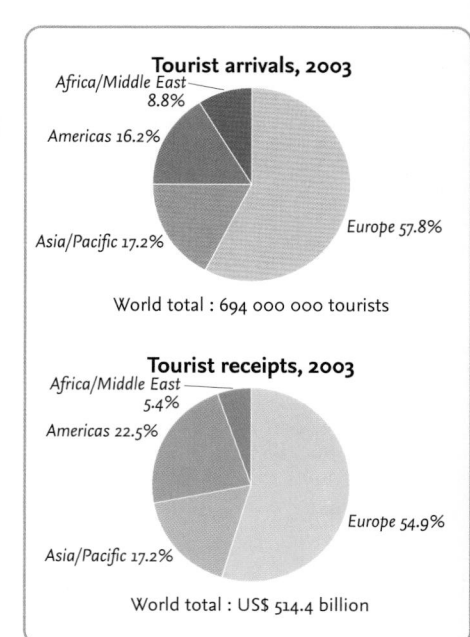

Tourist arrivals, 2003

Africa/Middle East 8.8%

Americas 16.2%

Asia/Pacific 17.2%

Europe 57.8%

World total : 694 000 000 tourists

Tourist receipts, 2003

Africa/Middle East 5.4%

Americas 22.5%

Asia/Pacific 17.2%

Europe 54.9%

World total : US$ 514.4 billion

2 International Tourist Arrivals

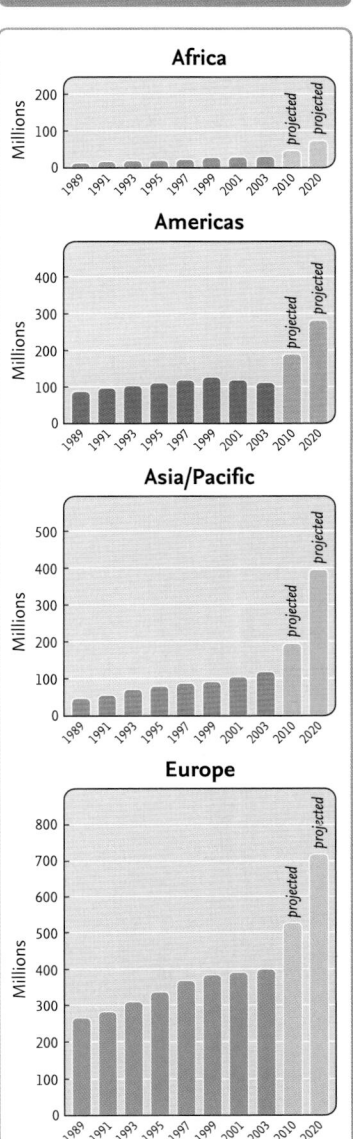

Africa

Americas

Asia/Pacific

Europe

RUSSIAN FEDERATION

KAZAKHSTAN

MONGOLIA

UZBEKISTAN
TURKMEN-
ISTAN
KYRGYZSTAN
TAJIKISTAN

KEY
Aleppo
JOR.
SYRIA
IRAQ
IRAN
AFGHAN-
ISTAN
PAKISTAN

CHINA

N. KOREA

S. KOREA

JAPAN

Tōkyō

PACIFIC

OCEAN

Beijing
Great Wall
Xi'an
Shanghai

Petra
Pyramids
KUWAIT
Red Sea
SAUDI
Abu Dhabi
QATAR
BAHRAIN
U.A.E.
ARABIA
OMAN
YEMEN
ERITREA

NEPAL
BHUTAN
BANGLA-
DESH

Agra/Taj Mahal
Jaipur

INDIA

MYANMAR
LAOS
VIETNAM

Hong
Kong

TAIWAN

Chiang Mai
THAILAND

Goa
Bangkok
CAMBODIA

PHILIPPINES

Northern
Marianas
(USA)

MARSHALL
ISLANDS

DJIBOUTI

ETHIOPIA

SOMALIA

Phuket
Koh Sumai

Sri
Lanka

Maldives

BRUNEI
MALAYSIA
Mt Kinabalu

Singapore

PALAU

FED. STATES OF
MICRONESIA

NAURU

KIRIBATI

KENYA
East African
National Parks
Mombasa

Seychelles

INDIAN

OCEAN

I N D O N E S I A

PAPUA
NEW
GUINEA

SOLOMON
ISLANDS

TUVALU

ANZANIA

Bali

MOZAMBIQUE

Comoros

MADAGASCAR
Mauritius
Reunion

VANUATU

Fiji

ke Kariba
BABWE
inge
onal
Kruger
National Park
SWAZILAND
Durban

AUSTRALIA

Uluru

Great Barrier Reef
Marine Park
New Caledonia
(Fr.)

Gold Coast

Blue Mountains

North
Island

NEW
ZEALAND
South
Island

Kerguelen
(Fr.)

World's top 10 tourist destinations, 2003

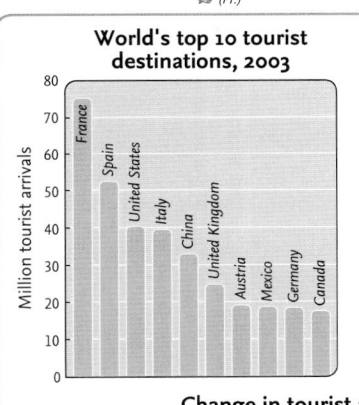

(Million tourist arrivals: France, Spain, United States, Italy, China, United Kingdom, Austria, Mexico, Germany, Canada)

World's top 10 tourist destinations (tourist receipts), 2003

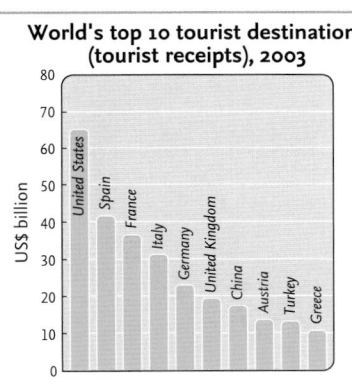

(US$ billion: United States, Spain, France, Italy, Germany, United Kingdom, China, Austria, Turkey, Greece)

Change in tourist arrivals (percentage)

Country	2002/2001	2003/2002
France	2.4	-2.6
Spain	4.5	0.3
United States	-6.7	-3.6
Italy	0.6	-0.5
China	11	-10.3
United Kingdom	5.9	2.6
Austria	2.4	2.6
Mexico	4.6	-4.9
Germany	0.6	2.4
Canada	1.9	-12.7

4 Tourism in the Future

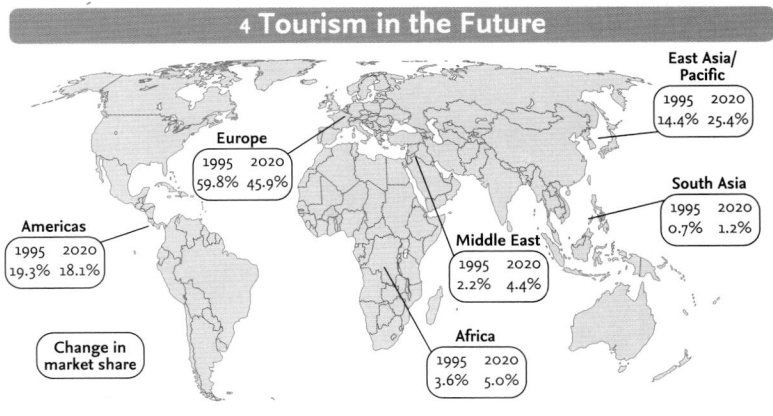

East Asia/Pacific	
1995	2020
14.4%	25.4%

Europe	
1995	2020
59.8%	45.9%

South Asia	
1995	2020
0.7%	1.2%

Americas	
1995	2020
19.3%	18.1%

Middle East	
1995	2020
2.2%	4.4%

Africa	
1995	2020
3.6%	5.0%

Change in
market share

Tourist arrivals forecast 1995-2020 (millions)

	1995	2010	2020	Average annual growth rate (%)
World	565.4	1006.4	1561.1	4.1
Africa	20.2	47.0	77.3	5.5
Americas	108.9	190.4	282.3	3.9
East Asia/Pacific	81.4	195.2	397.2	6.5
Europe	338.4	527.3	717.0	3.0
Middle East	12.4	35.9	68.5	7.1
South Asia	4.2	10.6	18.8	6.2

1 Telephone Lines

Top twenty internet server providers (ISPs)

Internet service provider	Web address	Subscribers (thousands)
AOL (USA)	www.aol.com	20 500
T-Online (Germany)	www.t-online.de	4 151
Nifty-Serve (Japan)	www.nifty.com	3 500
EarthLink (USA)	www.earthlink.com	3 122
Biglobe (Japan)	www.biglobe.ne.jp	2 720
MSN (USA)	www.msn.com	2 700
Chollian (South Korea)	www.chollian.net	2 000
Tin.it (Italy)	www.tin.it	1 990
Freeserve (UK)	www.freeserve.com	1 575
AT&T WorldNet (USA)	www.att.net	1 500
Prodigy (USA)	www.prodigy.com	1 502
NetZero (USA)	www.netzero.com	1 450
Terra Networks (Spain)	www.terra.es	1 317
HiNet (Taiwan-China)	www.hinet.net	1 200
Wanadoo (France)	www.wanadoo.fr	1 124
AltaVista	www.microav.com	750
Freei (USA)	www.freei.com	750
SBC Internet Services	www.sbc.com	720
Telia Internet (Sweden)	www.telia.se	613
Netvigator (Hong Kong SAR)	www.netvigator.com	561

Total telephone lines, 2003

Africa	24 711 900
Americas	290 146 600
Asia	493 050 300
Europe	326 545 700
Oceania	12 889 100
World	**1 147 343 600**

Telephone lines per 100 people

- over 49.9
- 30 – 49.9
- 10 – 29.9
- 0 – 9.9
- no data

Scale 1 : 110 000 000

International Telecommunication Union
www.itu.int
TeleGeography
www.telegeography.com

2 Internet Users

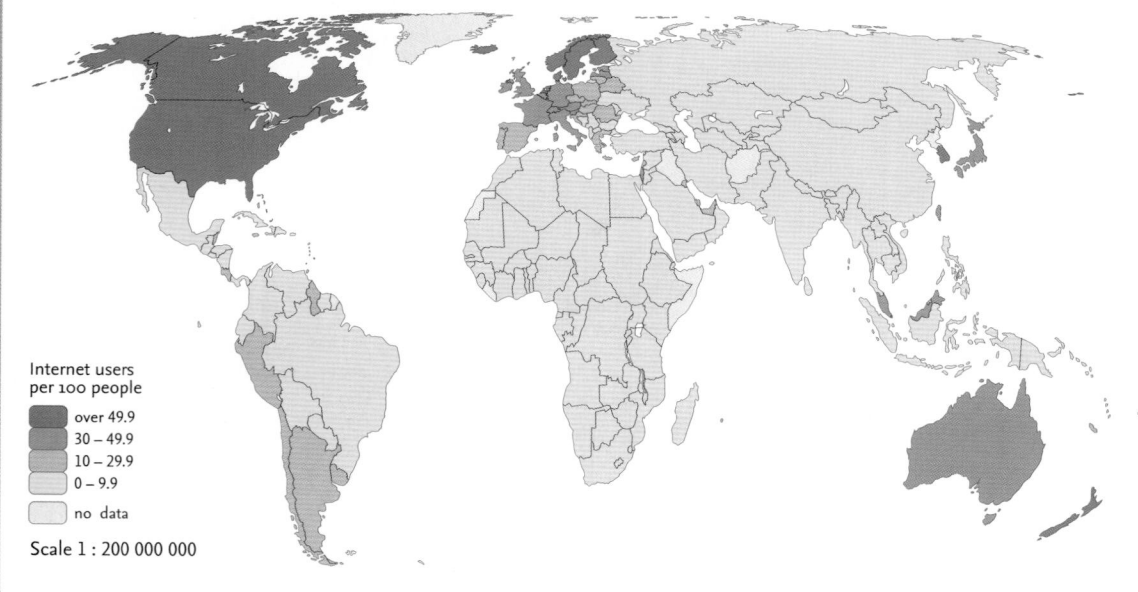

Internet users
per 100 people

- over 49.9
- 30 – 49.9
- 10 – 29.9
- 0 – 9.9
- no data

Scale 1 : 200 000 000

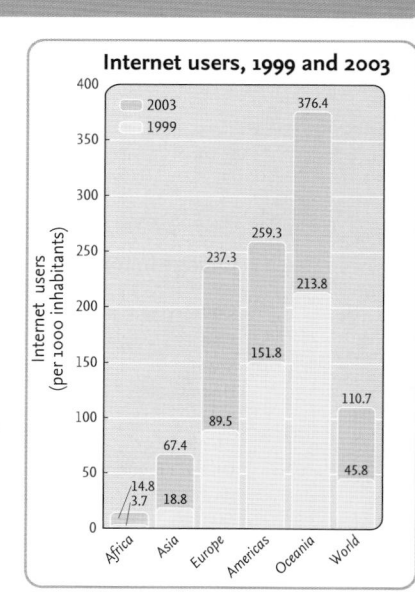

Internet users, 1999 and 2003

Internet users (per 1000 inhabitants)

- 2003
- 1999

	1999	2003
Africa	3.7	14.8
Asia	18.8	67.4
Europe	89.5	237.3
Americas	151.8	259.3
Oceania	213.8	376.4
World	45.8	110.7

Telephone main lines, 2003

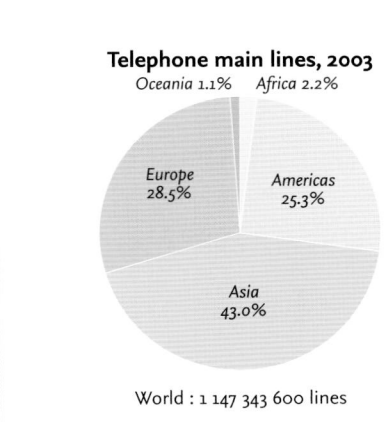

Oceania 1.1% *Africa* 2.2%
Europe 28.5% Americas 25.3%
Asia 43.0%

World : 1 147 343 600 lines

Internet users, 2003

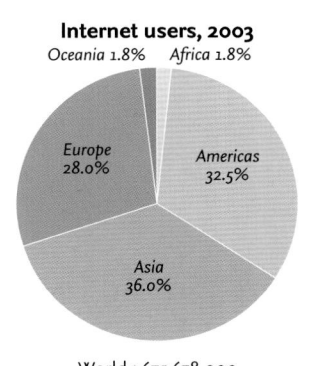

Oceania 1.8% *Africa* 1.8%
Europe 28.0% Americas 32.5%
Asia 36.0%

World : 675 678 000

World communication equipment, 1976 – 2003

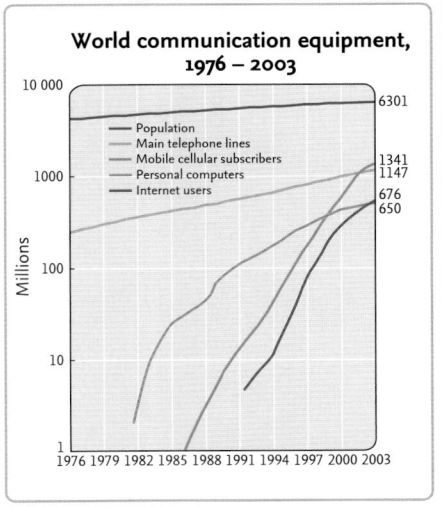

- Population
- Main telephone lines
- Mobile cellular subscribers
- Personal computers
- Internet users

Millions

6301
1341
1147
676
650

10 000
1000
100
10

1976 1979 1982 1985 1988 1991 1994 1997 2000 2003

Cellular subscribers, 2003

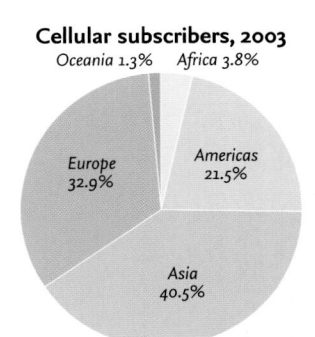

Oceania 1.3% *Africa* 3.8%
Europe 32.9% Americas 21.5%
Asia 40.5%

World : 1 340 668 000

3 Geostationary Communication Satellites

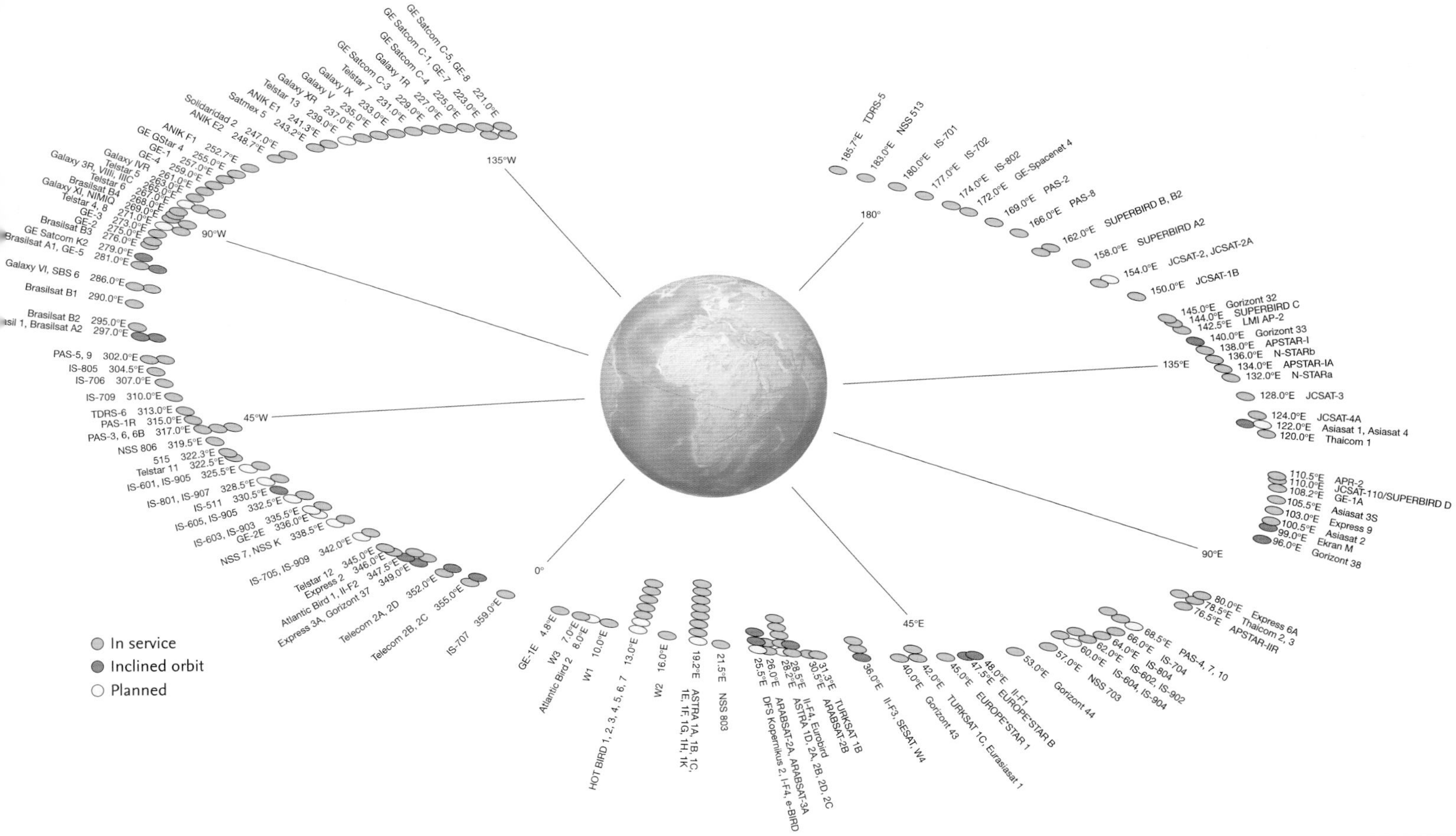

GE Satcom C-5, GE-8 221.0°E
GE Satcom C-1, GE-7 223.0°E
GE Satcom C-4 227.0°E
Galaxy IX 229.0°E
GE Satcom C-3 231.0°E
Telstar 7 233.0°E
Galaxy V 235.0°E
Galaxy XR 237.0°E
Telstar 13 239.0°E
Satmex 5 241.3°E
Solidaridad 2 247.0°E
ANIK E1 243.2°E
ANIK E2 248.7°E
GE GStar 4 252.7°E
ANIK F1 255.0°E
GE-4 257.0°E
GE-1 259.0°E
Galaxy IVR 263.0°E
Telstar 5 265.0°E
Galaxy 3R, VIIIi, IIIC 268.0°E
Brasilsat B4 268.5°E
Galaxy XI, NIMIQ 269.0°E
Telstar 4, 8 271.0°E
GE-3 273.0°E
Brasilsat B3 275.0°E
GE Satcom K2 276.0°E
Brasilsat A1, GE-5 279.0°E
Galaxy VI, SBS 6 281.0°E
Brasilsat B1 286.0°E
Brasilsat B2 290.0°E
Brasil 1, Brasilsat A2 295.0°E
297.0°E
PAS-5, 9 302.0°E
IS-805 304.5°E
IS-706 307.0°E
IS-709 310.0°E
TDRS-6 313.0°E
PAS-1R 315.0°E
PAS-3, 6, 6B 317.0°E
NSS 806 319.5°E
Telstar 11 322.3°E
515 322.5°E
IS-601, IS-905 325.5°E
IS-801, IS-907 328.5°E
IS-511 330.5°E
IS-605, IS-905 332.5°E
IS-603, IS-903 336.0°E
GE-2E 336.0°E
NSS 7, NSS K 338.5°E
IS-705, IS-909 342.0°E
Telstar 12 345.0°E
Express 2 346.0°E
Atlantic Bird 1, II-F2 347.5°E
Express 3A, Gorizont 37 349.0°E
Telecom 2A, 2D 352.0°E
Telecom 2B, 2C 355.0°E
IS-707 359.0°E
GE-1E 4.8°E
W3 7.0°E
Atlantic Bird 2 8.0°E
W1 10.0°E
HOT BIRD 1, 2, 3, 4, 5, 6, 7 13.0°E
W2 16.0°E
ASTRA 1A, 1B, 1C, 1E, 1F, 1G, 1H, 1K 19.2°E
NSS 803 21.5°E
DFS Kopernikus 2, I-F4, e-BIRD 23.5°E
ARABSAT-2A, ARABSAT-3A 26.0°E
ARABSAT-1D, 2A 28.2°E
ARABSAT 1B 28.5°E
TURKSAT 1B 31.3°E
Eurobird 33.0°E
II-F4, 28, 2B, 2C 36.0°E
II-F3, SESAT, W4 40.0°E
Gorizont 43 42.0°E
TURKSAT 1C, Eurasiasat 1 45.0°E
EUROPE*STAR 1C 47.5°E
II-F1, EUROPE*STAR B 48.0°E
Gorizont 44 53.0°E
NSS 703 57.0°E
IS-804 60.0°E
IS-604, IS-902 62.0°E
IS-902, IS-904 64.0°E
Thaicom 2, 3 66.0°E
APSTAR-IIR 76.5°E
PAS-4, 7, 10 68.5°E
Express 6A 80.0°E
Gorizont 38 96.0°E
Ekran M 99.0°E
Asiasat 2 100.5°E
Express 9 103.0°E
Asiasat 3S 105.5°E
GE-1A 108.2°E
JCSAT-110/SUPERBIRD D 110.0°E
APR-2 110.5°E
Thaicom 1 120.0°E
Asiasat 1, Asiasat 4 122.0°E
JCSAT-4A 124.0°E
JCSAT-3 128.0°E
N-STARa 132.0°E
APSTAR-IA 134.0°E
N-STARb 136.0°E
APSTAR-I 138.0°E
Gorizont 33 140.0°E
LMI AP-2 142.5°E
SUPERBIRD C 144.0°E
Gorizont 32 145.0°E
JCSAT-1B 150.0°E
JCSAT-2, JCSAT-2A 154.0°E
SUPERBIRD A2 158.0°E
SUPERBIRD B, B2 162.0°E
PAS-8 166.0°E
PAS-2 169.0°E
GE-Spacenet 4 172.0°E
IS-802 174.0°E
IS-702 177.0°E
IS-701 180.0°E
NSS 513 183.0°E
TDRS-5 185.7°E

135°W
180°
90°W
45°W
0°
45°E
90°E
135°E

- In service
- Inclined orbit
- Planned

Flag	Country	Capital city	Population total 2003	Density persons per sq km 2003	Birth rate per 1000 population 2002	Death rate per 1000 population 2002	Life expectancy in years 2002	Population change average % per annum 2000-2005	Urban population % 2002
			Population						
	Afghanistan	Kābul	23 897 000	37	49	21	43	3.9	23
	Albania	Tirana	3 166 000	110	17	6	74	0.7	44
	Algeria	Algiers	31 800 000	13	22	5	71	1.7	58
	Angola	Luanda	13 625 000	11	47	19	47	3.2	36
	Antigua & Barbuda	St John's	73 000	165	...	...	...	0.5	37
	Argentina	Buenos Aires	38 428 000	14	19	8	74	1.2	89
	Armenia	Yerevan	3 061 000	103	12	7	75	-0.5	67
	Australia	Canberra	19 731 000	3	13	8	79	1.0	92
	Austria	Vienna	8 116 000	97	9	10	79	0.1	68
	Azerbaijan	Baku	8 370 000	97	16	7	65	0.9	52
	Bahamas, The	Nassau	314 000	23	18	8	70	1.1	89
	Bahrain	Manama	724 000	1 048	21	4	73	2.2	93
	Bangladesh	Dhaka	146 736 000	1 019	28	8	62	2.0	26
	Barbados	Bridgetown	270 000	628	14	8	75	0.4	51
	Belarus	Minsk	9 895 000	48	9	14	68	-0.5	70
	Belgium	Brussels	10 318 000	338	10	10	79	0.2	98
	Belize	Belmopan	256 000	11	25	4	74	2.1	48
	Benin	Porto-Novo	6 736 000	60	38	13	53	2.7	44
	Bhutan	Thimphu	2 257 000	48	37	9	63	3.0	8
	Bolivia	La Paz/Sucre	8 808 000	8	29	8	64	1.9	63
	Bosnia & Herzegovina	Sarajevo	4 161 000	81	12	8	74	1.1	44
	Botswana	Gaborone	1 785 000	3	30	23	38	0.9	50
	Brazil	Brasília	178 470 000	21	19	7	69	1.2	82
	Brunei	Bandar Seri Begawan	358 000	62	19	3	77	2.3	73
	Bulgaria	Sofia	7 897 000	71	9	14	72	-0.9	68
	Burkina	Ouagadougou	13 002 000	47	43	19	43	3.0	17
	Burundi	Bujumbura	6 825 000	245	39	20	42	3.1	10
	Cambodia	Phnom Penh	14 144 000	78	27	12	54	2.4	18
	Cameroon	Yaoundé	16 018 000	34	36	16	48	1.8	50
	Canada	Ottawa	31 510 000	3	11	8	79	0.8	79
	Cape Verde	Praia	463 000	115	31	5	69	2.0	64
	Central African Republic	Bangui	3 865 000	6	36	20	42	1.3	42
	Chad	Ndjamena	8 598 000	7	45	16	48	3.0	25
	Chile	Santiago	15 805 000	21	16	6	76	1.2	86
	China	Beijing	1 304 196 000	135	15	8	71	0.7	38
	Colombia	Bogotá	44 222 000	39	21	6	72	1.6	76
	Comoros	Moroni	768 000	412	32	8	61	2.8	34
	Congo	Brazzaville	3 724 000	11	41	14	52	2.6	67
	Congo, Dem. Rep. of	Kinshasa	52 771 000	22	45	18	45	2.9	...
	Costa Rica	San José	4 173 000	82	20	4	78	1.9	60
	Côte d'Ivoire	Yamoussoukro	16 631 000	52	37	17	45	1.6	45
	Croatia	Zagreb	4 428 000	78	10	12	74	-0.2	59
	Cuba	Havana	11 300 000	102	12	8	77	0.3	76
	Cyprus	Nicosia	802 000	87	13	8	78	0.8	71
	Czech Republic	Prague	10 236 000	130	9	11	75	-0.1	75
	Denmark	Copenhagen	5 364 000	125	12	12	77	0.2	85
	Djibouti	Djibouti	703 000	30	36	20	44	1.6	84

Land		Education and Health			Development		Communications			Country	Time Zones
Area sq km	Forest 'ooo sq km 2000	Adult literacy % 2002	Doctors per 1000 population 1996-2002	Food intake calories per capita per day 1999	Energy consumption million tonnes of oil equivalent 2001	GNI per capita US$ 2002	Telephone lines per 100 population 2001	Cell phones per 100 population 2001	Internet connections per 1000 population 2001		+ or - GMT
652 225	14	...	0.11	1 755	...	...	...	...	...	Afghanistan	+4¹/₂
28 748	10	85.9	1.39	2 717	1.4	1 380	5.0	8.8	2.5	Albania	+1
2 381 741	21	68.9	1.00	2 966	16.4	1 720	6.0	0.3	1.9	Algeria	+1
1 246 700	698	...	0.08	1 873	6.6	660	0.6	0.6	4.4	Angola	+1
442	...	...	1.14	...	...	9 390	47.4	31.8	65.2	Antigua & Barbuda	-4
2 766 889	346	97	...	3 177	43.8	4 060	21.6	18.6	80.0	Argentina	-3
29 800	4	98.6	2.86	2 167	1.4	790	14.0	0.7	142.1	Armenia	+5
7 692 024	1 545	100	2.50	3 150	73.0	19 740	52.0	57.8	372.3	Australia	+8 to +10¹/₂
83 855	39	100	3.20	3 639	25.8	23 390	46.8	80.7	319.4	Austria	+1
86 600	11	...	3.59	2 224	6.5	710	11.1	8.0	3.2	Azerbaijan	+4
13 939	...	95.6	1.52	...	...	...	40.0	19.7	55.0	Bahamas, The	-5
691	...	88.5	1.00	...	3.1	...	24.7	42.5	198.9	Bahrain	+3
143 998	13	41.1	0.20	2 201	16.9	360	0.4	0.4	1.1	Bangladesh	+6
430	...	99.7	...	...	...	...	46.3	10.6	37.4	Barbados	-4
207 600	94	99.7	4.50	3 171	18.1	1 360	27.9	1.4	41.2	Belarus	+3
30 520	7	100	3.90	...	43.1	23 250	49.3	74.7	280.0	Belgium	+1
22 965	13	93.8	0.55	2 889	...	2 960	14.4	11.6	73.8	Belize	-6
112 620	27	39.8	...	2 489	17.5	380	0.9	1.9	3.9	Benin	+1
46 620	30	...	...	...	...	590	2.0	...	3.6	Bhutan	+6
1 098 581	531	86.6	1.30	2 237	2.9	900	6.2	9.0	14.6	Bolivia	-4
51 130	23	...	1.45	2 960	2.7	1 270	11.1	5.7	11.1	Bosnia & Herzegovina	+1
581 370	124	78.9	...	2 288	...	2 980	9.3	16.7	15.4	Botswana	+2
8 514 879	5 439	87.7	1.27	3 012	156.4	2 850	21.8	16.7	46.6	Brazil	-2 to -5
5 765	...	91.5	0.85	...	0.6	...	24.5	28.9	104.5	Brunei	+8
110 994	37	98.6	3.44	2 847	9.8	1 790	35.9	19.1	74.6	Bulgaria	+2
274 200	71	25.7	0.04	2 376	...	220	0.5	0.6	1.7	Burkina	GMT
27 835	1	50.4	...	1 628	...	100	0.3	0.3	0.9	Burundi	+2
181 000	93	69.4	0.30	2 000	...	280	0.3	1.7	0.7	Cambodia	+7
475 442	239	73.5	0.07	2 260	6.1	560	0.7	2.0	3.0	Cameroon	+1
9 984 670	2 446	100	2.10	3 161	248.2	22 300	65.5	32.0	435.3	Canada	-3¹/₂ to -8
4 033	...	75.7	0.17	...	...	1 290	14.3	7.2	27.5	Cape Verde	-1
622 436	229	49.6	...	1 978	...	260	0.3	0.3	0.5	Central African Republic	+1
1 284 000	127	45.8	...	2 206	...	220	0.1	0.3	0.5	Chad	+1
756 945	155	96.1	...	2 858	18.3	4 260	23.9	34.0	200.2	Chile	-4
9 562 000	1 635	86.4	1.44	3 044	785.4	940	13.8	11.2	26.0	China	+8
1 141 748	496	92.2	1.16	2 567	22.9	1 830	17.1	7.6	27.0	Colombia	-5
1 862	...	56.2	0.07	...	...	390	1.2	...	3.4	Comoros	+3
342 000	221	82.8	...	2 212	0.7	700	0.7	4.8	0.2	Congo	+1
2 345 410	1 352	64.1	0.07	1 637	14.3	90	0.0	0.3	0.1	Congo, Dem. Rep. of	+1 to +2
51 100	20	95.8	0.90	2 761	2.6	4 100	23.0	7.6	93.4	Costa Rica	-6
322 463	71	50.7	0.09	2 582	4.2	610	1.8	4.5	4.3	Côte d'Ivoire	GMT
56 538	18	98.5	2.38	2 617	6.1	4 640	36.5	37.7	55.9	Croatia	+1
110 860	23	96.9	5.30	2 490	10.6	...	5.1	0.1	10.7	Cuba	-4
9 251	...	97.5	2.55	...	1.8	...	64.3	46.4	221.6	Cyprus	+2
78 864	26	100	3.40	3 241	25.6	5 560	37.4	65.9	136.3	Czech Republic	+1
43 075	5	100	3.40	3 317	15.2	30 290	72.3	73.7	447.2	Denmark	+1
23 200	...	66.5	0.14	...	...	900	1.5	0.5	5.1	Djibouti	+3

no data available

Flag	Key Information		Population						
	Country	Capital city	Population total 2003	Density persons per sq km 2003	Birth rate per 1000 population 2002	Death rate per 1000 population 2002	Life expectancy in years 2002	Population change average % per annum 2000-2005	Urban population % 2002
	Dominica	Roseau	79 000	105	18	6	77	0.3	72
	Dominican Republic	Santo Domingo	8 745 000	181	23	7	67	1.5	67
	East Timor	Dili	778 000	52	43	...	...	4.0	8
	Ecuador	Quito	13 003 000	48	24	6	70	1.5	64
	Egypt	Cairo	71 931 000	72	24	6	69	2.0	43
	El Salvador	San Salvador	6 515 000	310	26	6	70	1.6	62
	Equatorial Guinea	Malabo	494 000	18	41	15	52	2.7	50
	Eritrea	Asmara	4 141 000	35	38	13	51	3.7	20
	Estonia	Tallinn	1 323 000	29	9	14	71	-1.1	70
	Ethiopia	Addis Ababa	70 678 000	62	42	20	42	2.5	16
	Fiji	Suva	839 000	46	22	6	70	1.0	51
	Finland	Helsinki	5 207 000	15	11	10	78	0.2	59
	France	Paris	60 144 000	111	13	10	79	0.5	76
	Gabon	Libreville	1 329 000	5	35	15	53	1.8	83
	Gambia, The	Banjul	1 426 000	126	37	14	53	2.7	32
	Georgia	T'bilisi	5 126 000	74	8	10	73	-0.9	57
	Germany	Berlin	82 476 000	231	9	11	78	0.1	88
	Ghana	Accra	20 922 000	88	29	13	55	2.2	37
	Greece	Athens	10 976 000	83	9	11	78	0.1	61
	Grenada	St George's	80 000	212	25	7	73	-0.3	39
	Guatemala	Guatemala City	12 347 000	113	33	7	65	2.6	40
	Guinea	Conakry	8 480 000	34	38	17	46	1.6	28
	Guinea-Bissau	Bissau	1 493 000	41	39	20	45	3.0	33
	Guyana	Georgetown	765 000	4	22	10	62	0.2	37
	Haiti	Port-au-Prince	8 326 000	300	32	14	52	1.3	37
	Honduras	Tegucigalpa	6 941 000	62	30	6	66	2.3	55
	Hungary	Budapest	9 877 000	106	10	14	72	-0.5	65
	Iceland	Reykjavík	290 000	3	13	7	80	0.8	93
	India	New Delhi	1 065 462 000	348	24	9	63	1.5	28
	Indonesia	Jakarta	219 883 000	115	20	7	67	1.3	43
	Iran	Tehrān	68 920 000	42	22	6	69	1.2	65
	Iraq	Baghdād	25 175 000	57	29	8	63	2.7	68
	Ireland	Dublin	3 956 000	56	14	8	77	1.1	60
	Israel	*Jerusalem	6 433 000	310	20	6	79	2.0	92
	Italy	Rome	57 423 000	191	9	11	78	-0.1	67
	Jamaica	Kingston	2 651 000	241	20	6	76	0.9	57
	Japan	Tōkyō	127 654 000	338	9	9	81	0.1	79
	Jordan	'Ammān	5 473 000	61	28	4	72	2.7	79
	Kazakhstan	Astana	15 433 000	6	15	12	62	-0.4	56
	Kenya	Nairobi	31 987 000	55	35	16	46	1.5	35
	Kiribati	Bairiki	88 000	123	28	7	63	1.4	39
	Kuwait	Kuwait	2 521 000	141	20	3	77	3.5	96
	Kyrgyzstan	Bishkek	5 138 000	26	19	8	65	1.4	34
	Laos	Vientiane	5 657 000	24	36	12	55	2.3	20
	Latvia	Rīga	2 307 000	36	8	14	70	-0.9	60
	Lebanon	Beirut	3 653 000	350	19	6	71	1.6	90
	Lesotho	Maseru	1 802 000	59	31	20	43	0.1	30

* Jerusalem - not internationally recognised.

Land		Education and Health			Development		Communications				
Area sq km	Forest 'ooo sq km 2000	Adult literacy % 2002	Doctors per 1000 population 1996-2002	Food intake calories per capita per day 1999	Energy consumption million tonnes of oil equivalent 2001	GNI per capita US$ 2002	Telephone lines per 100 population 2001	Cell phones per 100 population 2001	Internet connections per 1000 population 2001	Country	Time Zones + or - GMT
750	...	...	0.49	...	...	3 180	29.1	1.6	77.8	Dominica	-4
48 442	14	84.4	2.16	2 334	5.4	2 320	11.0	14.7	21.5	Dominican Republic	-4
14 874	...	...	...	...	...	...	...	...	...	East Timor	+9
272 045	106	92.1	1.70	2 679	6.7	1 450	10.4	6.7	25.4	Ecuador	-5
1 000 250	1	56.9	1.60	3 323	33.6	1 470	10.3	4.3	9.3	Egypt	+2
21 041	1	79.7	1.07	2 463	3.0	2 080	9.3	12.5	8.0	El Salvador	-6
28 051	18	97.8	0.25	...	...	...	1.5	3.2	1.9	Equatorial Guinea	+1
117 400	16	57.7	0.03	1 646	0.6	160	0.8	...	2.6	Eritrea	+3
45 200	21	99.8	3.13	3 154	2.7	4 130	35.2	45.5	300.5	Estonia	+2
1 133 880	46	41.5	...	1 803	18.5	100	0.5	0.0	0.4	Ethiopia	+3
18 330	8	93.5	...	2 934	...	2 160	11.0	9.3	18.3	Fiji	+12
338 145	219	100	3.10	3 143	25.2	23 510	54.8	77.8	430.3	Finland	+2
543 965	153	100	3.30	3 575	173.8	22 010	57.4	60.5	263.8	France	+1
267 667	218	...	...	2 487	1.5	3 120	3.0	20.5	13.5	Gabon	+1
11 295	5	38.9	...	2 598	...	280	2.6	3.2	13.5	Gambia, The	GMT
69 700	30	100	3.88	2 347	2.0	650	15.9	5.4	4.6	Georgia	+4
357 022	107	100	3.30	3 411	246.0	22 670	63.5	68.3	364.3	Germany	+1
238 537	63	73.8	0.06	2 590	6.3	270	1.2	0.9	1.9	Ghana	GMT
131 957	36	97.4	4.40	3 689	20.1	11 660	52.9	75.1	132.1	Greece	+2
378	...	...	0.50	...	...	3 500	32.8	6.4	52.0	Grenada	-4
108 890	29	69.9	0.93	2 331	6.3	1 750	6.5	9.7	17.1	Guatemala	-6
245 857	69	...	...	2 133	...	410	0.3	0.7	1.9	Guinea	GMT
36 125	22	41	0.17	2 245	...	150	1.0	...	3.3	Guinea-Bissau	GMT
214 969	169	98.7	0.18	2 569	...	840	9.2	8.7	109.2	Guyana	-4
27 750	1	51.9	...	1 978	1.8	440	1.0	1.1	3.6	Haiti	-5
112 088	54	76.2	0.83	2 396	2.9	920	4.7	3.6	6.2	Honduras	-6
93 030	18	99.4	2.90	3 437	17.8	5 280	37.4	49.8	148.4	Hungary	+1
102 820	0	100	3.50	3 313	2.3	27 970	66.4	82.0	679.4	Iceland	GMT
3 064 898	641	58.8	...	2 417	379.7	480	3.4	0.6	6.8	India	+5$\frac{1}{2}$
1 919 445	1 050	87.9	...	2 931	117.5	710	3.7	2.5	18.6	Indonesia	+7 to +9
1 648 000	73	78.1	0.85	2 898	99.3	1 710	16.0	2.7	6.2	Iran	3$\frac{1}{2}$
438 317	8	40.1	0.55	2 446	23.2	...	...	...	...	Iraq	+3
70 282	7	100	2.40	3 649	11.7	23 870	48.5	72.9	233.1	Ireland	GMT
20 770	1	95.3	3.75	3 542	13.4	...	47.6	80.8	230.5	Israel	+2
301 245	100	98.6	4.30	3 629	134.1	18 960	47.1	83.9	275.8	Italy	+1
10 991	3	87.6	1.40	2 708	2.3	2 820	19.7	26.9	38.5	Jamaica	-5
377 727	241	100	1.90	2 782	342.1	33 550	59.7	58.8	454.7	Japan	+9
89 206	1	90.9	1.66	2 834	3.7	1 760	12.7	14.4	40.9	Jordan	+2
2 717 300	121	99.4	3.61	2 181	21.5	1 510	11.3	3.6	6.2	Kazakhstan	+4 to +6
582 646	171	84.3	...	1 886	11.0	360	1.0	1.6	16.0	Kenya	+3
717	...	...	0.30	...	...	810	4.0	0.5	25.0	Kiribati	+12 to +14
17 818	0	82.9	1.89	3 167	13.7	...	24.0	24.8	101.5	Kuwait	+3
198 500	10	...	2.60	2 833	1.6	290	7.7	0.5	10.6	Kyrgyzstan	+5
236 800	126	66.4	0.24	2 152	...	310	0.9	0.5	1.8	Laos	+7
63 700	29	99.8	2.91	2 904	3.7	3 480	30.8	27.9	72.3	Latvia	+2
10 452	0	86.9	2.10	3 256	4.0	3 990	19.5	21.3	85.8	Lebanon	+2
30 355	0	84.4	...	2 300	...	470	1.0	1.5	2.3	Lesotho	+2

, no data available

	Key Information		Population						
Flag	Country	Capital city	Population total 2003	Density persons per sq km 2003	Birth rate per 1000 population 2002	Death rate per 1000 population 2002	Life expectancy in years 2002	Population change average % per annum 2000-2005	Urban population % 2002
	Liberia	Monrovia	3 367 000	30	43	20	47	4.1	46
	Libya	Tripoli	5 551 000	3	27	4	72	1.9	88
	Liechtenstein	Vaduz	34 000	213	...	...	...	0.9	22
	Lithuania	Vilnius	3 444 000	53	10	12	73	-0.6	69
	Luxembourg	Luxembourg	453 000	175	12	10	77	1.3	92
	Macedonia	Skopje	2 056 000	80	13	9	73	0.5	60
	Madagascar	Antananarivo	17 404 000	30	39	12	55	2.8	31
	Malawi	Lilongwe	12 105 000	102	45	25	38	2.0	16
	Malaysia	Kuala Lumpur/Putrajaya	24 425 000	73	22	4	73	1.9	59
	Maldives	Male	318 000	1 067	29	6	69	3.0	29
	Mali	Bamako	13 007 000	10	46	21	41	3.0	32
	Malta	Valletta	394 000	1 247	12	8	78	0.4	91
	Marshall Islands	Dalap-Uliga-Darrit	53 000	293	...	...	...	1.2	66
	Mauritania	Nouakchott	2 893 000	3	40	15	51	3.0	60
	Mauritius	Port Louis	1 221 000	599	17	7	73	1.0	42
	Mexico	Mexico City	103 457 000	52	22	5	74	1.5	75
	Micronesia	Palikir	109 000	155	25	6	69	0.8	29
	Moldova	Chişinău	4 267 000	127	11	13	67	-0.1	42
	Mongolia	Ulan Bator	2 594 000	2	23	6	65	1.3	57
	Morocco	Rabat	30 566 000	68	21	6	68	1.6	57
	Mozambique	Maputo	18 863 000	24	40	21	41	1.8	34
	Myanmar	Yangôn	49 485 000	73	23	12	57	1.3	29
	Namibia	Windhoek	1 987 000	2	35	21	42	1.4	32
	Nepal	Kathmandu	25 164 000	171	32	10	60	2.2	13
	Netherlands	Amsterdam/The Hague	16 149 000	389	12	9	78	0.5	90
	New Zealand	Wellington	3 875 000	14	14	8	78	0.8	86
	Nicaragua	Managua	5 466 000	42	29	5	69	2.4	57
	Niger	Niamey	11 972 000	9	49	20	46	3.6	22
	Nigeria	Abuja	124 009 000	134	39	17	45	2.5	46
	North Korea	P'yŏngyang	22 664 000	188	18	11	62	0.5	61
	Norway	Oslo	4 533 000	14	13	10	79	0.4	75
	Oman	Muscat	2 851 000	9	26	3	74	2.9	77
	Pakistan	Islamabad	153 578 000	191	33	8	64	2.4	34
	Palau	Koror	20 000	40	...	...	...	2.1	70
	Panama	Panama City	3 120 000	40	20	5	75	1.8	57
	Papua New Guinea	Port Moresby	5 711 000	12	32	10	57	2.2	18
	Paraguay	Asunción	5 878 000	14	30	5	71	2.4	57
	Peru	Lima	27 167 000	21	22	6	70	1.5	74
	Philippines	Manila	79 999 000	267	26	6	70	1.8	60
	Poland	Warsaw	38 587 000	123	10	10	74	-0.1	63
	Portugal	Lisbon	10 062 000	113	11	11	76	0.1	67
	Qatar	Doha	610 000	53	14	4	75	1.5	93
	Romania	Bucharest	22 334 000	94	10	13	70	-0.2	56
	Russian Federation	Moscow	143 246 000	8	10	15	66	-0.6	73
	Rwanda	Kigali	8 387 000	318	44	22	40	2.2	6
	St Kitts & Nevis	Basseterre	42 000	161	17	11	71	-0.3	35
	St Lucia	Castries	149 000	242	19	6	72	0.8	38

Land		Education and Health			Development		Communications			Country	Time Zones + or - GMT
Area sq km	Forest '000 sq km 2000	Adult literacy % 2002	Doctors per 1000 population 1996-2002	Food intake calories per capita per day 1999	Energy consumption million tonnes of oil equivalent 2001	GNI per capita US$ 2002	Telephone lines per 100 population 2001	Cell phones per 100 population 2001	Internet connections per 1000 population 2001		
111 369	35	55.9	0.02	2 089	...	150	...	...	...	Liberia	GMT
1 759 540	4	81.7	1.28	3 277	10.8	...	10.9	0.9	3.6	Libya	+2
160	...	...	...	...	...	...	...	...	...	Liechtenstein	+1
65 200	20	99.6	4.03	2 959	4.6	3 660	31.3	25.3	67.9	Lithuania	+2
2 586	...	100	2.50	...	3.8	38 830	78.3	96.7	226.6	Luxembourg	+1
25 713	9	...	2.19	2 878	1.4	1 700	26.4	10.9	34.3	Macedonia	+1
587 041	117	68.1	0.14	1 994	...	240	0.4	0.9	2.1	Madagascar	+3
118 484	26	61.8	...	2 164	...	160	0.5	0.5	1.7	Malawi	+2
332 965	193	88.4	0.66	2 947	32.5	3 540	19.9	30.0	239.5	Malaysia	+8
298	...	97.2	...	...	...	2 090	10.1	6.8	37.0	Maldives	+5
1 240 140	132	27.2	0.06	2 314	...	240	0.4	0.4	2.6	Mali	GMT
316	...	96.6	2.91	...	0.4	...	53.0	35.4	252.6	Malta	+1
181	...	...	0.42	...	...	2 350	6.0	0.1	12.9	Marshall Islands	+12
1 030 700	3	41.2	...	2 703	...	410	0.7	0.3	2.6	Mauritania	GMT
2 040	...	85.3	...	...	...	3 850	25.6	25.0	131.7	Mauritius	+4
1 972 545	552	91.7	1.50	3 168	93.2	5 910	13.7	21.7	36.2	Mexico	-6 to -8
701	...	...	0.57	...	...	1 980	8.3	...	33.8	Micronesia	+10 to +11
33 700	3	99.1	2.71	2 728	1.4	460	15.4	4.8	13.7	Moldova	+2
1 565 000	106	98.5	2.43	1 963	...	440	4.8	7.6	15.6	Mongolia	+8
446 550	30	50.7	0.46	3 010	8.4	1 190	3.9	15.7	13.2	Morocco	GMT
799 380	306	46.5	...	1 939	6.5	210	0.4	0.8	0.7	Mozambique	+2
676 577	344	85.3	0.30	2 803	11.1	...	0.6	0.0	0.2	Myanmar	+6½
824 292	80	83.3	0.30	2 096	1.1	1 780	6.6	5.6	25.2	Namibia	+2
147 181	39	44	0.04	2 264	8.4	230	1.3	0.1	2.5	Nepal	5¾
41 526	4	100	3.30	3 243	60.3	23 960	62.1	73.9	329.2	Netherlands	+1
270 534	79	100	2.20	3 152	13.7	13 710	47.1	62.1	280.7	New Zealand	+12 to +12¾
130 000	33	67.1	0.86	2 314	2.2	...	3.1	3.0	9.9	Nicaragua	-6
1 267 000	13	17.1	0.03	2 064	...	170	0.2	0.0	1.1	Niger	+1
923 768	135	66.8	...	2 833	85.5	290	0.4	0.3	1.8	Nigeria	+1
120 538	82	...	...	2 100	17.6	...	...	...	...	North Korea	+9
323 878	89	100	3.00	3 425	21.2	37 850	72.0	82.5	596.3	Norway	+1
309 500	0	74.4	1.33	...	5.5	...	9.0	12.4	45.8	Oman	+4
803 940	24	44.9	0.57	2 462	52.1	410	2.4	0.6	3.5	Pakistan	+5
497	...	...	...	...	...	7 140	...	...	...	Palau	+9
77 082	29	92.3	...	2 496	1.9	4 020	14.8	20.7	31.7	Panama	-5
462 840	306	65.3	0.07	2 186	...	530	1.4	0.2	28.1	Papua New Guinea	+10
406 752	234	93.7	1.10	2 588	3.5	1 170	5.1	20.4	10.6	Paraguay	-4
1 285 216	652	90.5	0.93	2 621	10.6	2 050	7.8	5.9	115.0	Peru	-5
300 000	58	95.4	1.23	2 357	24.9	1 020	4.0	13.7	25.9	Philippines	+8
312 683	90	99.7	2.20	3 368	59.0	4 570	29.5	26.0	98.4	Poland	+1
88 940	37	92.9	3.20	3 768	19.6	10 840	42.7	77.4	349.4	Portugal	GMT
11 437	...	82.1	1.26	...	9.1	...	27.5	29.3	65.6	Qatar	+3
237 500	64	98.3	1.89	3 254	24.3	1 850	18.3	17.2	44.7	Romania	+2
17 075 400	8 514	99.6	4.20	2 879	427.5	2 140	24.3	3.8	29.3	Russian Federation	+2 to +12
26 338	3	69.2	...	2 011	...	230	0.3	0.8	2.5	Rwanda	+2
261	...	...	1.17	...	...	6 370	56.9	3.1	51.6	St Kitts & Nevis	-4
616	...	...	0.47	...	...	3 840	...	...	...	St Lucia	-4

. no data available

Flag	Country	Capital city	Population total 2003	Density persons per sq km 2003	Birth rate per 1000 population 2002	Death rate per 1000 population 2002	Life expectancy in years 2002	Population change average % per annum 2000-2005	Urban population % 2002
	St Vincent & the Grenadines	Kingstown	120 000	308	18	6	73	0.6	57
	Samoa	Apia	178 000	63	29	6	69	1.0	23
	São Tomé & Príncipe	São Tomé	161 000	167	31	9	66	2.5	48
	Saudi Arabia	Riyadh	24 217 000	11	32	4	73	2.9	87
	Senegal	Dakar	10 095 000	51	35	13	52	2.4	49
	Serbia & Montenegro	Belgrade	10 527 000	103	12	12	73	-0.1	52
	Seychelles	Victoria	81 000	178	19	7	73	0.9	65
	Sierra Leone	Freetown	4 971 000	69	44	25	37	3.8	38
	Singapore	Singapore	4 253 000	6 656	12	5	...	1.7	100
	Slovakia	Bratislava	5 402 000	110	11	10	73	0.1	58
	Slovenia	Ljubljana	1 984 000	98	9	10	76	-0.1	49
	Solomon Islands	Honiara	477 000	17	39	5	69	2.9	21
	Somalia	Mogadishu	9 890 000	16	50	17	47	4.2	28
	South Africa, Republic of	Pretoria/Cape Town	45 026 000	37	25	20	46	0.6	58
	South Korea	Seoul	47 700 000	480	12	7	74	0.6	83
	Spain	Madrid	41 060 000	81	10	10	78	0.2	78
	Sri Lanka	Sri Jayewardenepura Kotte	19 065 000	291	18	6	74	0.8	23
	Sudan	Khartoum	33 610 000	13	33	10	58	2.2	38
	Suriname	Paramaribo	436 000	3	21	6	70	0.8	75
	Swaziland	Mbabane	1 077 000	62	35	18	44	0.8	27
	Sweden	Stockholm	8 876 000	20	11	11	80	0.1	83
	Switzerland	Bern	7 169 000	174	9	9	80	-0.1	68
	Syria	Damascus	17 800 000	96	29	4	70	2.4	52
	Taiwan	T'aipei	22 548 000	623	...	...	...	...	...
	Tajikistan	Dushanbe	6 245 000	44	23	7	67	0.9	28
	Tanzania	Dodoma	36 977 000	39	38	18	43	1.9	34
	Thailand	Bangkok	62 833 000	122	15	8	69	1.0	20
	Togo	Lomé	4 909 000	86	34	15	50	2.3	35
	Tonga	Nuku'alofa	104 000	139	23	8	71	1.0	33
	Trinidad & Tobago	Port of Spain	1 303 000	254	16	7	72	0.3	75
	Tunisia	Tunis	9 832 000	60	18	6	73	1.1	67
	Turkey	Ankara	71 325 000	92	20	7	70	1.4	67
	Turkmenistan	Ashgabat	4 867 000	10	20	7	65	1.5	45
	Tuvalu	Vaiaku	11 000	440	...	...	...	1.2	...
	Uganda	Kampala	25 827 000	107	44	18	43	3.2	15
	Ukraine	Kiev	48 523 000	80	9	15	68	-0.8	68
	United Arab Emirates	Abu Dhabi	2 995 000	39	17	4	75	1.9	88
	United Kingdom	London	59 251 000	241	11	11	77	0.3	90
	United States of America	Washington	294 043 000	30	14	9	78	1.0	78
	Uruguay	Montevideo	3 415 000	19	16	10	75	0.7	92
	Uzbekistan	Tashkent	26 093 000	58	20	6	67	1.5	37
	Vanuatu	Port Vila	212 000	17	32	5	69	2.4	23
	Venezuela	Caracas	25 699 000	28	23	5	74	1.9	87
	Vietnam	Ha Nôi	81 377 000	247	19	6	70	1.4	25
	Yemen	Şan'ā'	20 010 000	38	41	10	57	3.5	25
	Zambia	Lusaka	10 812 000	14	39	23	37	1.2	40
	Zimbabwe	Harare	12 891 000	33	29	21	39	0.5	37

Land		Education and Health			Development		Communications				
Area sq km	Forest 'ooo sq km 2000	Adult literacy % 2002	Doctors per 1000 population 1996-2002	Food intake calories per capita per day 1999	Energy consumption million tonnes of oil equivalent 2001	GNI per capita US$ 2002	Telephone lines per 100 population 2001	Cell phones per 100 population 2001	Internet connections per 1000 population 2001	Country	Time Zones + or - GMT
389	...	...	0.88	...	...	2 820	22.0	2.1	30.9	St Vincent & the Grenadines	-4
2 831	...	98.7	0.34	...	...	1 420	5.6	1.7	16.7	Samoa	-11
964	...	...	0.47	...	...	290	3.6	...	60.0	São Tomé & Príncipe	GMT
2 200 000	15	77.9	1.66	2 953	68.5	...	14.5	11.3	13.4	Saudi Arabia	+3
196 720	62	39.3	0.10	2 307	2.4	470	2.5	4.0	10.4	Senegal	GMT
102 173	29	...	2.13	2 805	10.1	1 400	22.9	18.7	56.2	Serbia & Montenegro	+1
455	...	...	1.32	...	...	...	26.7	55.2	112.5	Seychelles	+4
71 740	11	...	0.07	2 017	...	140	0.5	0.6	1.4	Sierra Leone	GMT
639	0	92.8	1.63	...	10.6	20 690	47.1	72.4	605.2	Singapore	+8
49 035	22	100	3.60	3 101	11.7	3 950	28.8	39.7	120.3	Slovakia	+1
20 251	11	99.7	2.19	3 089	4.9	9 810	40.1	76.0	300.8	Slovenia	+1
28 370	25	...	...	2 222	...	570	1.6	0.2	4.3	Solomon Islands	+11
637 657	75	...	0.04	1 555	...	...	...	...	...	Somalia	+3
1 219 080	89	86	0.56	2 805	56.4	2 600	11.4	21.0	70.1	South Africa, Republic of	+2
99 274	62	98	1.40	3 073	130.3	9 930	47.6	60.8	510.7	South Korea	+9
504 782	144	97.8	3.30	3 353	93.3	14 430	43.1	65.5	182.8	Spain	+1
65 610	19	92.1	0.37	2 411	7.3	840	4.3	3.8	7.9	Sri Lanka	+6
2 505 813	616	59.9	0.09	2 360	9.1	350	1.4	0.3	1.8	Sudan	+3
163 820	141	...	0.25	2 604	...	1 960	17.6	19.1	33.0	Suriname	-3
17 364	...	80.9	0.15	...	...	1 180	3.1	6.5	13.7	Swaziland	+2
449 964	271	100	3.00	3 141	34.8	24 820	73.9	79.0	516.3	Sweden	+1
41 293	12	100	3.50	3 258	21.6	37 930	71.8	72.4	404.0	Switzerland	+1
185 180	5	76.1	1.30	3 272	13.5	1 130	10.9	1.2	3.6	Syria	+2
36 179	...	...	...	...	54.8	...	57.3	96.6	349.0	Taiwan	+8
143 100	4	99.3	2.12	1 927	2.7	180	3.6	0.0	0.5	Tajikistan	+5
945 087	388	77.1	...	1 940	12.4	280	0.4	1.2	8.3	Tanzania	+3
513 115	148	95.8	0.37	2 411	53.4	1 980	9.4	11.9	55.6	Thailand	+7
56 785	5	56.6	...	2 528	1.0	270	1.0	2.0	10.7	Togo	GMT
748	...	...	0.44	...	...	1 410	9.9	0.1	10.2	Tonga	+13
5 130	3	98.5	0.82	2 703	5.6	6 490	24.0	17.3	92.3	Trinidad & Tobago	-4
164 150	5	63.2	0.70	3 388	6.3	2 000	10.9	4.0	41.2	Tunisia	+1
779 452	102	86	1.30	3 469	51.8	2 500	28.5	30.2	37.7	Turkey	+2
488 100	38	...	3.00	2 746	9.8	1 200	8.0	0.2	1.7	Turkmenistan	+5
25	...	...	...	...	...	...	...	...	...	Tuvalu	+12
241 038	42	68.9	...	2 238	...	250	0.3	1.4	2.7	Uganda	+3
603 700	96	99.6	2.98	2 809	87.0	770	21.2	4.4	11.9	Ukraine	+2
77 700	3	77.3	1.81	3 182	19.2	...	39.7	72.0	339.2	United Arab Emirates	+4
243 609	28	100	2.00	3 318	161.4	25 250	58.8	78.3	399.5	United Kingdom	GMT
9 826 635	2 260	100	2.70	3 754	1 540.6	35 060	66.5	44.4	499.5	United States	-5 to -10
176 215	13	97.7	...	2 862	2.4	4 370	28.3	15.5	119.0	Uruguay	-3
447 400	20	99.3	2.93	2 871	37.8	450	6.6	0.3	5.9	Uzbekistan	+5
12 190	...	...	0.12	...	...	1 080	3.4	0.2	27.4	Vanuatu	+11
912 050	495	93.1	2.36	2 229	37.0	4 090	11.2	26.4	52.8	Venezuela	-4
329 565	98	92.9	0.48	2 564	35.3	430	3.8	1.5	4.9	Vietnam	+7
527 968	4	49	0.20	2 002	2.9	490	2.2	0.8	0.9	Yemen	+3
752 614	312	79.9	...	1 934	5.1	330	0.8	0.9	2.4	Zambia	+2
390 759	190	90	...	2 076	8.3	...	1.9	2.4	7.3	Zimbabwe	+2

no data available

How to use the Index

All the names on the maps in this atlas, except some of those on the special topic maps, are included in the index.

The names are arranged in **alphabetical order.** Where the name has more than one word the separate words are considered as one to decide the position of the name in the index:

Thetford
Thetford Mines
The Trossachs
The Wash
The Weald
Thiers

Where there is more than one place with the same name, the country name is used to decide the order:

London Canada
London England

If both places are in the same country, the county or state name is also used:

Avon *r.* Bristol England
Avon *r.* Dorset England

Each entry in the index starts with the name of the place or feature, followed by the name of the country or region in which it is located. This is followed by the number of the most appropriate page on which the name appears, usually the largest scale map. Next comes the alphanumeric reference followed by the latitude and longitude.

Names of physical features such as rivers, capes, mountains etc are followed by a description. The descriptions are usually shortened to one or two letters, these abbreviations are keyed below. Town names are followed by a description only when the name may be confused with that of a physical feature:

Big Spring *town*

To help to distinguish the different parts of each entry, different styles of type are used:

place name   country name   alphanumeric
           or   grid reference
     region name

description   page   latitude/
(if any)   number   longitude

Thames   *r.*   England   **11 F2**   51.27N 0.21E

To use the **alphanumeric grid reference** to find a feature on the map, first find the correct page and then look at the coloured letters printed outside the frame along the top, bottom and sides of the map.
When you have found the correct letter and number follow the grid boxes up and along until you find the correct grid box in which the feature appears. You must then search the grid box until you find the name of the feature.

The **latitude and longitude reference** gives a more exact description of the position of the feature.

Page 6 of the atlas describes lines of latitude and lines of longitude, and explains how they are numbered and divided into degrees and minutes. Each name in the index has a different latitude and longitude reference, so the feature can be located accurately. The lines of latitude and lines of longitude shown on each map are numbered in degrees. These numbers are printed in black along the top, bottom and sides of the map frame.

The drawing above shows part of the map on page 41 and the lines of latitude and lines of longitude.

The index entry for Wexford is given as follows

Wexford   Rep. of Ire.   **41 E2**   52.20N 6.28W

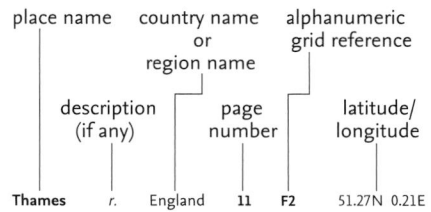

To locate Wexford, first find latitude 52N and estimate 20 minutes north from 52 degrees to find 52.20N, then find longitude 6W and estimate 28 minutes west from 6 degrees to find 6.28W. The symbol for the town of Wexford is where latitude 52.20N and longitude 6.28W meet.

On maps at a smaller scale than the map of Ireland, it is not possible to show every line of latitude and longitude. Only every 5 or 10 degrees of latitude and longitude may be shown. On these maps you must estimate the degrees and minutes to find the exact location of a feature.

Abbreviations

A. and B	Argyll and Bute
Afgh.	Afghanistan
Ala.	Alabama
Ang.	Angus
b.	bay
Baja Calif.	Baja California
Bangl.	Bangladesh
Bos.-Herz.	Bosnia-Herzegovina
Brist.	Bristol
c.	cape
Cambs.	Cambridgeshire
C.A.R.	Central African Republic
Colo.	Colorado
Corn.	Cornwall
Cumb.	Cumbria
Czech Rep.	Czech Republic
d.	internal division e.g. county, state
Del.	Delaware
Dem. Rep. Congo	Democratic Republic of Congo
Derbys.	Derbyshire
des.	desert
Dev.	Devon
Dom. Rep.	Dominican Republic
Don.	Donegal
Dor.	Dorset
Dur.	Durham
Equat. Guinea	Equatorial Guinea
Ess.	Essex
est.	estuary
E. Sussex	East Sussex
E. Yorks.	East Riding of Yorkshire
f.	physical feature, e.g. valley, plain, geographic area
Falk.	Falkirk
for.	forest
g.	gulf
Ga.	Georgia
Glos.	Gloucestershire
Hants.	Hampshire
High.	Highland
hd	headland

i.	island
Ill.	Illinois
I. o. W.	Isle of Wight
is	islands
l.	lake
La.	Louisiana
Lancs.	Lancashire
Leics.	Leicestershire
Lincs.	Lincolnshire
Lux.	Luxembourg
Man.	Manitoba
Mass.	Massachusetts
Me.	Maine
Mich.	Michigan
Minn.	Minnesota
Miss.	Mississippi
Mo.	Missouri
Mor.	Moray
mt.	mountain
mts	mountains
N. Africa	North Africa
N. America	North America
N. Atlantic Oc.	North Atlantic Ocean
nat. park	National Park
nature res.	Nature Reserve
N. C.	North Carolina
Neth.	Netherlands
Neth. Antilles	Netherlands Antilles
Nev.	Nevada
New.	Newport
Nfld. and Lab.	Newfoundland and Labrador
N. Korea	North Korea
N. M.	New Mexico
N. Mariana Is	Northern Marianas Islands
Norf.	Norfolk
Northum.	Northumberland
Notts.	Nottinghamshire
N. Pacific Oc.	North Pacific Ocean
N. Y.	New York
Oh.	Ohio
Oreg.	Oregon
Orkn.	Orkney
Oxon.	Oxfordshire

Pacific Oc.	Pacific Ocean
P. and K.	Perth and Kinross
P'boro.	Peterborough
Pem.	Pembrokeshire
pen.	peninsula
P.N.G.	Papua New Guinea
pt	point
r.	river
r. mouth	river mouth
Rep. of Ireland	Republic of Ireland
resr	reservoir
Rus. Fed.	Russian Federation
S. Africa	South Africa
S. America	South America
S. Atlantic Oc.	South Atlantic Ocean
S. C.	South Carolina
S. China Sea	South China Sea
Shetl.	Shetland
S. Korea	South Korea
S.M.	Serbia and Montenegro
Som.	Somerset
Southern Oc.	Southern Ocean
S. Pacific Oc.	South Pacific Ocean
str.	strait
Suff.	Suffolk
Switz.	Switzerland
T. and W.	Tyne and Wear
Tel. Wre.	Telford and Wrekin
Tex.	Texas
Tipp.	Tipperary
U.A.E.	United Arab Emirates
U.K.	United Kingdom
U.S.A.	United States of America
Va.	Virginia
vol.	volcano
Vt.	Vermont
Water.	Waterford
Warwicks.	Warwickshire
Wick.	Wicklow
W. Isles	Western Isles
W. Va.	West Virginia
Wyo.	Wyoming

Index 145

r. France 11 H2 ....51.00N 2.07E
benraa Denmark 40 B1 ....55.02N 9.25E
chen Germany 54 B4 ....50.46N 6.05E
lborg Denmark 40 B2 ....57.03N 9.55E
len Germany 54 D3 ....48.50N 10.06E
lst Belgium 42 D3 ....50.56N 4.03E
ädån Iran 95 G6 ....30.20N 48.15E
ädeh Iran 95 H6 ....31.08N 52.36E
adla Algeria 84 D5 ....31.00N 2.43W
akan Rus. Fed. 59 K3 ......53.42N 91.25E
ancay Peru 76 F5 ....13.39S 72.52W
arqü Iran 95 H6 ....31.06N 53.13E
ashiri Japan 106 D4 ......44.01N 144.15E
aya, Lake Ethiopia 85 H2 ....6.19N 37.53E
aza Rus. Fed. 102 G8 ......52.40N 90.06E
beville France 44 D7 ....50.06N 1.50E
beyfeale Rep. of Ireland 41 B2 ...52.23N 9.18W
bey Head Scotland 17 F2 ....54.46N 3.58W
beyleix Rep. of Ireland 41 D2 ...52.55N 7.21W
bottabad Pakistan 95 L6 .....34.13N 73.17E
éché Chad 85 G3 ....13.50N 20.49E
eokuta Nigeria 84 E2 ....7.07N 3.18E
eraeron Wales 12 C4 ......52.15N 4.15W
erchirder Scotland 19 G2 ....57.34N 2.38W
erdare Wales 12 D3 ....51.43N 3.27W
erdare Range mts Kenya 87 B2 ...0.21S 36.19E
erdaron Wales 12 C4 ......52.48N 4.43W
erdeen Scotland 19 G2 .....57.09N 2.06W
erdeen d. Scotland 8 D5 ....57.10N 2.11W
erdeenshire d. Scotland 8 D5 ...57.21N 2.32W
erfeldy Scotland 19 F1 .....56.37N 3.52W
erford England 15 F2 ......53.50N 1.21W
erfoyle Scotland 16 E4 .....56.11N 4.23W
ergavenny Wales 12 D3 ....51.49N 3.01W
ergele Wales 12 D5 ......53.17N 3.35W
erlour Scotland 19 F2 ......57.29N 3.13W
erporth Wales 12 C4 ......52.08N 4.33W
ersoch Wales 12 C4 ......52.50N 4.30W
ertillery Wales 12 D3 ......51.44N 3.08W
erystwyth Wales 12 C4 ....52.25N 4.05W
hä Saudi Arabia 94 F3 .....18.14N 42.27E
idjan Côte d'Ivoire 84 D2 ....5.21N 4.02W
ilene U.S.A. 64 G3 ....32.26N 99.45W
ingdon England 10 D2 .....51.40N 1.17W
ington Scotland 17 F3 ......55.30N 3.41W
itibi, Lake Canada 65 J6 ....48.55N 80.01W
oyne Scotland 19 G2 ......57.05N 2.47W
qaiq Saudi Arabia 95 G5 ....25.56N 49.42E
rolhos Bank f. S. Atlantic Oc. 109 R4 ...19.28S 38.59W
ü 'Arïsh Saudi Arabia 94 F3 ...16.59N 42.45E
u Dhabi U.A.E. 95 H4 ......24.28N 54.20E
u Hamed Sudan 85 H3 .....19.30N 33.24E
uja Nigeria 84 E2 ....9.06N 7.19E
ü Kamãl Syria 94 F7 ....34.26N 40.56E
unã r. Bolivia 76 G6 ....9.43S 65.26W
unã Brazil 76 G6 ....9.44S 65.20W
ü Nujaym Libya 53 G3 .....30.28N 15.27E
ü Sunbul Egypt 94 D4 .....22.26N 31.39E
yad Sudan 94 C2 ....13.46N 26.26E
Cañiza Spain 48 A5 ....42.13N 8.16W
caponeta Mexico 70 C5 .....22.30N 105.25W
apulco Mexico 70 E4 ....16.55N 99.52W
ariguá Venezuela 72 C7 .....9.33N 69.11W
cra Ghana 84 D2 ....5.35N 0.14W
ccrington England 15 E2 .....53.45N 2.22W
cheloös r. Greece 56 D4 ....38.20N 21.06E
chill Island Rep. of Ireland 41 A3 ...53.56N 10.00W
chinsk Rus. Fed. 59 K3 .....56.17N 90.34E
Chralaig mt. Scotland 18 D2 ...57.11N 5.09W
cklins Island Bahamas 71 J5 ...22.18N 74.08W
cle England 11 J3 ....52.38N 1.33E
concagua, Cerro mt. Argentina 73 B3 ...32.38S 70.01W
Coruña Spain 48 A5 ....43.22N 8.23W
re d. Brazil 76 F6 ....9.06S 70.25W
cre r. Brazil 76 G5 ....10.07S 67.52W
ctéon, Groupe is French Polynesia 109 K4 ...21.20S 135.57W
daja r. Spain 48 C4 ....41.33N 4.51W
dam's Peak Sri Lanka 96 F2 ...6.49N 80.28E
dana Turkey 57 K5 ....36.59N 35.19E
dapazarı Turkey 57 I5 ......40.47N 30.23E
la Terra Ethiopia 87 C4 .....6.37N 40.56E
dda r. Italy 50 C6 ....45.08N 9.53E
d Dahnã' des. Saudi Arabia 95 G5 ...20.40N 46.52E
d Dakhla Western Sahara 84 C4 ...23.42N 15.56W
dderbury England 10 D3 .....52.01N 1.19W
d Dir'iyah Saudi Arabia 95 G4 ...24.45N 46.34E
ddis Ababa Ethiopia 85 H2 ....9.01N 38.45E
d Dïwänïyah Iraq 94 F6 .....31.59N 44.59E
delaide Australia 110 C3 ....34.56S 138.40E
den Yemen 94 F2 ....12.49N 44.59E
den, Gulf of Somalia/Yemen 85 I3 ...11.44N 45.16E
di i. Indonesia 105 J3 ......4.15S 133.27E
dï Ark'ay Ethiopia 94 E2 ....13.24N 38.03E
dige r. Italy 50 E6 ....45.08N 12.18E
digrat Ethiopia 94 E2 ......14.16N 39.29E
dilanga Ethiopia 87 A3 .....2.43N 33.28E
di Ugri Eritrea 94 E2 ......14.52N 38.48E
diyaman Turkey 57 M3 .....37.46N 38.17E
dmiralty Islands P.N.G. 110 D6 ...1.44S 146.17E
dour r. France 44 C3 ......43.32N 1.31W
driatic Sea Europe 50 E6 ....44.19N 13.24E
dwa Ethiopia 85 H3 ....14.09N 38.52E
dwick le Street England 15 F2 ...53.34N 1.12W
dycha r. Rus. Fed. 59 O4 ....66.42N 136.32E
egean Sea Greece/Turkey 56 F4 ...39.00N 24.51E
ghanistan Asia 95 K6 ......33.53N 65.52E
madow Somalia 87 C3 .....0.32N 42.04E
frica 82
fyon Turkey 57 I4 ....38.46N 30.33E
gadez Niger 84 E3 ....16.57N 7.59E
gadir Morocco 84 D5 ......30.27N 9.37W
gano r. Japan 106 C3 ......37.58N 139.02E
gartala India 97 H5 ....23.50N 91.16E
gde France 44 E3 ....43.18N 3.28E
gen France 44 D4 ....44.12N 0.38E
gere Maryam Ethiopia 87 B4 ...5.38N 38.13E
gios Dimitrios Greece 56 E3 ...37.49N 23.51E
gios Efstratios i. Greece 56 F4 ...39.30N 25.01E
gios Konstantinos Greece 56 E4 ...38.45N 22.51E
gios Nikolaos Greece 56 F2 ...35.12N 25.43E
girwat Hills Sudan 94 E3 ....16.26N 35.03E
gra India 96 E6 ....27.09N 78.02E
gri Turkey 94 F7 ....39.43N 43.04E
grigento mt. Italy 50 E3 ....37.18N 13.35E
grihan i. N. Mariana Is 105 L7 ...18.46N 145.42E
guadulce Panama 71 H2 ....8.12N 80.33W
guascalientes Mexico 70 D5 ...21.51N 102.21W
guascalientes d. Mexico 70 D5 ...21.57N 102.11W
guilar de Campóo Spain 48 C5 ...42.47N 4.14W
guilas Spain 48 E2 ....37.25N 1.35W

Agulhas, Cape S. Africa 86 B1 ...34.50S 20.03E
Ahar Iran 95 G7 ...38.27N 47.02E
Ahaus Germany 42 G5 ...52.05N 7.01E
Ahmadabad India 96 D5 ...23.03N 72.37E
Ahmadpur East Pakistan 96 D6 ...29.10N 71.22E
Ahväz Iran 95 G6 ...31.15N 48.40E
Aigialousa Cyprus 57 K2 ...35.31N 34.11E
Aigina i. Greece 56 E3 ...37.41N 23.31E
Ailsa Craig i. Scotland 16 D3 ...55.15N 5.06W
Aïn Beïda Algeria 52 E4 ...35.47N 7.25E
'Aïn Ben Tili Mauritania 84 D4 ...25.58N 9.31W
Aïn Sefra Algeria 84 D5 ...32.42N 0.35W
Aïr, Massif de l' mts Niger 84 E3 ...18.46N 8.15E
Airdrie Canada 62 G3 ...51.17N 114.01W
Airdrie Scotland 17 F3 ...55.52N 3.58W
Aisne r. France 44 E6 ...49.26N 2.51E
Aitape P.N.G. 105 K3 ...3.09S 142.22E
Aitutaki i. Cook Is 109 J4 ...18.52S 159.44W
Aix-en-Provence France 44 F3 ...43.32N 5.27E
Aizkraukle Latvia 55 K7 ...56.36N 25.15E
Aizu-wakamatsu Japan 106 C3 ...37.29N 139.56E
Ajaccio France 44 H2 ...41.55N 8.44E
Ajdäbïyä Libya 85 G5 ...30.45N 20.13E
Akçakale Turkey 57 M3 ...36.43N 38.57E
Akdağmadeni Turkey 57 K4 ...39.39N 35.54E
Akhdar, Al Jabal al mts Libya 53 H3 ...31.46N 20.46E
Akhdar, Jabal mts Oman 95 I4 ...23.22N 57.00E
Akhisar Turkey 57 G4 ...38.55N 27.50E
Akimiski Island Canada 63 J3 ...53.08N 81.17W
Akita Japan 106 D3 ...39.43N 140.07E
Akkajaure l. Sweden 40 D4 ...67.41N 17.29E
Aknoul Morocco 48 D1 ...34.38N 3.51W
Akordat Eritrea 85 H3 ...15.31N 37.54E
Akpatok Island Canada 63 L4 ...60.24N 67.45W
Akranes Iceland 40 X2 ...64.19N 22.05W
Akron U.S.A. 65 J5 ...41.07N 81.33W
Aksai Chin Asia 96 E8 ...35.08N 79.11E
Aksaray Turkey 57 K4 ...38.23N 34.02E
Akşehir Turkey 57 I4 ...38.21N 31.24E
Aksu China 102 E6 ...41.06N 80.21E
Äksum Ethiopia 94 E2 ...14.07N 38.46E
Aktau Kazakhstan 58 G2 ...43.39N 51.12E
Aktobe Kazakhstan 58 G3 ...50.13N 57.10E
Aktogay Kazakhstan 58 I2 ...47.06N 79.42E
Akureyri Iceland 40 Y2 ...65.41N 18.07W
Alabama d. U.S.A. 65 I3 ...32.41N 86.42W
Alabama r. U.S.A. 65 I3 ...31.09N 87.57W
Alagoas d. Brazil 77 M6 ...9.33S 36.46W
Alagoinhas Brazil 77 M5 ...12.07S 38.17W
Al Ahmadï Kuwait 95 G5 ...29.04N 48.02E
Alakol', Ozero l. Kazakhstan 102 E7 ...46.03N 81.30E
Alakurtti Rus. Fed. 40 G4 ...66.58N 30.20E
Alamagan i. N. Mariana Is 105 L7 ...17.35N 145.52E
Åland Islands Finland 40 D3 ...60.28N 19.53E
Alanya Turkey 57 J3 ...36.33N 32.00E
Al 'Aqabah Jordan 94 E5 ...29.31N 35.01E
Al Artäwïyah Saudi Arabia 95 G5 ...26.30N 45.21E
Alaşehir Turkey 57 H4 ...38.21N 28.30E
Alaska d. U.S.A. 62 D4 ...63.41N 143.49W
Alaska, Gulf of U.S.A. 62 D3 ...58.10N 147.57W
Alaska Peninsula U.S.A. 62 C3 ...55.18N 162.25W
Alaska Range mts U.S.A. 62 D4 ...63.19N 148.01W
Alausí Ecuador 76 E7 ...2.10S 78.52W
Alavus Finland 40 E3 ...62.35N 23.36E
Alaw, Llyn resr Wales 12 C5 ...53.21N 4.25W
Albacete Spain 48 E3 ...39.00N 1.50W
Alba Iulia Romania 56 E8 ...46.05N 23.36E
Albania Europe 56 C5 ...41.06N 19.34E
Albany Australia 110 A3 ...34.58S 117.54E
Albany r. Canada 63 J3 ...52.08N 81.59W
Albany U.S.A. 65 L5 ...42.40N 73.46W
Albatross Bay Australia 105 K1 ...12.41S 141.44E
Al Bawïtï Egypt 85 G4 ...28.21N 28.50E
Al Bayda' Libya 85 G5 ...32.44N 21.44E
Albenga Italy 50 C6 ...44.03N 8.13E
Alberche r. Spain 48 C3 ...39.58N 4.46W
Albert France 42 B2 ...49.59N 2.39E
Albert, Lake Dem. Rep. Congo/Uganda 86 C5 ...1.43N 30.52E
Alberta d. Canada 62 G3 ...52.45N 113.59W
Albert Lea U.S.A. 65 H5 ...43.39N 93.22W
Albert Nile r. Sudan/Uganda 85 H2 ...3.36N 32.02E
Albi France 44 E3 ...43.56N 2.08E
Al Biyädh f. Saudi Arabia 95 G4 ...20.57N 46.14E
Alborán, Isla de i. Spain 48 D1 ...35.57N 3.02W
Albuquerque U.S.A. 64 E4 ...35.07N 106.38W
Al Buraymï Oman 95 I4 ...24.14N 55.46E
Albury Australia 110 D3 ...36.03S 146.54E
Alcalá de Henares Spain 48 D4 ...40.29N 3.21W
Alcalá la Real Spain 48 D2 ...37.28N 3.55W
Alcañiz Spain 48 E4 ...41.03N 0.07W
Alcázar de San Juan Spain 48 D3 ...39.23N 3.11W
Alcester England 10 D3 ...52.13N 1.52W
Alcoy-Alcoi Spain 48 E3 ...38.42N 0.27W
Alcúdia Spain 48 G3 ...39.52N 3.08E
Aldabra Islands Seychelles 85 I1 ...9.16S 46.30E
Aldan Rus. Fed. 59 N4 ...58.36N 125.28E
Aldan r. Rus. Fed. 59 N4 ...63.32N 128.46E
Aldbrough England 15 G2 ...53.50N 0.07W
Aldeburgh England 11 G3 ...52.09N 1.36E
Alderley Edge England 15 E2 ...53.18N 2.15W
Alderney i. Channel Is 13 Z9 ...49.42N 2.15W
Aldershot England 10 E2 ...51.15N 0.45W
Aldingham England 14 D3 ...54.08N 3.06W
Aldridge England 10 D3 ...52.36N 1.55W
Aleksandrovsk-Sakhalinskiy Rus. Fed. 59 P3 ...51.08N 142.21E
Aleksin Rus. Fed. 55 Q6 ...54.31N 37.05E
Alençon France 44 D6 ...48.26N 0.06E
Aleppo Syria 94 E7 ...36.12N 37.09E
Alès France 44 F4 ...44.08N 4.05E
Aleşd Romania 46 F1 ...47.03N 22.25E
Alessandria Italy 50 C6 ...44.55N 8.38E
Ålesund Norway 40 A3 ...62.28N 6.12E
Aleutian Basin f. Bering Sea 108 H9 ...57.54N 179.12E
Aleutian Islands U.S.A. 62 A3 ...53.03N 176.15W
Aleutian Range mts U.S.A. 62 C3 ...56.10N 159.17W
Aleutian Trench f. N. Pacific Oc. 108 I9 ...49.44N 178.54W
Alexander Archipelago is U.S.A. 62 E3 ...57.59N 137.33W
Alexandra, Cape S. Atlantic Oc. 73 F1 ...54.05S 37.58W
Alexandria Egypt 85 G5 ...31.13N 29.56E
Alexandria Romania 56 F6 ...43.58N 25.20E
Alexandria Scotland 16 E3 ...55.59N 4.35W
Alexandria La. U.S.A. 65 H3 ...31.17N 92.28W
Alexandria Va. U.S.A. 65 K4 ...38.48N 77.05W
Alexandroupoli Greece 56 F5 ...40.51N 25.53E
Aleysk Rus. Fed. 102 E8 ...52.30N 82.51E
Al Fayyum Egypt 85 H4 ...29.18N 30.51E
Alford England 15 H2 ...53.15N 0.10E
Alfreton England 15 F2 ...53.06N 1.23W
Algarve f. Portugal 48 A2 ...37.16N 8.07W
Algeciras Spain 48 C2 ...36.07N 5.27W
Algeria Africa 84 E4 ...30.15N 3.31E
Al Ghaydah Yemen 95 H3 ...16.14N 52.13E
Al Ghurdaqah Egypt 53 J2 ...27.12N 33.48E

Al Ghwaybiyah Saudi Arabia 95 G5 ...25.14N 49.43E
Algiers Algeria 84 E5 ...36.46N 3.04E
Algorta Spain 48 D5 ...43.21N 2.59W
Al Hasakah Syria 94 F7 ...36.30N 40.44E
Al Hibäk des. Saudi Arabia 95 H3 ...19.30N 52.27E
Al Hoceima Morocco 52 C4 ...35.15N 3.56W
Al Hufüf Saudi Arabia 95 G5 ...25.22N 49.35E
Aliağa Turkey 56 G4 ...38.47N 26.58E
Aliakmonas r. Greece 56 E5 ...40.28N 22.38E
Äli Bayramlï Azerbaijan 95 G7 ...39.56N 48.56E
Alicante Spain 48 E3 ...38.21N 0.28W
Alice Springs town Australia 110 C4 ...23.42S 133.52E
Al Ismä'ïlïyah Egypt 53 J3 ...30.35N 32.17E
Al Jaghbüb Libya 85 G4 ...29.43N 24.31E
Al Jahrah Kuwait 95 G5 ...29.20N 47.41E
Al Jawf Libya 85 G4 ...24.14N 23.24E
Al Jawf Saudi Arabia 94 E5 ...29.47N 39.55E
Al Jawsh Libya 52 F3 ...32.01N 11.42E
Al Jubayl Saudi Arabia 95 G5 ...27.00N 49.38E
Aljustrel Portugal 48 A2 ...37.53N 8.10W
Al Karak Jordan 94 E6 ...31.10N 35.42E
Al Khäbürah Oman 95 I4 ...23.58N 57.06E
Al Khärijah Egypt 85 H4 ...25.25N 30.31E
Al Khasab Oman 95 I5 ...26.11N 56.14E
Al Khums Libya 52 F3 ...32.35N 14.22E
Alkmaar Neth. 42 D5 ...52.38N 4.45E
Al Küt Iraq 95 G6 ...32.31N 45.47E
Allahabad India 96 F6 ...25.25N 81.52E
Allakh-Yun' Rus. Fed. 59 O4 ...60.35N 138.03E
Allegheny r. U.S.A. 65 K5 ...40.27N 79.59W
Allegheny Mountains U.S.A. 65 J4 ...36.46N 82.22W
Allen, Lough l. Rep. of Ireland 41 C4 ...54.09N 8.03W
Allendale Town England 15 E3 ...54.54N 2.15W
Allentown U.S.A. 65 K5 ...40.37N 75.30W
Alleppey India 96 E2 ...9.30N 76.21E
Aller r. Germany 54 D5 ...52.57N 9.11E
Allinge-Sandvig Denmark 46 B5 ...55.16N 14.49E
Al Lïth Saudi Arabia 94 F4 ...20.10N 40.16E
Alloa Scotland 17 F4 ...56.07N 3.47W
Almansa Spain 48 E3 ...38.52N 1.05W
Al Mansürah Egypt 53 J3 ...31.02N 31.23E
Almanzor mt. Spain 48 C4 ...40.15N 5.18W
Al Marj Libya 85 G4 ...32.29N 20.50E
Almaty Kazakhstan 58 I2 ...43.16N 77.01E
Almeirim Brazil 77 J7 ...1.30S 52.35W
Almendra, Embalse de resr Spain 48 B4 ...41.17N 6.14W
Almería Spain 48 D2 ...36.50N 2.27W
Almina, Punta pt Spain 48 C1 ...35.54N 5.16W
Al Minyä Egypt 85 H4 ...28.03N 30.45E
Almodôvar Portugal 48 A2 ...37.31N 8.04W
Almond r. Scotland 17 F4 ...56.25N 3.28W
Al Mudawwara Jordan 94 E5 ...29.19N 36.02E
Almuñécar Spain 48 D2 ...36.44N 3.41W
Alnwick England 15 F4 ...55.25N 1.42W
Alofi Niue 108 I4 ...19.03S 169.54W
Aloi Uganda 87 A3 ...2.16N 33.09E
Alor i. Indonesia 105 G2 ...8.17S 124.45E
Alor Setar Malaysia 104 C5 ...6.08N 100.22E
Alpena U.S.A. 65 J6 ...45.03N 83.27W
Alpine U.S.A. 64 F3 ...30.18N 103.35W
Alps mts Europe 52 F6 ...46.00N 7.30E
Al Qa'ämïyät f. Saudi Arabia 95 G3 ...17.59N 47.47E
Al Qaddähïyah Libya 52 G3 ...31.22N 15.12E
Al Qämishlï Syria 94 F7 ...37.03N 41.13E
Al Qaryatayn Syria 57 L2 ...34.13N 37.14E
Al Qunfidhah Saudi Arabia 94 F3 ...19.09N 41.04E
Al Quşayr Egypt 85 H4 ...26.07N 34.13E
Alsace d. France 42 G1 ...48.22N 7.24E
Alsager England 15 E2 ...53.06N 2.18W
Alston England 15 E3 ...54.49N 2.26W
Altaelva r. Norway 40 E5 ...69.57N 23.20E
Altai Mountains Asia 102 F7 ...48.55N 87.16E
Altamira Brazil 77 J7 ...3.14S 52.14W
Altamura Italy 50 G4 ...40.49N 16.34E
Altay China 102 F7 ...47.48N 88.10E
Altay Mongolia 102 H7 ...46.18N 96.15E
Altiplano f. Bolivia 76 G4 ...16.24S 69.39W
Altiplano Mexicano f. N. America 60 I5 ...24.00N 105.00W
Alton England 10 E2 ...51.09N 0.58W
Altoona U.S.A. 65 K5 ...40.30N 78.24W
Altötting Germany 54 E3 ...48.14N 12.41E
Altrincham England 15 E2 ...53.23N 2.21W
Altun Shan mts China 102 F5 ...37.45N 86.38E
Al 'Uqaylah Libya 53 G3 ...30.13N 19.12E
Al 'Uwaynät Libya 94 B4 ...21.46N 24.51E
Älvdalen Sweden 40 C3 ...61.13N 14.04E
Alveley England 10 C3 ...52.27N 2.21W
Älvsborn Sweden 40 E4 ...65.40N 21.00E
Al Wajh Saudi Arabia 94 E5 ...26.17N 36.25E
Alwen Reservoir Wales 12 D5 ...53.05N 3.35W
Al Widyän f. Iraq/Saudi Arabia 94 F6 ...32.09N 40.22E
Alyth Scotland 19 F1 ...56.38N 3.14W
Alytus Lithuania 46 G5 ...54.24N 24.03E
Amadeus, Lake Australia 110 C4 ...24.50S 131.09E
Amadjuak Lake Canada 63 K4 ...64.57N 71.09W
Amadora Portugal 48 A3 ...38.46N 9.14W
Åmål Sweden 40 C2 ...59.03N 12.44E
Amamapare Indonesia 105 J3 ...4.54S 136.58E
Amami-Ō-shima i. Japan 106 A1 ...28.13N 129.08E
Amapá Brazil 77 J8 ...2.02N 50.50W
Amapá d. Brazil 77 J8 ...1.29N 51.50W
Amasra Turkey 57 J5 ...41.45N 32.23E
Amasya Turkey 57 K5 ...40.39N 35.50E
Amazon r. S. America 72 D7 ...0.01N 50.37W
Amazon, Mouths of the Brazil 77 K8 ...0.41N 49.28W
Amazonas d. Brazil 76 G7 ...4.48S 64.00W
Ambarchik Rus. Fed. 59 R4 ...69.35N 162.13E
Ambato Ecuador 76 E7 ...1.16S 78.39W
Ambergate England 15 F2 ...53.04N 1.29W
Ambergris Cay i. Belize 70 G4 ...18.08N 87.52W
Amble England 15 F4 ...55.20N 1.35W
Ambleside England 14 E3 ...54.26N 2.58W
Ambon Indonesia 105 H3 ...3.43S 128.11E
Amboseli National Park Kenya 87 B2 ...2.37S 37.14E
Ambrym i. Vanuatu 111 F5 ...16.12S 168.13E
Ameland i. Neth. 42 E6 ...53.28N 5.48E
American Samoa is S. Pacific Oc. 108 I5 ...12.00S 170.00W
Amersfoort Neth. 42 E5 ...52.09N 5.23E
Amersham England 11 E2 ...51.41N 0.36W
Amesbury England 10 D2 ...51.10N 1.47W
Amga r. Rus. Fed. 59 N4 ...62.38N 134.20E
Amgun' r. Rus. Fed. 59 O3 ...53.01N 139.38E
Amiens France 44 E6 ...49.54N 2.18E
Amino Ethiopia 87 C4 ...4.21N 41.63E
Amlwch Wales 12 C5 ...53.25N 4.21W
Ammanford Wales 12 D3 ...51.48N 3.59W
Amol Iran 95 H7 ...36.27N 52.20E
Amorgos i. Greece 56 F3 ...36.49N 25.54E
Amos Canada 63 K2 ...48.34N 78.08W

Ampthill England 11 E3 ...52.02N 0.30W
Amravati India 96 E5 ...20.56N 77.51E
Amritsar India 96 D7 ...31.34N 74.56E
Amstelveen Neth. 42 D5 ...52.19N 4.52E
Amsterdam Neth. 42 D5 ...52.23N 4.54E
Amstetten Austria 54 F3 ...48.08N 14.52E
Amu Darya r. Asia 58 H2 ...43.50N 59.00E
Amund Ringnes Island Canada 63 I5 ...78.00N 96.00W
Amuntai Indonesia 104 F3 ...2.25S 115.13E
Amur r. Rus. Fed. 59 P3 ...53.17N 140.37E
Anabar r. Rus. Fed. 59 M5 ...73.13N 113.31E
Anadolu Dağları mts Turkey 57 L5 ...40.59N 36.11E
Anadyr' Rus. Fed. 59 S4 ...64.44N 177.20E
Anadyrskiy Zaliv b. Rus. Fed. 59 T4 ...63.56N 177.42W
'Änah Iraq 94 F6 ...34.25N 41.56E
Anambas, Kepulauan is Indonesia 104 D4 ...3.17N 105.55E
Anamur Turkey 57 J3 ...36.06N 32.50E
Anapa Rus. Fed. 57 L4 ...44.54N 37.20E
Anápolis Brazil 77 K4 ...16.20S 48.55W
Anatahan i. N. Mariana Is 105 L7 ...16.21N 145.42E
Anatolia f. Turkey 57 J4 ...38.58N 33.19E
Anchorage U.S.A. 62 D4 ...61.12N 149.52W
Ancona Italy 50 E5 ...43.37N 13.31E
Andalsnes Norway 40 A3 ...62.34N 7.42E
Andaman Islands India 97 H3 ...12.46N 93.17E
Andaman Sea Indian Oc. 97 I3 ...11.33N 95.19E
Anderlecht Belgium 42 D3 ...50.49N 4.18E
Andermatt Switz. 54 C2 ...46.38N 8.36E
Anderson r. Canada 62 F4 ...69.42N 128.56W
Anderson U.S.A. 62 D4 ...64.22N 149.12W
Andes mts S. America 73 B6 ...9.10S 77.03W
Andfjorden str. Norway 40 D5 ...68.53N 16.04E
Andhra Pradesh d. India 96 E4 ...16.03N 79.11E
Andkhvoy Afgh. 95 K7 ...36.59N 65.08E
Andong S. Korea 106 A3 ...36.33N 128.43E
Andorra Europe 48 F5 ...42.32N 1.35E
Andorra la Vella Andorra 48 F5 ...42.31N 1.32E
Andover England 10 D2 ...51.12N 1.29W
Andøya i. Norway 40 C5 ...69.11N 15.48E
Andreas Isle of Man 14 C3 ...54.22N 4.27W
Andria Italy 50 G4 ...41.14N 16.18E
Andros i. Bahamas 71 I5 ...24.25N 78.09W
Andros i. Greece 56 F3 ...37.53N 24.57E
Andújar Spain 48 C3 ...38.02N 4.03W
Anéfis Mali 84 E3 ...18.02N 0.32E
Anegada i. Virgin Is (U.K.) 71 L4 ...18.44N 64.19W
Aneto mt. Spain 48 F5 ...42.38N 0.39E
Angara r. Rus. Fed. 59 K3 ...58.05N 92.59E
Angarsk Rus. Fed. 103 I8 ...52.24N 103.45E
Ånge Sweden 40 C3 ...62.31N 15.40E
Ángel de la Guarda, Isla i. Mexico 70 B6 ...29.25N 113.24W
Ångelholm Sweden 40 C2 ...56.15N 12.52E
Angers France 44 C5 ...47.28N 0.33W
Anglesey i. Wales 12 C5 ...53.18N 4.23W
Angola Africa 86 A3 ...11.40S 17.34E
Angola Basin f. Atlantic Oc. 117 J5 ...15.00S 0.00E
Angoulême France 44 D4 ...45.39N 0.10E
Angren Uzbekistan 102 C6 ...41.02N 70.07E
Anguilla i. Central America 71 L4 ...18.14N 63.02W
Angus d. Scotland 8 D5 ...56.43N 2.55W
Anhui d. China 103 L4 ...32.10N 117.07E
Ankara Turkey 57 J4 ...39.56N 32.50E
Anlaby England 15 G2 ...53.45N 0.26W
Annaba Algeria 84 E5 ...36.54N 7.46E
An Nabk Syria 57 L2 ...34.01N 36.44E
An Nafüd des. Saudi Arabia 94 F5 ...28.28N 41.17E
An Najaf Iraq 94 F6 ...31.59N 44.20E
Annalee r. Rep. of Ireland 41 D4 ...54.02N 7.23W
Annalong Northern Ireland 16 D2 ...54.06N 5.54W
Annan Scotland 17 F2 ...54.59N 3.15W
Annan r. Scotland 17 F2 ...54.59N 3.16W
Annapurna mt. Nepal 96 F6 ...28.34N 83.49E
Ann Arbor U.S.A. 65 J5 ...42.17N 83.45W
An Näşirïyah Iraq 95 G6 ...31.01N 46.14E
An Nawfalïyah Libya 53 G3 ...30.51N 17.52E
Annecy France 44 G4 ...45.54N 6.08E
Anniston U.S.A. 65 I3 ...33.39N 85.43W
An Nu'ayrïyah Saudi Arabia 95 G5 ...27.29N 48.26E
An Nu'ayrïyah, Jabal mts Syria 57 L2 ...35.15N 36.05E
Ansbach Germany 54 D3 ...49.18N 10.36E
Anshan China 103 M6 ...41.06N 123.02E
Anshun China 103 J3 ...26.15N 105.57E
Anstruther Scotland 17 G4 ...56.13N 2.42W
Antakya Turkey 57 L3 ...36.11N 36.07E
Antalya Turkey 57 I3 ...36.53N 30.41E
Antalya Körfezi g. Turkey 57 I3 ...36.40N 30.58E
Antananarivo Madagascar 86 D3 ...18.54S 47.33E
Antarctica 112
Antarctic Peninsula f. Antarctica 116 F2 ...65.00S 64.00W
An Teallach mt. Scotland 18 D2 ...57.48N 5.16W
Antequera Spain 48 C2 ...37.02N 4.33W
Antibes France 44 G3 ...43.35N 7.07E
Anticosti, Île d' i. Canada 63 L2 ...49.27N 62.59W
Antigua i. Antigua 71 L4 ...17.02N 61.43W
Antigua and Barbuda Central America 71 L4 ...17.20N 61.20W
Antikythira i. Greece 56 E3 ...35.52N 23.20E
Antipodes Islands New Zealand 111 G2 ...49.39S 178.44E
Antofagasta Chile 73 B5 ...23.37S 70.22W
Antrim Northern Ireland 16 C2 ...54.43N 6.12W
Antrim d. Northern Ireland 9 B4 ...54.43N 6.16W
Antrim r. Northern Ireland 16 C2 ...54.59N 6.22W
Antrim Hills Northern Ireland 16 C3 ...55.05N 6.16W
Antsirabe Madagascar 86 D3 ...19.53S 47.03E
Antsirañana Madagascar 86 D3 ...12.19S 49.17E
Antsohihy Madagascar 86 D3 ...14.53S 47.59E
Antwerp Belgium 42 D4 ...51.12N 4.26E
Antwerpen d. Belgium 42 D4 ...51.17N 4.46E
Anxi China 102 H6 ...40.27N 95.48E
Anyang China 103 K5 ...36.04N 114.22E
Anzhero-Sudzhensk Rus. Fed. 58 J3 ...56.08N 86.01E
Aomori Japan 106 D4 ...40.49N 140.45E
Aoraki mt. New Zealand 111 G2 ...43.37S 170.08E
Aosta Italy 50 B6 ...45.44N 7.20E
Apa r. Brazil 77 I3 ...22.07S 57.57W
Apalachee Bay U.S.A. 65 J2 ...29.59N 84.06W
Apaporis r. Colombia 76 G7 ...1.04S 69.26W
Aparri Phil. 105 G7 ...18.21N 121.40E
Apatity Rus. Fed. 40 H4 ...67.34N 33.23E
Apeldoorn Neth. 42 E5 ...52.12N 5.58E
Apennines mts Italy 50 D6 ...44.37N 9.47E
Apia Samoa 108 I5 ...13.50S 171.44W
Aporé r. Brazil 77 J3 ...19.25S 50.59W
Apostolos Andreas, Cape Cyprus 57 K2 ...35.41N 34.35E
Appalachian Mountains U.S.A. 65 J4 ...36.08N 83.01W
Appleby-in-Westmorland England 15 E3 ...54.35N 2.29W
Appledore England 13 C3 ...51.03N 4.12W
Apucarana Brazil 77 J2 ...23.34S 51.27W
Apurímac r. Peru 76 F5 ...12.16S 73.54W
Aqaba, Gulf of Asia 94 D5 ...29.19N 34.54E
Ara Arba Ethiopia 87 C4 ...5.53N 41.26E
Arabian Peninsula Asia 85 I4 ...24.00N 45.00E
Arabian Sea Indian Oc. 90 F4 ...18.08N 66.38E
Aracaju Brazil 77 M5 ...10.52S 37.03W

Aracati Brazil 77 M7 . . . . .4.33S 37.42W
Araçatuba Brazil 77 J3 . . . . .21.12S 50.22W
Aracena, Sierra de *hills* Spain 48 B2 . . . .37.51N 7.07W
Arad Romania 56 D8 . . . . .46.11N 21.21E
Arafura Sea Australia/Indonesia 110 C6 . . . .9.04S 132.58E
Aragón r. Spain 48 E5 . . . . .42.13N 1.45W
Araguaia r. Brazil 77 K6 . . . . .5.24S 48.41W
Araguaína Brazil 77 K6 . . . . .7.20S 48.15W
Araguari Brazil 77 K4 . . . . .18.38S 48.09W
Arak Algeria 84 E4 . . . . .25.18N 3.39E
Arāk Iran 95 G6 .34.05N 49.42E
Arakan Yoma *mts* Myanmar 97 H5 . . . . .20.18N 94.07E
Aral Sea Kazakhstan/Uzbekistan 58 H2 . . . .45.07N 60.05E
Aral'sk Kazakhstan 58 H2 . . . . .46.46N 61.43E
Aranda de Duero Spain 48 D4 . . . . .41.41N 3.40W
Aran Island Rep. of Ireland 41 C4 . . . . . . .54.59N 8.35W
Aran Islands Rep. of Ireland 41 B3 . . . . . .53.07N 9.44W
Aranjuez Spain 48 D4 . . . . .40.02N 3.36W
Arapgir Turkey 57 M4 . . . . .39.02N 38.29E
Arapiraca Brazil 77 M6 . . . . .9.44S 36.37W
Arapis, Akra *pt* Greece 56 F5 . . . . .40.27N 24.00E
'Ar'ar Saudi Arabia 94 F4 . . . . .30.58N 40.58E
Araraquara Brazil 77 K3 . . . . .21.47S 48.06W
Ararat, Mount Turkey 58 F1 . . . . .39.45N 44.15E
Ārba Minch Ethiopia 87 B4 . . . . .5.59N 37.32E
Arbīl Iraq 94 F7 .36.11N 44.01E
Arboga Sweden 40 C2 . . . . .59.23N 15.51E
Arbroath Scotland 17 G4 . . . . .56.34N 2.35W
Arbu Lut, Dasht-e *des.* Afgh. 95 J5 . . . . .29.57N 63.56E
Arcachon France 44 C4 . . . . .44.40N 1.10W
Archangel Rus. Fed. 58 F4 . . . . .64.33N 40.33E
Arctic Bay *town* Canada 63 J5 . . . . .72.55N 85.10W
Arctic Ocean 112
Arctic Red r. Canada 62 E4 . . . . .67.27N 133.44W
Ardabīl Iran 95 G7 . . . . .38.14N 48.15E
Ardas r. Greece 56 G5 . . . . .41.40N 26.30E
Ardèche r. France 44 F4 . . . . .44.16N 4.39E
Ardennes f. Belgium 42 D2 . . . . .49.56N 4.52E
Ardestān Iran 95 H6 . . . . .33.20N 52.21E
Ardglass Northern Ireland 16 D2 . . . . . . .54.15N 5.36W
Ardila r. Portugal 48 B3 . . . . .38.10N 7.28W
Ardnamurchan, Point of Scotland 18 C1 . . .56.43N 6.13W
Ardrishaig Scotland 16 D4 . . . . .56.01N 5.27W
Ardrossan Scotland 16 E3 . . . . .55.39N 4.49W
Ards d. Northern Ireland 9 C4 . . . . .54.28N 5.37W
Ards Peninsula Northern Ireland 16 D2 . . . .54.30N 5.25W
Ardvasar Scotland 18 D2 . . . . .57.03N 5.55W
Arena, Point U.S.A. 64 B4 . . . . .38.57N 123.44W
Arendal Norway 40 B2 . . . . .58.27N 8.46E
Arenig Fawr *hill* Wales 12 D4 . . . . .52.55N 3.45W
Arequipa Peru 76 F4 . . . . .16.23S 71.32W
Arezzo Italy 50 D5 . . . . .43.27N 11.53E
Arganda Spain 48 D4 . . . . .40.18N 3.30W
Argentan France 44 C6 . . . . .48.45N 0.01W
Argentina S. America 73 C3 . . . . .35.00S 68.00W
Argentine Rise f. S. Atlantic Oc. 109 Q3 . . .39.32S 53.02W
Argentino, Lago l. Argentina 73 B1 . . . . . .50.20S 72.51W
Argenton-sur-Creuse France 44 D5 . . . . . .46.36N 1.31E
Arges r. Romania 56 G7 . . . . .44.04N 26.37E
Argun' r. China/Rus. Fed. 103 M8 . . . . . . .53.18N 121.28E
Argyle, Lake Australia 110 B5 . . . . .16.37S 128.41E
Argyll f. Scotland 16 D4 . . . . .56.08N 5.19W
Argyll and Bute d. Scotland 8 C4 . . . . . . .55.46N 5.25W
Århus Denmark 40 B2 . . . . .56.09N 10.12E
Arica Chile 72 B5 . . . . .18.29S 70.20W
Arienas, Loch l. Scotland 16 D4 . . . . .56.35N 5.46W
Arinos r. Brazil 77 I5 . . . . .10.25S 58.13W
Aripuanã r. Brazil 77 H6 . . . . .5.07S 60.22W
Ariquemes Brazil 76 H6 . . . . .9.59S 63.05W
Arisaig Scotland 18 D1 . . . . .56.55N 5.50W
Arisaig, Sound of *str.* Scotland 18 D1 . . . .56.51N 5.56W
Arizona d. U.S.A. 64 D3 . . . . .34.11N 111.37W
Arkadelphia U.S.A. 65 H3 . . . . .34.09N 93.03W
Arkaig, Loch l. Scotland 18 D1 . . . . .56.58N 5.13W
Arkansas d. U.S.A. 65 H4 . . . . .35.49N 92.00W
Arkansas r. U.S.A. 65 H3 . . . . .33.49N 91.08W
Arkansas City U.S.A. 64 G4 . . . . .37.04N 97.03W
Arklow Rep. of Ireland 41 E2 . . . . .52.48N 6.10W
Arkona, Kap c. Germany 54 E6 . . . . .54.41N 13.27E
Arles France 44 F3 . . . . .43.41N 4.38E
Arlit Niger 84 E3 . . . . .18.42N 7.21E
Arlon Belgium 42 E2 . . . . .49.41N 5.49E
Armagh Northern Ireland 16 C2 . . . . .54.20N 6.39W
Armagh d. Northern Ireland 9 B4 . . . . .54.19N 6.39W
Armagh f. Northern Ireland 41 E4 . . . . . . .54.18N 6.39W
Armant Egypt 53 J2 . . . . .25.37N 32.32E
Armavir Rus. Fed. 53 L6 . . . . .45.01N 41.06E
Armenia Asia 58 F2 . . . . .40.26N 44.30E
Armenia Colombia 72 B7 . . . . .4.30N 75.39W
Armidale Australia 110 E3 . . . . .30.32S 151.41E
Armyans'k Ukraine 57 J8 . . . . .46.07N 33.41E
Arnauti, Cape Cyprus 57 J2 . . . . .35.06N 32.16E
Arnhem Neth. 42 E4 . . . . .51.59N 5.56E
Arnhem, Cape Australia 110 C5 . . . . .12.19S 136.58E
Arnhem Land f. Australia 110 C5 . . . . .13.26S 133.57E
Arno r. Italy 50 D5 . . . . .43.41N 10.16E
Arnsberg Germany 54 C4 . . . . .51.23N 8.04E
Ar Ramādī Iraq 94 F6 . . . . .33.23N 43.16E
Arran i. Scotland 16 D3 . . . . .55.35N 5.20W
Ar Raqqah Syria 94 E7 . . . . .35.57N 39.01E
Arras France 44 E7 . . . . .50.17N 2.46E
Arrecife Canary Islands 48 Z2 . . . . .28.57N 13.33W
Arriagá Mexico 70 F4 . . . . .16.16N 93.52W
Arrieta Canary Islands 48 Z2 . . . . .29.08N 13.28W
Ar Rimāl f. Saudi Arabia 95 H4 . . . . .21.43N 52.53E
Arrochar Scotland 16 E4 . . . . .56.12N 4.44W
Ar Ruṭbah Iraq 94 F6 . . . . .33.01N 40.11E
Arta Greece 56 D4 . . . . .39.10N 20.59E
Artesia U.S.A. 64 F3 . . . . .32.52N 104.25W
Artigas Uruguay 77 I1 . . . . .30.24S 56.29W
Artois f. France 42 A3 . . . . .50.40N 1.55E
Artois, Collines de l' *hills* France 11 G1 . . .50.33N 1.54E
Artsyz Ukraine 57 H7 . . . . .45.59N 29.27E
Aru, Kepulauan is Indonesia 105 I2 . . . . . . .6.09S 134.08E
Aruba i. Central America 71 K3 . . . . .12.30N 69.56W
Arunachal Pradesh d. India 97 H6 . . . . . . .27.28N 92.48E
Arundel England 11 E1 . . . . .50.51N 0.33W
Arusha Tanzania 86 C4 . . . . .3.22S 36.37E
Arusha d. Tanzania 87 B2 . . . . .3.51S 36.39E
Aruwimi r. Dem. Rep. Congo 86 B5 . . . . . . .1.14N 23.38E
Arvayheer Mongolia 103 I7 . . . . .46.08N 102.47E
Arviat Canada 63 I4 . . . . .61.12N 94.09W
Arvidsjaur Sweden 40 D4 . . . . .65.35N 19.12E
Arvika Sweden 40 C2 . . . . .59.39N 12.37E
Arzamas Rus. Fed. 58 F3 . . . . .55.23N 43.45E
Asad, Buḩayrat al *resr* Syria 57 M3 . . . . . .36.05N 38.03E
Asahi-dake *vol.* Japan 106 D4 . . . . .43.41N 142.54E
Asahikawa Japan 106 D4 . . . . .43.46N 142.22E
Asansol India 96 G5 . . . . .23.41N 87.01E
Ascension Island Atlantic Oc. 82 B4 . . . . . .8.00S 14.00W
Ascoli Piceno Italy 50 E5 . . . . .42.52N 13.33E
Åsele Sweden 40 D4 . . . . .64.10N 17.22E
Asenovgrad Bulgaria 56 F6 . . . . .42.00N 24.52E
Asforby England 10 E3 . . . . .52.46N 0.57W

Ashbourne England 15 F2 . . . . .53.01N 1.44W
Ashbourne Rep. of Ireland 41 E3 . . . . .53.31N 6.23W
Ashburton *watercourse* Australia 110 A4 . . .21.43S 114.54E
Ashburton England 13 D2 . . . . .50.31N 3.45W
Ashby de la Zouch England 10 D3 . . . . . . .52.45N 1.28W
Ashford England 11 F2 . . . . .51.09N 0.53E
Ashgabat Turkmenistan 58 G1 . . . . .37.53N 58.21E
Ashington England 15 F4 . . . . .55.11N 1.34W
Ashland U.S.A. 65 H6 . . . . .46.35N 90.53W
Ashmore and Cartier Islands Australia 110 B5 . .12.38S 122.40E
Ashmyany Belarus 46 G5 . . . . .54.25N 25.56E
Ash Shiḩr Yemen 95 G2 . . . . .14.49N 49.45E
Ashton-under-Lyne England 15 E2 . . . . . . .53.30N 2.06W
Asia 90
Asilah Morocco 48 B1 . . . . .35.28N 6.02W
Asinara, Golfo dell' b. Italy 50 C4 . . . . . . .40.59N 8.31E
Asipovichy Belarus 55 M5 . . . . .53.18N 28.38E
'Asīr f. Saudi Arabia 94 F4 . . . . .20.53N 40.14E
Askern England 15 F2 . . . . .53.37N 1.09W
Askim Norway 40 B2 . . . . .59.35N 11.10E
Asmara Eritrea 85 H3 . . . . .15.20N 38.56E
Åsnen l. Sweden 40 C2 . . . . .56.37N 14.50E
Aspang-Markt Austria 54 G2 . . . . .47.33N 16.05E
Aspatria England 14 D3 . . . . .54.46N 3.20W
Aspen U.S.A. 64 E4 . . . . .39.11N 106.49W
Assab Eritrea 85 I3 . . . . .12.59N 42.43E
Assam d. India 97 H6 . . . . .26.14N 91.22E
As Samāwah Iraq 94 G6 . . . . .31.15N 45.19E
As Sarīr f. Libya 53 H2 . . . . .27.02N 21.36E
Assen Neth. 42 F6 . . . . .53.00N 6.33E
As Sidrah Libya 53 G3 . . . . .30.38N 18.18E
As Sulaymānīyah Iraq 94 G7 . . . . .35.32N 45.27E
As Sūq Saudi Arabia 94 F4 . . . . .21.57N 41.59E
Assumption i. Seychelles 86 D4 . . . . .9.30S 47.20E
Assynt, Loch l. Scotland 18 D3 . . . . .58.11N 5.05W
Astana Kazakhstan 58 I3 . . . . .51.09N 71.27E
Āstārā Iran 95 G7 . . . . .38.27N 48.52E
Asti Italy 50 C6 .44.54N 8.13E
Astorga Spain 48 B5 . . . . .42.28N 6.03W
Astoria U.S.A. 64 B6 . . . . .46.08N 123.46W
Astove i. Seychelles 86 D4 . . . . .10.05S 47.40E
Astrakhan' Rus. Fed. 58 F2 . . . . .46.22N 48.03E
Astravyets Belarus 46 G5 . . . . .54.36N 25.56E
Asuncion i. N. Mariana Is 105 L7 . . . . .19.40N 145.25E
Asunción Paraguay 77 I2 . . . . .25.16S 57.39W
Aswān Egypt 85 H4 . . . . .24.02N 32.56E
Asyūṭ Egypt 85 H4 . . . . .27.07N 31.08E
Atacama, Salar de f. Chile 76 G3 . . . . .23.23S 68.18W
Atacama Desert Chile 73 C4 . . . . .26.13S 69.39W
Atafu i. Tokelau 108 I5 . . . . .8.33S 172.30W
Atâr Mauritania 84 C4 . . . . .20.32N 13.03W
Atasu Kazakhstan 58 I2 . . . . .48.42N 71.37E
Atatürk Baraji *resr* Turkey 57 M3 . . . . . . .37.28N 38.26E
Atbara Sudan 85 H3 . . . . .17.43N 33.55E
Atbara r. Sudan 85 H3 . . . . .17.40N 33.58E
Ath Belgium 42 C3 . . . . .50.38N 3.47E
Athabasca r. Canada 62 G3 . . . . .58.28N 111.09W
Athabasca, Lake Canada 62 H3 . . . . .59.17N 109.24W
Athboy Rep. of Ireland 41 E3 . . . . .53.37N 6.55W
Athenry Rep. of Ireland 41 C3 . . . . .53.18N 8.45W
Athens Greece 56 E3 . . . . .37.59N 23.43E
Atherstone England 10 D3 . . . . .52.35N 1.33W
Athi r. Kenya 87 B2 . . . . .2.57S 38.31E
Athi Plains f. Kenya 87 B2 . . . . .1.30S 36.50E
Athi River *town* Kenya 87 B2 . . . . .1.27S 36.58E
Athlone Rep. of Ireland 41 D3 . . . . .53.25N 7.57W
Atholl, Forest of Scotland 19 E1 . . . . .56.51N 4.10W
Athos mt. Greece 56 F5 . . . . .40.10N 24.19E
Athy Rep. of Ireland 41 E2 . . . . .52.59N 6.59W
Ati Chad 85 F3 . . . . .13.14N 18.20E
Atikokan Canada 65 H6 . . . . .48.45N 91.37W
Atiu i. Cook Is 109 J4 . . . . .19.59S 158.07W
Atlanta U.S.A. 65 J3 . . . . .33.46N 84.22W
Atlantic City U.S.A. 65 L4 . . . . .39.21N 74.26W
Atlantic Ocean 116 G7
Atlas Mountains Africa 84 D5 . . . . .30.13N 7.41W
Atlas Saharien *mts* Algeria 84 E5 . . . . . . .32.41N 0.20E
Aṭ Ṭā'if Saudi Arabia 94 F4 . . . . .21.15N 40.20E
Attleborough England 11 G3 . . . . .52.31N 1.01E
Atyrau Kazakhstan 58 G2 . . . . .47.08N 51.56E
Aube r. France 44 E6 . . . . .48.34N 3.43E
Auchterarder Scotland 17 F4 . . . . .56.18N 3.42W
Auchtermuchty Scotland 17 F4 . . . . .56.18N 3.14W
Auckland New Zealand 111 G3 . . . . .36.52S 174.46E
Auckland Islands New Zealand 111 F1 . . . . .50.43S 166.12E
Auderville France 13 Z9 . . . . .49.43N 1.55W
Audlem England 10 C3 . . . . .52.59N 2.31W
Audo mts Ethiopia 87 C4 . . . . .6.46N 41.15E
Audruicq France 11 H1 . . . . .50.52N 2.05E
Aughton England 15 F2 . . . . .53.22N 1.19W
Augsburg Germany 54 D3 . . . . .48.22N 10.52E
Augusta Australia 110 A3 . . . . .34.20S 115.08E
Augusta U.S.A. 65 J3 . . . . .33.28N 82.02W
Augusta Me. U.S.A. 65 M5 . . . . .44.19N 69.46W
Aulnoye-Aymeries France 42 C3 . . . . .50.12N 3.51E
Aurangabad India 96 E4 . . . . .19.53N 75.24E
Aurich Germany 42 G6 . . . . .53.28N 7.30E
Aurora U.S.A. 64 F4 . . . . .39.43N 104.53W
Auskerry i. Scotland 19 G4 . . . . .59.02N 2.33W
Aus Maduli Sudan 87 C3 . . . . .2.16N 40.36E
Austin U.S.A. 64 G3 . . . . .30.16N 97.42W
Australia Oceania 110 B4 . . . . .27.17S 129.18E
Australian Capital Territory d. Australia 110 D3 . .35.27S 148.52E
Austria Europe 54 E2 . . . . .47.12N 13.26E
Authie r. France 11 G1 . . . . .50.22N 1.37E
Auvergne, Monts d' *mts* France 44 E4 . . . .45.45N 2.59E
Auxerre France 44 E5 . . . . .47.48N 3.35E
Avallon France 44 E5 . . . . .47.30N 3.54E
Avaré Brazil 77 K2 . . . . .38.43N 34.51E
Avarua Cook Is 109 J4 . . . . .21.13S 159.46W
Aveiro Portugal 48 A4 . . . . .40.39N 8.38W
Aveyron r. France 44 D4 . . . . .44.05N 1.16E
Avezzano Italy 50 E5 . . . . .42.02N 13.25E
Avignon France 44 F3 . . . . .43.57N 4.49E
Ávila Spain 48 C4 . . . . .40.40N 4.41W
Avilés Spain 48 C5 . . . . .43.33N 5.54W
Avon r. Brist. England 10 C2 . . . . .51.29N 2.40W
Avon r. Dor. England 10 D1 . . . . .50.44N 1.46W
Avon r. Glos. England 10 C3 . . . . .52.00N 2.10W
Avon r. Scotland 19 F2 . . . . .57.25N 3.22W
Avonmore r. Rep. of Ireland 12 A4 . . . . . . .52.48N 6.08W
Avonmouth England 10 C2 . . . . .51.30N 2.42W
Awara Plain f. Kenya 87 C3 . . . . .3.39N 40.54E
Āwash Ethiopia 87 B4 . . . . .8.57N 38.28E
Āwash r. Ethiopia 85 I2 . . . . .6.57N 40.16E
Awbārī Libya 84 F4 . . . . .26.34N 12.46E
Awbārī, Idhān *des.* Libya 52 F2 . . . . .28.00N 10.25E
Awe, Loch l. Scotland 16 D4 . . . . .56.16N 5.14W
Axe r. England 13 D2 . . . . .50.42N 3.04W
Axel Heiberg Island Canada 63 I5 . . . . . . .79.47N 91.17W
Axminster England 10 C1 . . . . .50.47N 2.59W

Ayacucho Peru 76 F5 . . . . .13.10S 74.13W
Ayagoz Kazakhstan 58 J2 . . . . .47.56N 80.23E
Ayan Rus. Fed. 59 O3 . . . . .56.26N 138.12E
Aydarko'l ko'li l. Uzbekistan 58 H2 . . . . . . .41.02N 66.33E
Aydın Turkey 57 G3 . . . . .37.50N 27.49E
Ayers Rock *hill* Australia 110 C4 . . . . .25.20S 131.05E
Aylesbury England 10 E2 . . . . .51.49N 0.48W
Aylesham England 11 G2 . . . . .51.14N 1.12E
Aylsham England 11 G3 . . . . .52.48N 1.15E
Ayr Scotland 16 E3 . . . . .55.28N 4.38W
Ayr r. Scotland 16 E3 . . . . .55.28N 4.38W
Ayr, Point of Wales 12 D5 . . . . .53.21N 3.18W
Ayre, Point of Isle of Man 14 C3 . . . . .54.25N 4.22W
Ayvalık Turkey 56 G4 . . . . .39.17N 26.41E
Azerbaijan Asia 58 F1 . . . . .40.23N 48.09E
Azogues Ecuador 76 E7 . . . . .2.44S 78.50W
Azov, Sea of Rus. Fed./Ukraine 58 E2 . . . .46.03N 36.47E
Azrou Morocco 52 B3 . . . . .33.26N 5.11W
Azuero, Península de *pen.* Panama 71 H2 . .7.39N 80.41W
Azul, Cordillera *mts* Peru 76 E6 . . . . .8.31S 75.56W
Az Zaqāzīq Egypt 53 J3 . . . . .30.35N 31.30E
Az Zarqā' Jordan 94 E6 . . . . .32.04N 36.05E

B

Baardheere Somalia 85 I2 . . . . .2.19N 42.18E
Bābā, Kūh-e mts Afgh. 95 K6 . . . . .34.48N 68.27E
Babadag Romania 57 H7 . . . . .44.54N 28.42E
Babaeski Turkey 56 G5 . . . . .41.26N 27.06E
Bāb al Mandab *str.* Africa/Asia 94 F2 . . . . .12.21N 43.26E
Babar i. Indonesia 105 H2 . . . . .7.57S 129.51E
Babbacombe Bay England 13 D2 . . . . .50.31N 3.28W
Babia Góra mt. Poland 46 D2 . . . . .49.35N 19.32E
Babo Indonesia 105 I3 . . . . .2.35S 133.21E
Babruysk Belarus 55 M5 . . . . .53.09N 29.14E
Bab-Termas *hill* Morocco 48 D1 . . . . .34.29N 3.53W
Babuyan Islands Phil. 105 G7 . . . . .19.13N 121.59E
Bacabal Brazil 77 L7 . . . . .4.16S 44.47W
Bacan i. Indonesia 105 H3 . . . . .0.44S 127.35E
Bacău Romania 55 L2 . . . . .46.34N 26.55E
Back r. Canada 63 I4 . . . . .66.32N 95.51W
Backwater Reservoir Scotland 19 F1 . . . . . .56.44N 3.13W
Bac Liêu Vietnam 104 D5 . . . . .9.15N 105.45E
Bacolod Phil. 105 G6 . . . . .10.37N 122.57E
Badajoz Spain 48 B3 . . . . .38.53N 6.57W
Baden-Baden Germany 54 C3 . . . . .48.45N 8.15E
Bad Neuenahr-Ahrweiler Germany 42 G3 . . .50.33N 7.07E
Badulla Sri Lanka 96 F2 . . . . .7.00N 81.01E
Baffin Bay *sea* Canada/Greenland 63 L5 . . .72.51N 66.20W
Baffin Island Canada 63 L4 . . . . .64.57N 68.47W
Bafoussam Cameroon 84 F2 . . . . .5.28N 10.26E
Bāfq Iran 95 I6 . . . . .31.34N 55.21E
Bafra Turkey 57 K5 . . . . .41.34N 35.55E
Bāft Iran 95 I5 . . . . .29.14N 56.36E
Bagé Brazil 77 J1 . . . . .31.20S 54.06W
Baggy Point England 13 C3 . . . . .51.08N 4.16W
Baghdad Iraq 94 F6 . . . . .33.18N 44.22E
Baghlān Afgh. 95 K7 . . . . .36.11N 68.47E
Bagrationovsk Rus. Fed. 46 E5 . . . . .54.23N 20.38E
Bahariya Oasis Egypt 94 D5 . . . . .27.56N 28.51E
Bahawalpur Pakistan 96 D6 . . . . .29.23N 71.45E
Bahia d. Brazil 77 L5 . . . . .14.28S 40.45W
Bahía, Islas de la is Honduras 71 G4 . . . . .16.13N 86.56W
Bahía Blanca Argentina 73 C3 . . . . .38.43S 62.18W
Bahía Negra Paraguay 77 I3 . . . . .20.11S 58.10W
Bahrain Asia 95 H5 . . . . .26.29N 50.51E
Baia Mare Romania 55 J2 . . . . .47.39N 23.35E
Baicheng China 103 M7 . . . . .45.29N 122.50E
Baie-Comeau Canada 63 L2 . . . . .49.13N 68.10W
Baikal, Lake Rus. Fed. 59 L3 . . . . .52.37N 107.12E
Bailieborough Rep. of Ireland 41 E3 . . . . . .53.55N 6.58W
Bain r. England 15 G2 . . . . .53.05N 0.11W
Bainbridge U.S.A. 65 J3 . . . . .30.54N 84.40W
Bairiki Kiribati 108 H6 . . . . .1.21N 172.57E
Bairnsdale Australia 110 D3 . . . . .37.51S 147.37E
Baiyuda Desert Sudan 94 D3 . . . . .18.03N 32.59E
Baja Hungary 54 H2 . . . . .46.12N 18.57E
Baja California d. Mexico 70 B6 . . . . .29.40N 115.07E
Baja California *pen.* Mexico 70 B6 . . . . . . .30.40N 115.41W
Baja California Sur d. Mexico 70 B6 . . . . . .25.19N 112.09W
Baker, Mount U.S.A. 64 B6 . . . . .48.46N 121.47W
Baker Island N. Pacific Oc. 108 I5 . . . . .0.13N 176.28W
Baker Lake Canada 63 I4 . . . . .64.09N 95.23W
Bakersfield U.S.A. 64 C4 . . . . .35.22N 118.59W
Bakharden Turkmenistan 95 I7 . . . . .38.27N 57.24E
Bakhtegan, Daryācheh-ye l. Iran 95 H5 . . . .29.18N 53.52E
Bakırköy Turkey 57 H5 . . . . .40.58N 28.51E
Bako Ethiopia 87 B4 . . . . .5.49N 36.37E
Baku Azerbaijan 58 F2 . . . . .40.22N 49.50E
Bala Wales 12 D4 . . . . .52.54N 3.36W
Bala, Cerros de *mts* Bolivia 76 G5 . . . . . . .13.49S 68.25W
Balabac Strait Malaysia/Phil. 104 F5 . . . . . .7.36N 116.45E
Bala Lake Wales 12 D4 . . . . .52.52N 3.39W
Balashikha Rus. Fed. 55 Q6 . . . . .55.49N 37.57E
Balaton l. Hungary 54 G2 . . . . .46.46N 17.32E
Balbina, Represa de *resr* Brazil 77 I7 . . . . .1.34S 59.27W
Balbriggan Rep. of Ireland 41 E3 . . . . .53.36N 6.11W
Baldock England 11 E2 . . . . .51.59N 0.11W
Baldy Peak U.S.A. 64 E3 . . . . .33.54N 109.34W
Balearic Islands Spain 48 F3 . . . . .39.28N 1.30E
Baleia, Ponta da *pt* Brazil 77 M4 . . . . . . .17.41S 39.09W
Baleine, Rivière à la r. Canada 63 L3 . . . . .57.57N 67.37W
Bale Mountains National Park Ethiopia 87 B4 . .7.01N 39.41E
Baleshwar India 96 G5 . . . . .21.30N 86.56E
Balestrieri, Punta mt. Italy 50 C4 . . . . .40.51N 9.10E
Bali i. Indonesia 104 E2 . . . . .8.41S 114.55E
Balıkesir Turkey 57 G4 . . . . .39.38N 27.52E
Balık r. Syria/Turkey 57 M2 . . . . .35.56N 39.03E
Balikpapan Indonesia 104 F3 . . . . .1.12S 116.49E
Balimo P.N.G. 105 K2 . . . . .7.59S 143.01E
Bali Sea Indonesia 104 E2 . . . . .7.31S 114.31E
Balintore Scotland 19 F2 . . . . .57.45N 3.54W
Balkan Mountains Bulgaria/S.M. 56 E6 . . . .43.23N 22.47E
Balkhash Kazakhstan 58 I2 . . . . .46.50N 74.59E
Balkhash, Lake Kazakhstan 58 I2 . . . . .45.30N 73.51E
Ballagan Point Rep. of Ireland 16 C1 . . . . . .53.59N 6.06W
Ballantrae Scotland 16 E3 . . . . .55.06N 5.00W
Ballarat Australia 110 D3 . . . . .37.35S 143.52E
Ballater Scotland 19 F2 . . . . .57.03N 3.02W
Ballena, Punta *pt* Chile 73 B4 . . . . .25.47S 70.47W
Ballencleuch Law *hill* Scotland 17 F3 . . . . .55.20N 3.41W
Ballina Rep. of Ireland 41 B4 . . . . .54.07N 9.10W
Ballinasloe Rep. of Ireland 41 C3 . . . . .53.20N 8.13W
Ballybay Rep. of Ireland 16 C2 . . . . .54.07N 6.54W
Ballybunnion Rep. of Ireland 41 B2 . . . . . . .52.31N 9.40W
Ballycastle Northern Ireland 16 C3 . . . . . . .55.12N 6.14W
Ballyclare Northern Ireland 16 D2 . . . . .54.45N 5.59W

Ballyhaunis Rep. of Ireland 41 C3 . . . . .53.46N 8.46W
Ballymena Northern Ireland 16 C2 . . . . .54.52N 6.16W
Ballymena d. Northern Ireland 8 B4 . . . . . . .54.53N 6.14W
Ballymoney Northern Ireland 16 C3 . . . . . . .55.04N 6.31W
Ballymoney d. Northern Ireland 8 B4 . . . . . .54.58N 6.28W
Ballynahinch Northern Ireland 16 D2 . . . . . .54.24N 5.53W
Ballyquintin Point Northern Ireland 16 D2 . . .54.19N 5.29W
Ballyshannon Rep. of Ireland 41 C4 . . . . . . .54.30N 8.12W
Balochistan f. Pakistan 96 B6 . . . . .27.30N 63.31W
Balsas Brazil 77 K6 . . . . .7.31S 46.00W
Balsas r. Mexico 70 D4 . . . . .17.57N 102.09W
Balta Ukraine 55 M2 . . . . .47.56N 29.37E
Baltasound Scotland 19 I5 . . . . .60.46N 0.52W
Bălți Moldova 53 I6 . . . . .47.47N 27.56E
Baltic Sea g. Europe 40 D1 . . . . .55.28N 16.46E
Baltimore U.S.A. 65 K4 . . . . .39.17N 76.37W
Baltiysk Rus. Fed. 46 D5 . . . . .54.39N 19.53E
Bam Iran 95 I5 . . . . .29.07N 58.22E
Bamaga Australia 110 D5 . . . . .10.53S 142.23E
Bamako Mali 84 D3 . . . . .12.38N 7.59W
Bamberg Germany 54 D3 . . . . .49.54N 10.53E
Bambili Dem. Rep. Congo 86 B5 . . . . .3.38N 26.07E
Bambouti C.A.R. 85 G2 . . . . .5.22N 27.12E
Bāmīan Afgh. 95 K6 . . . . .34.52N 67.49E
Bampton Dev. England 13 D2 . . . . .50.59N 3.29W
Bampton Oxon. England 10 D2 . . . . .51.43N 1.33W
Banaba i. Kiribati 108 H5 . . . . .0.49S 169.35E
Bañados del Izozog f. Bolivia 77 H4 . . . . . .18.20S 61.45W
Banagher Rep. of Ireland 41 D3 . . . . .53.11N 7.59W
Bananal, Ilha do i. Brazil 77 J5 . . . . .11.26S 50.19W
Banaz Turkey 57 H4 . . . . .38.44N 29.44E
Banbridge Northern Ireland 16 C2 . . . . .54.21N 6.16W
Banbridge d. Northern Ireland 9 B4 . . . . . . .54.20N 6.09W
Banbury England 10 D3 . . . . .52.04N 1.20W
Banchory Scotland 19 G2 . . . . .57.03N 2.29W
Banda, Kepulauan is Indonesia 105 H3 . . . .4.33S 129.53E
Banda Aceh Indonesia 104 B5 . . . . .5.30N 95.18E
Bandar-e 'Abbās Iran 95 I5 . . . . .27.11N 56.18E
Bandar-e Anzali Iran 95 G7 . . . . .37.26N 49.26E
Bandar-e Lengeh Iran 95 H5 . . . . .26.34N 54.53E
Bandar-e Torkeman Iran 95 H7 . . . . .36.54N 53.59E
Bandar Lampung Indonesia 104 D2 . . . . . . .5.27S 105.17E
Banda Sea Indonesia 105 I2 . . . . .5.40S 130.07E
Bandeiras, Pico de *mt.* Brazil 77 L3 . . . . . .20.26S 41.48W
Bandirma Turkey 57 G5 . . . . .40.21N 27.57
Bandon Rep. of Ireland 41 C1 . . . . .51.45N 8.44W
Bandon r. Rep. of Ireland 41 C1 . . . . .51.45N 8.38W
Bandundu Dem. Rep. Congo 86 A4 . . . . . . .3.17S 17.23
Bandung Indonesia 104 D2 . . . . .6.56S 107.35
Banff Canada 62 G3 . . . . .51.11N 115.35E
Banff Scotland 19 G2 . . . . .57.40N 2.31W
Bangalore India 96 E3 . . . . .12.57N 77.34
Bangassou C.A.R. 85 G2 . . . . .4.44N 22.50
Banggai, Kepulauan is Indonesia 105 G3 . . .1.59S 123.27
Bangka i. Indonesia 104 D3 . . . . .2.07S 106.17
Bangkok Thailand 104 C6 . . . . .13.44N 100.33
Bangladesh Asia 97 H5 . . . . .23.47N 89.49
Bangor Northern Ireland 16 D2 . . . . .54.39N 5.40W
Bangor U.S.A. 65 M5 . . . . .44.48N 68.47W
Bangor Wales 12 C5 . . . . .53.14N 4.08W
Bangui C.A.R. 85 F2 . . . . .4.20N 18.33
Bangweulu, Lake Zambia 86 B3 . . . . .11.13S 29.39
Bani r. Mali 84 D3 . . . . .14.30N 4.13W
Banī Mazār Egypt 53 J2 . . . . .28.29N 30.49
Banī Suwayf Egypt 53 J2 . . . . .29.05N 31.06
Banī Walīd Libya 52 F3 . . . . .31.47N 14.00
Bāniyās Syria 57 K2 . . . . .35.11N 35.57
Banja Luka Bos.-Herz. 56 B7 . . . . .44.46N 17.12
Banjarmasin Indonesia 104 E3 . . . . .3.23S 114.33
Banjul Gambia 84 C3 . . . . .13.27N 16.36
Banks Island Canada 62 F5 . . . . .73.06N 121.26W
Banks Islands Vanuatu 111 F3 . . . . .13.55S 167.13
Banmi Pakistan 95 L6 . . . . .33.00N 70.40
Bann r. Northern Ireland 16 C3 . . . . .55.09N 6.42W
Bann r. Rep. of Ireland 12 A4 . . . . .52.33N 6.33W
Bantry Rep. of Ireland 41 B1 . . . . .51.41N 9.27W
Bantry Bay Rep. of Ireland 41 B1 . . . . .51.34N 9.53W
Baoding China 103 L5 . . . . .38.46N 115.34E
Baoji China 103 J4 . . . . .34.21N 107.09
Baoshan China 103 H3 . . . . .25.07N 99.05
Baotou China 103 K6 . . . . .40.31N 110.08
Baotou Shan mt. China/N. Korea 106 A4 . . . .41.57N 128.08
Ba'qūbah Iraq 94 F6 . . . . .33.42N 44.38
Baquerizo Moreno Ecuador 76 C7 . . . . .0.54S 89.37W
Bar S.M. 56 C6 . . . . .42.05N 19.05
Bara Sudan 94 D2 . . . . .13.40N 30.21
Baracoa Cuba 71 J5 . . . . .20.21N 74.29W
Baranavichy Belarus 55 L5 . . . . .53.08N 26.02
Baranīs Egypt 53 K1 . . . . .23.53N 35.27
Barbacena Brazil 77 L3 . . . . .21.13S 43.45
Barbados Central America 71 M3 . . . . .13.09N 59.25W
Barbuda i. Antigua 71 L4 . . . . .17.39N 61.47W
Barcaldine Australia 110 D4 . . . . .23.32S 145.19
Barcelona Spain 48 G4 . . . . .41.25N 2.13
Barcelona Venezuela 72 C8 . . . . .10.06N 64.41W
Barcelos Brazil 76 H7 . . . . .0.58S 62.58W
Bárðarbunga *mt.* Iceland 40 Y2 . . . . .64.38N 17.32W
Bardejov Slovakia 46 E3 . . . . .49.18N 21.17
Bardney England 15 G2 . . . . .53.13N 0.19W
Bardsey Island Wales 12 C4 . . . . .52.45N 4.46W
Bardsey Sound *str.* Wales 12 C4 . . . . .52.47N 4.48W
Bareilly India 96 E6 . . . . .28.22N 79.27E
Barentsburg Arctic Oc. 58 C5 . . . . .77.49N 14.20E
Barents Sea Arctic Oc. 58 F5 . . . . .75.18N 42.16E
Barham England 11 G2 . . . . .51.12N 1.10E
Bari Italy 50 G4 .41.07N 16.52E
Barinas Venezuela 72 B7 . . . . .8.34N 70.11W
Baringo, Lake Kenya 87 B3 . . . . .0.33N 36.05E
Barisan, Pegunungan *mts* Indonesia 104 C3 . .1.12S 100.37E
Barkly Tableland f. Australia 110 C5 . . . . . .18.06S 135.25E
Bârlad Romania 56 H8 . . . . .46.13N 27.39
Barlee, Lake Australia 110 A4 . . . . .28.58S 119.40E
Barletta Italy 50 G4 . . . . .41.19N 16.17E
Barmer India 96 D6 . . . . .25.44N 71.26E
Barmouth Wales 12 C4 . . . . .52.43N 4.03W
Barmouth Bay Wales 12 C4 . . . . .52.43N 4.10W
Barnard Castle England 15 F3 . . . . .54.33N 1.55W
Barnaul Rus. Fed. 58 J3 . . . . .53.22N 83.49E
Barnet England 11 E2 . . . . .51.39N 0.12W
Barnoldswick England 15 E2 . . . . .53.55N 2.11W
Barnsley England 15 F2 . . . . .53.33N 1.29W
Barnstaple England 13 C3 . . . . .51.05N 4.03W
Barnstaple or Bideford Bay England 13 C3 . . .51.05N 4.23W
Barquisimeto Venezuela 72 C8 . . . . .10.03N 69.15W
Barra i. Scotland 18 B1 . . . . .56.59N 7.30W
Barra, Sound of *str.* Scotland 18 B2 . . . . . .57.04N 7.27W
Barra do Corda Brazil 77 K6 . . . . .5.29S 45.10W
Barra do Garças Brazil 77 J4 . . . . .15.53S 52.16W
Barranquilla Colombia 72 B8 . . . . .10.59N 74.51W
Barreiras Brazil 77 L5 . . . . .12.07S 44.53W
Barretos Brazil 77 K3 . . . . .20.35S 48.34W
Barrhead Scotland 16 E3 . . . . .55.48N 4.24W
Barrow r. Rep. of Ireland 41 E2 . . . . .52.23N 6.57W

arrow U.S.A. 62 C5 ....71.18N 156.43W
arrow, Point U.S.A. 62 C5 ....71.23N 156.22W
arrow-in-Furness England 14 D3 ....54.07N 3.13W
arry Wales 13 D3 ....51.24N 3.17W
arstow U.S.A. 64 C3 ....34.54N 117.01W
artin Turkey 57 J5 ....41.38N 32.21E
arton-upon-Humber England 15 G2 ....53.41N 0.27W
artoszyce Poland 46 E5 ....54.15N 20.49E
arysaw Belarus 55 M6 ....54.14N 28.31E
aschurch England 10 C3 ....52.47N 2.51W
asel Switz. 50 B7 ....47.33N 7.35E
asilan i. Phil. 105 G5 ....6.32N 121.52E
asildon England 11 F2 ....51.35N 0.29E
asingstoke England 10 D2 ....51.16N 1.06W
asra Iraq 95 G6 ....30.29N 47.48E
assein Myanmar 97 H4 ....16.45N 94.44E
assenthwaite Lake England 14 D3 ....54.40N 3.14W
asse-Terre Guadeloupe 71 L4 ....16.01N 61.44W
ass Rock i. Scotland 17 G4 ....56.05N 2.38W
ass Strait Australia 110 D3 ....39.43S 146.11E
astia France 44 H2 ....42.42N 9.27E
astogne Belgium 42 E3 ....50.00N 5.43E
ata Equat. Guinea 84 E2 ....1.50N 9.48E
atabanó, Golfo de b. Cuba 71 H5 ....22.16N 82.38W
atang China 103 H4 ....30.01N 99.08E
atang Indonesia 97 I6 ....6.57S 109.43E
atangas Phil. 105 G6 ....13.46N 121.01E
atan Islands Phil. 105 G8 ....20.46N 122.05E
atâdâmbâng Cambodia 104 C6 ....13.06N 103.14E
ath England 10 C2 ....51.23N 2.22W
ath and North East Somerset d. England 9 D2 ....51.21N 2.28W
athgate Scotland 17 F3 ....55.54N 3.39W
athurst Australia 110 D3 ....33.25S 149.34E
athurst Canada 63 L2 ....47.36N 65.39W
athurst Inlet Canada 62 H4 ....66.50N 108.10W
athurst Island Australia 110 C5 ....11.29S 130.11E
athurst Island Canada 63 I5 ....75.49N 98.59W
atley England 15 F2 ....53.43N 1.38W
atna Algeria 84 F5 ....35.32N 6.13E
aton Rouge U.S.A. 65 H3 ....30.27N 91.11W
atticaloa Sri Lanka 96 F2 ....7.42N 81.83E
attle England 11 F1 ....50.55N 0.29E
atu mt. Ethiopia 87 B4 ....6.51N 39.50E
atu, Pulau-pulau is Indonesia 104 B3 ....0.14S 98.16E
at'umi Georgia 58 F2 ....41.39N 41.38E
aubau Indonesia 105 G2 ....5.29S 122.37E
auchi Nigeria 84 E3 ....10.19N 9.50E
auru Brazil 77 K3 ....22.20S 49.05W
auska Latvia 55 K7 ....56.25N 24.13E
autzen Germany 54 F4 ....51.11N 14.26E
awean i. Indonesia 104 E2 ....5.48S 112.34E
ayamo Cuba 71 I5 ....20.22N 76.38W
ayanhongor Mongolia 103 I7 ....46.09N 100.41E
ayburt Turkey 57 N5 ....40.15N 40.14E
ay City Mich. U.S.A. 65 J5 ....43.35N 83.53W
ay City Tex. U.S.A. 65 G2 ....28.59N 96.02W
aydaratskaya Guba Rus. Fed. 58 H4 ....69.29N 66.01E
ayonne France 44 C3 ....43.29N 1.29W
ayreuth Germany 54 E3 ....49.56N 11.36E
ayy al Kabir, Wâdi watercourse Libya 52 G3 ....31.11N 15.53E
aza Spain 48 D2 ....37.30N 2.46W
eachy Head England 11 F1 ....50.44N 0.15E
eaconsfield England 10 E2 ....51.36N 0.39W
eagle Gulf Australia 105 H1 ....12.04S 129.55E
eaminster England 10 C1 ....50.49N 2.45W
eardmore Canada 65 I6 ....49.36N 87.58W
eata, Cabo c. Dom. Rep. 71 J4 ....17.38N 71.23W
eata, Isla i. Dom. Rep. 71 J4 ....17.36N 71.30W
eaufort Sea Canada/U.S.A. 62 F5 ....73.19N 129.52W
eaufort West S. Africa 86 B1 ....32.20S 22.36E
eauly Scotland 19 E2 ....57.29N 4.28W
eauly r. Scotland 19 E2 ....57.29N 4.27W
eauly Firth est. Scotland 19 E2 ....57.29N 4.27W
eaumaris Wales 12 C5 ....53.16N 4.05W
eaumont France 13 Z9 ....49.40N 1.50W
eaumont U.S.A. 65 H3 ....30.05N 94.09W
eaune France 44 F5 ....47.01N 4.50E
eauvais France 44 E6 ....49.26N 2.05E
eaver r. Canada 62 H3 ....55.22N 107.45W
eaver Creek town Canada 62 D4 ....62.23N 140.49W
ebington England 14 D2 ....53.21N 3.00W
eccles England 11 G3 ....52.28N 1.34E
ecerreá Spain 48 B5 ....42.51N 7.09W
échar Algeria 84 D5 ....31.36N 2.13W
eckingham England 15 G2 ....53.24N 0.49W
eckley U.S.A. 65 J4 ....37.47N 81.11W
edale England 15 F3 ....54.17N 1.35W
edelë England 85 H2 ....8.28N 36.21E
edford England 11 E3 ....52.08N 0.28W
edfordshire d. England 9 E3 ....52.03N 0.24W
edlington England 15 F4 ....55.08N 1.36W
edworth England 10 D3 ....52.29N 1.28W
eersheba Israel 53 J3 ....31.15N 34.48E
eeville U.S.A. 64 G2 ....28.25N 97.45W
eg, Lough l. Northern Ireland 16 C2 ....54.47N 6.27W
ei'an China 103 N7 ....48.11N 126.31E
eihai China 103 J2 ....21.27N 109.08E
eijing China 103 L5 ....39.52N 116.27E
einn an Oir hill Scotland 16 D3 ....55.54N 5.59W
einn Dearg mt. High. Scotland 18 E2 ....57.47N 4.56W
einn Dearg mt. P. and K. Scotland 19 F1 ....56.53N 3.53W
einn Heasgarnich mt. Scotland 16 E4 ....56.33N 4.36W
eira Mozambique 86 C3 ....19.50S 34.52E
eirut Lebanon 53 K3 ....33.52N 35.30E
eith Scotland 16 E3 ....55.45N 4.38W
eiuș Romania 55 J2 ....46.40N 22.23E
eja Portugal 48 B3 ....38.01N 7.52W
ejaïa Algeria 84 E5 ....36.44N 5.03E
éjar Spain 48 C4 ....40.24N 5.46W
ékés Hungary 46 E1 ....46.46N 21.07E
ékéscsaba Hungary 54 I2 ....46.41N 21.05E
ela Pakistan 96 C6 ....26.12N 66.21E
elarus r. Rus. Fed. 59 S4 ....65.32N 173.15E
ełchatów Poland 46 D3 ....51.22N 19.22E
elcher Islands Canada 63 K3 ....56.10N 78.47W
eledweyne Somalia 85 I2 ....4.44N 45.13E
elém Brazil 77 K7 ....1.26S 48.29W
elev Rus. Fed. 55 Q5 ....53.48N 36.10E
elfast Northern Ireland 16 D2 ....54.36N 5.55W
elfast d. Northern Ireland 9 C4 ....54.36N 5.55W
elfast Lough inlet Northern Ireland 16 D2 ....54.40N 5.52W
elford England 15 F4 ....55.36N 1.50W
elgium Europe 42 D3 ....51.00N 4.14E
elgorod Rus. Fed. 58 E3 ....50.35N 36.37E
elgrade S.M. 56 D7 ....44.48N 20.29E
elitung i. Indonesia 104 D3 ....2.47S 108.14E
elize town Belize 70 G4 ....17.31N 88.14W
elize Central America 70 G4 ....17.10N 88.18W
ellac France 44 D5 ....46.08N 1.03E
ellary India 96 E4 ....15.10N 76.53E

Belle-Île i. France 44 B5 ....47.19N 3.15W
Belle Isle, Strait of Canada 63 M3 ....51.16N 56.57W
Bellingham England 14 E4 ....55.09N 2.15W
Bellingham U.S.A. 64 B6 ....48.45N 122.28W
Bellinzona Switz. 50 C7 ....46.12N 9.01E
Belluno Italy 50 E7 ....46.08N 12.13E
Belmopan Belize 70 G4 ....17.14N 88.46W
Belmullet Rep. of Ireland 41 B4 ....54.14N 9.59W
Belo Horizonte Brazil 77 L4 ....19.55S 43.56W
Belper England 15 F2 ....53.02N 1.29W
Belukha, Gora mt. Kazakhstan/Rus. Fed. 58 J2 ....49.50N 86.41E
Belyy Rus. Fed. 55 O6 ....55.50N 32.57E
Bembridge England 10 D1 ....50.41N 1.05W
Bemidji U.S.A. 65 H6 ....47.27N 94.52W
Ben Alder mt. Scotland 19 E1 ....56.49N 4.28W
Benavente Spain 48 C5 ....42.00N 5.40W
Benbane Head Northern Ireland 16 C3 ....55.15N 6.30W
Benbecula i. Scotland 18 B2 ....57.27N 7.23W
Ben Cleuch hill Scotland 17 F4 ....56.11N 3.46W
Ben Cruachan mt. Scotland 16 D4 ....56.25N 5.08W
Bend U.S.A. 64 B5 ....44.04N 121.17W
Bendigo Australia 110 D3 ....36.46S 144.18E
Benešov Czech Rep. 54 F3 ....49.47N 14.42E
Bengal, Bay of sea Indian Oc. 96 G4 ....17.51N 88.40E
Bengbu China 103 L4 ....32.54N 117.23E
Benghazi Libya 85 G5 ....32.06N 20.04E
Bengkulu Indonesia 104 C3 ....3.45S 102.18E
Benguela Angola 86 A3 ....12.36S 13.21E
Ben Hope hill Scotland 19 E3 ....58.25N 4.36W
Beni r. Bolivia 76 G5 ....11.01S 66.07W
Benidorm Spain 48 E3 ....38.32N 0.08W
Beni Mellal Morocco 84 D5 ....32.17N 6.25W
Benin Africa 84 E3 ....8.26N 2.11E
Benin, Bight of g. Africa 84 E2 ....5.17N 3.27E
Benin City Nigeria 84 E2 ....6.19N 5.36E
Beni-Saf Algeria 52 C4 ....35.20N 1.21W
Benjamim Constant Brazil 76 G7 ....4.23S 69.58W
Ben Klibreck hill Scotland 19 E3 ....58.15N 4.24W
Ben Lawers mt. Scotland 16 E4 ....56.33N 4.13W
Ben Lomond hill Scotland 16 E4 ....56.11N 4.38W
Ben Loyal hill Scotland 19 E3 ....58.24N 4.27W
Ben Lui mt. Scotland 16 E4 ....56.24N 4.49W
Ben Macdui mt. Scotland 19 F2 ....57.05N 3.40W
Ben More mt. Scotland 16 D4 ....56.25N 6.00W
Ben More mt. Scotland 16 C4 ....56.25N 6.01W
Ben More Assynt hill Scotland 18 E3 ....58.08N 4.51W
Ben Nevis mt. Scotland 18 D1 ....56.48N 5.00W
Bentley England 15 F2 ....53.33N 1.09W
Benue r. Nigeria 84 E2 ....7.49N 6.48E
Ben Vorlich hill Scotland 16 E4 ....56.21N 4.13W
Ben Wyvis mt. Scotland 19 E2 ....57.41N 4.35W
Benxi China 103 M6 ....41.16N 123.45E
Beoraid, Loch l. Scotland 18 D1 ....56.58N 5.42W
Berat Albania 56 C5 ....40.42N 19.58E
Berau, Teluk b. Indonesia 105 I3 ....2.28S 132.36E
Berber Sudan 94 D3 ....18.00N 34.02E
Berbera Somalia 85 I3 ....10.24N 45.02E
Berbérati C.A.R. 84 F2 ....4.14N 15.47E
Berck France 11 G1 ....50.25N 1.35E
Berdyans'k Ukraine 53 K6 ....46.46N 36.48E
Berdychiv Ukraine 55 M3 ....49.53N 28.36E
Berehove Ukraine 55 J2 ....48.13N 22.38E
Berens River town Canada 62 I3 ....52.21N 97.01W
Berezhany Ukraine 55 J3 ....49.27N 24.56E
Berezivka Ukraine 55 N2 ....47.12N 30.55E
Berezniki Rus. Fed. 58 G3 ....59.25N 56.48E
Bergama Turkey 56 G4 ....39.07N 27.11E
Bergamo Italy 50 C6 ....45.42N 9.41E
Bergen Norway 40 A3 ....60.23N 5.22E
Bergerac France 44 D4 ....44.51N 0.29E
Bergisch Gladbach Germany 54 B4 ....50.58N 7.08E
Bering Sea N. Pacific Oc. 60 A7 ....60.00N 170.00E
Bering Strait Rus. Fed./U.S.A. 59 U4 ....66.18N 168.40W
Berkel r. Neth. 42 F5 ....52.08N 6.11E
Berkeley England 10 C2 ....51.41N 2.27W
Berkshire Downs hills England 10 D2 ....51.30N 1.20W
Berlin Germany 54 E5 ....52.31N 13.23E
Bermuda i. N. Atlantic Oc. 71 L7 ....32.24N 64.56W
Bern Switz. 50 B7 ....46.57N 7.27E
Berneray i. W. Isles Scotland 18 B1 ....57.43N 2.29W
Berneray i. W. Isles Scotland 18 B2 ....57.44N 7.18W
Beroun Czech Rep. 46 B2 ....49.58N 14.04E
Berounka r. Czech Rep. 46 B2 ....49.59N 14.22E
Berry Head England 13 D2 ....50.24N 3.29W
Bertoua Cameroon 84 F2 ....4.35N 13.41E
Beru atoll Kiribati 108 H5 ....1.17S 176.00E
Berwick-upon-Tweed England 15 E4 ....55.46N 2.00W
Besançon France 44 G5 ....47.15N 6.01E
Bessbrook Northern Ireland 16 C2 ....54.11N 6.24W
Betanzos Spain 48 A5 ....43.17N 8.12W
Beth, Oued r. Morocco 48 B1 ....34.25N 6.26W
Bethesda Wales 12 C5 ....53.11N 4.03W
Béthune France 42 B3 ....50.31N 2.38E
Betsiboka r. Madagascar 86 D3 ....15.58S 46.27E
Bettystown Rep. of Ireland 12 A5 ....53.42N 6.15W
Betws-y-coed Wales 12 D5 ....53.05N 3.48W
Beult r. England 11 F2 ....51.13N 0.25E
Beverley England 15 G2 ....53.51N 0.26W
Bewdley England 10 C3 ....52.23N 2.19W
Bewl Water resr England 11 F2 ....51.04N 0.23E
Bexhill England 11 F1 ....50.50N 0.29E
Beykoz Turkey 57 H5 ....41.07N 29.05E
Beyla Guinea 84 D2 ....8.41N 8.41W
Beyneu Kazakhstan 58 G2 ....45.18N 55.11E
Beypazarı Turkey 57 I5 ....40.10N 31.56E
Beyşehir Turkey 57 I3 ....37.42N 31.43E
Beyşehir Gölü l. Turkey 57 I3 ....37.42N 31.33E
Béziers France 44 E3 ....43.21N 3.13E
Bhagalpur India 96 G5 ....25.15N 86.56E
Bhamo Myanmar 97 I5 ....24.18N 97.17E
Bhavnagar India 96 D5 ....21.46N 72.14E
Bhima r. India 96 E4 ....16.26N 77.13E
Bhopal India 96 E5 ....23.15N 77.23E
Bhubaneshwar India 96 G5 ....20.13N 85.53E
Bhuj India 96 C5 ....23.11N 69.44E
Bhutan Asia 97 H6 ....27.30N 90.33E
Biak Indonesia 105 J3 ....1.12S 136.05E
Biak i. Indonesia 105 J3 ....0.59S 135.59E
Biała Podlaska Poland 46 F4 ....52.02N 23.07E
Białogard Poland 46 B4 ....53.59N 15.59E
Białystok Poland 46 F4 ....53.08N 23.10E
Biarritz France 44 C3 ....43.29N 1.33W
Bibai Japan 106 D4 ....43.18N 141.52E
Biberach an der Riß Germany 54 C3 ....48.06N 9.47E
Bicester England 10 D2 ....51.54N 1.09W
Bidar India 96 E4 ....17.54N 77.34E
Biddulph England 15 E2 ....53.07N 2.10W
Bidean nam Bian mt. Scotland 18 D1 ....56.39N 5.02W
Bideford England 13 C3 ....51.01N 4.12W
Biel Switz. 50 B7 ....47.09N 7.15E
Bielefeld Germany 54 C5 ....52.01N 8.32E
Biella Italy 50 C6 ....45.34N 8.04E
Bielsko-Biała Poland 46 D2 ....49.49N 19.03E
Bié Plateau f. Angola 82 E3 ....13.00S 16.00E

Bifoun Gabon 84 F1 ....0.15S 10.25E
Biga Turkey 56 G5 ....40.13N 27.13E
Bigbury Bay England 13 D2 ....50.15N 3.54W
Biggar Scotland 17 F3 ....55.37N 3.31W
Biggleswade England 11 E3 ....52.05N 0.16W
Bighorn r. U.S.A. 64 E6 ....46.10N 107.30W
Bighorn Mountains U.S.A. 64 E5 ....44.06N 106.55W
Big Spring U.S.A. 64 F3 ....32.16N 101.24W
Big Trout Lake town Canada 63 J3 ....53.49N 89.50W
Bihać Bos.-Herz. 56 A7 ....44.49N 15.53E
Bihar d. India 96 G5 ....25.13N 85.37E
Bihor, Vârful mt. Romania 55 J2 ....46.27N 22.44E
Bijapur India 96 E4 ....16.49N 75.48E
Bijeljina Bos.-Herz. 56 C7 ....44.46N 19.14E
Bijelo Polje S.M. 56 C6 ....43.02N 19.45E
Bikaner India 96 D6 ....28.00N 73.23E
Bilaspur India 102 E2 ....22.05N 82.09E
Bilaspur India 96 E7 ....31.17N 76.49E
Bila Tserkva Ukraine 55 N3 ....49.48N 30.07E
Bilbao Spain 48 D5 ....43.15N 2.54W
Bilecik Turkey 56 H5 ....40.09N 29.57E
Biłgoraj Poland 46 F3 ....50.33N 22.43E
Billericay England 11 F2 ....51.38N 0.25E
Billingham England 15 F3 ....54.37N 1.17W
Billinghay England 15 G2 ....53.05N 0.17W
Billings U.S.A. 64 E6 ....45.48N 108.27W
Billingshurst England 11 E2 ....51.01N 0.27W
Bill of Portland hd England 10 C1 ....50.30N 2.30W
Bilopillya Ukraine 55 P4 ....51.09N 34.20E
Biloxi U.S.A. 65 I3 ....30.24N 88.57W
Bilston Scotland 17 F3 ....55.52N 3.11W
Bilton England 15 G2 ....53.47N 0.15W
Bimini Islands Bahamas 71 I6 ....25.46N 79.14W
Bindura Zimbabwe 86 C3 ....17.18S 31.19E
Bingham England 10 E3 ....52.57N 0.57W
Binghamton U.S.A. 65 K5 ....42.06N 75.55W
Bingley England 15 F2 ....53.51N 1.50W
Bintulu Malaysia 104 E4 ....3.12N 113.03E
Bioco i. Equat. Guinea 84 E2 ....3.16N 8.31E
Birak Libya 52 F2 ....27.33N 14.16E
Birao C.A.R. 94 B2 ....10.15N 22.48E
Birecik Turkey 57 L3 ....37.01N 37.59E
Birhan mt. Ethiopia 85 H3 ....10.43N 37.52E
Birjand Iran 95 I6 ....32.53N 59.08E
Birkenhead England 14 D2 ....53.23N 3.01W
Birmingham England 10 D3 ....52.29N 1.53W
Birmingham U.S.A. 65 I3 ....33.32N 86.47W
Bîr Mogreïn Mauritania 84 C4 ....25.14N 11.34W
Birnin Konni Niger 84 E3 ....13.48N 5.14E
Birobidzhan Rus. Fed. 103 O7 ....48.45N 132.52E
Birr Rep. of Ireland 41 D3 ....53.06N 7.55W
Birsay Scotland 19 F4 ....59.08N 3.18W
Birstall England 15 F2 ....52.41N 1.07W
Biržai Lithuania 46 G6 ....56.12N 24.45E
Biscay, Bay of sea France/Spain 48 C6 ....45.40N 5.07W
Bischofshofen Austria 54 E2 ....47.26N 13.13E
Bishkek Kyrgyzstan 102 C6 ....42.54N 74.32E
Bisho S. Africa 86 B1 ....32.51S 27.24E
Bishop Auckland England 15 F3 ....54.40N 1.41W
Bishop's Lydeard England 13 D3 ....51.04N 3.11W
Bishop's Stortford England 11 F2 ....51.52N 0.10E
Bishop's Waltham England 10 D1 ....50.57N 1.13W
Bisina, Lake Uganda 87 A3 ....1.38N 33.57E
Biskra Algeria 84 E5 ....34.49N 5.44E
Bismarck U.S.A. 64 F6 ....46.50N 100.46W
Bismarck Sea P.N.G. 110 D6 ....4.01S 149.01E
Bissau Guinea-Bissau 84 C3 ....11.53N 15.38W
Bistra r. S.M. 56 D6 ....42.09N 20.59E
Bistrița Romania 55 K2 ....47.09N 24.30E
Bistrița r. Romania 55 L2 ....46.30N 26.58E
Bitburg Germany 42 F2 ....49.58N 6.32E
Bitola Macedonia 56 D5 ....41.01N 21.20E
Bitterroot Range mts U.S.A. 64 D6 ....47.16N 115.41W
Biwa-ko l. Japan 106 C3 ....35.09N 135.59E
Biysk Rus. Fed. 58 J3 ....52.31N 85.17E
Bizerte Tunisia 52 F4 ....37.16N 9.52E
Bjørnøya i. Arctic Oc. 58 C5 ....74.24N 19.07E
Blackburn England 14 E2 ....53.45N 2.29W
Blackburn with Darwen d. England 9 D3 ....53.41N 2.27W
Black Combe hill England 14 D3 ....54.15N 3.20W
Blackfield England 10 D1 ....50.49N 1.22W
Black Forest mts Germany 54 C2 ....47.56N 8.08E
Black Head England 13 B2 ....50.00N 5.07W
Black Hill England 15 F2 ....53.32N 1.53W
Black Isle pen. Scotland 19 E2 ....57.35N 4.19W
Black Mountains hills Wales 12 D3 ....51.58N 3.08W
Blackpool England 14 D2 ....53.49N 3.03W
Blackpool d. England 9 D3 ....53.50N 3.01W
Black Sea Asia/Europe 57 M6 ....43.21N 38.22E
Blacksod Bay Rep. of Ireland 41 A4 ....54.03N 10.03W
Black Volta r. Africa 84 D2 ....8.29N 0.51W
Blackwater r. England 11 F2 ....51.44N 0.41E
Blackwater r. Northern Ireland 16 C2 ....54.31N 6.34W
Blackwater r. Meath Rep. of Ireland 41 E3 ....53.39N 6.41W
Blackwater r. Water. Rep. of Ireland 41 D2 ....52.08N 7.51W
Blackwood Wales 12 D3 ....51.40N 3.12W
Blaenau Ffestiniog Wales 12 D4 ....52.59N 3.57W
Blaenau Gwent d. Wales 9 D2 ....51.46N 3.12W
Blaenavon Wales 12 D3 ....51.47N 3.06W
Blagdon England 10 C2 ....51.20N 2.43W
Blagoevgrad Bulgaria 56 E6 ....42.01N 23.06E
Blagoveshchensk Rus. Fed. 59 N3 ....50.17N 127.29E
Blair Atholl Scotland 19 F1 ....56.46N 3.51W
Blairgowrie Scotland 17 F4 ....56.35N 3.21W
Blanc, Mont mt. France/Italy 44 G4 ....45.50N 6.51E
Blanca, Bahía b. Argentina 73 C3 ....39.08S 61.47W
Blanche, Lake Australia 110 C4 ....29.15S 139.42E
Blanc Nez, Cap c. France 11 G1 ....50.56N 1.44E
Blanco, Cape U.S.A. 64 B5 ....42.51N 124.34W
Blandford Forum England 10 C1 ....50.51N 2.10W
Blanquilla, Isla i. Venezuela 71 L3 ....11.51N 64.35W
Blansko Czech Rep. 46 C2 ....49.22N 16.39E
Blantyre Malawi 86 C3 ....15.47S 35.02E
Blarney Rep. of Ireland 41 C1 ....51.56N 8.34W
Bletchley England 10 E2 ....51.59N 0.45W
Bloemfontein S. Africa 86 B2 ....29.07S 26.13E
Blois France 44 D5 ....47.35N 1.20E
Bloody Foreland pt Rep. of Ireland 41 C5 ....55.10N 8.18W
Bloomington U.S.A. 65 I5 ....40.29N 89.00W
Blue Mountains U.S.A. 64 C6 ....45.30N 118.30W
Blue Nile r. Sudan 85 H3 ....15.38N 32.30E
Blue Stack hill Rep. of Ireland 41 C4 ....54.46N 8.05W
Blue Stack Mountains hills Rep. of Ireland 41 C4 ....54.42N 8.13W
Blumenau Brazil 77 K2 ....26.52S 49.04W
Blyth Northum. England 15 F4 ....55.08N 1.30W
Blyth Notts. England 15 F2 ....53.22N 1.04W
Blytheville U.S.A. 65 I4 ....35.56N 89.52W
Boa Esperança, Açude resr Brazil 77 L6 ....6.58S 43.47W
Boa Vista Brazil 77 H8 ....2.51N 60.43W

Boa Vista i. Cape Verde 84 B3 ....16.05N 22.40W
Bobaomby, Tanjona c. Madagascar 86 D3 ....11.57S 49.15E
Bobo-Dioulasso Burkina 84 D3 ....11.11N 4.18W
Bóbr r. Poland 46 B4 ....52.03N 15.04E
Boby mt. Madagascar 86 D2 ....22.13S 46.54E
Bochnia Poland 46 E2 ....49.58N 20.26E
Bocholt Germany 54 B4 ....51.50N 6.36E
Boddam Scotland 19 H2 ....57.28N 1.47W
Bodélé f. Chad 85 F3 ....16.12N 16.17E
Boden Sweden 40 E4 ....65.49N 21.41E
Bodenham England 10 C3 ....52.09N 2.41W
Bodmin England 13 C2 ....50.28N 4.43W
Bodmin Moor f. England 13 C2 ....50.34N 4.36W
Bodø Norway 40 D4 ....67.17N 14.23E
Bodrum Turkey 56 G3 ....37.02N 27.25E
Boğazlıyan Turkey 57 K4 ....39.11N 35.15E
Boggeragh Mountains hills Rep. of Ireland 41 B2 ....52.01N 9.01W
Bogie r. Scotland 19 G2 ....57.27N 2.46W
Bognor Regis England 10 E1 ....50.47N 0.40W
Bogor Indonesia 104 D2 ....6.35S 106.45E
Bogotá Colombia 72 B7 ....4.38N 74.05W
Bo Hai g. China 103 L5 ....38.32N 119.14E
Bohain-en-Vermandois France 42 C2 ....49.59N 3.28E
Bohemian Forest mts Germany 54 E3 ....49.42N 12.27E
Bohol i. Phil. 105 G5 ....9.55N 124.16E
Bohu China 102 F6 ....41.55N 86.35E
Boise U.S.A. 64 C5 ....43.38N 116.11W
Bojnūrd Iran 95 I7 ....37.27N 57.19E
Bolhrad Ukraine 53 I6 ....45.41N 28.37E
Bolívar, Pico mt. Venezuela 71 J2 ....8.33N 70.59W
Bolivia S. America 76 H4 ....16.23S 64.00W
Bollnäs Sweden 40 D3 ....61.21N 16.24E
Bolmen l. Sweden 40 C2 ....56.52N 13.43E
Bologna Italy 50 D6 ....44.29N 11.22E
Bolsena, Lago di l. Italy 50 D5 ....42.36N 11.56E
Bol'shakovo Rus. Fed. 46 E5 ....54.53N 21.39E
Bol'shevik, Ostrov i. Rus. Fed. 59 L5 ....78.39N 102.16E
Bol'shoy Aluy r. Rus. Fed. 59 Q4 ....66.29N 159.26E
Bol'shoy Lyakhovskiy, Ostrov i. Rus. Fed. 59 P5 ....73.26N 142.14E
Bolsover England 15 F2 ....53.14N 1.17W
Bolt Head England 13 D2 ....50.12N 3.47W
Bolton England 15 E2 ....53.35N 2.26W
Bolu Turkey 57 I5 ....40.44N 31.36E
Bolus Head Rep. of Ireland 41 A1 ....51.47N 10.20W
Bolzano Italy 50 D7 ....46.29N 11.21E
Boma Dem. Rep. Congo 86 A4 ....5.48S 13.03E
Bømlo i. Norway 40 A2 ....59.45N 5.13E
Bon, Cap c. Tunisia 52 F4 ....37.04N 11.04E
Bonaire i. Neth. Antilles 71 K3 ....12.02N 68.12W
Bonar Bridge Scotland 19 E2 ....57.54N 4.21W
Bonavista Canada 63 M2 ....48.33N 52.43W
Bondoukou Côte d'Ivoire 84 D2 ....8.03N 2.48W
Bo'ness Scotland 17 F4 ....56.01N 3.36W
Bonete, Cerro mt. Bolivia 76 G2 ....21.46S 66.29W
Bonifacio France 44 H2 ....41.23N 9.10E
Bonifacio, Strait of France/Italy 44 H2 ....41.20N 9.05E
Bonin Islands Japan 108 F7 ....27.13N 141.44E
Bonn Germany 54 B4 ....50.44N 7.04E
Bonnyrigg Scotland 17 F3 ....55.52N 3.06W
Bontosunggu Indonesia 104 F2 ....5.41S 119.43E
Boothia, Gulf of Canada 63 J4 ....68.48N 86.41W
Boothia Peninsula Canada 63 I5 ....70.40N 94.39W
Bootle England 14 E2 ....53.27N 2.59W
Bor Turkey 57 K3 ....37.54N 34.33E
Borås Sweden 40 C2 ....57.44N 12.57E
Borāzjān Iran 95 H5 ....29.16N 51.12E
Bordeaux France 44 C4 ....44.51N 0.34W
Borden Island Canada 62 G5 ....78.31N 111.01W
Borden Peninsula Canada 63 J5 ....72.45N 82.32W
Bordj Messaouda Algeria 52 E3 ....30.10N 9.25E
Bordj Omer Driss Algeria 84 E4 ....28.11N 6.47E
Boreray i. Scotland 18 B2 ....57.42N 7.16W
Borgarnes Iceland 40 X2 ....64.32N 21.55W
Borken Germany 42 F4 ....51.50N 6.51E
Borkum i. Germany 42 F5 ....53.37N 6.44E
Borlänge Sweden 40 C3 ....60.29N 15.26E
Borneo i. Asia 104 E3 ....0.08N 113.25E
Bornholm i. Denmark 40 C1 ....55.09N 14.38E
Bornova Turkey 56 G4 ....38.27N 27.11E
Borodyanka Ukraine 55 M4 ....50.39N 29.56E
Boroughbridge England 15 F3 ....54.06N 1.24W
Borüjerd Iran 95 G6 ....33.53N 48.43E
Boryspil' Ukraine 55 N4 ....50.21N 30.58E
Borzna Ukraine 55 O4 ....51.15N 32.26E
Borzya Rus. Fed. 59 M3 ....50.11N 116.31E
Bosanska Dubica Bos.-Herz. 56 B7 ....45.11N 16.48E
Bose China 103 J3 ....23.54N 106.37E
Bosna r. Bos.-Herz. 56 C7 ....45.04N 18.29E
Bosnia-Herzegovina Europe 56 B7 ....44.23N 17.40E
Bosobolo Dem. Rep. Congo 86 A5 ....4.10N 19.52E
Bosporus str. Turkey 57 H5 ....41.20N 29.06E
Bossembélé C.A.R. 85 F2 ....5.15N 17.38E
Bosten Hu l. China 102 F6 ....41.53N 87.24E
Boston England 11 E3 ....52.59N 0.01W
Boston U.S.A. 65 L5 ....42.23N 71.06W
Boston Spa England 15 F2 ....53.54N 1.20W
Botevgrad Bulgaria 56 E6 ....42.54N 23.47E
Bothnia, Gulf of Finland/Sweden 40 D3 ....61.09N 19.15E
Botoșani Romania 55 L2 ....47.45N 26.39E
Botswana Africa 86 B2 ....24.56S 22.47E
Botte Donato, Monte mt. Italy 50 G3 ....39.17N 16.28E
Bottesford England 15 G2 ....53.33N 0.38W
Bouaké Côte d'Ivoire 84 D2 ....7.42N 5.03W
Bouar C.A.R. 84 F2 ....5.56N 15.35E
Bouârfa Morocco 84 D5 ....32.34N 1.56W
Bougainville Island P.N.G. 110 E6 ....6.04S 154.53E
Bouillon Belgium 42 E2 ....49.48N 5.06E
Boujdour Western Sahara 84 C4 ....26.08N 14.32W
Boulder U.S.A. 64 E5 ....40.02N 105.16W
Boulogne-Billancourt France 44 E6 ....48.50N 2.15E
Boulogne-sur-Mer France 44 D7 ....50.43N 1.37E
Bounty Islands New Zealand 111 H2 ....47.40S 179.02E
Bourg-en-Bresse France 44 F5 ....46.12N 5.14E
Bourges France 44 E5 ....47.05N 2.24E
Bourke Australia 110 D3 ....30.07S 145.54E
Bourne England 11 E3 ....52.46N 0.23W
Bournemouth England 10 D1 ....50.43N 1.53W
Bournemouth d. England 9 E2 ....50.45N 1.50W
Bou Saâda Algeria 52 D4 ....35.13N 4.11E
Bow r. Canada 64 D6 ....49.58N 111.41W
Bowes England 15 E3 ....54.31N 2.00W
Bowland, Forest of England 14 E2 ....53.59N 2.33W
Boxtel Neth. 42 E4 ....51.35N 5.20E
Boyabat Turkey 57 K5 ....41.28N 34.46E
Boyle Rep. of Ireland 41 C3 ....53.58N 8.18W
Boyne r. Rep. of Ireland 41 E3 ....53.43N 6.18W
Boyuibe Bolivia 76 H3 ....20.27S 63.20W
Bozeman U.S.A. 64 D6 ....45.42N 111.02W
Bozüyük Turkey 57 I4 ....39.55N 30.01E
Braan r. Scotland 19 F1 ....56.34N 3.36W
Brabant Wallon d. Belgium 42 D3 ....50.39N 4.35E
Brač i. Croatia 56 B6 ....43.17N 16.31E

Bracadale, Loch b. Scotland 18 C2 .....57.21N 6.33W
Bräcke Sweden 40 C3 .....62.46N 15.26E
Brackley England 10 D3 .....52.02N 1.08W
Bracknell England 10 E2 .....51.25N 0.45W
Bracknell Forest d. England 9 E2 .....51.24N 0.45W
Brad Romania 56 E8 .....46.07N 22.48E
Bradano r. Italy 50 G4 .....40.23N 16.51E
Bradford England 15 F2 .....53.48N 1.45W
Bradford-on-Avon England 10 C2 .....51.21N 2.15W
Braemar Scotland 19 F2 .....57.00N 3.24W
Braga Portugal 48 A4 .....41.33N 8.26W
Bragança Brazil 77 K7 .....1.00S 46.49W
Bragança Portugal 48 B4 .....41.49N 6.45W
Brahmapur India 96 F4 .....19.21N 84.52E
Brahmaputra r. China/India 102 G2 .....23.36N 90.31E
Brăila Romania 57 G2 .....45.17N 27.58E
Braintree England 11 F2 .....51.53N 0.33E
Brämön i. Sweden 40 D3 .....62.13N 17.45E
Brampton England 14 E3 .....54.57N 2.44W
Branco r. Brazil 77 H7 .....1.18S 61.52W
Brandenburg Germany 54 E5 .....52.25N 12.34E
Brandesburton England 15 G2 .....53.55N 0.18W
Brandon Canada 62 I2 .....49.51N 99.57W
Brandon England 11 F3 .....52.27N 0.37E
Brandon Head Rep. of Ireland 41 A2 .....52.17N 10.13W
Brandon Mountain hill Rep. of Ireland 41 A2 .....52.14N 10.15W
Braniewo Poland 46 D5 .....54.23N 19.49E
Bransgore England 10 D1 .....50.47N 1.44W
Brasília Brazil 77 K4 .....15.49S 47.55W
Brașov Romania 56 F7 .....45.40N 25.36E
Bratislava Slovakia 54 G3 .....48.09N 17.06E
Bratsk Rus. Fed. 59 L3 .....56.16N 101.41E
Braunau am Inn Austria 54 E3 .....48.16N 13.02E
Braunschweig Germany 54 D5 .....52.17N 10.32E
Braunton England 13 C3 .....51.06N 4.10W
Brawley U.S.A. 64 C3 .....32.58N 115.32W
Bray Rep. of Ireland 41 E3 .....53.12N 6.07W
Bray Head Rep. of Ireland 41 A1 .....51.52N 10.25W
Brazil S. America 77 I5 .....29.58S 54.33W
Brazil Basin f. Atlantic Oc. 116 H5 .....15.00S 30.00W
Brazilian Highlands mts Brazil 77 K5 .....17.00S 48.00W
Brazos r. U.S.A. 64 G2 .....28.52N 95.25W
Brazzaville Congo 84 F1 .....4.17S 15.11E
Breamish r. England 15 E4 .....55.41N 2.13W
Brechin Scotland 19 G1 .....56.44N 2.39W
Breckland f. England 11 F3 .....52.28N 0.39E
Břeclav Czech Rep. 54 G3 .....48.46N 16.53E
Brecon Wales 12 D3 .....51.57N 3.24W
Brecon Beacons f. Wales 12 D3 .....51.53N 3.26W
Breda Neth. 42 D4 .....51.35N 4.46E
Breiðafjörður b. Iceland 40 W2 .....65.03N 24.07W
Breiðdalsvík Iceland 40 Y2 .....64.48N 14.02W
Bremen Germany 54 C5 .....53.05N 8.51E
Bremerhaven Germany 54 C5 .....53.33N 8.35E
Brenner Pass Austria/Italy 50 D7 .....46.59N 11.32E
Brentwood England 11 F2 .....51.37N 0.19E
Brescia Italy 50 D6 .....45.32N 10.13E
Bressanone Italy 50 D7 .....46.43N 11.40E
Bressay i. Scotland 19 H5 .....60.16N 1.18W
Bressuire France 44 C5 .....46.49N 0.30W
Brest Belarus 55 J5 .....52.05N 23.40E
Brest France 44 A6 .....48.24N 4.30W
Bretton Wales 12 E5 .....53.10N 2.58W
Bria C.A.R. 85 G2 .....6.32N 21.59E
Briançon France 44 G4 .....44.54N 6.38E
Brianne, Llyn resr Wales 12 D4 .....52.08N 3.45W
Bride r. Rep. of Ireland 41 D2 .....52.04N 7.52W
Bridgend Wales 13 D3 .....51.30N 3.35W
Bridgend d. Wales 9 D2 .....51.34N 3.33W
Bridgeport U.S.A. 65 L5 .....41.12N 73.12W
Bridgetown Barbados 71 M3 .....13.05N 59.36W
Bridgnorth England 10 C3 .....52.32N 2.25W
Bridgwater England 13 D3 .....51.08N 3.00W
Bridgwater Bay England 13 D3 .....51.16N 3.19W
Bridlington England 15 G3 .....54.05N 0.12W
Bridlington Bay England 15 G3 .....54.03N 0.10W
Bridport England 10 C1 .....50.44N 2.45W
Brig Switz. 50 B7 .....46.19N 7.59E
Brigg England 15 G2 .....53.33N 0.29W
Brighstone England 10 D1 .....50.39N 1.23W
Brightlingsea England 11 G2 .....51.49N 1.01E
Brighton England 11 E1 .....50.49N 0.08W
Brighton and Hove d. England 9 E2 .....50.51N 0.08W
Brindisi Italy 50 G4 .....40.38N 17.56E
Brisbane Australia 110 E4 .....27.33S 153.03E
Bristol England 10 C2 .....51.27N 2.35W
Bristol d. England 9 D2 .....51.28N 2.36W
Bristol U.S.A. 65 J4 .....36.36N 82.10W
Bristol Bay U.S.A. 62 B3 .....57.22N 161.29W
Bristol Channel est. England 10 B2 .....51.20N 4.16W
British Columbia d. Canada 62 F3 .....51.49N 121.48W
British Empire Range mts Canada 63 J6 .....82.22N 80.08W
British Isles Europe 34 D3 .....54.00N 5.00W
Briton Ferry Wales 12 D3 .....51.38N 3.49W
Britstown S. Africa 86 B1 .....30.35S 23.30E
Brittany f. France 44 B6 .....48.10N 3.22W
Brittas Bay Rep. of Ireland 12 A4 .....52.52N 6.03W
Brive-la-Gaillarde France 44 D4 .....45.10N 1.32E
Brixham England 13 D2 .....50.24N 3.31W
Brno Czech Rep. 54 G3 .....49.11N 16.37E
Broad r. U.S.A. 65 J3 .....34.00N 81.04W
Broadback r. Canada 65 K7 .....51.21N 78.50W
Broad Bay Scotland 18 C3 .....58.15N 6.15W
Broad Law hill Scotland 17 F3 .....55.30N 3.21W
Broadstairs England 11 G2 .....51.22N 1.26E
Broadway England 10 D3 .....52.02N 1.51W
Broadwey England 10 C1 .....50.39N 2.28W
Broadwindsor England 10 C1 .....50.49N 2.48W
Brockenhurst England 10 D1 .....50.49N 1.34W
Brock Island Canada 62 G5 .....77.53N 114.21W
Brodeur Peninsula Canada 63 J5 .....71.50N 88.32W
Brodick Scotland 16 D3 .....55.35N 5.09W
Brodnica Poland 46 D4 .....53.16N 19.24E
Brody Ukraine 55 K4 .....50.05N 25.09E
Broken Hill town Australia 110 D3 .....31.55S 141.27E
Bromley England 11 F2 .....51.24N 0.01E
Bromsgrove England 10 C3 .....52.20N 2.04W
Bromyard England 10 C3 .....52.11N 2.30W
Brønderslev Denmark 40 B2 .....57.17N 9.58E
Brønnøysund Norway 40 C4 .....65.28N 12.12E
Brooke England 11 G3 .....52.33N 1.23E
Brooke's Point town Phil. 104 F5 .....8.50N 117.51E
Brookings U.S.A. 64 G5 .....44.19N 96.44W
Brooks Canada 64 D7 .....50.35N 111.54W
Brooks Range U.S.A. 62 D4 .....69.18N 144.41W
Broom, Loch inlet Scotland 18 D2 .....57.56N 5.19W
Broome Australia 110 B5 .....17.57S 122.14E
Brora Scotland 19 F3 .....58.01N 3.51W
Brora r. Scotland 19 F3 .....58.01N 3.50W
Brosna r. Rep. of Ireland 41 D3 .....53.14N 7.57W
Brotton England 15 G3 .....54.34N 0.56W
Brough Cumb. England 15 E3 .....54.32N 2.19W
Brough E. Yorks. England 15 G2 .....53.44N 0.34W
Brough Head Scotland 19 F4 .....59.08N 3.21W

Brough Ness pt Scotland 19 G3 .....58.44N 2.58W
Broughshane Northern Ireland 16 C2 .....54.54N 6.12W
Brownhills England 10 D3 .....52.39N 1.56W
Broxburn Scotland 17 F3 .....55.56N 3.28W
Bruay-la-Bussière France 42 B3 .....50.29N 2.33E
Brue r. England 10 C2 .....51.13N 2.59W
Brugge Belgium 42 C4 .....51.12N 3.15E
Brumado Brazil 77 L5 .....14.12S 41.34W
Brunei Asia 104 E4 .....5.06N 114.18E
Brunflo Sweden 40 C3 .....63.05N 14.51E
Brunswick U.S.A. 65 J3 .....31.09N 81.30W
Bruntál Czech Rep. 46 C2 .....49.59N 17.28E
Brussels Belgium 42 D3 .....50.50N 4.21E
Bruton England 10 C2 .....51.07N 2.27W
Bryansk Rus. Fed. 58 E3 .....53.15N 34.23E
Bryher i. England 13 A1 .....49.57N 6.23W
Brynamman Wales 12 D3 .....51.49N 3.52W
Brynmawr Wales 12 D3 .....51.48N 3.10W
Brzeg Poland 46 C3 .....50.51N 17.28E
Buca Turkey 56 G4 .....38.22N 27.11E
Bucaramanga Colombia 72 B7 .....7.05N 73.09W
Bucharest Romania 56 G7 .....44.26N 26.06E
Buckhaven Scotland 17 F4 .....56.11N 3.02W
Buckie Scotland 19 G2 .....57.41N 2.58W
Buckingham England 10 E2 .....51.59N 0.59W
Buckinghamshire d. England 9 E2 .....51.47N 0.56W
Buckley Wales 12 D5 .....53.10N 3.05W
Budapest Hungary 54 H2 .....47.30N 19.04E
Buddon Ness pt Scotland 17 G4 .....56.28N 2.43W
Bude England 13 C2 .....50.50N 4.32W
Bude Bay England 13 C2 .....50.50N 4.38W
Buenaventura Colombia 72 B7 .....3.52N 77.00W
Buenos Aires Argentina 73 D3 .....34.36S 58.24W
Buenos Aires, Lago l. Argentina/Chile 73 B2 .....46.31S 72.13W
Buffalo N. Y. U.S.A. 65 K5 .....42.53N 78.52W
Buffalo Wyo. U.S.A. 64 E5 .....44.20N 106.41W
Bug r. Poland 46 F3 .....51.30N 23.39E
Buhu r. Tanzania 87 A1 .....6.03S 35.20E
Builth Wells Wales 12 D4 .....52.09N 3.24W
Buir Nur l. Mongolia 103 L7 .....47.47N 117.53E
Bujumbura Burundi 85 G1 .....3.24S 29.22E
Bukavu Dem. Rep. Congo 86 B4 .....2.30S 28.49E
Bukittinggi Indonesia 104 C3 .....0.15S 100.20E
Bukoba Tanzania 86 C4 .....1.18S 31.48E
Bula Indonesia 105 I3 .....3.06S 130.28E
Bulawayo Zimbabwe 86 B2 .....20.09S 28.36E
Bulgan Mongolia 103 I7 .....48.48N 103.28E
Bulgaria Europe 56 F6 .....42.51N 25.15E
Bulun Rus. Fed. 59 N5 .....70.59N 127.16E
Buna Kenya 87 B3 .....2.47N 39.31E
Bunbury Australia 110 A3 .....33.20S 115.36E
Bunclody Rep. of Ireland 41 E2 .....52.39N 6.39W
Buncrana Rep. of Ireland 41 D5 .....55.09N 7.27W
Bunda Tanzania 87 A2 .....2.04S 33.56E
Bundaberg Australia 110 E4 .....24.52S 152.22E
Bundoran Rep. of Ireland 41 C4 .....54.28N 8.18W
Bungay England 11 G3 .....52.27N 1.27E
Bungoma Kenya 87 A3 .....0.34N 34.34E
Buôn Ma Thuột Vietnam 104 D6 .....12.38N 108.05E
Bura Kenya 87 B2 .....1.06S 39.57E
Buraydah Saudi Arabia 94 F5 .....26.20N 43.57E
Burbage England 10 D2 .....51.21N 1.40W
Burdur Turkey 57 I3 .....37.43N 30.17E
Bure r. England 11 G3 .....52.37N 1.43E
Burē Ethiopia 85 H3 .....10.50N 36.57E
Burford England 10 D2 .....51.48N 1.38W
Burgas Bulgaria 56 G6 .....42.30N 27.28E
Burgess Hill town England 11 E1 .....50.57N 0.08W
Burghausen Germany 54 E3 .....48.10N 12.50E
Burghead Scotland 19 F2 .....57.42N 3.29W
Burgh le Marsh England 15 H2 .....53.10N 0.14E
Burgos Spain 48 D5 .....42.21N 3.41W
Burhanpur India 96 E5 .....21.18N 76.14E
Burkina Africa 84 D3 .....11.39N 1.18W
Burlington Colo. U.S.A. 64 F4 .....39.19N 102.17W
Burlington Iowa U.S.A. 65 H5 .....40.49N 91.06W
Burlington Vt. U.S.A. 65 L5 .....44.28N 73.13W
Burnham England 10 E2 .....51.32N 0.39W
Burnham Market England 11 F3 .....52.57N 0.44E
Burnham-on-Crouch England 11 F2 .....51.38N 0.49E
Burnham-on-Sea England 10 C2 .....51.14N 2.59W
Burnie Australia 110 D1 .....41.03S 145.57E
Burniston England 15 G3 .....54.19N 0.27W
Burnley England 15 E2 .....53.47N 2.15W
Burns U.S.A. 64 C5 .....43.36N 119.03W
Burns Lake town Canada 62 F3 .....54.15N 125.46W
Burntisland Scotland 17 F4 .....56.04N 3.14W
Burntwood Green England 10 D3 .....52.41N 1.54W
Burray i. Scotland 19 H5 .....60.05N 1.22W
Burray i. Scotland 19 G3 .....58.51N 2.53W
Burro, Serranías del Mexico 70 D6 .....29.02N 102.00W
Burrow Head Scotland 16 E2 .....54.41N 4.23W
Burry Inlet Wales 12 C3 .....51.38N 4.18W
Burry Port Wales 12 C3 .....51.41N 4.16W
Bursa Turkey 57 H5 .....40.14N 29.03E
Bûr Safâjah Egypt 53 J2 .....26.45N 33.55E
Burscough Bridge England 14 E2 .....53.36N 2.51W
Burton-in-Kendal England 14 E3 .....54.11N 2.43W
Burton Latimer England 10 E3 .....52.22N 0.41W
Burton upon Trent England 10 D3 .....52.48N 1.38W
Buru i. Indonesia 105 H3 .....3.24S 126.35E
Burundi Africa 85 H1 .....3.36S 30.03E
Burwash Landing Canada 62 E4 .....61.21N 138.58W
Burwell England 11 F3 .....52.16N 0.20E
Burwick Scotland 19 G3 .....58.45N 2.58W
Bury England 15 E2 .....53.36N 2.18W
Bury St Edmunds England 11 F3 .....52.15N 0.44E
Bush r. Northern Ireland 16 C3 .....55.13N 6.31W
Bushbush r. Kenya/Somalia 87 C2 .....1.11S 41.49E
Büshehr Iran 95 H5 .....28.58N 50.51E
Bushmills Northern Ireland 16 C3 .....55.12N 6.31W
Busto Arsizio Italy 50 C6 .....45.37N 8.51E
Buta Dem. Rep. Congo 86 B5 .....2.49N 24.45E
Bute i. Scotland 16 D3 .....55.49N 5.06W
Bute, Sound of str. Scotland 16 D3 .....55.44N 5.19W
Buton i. Indonesia 105 G3 .....4.57S 123.00E
Butt of Lewis hd Scotland 18 C3 .....58.32N 6.17W
Butterworth Malaysia 104 C5 .....5.22N 100.22E
Buttevant Rep. of Ireland 41 C2 .....52.14N 8.40W
Butuan Phil. 105 H5 .....8.56N 125.32E
Buur Gaabo Somalia 87 C2 .....1.15S 41.49E
Buvuma Island Uganda 87 A3 .....0.10N 33.18E
Buxoro Uzbekistan 58 H1 .....39.46N 64.25E
Buxton England 15 F2 .....53.16N 1.55W
Büyük Ağrı Dağı mt. Turkey 94 F7 .....39.44N 44.15E
Büyükmenderes r. Turkey 57 G3 .....37.28N 27.11E
Buzău Romania 56 G7 .....45.09N 26.48E
Byarezina r. Belarus 55 K5 .....53.48N 25.58E
Byaroza Belarus 55 K5 .....52.32N 24.59E
Bydgoszcz Poland 46 D4 .....53.08N 18.02E
Byfield England 10 D3 .....52.11N 1.14W
Bylot Island Canada 63 K5 .....73.07N 79.01W
Byrranga, Gory mts Rus. Fed. 59 K5 .....74.25N 99.53E
Bytom Poland 46 D3 .....50.21N 18.55E

C

Caacupé Paraguay 77 I2 .....25.20S 57.05W
Cabanatuan Phil. 105 G7 .....15.31N 120.58E
Caban Coch Reservoir Wales 12 D4 .....52.15N 3.35W
Cabezas Bolivia 76 H4 .....18.46S 63.23W
Cabimas Venezuela 72 B8 .....10.23N 71.26W
Cabinda Angola 84 F1 .....5.33S 12.15E
Cabo Frio Brazil 73 E4 .....22.51S 42.02W
Cabonga, Réservoir Canada 65 K6 .....47.21N 76.32W
Cabo Pantoja Peru 76 E7 .....0.58S 75.13W
Cabora Bassa, Lake resr Mozambique 86 C3 .....15.46S 31.11E
Caborca Mexico 70 B7 .....30.44N 112.09W
Cabot Strait Canada 63 L2 .....47.39N 60.16W
Cabrera, Sierra de la mts Spain 48 B5 .....42.13N 6.51W
Cabriel r. Spain 48 E3 .....39.16N 1.04W
Cáceres Brazil 77 I4 .....16.03S 57.41W
Cáceres Spain 48 B3 .....39.29N 6.21W
Cachi, Nevados de mts Argentina 76 G3 .....24.48S 66.25W
Cachimbo, Serra do hills Brazil 77 J6 .....9.18S 54.11W
Cachoeiro de Itapemirim Brazil 77 L3 .....20.51S 41.08W
Cadillac U.S.A. 65 I5 .....44.14N 85.23W
Cádiz Spain 48 B2 .....36.32N 6.17W
Cádiz, Golfo de g. Spain 48 B2 .....36.44N 7.14W
Caen France 44 C6 .....49.11N 0.21W
Caerleon Wales 12 E3 .....51.37N 2.57W
Caernarfon Wales 12 C5 .....53.08N 4.16W
Caernarfon Bay Wales 12 C5 .....53.06N 4.34W
Caerphilly Wales 12 D3 .....51.35N 3.13W
Caerphilly d. Wales 9 D2 .....51.38N 3.11W
Caerwent Wales 12 E3 .....51.37N 2.46W
Cagayan de Oro Phil. 105 G5 .....8.29N 124.39E
Cagliari Italy 50 C3 .....39.13N 9.08E
Cagliari, Golfo di b. Italy 50 C3 .....39.07N 9.13E
Caha Mountains hills Rep. of Ireland 41 B1 .....51.41N 9.44W
Cahirciveen Rep. of Ireland 41 A1 .....51.57N 10.13W
Cahore Point Rep. of Ireland 41 E2 .....52.33N 6.11W
Cahors France 44 D4 .....44.28N 1.26E
Cahul Moldova 57 H7 .....45.54N 28.12E
Caia Mozambique 86 C3 .....17.50S 35.19E
Caiabis, Serra dos hills Brazil 77 I5 .....12.46S 56.21W
Caiapó, Serra do mts Brazil 77 J4 .....17.19S 52.31W
Caicos Islands Turks and Caicos Is 71 J5 .....21.45N 71.53W
Caimodorro mt. Spain 48 E4 .....40.32N 1.40W
Cairn Gorm mt. Scotland 19 F2 .....57.07N 3.39W
Cairngorm Mountains Scotland 19 F2 .....57.08N 3.45W
Cairnryan Scotland 16 D2 .....54.59N 5.02W
Cairns Australia 110 D5 .....16.54S 145.45E
Cairn Toul mt. Scotland 19 F2 .....57.03N 3.43W
Cairo Egypt 85 H5 .....30.01N 31.15E
Caister-on-Sea England 11 G3 .....52.39N 1.44E
Caistor England 15 G2 .....53.30N 0.19W
Caithness f. Scotland 19 F3 .....58.24N 3.22W
Cajamarca Peru 76 E6 .....7.11S 78.31W
Calabar Nigeria 84 E2 .....4.59N 8.19E
Calafat Romania 56 E6 .....43.59N 22.57E
Calais France 44 D7 .....50.57N 1.51E
Calais U.S.A. 65 M6 .....45.10N 67.18W
Calama Chile 73 C4 .....22.29S 68.56W
Calamian Group is Phil. 104 F6 .....11.59N 119.29E
Calamocha Spain 48 E4 .....40.56N 1.17W
Calanscio Sand Sea des. Libya 53 H3 .....30.11N 22.22E
Calapan Phil. 105 G6 .....13.24N 121.11E
Călărași Romania 56 G7 .....44.12N 27.19E
Calatayud Spain 48 E4 .....41.22N 1.37W
Calbayog Phil. 105 G6 .....12.05N 124.37E
Calcanhar, Ponta do pt Brazil 77 M6 .....5.07S 35.34W
Caldas da Rainha Portugal 48 A3 .....39.24N 9.08W
Caldey Island Wales 12 C3 .....51.38N 4.40W
Calf of Man i. Isle of Man 14 C3 .....54.04N 4.50W
Calgary Canada 62 G3 .....51.02N 114.04W
Cali Colombia 72 B7 .....3.22N 76.28W
Caliente U.S.A. 64 D4 .....37.37N 114.31W
California d. U.S.A. 64 B5 .....37.00N 120.00W
California, Gulf of Mexico 70 B7 .....30.51N 113.58W
Callan Rep. of Ireland 41 D2 .....52.32N 7.24W
Callander Scotland 16 E4 .....56.15N 4.13W
Callanish Scotland 18 C3 .....58.12N 6.45W
Callao Peru 76 E5 .....12.04S 77.08W
Callington England 13 C2 .....50.30N 4.19W
Calne England 10 C2 .....51.26N 2.00W
Caltanissetta Italy 50 F2 .....37.30N 14.03E
Calvi France 44 H3 .....42.34N 8.45E
Cam r. England 11 F3 .....52.20N 0.15E
Camaçari Brazil 77 M5 .....12.43S 38.15W
Camagüey Cuba 71 I5 .....21.23N 77.54W
Ca Mau, Mui c. Vietnam 104 C5 .....8.35N 104.45E
Camberley England 10 E2 .....51.20N 0.44W
Cambodia Asia 104 D6 .....13.05N 105.10E
Camborne England 13 B2 .....50.13N 5.18W
Cambrai France 42 C3 .....50.10N 3.14E
Cambrian Mountains Wales 12 D4 .....52.37N 3.40W
Cambridge England 11 F3 .....52.12N 0.07E
Cambridge Bay town Canada 62 H4 .....69.02N 105.14W
Cambridgeshire d. England 9 F3 .....52.25N 0.02E
Camelford England 13 C2 .....50.37N 4.41W
Cameroon Africa 84 F2 .....5.45N 12.41E
Cameroun, Mont vol. Cameroon 84 E2 .....4.12N 9.12E
Cametá Brazil 77 K7 .....2.13S 49.30W
Campbell Island New Zealand 108 H2 .....52.31S 169.01E
Campbell Plateau f. S. Pacific Oc. 108 H2 .....49.32S 170.53E
Campbell River town Canada 62 F3 .....50.01N 125.14W
Campbeltown Scotland 16 D3 .....55.25N 5.36W
Campeche Mexico 70 F4 .....19.51N 90.30W
Campeche d. Mexico 70 F4 .....18.53N 90.28W
Campeche, Bahía de b. Mexico 70 F4 .....19.30N 93.30W
Campina Grande Brazil 77 M6 .....7.14S 35.49W
Campinas Brazil 77 K3 .....22.55S 47.04W
Campo Grande Brazil 77 J3 .....20.24S 54.34W
Campobasso Italy 50 F4 .....41.34N 14.39E
Câmpulung Romania 56 F7 .....45.16N 25.03E
Câmpulung Moldovenesc Romania 55 K2 .....47.32N 25.30E
Camrose Canada 62 G3 .....53.01N 112.48W
Çan Turkey 56 G5 .....40.02N 27.02E
Canada N. America 62 H4 .....60.00N 105.00W
Canadian r. U.S.A. 64 G4 .....35.11N 95.52W
Canadian Shield f. N. America 60 K7 .....50.00N 80.00W
Çanakkale Turkey 56 G5 .....40.09N 26.24E
Canary Islands N. Atlantic Oc. 48 X2 .....30.08N 18.27W
Canaveral, Cape U.S.A. 65 J2 .....28.26N 80.36W
Canberra Australia 110 D3 .....35.19S 149.09E
Cancún Mexico 70 G5 .....21.10N 86.50W
Canelones Uruguay 77 I1 .....34.32S 56.17W
Caniapiscau r. Canada 63 L3 .....57.39N 69.25W
Caniapiscau, Lac l. Canada 63 K3 .....54.21N 70.31W
Canindé Brazil 77 M6 .....6.17S 42.49W
Canisp hill Scotland 18 D3 .....58.07N 5.03W
Çankaya Turkey 57 J4 .....39.53N 32.49E
Çankırı Turkey 57 J5 .....40.36N 33.36E
Canna i. Scotland 18 C2 .....57.04N 6.34W

Cannes France 44 G3 .....43.33N 7.01E
Cannock England 10 C3 .....52.41N 2.02W
Canoas Brazil 77 J2 .....29.54S 51.10W
Canora Canada 64 F7 .....51.39N 102.26W
Cantabrian Mountains Spain 48 C5 .....43.07N 4.13W
Canterbury England 11 G2 .....51.17N 1.05E
Cân Thơ Vietnam 104 D6 .....10.01N 105.46E
Canvey Island England 11 F2 .....51.31N 0.35E
Cao Bằng Vietnam 104 D8 .....22.41N 106.17E
Capbreton France 44 C3 .....43.39N 1.26W
Cape Breton Island Canada 63 L2 .....46.45N 60.24W
Cape Johnson Depth f. N. Pacific Oc. 108 E6 .....10.26N 126.39E
Capel St Mary England 11 G3 .....52.00N 1.03E
Cape Town S. Africa 86 A1 .....33.57S 18.28E
Cape Verde N. Atlantic Oc. 84 B3 .....15.47N 24.31W
Cape York Peninsula Australia 110 D5 .....12.33S 142.33E
Cap-Haïtien Haiti 71 J4 .....19.46N 72.15W
Capim r. Brazil 77 K7 .....1.30S 48.30W
Capitol Hill town N. Mariana Is 108 F7 .....15.12N 145.45E
Capraia, Isola di i. Italy 50 C5 .....43.04N 9.48E
Caprera, Isola di i. Italy 50 C4 .....41.13N 9.29E
Capri, Isola di i. Italy 50 F4 .....40.32N 14.13E
Capricorn Channel Australia 110 E4 .....22.20S 151.46E
Caprivi Strip f. Namibia 86 B3 .....18.11S 21.44E
Caquetá r. Colombia 72 C6 .....1.27S 69.25W
Carabaya, Cordillera de mts Peru 76 F5 .....13.27S 71.27W
Caracal Romania 56 F7 .....44.07N 24.21E
Caracas Venezuela 72 C8 .....10.28N 66.59W
Carajás, Serra dos hills Brazil 77 J6 .....5.43S 51.27W
Caransebeș Romania 56 E7 .....45.25N 22.14E
Caratasca, Laguna de lagoon Honduras 71 H4 .....15.07N 83.57W
Caratinga Brazil 77 L4 .....19.45S 42.04W
Caravaca de la Cruz Spain 48 E3 .....38.07N 1.51W
Carbonara, Capo c. Italy 50 C3 .....39.06N 9.32E
Carcassonne France 44 E3 .....43.13N 2.22E
Cardiff Wales 13 D3 .....51.29N 3.11W
Cardiff d. Wales 9 D2 .....51.30N 3.12W
Cardigan Wales 12 C4 .....52.05N 4.40W
Cardigan Bay Wales 12 C4 .....52.33N 4.32W
Carei Romania 55 J2 .....47.41N 22.28E
Carey, Lake Australia 110 B4 .....28.57S 122.21E
Caribbean Sea N. Atlantic Oc. 71 H4 .....19.03N 83.05W
Caribou Mountains Canada 62 G3 .....59.02N 115.22W
Cark Mountain Rep. of Ireland 16 B2 .....54.53N 7.52W
Carletonville S. Africa 86 B2 .....26.21S 27.24E
Carlingford Lough inlet Rep. of Ireland/U.K. 41 E4 .....54.05N 6.14W
Carlisle England 14 E3 .....54.54N 2.56W
Carlow Rep. of Ireland 41 E2 .....52.50N 6.56W
Carlow d. Rep. of Ireland 41 E2 .....52.47N 6.52W
Carluke Scotland 17 F3 .....55.44N 3.50W
Carmacks Canada 62 E4 .....62.05N 136.17W
Carmarthen Wales 12 C3 .....51.51N 4.19W
Carmarthen Bay Wales 12 C3 .....51.38N 4.32W
Carmarthenshire d. Wales 9 C2 .....51.57N 4.19W
Carmel Head Wales 12 C5 .....53.25N 4.34W
Carmen, Isla i. Mexico 70 B6 .....25.59N 111.09W
Carnac France 44 B5 .....47.35S 3.04W
Carn Deang hill Scotland 19 E2 .....57.06N 4.16W
Carndonagh Rep. of Ireland 16 B3 .....55.15N 7.15W
Carnedd Llywelyn mt. Wales 12 D5 .....53.10N 3.58W
Carnedd y Filiast hill Wales 12 D4 .....52.59N 3.41W
Carnegie, Lake Australia 110 B4 .....26.10S 122.54E
Carn Eighe mt. Scotland 18 D2 .....57.17N 5.07W
Carnforth England 14 E3 .....54.08N 2.46W
Carnic Alps mts Italy 50 E7 .....46.40N 12.48E
Car Nicobar i. India 97 H2 .....9.10N 92.47E
Carnlough Northern Ireland 16 D2 .....54.59N 5.59W
Carn Mòr hill Scotland 19 F2 .....57.15N 3.18W
Carn nan Gabhar mt. Scotland 19 F1 .....56.50N 3.41W
Carnot, Cape Australia 110 C3 .....34.55S 135.37E
Carnoustie Scotland 17 G4 .....56.30N 2.42W
Carnsore Point Rep. of Ireland 41 E2 .....52.10N 6.22W
Caroline Island atoll Kiribati 109 J5 .....9.58S 150.11W
Caroline Islands N. Pacific Oc. 108 F6 .....6.35N 144.24E
Carpathian Mountains Europe 55 J3 .....48.45N 23.45E
Carpentaria, Gulf of Australia 110 C5 .....14.06S 139.04E
Carpentras France 44 F4 .....44.04N 5.03E
Carra, Lough l. Rep. of Ireland 41 B3 .....53.44N 9.14W
Carrantuohill mt. Rep. of Ireland 41 B1 .....51.59N 9.44W
Carrara Italy 50 D6 .....44.04N 10.06E
Carrickfergus Northern Ireland 16 D2 .....54.43N 5.48W
Carrickfergus d. Northern Ireland 9 C4 .....54.44N 5.49W
Carrickmacross Rep. of Ireland 41 E3 .....53.59N 6.43W
Carrick-on-Shannon Rep. of Ireland 41 C3 .....53.56N 8.05W
Carrick-on-Suir Rep. of Ireland 41 D2 .....52.21N 7.25W
Carron r. Falk. Scotland 17 F4 .....56.02N 3.44W
Carron r. High. Scotland 18 D2 .....57.53N 4.22W
Carrowmore Lake Rep. of Ireland 41 B4 .....54.11N 9.47W
Carson City U.S.A. 64 C4 .....39.10N 119.46W
Carsphairn Scotland 16 E3 .....55.13N 4.16W
Cartagena Colombia 72 B8 .....10.23N 75.33W
Cartagena Spain 48 E2 .....37.36N 0.59W
Carteret France 13 Z9 .....49.23N 1.47W
Carterton England 10 D2 .....51.46N 1.36W
Cartmel England 14 E3 .....54.12N 2.57W
Caruaru Brazil 77 M6 .....8.13S 35.52W
Carvin France 42 B3 .....50.29N 2.57E
Casablanca Morocco 84 D5 .....33.35N 7.34W
Casa Grande U.S.A. 64 D3 .....32.53N 111.45W
Cascade Range mts Canada/U.S.A. 62 F2 .....41.49N 122.21W
Cascavel Brazil 77 J3 .....24.55S 53.28W
Caserta Italy 50 F4 .....41.04N 14.20E
Cashel Rep. of Ireland 41 D2 .....52.31N 7.53W
Casper U.S.A. 64 E5 .....42.52N 106.20W
Caspian Lowland f. Kazakhstan/Rus. Fed. 58 F2 .....44.15N 45.47E
Caspian Sea l. Asia/Europe 58 G2 .....42.00N 51.00E
Cassiar Mountains Canada 62 E3 .....59.40N 130.31W
Cassley r. Scotland 18 E2 .....57.58N 4.34W
Castanhal Brazil 77 K7 .....1.18S 47.54W
Castelló de la Plana Spain 48 E3 .....39.59N 0.02W
Castlebar Rep. of Ireland 41 B3 .....53.51N 9.17W
Castlebay Scotland 18 B1 .....56.57N 7.29W
Castleblayney Rep. of Ireland 41 E4 .....54.07N 6.43W
Castle Cary England 10 C2 .....51.05N 2.31W
Castlecomer Rep. of Ireland 41 D2 .....52.48N 7.13W
Castleconnell Rep. of Ireland 41 C2 .....52.43N 8.30W
Castlederg Northern Ireland 16 B2 .....54.42N 7.35W
Castle Donington England 10 D3 .....52.50N 1.20W
Castle Douglas Scotland 17 F2 .....54.56N 3.56W
Castleford England 15 F2 .....53.43N 1.21W
Castleisland Rep. of Ireland 41 B2 .....52.14N 9.27W
Castlereagh d. Northern Ireland 9 C4 .....54.33N 5.51W
Castletown Isle of Man 14 C3 .....54.05N 4.39W
Castres France 44 E3 .....43.36N 2.14E
Castries St Lucia 71 L3 .....14.00N 60.59W
Castro Verde Portugal 48 A2 .....37.42N 8.05W
Catacaos Peru 76 D6 .....5.18S 80.42W
Catamarca Argentina 73 C4 .....28.26S 65.45W
Catanduanes i. Phil. 105 G6 .....13.46N 124.14E
Catania Italy 50 F2 .....37.30N 15.05E
Catanzaro Italy 50 G3 .....38.55N 16.36E
Catarman Phil. 105 G6 .....12.29N 124.38E

aterham England 11 E2 ....51.17N 0.05W
at Island Bahamas 71 I5 ....24.28N 75.30W
atoche, Cabo c. Mexico 70 G5 ....21.37N 87.06W
atterick England 15 F3 ....54.23N 1.38W
auca r. Colombia 71 J2 ....8.54N 74.29W
aucaia Brazil 77 M7 ....3.42S 38.43W
aucasus mts Asia/Europe 58 F2 ....43.53N 40.00E
audry France 42 C3 ....50.07N 3.25E
avan Rep. of Ireland 41 D3 ....53.59N 7.22W
avan d. Rep. of Ireland 41 D3 ....53.57N 7.15W
awston England 11 G3 ....52.46N 1.10E
axias Brazil 77 L7 ....4.54S 43.19W
axias do Sul Brazil 77 J2 ....29.13S 51.11W
ayenne French Guiana 72 D7 ....4.53N 52.21W
ayman Brac i. Cayman Is 71 I4 ....19.43N 79.48W
ayman Islands Central America 71 H4 ....19.31N 81.51W
eará d. Brazil 77 M7 ....4.51S 39.03W
ebu Phil. 105 G6 ....10.17N 123.55E
ebu i. Phil. 105 G6 ....10.26N 123.53E
edar r. U.S.A. 65 J5 ....43.40N 84.23W
edar City U.S.A. 64 D4 ....37.41N 113.04W
edar Rapids town U.S.A. 65 H5 ....41.59N 91.40W
edros, Isla i. Mexico 70 A6 ....28.11N 115.20W
efalù Italy 50 F3 ....38.02N 14.02E
egléd Hungary 54 H2 ....47.10N 19.48E
elebes i. Indonesia 104 G3 ....2.01S 120.29E
elebes Sea Indonesia/Phil. 104 G4 ....3.03N 121.10E
elje Slovenia 54 F2 ....46.14N 15.15E
elle Germany 54 D5 ....52.38N 10.05E
eltic Sea Rep. of Ireland/U.K. 13 A2 ....50.54N 6.33W
elyn, Llyn l. Wales 12 D4 ....52.57N 3.43W
enderawasih, Teluk b. Indonesia 105 J3 ....2.05S 135.33E
entral d. Kenya 87 B2 ....0.42S 36.56S
entral, Cordillera mts Bolivia 76 G4 ....18.27S 66.22W
entral, Cordillera mts Colombia 72 B7 ....1.38N 76.51W
entral, Cordillera mts Peru 76 E5 ....10.02S 76.25W
entral African Republic Africa 85 G2 ....6.25N 20.12E
entral Pacific Basin f. Pacific Oc. 108 H6 ....3.53N 179.43E
entral Range mts P.N.G. 105 K3 ....4.57S 142.36E
entral Russian Upland hills Rus. Fed. 55 Q6 ....54.27N 36.28E
entral Siberian Plateau f. Rus. Fed. 59 M4 ....67.03N 110.35E
ephalonia i. Greece 56 D4 ....38.14N 20.21E
eredigion d. Wales 9 D3 ....52.19N 3.58W
ernavodă Romania 57 H7 ....44.21N 28.02E
erralvo, Isla i. Mexico 70 C5 ....24.10N 109.48W
erro de Pasco Peru 76 E5 ....10.42S 76.14W
ervo Spain 48 B5 ....43.41N 7.26W
eské Budějovice Czech Rep. 54 F3 ....48.59N 14.28E
etinje S.M. 56 C5 ....42.23N 18.55E
euta N. Africa 52 B4 ....35.53N 5.20W
évennes mts France 44 E3 ....43.50N 3.17E
eyhan Turkey 57 K3 ....37.01N 35.47E
eyhan r. Turkey 57 K3 ....36.42N 35.37E
hābahār Iran 95 J5 ....25.17N 60.38E
had Africa 85 F3 ....15.07N 18.13E
had, Lake Africa 84 F3 ....13.27N 14.24E
hadan Rus. Fed. 102 G8 ....51.18N 91.31E
hadron U.S.A. 64 F5 ....42.50N 102.57W
hagai Hills Afgh./Pakistan 96 B6 ....29.17N 63.23E
haghcharān Afgh. 95 K6 ....34.28N 65.03E
hagos Archipelago is. Indian Oc. 90 F2 ....7.00S 72.00E
hake Chake Tanzania 87 B1 ....5.15S 39.47E
hala Peru 76 F4 ....15.49S 74.12W
halbi Desert Kenya 87 B3 ....3.13N 37.14E
hale England 10 D1 ....50.36N 1.19W
halkida Greece 56 E4 ....38.27N 23.37E
hallenger Deep f. N. Pacific Oc. 117 Q6 ....11.17N 142.30E
hallenger Fracture Zone f. S. Pacific Oc. 108 M3
.........34.26S 113.31W
hâlons-en-Champagne France 44 F6 ....48.58N 4.22E
halon-sur-Saône France 44 F5 ....46.48N 4.51E
hālus Iran 95 H7 ....36.37N 51.26E
haman Pakistan 96 C7 ....30.55N 66.28E
hambéry France 44 F4 ....45.34N 5.55E
h'amo Häyk' l. Ethiopia 87 B4 ....5.49N 37.32E
hamonix-Mont-Blanc France 44 G4 ....45.55N 6.52E
hampagne-Ardenne d. France 42 D1 ....48.43N 4.15E
hampaign U.S.A. 65 I5 ....40.06N 88.17W
hampaqui, Cerro mt. Argentina 76 H1 ....31.59S 64.56W
hamplain, Lake Canada/U.S.A. 65 L5 ....44.23N 73.22W
hañaral Chile 76 F2 ....26.19S 70.41W
handalar r. U.S.A. 62 D4 ....66.36N 145.51W
handigarh India 96 E7 ....30.42N 76.48E
handigarh d. India 102 D4 ....30.43N 76.52E
handrapur India 96 E4 ....19.57N 79.21E
hangbai China 106 A4 ....41.25N 128.10E
hangchun China 103 N6 ....43.53N 125.20E
hangde China 103 K3 ....29.03N 111.42E
hang Jiang r. China 103 M4 ....31.24N 121.48E
hangsha China 103 K3 ....28.10N 112.59E
hangzhi China 103 K5 ....36.06N 113.09E
hangzhou China 103 L4 ....31.47N 119.59E
hania Greece 56 F2 ....35.30N 24.02E
hannel Islands English Channel 13 Z9 ....49.20N 2.37W
hannel Islands U.S.A. 64 C3 ....33.41N 119.26W
hannel-Port-aux-Basques Canada 63 M2 ....47.33N 59.01W
hannel Tunnel France/U.K. 11 G2 ....51.04N 1.24E
hanthaburi Thailand 104 C6 ....12.37N 102.08E
hantilly France 42 B2 ....49.12N 2.28E
hao Phraya r. Thailand 104 C6 ....13.40N 100.36E
haouèn Morocco 52 B4 ....35.11N 5.16W
hapala, Laguna de l. Mexico 70 D5 ....20.15N 103.04W
hapecó Brazil 77 J2 ....27.09S 52.39W
hapel-en-le-Frith England 15 F2 ....53.20N 1.54W
hapeltown England 15 F2 ....53.28N 1.28W
hapleau Canada 63 J2 ....47.51N 83.24W
hard England 10 C1 ....50.52N 2.58W
hari r. Chad 82 F3 ....13.00N 14.30E
hārīkär Afgh. 95 K7 ....35.02N 69.15E
harlbury England 10 D2 ....51.52N 1.29W
harleroi Belgium 42 D3 ....50.25N 4.27E
harles, Cape U.S.A. 65 K4 ....37.10N 75.58W
harleston S.C. U.S.A. 65 K3 ....32.48N 79.58W
harleston W. Va. U.S.A. 65 J4 ....38.21N 81.39W
harlestown Rep. of Ireland 41 C3 ....53.57N 8.47W
harleville-Mézières France 44 F6 ....49.46N 4.44E
harlotte U.S.A. 65 J4 ....35.14N 80.50W
harlottesville U.S.A. 65 K4 ....38.02N 78.30W
harlottetown Canada 63 L2 ....46.16N 63.09W
hartres France 44 D6 ....48.27N 1.30E
hassiron, Pointe de pt France 44 C5 ....46.03N 1.24W
hâteaubriant France 44 C5 ....47.43N 1.22W
hâteaudun France 44 D6 ....48.04N 1.20E
hâteauroux France 44 D5 ....46.48N 1.41E
hâteau-Thierry France 44 E6 ....49.03N 3.25E
hâtellerault France 44 D5 ....46.49N 0.33E
hatham England 11 F2 ....51.23N 0.31E
hatham Islands New Zealand 108 I3 ....43.24S 176.11W
hatham Rise f. S. Pacific Oc. 108 I3 ....42.18S 176.14W
hattahoochee r. U.S.A. 65 J3 ....30.55N 84.58W
hattanooga U.S.A. 65 I4 ....35.02N 85.21W
hatteris England 11 F3 ....52.27N 0.03E
haumont France 44 F6 ....48.07N 5.08E

Chauny France 42 C2 ....49.37N 3.13E
Chaves Brazil 77 K7 ....0.11S 49.58W
Cheadle England 10 D3 ....52.59N 1.59W
Cheb Czech Rep. 54 E4 ....50.05N 12.28E
Cheboksary Rus. Fed. 58 F3 ....56.09N 47.13E
Cheboygan U.S.A. 65 J6 ....45.39N 84.28W
Cheddar England 10 C2 ....51.17N 2.47W
Cheju-do i. S. Korea 103 N4 ....33.34N 126.43E
Chekhov Rus. Fed. 55 Q6 ....55.09N 37.28E
Cheleken Turkmenistan 95 H7 ....39.25N 53.01E
Chełm Poland 46 F3 ....51.08N 23.29E
Chelmer r. England 11 F2 ....51.45N 0.40E
Chelmno Poland 46 D4 ....53.21N 18.26E
Chelmsford England 11 F2 ....51.44N 0.29E
Cheltenham England 10 C2 ....51.54N 2.04W
Chelyabinsk Rus. Fed. 58 H3 ....55.11N 61.24E
Chemnitz Germany 54 E4 ....50.50N 12.56E
Ch'ench'a Ethiopia 87 B4 ....6.17N 37.38E
Chengde China 103 L6 ....40.52N 117.58E
Chengdu China 103 I4 ....30.43N 104.04E
Chennai India 96 F3 ....13.06N 80.16E
Chenzhou China 103 K3 ....25.44N 113.00E
Chepstow Wales 12 D3 ....51.38N 2.40W
Cher r. France 44 D5 ....47.20N 0.29E
Cherbourg France 44 C6 ....49.38N 1.37W
Cherchell Algeria 48 D4 ....36.32N 2.06E
Cherepovets Rus. Fed. 58 E3 ....59.08N 37.55E
Chergui, Chott ech l. Algeria 52 C3 ....34.03N 0.16W
Cherkasy Ukraine 55 O3 ....49.26N 32.05E
Cherkessk Rus. Fed. 53 L5 ....44.13N 42.03E
Chernihiv Ukraine 55 N4 ....51.29N 31.19E
Chernivtsi Ukraine 55 K3 ....48.19N 25.56E
Chernyakhovsk Rus. Fed. 46 E5 ....54.38N 21.49E
Chernyshevskiy Rus. Fed. 59 M4 ....62.56N 112.36E
Cherskogo, Khrebet mts Rus. Fed. 59 P4 ....63.42N 146.57E
Chervonohrad Ukraine 55 K4 ....50.23N 24.14E
Cherwell r. England 10 D2 ....51.44N 1.15W
Chesapeake Bay U.S.A. 65 K4 ....38.05N 76.14W
Chesham England 11 E2 ....51.43N 0.37W
Cheshire d. England 9 D3 ....53.13N 2.26W
Cheshskaya Guba b. Russian Fed. 35 I4 ....67.20N 46.30E
Cheshunt England 11 E2 ....51.42N 0.02W
Chesil Beach f. England 10 C1 ....50.38N 2.36W
Chester England 14 E2 ....53.12N 2.54W
Chesterfield England 15 F2 ....53.14N 1.25W
Chester-le-Street England 15 F3 ....54.52N 1.34W
Chetumal Mexico 70 G4 ....18.30N 88.18W
Cheviot Hills England 15 E4 ....55.12N 2.39W
Che'w Bahir l. Ethiopia 87 B4 ....4.40N 36.56E
Che'w Bahir Wildlife Reserve Ethiopia 87 B4 ....4.51N 36.51E
Chew Magna England 10 C2 ....51.22N 2.37W
Chew Valley Lake resr England 10 C2 ....51.20N 2.38W
Cheyenne U.S.A. 64 F5 ....41.09N 104.49W
Cheyenne r. U.S.A. 64 F5 ....44.44N 101.09W
Chhattisgarh d. India 96 F5 ....21.29N 81.46E
Chiai Taiwan 103 M2 ....23.29N 120.27E
Chiang Mai Thailand 104 B7 ....18.47N 98.59E
Chiang Rai Thailand 104 B7 ....19.55N 99.53E
Chiapas d. Mexico 70 F4 ....16.23N 92.17W
Chiba Japan 106 D3 ....35.37N 140.07E
Chibougamau Canada 63 K2 ....49.55N 74.22W
Chicago U.S.A. 65 I5 ....41.50N 87.38W
Chichester England 10 E1 ....50.50N 0.46W
Chiclayo Peru 76 E6 ....6.44S 79.51W
Chicoutimi Canada 63 K2 ....48.26N 71.03W
Chidley, Cape Canada 63 L4 ....60.26N 64.20W
Chiemsee l. Germany 54 E2 ....47.52N 12.28E
Chieti Italy 50 F5 ....42.21N 14.10E
Chifeng China 103 L6 ....42.11N 119.02E
Chiganak Kazakhstan 58 I2 ....45.10N 73.57E
Chihuahua Mexico 70 C6 ....28.38N 106.07W
Chihuahua d. Mexico 70 C6 ....29.10N 106.11W
Chile S. America 73 B3 ....34.06S 71.23W
Chile Basin f. S. Pacific Oc. 109 O3 ....31.51S 80.03W
Chile Rise f. S. Pacific Oc. 109 O3 ....41.37S 89.56W
Chilham England 11 F2 ....51.16N 0.58E
Chillán Chile 73 B3 ....36.37S 72.07W
Chiloé, Isla de i. Chile 73 B2 ....42.26S 74.29W
Chilpancingo Mexico 70 E4 ....17.33N 99.30W
Chiltern Hills England 10 E2 ....51.39N 0.50W
Chilung Taiwan 103 M3 ....25.07N 121.43E
Chimborazo mt. Ecuador 76 E7 ....1.27S 78.50W
Chimbote Peru 76 E6 ....9.03S 78.35W
Chimoio Mozambique 86 C3 ....19.07S 33.28E
China Asia 102 H3 ....38.39N 98.40E
Chindwin r. Myanmar 97 I5 ....21.27N 95.15E
Chingola Zambia 86 B3 ....12.33S 27.54E
Chinhoyi Zimbabwe 86 C3 ....17.21S 30.11E
Chinju S. Korea 106 A3 ....35.10N 128.05E
Chinook Trough f. N. Pacific Oc. 108 I8 ....41.53N 179.40W
Chioggia Italy 50 E6 ....45.12N 12.16E
Chios Greece 56 G4 ....38.22N 26.08E
Chios i. Greece 56 F4 ....38.24N 25.58E
Chipata Zambia 86 C3 ....13.37S 32.38E
Chippenham England 10 C2 ....51.27N 2.07W
Chipping Campden England 10 D3 ....52.03N 1.47W
Chipping Norton England 10 D2 ....51.57N 1.32W
Chipping Ongar England 11 F2 ....51.42N 0.15E
Chipping Sodbury England 10 C2 ....51.32N 2.23W
Chiriquí, Golfo de b. Panama 71 H2 ....8.02N 82.04W
Chirk Wales 12 D4 ....52.56N 3.03W
Chirnside Scotland 17 G3 ....55.48N 2.12W
Chirripo mt. Costa Rica 71 H2 ....9.30N 83.30W
Chisasibi Canada 63 K3 ....53.49N 78.59W
Chişinău Moldova 55 M2 ....47.02N 28.50E
Chita Rus. Fed. 59 M3 ....51.54N 113.27E
Chitambo Zambia 86 C3 ....12.54S 30.37E
Chitradurga India 96 E3 ....14.14N 76.22E
Chitral Pakistan 96 D8 ....35.53N 71.47E
Chittagong Bangl. 97 H5 ....22.20N 91.49E
Chittoor India 96 E3 ....13.12N 79.05E
Chitungwiza Zimbabwe 86 C3 ....18.01S 31.04E
Chojnice Poland 46 C4 ....53.42N 17.34E
Chomutov Czech Rep. 54 E4 ....50.28N 13.24E
Chon Buri Thailand 104 C6 ....13.24N 101.01E
Ch'ŏngjin N. Korea 103 N6 ....41.46N 129.45E
Chongqing China 103 J3 ....29.30N 106.15E
Chongqing d. China 103 J4 ....30.04N 107.39E
Chŏnju S. Korea 103 N5 ....35.51N 127.09E
Chonos, Archipélago de los is. Chile 73 B2 ....44.59S 75.31W
Chorley England 14 E2 ....53.39N 2.38W
Chornobyl' Ukraine 55 N4 ....51.16N 30.14E
Chornomors'ke Ukraine 57 J7 ....45.30N 32.43E
Chortkiv Ukraine 55 K3 ....49.00N 25.44E
Chōshi Japan 106 D3 ....35.44N 140.49E
Choszczno Poland 46 B4 ....53.10N 15.26E
Choûm Mauritania 84 C4 ....21.20N 12.59W
Choybalsan Mongolia 103 K7 ....47.57N 114.34E
Chřiby hills Czech Rep. 46 C2 ....49.05N 17.11E
Christchurch England 10 D1 ....50.44N 1.47W
Christchurch New Zealand 111 G2 ....43.32S 172.37E
Christmas Island Indian Oc. 104 D1 ....10.30S 105.44E
Chūgoku-sanchi mts Japan 106 B2 ....34.45N 132.19E

Chukchi Sea Rus. Fed./U.S.A. 59 T4 ....69.12N 171.31W
Chukotskiy Poluostrov pen. Rus. Fed. 59 T4 ....65.58N 175.16W
Chulmleigh England 13 D2 ....50.55N 3.52W
Chumba Ethiopia 87 B4 ....4.30N 38.16E
Chumphon Thailand 104 B6 ....10.31N 99.13E
Ch'unch'ŏn S. Korea 103 N5 ....37.52N 127.46E
Chunya r. Rus. Fed. 59 K4 ....61.36N 96.31E
Chur Switz. 50 C7 ....46.51N 9.32E
Churchill Canada 63 I3 ....58.44N 94.05W
Churchill r. Man. Canada 63 I3 ....58.11N 94.23W
Churchill r. Nfld. and Lab. Canada 63 L3 ....53.16N 60.14W
Churchill, Cape Canada 63 I3 ....58.45N 93.16W
Church Stretton England 10 C3 ....52.32N 2.48W
Chuuk is Micronesia 108 G6 ....7.22N 151.37E
Chuxiong China 103 I3 ....25.02N 101.32E
Chyulu Range mts Kenya 87 B2 ....2.34S 37.41E
Ciechanów Poland 46 E4 ....52.53N 20.38E
Ciego de Ávila Cuba 71 I5 ....21.50N 78.45W
Cienfuegos Cuba 71 H5 ....22.10N 80.25W
Cigüela r. Spain 48 D3 ....39.08N 3.43W
Cihanbeyli Turkey 57 J4 ....38.40N 32.56E
Cilacap Indonesia 104 D2 ....7.41S 109.00E
Cimone, Monte mt. Italy 50 D6 ....44.11N 10.42E
Cinca r. Spain 48 F4 ....41.26N 0.21E
Cincinnati U.S.A. 65 J4 ....39.06N 84.32W
Cinderford England 10 C2 ....51.49N 2.30W
Ciney Belgium 42 D3 ....50.18N 5.06E
Cinto, Monte mt. France 44 H3 ....42.23N 8.56E
Cirebon Indonesia 104 D2 ....6.45S 108.34E
Cirencester England 10 D2 ....51.43N 1.58W
Ciudad Bolívar Venezuela 72 C7 ....8.01N 63.35W
Ciudad del Carmen Mexico 70 F4 ....18.39N 91.51W
Ciudad Delicias Mexico 70 C6 ....28.10N 105.30W
Ciudad de Valles Mexico 70 E5 ....21.59N 99.00W
Ciudad Guayana Venezuela 72 C7 ....8.20N 62.37W
Ciudad Ixtepec Mexico 70 E4 ....16.35N 95.06W
Ciudad Juárez Mexico 70 C7 ....31.44N 106.28W
Ciudad Madero Mexico 70 E5 ....22.19N 97.51W
Ciudad Obregón Mexico 70 C6 ....27.28N 109.57W
Ciudad Real Spain 48 D3 ....38.59N 3.54W
Ciudad Rodrigo Spain 48 B4 ....40.36N 6.31W
Ciudad Victoria Mexico 70 E5 ....23.45N 99.08W
Ciutadella de Menorca Spain 48 G4 ....40.00N 3.52E
Civitavecchia Italy 50 D5 ....42.05N 11.48E
Çivril Turkey 57 H4 ....38.18N 29.43E
Clackmannanshire d. Scotland 8 D5 ....56.09N 3.45W
Clacton-on-Sea England 11 G2 ....51.47N 1.09E
Claonaig Scotland 16 D3 ....55.45N 5.24W
Clara Rep. of Ireland 41 D3 ....53.20N 7.37W
Clare r. Rep. of Ireland 41 C3 ....53.20N 7.37W
Clare Rep. of Ireland 41 C2 ....52.53N 8.50W
Clare d. Rep. of Ireland 41 B3 ....53.19N 9.03W
Clare Island Rep. of Ireland 41 A3 ....53.49N 10.01W
Claremorris Rep. of Ireland 41 C3 ....53.43N 8.59W
Clarksville U.S.A. 65 I4 ....36.32N 87.20W
Claro r. Brazil 77 J4 ....19.07S 50.39W
Clay Cross England 15 F2 ....53.10N 1.25W
Claydon England 11 G3 ....52.06N 1.07E
Clay Head Isle of Man 14 C3 ....54.12N 4.23W
Clayton U.S.A. 64 F4 ....36.28N 103.12W
Clear, Cape Rep. of Ireland 41 B1 ....51.25N 9.31W
Clear Island Rep. of Ireland 41 B1 ....51.26N 9.28W
Cleator Moor England 14 D3 ....54.31N 3.31W
Cleethorpes England 15 G2 ....53.33N 0.02W
Cleobury Mortimer England 10 C3 ....52.23N 2.29W
Clermont France 42 B2 ....49.23N 2.25E
Clermont-Ferrand France 44 E4 ....45.46N 3.05E
Clevedon England 10 C2 ....51.26N 2.51W
Cleveland U.S.A. 65 J5 ....41.30N 81.41W
Cleveland Hills England 15 F3 ....54.22N 1.13W
Cleveleys England 14 D2 ....53.53N 3.02W
Clew Bay Rep. of Ireland 41 B3 ....53.48N 9.47W
Cliffe England 11 F2 ....51.28N 0.30E
Clinton U.S.A. 65 H4 ....35.30N 98.58W
Clipperton, Île N. Pacific Oc. 109 M6 ....10.21N 109.19W
Clisham hill Scotland 18 C2 ....57.58N 6.49W
Clitheroe England 14 E2 ....53.52N 2.23W
Clogher Head Rep. of Ireland 41 E3 ....53.48N 6.13W
Clonakilty Rep. of Ireland 41 C1 ....51.37N 8.53W
Clones Rep. of Ireland 41 D4 ....54.10N 7.13W
Clonmel Rep. of Ireland 41 D2 ....52.21N 7.43W
Cloud Peak U.S.A. 64 E5 ....44.24N 107.01W
Clovis U.S.A. 64 F3 ....34.27N 103.12W
Cluanie, Loch l. Scotland 18 D2 ....57.09N 5.07W
Cluj-Napoca Romania 55 J2 ....46.46N 23.36E
Clun England 10 C3 ....52.26N 3.02W
Clydach Wales 12 D3 ....51.42N 3.54W
Clyde r. Scotland 17 F3 ....55.55N 4.29W
Clyde, Firth of est. Scotland 16 E3 ....55.25N 4.59W
Clydebank Scotland 16 E3 ....55.54N 4.24W
Clyde River town Canada 63 L5 ....70.23N 68.31W
Coahuila d. Mexico 70 D6 ....27.30N 102.24W
Coalville England 10 D3 ....52.43N 1.22W
Coari Brazil 76 H7 ....4.08S 63.07W
Coari r. Brazil 76 H7 ....4.26S 63.30W
Coast d. Kenya 87 C2 ....2.40S 40.07E
Coastal Plain f. U.S.A. 65 H3 ....30.25N 94.23W
Coast Mountains Canada 62 F3 ....52.40N 127.48W
Coast Ranges mts U.S.A. 64 B5 ....40.40N 123.39W
Coatbridge Scotland 17 F3 ....55.52N 4.01W
Coats Island Canada 63 J4 ....62.41N 82.53W
Coatzacoalcos Mexico 70 F4 ....18.08N 94.26W
Cobh Rep. of Ireland 41 C1 ....51.51N 8.18W
Cobija Bolivia 76 G5 ....11.03S 68.47W
Cochabamba Bolivia 76 G4 ....17.25S 66.11W
Cochin India 96 E2 ....9.55N 76.14E
Cochrane Canada 65 J6 ....49.04N 81.03W
Cockburnspath Scotland 17 G3 ....55.56N 2.22W
Cockermouth England 14 D3 ....54.40N 3.22W
Coco r. Honduras/Nicaragua 71 H3 ....14.59N 83.15W
Coco, Isla de i. N. Pacific Oc. 60 K2 ....5.32N 87.04W
Cocos Islands Indian Oc. 108 C6 ....0.02N 91.02E
Cocos Islands Indian Oc. 104 B1 ....11.56S 96.56E
Cocos Ridge f. N. Pacific Oc. 109 O6 ....0.42N 89.55W
Cocuy, Sierra Nevada del mt. Colombia 71 J2 ....6.28N 72.19W
Cod, Cape U.S.A. 65 L5 ....41.58N 70.01W
Coddington England 15 G2 ....53.05N 0.45W
Codó Brazil 77 L7 ....4.28S 43.50W
Codsall England 10 C3 ....52.38N 2.11W
Coeur d'Alene U.S.A. 64 C6 ....47.41N 116.47W
Coffs Harbour Australia 110 E3 ....30.19S 153.06E
Coggeshall England 11 F2 ....51.52N 0.42E
Coiba, Isla de i. Panama 71 H2 ....7.27N 81.51W
Coigeach, Rubha pt Scotland 18 D3 ....58.06N 5.28W
Coihaique Chile 73 B2 ....45.36S 72.05W
Coimbatore India 96 E3 ....10.59N 76.57E
Coimbra Portugal 48 A4 ....40.13N 8.25W
Coipasa, Salar de f. Bolivia 76 G4 ....19.26S 68.07W
Colatina Brazil 77 L4 ....19.35S 40.38W
Colchester England 11 F2 ....51.53N 0.54E
Coldstream Scotland 17 G3 ....55.39N 2.15W
Coleford England 10 C2 ....51.48N 2.37W
Coleraine Northern Ireland 16 C3 ....55.08N 6.40W
Coleraine d. Northern Ireland 8 B4 ....54.58N 6.41W
Colima Mexico 70 D4 ....19.14N 103.45W

Colima d. Mexico 70 D4 ....19.03N 103.59W
Coima, Nevado de vol. Mexico 70 D4 ....19.33N 103.37W
Coll i. Scotland 18 C3 ....56.36N 6.36W
Collier Bay Australia 110 B5 ....16.15S 124.15E
Colmar France 44 G6 ....48.05N 7.21E
Colne England 15 E2 ....53.51N 2.11W
Colne r. England 11 F2 ....51.51N 0.57E
Cologne Germany 54 B4 ....50.56N 6.57E
Colombia S. America 72 B7 ....3.45N 72.22W
Colombo Sri Lanka 96 E2 ....6.56N 79.50E
Colón Panama 71 I2 ....9.22N 79.55W
Colonsay i. Scotland 16 C4 ....56.05N 6.15W
Colorado r. Argentina 73 C3 ....39.42S 62.07W
Colorado d. U.S.A. 64 E4 ....39.02N 105.31W
Colorado r. Mexico/U.S.A. 64 C3 ....31.56N 115.01W
Colorado r. U.S.A. 64 G2 ....28.40N 96.01W
Colorado Plateau f. U.S.A. 64 E4 ....37.27N 109.54W
Colorado Springs town U.S.A. 64 F4 ....38.52N 104.47W
Coltishall England 11 G3 ....52.44N 1.22E
Columbia U.S.A. 65 J3 ....33.59N 81.01W
Columbia r. U.S.A. 64 B6 ....46.11N 123.23W
Columbia, Mount Canada 62 G3 ....52.08N 117.25W
Columbus Ga. U.S.A. 65 J3 ....32.32N 84.59W
Columbus Miss. U.S.A. 65 I3 ....33.33N 88.25W
Columbus Oh. U.S.A. 65 J4 ....39.58N 83.00W
Colville r. U.S.A. 62 C4 ....70.20N 150.32W
Colwyn Bay town Wales 12 D5 ....53.18N 3.43W
Comacchio Italy 50 E6 ....44.41N 12.11E
Combe Martin England 13 C3 ....51.12N 4.01W
Comber Northern Ireland 16 D4 ....54.33N 5.44W
Comeragh Mountains Rep. of Ireland 41 D2 ....52.18N 7.39W
Como Italy 50 C6 ....45.48N 9.05E
Como, Lake Italy 50 C6 ....45.57N 9.11E
Comodoro Rivadavia Argentina 73 C2 ....45.56S 67.30W
Comorin, Cape India 90 G3 ....8.04N 77.35E
Comoros Africa 86 D3 ....11.50S 44.17E
Compiègne France 42 B2 ....49.25N 2.50E
Comrat Moldova 57 H8 ....46.18N 28.40E
Comrie Scotland 17 F4 ....56.23N 3.59W
Conakry Guinea 84 C2 ....9.31N 13.42W
Concarneau France 44 B5 ....47.53N 3.55W
Concepción Argentina 76 G2 ....27.18S 65.38W
Concepción Chile 73 B3 ....36.50S 73.04W
Conception, Point U.S.A. 64 B3 ....34.27N 120.26W
Conchos r. Mexico 70 D6 ....29.35N 104.29W
Concord U.S.A. 65 L5 ....43.12N 71.33W
Concordia Argentina 73 D3 ....31.23S 57.59W
Condor, Cordillera del mts Ecuador/Peru 76 E7 ....4.17S 78.34W
Congleton England 15 E2 ....53.10N 2.13W
Congo Africa 84 F1 ....2.24S 15.10E
Congo r. Congo/Dem. Rep. Congo 86 A4 ....6.05S 12.26E
Congo, Democratic Republic of Africa 86 B4 ....3.43S 22.17E
Congo Basin f. Africa 82 F4 ....1.00S 20.00E
Coningsby England 15 G2 ....53.06N 0.10W
Coniston England 14 D3 ....54.22N 3.05W
Coniston Water l. England 14 D3 ....54.19N 3.04W
Conn, Lough l. Rep. of Ireland 41 B4 ....54.01N 9.16W
Connah's Quay Wales 12 D5 ....53.13N 3.04W
Connecticut d. U.S.A. 65 L5 ....41.41N 72.36W
Connecticut r. U.S.A. 65 L5 ....41.16N 72.22W
Connemara f. Rep. of Ireland 41 B3 ....53.28N 9.52W
Conon Bridge Scotland 19 E2 ....57.34N 4.26W
Consett England 15 F3 ....54.51N 1.50W
Con Son i. Vietnam 104 D5 ....8.42N 106.40E
Constance, Lake Germany/Switz. 54 C2 ....47.40N 9.17E
Constanța Romania 57 H7 ....44.11N 28.37E
Constantine Algeria 84 E5 ....36.23N 6.38E
Conwy Wales 12 D5 ....53.17N 3.50W
Conwy d. Wales 9 D3 ....53.10N 3.37W
Conwy r. Wales 12 D5 ....53.14N 3.48W
Conwy Bay Wales 12 D5 ....53.16N 4.02W
Cook, Mount New Zealand 111 G2 ....43.37S 170.08E
Cook Islands S. Pacific Oc. 108 J4 ....20.05S 160.06W
Cookstown Northern Ireland 16 C2 ....54.38N 6.44W
Cookstown d. Northern Ireland 9 B4 ....54.39N 6.44W
Cook Strait New Zealand 111 G2 ....40.32S 174.01E
Cooktown Australia 110 D5 ....15.28S 145.17E
Coolangatta Australia 110 E4 ....28.10S 153.31E
Cooper Creek watercourse Australia 110 C4 ....28.29S 137.43E
Coos Bay town U.S.A. 64 B5 ....43.21N 124.12W
Copenhagen Denmark 40 C1 ....55.40N 12.34E
Copiapó Chile 73 B4 ....27.18S 70.23W
Copinsay i. Scotland 19 G3 ....58.54N 2.40W
Coquimbo Chile 76 F2 ....29.58S 71.20W
Corabia Romania 56 F6 ....43.47N 24.29E
Coral Harbour Canada 63 J4 ....64.12N 83.19W
Coral Sea S. Pacific Oc. 110 E5 ....13.27S 151.06E
Coral Sea Basin f. S. Pacific Oc. 108 G5 ....13.23S 152.14E
Coral Sea Islands Territory Australia 110 E5 ....15.01S 150.43E
Corbie France 42 B2 ....49.55N 2.31E
Corbridge England 15 E3 ....54.58N 2.01W
Corby England 10 E3 ....52.29N 0.41W
Córdoba Argentina 73 C3 ....31.24S 64.11W
Córdoba Mexico 70 E4 ....18.55N 96.53W
Córdoba Spain 48 C2 ....37.53N 4.46W
Córdoba, Sierras de mts Argentina 73 C3 ....32.55S 64.22W
Corfe Castle England 10 C1 ....50.38N 2.03W
Corfu i. Greece 56 C4 ....39.36N 19.47E
Corigliano Calabro Italy 50 G3 ....39.35N 16.32E
Corinth Greece 56 E3 ....37.56N 22.55E
Corixa Grande r. Bolivia/Brazil 77 I4 ....17.30S 57.56W
Cork Rep. of Ireland 41 C1 ....51.54N 8.28W
Cork d. Rep. of Ireland 41 C2 ....52.01N 8.39W
Çorlu Turkey 57 G5 ....41.09N 27.48E
Corner Brook Canada 63 M2 ....48.54N 57.47W
Corno, Monte mt. Italy 50 E5 ....42.28N 13.34E
Cornwall d. England 9 C2 ....50.32N 4.33W
Cornwall, Cape England 13 B2 ....50.08N 5.47W
Cornwallis Island Canada 63 I5 ....75.08N 94.56W
Coro Venezuela 72 C8 ....11.23N 69.40W
Coronado, Bahía de b. Costa Rica 71 H2 ....8.55N 83.48W
Coronation Gulf Canada 62 H4 ....68.08N 112.32W
Coronel Oviedo Paraguay 77 I2 ....25.21S 56.27W
Corpus Christi U.S.A. 64 G2 ....27.44N 97.27W
Corral de Cantos mt. Spain 48 C3 ....39.34N 4.27W
Corrente Brazil 77 L5 ....10.28S 45.07W
Corrib, Lough l. Rep. of Ireland 41 B3 ....53.27N 9.19W
Corrientes Argentina 73 D4 ....27.27S 58.46W
Corrientes, Cabo c. Mexico 70 C5 ....20.26N 105.42W
Corse, Cap c. France 44 H3 ....43.02N 9.22E
Corserine hill Scotland 16 E3 ....55.09N 4.21W
Corsham England 10 C2 ....51.26N 2.11W
Corsica i. France 44 H3 ....42.20N 8.29E
Corte France 44 H3 ....42.18N 9.09E
Cortegana Spain 48 B2 ....37.55N 6.49W
Cortina d'Ampezzo Italy 50 E7 ....46.32N 12.08E
Corton England 11 G3 ....52.31N 1.45E
Çorum Turkey 57 K5 ....40.33N 34.57E
Corumbá Brazil 77 I4 ....19.00S 57.37W
Corwen Wales 12 D4 ....52.59N 3.22W
Cosenza Italy 50 G3 ....39.18N 16.15E
Cosmoledo Islands Seychelles 86 D4 ....9.30S 49.00E
Cosne-Cours-sur-Loire France 44 E5 ....47.25N 2.56E

Costa Blanca f. Spain 48 E3 ....38.03N 0.20W
Costa Brava f. Spain 48 G4 ....41.28N 3.05E
Costa del Sol f. Spain 48 C2 ....36.25N 5.06W
Costa de Mosquitos f. Nicaragua 71 H3 ....12.08N 83.52W
Costa Rica Central America 71 H3 ....10.08N 84.19W
Cotabato Phil. 105 G5 ....7.13N 124.14E
Côte d'Azur f. France 44 G3 ....43.33N 7.13E
Côte d'Ivoire Africa 84 D2 ....7.35N 4.22E
Cothi r. Wales 12 C3 ....51.52N 4.10W
Cotonou Benin 84 E2 ....6.21N 2.27E
Cotopaxi, Volcán vol. Ecuador 76 E7 ......0.39S 78.26W
Cotswold Hills England 10 C2 ....51.36N 2.15W
Cottbus Germany 54 F4 ....51.45N 14.21E
Cottenham England 11 F3 ....52.17N 0.08E
Cottesmore England 10 E3 ....52.43N 0.40W
Coulogne France 42 A3 ....50.55N 1.53E
Coupar Angus Scotland 17 F4 ....56.33N 3.16E
Courland Lagoon b. Lithuania/Rus. Fed. 40 E1 ..55.16N 21.06E
Coutances France 44 C6 ....49.03N 1.27W
Coventry England 10 D3 ....52.24N 1.31W
Covilhã Portugal 48 B4 ....40.17N 7.29W
Cowan, Lake Australia 110 B3 ....31.45S 121.59E
Cowbridge Wales 13 D3 ....51.28N 3.27W
Cowdenbeath Scotland 17 F4 ....56.07N 3.20W
Cowes England 10 D1 ....50.46N 1.18W
Cowfold England 11 E2 ....50.59N 0.16W
Cow Green Reservoir England 15 E3 ......54.40N 2.20W
Coxim Brazil 77 J4 ....18.30S 54.44W
Cox's Bazar Bangl. 97 H5 ....21.27N 91.59E
Cozumel, Isla de i. Mexico 70 G5 ....20.22N 86.53W
Craig U.S.A. 64 E5 ....40.31N 107.32W
Craigavon Northern Ireland 16 C2 ....54.26N 6.21W
Craigavon d. Northern Ireland 9 B4 ....54.29N 6.22W
Craig Goch Reservoir Wales 12 D4 ....52.19N 3.37W
Craignure Scotland 16 D4 ....56.28N 5.43W
Crail Scotland 17 G4 ....56.16N 2.38W
Craiova Romania 56 E7 ....44.19N 23.48E
Cramlington England 15 F4 ....55.05N 1.35W
Cranbrook Canada 62 G2 ....49.32N 115.45W
Cranleigh England 11 E2 ....51.08N 0.29W
Crawley England 11 E2 ....51.07N 0.11W
Creag Meagaidh mt. Scotland 19 E1 ......56.57N 4.36W
Credenhill England 10 C3 ....52.05N 2.48W
Crediton England 13 D2 ....50.48N 3.39W
Cree Lake Canada 62 H3 ....57.31N 106.29W
Creil France 42 B2 ....49.16N 2.29E
Cremona Italy 50 D6 ....45.08N 10.01E
Crépy-en-Valois France 42 B2 ....49.14N 2.53E
Cres i. Croatia 56 A7 ....44.51N 14.28E
Crescent City U.S.A. 64 B5 ....41.47N 124.09W
Creston U.S.A. 65 H5 ....41.03N 94.22W
Creswell England 15 F2 ....53.16N 1.13W
Crete i. Greece 56 G2 ....35.28N 24.41E
Creuse r. France 44 D5 ....47.00N 0.34E
Crewe England 15 E2 ....53.06N 2.26W
Crewkerne England 10 C1 ....50.53N 2.48W
Crianlarich Scotland 16 E4 ....56.24N 4.37W
Criccieth Wales 12 C4 ....52.55N 4.14W
Criciúma Brazil 77 K2 ....28.45S 49.25W
Crickhowell Wales 12 D3 ....51.51N 3.08W
Crieff Scotland 17 F4 ....56.23N 3.50W
Criffel hill Scotland 17 F2 ....54.57N 3.38W
Crimea pen. Ukraine 53 J6 ....45.20N 34.05E
Crimond Scotland 19 H2 ....57.36N 1.55W
Croatia Europe 56 B7 ....45.02N 15.14E
Croisilles France 11 H1 ....50.12N 2.53E
Croker Island Australia 105 I1 ....11.04S 132.38E
Cromarty Scotland 19 E2 ....57.41N 4.02W
Cromarty Firth est. Scotland 19 E2 ......57.38N 4.19W
Cromdale, Hills of Scotland 19 F2 ....57.19N 3.31W
Cromer England 11 G3 ....52.56N 1.18E
Cronamuck Mountain hill Rep. of Ireland 16 B2 ..54.54N 7.51W
Crook England 15 F3 ....54.43N 1.45W
Crooked Island Bahamas 71 J5 ....22.48N 74.14W
Crooked Island Passage str. Bahamas 71 J5 ..22.29N 74.55W
Croom Rep. of Ireland 41 C2 ....52.31N 8.43W
Crosby England 14 D2 ....53.29N 3.02W
Cross Fell hill England 15 E3 ....54.42N 2.29W
Crossett Northern Ireland 16 D2 ....54.24N 5.45W
Crossmaglen Northern Ireland 16 C2 ....54.04N 6.36W
Crotone Italy 50 G3 ....39.05N 17.08E
Crouch r. England 11 F2 ....51.38N 0.56E
Crowborough England 11 F2 ....51.04N 0.10E
Crowland England 11 E3 ....52.41N 0.10W
Crowle England 15 G2 ....53.37N 0.50W
Crowthorne England 10 E2 ....51.22N 0.48W
Croyde England 13 C3 ....51.08N 4.13W
Croydon England 11 E2 ....51.23N 0.06W
Crozet Islands Indian Oc. 117 L3 ....47.00S 52.00E
Cruden Bay town Scotland 19 H2 ....57.25N 1.51W
Crumlin Northern Ireland 16 C2 ....54.38N 6.13W
Cruz, Cabo c. Cuba 71 I4 ....19.51N 77.43W
Cruzeiro do Sul Brazil 76 F6 ....7.41S 72.40W
Cuando r. Angola/Zambia 86 B3 ....17.39S 23.24E
Cuanza r. Angola 86 A4 ....9.21S 13.08E
Cuauhtémoc Mexico 70 C6 ....28.24N 106.53W
Cuba Central America 71 H5 ....21.18N 80.06W
Cubango r. Angola/Namibia 86 B3 ....18.01S 21.26E
Cuckfield England 11 E2 ....51.00N 0.09W
Cúcuta Colombia 72 B7 ....7.53N 72.31W
Cuddalore India 96 E3 ....11.42N 79.43E
Cuddapah India 96 E3 ....14.29N 78.48E
Cuenca Ecuador 76 E7 ....2.53S 79.00W
Cuenca Spain 48 D4 ....40.04N 2.08W
Cuenca, Serranía de mts Spain 48 D4 ....40.38N 2.08W
Cuernavaca Mexico 70 E4 ....18.56N 99.11W
Cuiabá Brazil 77 I4 ....15.33S 56.04W
Cuiabá r. Brazil 77 I4 ....17.19S 56.41W
Cuilcagh hill Rep. of Ireland/U.K. 16 B2 ..54.12N 7.49W
Cuillin Hills Scotland 18 C2 ....57.14N 6.17W
Cuillin Sound str. Scotland 18 C2 ....57.08N 6.21W
Culiacán Mexico 70 C5 ....24.47N 107.27W
Cullen Scotland 19 G2 ....57.41N 2.49W
Cullera Spain 48 E3 ....39.10N 0.13W
Cullompton England 13 D2 ....50.51N 3.23W
Cullybackey Northern Ireland 16 C2 ......54.53N 6.21W
Cul Mòr hill Scotland 18 D3 ....58.03N 5.07W
Culuene r. Brazil 77 I5 ....11.11S 53.09W
Culzean Bay Scotland 16 E3 ....55.22N 4.49W
Cumaná Venezuela 72 C8 ....10.24N 64.09W
Cumbal, Nevado de vol. Colombia 76 E8 ..0.57N 77.51W
Cumberland r. U.S.A. 65 I4 ....36.30N 87.49W
Cumberland Sound str. Canada 63 L4 ....64.08N 63.14W
Cumbria d. England 9 D4 ....54.42N 3.17W
Cumnock Scotland 16 E3 ....55.27N 4.16W
Cunene r. Angola 86 A3 ....17.15S 11.46E
Cuneo Italy 50 B6 ....44.24N 7.33E
Cupar Scotland 19 G2 ....56.19N 3.01W
Cupica, Golfo de b. Colombia 71 I2 ....6.25N 77.46W
Curaçao i. Neth. Antilles 71 K3 ....12.12N 69.04W
Curaray r. Ecuador 76 F7 ....2.25S 74.06W
Curitiba Brazil 77 K2 ....25.28S 49.17W
Curuá r. Brazil 77 J6 ....5.25S 54.21W

Cusco Peru 76 F5 ....13.31S 71.59W
Cushendall Northern Ireland 16 C3 ......55.05N 6.04W
Cuttack India 96 G5 ....20.27N 85.55E
Cuxhaven Germany 54 C5 ....53.52N 8.42E
Cuyo Islands Phil. 105 G6 ....11.11N 121.10E
Cwmbrân Wales 13 D3 ....51.39N 3.02W
Cyclades is Greece 56 F3 ....37.14N 24.37E
Cyprus Asia 57 J2 ....35.38N 33.17E
Cyrenaica f. Libya 53 H3 ....31.06N 22.24E
Czech Republic Europe 54 F3 ....49.38N 15.37E
Czersk Poland 46 C4 ....53.48N 17.59E
Częstochowa Poland 46 D3 ....50.48N 19.07E

D

Dąbrowa Górnicza Poland 46 D3 ....50.21N 19.15E
Dachau Germany 54 D3 ....48.15N 11.27E
Dagupan Phil. 104 G7 ....16.04N 120.21E
Da Hinggan Ling mts China 103 L6 ......43.33N 117.52E
Dahlak Archipelago is Eritrea 94 F3 ......15.58N 40.04E
Dahm, Ramlat des. Saudi Arabia/Yemen 94 G3 ..17.09N 45.00E
Dailly Scotland 16 E3 ....55.17N 4.43W
Dakar Senegal 84 C3 ....14.43N 17.28W
Dakhla Oasis Egypt 94 C5 ....25.25N 28.53E
Dakol'ka r. Belarus 55 M5 ....52.08N 28.52E
Dakoro Niger 84 E3 ....14.32N 6.43E
Dalaman Turkey 57 H3 ....36.47N 28.48E
Đa Lat Vietnam 104 D6 ....11.56N 108.26E
Dalbandin Pakistan 95 J5 ....28.56N 64.30E
Dalbeattie Scotland 17 F2 ....54.56N 3.49W
Dali China 103 I3 ....25.33N 100.13E
Dalian China 103 M5 ....38.51N 121.37E
Dalkeith Scotland 17 F3 ....55.54N 3.04W
Dallas U.S.A. 64 G3 ....32.46N 96.48W
Dalmally Scotland 16 E4 ....56.24N 4.58W
Dalmatia f. Bos.-Herz./Croatia 56 A7 ....44.01N 15.30E
Dalmellington Scotland 16 E3 ....55.19N 4.24W
Dal'negorsk Rus. Fed. 106 C4 ....44.28N 135.30E
Daloa Côte d'Ivoire 84 D2 ....6.54N 6.28W
Dalry Scotland 16 E3 ....55.43N 4.43W
Dalrymple Scotland 16 E3 ....55.24N 4.36W
Dalrymple, Mount Australia 110 D4 ....20.59S 148.37E
Dalton U.S.A. 65 J3 ....34.49N 84.56W
Dalton-in-Furness England 14 D3 ....54.09N 3.11W
Daly r. Australia 110 C5 ....13.31S 130.28E
Daman India 96 D5 ....20.24N 72.58E
Damanhûr Egypt 53 J3 ....31.02N 30.28E
Damar i. Indonesia 105 H2 ....7.07S 128.40E
Damaraland f. Namibia 86 A2 ....21.58S 17.06E
Damascus Syria 94 E6 ....33.30N 36.20E
Damāvand, Qolleh-ye mt. Iran 95 H7 ....35.58N 52.07E
Damghan Iran 95 H7 ....36.09N 54.19E
Dammam Saudi Arabia 95 H5 ....26.24N 50.10E
Dampier Australia 110 A4 ....20.41S 116.47E
Dampir, Selat str. Indonesia 105 I3 ......0.40S 130.43E
Đa Nẵng Vietnam 104 D7 ....16.01N 108.12E
Dande r. Ethiopia 87 B4 ....4.44N 36.25E
Dandong China 103 M6 ....40.06N 124.22E
Dane r. England 15 E2 ....53.16N 2.31W
Danger Island Indian Oc. 108 A5 ....6.24S 71.17E
Dangla Bulgaria/Croatia/S.M. 53 I6 ......45.26N 29.38E
Danube Delta Romania/Ukraine 57 H7 ..45.11N 29.13E
Danville U.S.A. 65 K4 ....36.35N 79.24W
Dapaong Togo 84 E3 ....10.53N 0.15E
Da Qaidam Zhen China 102 H5 ....37.49N 95.18E
Daqing China 103 N7 ....46.28N 125.01E
Dar'ā Syria 94 E6 ....32.38N 36.07E
Dārāb Iran 95 H5 ....28.45N 54.32E
Darabani Romania 55 L3 ....48.11N 26.36E
Daraj Libya 84 F5 ....30.10N 10.28E
Darbhanga India 96 G6 ....26.10N 85.57E
Dardanelles str. Turkey 56 G5 ....40.12N 26.25E
Dar es Salaam Tanzania 86 C4 ....6.48S 39.16E
Darhan Mongolia 103 J7 ....49.23N 105.49E
Darién, Golfo del g. Colombia 72 B7 ......8.56N 77.01W
Darjiling India 96 G6 ....27.02N 88.19E
Darling r. Australia 110 D3 ....34.05S 141.56E
Darling Downs hills Australia 110 D4 ....27.58S 149.54E
Darlington England 15 F3 ....54.31N 1.33W
Darlington d. England 9 E4 ....54.33N 1.34W
Darmstadt Germany 44 H6 ....49.52N 8.38E
Darnah Libya 85 G5 ....32.42N 22.40E
Dart r. England 13 D2 ....50.25N 3.39W
Dartford England 11 F2 ....51.27N 0.13E
Dartmoor hills England 13 C2 ....50.36N 4.01W
Dartmouth Canada 65 N5 ....44.41N 63.35W
Dartmouth England 13 D2 ....50.21N 3.35W
Darton England 15 F2 ....53.35N 1.31W
Daru P.N.G. 105 K2 ....9.03S 143.12E
Darvel England 16 E2 ....53.42N 2.28W
Darwin Australia 110 C5 ....12.27S 130.51E
Datong China 103 K6 ....40.03N 113.20E
Daud Khel Pakistan 95 L6 ....32.51N 71.37E
Daugava r. Latvia 40 F1 ....57.03N 24.04E
Daugavpils Latvia 40 F1 ....55.53N 26.31E
Dauphin Canada 62 H3 ....51.09N 100.02W
Dauphiné f. France 44 F4 ....45.21N 6.17E
Davangere India 96 E3 ....14.27N 75.51E
Davao Phil. 105 H5 ....7.05N 125.34E
Davao Gulf Phil. 105 H5 ....6.22N 125.49E
Davenport U.S.A. 65 H5 ....41.32N 90.33W
Daventry England 10 D3 ....52.15N 1.10W
David Panama 71 H2 ....8.27N 82.25W
Davis Strait Canada/Greenland 63 M4 ....63.48N 56.19W
Davos Switz. 50 C7 ....46.48N 9.49E
Dawa Wenz r. Ethiopia 87 C4 ....4.09N 42.04E
Dawlish England 13 D2 ....50.35N 3.28W
Dawqah Oman 95 H3 ....18.37N 54.04E
Dawson Canada 62 E4 ....64.04N 139.24W
Dawson Creek town Canada 62 F3 ....55.46N 120.17W
Daxian China 97 K7 ....31.05N 107.26E
Dayr az Zawr Syria 94 F7 ....35.19N 40.06E
Dayton U.S.A. 65 J4 ....39.45N 84.11W
Daytona Beach town U.S.A. 65 J2 ....29.08N 81.05W
Dazhou China 103 J4 ....31.12N 107.28E
Dead Sea l. Asia 94 E6 ....31.08N 35.27E
Deal England 11 G2 ....51.13N 1.24E
Dean, Forest of England 10 C2 ....51.48N 2.32W
Dearne r. England 15 F2 ....53.29N 1.14W
Death Valley f. U.S.A. 64 C4 ....36.34N 117.01W
Debak Malaysia 104 E4 ....1.31N 111.29E
Debar Macedonia 56 D5 ....41.31N 20.31E
Debenham England 11 G3 ....52.14N 1.11E
Debrecen Hungary 55 J2 ....47.32N 21.37E
Debre Zeyit Ethiopia 86 C5 ....8.45N 38.57E
Decatur U.S.A. 65 I3 ....34.37N 86.59W
Deccan f. India 96 E4 ....18.40N 77.05E
Děčín Czech Rep. 54 F4 ....50.48N 14.13E
Dee r. Scotland 19 G2 ....57.09N 2.05W
Dee r. Wales 12 D5 ....53.13N 3.01W
Dee est. Wales 12 D5 ....53.18N 3.09W
Deele r. Rep. of Ireland 16 B2 ....54.51N 7.28W
Degodia f. Ethiopia 87 C4 ....4.13N 41.24E

De Grey r. Australia 110 A4 ....20.19S 119.14E
Dehra Dun India 96 E7 ....30.20N 78.05E
Dej Romania 55 J2 ....47.09N 23.53E
Delano Peak U.S.A. 64 D4 ....38.23N 112.21W
Delap-Uliga-Djarrit Marshall Is 108 H6 ..7.07N 171.22E
Delārām Afgh. 95 J6 ....32.11N 63.28E
Delaware r. U.S.A. 65 K4 ....38.58N 75.28W
Delft Neth. 42 D5 ....52.01N 4.21E
Delfzijl Neth. 42 F6 ....53.20N 6.55E
Delgado, Cabo c. Mozambique 86 D3 ....10.41S 40.36E
Delhi India 96 E6 ....28.38N 77.17E
Delhi d. India 102 D3 ....28.38N 77.08E
Delice r. Turkey 57 K5 ....40.31N 34.13E
Del Rio U.S.A. 64 F2 ....29.21N 100.54W
Demanda, Sierra de la mts Spain 48 D5 ..42.13N 3.27W
Deming U.S.A. 64 E3 ....32.16N 107.45W
Demirci Turkey 57 H4 ....39.02N 28.39E
Demirkazık Tepe mt. Turkey 57 K3 ......37.48N 35.09E
Demmin Germany 46 A4 ....53.54N 13.03E
Denakil f. Africa 85 I3 ....14.27N 40.44E
Denbigh Wales 12 D5 ....53.11N 3.25W
Denbighshire d. Wales 9 D3 ....53.06N 3.20W
Den Burg Neth. 42 D6 ....53.03N 4.49E
Dendermonde Belgium 42 D4 ....51.01N 4.07E
Den Helder Neth. 42 D5 ....52.58N 4.46E
Denizli Turkey 57 H3 ....37.45N 29.05E
Denmark Europe 40 B2 ....56.13N 10.09E
Denmark Strait Greenland/Iceland 63 P4 ..66.11N 28.09W
Denny Scotland 17 F4 ....56.01N 3.54W
Denpasar Indonesia 104 F2 ....8.41S 115.10E
Denton U.S.A. 64 G3 ....33.15N 97.08W
D'Entrecasteaux Islands P.N.G. 110 E6 ..9.38S 151.02E
Denver U.S.A. 64 E4 ....39.45N 105.02W
Dêqên China 103 H3 ....28.26N 98.50E
Dera Ghazi Khan Pakistan 96 D7 ....30.05N 70.44E
Dera Ismail Khan Pakistan 96 D7 ....31.51N 70.56E
Derby Australia 110 B5 ....17.19S 123.38E
Derby England 10 D3 ....52.55N 1.28W
Derby d. England 9 E3 ....52.55N 1.28W
Derbyshire d. England 9 E3 ....53.11N 1.36W
Dereham England 11 F3 ....52.41N 0.56E
Derg r. Rep. of Ireland/U.K. 41 D4 ....54.44N 7.26W
Derg, Lough l. Don. Rep. of Ireland 41 C4 ..54.37N 7.51W
Derg, Lough l. Tipp. Rep. of Ireland 41 C3 ..52.54N 8.28W
Derry d. Northern Ireland 8 B4 ....54.56N 7.10W
Derry r. Rep. of Ireland 41 C2 ....52.21N 6.40W
Derryveagh Mountains Rep. of Ireland 41 C4 ..54.56N 8.14W
Derwent r. England 11 F3 ....52.51N 0.31E
Derwent r. Derbys. England 15 F2 ....53.25N 1.44W
Derwent Reservoir Derbys. England 15 F2 ..53.25N 1.44W
Derwent Reservoir Dur. England 15 F3 ....54.52N 1.58W
Derwent Water l. England 14 D3 ....54.34N 3.10W
Desaguadero r. Argentina 73 C3 ....34.03S 66.43W
Desaguadero r. Bolivia 76 G4 ....16.40S 69.01W
Désappointement, Îles du is French Polynesia 109 K5
..................13.59S 141.06W
Desē Ethiopia 85 H3 ....11.07N 39.38E
Deseado Argentina 73 C2 ....47.45S 65.55W
Des Moines U.S.A. 65 H5 ....41.36N 93.37W
Des Moines r. U.S.A. 65 H5 ....40.23N 91.28W
Desna r. Rus. Fed./Ukraine 55 M3 ....49.19N 28.31E
Desna r. Ukraine 55 N4 ....50.32N 30.33E
Dessau Germany 54 E4 ....51.50N 12.15E
Detroit U.S.A. 65 J5 ....42.19N 83.04W
Deva Romania 56 E7 ....45.54N 22.55E
Deventer Neth. 42 F5 ....52.15N 6.10E
Deveron r. Scotland 19 G2 ....57.40N 2.31W
Devil's Bit Mountain hill Rep. of Ireland 41 D2 ..52.49N 7.55W
Devil's Bridge Wales 12 D4 ....52.23N 3.51W
Devil's Lake town U.S.A. 64 G6 ....48.02N 98.46W
Devizes England 10 D2 ....51.21N 1.59W
Devon d. England 9 D2 ....50.32N 3.51W
Devon r. England 15 G2 ....53.04N 0.50W
Devon r. Scotland 17 F4 ....56.11N 3.51W
Devon Island Canada 63 I5 ....75.20N 91.06W
Devonport Australia 110 D2 ....41.11S 146.20E
Devrez r. Turkey 57 K5 ....41.27N 35.01E
Dewsbury England 15 F2 ....53.41N 1.38W
Dezfūl Iran 95 G6 ....32.23N 48.24E
Dezhou China 103 L5 ....37.25N 116.19E
Dhahran Saudi Arabia 95 H5 ....26.19N 50.07E
Dhamār Yemen 94 F2 ....14.34N 44.26E
Dhanbad India 96 G5 ....23.47N 86.25E
Dharwad India 96 E3 ....15.27N 75.04E
Dhaulagiri mt. Nepal 96 F6 ....28.40N 83.28E
Dhule India 96 E5 ....20.54N 74.47E
Diablo, Picacho del mt. Mexico 70 A7 ....30.59N 115.24W
Diamantina watercourse Australia 110 C4 ..26.30S 139.22E
Diamantina, Chapada f. Brazil 77 L5 ......14.21S 43.09W
Diamantina Deep f. Indian Oc. 108 C3 ....35.42S 104.20E
Dibrugarh India 97 I6 ....27.27N 94.55E
Dickinson U.S.A. 64 F6 ....46.53N 102.48W
Dida Galgalu f. Kenya 87 B3 ....3.11N 38.06E
Didcot England 10 D2 ....51.36N 1.15W
Diekirch d. Lux. 42 E2 ....49.59N 5.59E
Dieppe France 44 D6 ....49.55N 1.05E
Diest Belgium 42 E3 ....50.59N 5.03E
Digne-les-Bains France 44 G4 ....44.06N 6.15E
Dijon France 44 F5 ....47.20N 5.03E
Diksmuide Belgium 42 B4 ....51.02N 2.52E
Dili East Timor 105 H2 ....8.35S 125.36E
Dillon U.S.A. 64 D6 ....45.13N 112.37W
Dimapur India 97 H6 ....25.54N 93.47E
Dimitrovgrad Bulgaria 56 F6 ....42.03N 25.35E
Dinajpur Bangl. 96 G6 ....25.38N 88.40E
Dinan France 44 B6 ....48.27N 2.03W
Dinant Belgium 42 D3 ....50.16N 4.56E
Dinar Turkey 57 I4 ....38.04N 30.10E
Dīnār, Kūh-e mt. Iran 95 H6 ....30.49N 51.32E
Dinard France 44 B6 ....48.38N 2.04W
Dinaric Alps mts Bos.-Herz./Croatia 56 B7 ..44.13N 16.16E
Dindigul India 96 E3 ....10.22N 78.02E
Dingle Rep. of Ireland 41 A2 ....52.08N 10.16W
Dingle Bay Rep. of Ireland 41 A2 ....52.04N 10.21W
Dingwall Canada 19 E2 ....46.54N 60.29W
Dipolog Phil. 105 G5 ....8.39N 123.26E
Dirē Dawa Ethiopia 85 I3 ....9.34N 41.53E
Dirranbandi Australia 110 D4 ....28.34S 148.14E
Disappointment, Cape S. Atlantic Oc. 73 F1 ..54.51S 36.07W
Disappointment, Lake Australia 110 B4 ..23.30S 122.40E
Disko i. Greenland 63 M4 ....69.44N 53.33W
Diss England 11 G3 ....52.23N 1.07E
Distington England 14 D3 ....54.36N 3.32W
Distrito Federal d. Brazil 77 K4 ....15.56S 47.39W
Distrito Federal d. Mexico 70 E4 ....19.25N 99.09W
Diu India 96 D5 ....20.40N 71.03E
Divinópolis Brazil 77 L3 ....20.09S 44.53W
Divnoye Rus. Fed. 53 L6 ....45.55N 43.20E
Divriği Turkey 57 M4 ....39.22N 38.06E

Dixon Entrance str. Canada/U.S.A. 62 E3 ..54.18N 133.28W
Diyarbakır Turkey 53 L4 ....37.55N 40.14E
Djado, Plateau du f. Niger 84 F4 ....21.30N 12.53E
Djelfa Algeria 84 E5 ....34.38N 3.16E
Djibouti Africa 85 I3 ....11.34N 42.25E
Djibouti town Djibouti 85 I3 ....11.32N 43.09E
Djouce Mountain hill Rep. of Ireland 12 A5 ..53.08N 6.15W
Dnieper r. Belarus 55 N4 ....51.16N 30.34E
Dnieper r. Ukraine 55 O2 ....46.30N 32.19E
Dniester r. Moldova 55 N2 ....46.25N 30.11E
Dniester r. Ukraine 55 M3 ....48.06N 28.30E
Dniprodzerzhyns'k Ukraine 55 P3 ....48.30N 34.39E
Dnipropetrovs'k Ukraine 55 P3 ....48.30N 35.05E
Dniprorudne Ukraine 55 P2 ....47.23N 34.58E
Doba Chad 85 F2 ....8.40N 16.51E
Doberai Peninsula Indonesia 105 I3 ......1.19S 132.27E
Doboj Bos. 56 C7 ....44.45N 18.06E
Dobrich Bulgaria 57 G6 ....43.33N 27.49E
Dobskie, Jezioro l. Poland 46 E5 ....54.04N 21.36E
Dochart r. Scotland 16 E4 ....56.28N 4.18W
Docking England 11 F3 ....52.54N 0.38E
Dodecanese is Greece 56 G2 ....37.57N 27.47E
Dodge City U.S.A. 64 F4 ....37.46N 100.03W
Dodman Point England 13 C2 ....50.13N 4.48W
Dodoma Tanzania 86 C4 ....6.10S 35.45E
Doetinchem Neth. 42 F4 ....51.58N 6.17E
Doha Qatar 95 H5 ....25.17N 51.33E
Dokkum Neth. 42 E6 ....53.19N 5.59E
Dolbenmaen Wales 12 C4 ....52.58N 4.14W
Dole France 44 F5 ....47.06N 5.30E
Dolgellau Wales 12 D4 ....52.45N 3.53W
Dolomites mts Italy 50 D6 ....45.42N 11.37E
Dolo Odo Ethiopia 87 C4 ....4.09N 42.03E
Dolyna Ukraine 55 J3 ....48.58N 23.59E
Dolyns'ka Ukraine 55 O3 ....48.07N 32.46E
Dominica Central America 71 L4 ....15.18N 61.15W
Dominican Republic Central America 71 J4 ..18.57N 70.23W
Don r. Rus. Fed. 35 H2 ....47.06N 39.16E
Don r. Scotland 19 G2 ....57.10N 2.05W
Donaghadee Northern Ireland 16 D2 ....54.38N 5.32W
Doncaster England 15 F2 ....53.31N 1.08W
Dondo Angola 86 A4 ....9.41S 14.27E
Donegal Rep. of Ireland 41 C4 ....54.39N 8.07W
Donegal d. Rep. of Ireland 41 C4 ....54.56N 8.07W
Donegal Bay Rep. of Ireland 41 C4 ....54.31N 8.21W
Donegal Point Rep. of Ireland 41 B2 ......52.43N 9.38W
Donets'k Ukraine 53 K6 ....47.59N 37.47E
Dongara Australia 110 A4 ....29.17S 114.54E
Dongfang China 103 J1 ....19.03N 108.39E
Dongfanghong China 106 B5 ....46.10N 133.02E
Dong Hoi Vietnam 104 D7 ....17.26N 106.36E
Dongotona Mountains Sudan 87 A4 ......4.12N 33.08E
Dongting Hu l. China 103 K3 ....29.20N 112.57E
Donostia-San Sebastián Spain 48 E5 ....43.19N 1.59W
Doon r. Scotland 16 E3 ....55.26N 4.39W
Doon, Loch l. Scotland 16 E3 ....55.15N 4.24W
Dorchester England 10 C1 ....50.43N 2.26W
Dordogne r. France 44 C4 ....45.00N 0.29E
Dordrecht Neth. 42 D4 ....51.48N 4.41E
Dorking England 11 E2 ....51.14N 0.20W
Dornbirn Austria 54 C2 ....47.26N 9.45E
Dornoch Scotland 19 E2 ....57.53N 4.02W
Dornoch Firth est. Scotland 19 E2 ....57.51N 4.04W
Döröö Nuur l. Mongolia 102 G7 ....47.33N 93.37E
Dorsale Camerounaise f. Cameroon/Nigeria 84 F2
..................5.59N 10.49E
Dorset d. England 9 D2 ....50.53N 2.18W
Dortmund Germany 54 B4 ....51.30N 7.27E
Dos Bahías, Cabo c. Argentina 73 C2 ....44.56S 65.32W
Dosso Niger 84 E3 ....13.03N 3.12E
Dothan U.S.A. 65 I3 ....31.14N 85.24W
Douai France 44 E7 ....50.23N 3.05E
Douala Cameroon 84 F2 ....4.03N 9.42E
Douglas Isle of Man 14 C3 ....54.09N 4.29W
Douglas Scotland 17 F3 ....55.33N 3.51W
Douglas U.S.A. 64 E3 ....31.20N 109.33W
Doullens France 42 B3 ....50.09N 2.21E
Doune Scotland 17 E4 ....56.11N 4.03W
Dounreay Scotland 19 F3 ....58.35N 3.45W
Dourados Brazil 77 J3 ....22.13S 54.49W
Douro r. Portugal 48 A4 ....41.09N 8.34W
Dove r. Derbys. England 10 D4 ....52.50N 1.35W
Dove r. Suff. England 11 G3 ....52.21N 1.11E
Dover England 11 G2 ....51.08N 1.19E
Dover U.S.A. 65 K4 ....39.09N 75.32W
Dover, Strait of France/U.K. 11 G1 ....50.53N 1.28E
Down d. Northern Ireland 9 C4 ....54.17N 5.32W
Down r. Northern Ireland 41 B4 ....54.20N 5.55W
Downham Market England 11 F3 ....52.36N 0.23E
Downpatrick Northern Ireland 16 D2 ....54.19N 5.42W
Downpatrick Head Rep. of Ireland 41 B4 ..54.20N 9.20W
Downton England 10 D1 ....50.59N 1.45W
Dowshī Afgh. 95 K7 ....35.38N 68.46E
Drãa, Hammada du f. Algeria 52 B2 ......28.29N 8.17W
Drachten Neth. 42 F6 ....53.06N 6.06E
Draguignan France 44 G3 ....43.32N 6.28E
Drahichyn Belarus 55 K5 ....52.11N 25.08E
Drakensberg mts Lesotho/S. Africa 86 B2 ..29.59S 28.56E
Drama Greece 56 F5 ....41.09N 24.08E
Drammen Norway 40 B2 ....59.45N 10.12E
Draperstown Northern Ireland 16 C2 ....54.48N 6.46W
Drau r. Austria 54 F2 ....46.38N 14.57E
Drava r. Europe 56 C7 ....45.33N 18.56E
Drenthe d. Neth. 42 F5 ....52.53N 6.43E
Dresden Germany 54 E4 ....51.03N 13.45E
Dreux France 44 D6 ....48.44N 1.23E
Drina r. Bos.-Herz./S.M. 56 C7 ....44.55N 19.22E
Drobeta-Turnu Severin Romania 56 E7 ..44.37N 22.40E
Drogheda Rep. of Ireland 41 E3 ....53.43N 6.21W
Drohobych Ukraine 55 J3 ....49.22N 23.32E
Droitwich Spa England 10 C3 ....52.16N 2.09W
Dromore Northern Ireland 16 C2 ....54.25N 6.08W
Dronfield England 15 F2 ....53.18N 1.28W
Drosh Pakistan 95 L7 ....35.33N 71.50E
Drumheller Canada 62 G3 ....51.27N 112.42W
Drummore Scotland 16 E2 ....54.41N 4.54W
Drumen Scotland 16 E4 ....56.04N 4.27W
Druskininkai Lithuania 46 G4 ....53.59N 24.01E
Druts' r. Belarus 55 N5 ....53.03N 30.03E
Drygarn Fawr hill Wales 12 D4 ....52.13N 3.40W
Drymen Scotland 16 E4 ....56.04N 4.27W
Duarte, Pico mt. Dom. Rep. 71 J4 ....19.03N 70.59W
Ḍubā Saudi Arabia 94 E5 ....27.20N 35.45E
Dubawnt Lake Canada 62 H4 ....63.05N 101.38W
Dubbo Australia 110 D3 ....32.16S 148.39E
Dublin Rep. of Ireland 41 E3 ....53.20N 6.16W
Dublin d. Rep. of Ireland 41 E3 ....53.24N 6.18W
Dublin Bay Rep. of Ireland 41 E3 ....53.21N 6.10W
Dubno Ukraine 55 K4 ....50.25N 25.43E
Dubrovnik Croatia 56 C6 ....42.39N 18.06E
Dubrovytsya Ukraine 55 L4 ....51.34N 26.34E
Dubysa r. Lithuania 46 F5 ....55.04N 23.25E
Ducie Island atoll S. Pacific Oc. 109 L4 ..24.40S 124.48W

Dudinka Rus. Fed. 59 J4 ....69.22N 86.11E
Dudley England 10 C3 ....52.31N 2.05W
Duero r. Spain 48 B4 ....41.02N 6.56W
Dufftown Scotland 19 F2 ....57.27N 3.08W
Dufourspitze mt. Italy/Switz. 50 B6 ....45.57N 7.53E
Dugi Otok i. Croatia 56 A7 ....44.01N 15.01E
Duisburg Germany 54 B4 ....51.28N 6.47E
Dukhān Qatar 95 H5 ....25.25N 50.47E
Dulce r. Argentina 76 H1 ....30.33S 62.34W
Duluth U.S.A. 65 H6 ....46.45N 92.07W
Dulverton England 13 D3 ....51.02N 3.33W
Dumas U.S.A. 64 F4 ....35.53N 101.59W
Dumbarton Scotland 16 E3 ....55.57N 4.34W
Dumbier mt. Slovakia 46 D2 ....48.57N 19.39E
Dumfries Scotland 17 F2 ....55.04N 3.16W
Dumfries and Galloway d. Scotland 8 D4 ....55.09N 3.46W
Dumyāṭ Egypt 53 J3 ....31.25N 31.49E
Dunaff Head Rep. of Ireland 16 B3 ....55.18N 7.31W
Dunany Point Rep. of Ireland 41 E3 ....53.52N 6.14W
Dunaújváros Hungary 54 H2 ....46.59N 18.56E
Dunbar Scotland 17 G4 ....56.00N 2.31W
Dunblane Scotland 17 F4 ....56.11N 3.58W
Duncansby Head Scotland 19 F3 ....58.39N 3.01W
Dunchurch England 10 D3 ....52.21N 1.17W
Dundalk Rep. of Ireland 41 E4 ....54.00N 6.24W
Dundalk Bay Rep. of Ireland 41 E3 ....53.57N 6.13W
Dundee Scotland 17 G4 ....56.28N 2.58W
Dundee d. Scotland 8 D5 ....56.29N 2.59W
Dundonald Northern Ireland 16 D2 ....54.36N 5.48W
Dundrum Bay Northern Ireland 16 D2 ....54.13N 5.46W
Dunedin New Zealand 111 G2 ....45.53S 170.30E
Dunfermline Scotland 17 F4 ....56.04N 3.27W
Dungannon Northern Ireland 16 C2 ....54.30N 6.46W
Dungannon d. Northern Ireland 9 B4 ....54.28N 6.52W
Dungarvan Rep. of Ireland 41 D2 ....52.05N 7.38W
Dungeness hd England 11 F1 ....50.55N 0.59E
Dungiven Northern Ireland 16 C2 ....54.55N 6.55W
Dungun Malaysia 104 C4 ....4.46N 103.23E
Dungunab Sudan 94 E4 ....21.04N 37.04E
Dunholme England 15 G2 ....53.18N 0.28W
Dunhua China 106 A4 ....43.22N 128.14E
Dunhuang China 102 G6 ....40.07N 94.40E
Dunkery Beacon hill England 13 D3 ....51.10N 3.35W
Dunkirk France 44 E7 ....51.02N 2.22E
Dún Laoghaire Rep. of Ireland 41 E3 ....53.17N 6.08W
Dunleer Rep. of Ireland 41 E3 ....53.50N 6.23W
Dunloy Northern Ireland 16 C3 ....55.00N 6.24W
Dunmore East Rep. of Ireland 41 E2 ....52.09N 6.59W
Dunmurry Northern Ireland 16 D2 ....54.33N 5.59W
Dunnet Bay Scotland 19 F3 ....58.37N 3.24W
Dunnet Head Scotland 19 F3 ....58.41N 3.23W
Dunoon Scotland 16 E3 ....55.57N 4.56W
Duns Scotland 17 G3 ....55.47N 2.21W
Dunstable England 11 E2 ....51.53N 0.31W
Dunvegan, Loch b. Scotland 18 C2 ....57.31N 6.41W
Durance r. France 44 F5 ....43.55N 4.45E
Durango Mexico 70 D5 ....24.02N 104.43W
Durango d. Mexico 70 D5 ....24.44N 104.59W
Durango U.S.A. 64 E4 ....37.16N 107.52W
Durazno Uruguay 77 I1 ....33.25S 56.31W
Durban S. Africa 86 C2 ....29.51S 31.02E
Düren Germany 42 F3 ....50.48N 6.29E
Durham England 15 F3 ....54.47N 1.35W
Durham d. England 9 D4 ....54.42N 2.09W
Durham U.S.A. 65 K4 ....35.59N 78.54W
Durmitor mt. S.M. 56 C6 ....43.07N 19.03E
Durness Scotland 18 E3 ....58.34N 4.45W
Durness, Kyle of inlet Scotland 18 E3 ....58.34N 4.47W
Durrës Albania 56 C5 ....41.19N 19.27E
Dursey Head Rep. of Ireland 41 A1 ....51.35N 10.13W
Dursley England 10 C2 ....51.41N 2.21W
Dushanbe Tajikistan 96 C8 ....38.38N 68.51E
Düsseldorf Germany 54 B4 ....51.13N 6.47E
Duyun China 103 J3 ....26.13N 107.32E
Düzce Turkey 57 I5 ....40.50N 31.09E
Dyat'kovo Rus. Fed. 55 P5 ....53.36N 34.21E
Dyce Scotland 19 G2 ....57.12N 2.11W
Dyer, Cape Canada 63 L4 ....66.39N 61.16W
Dyfi r. Wales 12 D4 ....52.33N 3.56W
Dylewska Góra hill Poland 46 D4 ....53.34N 19.57E
Dymchurch England 11 F2 ....51.01N 0.59E
Dymock England 10 C2 ....51.58N 2.27W
Dzerzhinsk Rus. Fed. 58 F3 ....56.14N 43.28E
Dzhankoy Ukraine 53 J6 ....45.43N 34.24E
Dzhugdzhur, Khrebet mts Rus. Fed. 59 O3 ......55.53N 135.07E
Działdowo Poland 46 E4 ....53.15N 20.11E
Dzisna r. Belarus 55 M6 ....55.33N 28.13E

E

Ealing England 11 E2 ....51.31N 0.18W
Earlston Scotland 17 G3 ....55.38N 2.41W
Earn r. Scotland 17 F4 ....56.20N 3.20W
Earn, Loch l. Scotland 16 E4 ....56.23N 4.15W
Easington England 15 F3 ....54.47N 1.21W
Easingwold England 15 F3 ....54.07N 1.11W
East Anglian Heights hills England 11 F3 .....52.03N 0.15E
East Ayrshire d. Scotland 8 C4 ....55.29N 4.15W
Eastbourne England 11 F1 ....50.46N 0.18E
East Cape New Zealand 111 G3 ....37.40S 178.33E
East Caroline Basin f. N. Pacific Oc. 108 F6 ..2.08N 148.16E
East China Sea N. Pacific Oc. 103 N4 ....31.00N 127.22E
East Dunbartonshire d. Scotland 8 C4 ....55.58N 4.12W
Easter Island S. Pacific Oc. 109 M4 ....27.05S 109.17W
Eastern d. Kenya 87 B3 ....0.23S 37.55E
Eastern Desert Egypt 53 J2 ....26.39N 32.50E
Eastern Equatoria d. Sudan 87 A4 ....5.45N 33.19E
Eastern Ghats mts India 96 F4 ....11.54N 77.22E
Eastern Ross f. Scotland 18 E2 ....57.49N 4.24W
East Falkland i. Falkland Is 73 D1 ....52.11S 57.55W
East Fen f. England 15 H2 ....53.05N 0.04E
Eastfield England 15 G3 ....54.15N 0.24W
East Frisian Islands Germany 54 B5 ....53.45N 7.00E
East Grinstead England 11 E2 ....51.08N 0.01W
East Indiaman Ridge f. Indian Oc. 108 C4 .....23.28S 91.17E
East Kilbride Scotland 16 E3 ....55.46N 4.10W
Eastleigh England 10 D1 ....50.58N 1.22W
East Linton Scotland 17 G3 ....55.59N 2.39W
East Loch Tarbert inlet Scotland 18 C2 ....57.51N 6.46W
East London S. Africa 86 B1 ....33.01S 27.56E
East Looe England 13 C2 ....50.21N 4.27W
East Lothian d. Scotland 8 D4 ....55.55N 2.40W
Eastmain Canada 63 K3 ....52.14N 78.30W
Eastmain r. Canada 63 K3 ....52.14N 78.30W
Easton England 13 E2 ....50.33N 2.26W
East Pacific Rise f. S. Pacific Oc. 109 M4 ...18.04N 107.07W
East Renfrewshire d. Scotland 8 C3 ....55.46N 4.21W
Eastry England 11 G2 ....51.15N 1.18E
East Sea N. Pacific Oc. 106 B3 ....39.13N 133.37E

East Siberian Sea Rus. Fed. 59 P5 ....72.59N 148.21E
East Sussex d. England 9 F2 ....50.53N 0.17E
East Timor Asia 105 H2 ....8.57S 125.59E
Eastwood England 15 F2 ....53.01N 1.18W
Eaton Socon England 11 E3 ....52.13N 0.17W
Eau Claire U.S.A. 65 H5 ....44.49N 91.31W
Eau Claire, Lac à l' l. Canada 63 K3 ....56.13N 74.07W
Eauripik atoll Micronesia 105 K5 ....6.43N 143.04E
Eauripik Rise-New Guinea Rise f. N. Pacific Oc. 108 F6
                                             8.13N 141.00E
Ebbw Vale Wales 12 D3 ....51.47N 3.12W
Eberswalde-Finow Germany 54 E5 ....52.50N 13.49E
Ebinur Hu l. China 102 E6 ....44.46N 82.51E
Ebro r. Spain 48 F4 ....40.43N 0.51E
Ecclefechan Scotland 17 F3 ....55.04N 3.16W
Eccleshall England 10 C3 ....52.52N 2.15W
Ech Chélif Algeria 84 E5 ....36.09N 1.17E
Écija Spain 48 C2 ....37.33N 5.04W
Eck, Loch l. Scotland 16 E4 ....56.04N 4.59W
Eckington England 10 C3 ....52.04N 2.07W
Ecuador S. America 76 E7 ....1.08S 78.05W
Eday i. Scotland 19 G4 ....59.11N 2.50W
Ed Da'ein Sudan 94 C2 ....11.27N 26.09E
Ed Damazin Sudan 85 H3 ....11.47N 34.20E
Ed Damer Sudan 94 D3 ....17.26N 33.58E
Ed Debba Sudan 94 D3 ....18.00N 30.55E
Ed Dueim Sudan 94 D2 ....13.57N 32.17E
Eden r. England 14 D3 ....54.57N 3.01W
Edessa Greece 56 E5 ....40.48N 22.04E
Edgeøya i. Arctic Oc. 58 D5 ....77.32N 22.45E
Edinburgh Scotland 17 F3 ....55.57N 3.11W
Edinburgh d. Scotland 8 D4 ....55.56N 3.17W
Edirne Turkey 56 G5 ....41.39N 26.34E
Edmonton Canada 62 G3 ....53.33N 113.33W
Edmundston Canada 63 L2 ....47.23N 68.20W
Edremit Turkey 56 G4 ....39.35N 27.00E
Edson Canada 62 G3 ....53.35N 116.25W
Edward, Lake Dem. Rep. Congo/Uganda 86 B4 ...0.17S 29.40E
Edwards Plateau f. U.S.A. 64 F3 ....30.28N 100.22W
Éfaté i. Vanuatu 111 F5 ....17.38S 168.30E
Effingham U.S.A. 65 I4 ....39.07N 88.33W
Eger Hungary 54 I2 ....47.54N 20.22E
Egilsay i. Scotland 19 G4 ....59.09N 2.55W
Egilsstaðir Iceland 40 Z2 ....65.16N 14.25W
Eğirdir Turkey 57 I3 ....37.51N 30.51E
Eğirdir Gölü l. Turkey 57 I3 ....37.59N 30.53E
Eglinton Northern Ireland 16 B3 ....55.02N 7.11W
Egmont, Mount Northern Ireland 16 B3 ....55.02N 7.11W
Egremont England 14 D3 ....54.29N 3.32W
Egvekinot Rus. Fed. 59 T4 ....66.20N 179.17W
Egypt Africa 85 G4 ....29.53N 31.16E
Eifel hills Germany 54 B4 ....50.10N 6.39E
Eigg i. Scotland 18 C1 ....56.54N 6.10W
Eighty Mile Beach f. Australia 110 B5 ....19.54S 120.10E
Eilat Israel 53 J2 ....29.33N 34.56E
Eindhoven Neth. 42 E4 ....51.26N 5.29E
Eisenhüttenstadt Germany 54 F5 ....52.09N 14.38E
Eishort, Loch inlet Scotland 18 D2 ....57.09N 5.59W
Ekibastuz Kazakhstan 102 D8 ....51.46N 75.27E
Ekostrovskaya Imandra, Ozero l. Rus. Fed. 40 H4
                                             67.29N 32.23E
Eksjö Sweden 40 C2 ....57.40N 14.59E
Elazığ Turkey 57 M4 ....38.39N 39.15E
Elba, Isola d' i. Italy 50 D5 ....42.50N 10.16E
El'ban Rus. Fed. 103 P8 ....50.03N 136.26E
Elbasan Albania 56 D5 ....41.07N 20.05E
El Bayadh Algeria 52 D3 ....33.41N 0.56E
Elbe r. Germany 54 D5 ....53.53N 9.05E
Elbert, Mount U.S.A. 64 E4 ....39.05N 106.25W
Elbistan Turkey 57 L4 ....38.12N 37.11E
Elbląg Poland 46 D5 ....54.10N 19.24E
El'brus mt. Rus. Fed. 58 F2 ....43.22N 42.25E
Elburz Mountains Iran 95 G7 ....36.52N 49.43E
El Callao Venezuela 71 L2 ....7.17N 61.47W
El Cerro Bolivia 77 H4 ....17.32S 61.36W
Elche-Elx Spain 48 E3 ....38.16N 0.41W
Elda Spain 48 E3 ....38.29N 0.47W
Eldama Ravine Kenya 87 A3 ....0.05N 35.44E
El Dera Kenya 87 B3 ....0.39N 38.43E
El Djouf des. Africa 82 C7 ....21.00N 8.00W
El Dorado U.S.A. 65 H3 ....33.13N 92.36W
Elemi Triangle Africa 87 A4 ....4.53N 35.11E
El Eulma Algeria 52 E4 ....36.07N 5.48E
Eleuthera i. Bahamas 71 I6 ....25.21N 76.22W
El Fasher Sudan 85 G3 ....13.36N 25.20E
El Geneina Sudan 85 G3 ....13.26N 22.26E
Elgin Scotland 19 F2 ....57.39N 3.19W
El'ginskiy Rus. Fed. 59 P4 ....64.32N 141.40E
El Goléa Algeria 84 E5 ....30.34N 2.58E
Elgon, Mount Kenya/Uganda 87 A3 ....1.08N 34.34E
El Hierro i. Canary Islands 48 X1 ....27.40N 17.56W
El Jadida Morocco 84 D5 ....33.12N 8.27W
Efk Poland 46 F4 ....53.50N 22.22E
Elkhovo Bulgaria 56 G6 ....42.11N 26.34E
Elko U.S.A. 64 C5 ....40.51N 115.46W
Ellef Ringnes Island Canada 63 H5 ....78.38N 101.56W
El Lēh Ethiopia 87 B3 ....3.45N 39.14E
Ellensburg U.S.A. 64 B6 ....46.59N 120.32W
Ellesmere England 10 C3 ....52.54N 2.54W
Ellesmere Island Canada 63 J5 ....77.10N 83.03W
Ellesmere Port England 14 E2 ....53.17N 2.54W
Ellice r. Canada 62 H4 ....67.56N 103.59W
Ellon Scotland 19 G2 ....57.22N 2.04W
Elmali Turkey 57 H3 ....36.44N 29.55E
El Meghaïer Algeria 52 E3 ....33.56N 5.56E
El Muglad Sudan 85 G3 ....11.01N 27.44E
El Obeid Sudan 85 H3 ....13.10N 30.11E
El Oued Algeria 52 E3 ....33.21N 6.54E
El Paso U.S.A. 64 E3 ....31.46N 106.24W
El Puerto de Santa María Spain 48 B2 ....36.36N 6.13W
El Salvador Central America 70 G3 ....13.22N 88.59W
El Tigre Venezuela 71 L2 ....8.52N 64.16W
Eluru India 96 F4 ....16.44N 81.09E
Elvas Portugal 48 B3 ....38.53N 7.10W
Elverum Norway 40 B3 ....60.53N 11.33E
El Wak Kenya 87 C3 ....2.47N 40.56E
Ely England 11 F3 ....52.24N 0.15E
Ely U.S.A. 64 D4 ....39.15N 114.53W
Ely, Isle of England 11 F3 ....52.27N 0.14E
Emāmrūd Iran 95 H7 ....36.24N 54.56E
Embu Kenya 87 B2 ....0.31S 37.26E
Emden Germany 54 B5 ....53.22N 7.13E
Emerson Canada 64 G6 ....49.02N 97.11W
Emi Koussi mt. Chad 85 F3 ....19.46N 18.34E
Emirdağ Turkey 57 I4 ....39.01N 31.09E
Emmeloord Neth. 42 E5 ....52.43N 5.45E
Emmen Neth. 42 F5 ....52.48N 6.55E
Emory Peak U.S.A. 64 F2 ....29.15N 103.18W
Emperor Seamount Chain f. N. Pacific Oc. 108 H9
                                             41.19N 167.06E
Emperor Trough f. N. Pacific Oc. 108 H9 ......46.06N 173.14E
Ems r. Germany 54 B5 ....53.18N 7.22E
Encarnación Paraguay 77 I2 ....27.17S 55.49W
Endeh Indonesia 105 G2 ....8.47S 121.38E

Endicott Mountains U.S.A. 62 C4 ....67.50N 152.33W
Enfield England 11 E2 ....51.39N 0.05W
Engel's Rus. Fed. 58 F3 ....51.29N 46.06E
Enggano i. Indonesia 104 C2 ....5.25S 102.20E
England d. U.K. 9 E3 ....52.48N 1.24W
English Channel France/U.K. 11 E1 ....49.59N 1.24W
En Nahud Sudan 85 G3 ....12.42N 28.25E
Ennerdale Water l. England 14 D3 ....54.30N 3.22W
Ennis Rep. of Ireland 41 C2 ....52.51N 8.59W
Enniscorthy Rep. of Ireland 41 E2 ....52.30N 6.34W
Enniskerry Rep. of Ireland 12 A5 ....53.11N 6.10W
Enniskillen Northern Ireland 16 B2 ....54.20N 7.37W
Ennistymon Rep. of Ireland 41 B2 ....52.56N 9.17W
Enns r. Austria 54 F3 ....48.14N 14.31E
Enschede Neth. 42 F5 ....52.13N 6.54E
Ensenada Mexico 70 A7 ....31.52N 116.37W
Enshi China 103 J4 ....30.13N 109.28E
Enugu Nigeria 84 E2 ....6.24N 7.31E
Envira r. Brazil 76 F6 ....7.31S 70.14W
Épernay France 42 C2 ....49.03N 3.58E
Épinal France 44 G6 ....48.11N 6.27E
Epomeo, Monte vol. Italy 50 E4 ....40.44N 13.53E
Epping England 11 F2 ....51.42N 0.07E
Eppynt, Mynydd hills Wales 12 D4 ....52.05N 3.28W
Epsom England 11 E2 ....51.20N 0.16W
Epworth England 15 G2 ....53.32N 0.49W
Eqlid Iran 95 H6 ....30.53N 52.42E
Equatorial Guinea Africa 84 E2 ....3.00N 8.36E
Équeurdreville-Hainneville France 13 Z9 .....49.39N 1.39W
Erbeskopf hill Germany 42 G2 ....49.43N 7.04E
Erciyes Dağı mt. Turkey 57 K4 ....38.32N 35.27E
Erdemli Turkey 57 K3 ....36.36N 34.19E
Erdi f. Chad 94 B3 ....19.02N 21.36E
Ereğli Konya Turkey 57 K3 ....37.30N 34.03E
Ereğli Zonguldak Turkey 57 I5 ....41.17N 31.25E
Erfurt Germany 54 D4 ....50.59N 11.02E
Ergani Turkey 57 M4 ....38.15N 39.46E
Ergene r. Turkey 56 G5 ....40.59N 26.22E
Ericht r. Scotland 17 F4 ....56.34N 3.15W
Ericht, Loch l. Scotland 19 E1 ....56.48N 4.25W
Erie U.S.A. 65 J5 ....42.07N 80.06W
Erie, Lake Canada/U.S.A. 63 J2 ....42.14N 80.53W
Eriskay i. Scotland 18 B2 ....57.04N 7.16W
Eritrea Africa 85 H3 ....15.57N 37.33E
Erlangen Germany 54 D3 ....49.35N 11.01E
Ermenek Turkey 57 J3 ....36.37N 32.54E
Ermoupoli Greece 56 F3 ....37.26N 24.56E
Erode India 96 E3 ....11.21N 77.43E
Er Rachidia Morocco 84 D5 ....31.54N 4.29W
Er Rahad Sudan 85 H3 ....12.44N 30.38E
Errigal hill Rep. of Ireland 41 C5 ....55.02N 8.07W
Erris Head Rep. of Ireland 41 A4 ....54.19N 10.01W
Errochty, Loch l. Scotland 19 E1 ....56.45N 4.11W
Erromango i. Vanuatu 111 F5 ....18.49S 168.58E
Erzgebirge mts Czech Rep./Germany 54 E4 .....50.33N 13.07E
Erzincan Turkey 94 F7 ....39.45N 39.29E
Erzurum Turkey 94 F7 ....39.53N 41.17E
Esbjerg Denmark 40 B1 ....55.28N 8.27E
Escanaba U.S.A. 65 I6 ....45.45N 87.03W
Escárcega Mexico 70 F4 ....18.39N 90.43W
Esch-sur-Alzette Lux. 42 E2 ....49.30N 5.59E
Eschweiler Germany 42 F3 ....50.49N 6.18E
Eşfahān Iran 95 H6 ....32.41N 51.39E
Esha Ness hd Scotland 19 H5 ....60.30N 1.37W
Esk r. Scotland 17 F3 ....55.56N 3.04W
Eske, Lough l. Rep. of Ireland 16 A2 ....54.42N 8.04W
Eski Gediz Turkey 57 H4 ....39.03N 29.25E
Eskilstuna Sweden 40 D2 ....59.22N 16.32E
Eskişehir Turkey 57 I4 ....39.47N 30.31E
Esla r. Spain 48 B4 ....41.30N 6.01W
Eslāmābād-e Gharb Iran 95 G6 ....34.06N 46.31E
Esmeraldas Ecuador 76 E8 ....0.55N 79.41W
Esperance Australia 110 B3 ....33.49S 121.52E
Espigüete mt. Spain 48 C5 ....42.57N 4.47W
Espinosa Brazil 77 L5 ....14.54S 42.46W
Espírito Santo d. Brazil 77 L4 ....19.31S 40.33W
Espíritu Santo i. Vanuatu 111 F5 ....15.16S 166.35E
Espoo Finland 40 F3 ....60.12N 24.40E
Esquel Argentina 73 B2 ....42.55S 71.20W
Essen Germany 54 B4 ....51.28N 7.03E
Essequibo r. Guyana 72 D7 ....6.23N 58.36W
Essex d. England 9 F2 ....51.51N 0.42E
Estados, Isla de los i. Argentina 73 C1 .....54.44S 64.16W
Estats, Pic d' mt. France/Spain 48 F5 ....42.40N 1.24E
Estevan Canada 62 H2 ....49.08N 102.59W
Estonia Europe 40 F2 ....58.44N 25.26E
Estrela, Serra da mts Portugal 48 B4 ....40.11N 7.57W
Estrella mt. Spain 48 D3 ....38.24N 3.36W
Estrondo, Serra hills Brazil 77 K6 ....9.08S 48.42W
Étaples France 44 D7 ....50.31N 1.39E
Ethiopia Africa 85 H2 ....6.30N 39.41E
Ethiopian Highlands f. Ethiopia 85 H2 ....8.49N 36.39E
Etimesğut Turkey 57 J4 ....39.56N 32.39E
Etive, Loch inlet Scotland 16 D4 ....56.27N 5.12W
Etna, Mount vol. Italy 50 F2 ....37.45N 15.00E
Etosha Pan f. Namibia 86 A3 ....18.52S 16.19E
Ettelbruck Lux. 42 F2 ....49.51N 6.06E
Ettrick Forest f. Scotland 17 F3 ....55.31N 3.05W
Ettrick Water r. Scotland 17 G3 ....55.34N 2.49W
Etwall England 10 D3 ....52.53N 1.36W
Eugene U.S.A. 64 B5 ....44.04N 123.05W
Eugenia, Punta pt Mexico 70 A6 ....27.51N 115.04W
Euphrates r. Asia 94 F6 ....30.59N 47.24E
Eureka U.S.A. 64 B5 ....40.48N 124.09W
Europa, Picos de mts Spain 48 C5 ....43.07N 5.01W
Europe 34
Evans, Lac l. Canada 63 K3 ....50.49N 77.07W
Evanston U.S.A. 64 D5 ....41.17N 110.56W
Evansville U.S.A. 65 I4 ....37.59N 87.32W
Evaton S. Africa 86 B2 ....26.32S 27.49E
Everest, Mount China/Nepal 102 F3 ....27.59N 86.55E
Everglades f. U.S.A. 65 J2 ....26.15N 81.02W
Evesham England 10 D3 ....52.06N 1.57W
Evesham, Vale of f. England 10 D3 ....52.05N 1.57W
Évora Portugal 48 B3 ....38.34N 7.54W
Évreux France 44 D6 ....49.01N 1.09E
Evvoia i. Greece 56 F4 ....38.19N 24.14E
Ewaso Ngiro r. North Eastern Kenya 87 B3 ....0.31N 41.04E
Ewaso Ngiro r. Rift Valley Kenya 87 B2 ......2.02S 36.07E
Ewe, Loch b. Scotland 18 D2 ....57.50N 5.40W
Exe r. England 13 D2 ....50.41N 3.29W
Exeter England 13 D2 ....50.43N 3.32W
Exminster England 13 D2 ....50.41N 3.30W
Exmoor hills England 13 D2 ....51.10N 3.46W
Exmouth England 13 D2 ....50.37N 3.25W
Exuma Cays is Bahamas 71 I5 ....24.30N 76.34W
Exuma Sound str. Bahamas 71 I5 ....24.17N 75.59W
Eyasi, Lake Tanzania 86 C4 ....3.38S 35.05E
Eye P'boro. England 11 E3 ....52.37N 0.11W
Eye Suff. England 11 G3 ....52.19N 1.09E
Eyemouth Scotland 17 G3 ....55.52N 2.05W

Eye Peninsula Scotland 18 C3 ....58.14N 6.14W
Eyre, Lake (North) Australia 110 C4 ....28.24S 137.16E
Eyre, Lake (South) Australia 110 C4 ....28.30S 137.25E
Ezine Turkey 56 G4 ....39.46N 26.19E

F

Faafxadhuun Somalia 87 C3 ....2.11N 41.37E
Faenza Italy 50 D6 ....44.17N 11.53E
Făgăraş Romania 56 F7 ....45.51N 24.59E
Fagatogo American Samoa 108 I5 ....14.17S 170.41W
Fagersta Sweden 40 C2 ....59.59N 15.49E
Fairbanks U.S.A. 62 D4 ....64.50N 147.47W
Fair Head Northern Ireland 16 C3 ....55.14N 6.08W
Fair Isle i. Scotland 19 H4 ....59.34N 1.38W
Fairmont U.S.A. 65 H5 ....43.39N 94.28W
Fairweather, Mount Canada/U.S.A. 62 E3 ......58.54N 137.29W
Fais i. Micronesia 105 K5 ....9.45N 140.33E
Faisalabad Pakistan 96 D7 ....31.24N 73.09E
Fakaofo atoll Tokelau 108 I5 ....9.23S 171.08W
Fakenham England 11 F3 ....52.50N 0.51E
Fakfak Indonesia 105 I3 ....2.55S 132.17E
Fal r. England 13 C2 ....50.14N 4.58W
Falcon Lake Mexico/U.S.A. 70 E6 ....26.53N 99.20W
Falkenberg Sweden 40 C2 ....56.55N 12.31E
Falkirk Scotland 17 F4 ....55.59N 3.47W
Falkirk d. Scotland 8 D4 ....55.59N 3.48W
Falkland Islands S. Atlantic Oc. 73 D1 ....50.55S 59.36W
Falköping Sweden 40 C2 ....58.10N 13.33E
Falmouth England 13 B2 ....50.09N 5.04W
Falmouth Bay England 13 B2 ....50.08N 5.04W
Falso, Cabo c. Mexico 70 C5 ....22.53N 109.59W
Falster i. Denmark 40 B1 ....54.49N 11.58E
Falun Sweden 40 C3 ....60.36N 15.38E
Famagusta Cyprus 57 J2 ....35.06N 33.57E
Famatina, Sierra de mts Argentina 76 G2 .....28.03S 68.06W
Fanad Head Rep. of Ireland 16 B3 ....55.17N 7.38W
Fane r. Rep. of Ireland 41 E3 ....53.57N 6.22W
Fannich, Loch l. Scotland 18 D2 ....57.39N 5.03W
Farafra Oasis Egypt 94 C5 ....26.43N 28.09E
Farāh Afgh. 95 J6 ....32.23N 62.07E
Farallon de Pajaros vol. N. Mariana Is 105 K8 ..20.32N 144.55E
Farasān, Jazā'ir is Saudi Arabia 94 F3 ....16.48N 41.41E
Fareham England 10 D1 ....50.51N 1.11W
Farewell, Cape New Zealand 111 G2 ....40.29S 172.40E
Fargo U.S.A. 64 G6 ....46.52N 96.49W
Farnborough England 10 E2 ....51.17N 0.45W
Farndon England 14 E2 ....53.05N 2.53W
Farne Islands England 15 F4 ....55.38N 1.36W
Farnham England 10 E2 ....51.13N 0.48W
Faro Portugal 48 B2 ....37.01N 7.56W
Fårö i. Sweden 40 D2 ....57.58N 19.22E
Faroe Islands Europe 34 D4 ....62.00N 7.00W
Farrāshband Iran 95 H5 ....28.52N 52.05E
Fasā Iran 95 H5 ....28.56N 53.38E
Fastiv Ukraine 55 M4 ....50.04N 29.55E
Fatehgarh India 96 E6 ....27.22N 79.36E
Faulquemont France 42 F2 ....49.03N 6.36E
Faversham England 11 F2 ....51.19N 0.53E
Faxaflói b. Iceland 40 X2 ....64.27N 22.58W
Fayetteville U.S.A. 65 K4 ....35.02N 78.53W
Fdérik Mauritania 84 C4 ....22.42N 12.44W
Feale r. Rep. of Ireland 41 B2 ....52.28N 9.38W
Fear, Cape U.S.A. 65 K3 ....33.51N 77.58W
Fehmarn i. Germany 54 D5 ....54.25N 11.07E
Feira de Santana Brazil 77 M5 ....12.12S 38.57W
Feldkirch Austria 54 C2 ....47.15N 9.36E
Felixstowe England 11 G2 ....51.58N 1.21E
Femunden l. Norway 40 B3 ....62.10N 11.48E
Feniton England 13 D2 ....50.47N 3.16W
Feodosiya Ukraine 53 K6 ....45.02N 35.22E
Ferdows Iran 95 I6 ....33.59N 58.10E
Fergus Falls town U.S.A. 64 G6 ....46.17N 96.07W
Ferkessédougou Côte d'Ivoire 84 D2 ....9.35N 5.13W
Fermanagh d. Northern Ireland 9 A4 ....54.27N 8.04W
Fermanagh f. Northern Ireland 41 D4 ....54.16N 7.35W
Fermoy Rep. of Ireland 41 C2 ....52.08N 8.17W
Ferndown England 10 D1 ....50.48N 1.54W
Ferrara Italy 50 D6 ....44.50N 11.38E
Ferrol Spain 48 A5 ....43.29N 8.13W
Ferryhill England 15 F3 ....54.41N 1.33W
Fès Morocco 84 D5 ....34.04N 4.57W
Fethaland, Point of Scotland 19 H5 ....60.39N 1.18W
Fethard Rep. of Ireland 41 D2 ....52.28N 7.42W
Fethiye Turkey 57 H3 ....36.37N 29.06E
Fetlar i. Scotland 19 I5 ....60.38N 0.49W
Feuilles, Rivière aux r. Canada 63 K3 ....58.46N 70.13W
Feyzābād Afgh. 95 L7 ....37.05N 70.41E
Fez Morocco 84 D5 ....34.04N 4.57W
Ffestiniog Wales 12 D4 ....52.58N 3.56W
Fianarantsoa Madagascar 86 D2 ....21.27S 47.07E
Fife d. Scotland 8 D5 ....56.16N 2.58W
Fife Ness pt Scotland 17 G4 ....56.16N 2.35W
Figeac France 44 D4 ....44.37N 2.01E
Figueira da Foz Portugal 48 A4 ....40.10N 8.51W
Figueres Spain 48 G5 ....42.16N 2.58E
Figuig Morocco 52 C3 ....32.09N 1.17W
Fiji S. Pacific Oc. 111 G5 ....17.51S 177.08E
Filadelfia Paraguay 77 H3 ....22.22S 60.03W
Filey England 15 G3 ....54.13N 0.18W
Filton England 10 C2 ....51.30N 2.35W
Filtu Ethiopia 87 C4 ....5.06N 40.38E
Findhorn r. Scotland 19 F2 ....57.38N 3.38W
Findhorn r. Scotland 19 F2 ....57.38N 3.38W
Finisterre, Cape Spain 48 A5 ....42.53N 9.15W
Finland Europe 40 F3 ....63.53S 26.54E
Finland, Gulf of Europe 40 E2 ....59.31N 22.42E
Finlay r. Canada 62 F3 ....56.41N 124.49W
Finn r. Rep. of Ireland 41 D4 ....54.50N 7.28W
Finspång Sweden 40 C2 ....58.42N 15.46E
Finstown Scotland 19 F4 ....59.00N 3.07W
Fintona Northern Ireland 16 B2 ....54.29N 7.19W
Fionn Loch l. Scotland 18 D2 ....57.46N 5.29W
Fionnphort Scotland 16 C4 ....56.19N 6.22W
Fisher Strait Canada 63 J4 ....63.14N 83.06W
Fishguard Wales 12 C3 ....51.59N 4.58W
Fishguard Bay Wales 12 C4 ....52.01N 4.58W
Fismes France 42 C2 ....49.18N 3.42E
Flagstaff U.S.A. 64 D4 ....35.12N 111.39W
Flamborough England 15 G3 ....54.07N 0.07W
Flamborough Head England 15 G3 ....54.07N 0.03W
Flannan Isles Scotland 18 B3 ....58.18N 7.39W
Flåsjön l. Sweden 40 C4 ....64.06N 15.53E
Flathead Lake U.S.A. 64 D6 ....47.52N 114.03W
Flat Holm i. Wales 13 D3 ....51.23N 3.07W
Fleet England 10 E2 ....51.17N 0.50W
Fleetwood England 14 D2 ....53.55N 3.02W
Flensburg Germany 54 C6 ....54.47N 9.25E
Flevoland d. Neth. 42 E5 ....52.17N 5.07E
Flinders r. Australia 110 D5 ....17.35S 140.35E
Flinders Island Australia 110 D3 ....39.56S 148.04E
Flinders Ranges mts Australia 110 C3 ....32.24S 137.57E
Flin Flon Canada 62 H3 ....54.46N 101.51W

Flint U.S.A. 65 J5 ....43.01N 83.42W
Flint Wales 12 D5 ....53.15N 3.08W
Flintshire d. Wales 9 D3 ....53.11N 3.07W
Florence Italy 50 D5 ....43.46N 11.16E
Florence U.S.A. 65 K3 ....34.11N 79.45W
Florencia Colombia 72 B7 ....1.36N 75.36W
Flores i. Indonesia 105 G2 ....8.29S 121.14E
Flores Sea Indonesia 104 F2 ....7.41S 119.59E
Floresta Brazil 77 M6 ....8.31S 38.32W
Florianópolis Brazil 77 K2 ....27.32S 48.32W
Florida d. U.S.A. 65 J3 ....30.12N 83.39W
Florida, Straits of Bahamas/U.S.A. 71 H5 ....23.59N 81.35W
Florida Keys is. U.S.A. 65 J1 ....24.41N 81.38W
Florina Greece 56 D5 ....40.46N 21.24E
Florø Norway 40 A3 ....61.36N 5.01E
Flotta i. Scotland 19 F3 ....58.50N 3.05W
Fly r. P.N.G. 105 K2 ....8.18S 142.36E
Foča Bos.-Herz. 56 C6 ....43.29N 18.45E
Fochabers Scotland 19 F2 ....57.37N 3.06W
Focşani Romania 56 G7 ....45.42N 27.11E
Foggia Italy 50 F4 ....41.28N 15.33E
Fogo i. Cape Verde 84 B3 ....14.59N 24.18W
Foinaven hill Scotland 18 E3 ....58.25N 4.53W
Foix France 44 D3 ....42.58N 1.36E
Foligno Italy 50 E5 ....42.57N 12.42E
Folkestone England 11 G2 ....51.05N 1.10E
Fonseca, Golfo de b. Central America 70 G3 ....13.03N 88.12W
Fontainebleau France 44 E6 ....48.25N 2.43E
Fontur pt Iceland 40 Z2 ....66.23N 14.32W
Førde Norway 40 A3 ....61.27N 5.52E
Fordingbridge England 10 D1 ....50.56N 1.47W
Foreland hd England 10 D1 ....50.41N 1.04W
Foreland Point England 13 D3 ....51.15N 3.47W
Forfar Scotland 19 G1 ....56.39N 2.53W
Forlì Italy 50 E6 ....44.14N 12.02E
Formby England 14 D2 ....53.34N 3.04W
Formentera i. Spain 48 F3 ....38.40N 1.24E
Formosa Argentina 73 D4 ....26.07S 58.12W
Formosa, Serra hills Brazil 77 I5 ....12.31S 55.28W
Forres Scotland 19 F2 ....57.37N 3.37W
Forssa Finland 40 E3 ....60.49N 23.39E
Fort Albany Canada 63 J3 ....52.13N 81.41W
Fortaleza Brazil 77 M7 ....3.43S 38.32W
Fort Augustus Scotland 18 E2 ....57.09N 4.41W
Fort Chipewyan Canada 62 G3 ....58.42N 111.07W
Fort Collins U.S.A. 64 E5 ....40.35N 105.05W
Fort-de-France Martinique 71 L3 ....14.37N 61.05W
Fortescue r. Australia 110 A4 ....21.02S 116.06E
Fort Frances Canada 63 I2 ....48.37N 93.24W
Fort Good Hope Canada 62 F4 ....66.16N 128.39W
Forth r. Scotland 16 E4 ....56.09N 3.52W
Forth, Firth of est. Scotland 17 F4 ....56.01N 3.13W
Fort Lauderdale U.S.A. 65 J2 ....26.04N 80.11W
Fort Liard Canada 62 F4 ....60.14N 123.24W
Fort McMurray Canada 62 G3 ....56.43N 111.21W
Fort McPherson Canada 62 E4 ....67.33N 134.44W
Fort Nelson Canada 62 F3 ....58.45N 122.39W
Fort Peck Reservoir U.S.A. 64 E6 ....47.47N 106.55W
Fort Pierce U.S.A. 65 J2 ....27.18N 80.24W
Fortrose Scotland 19 E2 ....57.35N 4.08W
Fort St John Canada 62 F3 ....56.15N 120.49W
Fort Severn Canada 63 J3 ....56.00N 87.39W
Fort-Shevchenko Kazakhstan 58 G2 ....44.29N 50.17E
Fort Simpson Canada 62 F4 ....61.52N 121.22W
Fort Smith Canada 62 G4 ....60.00N 112.13W
Fort Smith U.S.A. 65 H4 ....35.26N 94.24W
Fortuneswell England 10 C1 ....50.34N 2.27W
Fort Wayne U.S.A. 65 I5 ....41.04N 85.08W
Fort William Scotland 18 D1 ....56.49N 5.06W
Fort Worth U.S.A. 64 G3 ....32.46N 97.19W
Fort Yukon U.S.A. 62 D4 ....66.35N 145.13W
Foshan China 103 K2 ....23.03N 113.06E
Fossano Italy 50 B6 ....44.33N 7.43E
Fougères France 44 C6 ....48.21N 1.12W
Foula i. Scotland 19 G5 ....60.10N 2.10W
Foulness Point England 11 F2 ....51.37N 0.57E
Fouta Djallon f. Guinea 84 C3 ....11.26N 12.34W
Fowey r. England 13 C2 ....50.26N 4.41W
Foxe Basin g. Canada 63 K4 ....66.53N 78.58W
Foxe Channel Canada 63 J4 ....64.56N 81.03W
Foxe Peninsula Canada 63 K4 ....64.48N 77.03W
Foxford Rep. of Ireland 41 B3 ....53.58N 9.07W
Fox Islands U.S.A. 62 B3 ....52.45N 168.53W
Foyle r. Rep. of Ireland/U.K. 41 D4 ....54.53N 7.26W
Foyle, Lough inlet Rep. of Ireland/U.K. 41 D5 ....55.07N 7.08W
Foz do Iguaçu Brazil 77 J2 ....25.30S 54.32W
Framlingham England 11 G3 ....52.13N 1.21E
Franca Brazil 77 K3 ....20.32S 47.23W
France Europe 44 E5 ....46.57N 2.11E
Franceville Gabon 84 F1 ....1.37S 13.37E
Francistown Botswana 86 B2 ....21.10S 27.29E
Frankfort U.S.A. 65 J4 ....38.12N 84.49W
Frankfurt am Main Germany 54 C4 ....50.07N 8.41E
Frankfurt an der Oder Germany 54 F5 ....52.21N 14.33E
Franklin D. Roosevelt Lake resr U.S.A. 64 C6 ....48.16N 118.09W
Frantsa-Iosifa, Zemlya is Rus. Fed. 58 G5 ....79.40N 58.29E
Frasca, Capo della c. Italy 50 C3 ....39.46N 8.26E
Fraser r. Canada 62 F2 ....49.19N 121.38W
Fraserburgh Scotland 19 G2 ....57.42N 2.01W
Fraser Island Australia 110 E4 ....25.12S 153.11E
Freckleton England 14 E2 ....53.45N 2.52W
Fredericia Denmark 40 B1 ....55.34N 9.45E
Fredericton Canada 63 L2 ....45.57N 66.39W
Frederikshavn Denmark 40 B2 ....57.27N 10.32E
Fredrikstad Norway 40 B2 ....59.13N 10.56E
Freeport City Bahamas 71 I6 ....26.30N 78.45W
Freetown Sierra Leone 84 C2 ....8.28N 13.12W
Freiburg im Breisgau Germany 54 B3 ....48.00N 7.50E
Fréjus France 44 G3 ....43.26N 6.45E
Fremantle Australia 110 A3 ....32.05S 115.42E
French Guiana S. America 109 Q6 ....3.56N 53.03W
French Polynesia is S. Pacific Oc. 109 K4 ....18.43S 147.32W
Freshwater England 10 D1 ....50.41N 1.31W
Fresno U.S.A. 64 C4 ....36.46N 119.46W
Frévent France 11 H1 ....50.16N 2.17E
Freyming-Merlebach France 42 F2 ....49.09N 6.68E
Fria Guinea 84 C3 ....10.24N 13.35W
Friedrichshafen Germany 54 C2 ....47.39N 9.31E
Friesland d. Neth. 42 E6 ....53.08N 5.68E
Frinton-on-Sea England 11 G2 ....51.50N 1.15E
Frisa, Loch l. Scotland 16 C4 ....56.34N 6.06W
Frisian Islands Europe 34 G3 ....54.00N 7.00E
Frizington England 14 D3 ....54.32N 3.30W
Frobisher Bay Canada 63 L4 ....63.18N 67.31W
Frodsham England 14 E2 ....53.18N 2.44W
Frohavet b. Norway 40 B3 ....63.52N 9.12E
Frome England 10 C2 ....51.14N 2.19W
Frome r. England 10 C1 ....50.41N 2.05W
Frome, Lake Australia 110 C3 ....30.43S 139.48E
Frøya i. Norway 40 B3 ....63.41N 8.39E
Fruges France 11 H1 ....50.31N 2.08E
Frýdek-Místek Czech Rep. 54 H3 ....49.41N 18.21E
Fuenlabrada Spain 48 D4 ....40.17N 3.47W

Fuerteventura i. Canary Islands 48 Y2 ....28.36N 14.04W
Fujairah U.A.E. 95 I5 ....25.06N 56.21E
Fujian d. China 103 L3 ....25.52N 117.59E
Fuji-san vol. Japan 106 C3 ....35.22N 138.43E
Fukui Japan 106 C3 ....36.04N 136.13E
Fukuoka Japan 106 B2 ....33.35N 130.24E
Fukushima Japan 106 D3 ....37.45N 140.28E
Fulda Germany 54 C4 ....50.33N 9.41E
Fulford England 15 F2 ....53.56N 1.04W
Fulham England 11 E2 ....51.29N 0.13W
Fumay France 42 D2 ....49.59N 4.42E
Funafuti atoll Tuvalu 111 G6 ....8.25S 179.13E
Funchal Atlantic Oc. 84 C5 ....32.39N 16.54W
Fundy, Bay of Canada 63 L2 ....44.06N 67.03W
Fürth Germany 54 D3 ....49.29N 10.57E
Fushun China 103 M6 ....41.51N 123.50E
Fusong China 106 A4 ....42.20N 127.17E
Fuxin China 103 M6 ....42.02N 121.41E
Fuyu China 103 M7 ....47.44N 124.26E
Fuzhou Fujian China 103 L3 ....26.07N 119.21E
Fuzhou Jiangxi China 103 L3 ....27.58N 116.17E
Fyn i. Denmark 40 B1 ....55.38N 10.17E

G

Gaalkacyo Somalia 85 I2 ....6.46N 47.25E
Gabès Tunisia 52 F3 ....33.53N 10.07E
Gabès, Golfe de g. Tunisia 52 F3 ....34.08N 10.40E
Gabon Africa 84 F1 ....0.56S 11.32E
Gaborone Botswana 86 B2 ....24.38S 25.56E
Gabrovo Bulgaria 56 F6 ....42.53N 25.20E
Gadsden U.S.A. 65 I3 ....34.03N 86.04W
Gaer Wales 12 D3 ....51.53N 3.12W
Gaeta Italy 50 E4 ....41.13N 13.34E
Gaeta, Golfo di g. Italy 50 E4 ....41.06N 13.33E
Gaferut i. Micronesia 108 F6 ....9.15N 145.25E
Gafsa Tunisia 52 E3 ....34.26N 8.51E
Gagarin Rus. Fed. 55 P6 ....55.33N 35.01E
Gagnon Canada 63 L3 ....51.52N 68.07W
Gagra Georgia 57 N6 ....43.18N 40.16E
Gainesville U.S.A. 65 J2 ....29.36N 82.20W
Gainsborough England 15 G2 ....53.24N 0.46W
Gairdner, Lake Australia 110 C3 ....31.17S 135.38E
Gairloch Scotland 18 D2 ....57.44N 5.42W
Gair Loch b. Scotland 18 D2 ....57.43N 5.44W
Galana r. Kenya 87 C2 ....3.10S 40.08E
Galapagos Islands Ecuador 76 C7 ....0.03S 89.05W
Galapagos Rise f. Pacific Oc. 109 N5 ....8.25S 96.06W
Galashiels Scotland 17 G3 ....55.37N 2.49W
Galaţi Romania 57 H7 ....45.27N 28.03E
Gala Water r. Scotland 17 G3 ....55.36N 2.47W
Galdhøpiggen mt. Norway 40 B3 ....61.38N 8.19E
Galilee, Sea of l. Israel 53 K3 ....32.49N 35.37E
Gallabat Sudan 94 E2 ....12.57N 36.06E
Galle Sri Lanka 96 F2 ....6.04N 80.09E
Gallego Basin f. Pacific Oc. 109 M5 ....2.20S 117.59W
Galley Head Rep. of Ireland 41 C1 ....51.32N 8.57W
Gallinas, Punta pt Colombia 71 J3 ....12.27N 71.42W
Gallipoli Italy 50 H4 ....40.03N 18.00E
Gallipoli Turkey 56 G5 ....40.25N 26.39E
Gällivare Sweden 40 E4 ....67.08N 20.40E
Gallup U.S.A. 64 E4 ....35.30N 108.45W
Galole Kenya 87 C2 ....1.34S 40.01E
Galston Scotland 16 E3 ....55.36N 4.23W
Galtat Zemmour Western Sahara 84 C4 ....25.08N 12.24W
Galtee Mountains hills Rep. of Ireland 41 C2 ....52.19N 8.16W
Galveston U.S.A. 65 H2 ....29.15N 94.54W
Galveston Bay U.S.A. 65 H2 ....29.19N 94.46W
Galway Rep. of Ireland 41 B3 ....53.16N 9.03W
Galway d. Rep. of Ireland 41 B3 ....53.22N 9.16W
Galway Bay Rep. of Ireland 41 B3 ....53.12N 9.16W
Gambia Africa r. Gambia 84 C3 ....13.28N 16.35W
Gambier, Îles is French Polynesia 109 L4 ....22.56S 134.51W
Gamud mt. Ethiopia 87 B4 ....4.07N 38.02E
Gäncä Azerbaijan 58 F2 ....40.41N 46.22E
Gandadiwata, Bukit mt. Indonesia 104 F3 ....2.43S 119.25E
Gander Canada 63 M2 ....48.54N 54.17W
Gandhidham India 96 D5 ....23.06N 70.08E
Gandhinagar India 96 D5 ....23.14N 72.44E
Gandía Spain 48 E3 ....38.58N 0.10W
Ganges r. Bangl./India 96 H5 ....23.32N 90.08E
Ganges, Mouths of the Bangl./India 96 G5 ....21.17N 88.23E
Gannett Peak U.S.A. 64 E5 ....43.12N 109.39W
Gansu d. China 102 H6 ....40.01N 97.56E
Gantamaa Somalia 87 C3 ....4.28N 45.04E
Ganzhou China 103 K3 ....25.50N 114.53E
Gao Mali 84 D3 ....16.16N 0.02W
Gap France 44 G4 ....44.34N 6.05E
Gar China 102 E4 ....32.33N 80.05E
Gara, Lough l. Rep. of Ireland 41 C3 ....53.57N 8.28W
Garanhuns Brazil 77 M6 ....8.52S 36.22W
Garba Tula Kenya 87 B3 ....0.30N 38.31E
Garcia Sola, Embalse de resr Spain 48 C3 ....39.14N 5.02W
Gard r. France 44 F3 ....43.51N 4.37E
Garda, Lake Italy 50 D6 ....45.28N 10.33E
Garden City U.S.A. 64 F4 ....37.59N 100.53W
Gardēz Afgh. 95 K6 ....33.38N 69.09E
Garelochhead Scotland 16 E4 ....56.05N 4.50W
Garforth England 15 F2 ....53.48N 1.23W
Gargždai Lithuania 40 E1 ....55.43N 21.24E
Garissa Kenya 87 B2 ....0.25S 39.40E
Garmisch-Partenkirchen Germany 54 D2 ....47.30N 11.06E
Garonne r. France 44 C4 ....45.53N 0.32W
Garoua Cameroon 84 F2 ....9.19N 13.23E
Garron Point Northern Ireland 16 D3 ....55.03N 5.57W
Garry r. Scotland 18 E2 ....57.04N 4.46W
Garry, Loch l. Scotland 19 E1 ....56.48N 4.15W
Garsen Kenya 87 C2 ....2.16S 40.06E
Garstang England 14 E2 ....53.54N 2.46W
Garvagh Northern Ireland 16 C2 ....54.59N 6.41W
Garvie mts Scotland 19 E3 ....58.15N 4.49W
Gary U.S.A. 65 I5 ....41.35N 87.20W
Gascony, Gulf of France 44 B3 ....43.43N 2.00W
Gascoyne r. Australia 110 A4 ....24.44S 114.03E
Gashua Nigeria 84 F3 ....12.51N 11.04E
Gaspé Canada 63 L2 ....48.48N 64.32W
Gaspé, Péninsule de pen. Canada 63 L2 ....48.35N 65.31W
Gastonia U.S.A. 65 J4 ....35.17N 81.13W
Gata, Cabo de c. Spain 48 D2 ....36.43N 2.11W
Gatehouse of Fleet Scotland 16 E2 ....54.53N 4.11W
Gateshead England 15 F3 ....54.57N 1.36W
Gatineau r. Canada 65 K6 ....45.28N 75.42W
Gaya India 96 G5 ....24.48N 85.00E
Gaya Niger 84 E3 ....11.53N 3.28E
Gaza Asia 53 J3 ....31.22N 34.19E
Gaza town Gaza 94 D6 ....31.30N 34.28E
Gaziantep Turkey 57 L3 ....37.03N 37.21E
Gdańsk Poland 46 D5 ....54.22N 18.38E
Gdańsk, Gulf of Poland/Rus. Fed. 46 D5 ....54.32N 19.12E
Gdynia Poland 46 D5 ....54.31N 18.33E

Geal Charn hill Scotland 19 F2 ....57.12N 3.30W
Gedaref Sudan 85 H3 ....14.02N 35.23E
Gediz r. Turkey 57 G4 ....38.35N 26.48E
Gedo d. Somalia 87 C3 ....2.52N 41.47E
Geel Belgium 42 E4 ....51.09N 5.00E
Geelong Australia 110 D3 ....38.08S 144.21E
Gejiu China 103 I2 ....23.22N 103.09E
Gela Italy 50 F2 ....37.04N 14.15E
Gelderland d. Neth. 42 F5 ....52.04N 6.08E
Gelibolu see Gallipoli
Gelligaer Wales 12 D3 ....51.40N 3.15W
Gelsenkirchen Germany 54 B4 ....51.33N 7.06E
Gemlik Turkey 57 H5 ....40.25N 29.09E
Genalē Wenz r. Ethiopia 87 C4 ....4.10N 42.05E
General Santos Phil. 105 H5 ....6.08N 125.15E
Geneva Switz. 50 B7 ....46.13N 6.09E
Geneva, Lake France/Switz. 44 G5 ....46.22N 6.16E
Genil r. Spain 48 C2 ....37.42N 5.18W
Genk Belgium 42 E3 ....50.57N 5.31E
Genoa Italy 50 C6 ....44.25N 8.56E
Genoa, Gulf of Italy 50 C6 ....44.08N 8.57E
George r. Canada 63 L3 ....58.19N 65.55W
Georgetown Guyana 72 D7 ....6.49N 58.09W
George Town Malaysia 104 C5 ....5.26N 100.17E
Georgia Asia 58 F2 ....41.49N 43.59E
Georgia d. U.S.A. 65 J3 ....32.35N 83.28W
Georgian Bay Canada 63 J2 ....45.17N 80.51W
Georgina watercourse Australia 110 C4 ....24.54S 139.35E
Georgiyevka Kazakhstan 102 E7 ....49.16N 81.34E
Gera Germany 54 E4 ....50.53N 12.06E
Geral de Goiás, Serra hills Brazil 77 K5 ....11.38S 46.01W
Geraldton Australia 110 A4 ....28.46S 114.37E
Gerede Turkey 57 J5 ....40.48N 32.12E
Gereshk Afgh. 95 J6 ....31.51N 64.37E
Gerlachovský štít mt. Slovakia 54 I3 ....49.10N 20.07E
Germany Europe 54 D4 ....51.18N 10.22E
Gevgelija Macedonia 56 E5 ....41.09N 22.30E
Geyik Dağı mt. Turkey 57 J3 ....36.52N 32.11E
Geyve Turkey 57 I5 ....40.30N 30.15E
Gezira f. Sudan 82 G6 ....14.30N 33.00E
Ghadāmis Libya 84 E5 ....30.05N 9.34E
Ghaem Shahr Iran 95 H7 ....36.32N 52.39E
Ghaghara r. India 96 F6 ....25.42N 84.51E
Ghana Africa 84 D2 ....8.23N 0.47W
Ghardaïa Algeria 84 E5 ....32.20N 3.49E
Gharyān Libya 84 F4 ....32.11N 13.01E
Ghāt Libya 84 F4 ....25.10N 10.13E
Ghazaouet Algeria 52 C4 ....35.06N 1.51W
Ghaziabad India 96 E6 ....28.40N 77.25E
Ghazni Afgh. 95 K6 ....33.33N 68.27E
Ghent Belgium 42 C4 ....51.03N 3.43E
Gherla Romania 46 F1 ....47.03N 23.55E
Giant's Causeway f. Northern Ireland 16 C3 ....55.14N 6.31W
Gibraltar Gibraltar 48 C2 ....36.08N 5.21W
Gibraltar, Strait of Morocco/Spain 48 B1 ....35.50N 6.05W
Gibson Desert Australia 110 B4 ....24.46S 123.25E
Gīdolē Ethiopia 87 B4 ....5.38N 37.25E
Gien France 44 E5 ....47.41N 2.38E
Gießen Germany 54 C4 ....50.35N 8.41E
Gifu Japan 106 C3 ....35.25N 136.46E
Gigha i. Scotland 16 D3 ....55.41N 5.46W
Gijón-Xixón Spain 48 C5 ....43.32N 5.39W
Gila r. U.S.A. 64 D3 ....32.45N 114.31W
Gilbert Islands Kiribati 108 H6 ....1.31N 170.43E
Gilbert Ridge f. Pacific Oc. 108 H5 ....0.07S 172.43E
Gilgil Kenya 87 B2 ....0.29S 36.21E
Gilgit Jammu and Kashmir 96 D8 ....35.54N 74.21E
Gill, Lough l. Rep. of Ireland 41 C4 ....54.15N 8.25W
Gillette U.S.A. 64 E5 ....44.18N 105.29W
Gillingham Dor. England 10 C2 ....51.02N 2.17W
Gillingham Medway England 11 F2 ....51.23N 0.33E
Gilwern Wales 12 D3 ....51.49N 3.06W
Gimbala, Jebel mt. Sudan 94 B2 ....13.00N 24.20E
Giresun Turkey 57 M5 ....40.55N 38.23E
Girona Spain 48 G4 ....41.58N 2.49E
Gironde est. France 44 C4 ....45.31N 0.59W
Girvan Scotland 16 E3 ....55.15N 4.51W
Gisborne New Zealand 111 H3 ....38.39S 178.01E
Giurgiu Romania 56 F6 ....43.54N 25.57E
Giza Egypt 85 H4 ....29.59N 31.12E
Gizhiga Rus. Fed. 59 R4 ....62.01N 160.28E
Gjirokastër Albania 56 D5 ....40.04N 20.09E
Gjøvik Norway 40 B3 ....60.48N 10.41E
Gladstone Australia 110 E4 ....23.51S 151.18E
Glan r. Germany 42 G2 ....49.47N 7.42E
Glanton England 15 F4 ....55.25N 1.53W
Glasgow Scotland 16 E3 ....55.52N 4.15W
Glasgow d. Scotland 8 C4 ....55.52N 4.15W
Glass, Loch l. Scotland 19 E2 ....57.44N 4.31W
Glastonbury England 10 C2 ....51.09N 2.43W
Glenarm Northern Ireland 16 D2 ....54.58N 5.56W
Glendale U.S.A. 64 D3 ....33.32N 112.12W
Glengad Head Rep. of Ireland 41 D5 ....55.20N 7.10W
Glen Garry r. Scotland 18 D2 ....57.03N 5.05W
Glenluce Scotland 16 E2 ....54.53N 4.49W
Glen More f. Scotland 19 E2 ....57.09N 4.44W
Glen Moriston f. Scotland 18 E2 ....57.09N 4.52W
Glennallen U.S.A. 62 D4 ....62.09N 145.32W
Glenrothes Scotland 17 F4 ....56.12N 3.10W
Glen Shee f. Scotland 19 F1 ....56.48N 3.29W
Glinton England 15 F4 ....52.38N 0.18W
Gliwice Poland 46 D3 ....50.18N 18.40E
Głogów Poland 46 C4 ....51.40N 16.05E
Glomfjord Norway 40 C4 ....66.49N 13.57E
Glossop England 15 F2 ....53.27N 1.57W
Gloucester England 10 C2 ....51.52N 2.14W
Gloucestershire d. England 9 D2 ....51.49N 2.11W
Glusburn England 15 F2 ....53.54N 1.59W
Glyder Fawr mt. Wales 12 C5 ....53.06N 4.02W
Glynneath Wales 12 D3 ....51.45N 3.37W
Gmünd Austria 54 F3 ....48.47N 14.59E
Gniezno Poland 46 C4 ....52.32N 17.36E
Goa d. India 96 D4 ....15.24N 74.11E
Goat Fell hill Scotland 16 D3 ....55.37N 5.11W
Gobabis Namibia 86 A2 ....22.27S 18.58E
Gobi des. China/Mongolia 103 J6 ....44.59N 107.19E
Gobowen England 10 B3 ....52.54N 3.02W
Goch Germany 42 F4 ....51.40N 6.09E
Godalming England 11 E2 ....51.11N 0.37W
Godavari r. India 96 F4 ....16.57N 81.49E
Godmanchester England 11 E3 ....52.19N 0.10W
Goes Neth. 42 C4 ....51.30N 3.54E
Goiânia Brazil 77 K4 ....16.43S 49.16W
Goiás Brazil 77 J4 ....15.54S 50.04W
Goiás d. Brazil 77 J4 ....15.15S 49.38W
Gökçeada i. Turkey 56 F5 ....40.12N 25.48E
Gökova Turkey 57 L4 ....38.02N 36.38E
Gölcük Turkey 57 H5 ....40.43N 29.49E
Goldap Poland 46 E5 ....54.19N 22.19E
Gold Coast town Australia 110 E4 ....28.03S 153.26E
Golmud China 102 G5 ....36.21N 94.50E

Golpāyegān Iran 95 H6 ....33.23N 50.13E
Golspie Scotland 19 F2 ....57.58N 3.59W
Gómez Palacio Mexico 70 D6 ....25.35N 103.32W
Gonaïves Haiti 71 J4 ....19.27N 72.42W
Gonbad-e Kavus Iran 95 I7 ....37.14N 55.07E
Gonder Ethiopia 85 H3 ....12.39N 37.28E
Gondia India 96 F5 ....21.28N 80.12E
Gongga Shan mt. China 103 I3 ....29.57N 101.55E
Good Hope, Cape of S. Africa 86 A1 ....34.22S 18.29E
Goodwick Wales 12 C4 ....52.00N 4.59W
Goole England 15 G2 ....53.42N 0.53W
Göppingen Germany 54 C3 ....48.43N 9.39E
Gora mt. Rus. Fed. 58 H4 ....64.59N 60.03E
Góra Kalwaria Poland 46 E3 ....51.59N 21.13E
Gorakhpur India 96 F6 ....26.45N 83.25E
Gorebridge Scotland 17 F3 ....55.50N 3.03W
Gorey Rep. of Ireland 41 E2 ....52.40N 6.18W
Gorgān Iran 95 H7 ....36.50N 54.24E
Goris Armenia 95 G7 ....39.30N 46.20E
Gorizia Italy 50 E6 ....45.57N 13.36E
Gorlice Poland 46 E2 ....49.40N 21.10E
Görlitz Germany 54 F4 ....51.09N 14.59E
Gornji Vakuf Bos.-Herz. 56 B6 ....43.55N 17.36E
Gorno-Altaysk Rus. Fed. 102 F8 ....51.59N 85.55E
Gornyak Rus. Fed. 102 E8 ....50.59N 81.28E
Gorontalo Indonesia 105 G4 ....0.34N 123.01E
Gort Rep. of Ireland 41 C3 ....53.04N 8.49W
Gory mts Rus. Fed. 59 K4 ....69.06N 95.00E
Gorzów Wielkopolski Poland 46 B4 ....52.44N 15.14E
Gosberton England 11 E3 ....52.52N 0.10W
Gosford England 8 E4 ....33.25S 151.28E
Gosforth Cumb. England 14 D3 ....54.25N 3.27W
Gosforth T. and W. England 15 F4 ....55.00N 1.37W
Goshogawara Japan 106 D4 ....40.48N 140.26E
Gospić Croatia 56 A7 ....44.33N 15.23E
Gosport England 10 D1 ....50.48N 1.08W
Gostivar Macedonia 56 D5 ....41.47N 20.54E
Gotha Germany 54 D4 ....50.57N 10.42E
Gothenburg Sweden 40 B2 ....57.43N 11.58E
Gotland i. Sweden 40 D2 ....57.36N 18.52E
Göttingen Germany 54 C4 ....51.32N 9.56E
Gouda Neth. 42 D5 ....52.00N 4.42E
Gouin, Réservoir resr Canada 63 K2 ....48.39N 74.39W
Goulburn Australia 110 D3 ....34.47S 149.45E
Gourdon France 44 D4 ....44.45N 1.23E
Governador Valadares Brazil 77 L4 ....18.49S 41.57W
Gower pen. Wales 12 C3 ....51.36N 4.15W
Gowna, Lough l. Rep. of Ireland 41 D3 ....53.53N 7.35W
Goya Argentina 77 I2 ....29.08S 59.15W
Göynük Turkey 57 I5 ....40.24N 30.46E
Gozo i. Malta 50 F2 ....36.05N 14.15E
Gradaús, Serra dos hills Brazil 77 J6 ....8.30S 50.40W
Grafham Water resr England 11 E3 ....52.18N 0.19W
Grafton Australia 110 E4 ....29.41S 152.57E
Grafton U.S.A. 64 G6 ....48.24N 97.26W
Grahamstown S. Africa 86 B1 ....33.19S 26.32E
Grain England 11 F2 ....51.27N 0.43E
Grampian Mountains Scotland 19 E1 ....56.47N 4.37W
Granada Spain 48 D2 ....37.11N 3.36W
Gran Canaria i. Canary Islands 48 Y1 ....27.47N 15.23W
Gran Chaco f. Argentina/Paraguay 73 C4 ....27.08S 62.24W
Grand Bahama i. Bahamas 71 I6 ....26.34N 78.29W
Grand Canyon f. U.S.A. 64 D4 ....36.03N 112.09W
Grand Canyon town U.S.A. 64 D4 ....36.03N 112.09W
Grand Cayman i. Cayman Is 71 H4 ....19.23N 81.06W
Grande r. Brazil 77 L5 ....11.08S 43.10W
Grande, Bahía b. Argentina 73 C1 ....50.40S 68.18W
Grande Prairie Canada 62 G3 ....55.11N 118.47W
Grandes, Salinas f. Argentina 73 C3 ....30.24S 65.31W
Grand Falls - Windsor Canada 63 M2 ....48.53N 55.25W
Grand Forks U.S.A. 64 G6 ....47.55N 97.06W
Grand Island U.S.A. 64 G5 ....40.56N 98.23W
Grand Junction U.S.A. 64 E4 ....39.04N 108.33W
Grândola Portugal 48 A3 ....38.11N 8.34W
Grand Rapids town U.S.A. 65 I5 ....42.57N 85.40W
Grand Turk Turks and Caicos Is 71 J5 ....21.28N 71.08W
Grangemouth Scotland 17 F4 ....56.01N 3.43W
Grange-over-Sands England 14 E3 ....54.11N 2.55W
Gran Paradiso mt. Italy 50 B6 ....45.31N 7.16E
Gran Tarajal Canary Islands 48 Y2 ....28.12N 14.01W
Grantham England 11 E3 ....52.55N 0.39W
Grantown-on-Spey Scotland 19 F2 ....57.20N 3.36W
Grants Pass U.S.A. 64 B5 ....42.29N 123.19W
Grasse France 44 G3 ....43.39N 6.55E
Grassington England 15 F3 ....54.04N 1.59W
Grave, Pointe de pt France 44 C4 ....45.35N 1.04W
Gravelines France 11 H1 ....50.59N 2.08E
Gravesend England 11 F2 ....51.26N 0.22E
Grays England 11 F2 ....51.28N 0.20E
Graz Austria 54 F2 ....47.04N 15.27E
Great Abaco i. Bahamas 71 I6 ....26.08N 77.12W
Great Australian Bight g. Australia 110 B3 ....33.06S 129.50E
Great Baddow England 11 F2 ....51.43N 0.30E
Great Barrier Reef Australia 110 D5 ....11.25S 144.09E
Great Basin f. U.S.A. 64 C4 ....39.25N 116.09W
Great Bear Lake Canada 62 G4 ....66.03N 119.59W
Great Belt str. Denmark 54 D6 ....55.30N 10.52E
Great Bend U.S.A. 64 G4 ....38.23N 98.47W
Great Bernera i. Scotland 18 C3 ....58.14N 6.52W
Great Blasket Island Rep. of Ireland 41 A2 ....52.06N 10.32W
Great Clifton England 14 D3 ....54.39N 3.29W
Great Cumbrae i. Scotland 16 E3 ....55.47N 4.58W
Great Dividing Range mts Australia 110 D3 ....37.30S 144.27E
Great Driffield England 15 G3 ....54.00N 0.27W
Great Dunmow England 11 F2 ....51.52N 0.22E
Greater Antilles is Caribbean Sea 71 H5 ....21.05N 81.40W
Greater London d. England 9 E2 ....51.30N 0.11W
Greater Manchester d. England 9 D3 ....53.31N 2.22W
Great Exuma i. Bahamas 71 I5 ....23.35N 75.54W
Great Falls town U.S.A. 64 D6 ....47.30N 111.17W
Great Gonerby England 10 E3 ....52.56N 0.40W
Greatham England 15 F3 ....54.38N 1.14W
Great Harwood England 15 E2 ....53.47N 2.24W
Great Inagua i. Bahamas 71 J5 ....21.13N 73.26W
Great Karoo f. S. Africa 86 B1 ....32.29S 23.21E
Great Linford England 10 E3 ....52.04N 0.46W
Great Malvern England 10 C3 ....52.07N 2.19W
Great Namaqualand f. Namibia 86 A2 ....26.29S 16.25E
Great Nicobar i. India 97 H2 ....7.06N 94.08E
Great Ormes Head Wales 12 C5 ....53.21N 3.52W
Great Ouse r. England 11 F3 ....52.46N 0.23E
Great Plains f. N. America 60 I7 ....45.00N 100.00W
Great Rhos hill Wales 12 D4 ....52.16N 3.12W
Great Rift Valley f. Africa 82 G4 ....7.00S 33.00E
Great St Bernard Pass Italy/Switz. 50 B6 ....45.53N 7.11E
Great Salt Lake U.S.A. 64 D5 ....40.58N 112.26W
Great Sand Sea des. Egypt/Libya 53 H2 ....28.55S 24.22E
Great Sandy Desert Australia 110 B4 ....20.35S 125.36E
Great Shelford England 11 F3 ....52.09N 0.08E
Great Slave Lake Canada 62 G4 ....61.26N 114.35W
Great Stour r. England 11 G2 ....51.19N 1.14E
Great Torrington England 13 C2 ....50.57N 4.08W
Great Victoria Desert Australia 110 B4 ....28.43S 128.38E
Great Whernside hill England 15 F3 ....54.10N 1.59W

Great Yarmouth England 11 G3 ....52.36N 1.44E
Greco, Monte mt. Italy 50 E4 ....41.48N 13.59E
Gredos, Sierra de mts Spain 48 C4 ....40.08N 5.43W
Greece Europe 56 D4 ....39.03N 21.56E
Greeley U.S.A. 64 F5 ....40.25N 104.41W
Green r. U.S.A. 64 E4 ....38.12N 109.53W
Green Bay town U.S.A. 65 I5 ....44.30N 88.02W
Greenland i. N. America 63 N5 ....72.21N 41.01W
Greenlaw Scotland 17 G3 ....55.42N 2.28W
Greenock Scotland 16 E3 ....55.57N 4.46W
Greenore Point Rep. of Ireland 12 A4 ....52.14N 6.18W
Green River town U.S.A. 64 E5 ....41.36N 109.29W
Greensboro U.S.A. 65 K4 ....36.04N 79.48W
Greenstone Point Scotland 18 D2 ....57.56N 5.40W
Greenville Liberia 84 D2 ....5.01N 9.02W
Greenville Miss. U.S.A. 65 H3 ....33.22N 91.01W
Greenville S. C. U.S.A. 65 J3 ....34.50N 82.27W
Greenwich England 11 E2 ....51.29N 0.00W
Greifswald Germany 54 E6 ....54.05N 13.24E
Grená Denmark 40 B2 ....56.24N 10.54E
Grenada Central America 71 L3 ....12.03N 61.38W
Grenada France 44 E3 ....43.46N 1.18E
Grenoble France 44 F4 ....45.11N 5.44E
Gretna Scotland 17 F2 ....54.59N 3.04W
Greven Germany 42 G5 ....52.06N 7.38E
Grevena Greece 56 D5 ....40.05N 21.25E
Grevenmacher d. Lux. 42 F2 ....49.42N 6.21E
Grey Range hills Australia 110 D4 ....28.13S 142.35E
Grimsby England 15 G2 ....53.34N 0.04W
Grimsey i. Iceland 40 Y2 ....66.32N 17.59W
Gris Nez, Cap c. France 11 G1 ....50.52N 1.36E
Gritley Scotland 19 G3 ....58.56N 2.45W
Grodzisk Wielkopolski Poland 46 C4 ....52.13N 16.22E
Groningen Neth. 42 F6 ....53.13N 6.34E
Groningen d. Neth. 42 F6 ....53.16N 6.40E
Groote Eylandt i. Australia 110 C5 ....13.58S 137.09E
Grosser Speikkogel mt. Austria 54 F2 ....46.48N 14.58E
Grosseto Italy 50 D5 ....42.45N 11.07E
Großglockner mt. Austria 54 E2 ....47.05N 12.41E
Groundhog r. Canada 63 J2 ....49.40N 81.56W
Grozny Rus. Fed. 58 F2 ....43.19N 45.42E
Grudziądz Poland 46 D4 ....53.30N 18.46E
Gruinard Bay Scotland 18 D2 ....57.53N 5.32W
Gryfice Poland 46 B4 ....53.54N 15.12E
Gryfino Poland 46 B4 ....53.15N 14.29E
Gryfów Śląski Poland 46 B3 ....51.01N 15.25E
Guacanayabo, Golfo de b. Cuba 71 I5 ....20.31N 77.38W
Guadajoz r. Spain 48 C2 ....37.51N 4.51W
Guadalajara Mexico 70 D5 ....20.40N 103.24W
Guadalajara Spain 48 D4 ....40.38N 3.09W
Guadalcanal i. Solomon Is 111 F6 ....9.38S 160.05E
Guadalete r. Spain 48 B2 ....36.32N 6.14W
Guadalope r. Spain 48 E4 ....41.15N 0.02W
Guadalquivir r. Spain 48 B2 ....36.48N 6.21W
Guadalupe i. Mexico 64 C2 ....29.09N 118.23W
Guadalupe, Sierra de mts Spain 48 C3 ....39.20N 5.49W
Guadarrama, Sierra de mts Spain 48 C4 ....40.40N 4.10W
Guadeloupe i. Central America 71 L4 ....16.30N 61.29W
Guadiana r. Portugal/Spain 48 B2 ....37.11N 7.24W
Guadix Spain 48 D2 ....37.18N 3.07W
Guajira, Península de la pen. Colombia 72 B8 ....11.59N 71.45W
Guam i. N. Pacific Oc. 105 K6 ....13.29N 144.58E
Guanajuato Mexico 70 D5 ....21.01N 101.15W
Guanajuato d. Mexico 70 D5 ....21.16N 100.47W
Guanare Venezuela 71 K2 ....9.03N 69.44W
Guane Cuba 71 H5 ....22.13N 84.05W
Guangdong d. China 103 K6 ....13.29N 114.45E
Guangxi Zhuangzu Zizhiqu d. China 103 J2 ....23.52N 108.27E
Guangyuan China 103 J4 ....32.24N 105.51E
Guangzhou China 103 K3 ....23.09N 113.21E
Guanipa r. Venezuela 71 L2 ....9.53N 62.26W
Guantánamo Cuba 71 I5 ....20.07N 75.13W
Guaporé r. Bolivia/Brazil 76 G5 ....11.57S 65.04W
Guara, Sierra de mts Spain 48 E5 ....42.15N 0.20W
Guarapuava Brazil 77 J2 ....25.24S 51.29W
Guarda Portugal 48 B4 ....40.33N 7.16W
Guasave Mexico 70 C6 ....25.33N 108.30W
Guatemala Central America 70 F4 ....15.43N 90.16W
Guatemala City Guatemala 70 F4 ....14.37N 90.31W
Guaviare r. Colombia 72 C7 ....4.02N 67.45W
Guayaquil Ecuador 76 E7 ....2.10S 79.56W
Guayaquil, Golfo de g. Ecuador 76 D7 ....3.10S 80.53W
Guaymas Mexico 70 B6 ....27.57N 110.53W
Guba Ethiopia 85 H3 ....11.16N 35.17E
Gudbrandsdalen r. Norway 40 B3 ....61.58N 9.20E
Gudong r. China 106 A4 ....42.31N 128.03E
Guéckédou Guinea 84 C2 ....8.33N 10.11W
Guelma Algeria 52 E4 ....36.27N 7.29E
Guelmine Morocco 84 C4 ....28.59N 10.02W
Guéret France 44 D5 ....46.10N 1.53E
Guernsey i. Channel Is 13 Y9 ....49.29N 2.36W
Guerrero d. Mexico 70 D4 ....17.41N 100.48W
Gughe mt. Ethiopia 87 B4 ....6.08N 37.20E
Guiana Highlands mts Guyana/Venezuela 72 C7 ....6.18N 63.41W
Guildford England 11 E2 ....51.14N 0.34W
Guilin China 103 K3 ....25.17N 110.18E
Guinea Africa 84 C3 ....10.50N 11.28W
Guinea, Gulf of Africa 84 E2 ....2.31N 4.26E
Guinea-Bissau Africa 84 C3 ....11.54N 14.45W
Guînes France 42 A3 ....50.52N 1.52E
Güiria Venezuela 71 L3 ....10.33N 62.19W
Guisborough England 15 F3 ....54.32N 1.03W
Guise France 42 C2 ....49.54N 3.38E
Guiyang China 103 J3 ....26.33N 106.39E
Guizhou d. China 103 J3 ....26.59N 106.45E
Gujarat d. India 96 D5 ....22.51N 72.32E
Gujranwala Pakistan 96 D7 ....32.07N 74.13E
Gulbarga India 96 E4 ....17.20N 76.47E
Gullane Scotland 17 G4 ....56.02N 2.50W
Gulu Uganda 85 H2 ....2.44N 32.21E
Gumdag Turkmenistan 95 H7 ....39.11N 54.29E
Gümüşhane Turkey 57 M5 ....40.29N 39.28E
Guna India 96 E5 ....24.39N 77.19E
Guntur India 96 F4 ....16.19N 80.26E
Gurgueia r. Brazil 77 L6 ....6.51S 43.23W
Gurupi r. Brazil 77 K7 ....1.19S 46.11W
Gusau Nigeria 84 E3 ....12.15N 6.37E
Güstrow Rus. Fed. 46 F5 ....54.36N 22.12E
Güstrow Germany 54 E5 ....53.48N 12.11E
Guwahati India 97 H6 ....26.09N 91.46E
Guyana S. America 72 D7 ....5.09N 59.59W
Gwadar Pakistan 96 B6 ....25.09N 62.23E
Gwalior India 96 E6 ....26.13N 78.10E
Gwardafuy, Gees c. Somalia 85 J3 ....11.49N 51.16E
Gweebarra Bay Rep. of Ireland 41 C4 ....54.53N 8.30W
Gweru Zimbabwe 86 B3 ....19.27S 29.48E
Gwynedd d. Wales 9 C3 ....53.00N 4.02W
Gydan Peninsula Rus. Fed. 58 I5 ....70.08N 77.30E
Gyöngyös Hungary 54 H2 ....47.46N 19.56E
Györ Hungary 54 G2 ....47.41N 17.39E

Gypsumville Canada 62 I3 ....51.47N 98.37W
Gyula Hungary 46 E1 ....46.39N 21.16E
Gyumri Armenia 94 F8 ....40.47N 43.51E
Gyzylarbat Turkmenistan 58 G1 ....38.59N 56.17E

H

Haapajärvi Finland 40 F3 ....63.45N 25.20E
Haapsalu Estonia 40 E2 ....58.56N 23.31E
Haarlem Neth. 42 D5 ....52.22N 4.38E
Habaswein Kenya 87 B3 ....1.01N 39.30E
Habbān Yemen 95 G2 ....14.20N 47.05E
Hachijo-jima i. Japan 106 C2 ....33.07N 139.50E
Hachinohe Japan 106 D4 ....40.32N 141.31E
Hadd, Ra's al pt Oman 95 I4 ....22.30N 59.50E
Haddington Scotland 17 G3 ....55.58N 2.46W
Haderslev Denmark 40 B1 ....55.15N 9.29E
Had Kourt Morocco 48 C1 ....34.31N 5.48W
Hadleigh England 11 F3 ....52.03N 0.57E
Hadramawt f. Yemen 95 G3 ....15.07N 47.48E
Hadyach Ukraine 55 O4 ....50.22N 33.59E
Haeju N. Korea 103 N5 ....38.02N 125.45E
Hagadera Kenya 87 C3 ....0.02N 40.22E
Hagar Nish Plateau f. Eritrea 94 E3 ....17.03N 37.58E
Hagåtña Guam 108 F6 ....13.29N 144.45E
Hagen Germany 54 B4 ....51.22N 7.28E
Hag's Head Rep. of Ireland 41 B2 ....52.56N 9.29W
Hague, Cap de la c. France 13 Z9 ....49.44N 1.55W
Hai Tanzania 87 B2 ....3.25S 37.06E
Haifa Israel 53 J3 ....32.50N 34.58E
Haikou China 103 K2 ....20.01N 110.18E
Ḩā'il Saudi Arabia 94 F5 ....27.33N 41.41E
Hailsham England 11 F1 ....50.52N 0.15E
Hainan d. China 103 J1 ....19.09N 109.33E
Hainan i. China 103 D7 ....18.51N 110.29E
Hainaut d. Belgium 42 D3 ....50.29N 4.00E
Haines U.S.A. 62 E3 ....59.13N 135.25W
Hai Phong Vietnam 104 D8 ....20.48N 106.43E
Haiti Central America 71 J4 ....19.19N 73.30W
Haiya Sudan 85 H3 ....18.20N 36.23E
Hakodate Japan 106 D4 ....41.47N 140.44E
Halabja Iraq 95 G7 ....35.11N 45.56E
Ḩalāniyāt, Juzur al is Oman 95 I3 ....17.30N 56.11E
Halden Norway 40 B2 ....59.07N 11.25E
Halesowen England 10 C3 ....52.27N 2.03W
Halesworth England 11 G3 ....52.21N 1.30E
Halifax Canada 63 L2 ....44.39N 63.36W
Halifax England 15 F2 ....53.44N 1.51W
Halkirk Scotland 19 F3 ....58.31N 3.29W
Halladale r. Scotland 19 F3 ....58.33N 3.54W
Hall Beach town Canada 63 J4 ....68.42N 81.17W
Halle Belgium 42 D3 ....50.44N 4.14E
Halle Germany 54 D4 ....51.29N 11.59E
Hall Islands Micronesia 108 G6 ....8.55N 151.52E
Halls Creek town Australia 110 B5 ....18.17S 127.40E
Halmahera i. Indonesia 105 H4 ....1.06N 128.32E
Halmstad Sweden 40 C2 ....56.40N 12.52E
Halstead England 11 F2 ....51.57N 0.39E
Halton d. England 9 D3 ....53.20N 2.43W
Haltwhistle England 15 E3 ....54.58N 2.27W
Ham France 42 C2 ....49.45N 3.04E
Hamadan Iran 95 G6 ....34.46N 48.30E
Hamāh Syria 94 E7 ....35.08N 36.45E
Hamamatsu Japan 106 C2 ....34.42N 137.44E
Hamar Norway 40 B3 ....60.48N 11.05E
Hambleton Hills England 15 F3 ....54.19N 1.14W
Hamburg Germany 54 C5 ....53.34N 9.59E
Hämeenlinna Finland 40 F3 ....60.59N 24.27E
Hamersley Range mts Australia 110 A4 ....22.11S 116.31E
Hamhŭng N. Korea 103 N5 ....39.55N 127.33E
Hami China 102 G6 ....42.48N 93.27E
Hamilton Bermuda 71 L7 ....32.18N 64.46W
Hamilton Canada 63 K2 ....43.15N 79.51W
Hamilton New Zealand 111 G3 ....37.48S 175.16E
Hamilton Scotland 17 E3 ....55.47N 4.03W
Ḩamīm, Wādī al watercourse Libya 53 H3 ....30.04N 21.35E
Hamina Finland 40 F3 ....60.34N 27.12E
Hampshire d. England 9 E2 ....51.10N 1.13W
Hampshire Downs hills England 10 D2 ....51.20N 1.35W
Ḩamrā', Al Ḩamādah al f. Libya 52 F2 ....29.40N 11.48E
Hamstreet England 11 F2 ....51.04N 0.52E
Hanamaki Japan 106 D3 ....39.23N 141.07E
Hanang mt. Tanzania 87 A1 ....4.26S 35.23E
Hancock U.S.A. 65 I6 ....47.08N 88.36W
Handa Island Scotland 18 D3 ....58.23N 5.13W
Handan China 103 K5 ....36.35N 114.32E
Handeni Tanzania 87 B1 ....5.25S 38.02E
Hangzhou China 103 M4 ....30.15N 120.10E
Hanna Canada 64 D7 ....51.38N 111.56W
Hannover Germany 54 C5 ....52.23N 9.44E
Hanöbukten b. Sweden 54 F6 ....55.48N 14.37E
Ha Noi Vietnam 104 D8 ....21.01N 105.51E
Hantsavichy Belarus 55 L5 ....52.46N 26.27E
Hanzhong China 103 J4 ....33.04N 107.03E
Haparanda Sweden 40 F4 ....65.50N 24.08E
Happy Valley-Goose Bay town Canada 63 L3 ....53.19N 60.07W
Harare Zimbabwe 86 C3 ....17.49S 31.04E
Ḩarāsīs, Jiddat al des. Oman 95 I3 ....18.59N 55.33E
Harbin China 103 N7 ....45.40N 126.37E
Harderwijk Neth. 42 E5 ....52.21N 5.38E
Haren Germany 42 G5 ....52.48N 7.15E
Hargele Ethiopia 87 C4 ....5.11N 42.10E
Hargeysa Somalia 85 I2 ....9.32N 44.05E
Har Hu l. China 102 H5 ....38.18N 97.23E
Hari Rūd r. Afgh./Iran 95 J7 ....36.50N 60.58E
Harleston England 11 G3 ....52.24N 1.18E
Harlingen Neth. 42 E6 ....53.10N 5.25E
Harlow England 11 F2 ....51.46N 0.05E
Harney Basin U.S.A. 64 C5 ....43.23N 119.56W
Härnösand Sweden 40 D3 ....62.38N 17.56E
Har Nuur l. Mongolia 102 G7 ....48.02N 93.23E
Harpenden England 11 E2 ....51.49N 0.21W
Harray, Loch of l. Scotland 19 F4 ....59.01N 3.13W
Harricanaw r. Canada 63 K3 ....50.58N 79.33W
Harris, Sound of str. Scotland 18 B2 ....57.46N 7.10W
Harrisburg U.S.A. 65 K5 ....40.17N 76.54W
Harrison, Cape Canada 63 M3 ....54.56N 57.42W
Harrogate England 15 F2 ....54.00N 1.32W
Hârşova Romania 57 G7 ....44.41N 27.57E
Harstad Norway 40 D5 ....68.47N 16.32E
Harteigan mt. Norway 40 A3 ....60.12N 7.05E
Harter Fell hill England 14 E3 ....54.29N 2.52W
Hart Fell hill Scotland 17 F3 ....55.24N 3.24W
Hartford U.S.A. 65 L5 ....41.46N 72.42W
Hartland England 12 C3 ....50.59N 4.29W
Hartland Point England 13 C3 ....51.01N 4.33W
Hartlepool England 15 F3 ....54.41N 1.13W

Hartlepool d. England 9 E4 ....54.40N 1.15W
Har Us Nuur l. Mongolia 102 G7 ....47.53N 92.19E
Harwich England 11 G2 ....51.56N 1.16E
Haryana d. India 96 E6 ....29.11N 76.12E
Haslemere England 10 E2 ....51.05N 0.43W
Hasselt Belgium 42 E3 ....50.56N 5.20E
Hassi Messaoud Algeria 84 E5 ....31.41N 6.10E
Hässleholm Sweden 40 C2 ....56.10N 13.46E
Hastings England 11 F1 ....50.51N 0.35E
Ha Tinh Vietnam 104 D7 ....18.18N 105.55E
Hatfield England 15 G2 ....53.35N 0.59W
Hatteras, Cape U.S.A. 65 K4 ....35.14N 75.34W
Hattiesburg U.S.A. 65 I3 ....31.23N 89.19W
Hat Yai Thailand 104 C5 ....7.01N 100.26E
Haud f. Ethiopia 85 I2 ....8.37N 44.15E
Haugesund Norway 40 A2 ....59.24N 5.18E
Haukivesi l. Finland 40 G3 ....62.06N 28.28E
Haut Atlas mts Morocco 84 D5 ....30.51N 8.03W
Haut-Folin hill France 44 F5 ....46.59N 4.01E
Hauts Plateaux f. Algeria 52 C3 ....33.42N 0.42W
Havana Cuba 71 H5 ....23.07N 82.22W
Haverfordwest Wales 12 C3 ....51.48N 4.58W
Haverhill England 11 F3 ....52.05N 0.26E
Havlíčkův Brod Czech Rep. 46 B2 ....49.36N 15.34E
Havre U.S.A. 64 E6 ....48.32N 109.41W
Havre-St-Pierre Canada 63 L3 ....50.14N 63.28W
Hawaii i. U.S.A. 109 J7 ....20.02N 155.17W
Hawaiian Islands N. Pacific Oc. 108 I7 ....28.26N 174.25W
Hawaiian Ridge f. N. Pacific Oc. 108 I7 ....26.19N 178.56W
Hawarden Wales 12 D5 ....53.11N 3.02W
Hawes England 15 E3 ....54.18N 2.12W
Haweswater Reservoir England 14 E3 ....54.30N 2.48W
Hawick Scotland 17 G3 ....55.26N 2.47W
Hawke Bay New Zealand 111 G3 ....39.24S 177.23E
Hawkhurst England 11 F2 ....51.03N 0.31E
Haxby England 15 F3 ....54.01N 1.04W
Hay Australia 110 D3 ....34.31S 144.48E
Hay r. Canada 62 G4 ....60.48N 115.47W
Haydarābād Iran 94 G7 ....37.04N 45.05E
Haydon Bridge England 15 E3 ....54.59N 2.15W
Hayle England 13 B2 ....50.11N 5.25W
Haymā' Oman 95 I3 ....19.54N 56.13E
Hay-on-Wye Wales 12 D4 ....52.05N 3.07W
Hay River town Canada 62 G4 ....60.51N 115.40W
Hayshah, Sabkhat al f. Libya 53 G3 ....31.55N 15.19E
Haywards Heath England 11 E1 ....50.59N 0.06W
Hazarajat f. Afgh. 95 K6 ....32.29N 65.07E
Hazebrouck France 42 B3 ....50.43N 2.32E
Heacham England 11 F3 ....52.54N 0.30E
Headcorn England 11 F2 ....51.10N 0.38E
Heanor England 15 F2 ....53.01N 1.21W
Hearst Canada 65 J6 ....49.41N 83.41W
Heathfield England 11 F1 ....50.58N 0.16E
Hebei d. China 103 L5 ....38.33N 115.49E
Hebron Israel 53 J3 ....31.53N 34.49E
Hecate Strait Canada 62 E3 ....52.36N 130.27W
Hechi China 103 J2 ....24.38N 108.04E
Heckington England 11 E3 ....52.59N 0.18W
Hede Sweden 40 C3 ....62.25N 13.32E
Heerenveen Neth. 42 E5 ....52.58N 5.56E
Heerlen Neth. 42 E3 ....50.53N 5.58E
Hefei China 103 L4 ....31.51N 117.19E
Hegang China 103 O7 ....47.13N 130.13E
Heidelberg Germany 54 C3 ....49.24N 8.41E
Heighington England 15 G2 ....53.13N 0.27W
Heilbronn Germany 54 C3 ....49.08N 9.12E
Heilen, Loch l. Scotland 19 F3 ....58.36N 3.17W
Heilongjiang d. China 103 N7 ....46.55N 128.30E
Heilong Jiang r. China 103 O7 ....48.25N 134.59E
Heinola Finland 40 F3 ....61.12N 26.02E
Hekla vol. Iceland 40 Y1 ....63.59N 19.41W
Helena U.S.A. 64 D6 ....46.36N 112.01W
Helensburgh Scotland 16 E4 ....56.00N 4.44W
Helgoländer Bucht g. Germany 54 C6 ....54.10N 8.14E
Hellín Spain 48 E3 ....38.31N 1.41W
Helmand r. Afgh. 95 J6 ....31.13N 61.35E
Helmond Neth. 42 E4 ....51.28N 5.40E
Helmsdale Scotland 19 F3 ....58.07N 3.39W
Helmsdale r. Scotland 19 F3 ....58.07N 3.38W
Helmsley England 15 F3 ....54.15N 1.04W
Helsingborg Sweden 40 C2 ....56.03N 12.42E
Helsingør Denmark 54 E7 ....56.02N 12.36E
Helsinki Finland 40 F3 ....60.10N 24.57E
Helston England 13 B2 ....50.06N 5.16W
Helvellyn hill England 14 D3 ....54.32N 3.01W
Hemel Hempstead England 11 E2 ....51.45N 0.27W
Hemsworth England 15 F2 ....53.37N 1.21W
Henares r. Spain 48 D4 ....40.25N 3.29W
Henderson Island S. Pacific Oc. 109 L4 ....24.20S 128.20W
Hendon England 11 E2 ....51.35N 0.13W
Hengelo Neth. 42 F5 ....52.16N 6.48E
Hengoed Wales 12 D3 ....51.39N 3.14W
Henichesk Ukraine 53 J6 ....46.10N 34.48E
Henley-on-Thames England 10 E2 ....51.32N 0.54W
Hennef Germany 42 G3 ....50.47N 7.18E
Henrietta Maria, Cape Canada 63 J3 ....55.21N 82.13W
Henzada Myanmar 97 I4 ....17.36N 95.26E
Herāt Afgh. 95 J6 ....34.22N 62.11E
Hereford England 10 C3 ....52.03N 2.43W
Herefordshire d. England 9 D3 ....52.07N 2.40W
Herm i. Channel Is 13 Y9 ....49.28N 2.26W
Herma Ness hd Scotland 19 I5 ....60.51N 0.54W
Hermosillo Mexico 70 B6 ....29.04N 110.58W
Herne Germany 42 G4 ....51.32N 7.13E
Herne Bay town England 11 G2 ....51.22N 1.08E
Herning Denmark 40 B2 ....56.08N 8.58E
Hertford England 11 E2 ....51.48N 0.05W
Hertfordshire d. England 9 F2 ....51.51N 0.09E
Hesdin France 11 H1 ....50.22N 2.03E
Heswall England 14 D2 ....53.20N 3.06W
Hetton England 15 E3 ....54.01N 2.03W
Hexham England 15 E3 ....54.58N 2.07W
Heysham England 14 E3 ....54.02N 2.54W
Heywood England 15 E2 ....53.35N 2.13W
Hidaka-sanmyaku mts Japan 106 D4 ....42.49N 142.38E
Hidalgo d. Mexico 70 E5 ....20.35N 99.07W
Hidalgo del Parral Mexico 70 C6 ....26.55N 105.40W
Higashi-suidō str. Japan 106 A2 ....33.55N 129.23E
Higham Ferrers England 11 E3 ....52.18N 0.36W
Highbridge England 10 C2 ....51.13N 2.59W
Highclere England 10 D2 ....51.20N 1.22W
Highland d. Scotland 8 C5 ....57.38N 4.59W
High Peak hills England 15 F2 ....53.23N 1.54W
High Seat hill England 15 E3 ....54.24N 2.18W
Highworth England 10 D2 ....51.38N 1.43W
High Wycombe England 10 E2 ....51.38N 0.45W
Hiiumaa i. Estonia 40 E2 ....58.50N 22.24E
Hijaz f. Saudi Arabia 94 E5 ....24.28N 37.01E
Hilāl, Ra's al pt Libya 53 H3 ....32.54N 22.09E
Hildesheim Germany 54 C5 ....52.09N 9.57E

Hillah Iraq 94 F6 ....32.27N 44.24E
Hillerød Denmark 40 C1 ....55.56N 12.18E
Hillside Scotland 19 G1 ....56.45N 2.29W
Hillswick Scotland 19 H5 ....60.29N 1.29W
Hilpsford Point England 14 D3 ....54.02N 3.12W
Hilversum Neth. 42 E5 ....52.13N 5.11E
Himachal Pradesh d. India 96 E7 ....31.59N 77.23E
Himalaya mts Asia 96 E7 ....33.06N 76.46E
Hinckley England 10 D3 ....52.33N 1.23W
Hinderwell England 15 G3 ....54.32N 0.46W
Hindhead England 10 E2 ....51.07N 0.44W
Hindley England 14 E2 ....53.32N 2.35W
Hindu Kush mts Afgh./Pakistan 95 K6 ....34.58N 67.52E
Hinnøya i. Norway 40 C5 ....68.37N 15.58E
Hiraman watercourse Kenya 87 B2 ....1.08S 39.54E
Hirosaki Japan 106 D4 ....40.36N 140.28E
Hiroshima Japan 106 B2 ....34.22N 132.27E
Hirson France 42 D2 ....49.55N 4.05E
Hirwaun Wales 12 D3 ....51.44N 3.31W
Hispaniola i. Caribbean Sea 71 J5 ....20.18N 72.57W
Hitachi Japan 106 D3 ....36.35N 140.39E
Hitchin England 11 E2 ....51.57N 0.17W
Hitra i. Norway 40 B3 ....63.31N 8.49E
Hiva Oa i. French Polynesia 109 K5 ....9.47S 138.57W
Hjälmaren l. Sweden 40 C2 ....59.14N 15.51E
Hjørring Denmark 40 B2 ....57.28N 10.01E
Hlybokaye Belarus 55 L6 ....55.08N 27.40E
Hobart Australia 110 D2 ....42.52S 147.19E
Hobro Denmark 40 B2 ....56.38N 9.48E
Ho Chi Minh City Vietnam 104 D6 ....10.45N 106.42E
Hochschwab mt. Austria 54 F2 ....47.38N 15.09E
Hoddesdon England 11 E2 ....51.46N 0.01W
Hodeidah Yemen 94 F2 ....14.50N 42.54E
Hódmezővásárhely Hungary 54 I2 ....46.25N 20.21E
Hodna, Chott el f. Algeria 52 D4 ....35.27N 4.55E
Hodnet England 10 C3 ....52.51N 2.35W
Hoek van Holland Neth. 42 D4 ....51.58N 4.08E
Hof Germany 54 D4 ....50.19N 11.55E
Höfn Iceland 40 Z2 ....64.16N 15.13W
Hofsjökull ice cap Iceland 40 Y2 ....64.49N 18.52W
Hoggar f. Algeria 84 E4 ....23.10N 4.23E
Hohhot China 103 K6 ....40.43N 111.44E
Hokkaidō i. Japan 106 D4 ....43.33N 143.27E
Holbæk Denmark 40 B1 ....55.43N 11.44E
Holbeach England 11 F3 ....52.48N 0.01E
Holbeach Marsh England 11 F3 ....52.51N 0.02E
Holderness pen. England 15 G2 ....53.52N 0.18W
Holguín Cuba 71 I5 ....20.54N 76.14W
Hollabrunn Austria 54 G3 ....48.34N 16.05E
Holland Fen f. England 11 E3 ....52.59N 0.11W
Hollesley Bay England 11 G3 ....52.02N 1.28E
Hollington England 11 F1 ....50.53N 0.33E
Hollingworth England 15 F2 ....53.28N 1.59W
Holme-on-Spalding-Moor England 15 G2 ....53.50N 0.47W
Holmfirth England 15 F2 ....53.34N 1.47W
Holstebro Denmark 40 B2 ....56.21N 8.37E
Holsworthy England 13 C2 ....50.49N 4.21W
Holt England 11 G3 ....52.55N 1.05E
Holyhead Wales 12 C5 ....53.19N 4.38W
Holyhead Bay Wales 12 C5 ....53.22N 4.40W
Holy Island England 15 F4 ....55.41N 1.47W
Holy Island Wales 12 C5 ....53.15N 4.41W
Holywell Wales 12 D5 ....53.17N 3.13W
Homa Bay town Kenya 87 A2 ....0.32S 34.27E
Homāyunshahr Iran 95 H6 ....32.59N 50.23E
Homburg Germany 42 G2 ....49.19N 7.20E
Home Bay Canada 63 L4 ....68.52N 67.27W
Homs Syria 94 E6 ....34.44N 36.44E
Homyel' Belarus 55 N5 ....52.25N 31.01E
Honduras Central America 70 G3 ....14.47N 86.43W
Honduras, Gulf of Belize/Honduras 60 K3 ....16.20N 87.30W
Hønefoss Norway 40 B3 ....60.10N 10.14E
Hong Kong China 103 K2 ....22.16N 114.11E
Hong Kong d. China 103 K2 ....22.21N 114.19E
Honiara Solomon Is 111 E6 ....9.26S 159.57E
Honington England 13 D2 ....52.03N 3.11W
Honley England 15 F2 ....53.36N 1.48W
Honolulu U.S.A. 109 J7 ....21.19N 157.52W
Honshū i. Japan 106 B3 ....35.42N 133.20E
Hood, Mount vol. U.S.A. 64 B6 ....45.23N 121.42W
Hood Point Australia 110 A3 ....34.19S 119.33E
Hoogeveen Neth. 42 F5 ....52.43N 6.30E
Hook England 10 E2 ....51.17N 0.58W
Hook Head Rep. of Ireland 41 E2 ....52.07N 6.56W
Hoorn Neth. 42 E5 ....52.39N 5.04E
Hope, Loch l. Scotland 19 E3 ....58.27N 4.39W
Hope, Point U.S.A. 62 B4 ....68.21N 166.49W
Hopedale Canada 63 L3 ....55.27N 60.00W
Hörby Sweden 54 F6 ....55.51N 13.40E
Horizon Deep f. S. Pacific Oc. 108 I4 ....23.23S 174.48W
Horley England 11 E2 ....51.10N 0.10W
Hormuz, Strait of Iran/Oman 95 I5 ....26.35N 56.59E
Horn Austria 46 B2 ....48.40N 15.40E
Horn c. Iceland 40 X2 ....66.28N 22.29W
Horn, Cape Chile 73 C1 ....56.04S 67.17W
Hornavan l. Sweden 40 D4 ....66.11N 17.44E
Horncastle England 15 G2 ....53.12N 0.07W
Hornepayne Canada 65 J6 ....49.13N 84.47W
Hornsea England 15 G2 ....53.55N 0.10W
Horodnya Ukraine 55 N4 ....51.53N 31.36E
Horodok Ukraine 55 J3 ....49.47N 23.39E
Horokhiv Ukraine 55 J4 ....50.30N 24.46E
Horrabridge England 13 C2 ....50.31N 4.06W
Horsens Denmark 40 B1 ....55.52N 9.51E
Horsham Australia 110 D3 ....36.43S 142.13E
Horsham England 11 E2 ....51.04N 0.19W
Horten Norway 40 B2 ....59.25N 10.28E
Horwich England 14 E2 ....53.36N 2.33W
Hotan China 102 E5 ....37.07N 80.02E
Houffalize Belgium 42 E3 ....50.08N 5.48E
Houghton le Spring England 15 F3 ....54.50N 1.28W
Houghton Regis England 11 E2 ....51.54N 0.31W
Hourn, Loch inlet Scotland 18 D2 ....57.08N 5.42W
Houston U.S.A. 65 G2 ....29.43N 95.19W
Hovd Mongolia 102 G7 ....47.59N 91.41E
Hove England 11 E1 ....50.50N 0.10W
Hoveton England 11 G3 ....52.43N 1.25E
Hövsgöl Nuur l. Mongolia 103 I8 ....50.59N 100.42E
Howden England 15 G2 ....53.45N 0.52W
Howland Island N. Pacific Oc. 108 I6 ....0.48N 176.38W
Høy i. Scotland 19 F3 ....58.50N 3.16W
Høyanger Norway 40 A3 ....61.13N 6.04E
Hoyerswerda Germany 54 F4 ....51.27N 14.16E
Höytiäinen l. Finland 40 G3 ....62.46N 29.43E
Hradec Králové Czech Rep. 54 F4 ....50.13N 15.50E
Hrebinka Ukraine 55 O4 ....50.06N 32.26E
Hrodna Belarus 55 J5 ....53.41N 23.49E
Hsinchu Taiwan 103 M2 ....24.48N 120.58E
Huacho Peru 76 E5 ....11.09S 77.35W
Huaibei China 103 L4 ....33.57N 116.51E
Huainan China 103 L4 ....32.36N 117.02E
Huallaga r. Peru 76 E5 ....5.06S 75.40W
Huambo Angola 86 A3 ....12.46S 15.44E
Huancayo Peru 76 E5 ....12.03S 75.11W

Huang He r. China 103 L5 ....37.46N 118.57E
Huangshi China 103 L4 ....30.10N 115.08E
Huánuco Peru 76 E6 ....9.57S 76.14W
Huarmey Peru 76 E5 ....10.03S 78.11W
Huascarán, Nevado de mt. Peru 76 E6 ....9.09S 77.36W
Hubei d. China 103 K4 ....31.09N 113.06E
Hubli India 96 E4 ....15.18N 75.15E
Hucknall England 15 F2 ....53.02N 1.12W
Huddersfield England 15 F2 ....53.39N 1.47W
Hudiksvall Sweden 40 D3 ....61.43N 17.06E
Hudson r. U.S.A. 65 L5 ....40.54N 73.56W
Hudson Bay sea Canada 63 J3 ....59.05N 86.00W
Hudson Strait Canada 63 K4 ....63.31N 74.25W
Huê Vietnam 104 D7 ....16.26N 107.33E
Huelva Spain 48 B2 ....37.16N 6.55W
Huércal-Overa Spain 48 E2 ....37.23N 1.55W
Huesca Spain 48 E5 ....42.09N 0.25W
Huila, Nevado de vol. Colombia 76 E8 ....2.59N 75.57W
Hulin China 106 B5 ....45.42N 132.52E
Hull Canada 65 K6 ....45.27N 75.45W
Hulun Buir China 103 L7 ....49.04N 119.46E
Hulun Nur l. China 103 L7 ....48.32N 117.11E
Ḥulwān Egypt 53 J2 ....29.55N 31.18E
Humaitá Brazil 76 H6 ....7.33S 63.02W
Humber, Mouth of the England 15 H2 ....53.33N 0.06E
Humboldt r. U.S.A. 64 C5 ....40.04N 118.36W
Humenné Slovakia 46 E2 ....48.56N 21.54E
Humphreys Peak U.S.A. 64 D4 ....35.21N 111.40W
Húnaflói b. Iceland 40 X2 ....65.46N 20.50W
Hunan d. China 103 K3 ....27.26N 111.22E
Hunchun China 106 B4 ....42.52N 130.21E
Hunchun China 106 B4 ....42.38N 130.17E
Hungarian Plain f. Hungary 34 F2 ....46.30N 19.00E
Hungary Europe 54 F2 ....47.01N 18.59E
Hungerford England 10 D2 ....51.25N 1.31W
Hunish, Rubha pt Scotland 18 C2 ....57.42N 6.24W
Hunmanby England 15 G3 ....54.11N 0.19W
Hunsrück hills Germany 54 B3 ....49.47N 7.00E
Hunstanton England 11 F3 ....52.56N 0.30E
Huntingdon England 11 E3 ....52.20N 0.11W
Huntington U.S.A. 65 J4 ....38.25N 82.18W
Huntly Scotland 19 G2 ....57.27N 2.47W
Huntsville Ala. U.S.A. 65 I3 ....34.46N 86.34W
Huntsville Tex. U.S.A. 65 G3 ....30.42N 95.34W
Huri Hills Kenya 87 B3 ....3.23N 37.40E
Huron U.S.A. 64 G5 ....44.23N 98.13W
Huron, Lake Canada/U.S.A. 63 J2 ....44.39N 82.23W
Hurstpierpoint England 11 E1 ....50.56N 0.11W
Husum Germany 54 C6 ....54.29N 9.04E
Hutton Rudby England 15 F3 ....54.27N 1.17W
Huzhou China 103 M4 ....30.50N 120.08E
Hvannadalshnúkur vol. Iceland 40 Y2 ....64.01N 16.41W
Hvar i. Croatia 56 B6 ....43.08N 16.33E
Hyargas Nuur l. Mongolia 102 G7 ....49.02N 93.18E
Hyderabad India 96 E4 ....17.21N 78.25E
Hyderabad Pakistan 96 C6 ....25.21N 68.23E
Hyères France 44 G3 ....43.07N 6.08E
Hyesan N. Korea 106 B4 ....41.24N 128.11E
Hyrynsalmi Finland 40 G4 ....64.40N 28.29E
Hythe Hants. England 10 D1 ....50.52N 1.24W
Hythe Kent England 11 G2 ....51.04N 1.05E
Hyvinkää Finland 40 F3 ....60.38N 24.51E

I

Ialomiţa r. Romania 56 G7 ....44.43N 27.51E
Iar Connaught f. Rep. of Ireland 41 B3 ....53.21N 9.19W
Iaşi Romania 53 I6 ....47.10N 27.35E
Ibadan Nigeria 84 E2 ....7.24N 3.55E
Ibagué Colombia 72 B7 ....4.24N 75.13W
Ibar r. S.M. 56 D6 ....43.43N 20.45E
Ibarra Ecuador 76 E8 ....0.23N 78.04W
Ibb Yemen 94 F2 ....14.03N 44.09E
Ibiapaba, Serra da hills Brazil 77 L7 ....3.54S 41.00W
Ibiza Spain 48 F3 ....38.54N 1.27E
Ibiza i. Spain 48 F3 ....39.10N 1.39E
Ibrā' Oman 95 I4 ....22.41N 58.33E
Ibstock England 10 D3 ....52.42N 1.24W
Ica Peru 76 E5 ....14.04S 75.43W
Iceland Europe 40 X2 ....64.42N 18.19W
Ichinoseki Japan 106 D3 ....38.55N 141.07E
Icklesham England 11 F1 ....50.55N 0.40E
Idaho d. U.S.A. 64 D5 ....44.08N 114.08W
Idaho Falls town U.S.A. 64 D5 ....43.32N 112.01W
Idar-Oberstein Germany 42 G2 ....49.42N 7.18E
Idfū Egypt 53 J1 ....24.55N 32.49E
Idi mt. Greece 56 F2 ....35.13N 24.47E
Idlib Syria 57 L2 ....35.56N 36.38E
Ieper Belgium 42 B3 ....50.51N 2.53E
Iešjávri l. Norway 40 F5 ....69.39N 24.28E
Igan Malaysia 104 E4 ....2.51N 111.44E
Iganga Uganda 87 A3 ....0.37N 33.28E
Iggesund Sweden 40 D3 ....61.39N 17.05E
Iglesias Italy 50 C3 ....39.19N 8.32E
İğneada Burnu pt Turkey 57 H5 ....41.53N 28.03E
Igoumenitsa Greece 56 D4 ....39.30N 20.17E
Iguaçu r. Brazil 77 J2 ....25.36S 54.35W
Iguaçu Falls Argentina/Brazil 77 J2 ....25.38S 54.26W
Iguatu Brazil 77 M6 ....6.22S 39.17W
Iisalmi Finland 40 F3 ....63.34N 27.11E
IJmuiden Neth. 42 D5 ....52.27N 4.37E
IJssel r. Neth. 42 E5 ....52.35N 5.50E
IJsselmeer l. Neth. 42 E5 ....52.48N 5.20E
IJzer r. Belgium 11 H2 ....51.09N 2.44E
Ikaahuk Canada 62 F5 ....71.55N 125.05W
Ikaría i. Greece 56 G3 ....37.39N 26.13E
Iki i. Japan 106 A3 ....33.45N 129.39E
Ilagan Phil. 105 G7 ....17.06N 121.53E
Ilaisamis Kenya 87 B3 ....1.36N 37.47E
Ilchester England 10 C2 ....51.00N 2.41W
Ilebo Dem. Rep. Congo 86 B4 ....4.21S 20.36E
Île-de-France f. France 42 B1 ....48.39N 2.36E
Ileret Kenya 87 B4 ....4.18N 36.14E
Ilford England 11 F2 ....51.33N 0.05E
Ilfracombe England 13 C3 ....51.12N 4.07W
Ilhéus Brazil 77 M5 ....14.46S 39.02W
Iligan Phil. 105 G5 ....8.13N 124.15E
Ilkeston England 10 D3 ....52.58N 1.18W
Ilkley England 15 F2 ....53.56N 1.49W
Illinois d. U.S.A. 65 I4 ....39.52N 89.07W
Illinois r. U.S.A. 65 H4 ....38.56N 90.30W
Illizi Algeria 84 E4 ....26.29N 8.30E
Ilminster England 10 C1 ....50.56N 2.54W
Iloilo Phil. 105 G6 ....10.41N 122.32E
Ilorin Nigeria 84 E2 ....8.32N 4.35E
Iman r. Rus. Fed. 106 B5 ....45.57N 133.45E
Imatra Finland 40 G3 ....61.11N 28.47E
Immingham England 15 G2 ....53.37N 0.13W
Imola Italy 50 D6 ....44.21N 11.42E
Imperatriz Brazil 77 K6 ....5.33S 47.26W
Imola Italy 50 D6 ....44.21N 11.42E
Imperatriz Brazil 77 K6 ....5.33S 47.26W
Imphal India 97 H5 ....24.46N 93.56E
İmroz Turkey 56 F5 ....40.10N 25.55E

Inambari r. Peru 76 G5 ....12.44S 69.47W
Inari Finland 40 F5 ....68.57N 27.37E
Inarijärvi l. Finland 40 F5 ....68.57N 27.37E
Inchard, Loch b. Scotland 18 D3 ....58.27N 5.04W
İnch'înî Terara mt. Ethiopia 87 B4 ....4.35N 37.07E
Inchkeith i. Scotland 17 F4 ....56.02N 3.08W
Inch'ŏn S. Korea 103 N5 ....37.28N 126.39E
Indalsälven r. Sweden 40 D3 ....62.32N 17.24E
Independence U.S.A. 65 H4 ....39.07N 94.26W
India Asia 96 E5 ....22.00N 79.00E
Indiana d. U.S.A. 65 I5 ....40.09N 86.01W
Indianapolis U.S.A. 65 I4 ....39.46N 86.10W
Indian-Antarctic Ridge f. Southern Oc. 108 D2 ..49.49S 117.01E
Indian Ocean 117 M5
Indigirka r. Rus. Fed. 59 P5 ....71.28N 149.53E
Indonesia Asia 104 E2 ....4.12S 112.02E
Indore India 96 E5 ....22.40N 75.53E
Indre r. France 44 D5 ....47.14N 0.12E
Indus r. China/Pakistan 102 B3 ....23.56N 67.38E
Indus, Mouths of the Pakistan 96 C5 ....24.36N 66.36E
İnebolu Turkey 57 J5 ....41.58N 33.45E
İnegöl Turkey 57 H5 ....40.04N 29.30E
Infiernillo, Presa resr Mexico 70 D4 ....18.41N 101.57W
Infiesto Spain 48 C5 ....43.21N 5.20W
Ingatestone England 11 F2 ....51.40N 0.23E
Ingleborough hill England 15 E3 ....54.10N 2.24W
Ingleton England 15 E3 ....54.09N 2.28W
Ingoldmells England 15 H2 ....53.12N 0.20E
Ingolstadt Germany 54 D3 ....48.46N 11.27E
Inhambane Mozambique 86 C2 ....23.47S 35.31E
Inhul r. Ukraine 55 N2 ....46.58N 31.58E
Inhulets' r. Ukraine 55 O2 ....46.41N 32.49E
Inishbofin i. Rep. of Ireland 41 A3 ....53.38N 10.14W
Inisheer i. Rep. of Ireland 41 B3 ....53.04N 9.30W
Inishmaan i. Rep. of Ireland 41 B3 ....53.05N 9.33W
Inishmore i. Rep. of Ireland 41 B3 ....53.09N 9.47W
Inishmurray i. Rep. of Ireland 41 C4 ....54.26N 8.40W
Inishowen pen. Rep. of Ireland 41 D5 ....55.13N 7.17W
Inishowen Head Rep. of Ireland 16 C3 ....55.14N 6.55W
Inishtrahull i. Rep. of Ireland 41 D5 ....55.28N 7.13W
Inishtrahull Sound str. Rep. of Ireland 16 B3 ....55.25N 7.28W
Inishturk i. Rep. of Ireland 41 A3 ....53.42N 10.08W
Inn r. Europe 50 D7 ....46.55N 10.29E
Inner Mongolia d. China 103 I6 ....40.12N 103.26E
Inner Sound str. Scotland 18 D2 ....57.21N 5.57W
Innsbruck Austria 54 D2 ....47.16N 11.24E
Inny r. Rep. of Ireland 41 D3 ....53.33N 7.50W
Inowrocław Poland 46 D4 ....52.48N 18.16E
In Salah Algeria 84 E4 ....27.13N 2.25E
Insch Scotland 19 G2 ....57.20N 2.37W
International Falls town U.S.A. 65 H6 ....48.36N 93.25W
Inukjuak Canada 63 K3 ....58.28N 78.04W
Inuvik Canada 62 E4 ....68.24N 133.43W
Inveraray Scotland 16 D4 ....56.14N 5.04W
Inverbervie Scotland 19 G1 ....56.51N 2.17W
Invercargill New Zealand 111 F2 ....46.25S 168.22E
Inverclyde d. Scotland 8 C4 ....55.54N 4.44W
Invergordon Scotland 19 E2 ....57.42N 4.10W
Inverkeithing Scotland 17 F4 ....56.02N 3.24W
Inverness Scotland 19 E2 ....57.29N 4.13W
Inverurie Scotland 19 G2 ....57.17N 2.22W
Investigator Ridge f. Indian Oc. 108 C5 ....7.10S 98.15E
Ioannina Greece 56 D4 ....39.40N 20.51E
Iona i. Scotland 16 C4 ....56.19N 6.25W
Ionian Islands Greece 56 C4 ....39.26N 19.33E
Ionian Sea Greece/Italy 56 C4 ....38.11N 18.29E
Ios i. Greece 56 F3 ....36.44N 25.22E
Iowa d. U.S.A. 65 H5 ....42.12N 92.47W
Iowa City U.S.A. 65 H5 ....41.40N 91.32W
Ipatinga Brazil 77 L4 ....19.29S 42.28W
Ipoh Malaysia 104 C4 ....4.40N 101.04E
Ipswich England 11 G3 ....52.03N 1.09E
Iput' r. Belarus 55 N5 ....52.30N 31.37E
Iqaluit Canada 63 L4 ....63.45N 68.36W
Iquique Chile 73 B4 ....20.14S 70.07W
Iquitos Peru 76 F7 ....3.50S 73.13W
Iraklion Greece 56 F2 ....35.19N 25.08E
Iran Asia 95 H6 ....31.28N 55.05E
Iran, Pegunungan mts Indonesia 104 E4 ....1.47N 114.46E
Iranian Plateau f. Iran 90 E5 ....32.00N 55.00E
Īrānshahr Iran 95 J5 ....27.13N 60.42E
Irapuato Mexico 70 D5 ....20.41N 101.23W
Iraq Asia 94 F6 ....32.50N 42.21E
Irbid Jordan 94 E6 ....32.34N 35.51E
Ireland, Republic of Europe 41 D3 ....53.33N 7.43W
Ireland's Eye i. Rep. of Ireland 41 E3 ....53.24N 6.03W
Irgiz Kazakhstan 58 H2 ....48.36N 61.18E
Iringa Tanzania 86 C4 ....7.48S 35.43E
Iriri r. Brazil 77 J7 ....3.52S 52.37W
Irish Sea Rep. of Ireland/U.K. 41 F3 ....53.40N 5.11W
Irkutsk Rus. Fed. 59 L3 ....52.11N 104.09E
Iron Mountain U.S.A. 65 I6 ....45.49N 88.04W
Ironwood U.S.A. 65 H6 ....46.28N 90.09W
Irosin Phil. 105 G6 ....12.42N 124.00E
Irrawaddy r. Myanmar 97 I4 ....15.48N 95.05E
Irrawaddy, Mouths of the Myanmar 97 H4 ....15.35N 94.02E
Irsha r. Ukraine 55 M4 ....50.46N 29.35E
Irthing r. England 14 E3 ....54.55N 2.51W
Irtysh r. Kazakhstan/Rus. Fed. 58 H4 ....61.07N 68.50E
Irún Spain 48 E5 ....43.20N 1.48W
Irvine Scotland 16 E3 ....55.37N 4.40W
Isabela Phil. 105 G5 ....6.40N 121.59E
Isabela, Isla i. Ecuador 76 B7 ....0.41S 91.03W
Isabelia, Cordillera mts Nicaragua 71 G3 ....13.13N 85.59W
Ísafjörður Iceland 40 X2 ....66.05N 23.10W
Isar r. Germany 50 E8 ....48.49N 12.59E
Isbister Scotland 19 H5 ....60.36N 1.19W
Ischia, Isola d' i. Italy 50 E4 ....40.42N 13.51E
Ise Japan 106 C3 ....34.29N 136.43E
Isère, Pointe pt French Guiana 72 D7 ....5.47N 53.57W
Ishikari-wan b. Japan 106 D4 ....43.17N 140.58E
Ishim r. Kazakhstan/Rus. Fed. 58 I3 ....57.45N 71.10E
Ishinomaki Japan 106 D3 ....38.25N 141.17E
Isiolo Kenya 87 B3 ....0.22N 37.38E
Isiro Dem. Rep. Congo 86 B5 ....2.46N 27.36E
Iskenderun Turkey 57 L3 ....36.34N 36.08E
İskenderun Körfezi b. Turkey 57 K3 ....36.38N 35.54E
Iskŭr r. Bulgaria 56 F6 ....43.44N 24.27E
Isla r. Ang. Scotland 19 F1 ....56.32N 3.22W
Isla r. Mor. Scotland 19 G2 ....57.31N 2.47W
Islamabad Pakistan 96 D7 ....33.40N 73.08E
Island Magee pen. Northern Ireland 16 D2 ....54.50N 5.41W
Islay i. Scotland 16 C3 ....55.46N 6.11W
Isle of Anglesey d. Wales 9 C3 ....53.18N 4.23W
Isle of Wight d. England 9 E1 ....50.41N 1.17W
Isles of Scilly d. England 9 B1 ....49.55N 6.17W
Isnā Egypt 53 J2 ....25.16N 32.30E
Isparta Turkey 57 I3 ....37.46N 30.32E
Israel Asia 53 J3 ....32.12N 34.48E
İstanbul Turkey 57 H5 ....41.07N 28.58E
Istra pen. Croatia 54 E1 ....45.12N 13.53E
Itaberaba Brazil 77 L5 ....12.31S 40.17W

Itajaí Brazil 77 K2 ....26.52S 48.41W
Italy Europe 50 D6 ....41.46N 14.35E
Itambé, Pico de mt. Brazil 77 L4 ....18.23S 43.20W
Itapetininga Brazil 73 E4 ....23.36S 48.03W
Itapicuru r. Maranhão Brazil 77 L7 ....2.55S 44.16W
Itapicuru r. Sergipe Brazil 77 M5 ....11.48S 37.30W
Itapicuru Mirim Brazil 77 L7 ....3.24S 44.21W
Itiquira r. Brazil 77 I4 ....17.18S 56.20W
Itui r. Brazil 76 F6 ....4.23S 70.13W
Ituxi r. Brazil 76 H6 ....7.21S 64.52W
Iul'tin Rus. Fed. 59 T4 ....67.51N 178.47W
Ivaí r. Brazil 77 J3 ....23.14S 53.15W
Ivalo Finland 40 F5 ....68.39N 27.32E
Ivanava Belarus 46 G4 ....52.09N 25.32E
Ivano-Frankivs'k Ukraine 55 K3 ....48.55N 24.43E
Ivanovo Rus. Fed. 58 F3 ....56.59N 40.59E
Ivatsevichy Belarus 55 K5 ....52.43N 25.21E
Ivittuut Greenland 63 N4 ....61.13N 48.10W
Ivybridge England 13 D2 ....50.23N 3.55W
Iwaki Japan 106 D3 ....37.03N 140.53E
Iwo Nigeria 84 E2 ....7.38N 4.10E
Iwye Belarus 46 G4 ....53.55N 25.47E
Ixworth England 11 F3 ....52.18N 0.50E
Izabal, Lago de l. Guatemala 70 G4 ....15.36N 89.08W
Izhevsk Rus. Fed. 58 G3 ....56.48N 53.10E
Izmayil Ukraine 53 I6 ....45.21N 28.51E
İzmir Turkey 56 G4 ....38.24N 27.10E
İzmir Körfezi g. Turkey 56 G4 ....38.30N 26.44E
İzmit Turkey 57 H5 ....40.47N 29.55E
Izu-Ogasawara Trench f. N. Pacific Oc. 108 F8 ....34.34N 141.53E
Izu-shotō is Japan 106 C2 ....34.24N 139.14E

J

Jabalón r. Spain 48 C3 ....38.53N 4.05W
Jabalpur India 96 E5 ....23.10N 79.57E
Jablah Syria 57 K2 ....35.21N 35.56E
Jaboatão Brazil 77 N6 ....8.03S 34.55W
Jaca Spain 48 E5 ....42.34N 0.34W
Jacareacanga Brazil 77 I6 ....5.59S 57.33W
Jackson U.S.A. 65 H3 ....32.19N 90.12W
Jacksonville U.S.A. 65 J3 ....30.18N 81.42W
Jacmel Haiti 71 J4 ....18.16N 72.32W
Jacobabad Pakistan 96 C6 ....28.15N 68.29E
Jacuí r. Brazil 77 J1 ....30.03S 51.15W
Jacuípe r. Brazil 77 M5 ....12.33S 39.04W
Jādū Libya 52 F3 ....31.58N 12.04E
Jaén Spain 48 D2 ....37.46N 3.47W
Jaffna Sri Lanka 96 F2 ....9.41N 79.59E
Jagdalpur India 96 F4 ....19.04N 82.07E
Jahrom Iran 95 H5 ....28.31N 53.33E
Jaipur India 96 E6 ....26.51N 75.50E
Jaisalmer India 96 D6 ....26.52N 70.56E
Jajce Bos.-Herz. 56 B6 ....44.21N 17.16E
Jakarta Indonesia 104 D2 ....6.07S 106.48E
Jakobstad Finland 40 E3 ....63.40N 22.42E
Jalgaon India 96 E5 ....21.01N 75.41E
Jalisco d. Mexico 70 D4 ....19.59N 104.18W
Jalna India 96 E4 ....19.49N 75.57E
Jalón r. Spain 48 E4 ....41.47N 1.02W
Jālū Libya 85 G4 ....29.03N 21.33E
Jamaica Central America 71 I4 ....17.30N 77.19W
Jamaica Channel Haiti/Jamaica 71 I4 ....18.29N 75.24W
Jamanxim r. Brazil 77 I7 ....4.43S 56.24W
James r. U.S.A. 64 G5 ....42.48N 97.17W
James Bay Canada 63 J3 ....53.23N 80.25W
Jamestown U.S.A. 64 G6 ....46.53N 98.43W
Jammu India 96 D7 ....32.42N 74.56E
Jammu and Kashmir Asia 96 E7 ....34.06N 76.59E
Jamnagar India 96 D5 ....22.26N 70.06E
Jampur Pakistan 96 D6 ....29.37N 70.41E
Jämsänkoski Finland 40 F3 ....61.56N 25.11E
Jamshedpur India 96 G5 ....22.46N 86.12E
Jandía hill Canary Islands 48 Y2 ....28.06N 14.21W
Jan Mayen i. Arctic Oc. 34 D5 ....72.00N 8.00W
Janúaria Brazil 77 L4 ....15.29S 44.22W
Japan Asia 106 C3 ....34.48N 133.17E
Japan, Sea of N. Pacific Oc. 106 B3 ....39.13N 133.37E
Japan Trench f. N. Pacific Oc. 108 F8 ....34.52N 143.17E
Japurá r. Brazil 76 H7 ....3.06S 64.45W
Jardines de la Reina, Archipiélago de los is Cuba 71 I5 ....20.46N 79.01W
Jarocin Poland 46 C3 ....51.58N 17.31E
Jarosław Poland 46 F3 ....50.01N 22.40E
Järpen Sweden 40 C3 ....63.22N 13.28E
Järvenpää Finland 40 F3 ....60.29N 25.06E
Jarvis Island S. Pacific Oc. 108 J5 ....0.26S 160.02W
Jäsk Iran 95 I5 ....25.40N 57.47E
Jasło Poland 46 E2 ....49.45N 21.28E
Jasper Canada 62 G3 ....52.53N 118.05W
Jataí Brazil 77 J4 ....17.53S 51.44W
Jatapu r. Brazil 77 I7 ....2.22S 58.11W
Jaú Brazil 77 K3 ....22.16S 48.33W
Java i. Indonesia 104 D2 ....8.12S 107.16E
Java Ridge f. Indian Oc. 108 D5 ....8.48S 104.02E
Javarthushuu Mongolia 103 K7 ....48.55N 112.44E
Java Sea Indonesia 104 E3 ....4.56S 110.49E
Java Trench f. Indian Oc. 108 C5 ....8.48S 104.02E
Jawhar Somalia 85 I2 ....2.43N 45.27E
Jawor Poland 46 C3 ....51.03N 16.12E
Jaya, Puncak mt. Indonesia 105 J3 ....4.03S 137.12E
Jaz Mūriān, Hāmūn-e f. Iran 95 I5 ....27.32N 58.47E
Jebel Abyad Plateau f. Sudan 94 C3 ....19.25N 26.59E
Jeddah Saudi Arabia 94 E4 ....21.30N 39.08E
Jefferson City U.S.A. 65 H4 ....38.37N 92.11W
Jelenia Góra Poland 46 B3 ....50.55N 15.44E
Jember Indonesia 104 E2 ....8.05S 113.45E
Jena Germany 54 D4 ....50.56N 11.36E
Jendouba Tunisia 52 E4 ....36.28N 8.47E
Jequié Brazil 77 L5 ....13.48S 40.00W
Jequitinhonha r. Brazil 77 M4 ....15.51S 38.52W
Jérémie Haiti 71 J4 ....18.38N 74.09W
Jerez de la Frontera Spain 48 B2 ....36.41N 6.08W
Jerid, Chott el f. Tunisia 52 E3 ....33.38N 8.28E
Jersey i. Channel Is 13 Z8 ....49.11N 2.10W
Jerusalem Israel/West Bank 53 K3 ....31.47N 35.13E
Jesi Italy 50 E5 ....43.31N 13.14E
Jesup U.S.A. 65 J3 ....31.34N 81.59W
Jhang Pakistan 95 L6 ....31.17N 72.23E
Jhansi India 96 F6 ....25.26N 78.34E
Jharkhand d. India 96 G5 ....23.36N 85.06E
Jiamusi China 103 O7 ....46.48N 130.25E
Ji'an China 103 K3 ....27.09N 114.56E
Jiangxi d. China 103 L3 ....27.21N 115.22E
Jiaohe China 106 A4 ....43.43N 127.20E

Jiehkkevárri mt. Norway 40 D5 ....69.28N 19.51E
Jieznas Lithuania 46 G5 ....54.36N 24.10E
Jihlava Czech Rep. 54 F3 ....49.24N 15.36E
Jilf al Kabīr, Ḥaḍabat al f. Egypt 94 C4 ....23.12N 25.56E
Jilib Somalia 85 I2 ....0.30N 42.47E
Jilin China 103 N6 ....43.53N 126.33E
Jilin d. China 103 N6 ....43.33N 125.10E
Jīma Ethiopia 85 H2 ....7.40N 36.49E
Jiménez Mexico 70 D6 ....27.08N 104.57W
Jinan China 103 L5 ....36.38N 117.01E
Jindřichův Hradec Czech Rep. 46 B2 ....49.09N 15.01E
Jingdezhen China 103 L3 ....29.21N 117.21E
Jinghong China 103 I2 ....21.57N 100.52E
Jingmen China 103 K4 ....30.58N 112.10E
Jingzhou China 103 K4 ....30.17N 112.17E
Jinhua China 103 L3 ....29.10N 119.41E
Jining Nei Mongol China 103 K6 ....40.54N 113.06E
Jining Shandong China 103 L5 ....35.22N 116.29E
Jinja Uganda 85 H2 ....0.28N 33.14E
Jinka Ethiopia 87 B4 ....5.40N 36.39E
Jinzhou China 103 M6 ....41.02N 121.06E
Jiparaná r. Brazil 77 H6 ....8.09S 62.60W
Jipe, Lake Kenya/Tanzania 87 B2 ....3.35S 37.45E
Jiu r. Romania 56 E6 ....43.47N 23.48E
Jiujiang China 103 L3 ....29.43N 116.00E
Jiwani Pakistan 95 J5 ....25.07N 61.48E
Jixi China 103 O7 ....45.13N 130.53E
Jīzān Saudi Arabia 94 F3 ....16.56N 42.30E
João Pessoa Brazil 77 N6 ....7.05S 34.50W
Jodhpur India 96 D6 ....26.16N 73.07E
Joensuu Finland 40 G3 ....62.36N 29.46E
Jõetsu Japan 106 C3 ....37.10N 138.14E
Johannesburg S. Africa 86 B2 ....26.09S 27.59E
John o'Groats Scotland 19 F3 ....58.38N 3.04W
Johnston Wales 12 C3 ....51.45N 4.59W
Johnston Atoll N. Pacific Oc. 108 I7 ....16.42N 169.30W
Johnstone Scotland 16 E3 ....55.50N 4.31W
Johor Bahru Malaysia 104 C4 ....1.29N 103.46E
Joinville Brazil 77 K2 ....26.17S 48.51W
Jokkmokk Sweden 40 D4 ....66.37N 19.49E
Jolo i. Phil. 105 G5 ....5.57N 121.06E
Jonava Lithuania 46 G5 ....55.04N 24.17E
Jones Sound str. Canada 63 J5 ....75.58N 88.58W
Jonglei d. Sudan 85 H2 ....7.17N 32.12E
Jönköping Sweden 40 C2 ....57.46N 14.09E
Jonquière Canada 63 K2 ....48.25N 71.14W
Joplin U.S.A. 65 H4 ....37.12N 94.31W
Jordan Asia 94 E6 ....31.17N 36.26E
Jörn Sweden 40 E4 ....65.03N 20.03E
Jos Nigeria 84 E2 ....9.55N 8.53E
Joseph Bonaparte Gulf Australia 110 B5 ....14.08S 128.39E
Jos Plateau f. Nigeria 82 D5 ....10.00N 9.00E
Juan Fernández, Archipiélago is S. Pacific Oc. 109 O3 ....33.24S 80.02W
Juàzeiro Brazil 77 L6 ....9.25S 40.26W
Juàzeiro do Norte Brazil 77 M6 ....7.11S 39.14W
Juba Sudan 85 H2 ....4.53N 31.38E
Jubba r. Somalia 85 I1 ....0.15S 42.37E
Jubbada Hoose d. Somalia 87 C3 ....0.16N 41.53E
Júcar r. Spain 48 E3 ....39.09N 0.13W
Juchitán Mexico 70 E4 ....16.29N 95.02W
Judenburg Austria 54 F2 ....47.11N 14.41E
Juist i. Germany 42 G6 ....53.40N 7.01E
Juiz de Fora Brazil 77 L3 ....21.46S 43.21W
Juliaca Peru 76 F4 ....15.28S 70.11W
Junction City U.S.A. 64 G4 ....39.03N 96.50W
Juneau U.S.A. 62 E3 ....58.19N 134.23W
Jungfrau mt. Switz. 50 B7 ....46.33N 7.58E
Junggar Pendi basin China 102 F7 ....45.02N 87.38E
Jura mts France/Switz. 44 F4 ....45.38N 5.26E
Jura i. Scotland 16 D4 ....56.02N 5.56W
Jura, Sound of str. Scotland 16 D3 ....55.51N 5.49W
Jurbarkas Lithuania 46 F5 ....55.05N 22.46E
Jūrmala Latvia 55 J7 ....56.57N 23.40E
Juruá r. Brazil 76 G7 ....2.39S 65.48W
Juruena r. Brazil 77 I6 ....7.21S 58.08W
Jutaí r. Brazil 76 G7 ....2.45S 66.58W
Jutland pen. Denmark 48 N2 ....56.13N 9.08E
Juventud, Isla de la i. Cuba 71 H5 ....21.27N 82.50W
Jyväskylä Finland 40 F3 ....62.14N 25.44E

K

K2 mt. China/Jammu and Kashmir 102 D5 ....35.52N 76.34E
Kaambooni Somalia 87 C2 ....1.41S 41.34E
Kaambooni, Raas pt Somalia 87 C2 ....1.34S 41.38E
Kabaena i. Indonesia 105 G2 ....5.15S 121.50E
Kabarnet Kenya 87 A3 ....0.31N 35.45E
Kābul Afgh. 95 K6 ....34.30N 69.11E
Kabwe Zambia 86 B3 ....14.27S 28.26E
Kachagalau mt. Kenya 87 A3 ....2.20N 35.04E
Kachchh, Gulf of India 96 C5 ....22.35N 68.57E
Kachug Rus. Fed. 59 L3 ....53.54N 105.47E
Kadam mt. Uganda 87 A3 ....1.47N 34.44E
Kadavu i. Fiji 115 G5 ....19.00S 178.10E
Kadıköy Turkey 57 H5 ....40.59N 29.01E
Kadirli Turkey 57 L3 ....37.22N 36.05E
Kadugli Sudan 85 G3 ....11.01N 29.42E
Kaduna Nigeria 84 E3 ....10.30N 7.25E
Kaesŏng N. Korea 103 N5 ....37.58N 126.33E
Kafireas, Akra c. Greece 56 F4 ....38.10N 24.35E
Kaga Bandoro C.A.R. 85 F2 ....6.57N 19.11E
Kagoshima Japan 106 B2 ....31.34N 130.33E
Kahramanmaraş Turkey 57 L3 ....37.35N 36.56E
Kai, Kepulauan is Indonesia 105 I2 ....5.26S 132.59E
Kaifeng China 103 K4 ....34.43N 114.24E
Kaimana Indonesia 105 I3 ....3.42S 133.49E
Kairouan Tunisia 52 F4 ....35.41N 10.06E
Kaiserslautern Germany 54 B3 ....49.27N 7.46E
Kaiyuan China 103 I2 ....23.40N 103.14E
Kajaani Finland 40 F4 ....64.13N 27.43E
Kajiado Kenya 87 B2 ....1.50S 36.47E
Kakamega Kenya 87 A3 ....0.17N 34.45E
Kakhovs'ke Vodoskhovyshche resr Ukraine 55 O2 ....47.00N 33.42E
Kakinada India 96 F4 ....16.59N 82.19E
Kaktovik U.S.A. 62 D5 ....70.04N 143.44W
Kakuma Kenya 87 A3 ....3.40N 34.53E
Kalacha Dida Kenya 87 B3 ....3.07N 37.36E
Kalahari Desert Africa 86 B2 ....23.25S 22.18E
Kalajoki Finland 40 E4 ....64.15N 23.57E
Kalamaria Greece 56 E5 ....40.36N 22.57E
Kalamata Greece 56 E3 ....37.02N 22.07E
Kalāt Afgh. 95 K6 ....32.05N 66.58E
Kalecik Turkey 57 J5 ....40.05N 33.26E
Kalemie Dem. Rep. Congo 86 B4 ....5.56S 29.08E
Kalgoorlie Australia 110 B3 ....30.50S 121.30E
Kaliakra, Nos pt Bulgaria 57 H6 ....43.22N 28.28E
Kalimantan f. Indonesia 104 E4 ....2.10S 111.35E
Kaliningrad Rus. Fed. 46 E5 ....54.42N 20.31E
Kalinkavichy Belarus 55 M5 ....52.08N 29.15E

Kalispell U.S.A. 64 D6 ....48.11N 114.19W
Kalisz Poland 46 D3 ....51.46N 18.05E
Kalixälven r. Sweden 40 E4 ....65.51N 23.08E
Kallavesi l. Finland 40 F3 ....62.47N 27.47E
Kallsjön l. Sweden 40 C3 ....63.37N 13.00E
Kalmar Sweden 40 D2 ....56.40N 16.22E
Kaltag U.S.A. 62 C4 ....64.20N 158.52W
Kaluga Rus. Fed. 58 E3 ....54.31N 36.16E
Kalundborg Denmark 40 B1 ....55.41N 11.06E
Kalush Ukraine 55 K3 ....49.02N 24.22E
Kama r. Rus. Fed. 58 G3 ....56.01N 53.46E
Kamaishi Japan 106 D3 ....39.16N 141.53E
Kaman Turkey 57 J4 ....39.22N 33.43E
Kamchatka Basin f. Bering Sea 108 H9 ..57.09N 166.28E
Kamchatka Peninsula Rus. Fed. 59 Q3 ..56.10N 159.12E
Kamenskoye Rus. Fed. 59 R4 ......62.33N 166.10E
Kamensk-Ural'skiy Rus. Fed. 58 H3 ....56.28N 61.48E
Kamina Dem. Rep. Congo 86 B4 ......8.44S 24.57E
Kamin'-Kashyrs'kyy Ukraine 55 K4 ....51.37N 24.58E
Kamloops Canada 62 F3 ....50.41N 120.21W
Kampala Uganda 85 H2 ....0.20N 32.34E
Kampen Neth. 42 E5 ....52.33N 5.55E
Kâmpóng Cham Cambodia 104 D6 ....11.59N 105.26E
Kâmpôt Cambodia 104 C6 ....10.36N 104.12E
Kamuli Uganda 87 A3 ....0.54N 33.06E
Kam''yanets'-Podil's'kyy Ukraine 55 L3 ..48.41N 26.35E
Kam''yanka-Buz'ka Ukraine 46 G3 ....50.06N 24.21E
Kamyshin Rus. Fed. 58 F3 ....50.06N 45.25E
Kananga Dem. Rep. Congo 86 B4 ......5.51S 22.22E
Kanazawa Japan 106 C3 ....36.34N 136.39E
Kanchipuram India 96 E3 ....12.51N 79.43E
Kandahār Afgh. 95 K6 ....31.37N 65.47E
Kandalaksha Rus. Fed. 40 H4 ......67.10N 32.22E
Kandalakshskiy Zaliv g. Rus. Fed. 40 H4 ..66.38N 33.25E
Kandıra Turkey 57 I5 ....41.04N 30.08E
Kandy Sri Lanka 96 F2 ....7.19N 80.34E
Kandyagash Kazakhstan 58 G2 ......49.27N 57.21E
Kangal Turkey 57 L4 ....39.14N 37.23E
Kangān Iran 95 H5 ....27.50N 52.05E
Kangaroo Island Australia 110 C3 ....35.48S 137.11E
Kangāvar Iran 95 G6 ....34.29N 47.51E
Kangchenjunga mt. India/Nepal 96 G6 ..27.41N 88.12E
Kangean, Kepulauan is Indonesia 104 F2 ..6.56S 115.12E
Kangertittivaq str. Greenland 63 P5 ....70.31N 24.44W
Kangetet Kenya 87 B3 ....1.58N 36.03E
Kangiqsualujjuaq Canada 63 L3 ....58.35N 65.45W
Kangiqsujuaq Canada 63 K4 ....61.34N 71.56W
Kangmar China 97 G3 ....28.30N 89.33E
Kangnŭng S. Korea 106 A3 ....37.46N 128.52E
Kanin, Poluostrov pen. Rus. Fed. 58 F4 ..68.00N 45.00E
Kankaanpää Finland 40 E3 ....61.49N 22.25E
Kankakee U.S.A. 65 I5 ....41.07N 87.51W
Kankan Guinea 84 D3 ....10.23N 9.19W
Kanker India 96 F5 ....20.16N 81.32E
Kano Nigeria 84 E3 ....12.01N 8.31E
Kanpur India 96 F6 ....26.27N 80.24E
Kansas d. U.S.A. 64 G4 ....38.35N 98.34W
Kansas r. U.S.A. 64 H4 ....39.07N 94.40W
Kansas City U.S.A. 65 H4 ....39.11N 94.45W
Kansk Rus. Fed. 59 K3 ....56.10N 95.43E
Kanta mt. Ethiopia 87 A4 ....6.10N 35.35E
Kantchari Burkina 84 E3 ....12.29N 1.30E
Kanton atoll Kiribati 108 I5 ......2.44S 171.42W
Kanye Botswana 86 B2 ....24.58S 25.21E
Kaohsiung Taiwan 103 M2 ....22.39N 120.20E
Kaokoveld f. Namibia 86 A3 ......17.41S 12.33E
Kaolack Senegal 84 C3 ....14.09N 16.04W
Kapchorwa Uganda 87 A3 ....1.27N 34.29E
Kapenguria Kenya 87 A3 ....1.21N 35.07E
Kapingamarangi Rise f. N. Pacific Oc. 108 G6 ..6.41N 150.16E
Kapoeta Sudan 87 A4 ....4.47N 33.35E
Kaposvár Hungary 54 G2 ....46.22N 17.48E
Kapsabet Kenya 87 A3 ....0.13N 35.08E
Kapuskasing Canada 63 J2 ....49.26N 82.26W
Kaputir Kenya 87 A3 ....2.05N 35.28E
Kara-Bogaz-Gol, Zaliv b. Turkmenistan 58 G2 ..41.24N 53.32E
Karabük Turkey 57 J5 ....41.11N 32.38E
Karabutak Kazakhstan 58 H2 ......49.55N 60.09E
Karachi Pakistan 96 C5 ....24.51N 67.03E
Karaganda Kazakhstan 58 I2 ......49.52N 73.04E
Karaginskiy Zaliv b. Rus. Fed. 59 R3 ..59.32N 164.48E
Karaj Iran 95 H7 ....35.45N 50.58E
Karakelong i. Indonesia 105 H4 ....4.22N 126.43E
Karakoram Range mts Asia 96 D8 ..36.18N 74.54E
Karakum Desert Turkmenistan 58 G2 ..38.58N 60.05E
Karaman Turkey 57 J3 ....37.11N 33.13E
Karamay China 102 E7 ....45.31N 84.54E
Karand Iran 95 G6 ....34.14N 46.16E
Karapınar Turkey 57 J3 ....37.43N 33.33E
Karasburg Namibia 86 A2 ....28.01S 18.45E
Kara Sea Rus. Fed. 58 I5 ....74.13N 71.44E
Karasuk Rus. Fed. 58 I3 ....53.43N 78.03E
Karbalā' Iraq 94 F6 ....32.36N 44.01E
Karcag Hungary 54 I2 ....47.19N 20.55E
Karditsa Greece 56 D4 ....39.21N 21.55E
Kärdla Estonia 40 E2 ....58.59N 22.45E
Kareima Sudan 85 H3 ....18.31N 31.49E
Kariba, Lake resr Zambia/Zimbabwe 86 B3 ..17.37S 27.17E
Karimata, Selat str. Indonesia 104 D3 ..1.50S 108.08E
Karimata, Kepulauan is Indonesia 104 D3 ..1.20S 109.00E
Karkinits'ka Zatoka g. Ukraine 53 J6 ..45.27N 32.11E
Karlovac Croatia 56 A7 ....45.29N 15.33E
Karlovo Bulgaria 56 F6 ....42.39N 24.48E
Karlovy Vary Czech Rep. 54 E4 ....50.14N 12.53E
Karlshamn Sweden 40 C2 ....56.11N 14.52E
Karlskoga Sweden 40 C2 ....59.20N 14.33E
Karlskrona Sweden 40 C2 ....56.10N 15.38E
Karlsruhe Germany 54 C3 ....49.01N 8.24E
Karlstad Sweden 40 C2 ....59.23N 13.31E
Karmøy i. Norway 40 A2 ....59.11N 5.15E
Karnataka d. India 96 E4 ....15.37N 75.29E
Karnobat Bulgaria 56 G6 ....42.38N 26.59E
Karora Eritrea 85 H3 ....17.41N 38.23E
Karpathos i. Greece 56 G2 ......35.29N 27.10E
Karpenisi Greece 56 D4 ....38.55N 21.48E
Kārsava Latvia 55 K7 ....56.47N 27.40E
Karşıyaka Turkey 56 G4 ....38.27N 27.06E
Karstula Finland 40 F3 ....62.53N 24.48E
Kartal Turkey 57 H5 ....40.54N 29.11E
Karungu Bay Kenya 87 A2 ....0.55S 33.59E
Karymskoye Rus. Fed. 59 M3 ......51.30N 114.25E
Kaş Turkey 57 H3 ....36.12N 29.37E
Kasaï r. Dem. Rep. Congo 86 A4 ....3.02S 16.58E
Kasama Zambia 86 C4 ....10.12S 31.12E
Kasese Uganda 85 H2 ....0.12N 30.05E
Kāshān Iran 95 H6 ....33.58N 51.30E
Kashi China 102 D5 ....39.29N 76.03E
Kashiwazaki Japan 106 C3 ....37.22N 138.34E
Kāshmar Iran 95 I7 ....35.10N 58.22E
Kasos i. Greece 56 G2 ....35.22N 26.55E
Kassala Sudan 85 H3 ....15.24N 36.20E
Kassel Germany 54 C4 ....51.19N 9.30E
Kasserine Tunisia 52 E4 ....35.11N 8.50E
Kastamonu Turkey 57 J5 ....41.22N 33.46E

Kastelli Greece 56 E2 ....35.30N 23.38E
Kastoria Greece 56 D5 ....40.31N 21.16E
Kastsyukovichy Belarus 55 O5 ....53.21N 32.09E
Katakwi Uganda 87 A3 ....1.54N 33.56E
Katerini Greece 56 E5 ....40.16N 22.31E
Katesh Tanzania 87 A1 ....4.32S 35.26E
Kate's Needle mt. Canada/U.S.A. 62 E3 ..57.02N 132.02W
Katha Myanmar 97 I5 ....24.11N 96.20E
Katherine Australia 110 C5 ......14.28S 132.18E
Kathmandu Nepal 96 G6 ....27.42N 85.18E
Kathua watercourse Kenya 87 B2 ..1.23S 39.09E
Katima Mulilo Namibia 86 B3 ....17.32S 24.15E
Katowice Poland 46 D3 ....50.16N 19.01E
Katrine, Loch l. Scotland 16 E4 ..56.15N 4.34W
Katrineholm Sweden 40 D2 ......58.59N 16.14E
Kattegat str. Denmark/Sweden 40 B2 ..56.49N 11.21E
Kauai i. U.S.A. 109 J7 ....22.10N 159.43W
Kauhajoki Finland 40 E3 ....62.25N 22.11E
Kaunas Lithuania 40 E1 ....54.54N 23.55E
Kaura-Namoda Nigeria 84 E3 ....12.37N 6.35E
Kavala Greece 56 F5 ....40.56N 24.23E
Kavarna Bulgaria 57 H6 ....43.26N 28.19E
Kavīr, Dasht-e des. Iran 95 H6 ..34.36N 54.41E
Kawasaki Japan 106 C3 ....35.32N 139.43E
Kawm Umbū Egypt 53 J1 ....24.28N 32.55E
Kayes Mali 84 C3 ....14.26N 11.27W
Kayseri Turkey 57 K4 ....38.43N 35.29E
Kazach'ye Rus. Fed. 59 O5 ......70.45N 136.09E
Kazakhstan Asia 58 H2 ....49.18N 82.53E
Kazan' Rus. Fed. 58 F3 ....55.47N 49.07E
Kazanlŭk Bulgaria 56 F6 ....42.37N 25.23E
Kāzerūn Iran 95 H5 ....29.37N 51.39E
Kazincbarcika Hungary 46 E2 ....48.16N 20.39E
Kea i. Greece 56 F3 ....37.38N 24.24E
Keady Northern Ireland 16 C2 ....54.15N 6.42W
Kearney U.S.A. 64 G5 ....40.43N 99.05W
Keban Baraji resr Turkey 57 M4 ..38.53N 38.55E
Kebkabiya Sudan 94 B2 ....13.37N 24.06E
Kebnekaise mt. Sweden 40 D4 ....67.55N 18.31E
Kebock Head Scotland 18 C3 ....58.03N 6.21W
Keçiören Turkey 57 J5 ....40.00N 32.50E
Kecskemét Hungary 54 H2 ....46.55N 19.42E
Kėdainiai Lithuania 40 E1 ....55.17N 23.59E
Kędzierzyn-Koźle Poland 46 D3 ..50.20N 18.13E
Keen, Mount hill Scotland 19 G1 ..56.58N 2.59W
Keetmanshoop Namibia 86 A2 ....26.35S 18.09E
Keewatin Canada 63 H6 ....49.46N 94.34W
Keflavík Iceland 40 X2 ....64.00N 22.34W
Kegworth England 10 D3 ....52.50N 1.17W
Keighley England 15 F2 ....53.52N 1.55W
Keitele l. Finland 40 F3 ....62.52N 26.00E
Keith Scotland 19 G2 ....57.33N 2.57W
Kelibia Tunisia 50 F2 ....36.51N 11.04E
Kelifskiy Uzboy f. Turkmenistan 95 J7 ..38.07N 63.33E
Kelkit r. Turkey 57 L5 ....40.51N 36.26E
Kellett, Cape Canada 62 F5 ......71.59N 125.59W
Kells Rep. of Ireland 41 E3 ......53.44N 6.52W
Kelmė Lithuania 46 F5 ....55.38N 22.56E
Kelo Chad 84 F2 ....9.18N 15.49E
Kelowna Canada 62 G2 ....49.53N 119.29W
Kelso Scotland 17 G3 ....55.36N 2.26W
Keluang Malaysia 104 C4 ....1.59N 103.19E
Kelvedon England 11 F2 ....51.50N 0.42E
Kem' Rus. Fed. 58 E4 ....64.57N 34.34E
Kemerovo Rus. Fed. 58 J3 ....55.23N 86.01E
Kemi Finland 40 F4 ....65.46N 24.33E
Kemijärvi Finland 40 F4 ....66.43N 27.23E
Kemijärvi l. Finland 40 F4 ......66.35N 27.25E
Kemijoki r. Finland 40 F4 ....65.47N 24.32E
Kemnay Scotland 19 G2 ....57.14N 2.27W
Kempston England 11 E3 ....52.07N 0.30W
Kempten Germany 54 D2 ....47.43N 10.18E
Kenai U.S.A. 62 C3 ....60.35N 151.16W
Kenamuke Swamp f. Sudan 87 A4 ..5.25N 34.00E
Kendal England 14 E3 ....54.20N 2.45W
Kendari Indonesia 105 G3 ......3.59S 122.35E
Kendawangan Indonesia 104 E3 ..2.30S 110.14E
Kengtung Myanmar 97 I5 ....21.18N 99.38E
Kenilworth England 10 D3 ......52.21N 1.35W
Kénitra Morocco 84 D5 ....34.16N 6.33W
Kenmare Rep. of Ireland 41 B1 ..51.53N 9.35W
Kenmare River inlet Rep. of Ireland 41 A1 ..51.43N 10.03W
Kennet r. England 10 E2 ....51.27N 0.57W
Kenora Canada 63 I2 ....49.47N 94.30W
Kent d. England 9 F2 ....51.12N 0.37E
Kent r. England 14 E3 ....54.15N 2.48W
Kentucky d. U.S.A. 65 J4 ....37.24N 84.54W
Kentucky r. U.S.A. 65 I4 ....38.41N 85.10W
Kenya Africa 87 B3 ....0.59N 37.32E
Kenya, Mount Kenya 87 B2 ......0.08S 37.18E
Kępno Poland 46 C3 ....51.17N 17.59E
Kerala d. India 96 E3 ....11.31N 75.51E
Kerch Ukraine 53 K6 ....45.22N 36.29E
Kerema P.N.G. 110 D6 ....7.56S 145.48E
Keren Eritrea 94 E3 ....15.46N 38.28E
Kericho Kenya 87 A2 ....0.22S 35.15E
Kerinci, Gunung vol. Indonesia 104 C3 ..1.42S 101.15E
Kerio watercourse Kenya 87 B3 ..2.56N 36.11E
Kerio Valley f. Kenya 87 A3 ....1.10N 35.45E
Kerki Turkmenistan 95 K7 ......37.51N 65.13E
Kerkyra Greece 56 C4 ....39.37N 19.55E
Kerma Sudan 94 D3 ....19.37N 30.26E
Kermadec Islands S. Pacific Oc. 108 I3 ..30.19S 178.19W
Kermadec Trench f. S. Pacific Oc. 108 I3 ..34.29S 177.56W
Kermān Iran 95 I6 ....30.17N 57.04E
Kermān Desert Iran 95 I5 ......28.27N 59.19E
Kermānshāh Iran 95 G6 ....34.19N 47.02E
Kerry d. Rep. of Ireland 41 B2 ..52.09N 9.28W
Kerry Head Rep. of Ireland 41 B2 ..52.25N 9.57W
Kesan Turkey 56 G5 ....40.51N 26.37E
Kesennuma Japan 106 D3 ....38.54N 141.33E
Kessingland England 11 G3 ......52.25N 1.43E
Keswick England 14 D3 ....54.36N 3.07W
Ketapang Indonesia 104 E3 ......1.50S 110.00E
Ketchikan U.S.A. 62 E3 ....55.20N 131.38W
Kettering England 11 E3 ....52.24N 0.44W
Keweenaw Bay U.S.A. 65 I6 ......46.52N 88.26W
Key, Lough l. Rep. of Ireland 41 C4 ..54.01N 8.15W
Keyala Sudan 87 A4 ....4.29N 32.51E
Keynsham England 10 C2 ....51.25N 2.30W
Kežmarok Slovakia 46 E4 ....49.09N 20.26E
Khabarovsk Rus. Fed. 59 O2 ....48.30N 135.08E
Khadyzhensk Rus. Fed. 57 M7 ..44.25N 39.32E
Khairpur Pakistan 102 B3 ......27.31N 68.49E
Khambhat, Gulf of India 96 D4 ..20.59N 71.29E
Khānābād Afgh. 95 K7 ....36.42N 69.09E
Khandwa India 96 E5 ....21.49N 76.21E
Khanewal Pakistan 96 L6 ....30.19N 71.59E
Khanka, Lake China/Rus. Fed. 103 O6 ..44.54N 132.45E
Khantayskoye, Ozero l. Rus. Fed. 59 K4 ..68.25N 91.57E
Khanty-Mansiysk Rus. Fed. 58 H4 ..61.05N 69.01E

Kharagpur India 96 G5 ....22.20N 87.20E
Kharkiv Ukraine 55 Q3 ....49.59N 36.16E
Khartoum Sudan 85 H3 ....15.32N 32.32E
Khāsh Iran 95 J5 ....28.12N 61.14E
Khashm el Girba Sudan 94 E2 ....14.56N 35.51E
Khaskovo Bulgaria 56 F5 ....41.56N 25.32E
Khatanga Rus. Fed. 59 L5 ......71.57N 102.24E
Khatangskiy Zaliv b. Rus. Fed. 59 L5 ..73.19N 107.17E
Khayelitsha S. Africa 86 A1 ....34.05S 18.39E
Khenchela Algeria 52 E4 ....35.26N 7.10E
Khenifra Morocco 52 B3 ....32.58N 5.37W
Kherson Ukraine 53 J6 ....46.39N 32.37E
Kheta r. Rus. Fed. 59 L5 ....71.55N 102.04E
Khimki Rus. Fed. 55 Q6 ....55.53N 37.26E
Khmel'nyts'kyy Ukraine 55 L3 ..49.25N 26.59E
Khon Kaen Thailand 104 C7 ....16.27N 102.52E
Khorinsk Rus. Fed. 103 J8 ......52.09N 109.48E
Khorramābād Iran 95 G6 ....33.27N 48.19E
Khorugh Tajikistan 95 L7 ......37.29N 71.35E
Khouribga Morocco 52 B3 ......32.53N 6.55W
Khowst Afgh. 95 K6 ....33.21N 69.59E
Khŭjand Tajikistan 102 B6 ......40.15N 69.38E
Khulna Bangl. 97 G5 ....22.50N 89.33E
Khunsar Iran 95 H6 ....33.10N 50.17E
Khust Ukraine 55 J3 ....48.10N 23.18E
Khvoy Iran 94 F7 ....38.33N 44.58E
Khyber Pass Afgh./Pakistan 95 L6 ..34.08N 71.12E
Kiambu Kenya 87 B2 ....1.13S 36.45E
Kiantajärvi l. Finland 40 G4 ....64.58N 29.06E
Kibaya Tanzania 87 B1 ....5.17S 36.33E
Kibre Mengist Ethiopia 87 B4 ..5.52N 38.57E
Kičevo Macedonia 56 D5 ....41.30N 20.58E
Kidderminster England 10 C3 ....52.23N 2.15W
Kidepo Valley National Park Uganda 87 A3 ..3.51N 33.48E
Kidsgrove England 15 E2 ....53.05N 2.14W
Kidwelly Wales 12 C3 ....51.44N 4.18W
Kiel Germany 54 D6 ....54.19N 10.08E
Kiel Canal Germany 40 B1 ......54.10N 9.27E
Kielce Poland 46 E3 ....50.51N 20.37E
Kielder Water resr England 15 E4 ..55.12N 2.34W
Kieler Bucht b. Germany 54 D6 ..54.27N 10.41E
Kiev Ukraine 55 N4 ....50.26N 30.34E
Kigali Rwanda 85 H1 ....1.59S 30.05E
Kigoma Tanzania 87 A1 ....4.51S 29.40E
Kii-sui̇do str. Japan 106 B2 ....33.57N 134.49E
Kikinda S.M. 56 D7 ....45.50N 20.28E
Kikori P.N.G. 110 D6 ....7.22S 144.14E
Kikwit Dem. Rep. Congo 86 A4 ..5.03S 18.50E
Kilbrannan Sound str. Scotland 16 D3 ..55.25N 5.27W
Kilcoole Rep. of Ireland 41 E3 ..53.06N 6.03W
Kilcormac Rep. of Ireland 41 D3 ..53.10N 7.44W
Kilcullen Rep. of Ireland 41 E3 ..53.08N 6.45W
Kildare Rep. of Ireland 41 E3 ..53.09N 6.55W
Kildare d. Rep. of Ireland 41 E3 ..53.17N 6.47W
Kilfi Kenya 87 B2 ....3.36S 39.51E
Kilimanjaro d. Tanzania 87 B2 ..3.15S 37.23E
Kilimanjaro vol. Tanzania 86 C4 ..3.03S 37.21E
Kilimanjaro National Park Tanzania 87 B2 ..3.01S 37.13E
Kilis Turkey 57 L3 ....36.43N 37.07E
Kilkee Rep. of Ireland 41 B2 ....52.41N 9.38W
Kilkeel Northern Ireland 16 D2 ..54.04N 5.59W
Kilkenny Rep. of Ireland 41 D2 ..52.39N 7.15W
Kilkenny d. Rep. of Ireland 41 D2 ..52.41N 7.14W
Kilkis Greece 56 E5 ....40.59N 22.52E
Killala Bay Rep. of Ireland 41 B4 ..54.16N 9.08W
Killarney Rep. of Ireland 41 B2 ..52.03N 9.30W
Killeen U.S.A. 64 G3 ....31.08N 97.44W
Killin Scotland 16 E4 ....56.28N 4.19W
Killorglin Rep. of Ireland 41 B2 ..52.06N 9.47W
Killybegs Rep. of Ireland 41 C4 ..54.38N 8.27W
Kilmallock Rep. of Ireland 41 C2 ..52.24N 8.35W
Kilmarnock Scotland 16 E3 ......55.37N 4.30W
Kilmelford Scotland 16 D4 ......56.16N 5.28W
Kilmichael Point Rep. of Ireland 41 E2 ..52.44N 6.08W
Kilrea Northern Ireland 16 C2 ..54.57N 6.33W
Kilrush Rep. of Ireland 41 B2 ..52.38N 9.29W
Kilsyth Scotland 17 E3 ....55.59N 4.03W
Kilwinning Scotland 16 E3 ......55.39N 4.42W
Kimberley S. Africa 86 B2 ......28.44S 24.46E
Kimberley Plateau f. Australia 110 B5 ..17.26S 127.05E
Kimch'aek N. Korea 103 N6 ....40.41N 129.12E
Kinabalu, Gunung mt. Malaysia 104 F5 ..6.04N 116.33E
Kinango Kenya 87 B1 ....4.08S 39.20E
Kinder Scout hill England 15 F2 ..53.23N 1.52W
Kindersley Canada 64 E7 ....51.28N 109.10W
Kindu Dem. Rep. Congo 86 B4 ..2.57S 25.53E
King Island Australia 110 D3 ....39.50S 143.58E
Kingman U.S.A. 64 D4 ....35.14N 114.02W
Kingsbridge England 13 D2 ......50.17N 3.47W
Kingsclere England 10 D2 ......51.19N 1.14W
Kingscourt Rep. of Ireland 41 E3 ..53.54N 6.48W
King's Lynn England 11 F3 ......52.45N 0.24E
Kingsmill Group is Kiribati 111 G6 ..1.37S 175.52E
Kingsnorth England 11 F2 ......51.07N 0.52E
Kings Peak U.S.A. 64 D5 ....40.45N 110.23W
Kingston Canada 63 K2 ....44.14N 76.30W
Kingston Jamaica 71 I4 ....18.00N 76.47W
Kingston upon Hull England 15 G2 ..53.45N 0.20W
Kingston upon Hull d. England 9 E3 ..53.46N 0.19W
Kingston upon Thames England 11 E2 ..51.25N 0.18W
Kingstown St Vincent 71 L3 ......13.10N 61.15W
Kingsville U.S.A. 64 G2 ....27.27N 97.47W
Kingswood England 10 C2 ......51.28N 2.30W
Kings Worthy England 10 D2 ....51.06N 1.18W
Kington England 10 B3 ....52.12N 3.02W
Kingussie Scotland 19 E2 ......57.05N 4.03W
King William Island Canada 63 I4 ..69.10N 97.45W
Kinlochbervie Scotland 18 D3 ..58.28N 5.03W
Kinlocheven Scotland 18 E1 ....56.43N 4.58W
Kinloss Scotland 19 F2 ....57.38N 3.34W
Kinna Sweden 40 C2 ....57.31N 12.40E
Kinnegad Rep. of Ireland 41 D3 ..53.27N 7.06W
Kinross Scotland 17 F4 ....56.12N 3.25W
Kinsale Rep. of Ireland 41 C1 ..51.42N 8.31W
Kinshasa Dem. Rep. Congo 86 A4 ..4.22S 15.23E
Kintore Scotland 19 G2 ....57.14N 2.21W
Kintyre pen. Scotland 16 D3 ....55.30N 5.39W
Kipini Kenya 87 C2 ....2.30S 40.32E
Kircubbin Northern Ireland 16 D2 ..54.29N 5.31W
Kiribati Pacific Oc. 108 I5 ......6.00S 164.59W
Kırıkhan Turkey 57 L3 ....36.29N 36.22E
Kırıkkale Turkey 57 J4 ....39.50N 33.30E
Kiritimati atoll Kiribati 109 J6 ..1.44N 157.13W
Kirkbean Scotland 17 F2 ....54.55N 3.36W
Kirkby England 14 E2 ....53.29N 2.54W
Kirkby in Ashfield England 15 F2 ..53.06N 1.16W
Kirkby Lonsdale England 14 E3 ..54.13N 2.36W
Kirkbymoorside England 15 G3 ..54.16N 0.56W
Kirkby Stephen England 15 E3 ..54.29N 2.21W
Kirkcaldy Scotland 17 F4 ......56.07N 3.09W
Kirkcolm Scotland 16 D2 ......54.58N 5.05W
Kirkconnel Scotland 17 E3 ......55.23N 4.00W
Kirkcudbright Scotland 17 E2 ..54.50N 4.03W
Kirkenes Norway 40 G5 ....69.43N 30.01E

Kirkham England 14 E2 ....53.47N 2.52W
Kirkintilloch Scotland 16 E3 ....55.56N 4.09W
Kirkkonummi Finland 40 F3 ....60.07N 24.27E
Kirkland Lake town Canada 63 J2 ..48.10N 80.02W
Kırklareli Turkey 56 G5 ....41.44N 27.13E
Kirk Michael Isle of Man 14 C3 ..54.17N 4.35W
Kirkūk Iraq 94 F7 ....35.24N 44.24E
Kirkwall Scotland 19 G3 ....58.59N 2.58W
Kirov Rus. Fed. 55 P6 ....54.04N 34.20E
Kirovohrad Ukraine 55 O3 ......48.30N 32.16E
Kirovsk Rus. Fed. 40 G2 ....59.52N 30.59E
Kirovsk Rus. Fed. 40 H4 ....67.37N 33.40E
Kirriemuir Scotland 19 F1 ......56.41N 3.00W
Kırşehir Turkey 57 J4 ....39.09N 34.09E
Kirtlington England 10 D2 ......51.52N 1.16W
Kirton in Lindsey England 15 G2 ..53.29N 0.35W
Kiruna Sweden 40 E4 ....67.51N 20.24E
Kisangani Dem. Rep. Congo 86 B5 ..0.34N 25.11E
Kisii Kenya 87 A2 ....0.42S 34.46E
Kislovodsk Rus. Fed. 53 L5 ....43.55N 42.44E
Kismaayo Somalia 85 I1 ....0.19S 42.31E
Kisoro Uganda 85 G1 ....1.17S 29.45E
Kisumu Kenya 87 A2 ....0.04S 34.47E
Kita-Kyūshū Japan 106 B2 ......33.52N 130.50E
Kitale Kenya 87 A3 ....1.01N 35.00E
Kitami Japan 106 D4 ....43.49N 143.53E
Kitgum Uganda 87 A3 ....3.16N 32.53E
Kitimat Canada 62 F3 ....54.03N 128.39W
Kittilä Finland 40 F4 ....67.38N 24.54E
Kitui Kenya 87 B2 ....1.22S 38.00E
Kitwe Zambia 86 B3 ....12.48S 28.12E
Kiurvesi Finland 40 F3 ....63.39N 26.38E
Kivu, Lake Dem. Rep. Congo/Rwanda 86 B4 ..1.55S 29.09E
Kızıl Dağı mt. Turkey 57 M4 ..39.57N 38.12E
Kızılırmak r. Turkey 57 K5 ....41.49N 35.54E
Kladno Czech Rep. 54 F4 ......50.09N 14.08E
Klagenfurt Austria 54 F2 ......46.38N 14.19E
Klaipėda Lithuania 40 E1 ......55.43N 21.09E
Klamath r. U.S.A. 64 B5 ......41.27N 124.02W
Klamath Falls town U.S.A. 64 B5 ..42.15N 121.46W
Klazienaveen Neth. 42 F5 ......52.44N 6.59E
Kleve Germany 42 F4 ....51.47N 6.08E
Klimovo Rus. Fed. 55 O5 ......52.23N 32.12E
Klintsy Rus. Fed. 55 O5 ....52.45N 32.15E
Kłodzko Poland 46 C3 ....50.26N 16.39E
Kluczbork Poland 46 D3 ....50.58N 18.13E
Klyuchevskaya, Sopka vol. Rus. Fed. 59 R3 ..56.01N 160.41E
Knaresborough England 15 F3 ..54.01N 1.28W
Knighton Wales 12 D4 ....52.20N 3.03W
Knin Croatia 56 B7 ....44.03N 16.12E
Knockaboy hill Rep. of Ireland 41 B1 ..51.48N 9.26W
Knockadoon Head Rep. of Ireland 41 D1 ..51.53N 7.52W
Knockalongy hill Rep. of Ireland 41 C4 ..54.12N 8.45W
Knock Hill Scotland 19 G2 ......57.35N 2.46W
Knocklayd hill Northern Ireland 16 C3 ..55.10N 6.15W
Knockmealdown Mountains hills Rep. of Ireland 41 C2 ..52.14N 8.04W
Knottingley England 15 F2 ......53.42N 1.15W
Knowle England 10 D3 ....52.23N 1.44W
Knoxville U.S.A. 65 J4 ....35.59N 83.56W
Knutsford England 15 E2 ......53.18N 2.22W
Kōbe Japan 106 C2 ....34.41N 135.11E
Koblenz Germany 54 B4 ....50.21N 7.35E
Kobroör i. Indonesia 105 I2 ....6.07S 134.30E
Kobryn Belarus 55 K5 ....52.12N 24.20E
Kočani Macedonia 56 E5 ....41.55N 22.23E
Kōchi Japan 106 B2 ....33.33N 133.32E
Kodiak U.S.A. 62 C3 ....57.46N 152.30W
Kodiak Island U.S.A. 62 C3 ....57.26N 153.20W
Kōfu Japan 106 C3 ....35.39N 138.34E
Køge Denmark 40 C1 ....55.27N 12.11E
Kohat Pakistan 95 L6 ....33.37N 71.30E
Kokand Uzbekistan 102 C6 ....40.31N 70.57E
Kokkola Finland 40 E3 ....63.51N 23.08E
Kokpekti Kazakhstan 102 E7 ..48.46N 82.21E
Kokshetau Kazakhstan 58 H3 ..53.17N 69.23E
Kola Rus. Fed. 40 H5 ....68.52N 33.03E
Kolaka Indonesia 105 G3 ......4.03S 121.38E
Kola Peninsula Rus. Fed. 58 E4 ..67.29N 34.49E
Kolding Denmark 40 B1 ....55.29N 9.30E
Kolguyev, Ostrov i. Rus. Fed. 58 F4 ..69.07N 49.03E
Kolhapur India 96 D4 ....16.40N 74.19E
Kolkata India 96 G5 ....22.32N 88.21E
Kolobrzeg Poland 46 C5 ......54.11N 15.35E
Kolomna Rus. Fed. 55 Q6 ......55.05N 38.50E
Kolomyya Ukraine 55 K3 ......48.32N 25.02E
Koluli Eritrea 94 F2 ....14.24N 40.20E
Kolvitskoye, Ozero l. Rus. Fed. 40 H4 ..67.04N 33.36E
Kolwezi Dem. Rep. Congo 86 B3 ..10.42S 25.28E
Kolyma r. Rus. Fed. 59 R4 ......69.22N 161.24E
Kolymskiy, Khrebet mts Rus. Fed. 59 R4 ..66.50N 167.12E
Komatsu Japan 106 C3 ....36.23N 136.28E
Kome Island Uganda 87 A2 ......0.06S 32.49E
Komotini Greece 56 F5 ....41.07N 25.24E
Komsomolets, Ostrov i. Rus. Fed. 59 K6 ..80.42N 94.20E
Komsomol's'k Ukraine 55 O3 ..49.01N 33.39E
Komsomol'sk-na-Amure Rus. Fed. 59 O3 ..50.36N 136.55E
Kondoa Tanzania 87 A1 ....4.55S 35.47E
Kong Christian IX Land f. Greenland 63 O4 ..66.49N 37.44W
Kongsberg Norway 40 B2 ......59.40N 9.39E
Kongsvinger Norway 40 C3 ....60.10N 12.00E
Konin Poland 46 D4 ....52.14N 18.15E
Konotop Ukraine 55 O4 ....51.14N 33.12E
Konso Ethiopia 87 B4 ....5.17N 37.29E
Konstanz Germany 54 C2 ......47.40N 9.10E
Konya Turkey 57 J3 ....37.52N 32.29E
Köping Sweden 40 D2 ....59.31N 16.00E
Koprivnica Croatia 54 G2 ......46.10N 16.50E
Kora National Park Kenya 87 B2 ..0.30S 39.00E
Korçë Albania 56 D5 ....40.38N 20.47E
Korčula i. Croatia 56 B6 ......42.54N 16.56E
Korea Bay China/N. Korea 103 M5 ..39.05N 124.20E
Korea Strait Japan/S. Korea 106 A2 ..34.25N 128.36E
Körfez Turkey 57 H5 ....40.47N 29.42E
Korinthiakos Kolpos str. Greece 56 E4 ..38.16N 22.11E
Köriyama Japan 106 D3 ....37.24N 140.22E
Korkuteli Turkey 57 I3 ....37.04N 30.11E
Korogwe Tanzania 87 B1 ......5.09S 38.30E
Koror Palau 105 I5 ....7.21N 134.28E
Körös r. Hungary 46 I2 ....46.42N 20.11E
Korosten' Ukraine 55 M4 ......50.57N 28.39E
Koro Toro Chad 85 F3 ....16.05N 18.30E
Korsakov Rus. Fed. 59 P2 ......46.38N 142.45E
Korsze Poland 46 E5 ....54.11N 21.08E
Kortrijk Belgium 42 C3 ....50.49N 3.16E
Koryakskiy Khrebet mts Rus. Fed. 59 S4 ..62.59N 177.49E
Kos i. Greece 56 G3 ....36.46N 27.07E
Kościan Poland 46 C4 ....52.05N 16.39E
Kościerzyna Poland 46 C5 ......54.07N 17.59E
Kosciuszko, Mount Australia 110 D3 ..36.28S 148.15E
Košice Slovakia 54 I3 ....48.43N 21.16E
Kosovska Mitrovica S.M. 56 D6 ..42.52N 20.52E
Kosrae atoll Micronesia 108 G6 ..5.19N 163.04E
Kostanay Kazakhstan 58 H3 ....53.12N 63.40E

Kosti Sudan 85 H3 ....13.09N 32.38E
Kostroma Rus. Fed. 58 F3 ....57.46N 40.58E
Kostrzyn Poland 46 B4 ....52.35N 14.39E
Koszalin Poland 46 C5 ....54.11N 16.11E
Kota India 96 E6 ....25.10N 75.57E
Kota Bharu Malaysia 104 C5 ....6.08N 102.16E
Kotabumi Indonesia 104 C3 ....4.51S 104.55E
Kota Kinabalu Malaysia 104 F5 ....5.58N 116.05E
Kotel'nyy Rus. Fed. 59 O5 ....76.00N 137.59E
Kotel'nyy, Ostrov i. Rus. Fed. 59 O5 ....75.07N 139.31E
Kotido Uganda 87 A3 ....2.59N 34.06E
Kotlas Rus. Fed. 58 F4 ....61.16N 46.38E
Kötlutangi pt Iceland 40 Y1 ....63.24N 18.45W
Kotuy r. Rus. Fed. 59 L5 ....71.55N 102.06E
Kotzebue U.S.A. 62 B4 ....66.53N 162.32W
Kotzebue Sound str. U.S.A. 62 B4 ....66.33N 163.11W
Koundâra Guinea 84 C3 ....12.30N 13.19W
Kouvola Finland 40 F3 ....60.52N 26.42E
Kovel' Ukraine 55 K4 ....51.13N 24.43E
Kowloon China 104 E8 ....22.20N 114.13E
Kozan Turkey 57 K3 ....37.28N 35.48E
Kozani Greece 56 D3 ....40.18N 21.48E
Kozhikode India 96 E3 ....11.15N 75.45E
Kozyatyn Ukraine 55 M3 ....49.42N 28.49E
Krabi Thailand 104 B5 ....8.05N 98.56E
Krâchéh Cambodia 104 D6 ....12.27N 106.03E
Kragujevac S.M. 56 D7 ....44.01N 20.55E
Kraków Poland 46 D3 ....50.03N 19.56E
Kraljevo S.M. 53 H5 ....43.43N 20.41E
Kramfors Sweden 40 D3 ....62.56N 17.46E
Kranj Slovenia 54 F2 ....46.15N 14.21E
Krasino Rus. Fed. 58 G5 ....70.44N 54.28E
Krasnoarmiys'k Ukraine 53 K6 ....48.17N 37.10E
Krasnodar Rus. Fed. 58 E2 ....45.02N 38.59E
Krasnohrad Ukraine 55 P3 ....49.22N 35.28E
Krasnoperekops'k Ukraine 57 J7 ....45.57N 33.49E
Krasnoyarsk Rus. Fed. 59 K3 ....56.03N 92.50E
Krefeld Germany 54 B4 ....51.20N 6.33E
Kremenchuk Ukraine 55 O3 ....49.04N 33.25E
Kremenchuts'ka Vodoskhovyshche resr Ukraine 55 O3
..............49.18N 32.42E
Křemešník hill Czech Rep. 46 B2 ....49.24N 15.20E
Kretinga Lithuania 46 E5 ....55.53N 21.14E
Krishna r. India 96 F4 ....16.01N 80.53E
Kristiansand Norway 40 A2 ....58.08N 7.59E
Kristianstad Sweden 40 C2 ....56.02N 14.10E
Kristiansund Norway 40 A3 ....63.07N 7.45E
Kristinehamn Sweden 40 C2 ....59.19N 14.07E
Krk i. Croatia 56 A7 ....45.02N 14.47E
Kropotkin Rus. Fed. 53 L6 ....45.26N 40.34E
Krosno Poland 46 E3 ....49.41N 21.46E
Krotoszyn Poland 46 C3 ....51.42N 17.27E
Kruševac S.M. 56 D6 ....43.35N 21.19E
Krychaw Belarus 55 N5 ....53.44N 31.43E
Krymsk Rus. Fed. 57 L7 ....44.55N 37.59E
Krytiko Pelagos sea Greece 56 F3 ....36.11N 26.57E
Kryvyy Rih Ukraine 55 O2 ....47.54N 33.21E
Ksabi Algeria 84 D4 ....28.54N 0.47W
Ksar el Boukhari Algeria 52 D4 ....35.52N 2.45E
Ksar el Kebir Morocco 52 B4 ....35.01N 5.54W
Kuala Lumpur Malaysia 104 C4 ....3.06N 101.42E
Kuala Terengganu Malaysia 104 C5 ....5.19N 103.07E
Kuantan Malaysia 104 C4 ....3.50N 103.21E
Kuban' r. Rus. Fed. 57 L7 ....45.19N 37.22E
Kuching Malaysia 104 E4 ....1.32N 110.20E
Kugluktuk Canada 62 G4 ....67.46N 115.07W
Kuhmo Finland 40 G4 ....64.07N 29.30E
Kuito Angola 86 A3 ....12.23S 16.57E
Kujū-san vol. Japan 106 B2 ....33.05N 131.16E
Kūl r. Iran 95 I5 ....27.04N 55.44E
Kulal, Mount Kenya 87 B3 ....2.42N 36.58E
Kuldīga Latvia 46 E2 ....56.58N 21.59E
Külob Tajikistan 95 K7 ....37.54N 69.51E
Kulunda Rus. Fed. 102 D8 ....52.33N 78.56E
Kulundinskoye, Ozero l. Rus. Fed. 102 D8 ....53.08N 79.46E
Kumamoto Japan 106 B2 ....32.47N 130.43E
Kumanovo Macedonia 56 D6 ....42.08N 21.43E
Kumasi Ghana 84 D2 ....6.4N 1.38W
Kumbakonam India 96 E3 ....10.58N 79.23E
Kumertau Rus. Fed. 58 G3 ....52.44N 55.46E
Kumla Sweden 40 C2 ....59.07N 15.10E
Kumo Nigeria 84 F3 ....10.06N 11.11E
Kunashir, Ostrov i. Rus. Fed. 106 E4 ....44.13N 146.23E
Kunlun Shan mts China 102 D5 ....36.11N 78.10E
Kunming China 103 I3 ....25.02N 102.44E
Kuohijärvi l. Finland 40 Y3 ....61.12N 24.59E
Kuopio Finland 40 F3 ....62.53N 27.41E
Kupa r. Croatia/Slovenia 56 B7 ....45.28N 16.25E
Kupang Indonesia 105 G1 ....10.12S 123.35E
Kupiškis Lithuania 40 F1 ....55.49N 24.59E
Kuqa China 102 E3 ....41.38N 83.01E
Kürdzhali Bulgaria 56 F5 ....41.38N 25.22E
Kure Atoll U.S.A. 108 I7 ....28.20N 178.17W
Kuressaare Estonia 40 E2 ....58.16N 22.29E
Kurgan Rus. Fed. 58 H3 ....55.28N 65.23E
Kurikka Finland 40 E3 ....62.37N 22.25E
Kuril Basin f. N. Pacific Oc. 108 F9 ....45.53N 145.16E
Kuril Islands Rus. Fed. 59 P2 ....46.04N 148.33E
Kuril'sk Rus. Fed. 59 P2 ....45.13N 147.57E
Kuril Trench f. N. Pacific Oc. 117 Q8 ....41.44N 146.31E
Kurmuk Sudan 85 H3 ....10.31N 34.16E
Kurnool India 96 E3 ....15.49N 77.59E
Kursk Rus. Fed. 58 E3 ....51.45N 36.12E
Kuršumlija S.M. 56 D6 ....43.08N 21.17E
Kurume Japan 106 B2 ....33.18N 130.31E
Kurun r. Sudan 87 A4 ....5.37N 34.33E
Kurunegala Sri Lanka 96 F2 ....7.30N 80.19E
Kuşadası Turkey 56 G3 ....37.52N 27.15E
Kushiro Japan 106 D4 ....42.59N 144.23E
Kuskokwim Mountains U.S.A. 62 C4 ....64.24N 155.17W
Kütahya Turkey 57 H4 ....39.25N 29.59E
Kutno Poland 46 D4 ....52.14N 19.22E
Kuujjuaq Canada 63 L3 ....58.10N 68.13W
Kuusamo Finland 40 G4 ....65.58N 29.09E
Kuwait Asia 95 G5 ....29.22N 47.08E
Kuwait town Kuwait 95 G5 ....29.18N 47.55E
Kuytun China 102 E3 ....44.20N 84.55E
Kuznetsk Rus. Fed. 58 F3 ....53.07N 46.37E
Kvaløya r. Norway 40 D5 ....69.38N 18.30E
Kwale Kenya 87 B1 ....4.12S 39.27E
KwaMashu S. Africa 86 C2 ....29.44S 30.59E
Kwa Mtoro Tanzania 87 A1 ....5.15S 35.25E
Kwangju S. Korea 103 N5 ....35.09N 126.54E
Kwania, Lake Uganda 85 H2 ....1.46N 32.63E
Kwanobuhle S. Africa 86 B1 ....33.48S 25.24E
Kwilu r. Angola/Dem. Rep. Congo 86 A4 ....3.23S 17.22E
Kwoka mt. Indonesia 105 I3 ....0.38S 132.28E
Kyakhta Rus. Fed. 59 L3 ....50.21N 106.30E
Kybartai Lithuania 46 F5 ....54.38N 22.46E
Kyle of Lochalsh Scotland 18 D2 ....57.17N 5.43W
Kyle of Tongue inlet Scotland 19 E3 ....58.28N 4.27W
Kyllíni mt. Greece 56 E3 ....37.56N 22.24E
Kyoga, Lake Uganda 85 H2 ....1.28N 32.53E

Kyōto Japan 106 C2 ....34.59N 135.46E
Kyparissia Greece 56 D3 ....37.15N 21.41E
Kypshak, Ozero l. Kazakhstan 58 H3 ....50.09N 68.23E
Kyrenia Cyprus 57 J2 ....35.20N 33.19E
Kyrgyzstan Asia 102 C6 ....41.47N 74.37E
Kythira i. Greece 56 E3 ....36.16N 22.55E
Kythnos i. Greece 56 F3 ....37.26N 24.27E
Kyūshū i. Japan 106 B2 ....32.20N 130.50E
Kyushu-Palau Ridge f. N. Pacific Oc. 108 F7 ....27.44N 135.16E
Kyustendil Bulgaria 56 E6 ....42.17N 22.41E
Kyyivs'ke Vodoskhovyshche resr Ukraine 55 N4 ....50.54N 30.30E
Kyzyl Rus. Fed. 59 K3 ....51.43N 94.24E
Kyzylorda Kazakhstan 58 H2 ....44.51N 65.30E

L

Laâyoune Western Sahara 84 C4 ....27.09N 13.12W
La Banda Argentina 76 H2 ....27.41S 64.15W
Labé Guinea 84 C3 ....11.20N 12.18W
Labrador f. Canada 63 L3 ....54.04N 62.29W
Labrador City Canada 63 L3 ....52.59N 66.54W
Labrador Sea Canada/Greenland 63 M4 ....60.07N 56.06W
Laccadive Islands India 96 E3 ....10.59N 72.11E
Laceby England 15 G2 ....53.32N 0.10W
Lachlan r. Australia 110 D3 ....34.21S 143.57E
La Crosse U.S.A. 65 H5 ....43.48N 91.12W
Ladhar Bheinn mt. Scotland 18 D2 ....57.05N 5.35W
Ladoga, Lake Rus. Fed. 58 E4 ....60.48N 31.27E
Ladybank Scotland 17 F4 ....56.17N 3.08W
Ladybower Reservoir England 15 F2 ....53.23N 1.45W
Ladysmith S. Africa 86 B2 ....28.34S 29.47E
Lae P.N.G. 110 D6 ....6.43S 147.00E
Læsø i. Denmark 40 B2 ....57.15N 11.05E
Lafayette U.S.A. 65 H3 ....30.14N 92.03W
Lagan r. Northern Ireland 16 D2 ....54.37N 5.54W
Laggan, Loch l. Scotland 19 E1 ....56.56N 4.31W
Lagh Bogal watercourse Kenya/Somalia 87 C3 ....0.42N 40.57E
Lagh Bor watercourse Kenya/Somalia 87 C3 ....0.31N 42.04E
Lagh Dima watercourse Kenya/Somalia 87 C3 ....0.31N 41.03E
Lagh Kutulo watercourse Kenya/Somalia 87 C3 ....2.04N 40.58E
Laghouat Algeria 84 E5 ....33.42N 2.53E
Lagh Walde watercourse Ethiopia/Kenya 87 B3 ....2.38N 38.53E
La Gomera i. Canary Islands 48 X2 ....28.14N 17.18W
Lagos Nigeria 84 E2 ....6.26N 3.20E
Lagos Portugal 48 A2 ....37.06N 8.41W
La Grande U.S.A. 64 C6 ....45.19N 118.02W
La Grande 2, Réservoir Canada 63 K3 ....53.52N 76.54W
La Grande 3, Réservoir Canada 63 K3 ....53.36N 75.18W
La Grande 4, Réservoir Canada 63 K3 ....54.13N 73.17W
La Gran Sabana f. Venezuela 71 L2 ....5.13N 61.40W
Lahad Datu Malaysia 104 F5 ....5.02N 118.20E
Lahat Indonesia 104 C3 ....3.46S 103.34E
Lahij Yemen 94 F2 ....13.02N 44.50E
Lāhījān Iran 95 G7 ....37.11N 49.56E
Lahti Finland 40 F3 ....60.59N 25.41E
Laidon, Loch l. Scotland 19 E1 ....56.39N 4.39W
Laihia Finland 40 E3 ....62.58N 22.01E
Lainioälven r. Sweden 40 E4 ....67.22N 22.39E
Lairg Scotland 19 E3 ....58.01N 4.24W
Lajes Brazil 77 J2 ....27.44S 50.19W
Lake City U.S.A. 65 J3 ....30.10N 82.39W
Lake District f. England 14 D3 ....54.30N 3.10W
Lakeland U.S.A. 65 J2 ....27.59N 81.58W
Lakki Pakistan 95 L6 ....32.35N 70.58E
Lakonikos Kolpos b. Greece 56 E3 ....36.32N 22.42E
Laksefjorden str. Norway 40 F5 ....70.52N 27.00E
Lakshadweep d. India 96 D3 ....10.35N 73.13E
La Línea de la Concepción Spain 48 C2 ....36.10N 5.21W
La Louvière Belgium 42 D3 ....50.28N 4.11E
La Mancha f. Spain 48 D3 ....39.15N 2.58W
Lamar U.S.A. 64 F4 ....38.06N 102.38W
Lamard Iran 95 H5 ....27.22N 53.08E
La Marmora, Punta mt. Italy 50 C3 ....39.59N 9.20E
La Martre, Lac l. Canada 62 G4 ....63.19N 118.02W
Lambay Island Rep. of Ireland 41 F3 ....53.29N 5.59W
Lambourn England 10 D2 ....51.30N 1.32W
Lambourn Downs hills England 10 D2 ....51.32N 1.32W
Lamego Portugal 48 B4 ....41.06N 7.48W
Lamia Greece 56 E4 ....38.54N 22.25E
Lamlash Scotland 16 D3 ....55.32N 5.07W
Lammermuir Hills Scotland 17 G3 ....55.49N 2.50W
Lampang Thailand 104 B7 ....18.16N 99.32E
Lampeter Wales 12 C4 ....52.07N 4.05W
Lamu Kenya 87 C2 ....2.18S 40.52E
Lamu Island Kenya 87 C2 ....2.19S 40.50E
Lanark Scotland 17 F3 ....55.40N 3.47W
Lancashire d. England 9 D3 ....53.57N 2.51W
Lancaster England 14 E3 ....54.03N 2.48W
Lancaster U.S.A. 65 K5 ....40.03N 76.19W
Lancaster Canal England 14 E3 ....53.59N 2.48W
Lancaster Sound str. Canada 63 J5 ....74.15N 89.18W
Landeck Austria 54 D2 ....47.08N 10.34E
Lander U.S.A. 64 E5 ....42.50N 108.42W
Landes f. France 44 C4 ....44.48N 0.55W
Landguard Point England 11 G2 ....51.56N 1.19E
Land's End England 13 B2 ....50.03N 5.46W
Landshut Germany 54 E3 ....48.33N 12.10E
Landskrona Sweden 54 E6 ....55.52N 12.50E
Lanesborough Rep. of Ireland 41 D3 ....53.40N 7.59W
Langavat, Loch l. W. Isles Scotland 18 C3 ....57.48N 6.59W
Langavat, Loch l. W. Isles Scotland 18 C3 ....58.02N 6.49W
Langeland i. Denmark 40 B1 ....55.02N 10.55E
Langeoog i. Germany 42 G6 ....53.46N 7.36E
Langholm Scotland 17 F3 ....55.09N 2.59W
Langøya i. Norway 40 C5 ....68.44N 14.27E
Langport England 10 C2 ....51.02N 2.50W
Langres France 44 F5 ....47.52N 5.20E
Langsa Indonesia 104 B4 ....4.25S 97.52E
Langstrothdale Chase hills England 15 E3 ....54.13N 2.18W
Languedoc f. France 44 D3 ....43.10N 1.57E
Lanivet England 13 C2 ....50.26N 4.46W
Länkäran Azerbaijan 95 G7 ....38.45N 48.51E
Lannion France 44 B6 ....48.44N 3.27W
Lanzarote i. Canary Islands 48 Z2 ....29.09N 13.35W
Lanzhou China 103 I5 ....36.04N 103.43E
Laoag Phil. 104 G7 ....18.14N 120.36E
Lao Cai Vietnam 104 C8 ....22.28N 103.57E
Laois d. Rep. of Ireland 41 D2 ....52.57N 7.23W
Laon France 44 E6 ....49.34N 3.38E
Laos Asia 104 C7 ....19.30N 103.01E
La Palma i. Canary Islands 48 X2 ....28.33N 17.44W
La Palma Panama 71 I2 ....8.21N 78.11W
La Palma del Condado Spain 48 B2 ....37.23N 6.33W
La Paragua Venezuela 71 L2 ....6.50N 63.19W
La Paz Bolivia 76 G4 ....16.30S 68.10W
La Paz Mexico 70 B5 ....24.08N 110.17W
La Pérouse Strait Japan/Rus. Fed. 106 D5 ....45.35N 141.33E
La Plata Argentina 73 D3 ....34.55S 57.58W
La Plata, Río de plat. Argentina/Uruguay 73 D3 ....35.15S 57.08W
Lappajärvi l. Finland 40 E3 ....63.07N 23.41E
Lappeenranta Finland 40 G3 ....61.03N 28.11E

Lappland f. Europe 40 D4 ....67.12N 18.37E
Laptev Sea Rus. Fed. 59 N5 ....76.05N 125.40E
Lapua Finland 40 E3 ....62.58N 23.00E
L'Aquila Italy 50 E5 ....42.22N 13.24E
Larache Morocco 52 B4 ....35.12N 6.09W
Laramie U.S.A. 64 E5 ....41.20N 105.36W
Laredo U.S.A. 64 G2 ....27.30N 99.30W
La Rioja Argentina 73 C4 ....29.25S 66.51W
Larisa Greece 56 E4 ....39.38N 22.25E
Larkana Pakistan 96 C6 ....27.31N 68.15E
Larnaca Cyprus 57 J2 ....34.55N 33.38E
Larne Northern Ireland 16 D2 ....54.51N 5.49W
Larne d. Northern Ireland 8 C4 ....54.55N 5.43W
Larne Lough inlet Northern Ireland 16 D2 ....54.49N 5.47W
La Rochelle France 44 C5 ....46.10N 1.09W
La Roche-sur-Yon France 44 C5 ....46.40N 1.25W
La Ronge Canada 62 H3 ....55.06N 105.17W
Larvik Norway 40 B2 ....59.03N 10.05E
La Sagra f. Spain 48 D4 ....40.05N 3.56W
La Sagra mt. Spain 48 D2 ....37.58N 2.35W
Las Cruces U.S.A. 64 E3 ....32.19N 106.47W
La Serena Chile 73 B4 ....29.53S 71.16W
Lashio Myanmar 97 I5 ....22.57N 97.44E
Las Marismas marsh Spain 48 B2 ....37.07N 6.35W
Las Palmas de Gran Canaria Canary Islands 48 Y2
..............28.06N 15.26W
La Spezia Italy 50 C6 ....44.07N 9.49E
Las Tórtolas, Cerro mt. Chile 73 C4 ....29.56S 69.52W
Las Tunas Cuba 71 I5 ....20.57N 76.57W
Las Vegas U.S.A. 64 C4 ....36.10N 115.09W
Las Villuercas mt. Spain 48 C3 ....39.29N 5.23W
Latacunga Ecuador 76 E7 ....0.58S 78.37W
Latakia Syria 94 E7 ....35.31N 35.47E
Latheron Scotland 19 F3 ....58.17N 3.22W
Latina Italy 50 E4 ....41.28N 12.54E
La Tortuga, Isla i. Venezuela 71 K3 ....10.58N 65.17W
La Tuque Canada 65 L6 ....47.27N 72.47W
Latvia Europe 40 E2 ....56.47N 23.49E
Lauchhammer Germany 54 E4 ....51.30N 13.46E
Launceston Australia 110 D2 ....41.27S 147.09E
Launceston England 13 C2 ....50.38N 4.21W
Laurencekirk Scotland 19 G1 ....56.50N 2.28W
Lausanne Switz. 50 H7 ....46.32N 6.39E
Laut i. Indonesia 104 F3 ....3.39S 116.18E
Laval France 44 C6 ....48.04N 0.46W
Lavenham England 11 F3 ....52.06N 0.48E
Lawton U.S.A. 64 G3 ....34.37N 98.24W
Lawz, Jabal al mt. Saudi Arabia 53 K2 ....28.39N 35.18E
Laxey Isle of Man 14 C3 ....54.14N 4.24W
Laxford, Loch inlet Scotland 18 D3 ....58.25N 5.08W
Laysan Island U.S.A. 108 I7 ....25.47N 171.43W
Lázaro Cárdenas Baja Calif. Mexico 70 A7 ....30.30N 115.56W
Lázaro Cárdenas Michoacán Mexico 70 D4 ....17.57N 102.12W
Leader Water r. Scotland 17 G3 ....55.36N 2.40W
Leane, Lough l. Rep. of Ireland 41 B2 ....52.02N 9.34W
Leatherhead England 11 E2 ....51.17N 0.19W
Lebanon Asia 53 K3 ....34.00N 35.20E
Lębork Poland 46 C5 ....54.32N 17.45E
Łebsko, Jezioro lagoon Poland 46 C5 ....54.43N 17.30E
Lecce Italy 50 H4 ....40.20N 18.11E
Lech r. Austria/Germany 54 D2 ....47.32N 10.40E
Lechlade England 10 D2 ....51.42N 1.41W
Le Croisic France 44 B5 ....47.18N 2.31W
Ledbury England 10 C3 ....52.02N 2.25W
Lee r. Rep. of Ireland 41 C1 ....51.54N 8.25W
Leeds England 15 F2 ....53.48N 1.33W
Leek England 15 E2 ....53.07N 2.01W
Leeming England 15 F3 ....54.17N 1.33W
Lee Moor England 13 C2 ....50.26N 4.01W
Leeuwarden Neth. 42 E6 ....53.12N 5.48E
Leeuwin, Cape Australia 110 A3 ....34.23S 115.09E
Leeward Islands Caribbean Sea 71 L4 ....18.59N 64.04W
Lefkada i. Greece 56 D4 ....38.45N 20.35E
Legaspi Phil. 105 G6 ....13.08N 123.44E
Legionowo Poland 46 E4 ....52.25N 20.58E
Legnica Poland 46 C3 ....51.13N 16.10E
Leh India 96 F7 ....34.09N 77.36E
Le Havre France 44 D6 ....49.30N 0.08E
Leiah Pakistan 95 L6 ....30.58N 70.58E
Leicester England 10 D3 ....52.38N 1.08W
Leicester d. England 9 E3 ....52.39N 1.07W
Leicestershire d. England 9 E3 ....52.37N 0.59W
Leichhardt r. Australia 110 C5 ....17.35S 139.44E
Leiden Neth. 42 D5 ....52.10N 4.30E
Leigh England 14 E2 ....53.30N 2.31W
Leighton Buzzard England 10 E2 ....51.55N 0.40W
Leinster, Mount hill Rep. of Ireland 41 E2 ....52.37N 6.47W
Leipzig Germany 54 E4 ....51.21N 12.23E
Leiston England 11 G3 ....52.13N 1.35E
Leith Scotland 17 F3 ....55.59N 3.10W
Leith Hill England 11 E2 ....51.11N 0.22W
Leitrim d. Rep. of Ireland 41 C4 ....54.19N 8.13W
Leixlip Rep. of Ireland 41 E3 ....53.22N 6.29W
Leizhou Bandao pen. China 103 J2 ....21.03N 109.41E
Lek r. Neth. 42 D4 ....51.54N 4.34E
Leka Norway 40 B4 ....65.05N 11.44E
Leksozero, Ozero l. Rus. Fed. 40 G3 ....63.51N 30.48E
Lelystad Neth. 42 E5 ....52.32N 5.29E
Le Mans France 44 D6 ....48.00N 0.12E
Lena r. Rus. Fed. 59 N5 ....72.20N 126.37E
Lens France 44 E7 ....50.26N 2.50E
Lensk Rus. Fed. 59 M4 ....60.44N 114.53E
Leoben Austria 54 F2 ....47.23N 15.06E
Leominster England 10 C3 ....52.14N 2.44W
León Mexico 70 D5 ....21.07N 101.44W
León Spain 48 C5 ....42.36N 5.34W
Le Puy-en-Velay France 44 E4 ....45.03N 3.53E
Lerum Sweden 40 C2 ....57.46N 12.17E
Lerwick Scotland 19 H5 ....60.09N 1.09W
Lesatima mt. Kenya 87 B2 ....0.21S 36.37E
Lesbos i. Greece 56 F4 ....39.08N 25.56E
Les Cayes Haiti 71 J4 ....18.14N 73.47W
Leshan China 103 I3 ....29.37N 103.44E
Leskovac S.M. 56 D6 ....42.59N 21.56E
Lesotho Africa 86 B2 ....29.38S 28.26E
Lesozavodsk Rus. Fed. 106 B5 ....45.33N 133.23E
Les Pieux France 13 Z9 ....49.31N 1.48W
Les Sables-d'Olonne France 44 C5 ....46.30N 1.46W
Lesser Antilles is Caribbean Sea 71 K3 ....12.28N 67.66W
Lesser Slave Lake Canada 62 G3 ....55.28N 115.29W
Lestijärvi l. Finland 40 F3 ....63.28N 24.47E
Leszno Poland 46 C3 ....51.51N 16.35E
Leti, Kepulauan is Indonesia 105 H2 ....8.13S 127.58E
Letterkenny Rep. of Ireland 41 D4 ....54.57N 7.43W
Leuchars Scotland 17 G4 ....56.23N 2.53W
Leuser, Gunung mt. Indonesia 104 B4 ....3.49N 97.11E
Leuven Belgium 42 D3 ....50.52N 4.43E
Levadeia Greece 56 E4 ....38.23S 115.09E
Leven England 15 G2 ....53.54N 0.18W
Leven Scotland 17 G4 ....56.12N 2.59W

Leven, Loch inlet Scotland 18 D1 ....56.41N 5.06W
Leven, Loch l. Scotland 17 F4 ....56.12N 3.23W
Levens England 14 E3 ....54.16N 2.47W
Leverkusen Germany 54 B4 ....51.03N 6.59E
Lewes England 11 F1 ....50.52N 0.01E
Lewis, Isle of l. Scotland 18 C3 ....58.09N 6.59W
Lexington U.S.A. 65 J4 ....38.02N 84.31W
Leyburn England 15 F3 ....54.19N 1.50W
Leyland England 14 E2 ....53.42N 2.42W
Leyte i. Phil. 105 G6 ....11.05N 124.31E
Lezhë Albania 56 C5 ....41.46N 19.39E
L'gov Rus. Fed. 55 P4 ....51.39N 35.16E
Lharigarbo China 102 G4 ....32.15N 91.43E
Lhasa China 102 G3 ....29.39N 91.05E
Lhazê China 102 F3 ....29.08N 87.36E
Lhokseumawe Indonesia 104 B5 ....5.09N 97.08E
L'Hospitalet de Llobregat Spain 48 G4 ....41.22N 2.08E
Lianyungang China 103 L4 ....34.37N 119.11E
Liaoning d. China 103 M6 ....41.30N 122.45E
Liaoyuan China 103 N6 ....42.54N 125.08E
Liard r. Canada 62 F4 ....61.51N 121.17W
Libenge Dem. Rep. Congo 86 A5 ....3.40N 18.38E
Liberal U.S.A. 64 F4 ....37.03N 100.57W
Liberec Czech Rep. 54 F4 ....50.45N 15.03E
Liberia Africa 84 D2 ....6.52N 9.55W
Libin Belgium 42 E2 ....49.59N 5.16E
Liboi Kenya 87 C3 ....0.20N 40.54E
Libourne France 44 C4 ....44.55N 0.14W
Libreville Gabon 84 E2 ....0.28N 9.27E
Libya Africa 84 F4 ....26.07N 17.09E
Libyan Desert Egypt/Libya 85 G4 ....24.51N 25.00E
Libyan Plateau f. Egypt/Libya 53 I3 ....30.59N 25.49E
Lichfield England 10 D3 ....52.41N 1.50W
Lichinga Mozambique 86 C3 ....13.17S 35.14E
Lida Belarus 55 K5 ....53.53N 25.19E
Liddel r. Scotland 17 G3 ....55.04N 2.57W
Lidköping Sweden 40 C2 ....58.30N 13.11E
Liechtenstein Europe 44 H5 ....47.07N 9.36E
Liège Belgium 42 E3 ....50.38N 5.35E
Liège d. Belgium 42 E3 ....50.29N 5.42E
Lieksa Finland 40 G3 ....63.19N 30.02E
Lienz Austria 54 E2 ....46.50N 12.46E
Liepāja Latvia 40 E2 ....56.31N 21.01E
Liévin France 42 B3 ....50.25N 2.47E
Liezen Austria 50 F7 ....47.35N 14.15E
Liffey r. Rep. of Ireland 41 E3 ....53.21N 6.14W
Lifford Rep. of Ireland 41 D4 ....54.50N 7.29W
Ligurian Sea France/Italy 44 H3 ....43.30N 8.50E
Likasi Dem. Rep. Congo 86 B3 ....10.58S 26.47E
Lilla Edet Sweden 40 C2 ....58.08N 12.08E
Lille Belgium 42 D4 ....51.14N 4.50E
Lille France 44 E7 ....50.38N 3.04E
Lillehammer Norway 40 B3 ....61.06N 10.29E
Lilleshall England 10 C3 ....52.44N 2.24W
Lillestrøm Norway 40 B2 ....59.59N 11.02E
Lilongwe Malawi 86 C3 ....13.57S 33.47E
Lima Peru 76 E5 ....12.04S 77.03W
Limassol Cyprus 57 J2 ....34.41N 33.02E
Limavady Northern Ireland 16 C3 ....55.03N 6.57W
Limavady d. Northern Ireland 8 B4 ....54.57N 6.58W
Limburg d. Belgium 42 E4 ....51.04N 5.27E
Limburg d. Neth. 42 E4 ....51.15N 5.54E
Limerick Rep. of Ireland 41 C2 ....52.40N 8.37W
Limerick d. Rep. of Ireland 41 C2 ....52.29N 8.50W
Limingen l. Norway 40 C4 ....64.48N 13.33E
Limnos i. Greece 56 F4 ....39.51N 25.21E
Limoges France 44 D4 ....45.50N 1.15E
Limousin f. France 44 D4 ....45.34N 1.17E
Limoux France 44 E3 ....43.04N 2.13E
Limpopo r. S. Africa/Zimbabwe 86 C2 ....25.13S 33.32E
Linares Spain 48 D3 ....38.06N 3.37W
Lincoln England 15 G2 ....53.14N 0.32W
Lincoln U.S.A. 64 G5 ....40.51N 96.40W
Lincolnshire d. England 9 E3 ....53.07N 0.14W
Lincolnshire Wolds hills England 15 G2 ....53.30N 0.19W
Lindesnes c. Norway 40 A2 ....58.00N 7.06E
Lindfield England 11 E2 ....51.01N 0.05W
Lindi Tanzania 86 C4 ....9.59S 39.40E
Lindos Greece 57 H3 ....36.05N 28.05E
Line Islands Kiribati 109 J6 ....5.19N 161.36W
Linfen China 103 K5 ....36.05N 111.34E
Lingen Germany 54 B5 ....52.32N 7.19E
Lingfield England 11 E2 ....51.11N 0.01W
Lingga, Kepulauan is Indonesia 104 D3 ....0.02S 105.19E
Linhares Brazil 77 L4 ....19.27S 40.08W
Linköping Sweden 40 C2 ....58.25N 15.38E
Linkou China 106 B5 ....45.11N 130.11E
Linlithgow Scotland 17 F3 ....55.58N 3.36W
Linney Head Wales 12 B3 ....51.37N 5.05W
Linnhe, Loch inlet Scotland 16 D4 ....56.31N 5.33W
Linosa, Isola di i. Italy 50 E1 ....35.52N 12.50E
Linxia China 103 I5 ....35.31N 103.04E
Linz Austria 54 F3 ....48.19N 14.18E
Lions, Gulf of France 44 E3 ....43.00N 3.31E
Lipari, Isole is Italy 50 F3 ....38.39N 14.43E
Lipetsk Rus. Fed. 58 E3 ....52.37N 39.36E
Liphook England 10 E2 ....51.04N 0.48W
Lipova Romania 56 D8 ....46.05N 21.43E
Lippe r. Germany 42 F4 ....51.39N 6.36E
Lisala Dem. Rep. Congo 86 B5 ....2.10N 21.32E
Lisbon Portugal 48 A3 ....38.44N 9.08W
Lisburn Northern Ireland 16 C2 ....54.31N 6.02W
Lisburn d. Northern Ireland 9 B4 ....54.31N 6.04W
Liscannor Bay Rep. of Ireland 41 B2 ....52.55N 9.26W
Liskeard England 13 C2 ....50.27N 4.28W
Lismore Australia 110 E4 ....28.47S 153.19E
Lismore Rep. of Ireland 41 D2 ....52.08N 7.56W
Lisnaskea Northern Ireland 16 B2 ....54.15N 7.26W
Liss England 10 E2 ....51.03N 0.53W
Listowel Rep. of Ireland 41 B2 ....52.26N 9.29W
Lithuania Europe 55 J6 ....55.29N 23.45E
Little Abaco i. Bahamas 71 I6 ....26.50N 77.30W
Little Andaman i. India 97 H3 ....10.38N 92.31E
Little Belt str. Denmark 40 B1 ....55.15N 9.47E
Littleborough England 15 E2 ....53.39N 2.06W
Little Cayman i. Cayman Is 71 H4 ....19.42N 80.04W
Littlehampton England 11 E1 ....50.49N 0.32W
Little Inagua Island Bahamas 71 J5 ....21.31N 72.59W
Little Karoo f. S. Africa 86 B1 ....33.43S 20.46E
Little Minch str. Scotland 18 B2 ....57.32N 7.00W
Little Ouse r. England 11 F3 ....52.30N 0.22E
Little Rock town U.S.A. 65 H3 ....34.46N 92.18W
Littleport England 11 F3 ....52.27N 0.19E
Liuzhou China 103 J2 ....24.21N 109.22E
Liverpool England 14 E2 ....53.25N 2.55W
Liverpool Canada 65 N5 ....44.02N 64.43W
Livingston Scotland 17 F3 ....55.54N 3.31W
Livingstone Zambia 86 B3 ....17.52S 25.52E
Livorno Italy 50 D5 ....43.32N 10.19E
Lizard England 13 B1 ....49.58N 5.12W
Lizard Point England 13 B1 ....49.57N 5.17W
Ljubljana Slovenia 54 F2 ....46.03N 14.30E
Ljungan r. Sweden 40 D3 ....62.18N 17.23E
Ljungby Sweden 40 C2 ....56.51N 13.55E

Ljusdal Sweden 40 D3 ....61.50N 16.06E
Llanarth Wales 12 C4 ....52.12N 4.18W
Llanbadarn Fawr Wales 12 C4 ....52.24N 4.04W
Llanberis Wales 12 D3 ....53.07N 4.08W
Llandeilo Wales 12 D3 ....51.53N 3.59W
Llandovery Wales 12 C4 ....51.59N 3.48W
Llandrindod Wells Wales 12 D4 ....52.14N 3.23W
Llandudno Wales 12 D5 ....53.19N 3.50W
Llandwrog Wales 12 C5 ....53.05N 4.19W
Llandysul Wales 12 C4 ....52.03N 4.18W
Llanegwad Wales 12 C3 ....51.52N 4.09W
Llanelli Wales 12 C3 ....51.41N 4.10W
Llanes Spain 48 C5 ....43.25N 4.44W
Llanfair Caereinion Wales 12 D4 ....52.39N 3.20W
Llanfairfechan Wales 12 C5 ....53.15N 3.58W
Llanfairpwllgwyngyll Wales 12 C5 ....53.13N 4.12W
Llanfair-yn-neubwll Wales 12 C5 ....53.16N 4.33W
Llanfyllin Wales 12 D4 ....52.46N 3.16W
Llangefni Wales 12 C5 ....53.15N 4.19W
Llangeler Wales 12 C4 ....52.02N 4.22W
Llangelynin Wales 12 C4 ....52.39N 4.07W
Llangoed Wales 12 C5 ....53.18N 4.05W
Llangollen Wales 12 D4 ....52.58N 3.10W
Llangurig Wales 12 D4 ....52.24N 3.36W
Llanidloes Wales 12 D4 ....52.27N 3.32W
Llanllwchaiarn Wales 12 D4 ....52.32N 3.17W
Llanllyfni Wales 12 C5 ....53.03N 4.17W
Llanos f. Col./Venez. 72 C7 ....5.54N 69.50W
Llanrumney Wales 13 D3 ....51.31N 3.07W
Llanrwst Wales 12 D5 ....53.08N 3.48W
Llansannan Wales 12 D5 ....53.11N 3.36W
Llantrisant Wales 12 D3 ....51.33N 3.22W
Llantwit Major Wales 13 D3 ....51.25N 3.29W
Llanwnda Wales 12 C5 ....53.05N 4.17W
Llanwnog Wales 12 D4 ....52.32N 3.27W
Llanybydder Wales 12 C4 ....52.04N 4.09W
Llay Wales 12 D5 ....53.06N 3.00W
Lleida Spain 48 F4 ....41.36N 0.38E
Llerena Spain 48 B3 ....38.15N 6.01W
Lleyn Peninsula Wales 12 C4 ....52.51N 4.34W
Lloyd George, Mount Canada 62 F3 ....57.50N 124.57W
Lloydminster Canada 62 G3 ....53.17N 110.00W
Llullaillaco, Volcán vol. Chile 73 C4 ....24.42S 68.33W
Lobito Angola 86 A3 ....12.24S 13.32E
Lochaline Scotland 16 D4 ....56.32N 5.47W
Lochboisdale Scotland 18 B2 ....57.09N 7.19W
Lochgelly Scotland 17 F4 ....56.08N 3.18W
Lochgilphead Scotland 16 D4 ....56.02N 5.26W
Lochinver Scotland 18 D3 ....58.09N 5.14W
Lochmaben Scotland 17 F3 ....55.08N 3.26W
Lochmaddy Scotland 18 B2 ....57.36N 7.10W
Lochnagar mt. Scotland 19 F1 ....56.58N 3.15W
Lochranza Scotland 16 E3 ....55.42N 5.17W
Lochy, Loch l. Scotland 18 E1 ....56.56N 4.58W
Lockerbie Scotland 17 F3 ....55.07N 3.21W
Loddon England 11 G3 ....52.32N 1.29E
Lodwar Kenya 87 A3 ....3.06N 35.36E
Łódź Poland 46 D3 ....51.46N 19.27E
Lofoten is Norway 40 C5 ....68.06N 12.44E
Lofusa Sudan 87 A4 ....3.50N 33.10E
Logan, Mount Canada 62 C4 ....60.40N 140.02W
Loggerheads England 10 C3 ....52.55N 2.23W
Logone r. Cameroon/Chad 82 E6 ....12.10N 15.00E
Logroño Spain 48 D5 ....42.28N 2.26W
Loire r. France 44 B5 ....47.17N 2.07W
Loja Ecuador 76 E7 ....4.00S 79.14W
Loja Spain 48 C2 ....37.10N 4.09W
Lokan tekojärvi resr Finland 40 F4 ....67.56N 27.35E
Lokeren Belgium 42 D4 ....51.06N 4.00E
Lokichar Kenya 87 A3 ....2.22N 35.37E
Lokichokio Kenya 87 A4 ....4.14N 34.21E
Løkken Norway 40 B3 ....63.07N 9.42E
Lokoja Nigeria 84 E2 ....7.49N 6.44E
Lokwa Kangole Kenya 87 A3 ....3.32N 35.50E
Lolland i. Denmark 40 B1 ....54.47N 11.21E
Lollondo Tanzania 87 A2 ....2.01S 35.38E
Lom Bulgaria 56 E6 ....43.49N 23.14E
Lomami r. Dem. Rep. Congo 86 B5 ....0.47N 24.17E
Lombok i. Indonesia 104 F2 ....9.07S 116.13E
Lomé Togo 84 E2 ....6.09N 1.13E
Lommel Belgium 42 E4 ....51.14N 5.19E
Lomond, Loch l. Scotland 16 E4 ....56.04N 4.37W
Łomża Poland 46 F4 ....53.11N 22.05E
London Canada 63 J2 ....42.59N 81.14W
London England 11 E2 ....51.30N 0.07W
Londonderry Northern Ireland 16 B2 ....54.59N 7.20W
Londonderry d. Northern Ireland 41 E4 ....54.59N 6.51W
Londonderry, Cape Australia 110 B5 ....13.47S 126.53E
Long, Loch inlet Scotland 16 D4 ....56.06N 4.51W
Longa, Proliv str. Rus. Fed. 59 S5 ....70.10N 178.17E
Long Ashton England 10 C2 ....51.26N 2.39W
Long Beach town U.S.A. 64 C3 ....33.47N 118.20W
Long Bennington England 10 E3 ....52.59N 0.46W
Long Eaton England 10 D3 ....52.54N 1.16W
Longford Rep. of Ireland 41 D3 ....53.44N 7.48W
Longford d. Rep. of Ireland 41 D3 ....53.45N 7.41W
Longhorsley England 15 F4 ....55.15N 1.46W
Longhoughton England 15 F4 ....55.26N 1.37W
Longido Tanzania 87 B2 ....2.47S 36.42E
Long Island Bahamas 71 I5 ....23.18N 75.06W
Long Island U.S.A. 65 L5 ....40.49N 72.36W
Longlac Canada 63 J2 ....49.47N 86.33W
Longridge England 14 E2 ....53.50N 2.36W
Long Stratton England 11 G3 ....52.29N 1.14E
Longton England 14 E2 ....53.44N 2.48W
Longtown England 14 E4 ....55.00N 2.58W
Longuyon France 42 E2 ....49.27N 5.37E
Longview U.S.A. 65 H3 ....32.32N 94.44W
Long Xuyên Vietnam 104 D6 ....10.20N 105.25E
Longyearbyen Arctic Oc. 58 C5 ....77.59N 15.44E
Lons-le-Saunier France 42 F1 ....46.41N 5.33E
Lookout, Cape U.S.A. 65 K3 ....34.37N 76.33W
Loolmalasin vol. Tanzania 87 A2 ....3.02S 35.48E
Loop Head Rep. of Ireland 41 B2 ....52.33N 9.56W
Lop Nur l. China 102 G6 ....40.28N 90.20E
Lopphavet b. Norway 40 E5 ....70.21N 21.03E
Loralai Pakistan 95 K6 ....30.21N 68.43E
Lorca Spain 48 E2 ....37.41N 1.41W
Lord Howe Island Australia 111 E3 ....31.26S 158.57E
Lord Howe Rise f. S. Pacific Oc. 108 G4 ...27.46S 160.37E
Lorient France 44 B5 ....47.45N 3.22W
Lorn, Firth of est. Scotland 16 D4 ....56.15N 5.54W
Lorraine d. France 42 F1 ....48.48N 6.06E
Losai National Reserve Kenya 87 B3 ....1.11N 37.41E
Los Ángeles Chile 73 B3 ....37.28S 72.21W
Los Angeles U.S.A. 64 C3 ....34.01N 118.15W
Los Mochis Mexico 70 C6 ....25.48N 108.59W
Los Roques, Islas is Venezuela 71 K3 .....11.55N 66.39W
Lossie r. Scotland 19 F2 ....57.43N 3.17W
Lossiemouth Scotland 19 F2 ....57.43N 3.17W
Lostwithiel England 13 C2 ....50.24N 4.40W
Los Vilos Chile 76 F1 ....31.56S 71.29W
Lot r. France 44 D4 ....44.19N 0.20E

Lotagipi Swamp f. Kenya/Sudan 87 A4 ......4.44N 34.42E
Loth Scotland 19 G4 ....59.12N 2.41W
Lotikipi Plain f. Kenya/Sudan 87 A4 ....4.36N 34.38E
Lotta r. Finland/Rus. Fed. 40 G5 ....68.40N 30.14E
Lotuke mt. Sudan 87 A4 ....4.08N 33.51E
Louangnamtha Laos 104 C8 ....21.03N 101.29E
Louangphabang Laos 104 C7 ....19.54N 102.10E
Loughborough England 10 D3 ....52.46N 1.12W
Loughor r. Wales 12 C3 ....51.42N 4.03W
Loughrea Rep. of Ireland 41 C3 ....53.12N 8.35W
Loughton England 11 F2 ....51.39N 0.04E
Louisiana d. U.S.A. 65 H3 ....30.40N 91.56W
Louisville U.S.A. 65 I4 ....38.15N 85.46W
Louisville Ridge f. S. Pacific Oc. 108 I3 ...30.29S 173.10W
Loukhi Rus. Fed. 40 H4 ....66.04N 33.03E
Louny Czech Rep. 46 A3 ....50.21N 13.49E
Lourdes France 44 C3 ....43.06N 0.02W
Louth England 15 G2 ....53.22N 0.01W
Louth d. Rep. of Ireland 41 E3 ....53.53N 6.31W
Lovech Bulgaria 56 F6 ....43.09N 24.42E
Lovozero Rus. Fed. 40 H5 ....68.01N 34.59E
Lowell U.S.A. 65 L5 ....42.39N 71.19W
Lower Lough Erne l. Northern Ireland 16 B2 ...54.29N 7.51W
Lowestoft England 11 G3 ....52.29N 1.45E
Łowicz Poland 46 D4 ....52.07N 19.57E
Loyal, Loch l. Scotland 19 E3 ....58.25N 4.20W
Loyauté, Îles is New Caledonia 111 F4 ....20.23S 167.17E
Loyne, Loch l. Scotland 18 D2 ....57.06N 5.05W
Loznica S.M. 56 C7 ....44.33N 19.15E
Luanda Angola 86 A4 ....8.50S 13.14E
Luarca Spain 48 B5 ....43.32N 6.31W
Luau Angola 86 B3 ....10.42S 22.15E
Lubaczów Poland 46 F3 ....50.10N 23.08E
Lubango Angola 86 A3 ....14.55S 13.30E
Lubartów Poland 46 F3 ....51.28N 22.37E
Lubbock U.S.A. 64 F3 ....33.38N 101.51W
Lübeck Germany 54 D5 ....53.52N 10.42E
Lübecker Bucht b. Germany 54 D6 ....54.03N 10.47E
Lubin Poland 46 C3 ....51.24N 16.13E
Lublin Poland 46 F3 ....51.14N 22.35E
Lubnaig, Loch l. Scotland 16 E4 ....56.18N 4.19W
Lubny Ukraine 55 O4 ....50.01N 33.00E
Lubuklinggau Indonesia 104 C3 ....3.23S 102.56E
Lubumbashi Dem. Rep. Congo 86 B3 ....11.40S 27.29E
Lubutu Dem. Rep. Congo 86 B6 ....0.44S 26.35E
Lucan Rep. of Ireland 12 A5 ....53.21N 6.27W
Luce Bay Scotland 16 E2 ....54.47N 4.52W
Lucena Phil. 105 G6 ....13.56N 121.36E
Lucena Spain 48 C2 ....37.25N 4.29W
Lučenec Slovakia 54 H3 ....48.21N 19.41E
Lucerne Switz. 50 C7 ....47.03N 8.18E
Lucknow India 96 F6 ....26.51N 80.58E
Lüderitz Namibia 86 A2 ....26.40S 15.09E
Ludgershall England 10 D2 ....51.15N 1.37W
Ludhiana India 96 E7 ....30.54N 75.53E
Ludlow England 10 C3 ....52.22N 2.43W
Ludvika Sweden 40 C3 ....60.09N 15.12E
Ludwigsburg Germany 54 C3 ....48.54N 9.12E
Ludwigshafen am Rhein Germany 54 C3 ...49.28N 8.26E
Ludwigslust Germany 54 D5 ....53.20N 11.30E
Luena Angola 86 A3 ....11.47S 19.54E
Lufkin U.S.A. 65 H3 ....31.21N 94.44W
Luga Rus. Fed. 40 G2 ....58.43N 29.51E
Luga r. Rus. Fed. 40 G2 ....59.40N 28.18E
Lugano Switz. 50 C7 ....46.01N 8.57E
Lugg r. Wales 12 E4 ....52.02N 2.38W
Lugo Spain 48 B5 ....43.01N 7.33W
Lugoj Romania 56 D7 ....45.42N 21.55E
Luichart, Loch l. Scotland 18 E2 ....57.37N 4.48W
Luing i. Scotland 16 D4 ....56.14N 5.39W
Łuków Poland 46 F3 ....51.56N 22.24E
Luleå Sweden 40 E4 ....65.35N 22.10E
Luleälven r. Sweden 40 E4 ....65.35N 22.03E
Lüleburgaz Turkey 56 G5 ....41.25N 27.21E
Lumberton U.S.A. 65 K3 ....34.36N 79.05W
Lunan Bay Scotland 19 G1 ....56.39N 2.30W
Lund Sweden 40 C1 ....55.42N 13.12E
Lundy i. England 13 C3 ....51.11N 4.39W
Lune r. England 14 E3 ....54.03N 2.49W
Lüneburg Germany 54 D5 ....53.15N 10.25E
Lunéville France 44 G6 ....48.36N 6.30E
Luninyets Belarus 55 L5 ....52.14N 26.48E
Luoyang China 103 K4 ....34.38N 112.27E
Lupanshui China 103 I3 ....26.40N 104.48E
Lurgainn, Loch l. Scotland 18 D3 ....58.02N 5.14W
Lurgan Northern Ireland 16 C2 ....54.27N 6.19W
Lusaka Zambia 86 B3 ....15.23S 28.16E
Lushnjë Albania 56 C5 ....40.57N 19.42E
Lushoto Tanzania 87 B1 ....4.47S 38.18E
Lut, Dasht-e des. Iran 95 I6 ....30.47N 58.45E
Lutherstadt Wittenberg Germany 54 E4 ...51.52N 12.39E
Luton England 11 E2 ....51.53N 0.25W
Luton d. England 9 E2 ....51.54N 0.25W
Luts'k Ukraine 55 K4 ....50.45N 25.21E
Lutterworth England 10 D3 ....52.27N 1.12W
Luxembourg d. Belgium 42 E3 ....50.03N 5.27E
Luxembourg Europe 42 F2 ....49.49N 6.01E
Luxembourg town Lux. 42 F2 ....49.36N 6.08E
Luxor Egypt 85 H4 ....25.43N 32.39E
Luziânia Brazil 77 K4 ....16.17S 47.53W
Luzon i. Phil. 105 G7 ....15.24N 122.02E
Luzon Strait Phil. 104 G8 ....20.19N 121.07E
L'viv Ukraine 55 K3 ....49.50N 24.02E
Lycksele Sweden 40 D4 ....64.36N 18.41E
Lydd England 11 F1 ....50.57N 0.55E
Lydford England 13 C2 ....50.39N 4.06W
Lydney England 10 C2 ....51.44N 2.32W
Lyepyel' Belarus 55 M6 ....54.53N 28.42E
Lyme Bay England 10 C1 ....50.39N 2.59W
Lyme Regis England 10 C1 ....50.43N 2.56W
Lymington England 10 D1 ....50.45N 1.33W
Lynchburg U.S.A. 65 K4 ....37.24N 79.09W
Lyndhurst England 10 D1 ....50.52N 1.35W
Lynmouth England 13 D3 ....51.14N 3.50W
Lynn Lake town Canada 62 H3 ....56.51N 101.03W
Lynton England 13 D3 ....51.14N 3.50W
Lyon France 44 F4 ....45.45N 4.52E
Lytchett Minster England 10 C1 ....50.44N 2.03W
Lytham St Anne's England 14 D2 ....53.45N 3.02W
Lyubeshiv Ukraine 46 G3 ....51.46N 25.31E

M

Ma'ān Jordan 94 E6 ....30.12N 35.43E
Ma'arrat an Nu'mān Syria 57 L2 ....35.39N 36.40E
Maas r. Neth. 42 D4 ....51.43N 4.32E
Maaseik Belgium 42 E4 ....51.05N 5.48E
Maastricht Neth. 42 E3 ....50.51N 5.42E
Mabalane Mozambique 86 C2 ....23.50S 32.37E
Mablethorpe England 15 H2 ....53.20N 0.16E

Macaé Brazil 77 L3 ....22.22S 41.50W
Macará Ecuador 76 E7 ....4.24S 79.58W
Macas Ecuador 76 E7 ....2.19S 78.10W
Macassar Strait Indonesia 104 F3 ....1.35S 117.24E
Macau China 103 K2 ....22.15N 113.34E
Macclesfield England 15 E2 ....53.16N 2.07W
Macdonnell Ranges mts Australia 110 C4 ...23.33S 131.18E
Macduff Scotland 19 G2 ....57.40N 2.30W
Macedo de Cavaleiros Portugal 48 B4 ...41.32N 6.57W
Macedonia Europe 56 D5 ....41.31N 21.46E
Maceió Brazil 77 M6 ....9.36S 35.40W
Macgillycuddy's Reeks mts Rep. of Ireland 41 B1 ..51.57N 9.52W
Mach Pakistan 96 C6 ....29.52N 67.20E
Machakos Kenya 87 B2 ....1.31S 37.16E
Machala Ecuador 76 E7 ....3.17S 79.57W
Machilipatnam India 96 F4 ....16.11N 81.10E
Machrihanish Scotland 16 D3 ....55.25N 5.44W
Machynlleth Wales 12 D4 ....52.35N 3.51W
Mackay Australia 110 D4 ....21.10S 149.11E
Mackay, Lake Australia 110 B4 ....22.36S 128.28E
Mackenzie r. Canada 62 E4 ....69.15N 134.11W
Mackenzie King Island Canada 62 G5 ..77.42N 111.56W
Mackenzie Mountains Canada 62 E4 ...65.04N 133.03W
MacLeod, Lake Australia 110 A4 ....24.08S 113.43E
Mâcon France 44 F5 ....46.19N 4.50E
Macon U.S.A. 65 J3 ....32.53N 83.37W
Macquarie Island S. Pacific Oc. 108 G2 ..54.36S 158.58E
Macquarie Ridge f. S. Pacific Oc. 108 G2 ..55.50S 157.21E
Macroom Rep. of Ireland 41 C1 ....51.54N 8.58W
Madadeni S. Africa 86 C2 ....27.45S 30.02E
Madeira i. Brazil 77 I7 ....3.23S 58.47W
Madeira is N. Atlantic Oc. 84 C5 ....33.15N 16.57W
Madeley England 10 C3 ....52.38N 2.26W
Madera Mexico 70 C6 ....29.11N 108.11W
Madhya Pradesh d. India 96 E5 ....23.32N 78.56E
Madidi r. Bolivia 76 G5 ....12.34S 66.54W
Madison U.S.A. 65 I5 ....43.04N 89.23W
Mado Gashi Kenya 87 B3 ....0.42N 39.09E
Madona Latvia 55 L7 ....56.51N 26.13E
Madrakah, Ra's c. Oman 95 I3 ....19.01N 57.51E
Madre, Laguna lagoon Mexico 70 E6 ...25.06N 97.37W
Madre, Sierra mts C. America 60 J4 ....15.00N 90.00W
Madre de Dios Peru 76 F5 ....12.34S 70.05W
Madre de Dios r. Peru 72 G5 ....10.24S 66.07W
Madre del Sur, Sierra mts Mexico 70 D4 ...18.07N 101.24W
Madre Occidental, Sierra mts Mexico 70 C6 ...28.46N 108.51W
Madre Oriental, Sierra mts Mexico 70 D6 ...26.41N 101.44W
Madrid Spain 48 D4 ....40.26N 3.40W
Madura i. Indonesia 104 E2 ....7.02S 113.11E
Madurai India 96 E2 ....9.56N 78.07E
Maebashi Japan 106 C3 ....36.23N 139.04E
Maesteg Wales 12 D3 ....51.36N 3.40W
Maestra, Sierra mts Cuba 71 I4 ....19.54N 77.33W
Mafia Island Tanzania 86 C4 ....7.48S 39.52E
Mafraq Jordan 94 E6 ....32.17N 36.15E
Magadan Rus. Fed. 59 Q3 ....59.38N 151.00E
Magadi Kenya 87 B2 ....1.52S 36.19E
Magdalena r. Colombia 72 B8 ....11.06N 74.52W
Magdalena Mexico 70 B7 ....30.38N 110.59W
Magdeburg Germany 54 D5 ....52.07N 11.38E
Magellan, Strait of Chile 73 B1 ....53.42S 71.59W
Magerøya i. Norway 40 F5 ....70.59N 25.40E
Maggiorasca, Monte mt. Italy 50 C6 ...44.33N 9.30E
Maggiore, Lake Italy 50 C6 ....45.56N 8.36E
Maghera Northern Ireland 16 C2 ....54.50N 6.40W
Magherafelt Northern Ireland 16 C2 ...54.45N 6.36W
Magherafelt d. Northern Ireland 9 B4 ..54.49N 6.39W
Maghull England 14 E2 ....53.31N 2.57W
Magilligan Point Northern Ireland 16 C3 ...55.12N 6.56W
Magnitogorsk Rus. Fed. 58 G3 ....53.24N 59.08E
Mago National Park Ethiopia 87 B4 .....5.29N 36.17E
Maguarinho, Cabo c. Brazil 77 K7 ......0.19S 48.27W
Magwe Myanmar 97 H5 ....20.09N 94.56E
Mahābād Iran 95 G7 ....36.44N 45.41E
Mahajanga Madagascar 86 D3 ....15.41S 46.21E
Mahalevona Madagascar 86 D3 ....15.24S 49.53E
Maharashtra d. India 96 E4 ....19.24N 75.18E
Mahé i. Seychelles 85 J1 ....4.36S 55.24E
Mahilyow Belarus 55 N5 ....53.55N 30.20E
Mahón Spain 48 H3 ....39.53N 4.17E
Mahrāt, Jabal mt. Yemen 95 H3 ....17.07N 51.07E
Maicao Colombia 71 J3 ....11.25N 72.23W
Maidenhead England 10 E2 ....51.31N 0.43W
Maidstone England 11 F2 ....51.16N 0.31E
Maiduguri Nigeria 84 F3 ....11.50N 13.08E
Main r. Northern Ireland 16 C2 ....54.43N 6.18W
Mai-Ndombe, Lac l. Dem. Rep. Congo 86 A4 ...2.15S 18.22E
Maine d. U.S.A. 65 M6 ....45.20N 69.21W
Mainland i. Orkn. Scotland 19 F4 ....59.04N 3.15W
Mainland i. Shetl. Scotland 19 H5 ......60.21N 1.17W
Mainz Germany 54 C4 ....50.00N 8.16E
Maiquetía Venezuela 71 K3 ....10.32N 66.56W
Maíz, Islas del is Nicaragua 71 H3 .....12.10N 83.02W
Maizuru Japan 106 C3 ....35.28N 135.24E
Maja Jezercë mt. Albania 56 C6 ....42.26N 19.50E
Majene Indonesia 104 F3 ....3.30S 118.54E
Majī Ethiopia 87 A4 ....6.08N 35.37E
Major, Puig mt. Spain 48 G3 ....39.48N 2.49E
Majorca i. Spain 48 G3 ....39.57N 2.43E
Makale Indonesia 104 F3 ....3.06S 119.52E
Makarska Croatia 56 B6 ....43.18N 17.02E
Makassar Indonesia 104 F2 ....5.06S 119.27E
Makat Kazakhstan 58 G2 ....47.37N 53.14E
Makgadikgadi f. Botswana 86 B2 ......20.45S 25.35E
Makhachkala Rus. Fed. 58 F2 ....42.59N 47.30E
Makindu Kenya 87 B2 ....2.18S 37.50E
Makran f. Iran/Pakistan 95 J5 ....26.29N 60.27E
Makurdi Nigeria 84 E2 ....7.43N 8.33E
Makuyuni Tanzania 87 B2 ....3.33S 36.05E
Mala, Punta pt Panama 71 H2 ....7.27N 80.00W
Malabar Coast f. India 96 D3 ....12.16N 74.30E
Malabo Equat. Guinea 84 E2 ....3.45N 8.46E
Malacca, Strait of Indonesia/Malaysia 104 B5 ...5.41N 98.38E
Maladzyechna Belarus 55 L6 ....54.18N 26.52E
Málaga Spain 48 C2 ....36.43N 4.25W
Malahide Rep. of Ireland 41 E3 ....53.27N 6.09W
Malaita i. Solomon Is 111 F6 ....8.58S 161.09E
Malakal Sudan 85 H2 ....9.30N 31.40E
Malakula i. Vanuatu 111 F5 ....16.16S 167.19E
Malang Indonesia 104 E2 ....7.56S 112.40E
Mälaren l. Sweden 40 D2 ....59.27N 17.13E
Malatya Turkey 57 M4 ....38.20N 38.20E
Malawi Africa 86 C3 ....11.32S 33.43E
Malāyer Iran 95 G6 ....34.17N 48.48E
Malaysia Asia 104 D4 ....3.39N 108.45E
Malbork Poland 46 D5 ....54.02N 19.02E
Malden Island Kiribati 109 J5 ....4.02S 154.57W
Maldives Indian Oc. 96 D2 ....6.09N 72.23E

Maldon England 11 F2 ....51.44N 0.40E
Male Maldives 96 D1 ....4.18N 73.29E
Maleas, Akra pt Greece 56 E3 ....36.26N 23.12E
Malgomaj l. Sweden 40 D4 ....64.44N 16.15E
Mali Africa 84 D3 ....13.54N 5.34W
Malili Indonesia 105 G3 ....2.37S 121.07E
Malindi Kenya 87 C2 ....3.14S 40.06E
Malin Head Rep. of Ireland 41 D5 ......55.23N 7.24W
Malka Mari Kenya 87 C4 ....4.13N 40.47E
Mallaig Scotland 18 D2 ....57.00N 5.50W
Mallawī Egypt 53 J2 ....27.43N 30.50E
Mallow Rep. of Ireland 41 C2 ....52.08N 8.39W
Malmédy Belgium 42 F3 ....50.26N 6.02E
Malmesbury England 10 C2 ....51.35N 2.06W
Malmö Sweden 40 C1 ....55.36N 13.01E
Måløy Norway 40 A3 ....61.56N 5.07E
Malpas England 14 E2 ....53.01N 2.46W
Malpaso mt. Canary Islands 48 W1 ....27.44N 18.01W
Malpelo, Isla de i. N. Pacific Oc. 109 O6 ..3.59N 81.34W
Malta Europe 50 F1 ....35.49N 14.18E
Maltby England 15 F2 ....53.25N 1.12W
Malton England 15 G3 ....54.08N 0.48W
Malvern Hills England 10 C3 ....52.04N 2.20W
Malyy Anyuy r. Rus. Fed. 59 R4 ....68.27N 161.01E
Mama r. Rus. Fed. 59 P4 ....66.28N 143.13E
Mamelodi S. Africa 86 B2 ....25.42S 28.23E
Mamoré r. Bolivia/Brazil 76 G5 ....10.23S 65.21W
Mamuju Indonesia 104 F3 ....2.40S 118.51E
Man, Isle of d. Irish Sea 9 C4 ....54.15N 4.39W
Man, Isle of i. Irish Sea 16 E2 ....54.16N 4.41W
Manacapuru Brazil 77 H7 ....3.14S 60.35W
Manacor Spain 48 G3 ....39.34N 3.14E
Manado Indonesia 105 G4 ....1.33N 124.52E
Managua Nicaragua 71 G3 ....12.07N 86.17W
Manama Bahrain 95 H5 ....26.12N 50.35E
Mananjary Madagascar 86 D2 ....21.14S 48.20E
Manaus Brazil 77 H7 ....3.04S 60.00W
Manavgat Turkey 57 J3 ....36.48N 31.26E
Manchester England 15 E2 ....53.29N 2.15W
Manchuria f. China 103 M7 ....46.27N 123.48E
Mand r. India 95 H5 ....21.42N 83.15E
Mandala, Puncak mt. Indonesia 105 K3 ..4.43S 140.21E
Mandalay Myanmar 97 I5 ....21.59N 96.06E
Mandalgovĭ Mongolia 103 J7 ....45.42N 106.19E
Mandera Kenya 87 C3 ....3.53N 41.50E
Mandioré, Lagoa l. Bolivia/Brazil 77 I4 ...18.08S 57.32W
Manevychi Ukraine 46 G3 ....51.17N 25.32E
Manfredonia Italy 50 F4 ....41.38N 15.55E
Manfredonia, Golfo di g. Italy 56 B5 ..41.31N 16.05E
Mangaia i. Cook Is 109 J4 ....21.52S 157.52W
Mangalia Romania 57 H6 ....43.49N 28.34E
Mangalore India 96 D3 ....12.53N 74.51E
Mangaung S. Africa 86 B2 ....29.09S 26.16E
Mangoky r. Madagascar 86 D2 ....23.25S 45.25E
Mangole i. Indonesia 105 H3 ....1.51S 125.49E
Mangotsfield England 10 C2 ....51.29N 2.31W
Mangu Kenya 87 B2 ....0.59S 36.57E
Manicouagan, Réservoir Canada 63 L3 ...51.18N 68.18E
Manihiki atoll Cook Is 108 J5 ....10.30S 160.55W
Maniitsoq Greenland 63 M4 ....65.26N 52.55W
Manila Phil. 105 G6 ....14.34N 120.59E
Manipur d. India 97 H5 ....24.53N 93.56E
Manisa Turkey 56 G4 ....38.36N 27.25E
Manitoba d. Canada 62 I3 ....53.40N 98.06W
Manitoba, Lake Canada 62 I3 ....51.34N 99.04W
Manizales Colombia 72 B7 ....5.00N 75.30W
Manmad India 96 D5 ....20.15N 74.30E
Mannheim Germany 54 C3 ....49.29N 8.28E
Manningtree England 11 G2 ....51.57N 1.04E
Manokwari Indonesia 105 I3 ....0.52S 134.06E
Manorbier Wales 12 C3 ....51.39N 4.48W
Manorhamilton Rep. of Ireland 41 C4 ...54.18N 8.11W
Manra i. Kiribati 108 I5 ....4.26S 171.13W
Manresa Spain 48 F4 ....41.43N 1.50E
Mansa Zambia 86 B3 ....11.11S 28.53E
Mansel Island Canada 63 K4 ....62.05N 79.35W
Mansfield England 15 F2 ....53.09N 1.12W
Mansfield U.S.A. 65 J5 ....40.45N 82.32W
Manston England 10 C1 ....50.56N 2.16W
Manta Ecuador 76 D7 ....0.59S 80.42W
Mantua Italy 50 D6 ....45.09N 10.47E
Manukau New Zealand 111 G3 ....36.58S 174.56E
Manyara, Lake Tanzania 87 A2 ....3.42S 35.47E
Manzanares Spain 48 D3 ....39.00N 3.21W
Manzhouli China 103 L7 ....49.20N 117.29E
Maoke, Pegunungan mts Indonesia 105 J3 ...3.34S 135.25E
Mapinhane Mozambique 86 C2 ......22.17S 35.06E
Mapmakers Seamounts f. N. Pacific Oc. 108 H7 ..23.40N 165.39E
Mapuera r. Brazil 77 J2 ....1.05S 57.06W
Maputo Mozambique 86 C2 ....25.56S 32.34E
Mar, Serra do mts Brazil 77 J2 ....29.20S 50.12W
Mara d. Tanzania 87 A2 ....1.44S 34.21E
Maraba Brazil 77 K6 ....5.23S 49.08W
Maracá, Ilha de i. Brazil 77 J8 ....1.59N 50.22W
Maracaibo Venezuela 72 B8 ....10.40N 71.38W
Maracaibo, Lake inlet Venezuela 72 B7 ...9.45N 71.36W
Maracaju, Serra de hills Brazil 77 I3 ...21.59S 55.53W
Maracás, Chapada de hills Brazil 77 L5 ..13.22S 40.28W
Maracay Venezuela 72 C8 ....10.16N 67.35W
Marādah Libya 85 F4 ....29.12N 19.12E
Maradi Niger 84 E3 ....13.31N 7.07E
Marāgheh Iran 95 G7 ....37.23N 46.14E
Marajó, Ilha de i. Brazil 77 J7 ....0.45S 50.38W
Maralal Kenya 87 B3 ....1.06N 36.42E
Marand Iran 95 G7 ....38.26N 45.46E
Maranhão d. Brazil 77 K6 ....5.06S 45.19W
Marañón r. Peru 76 E7 ....4.27S 73.30W
Marathon Canada 65 I6 ....48.43N 86.23W
Marathonas Greece 56 E4 ....38.09N 23.58E
Marazion England 13 B2 ....50.07N 5.28W
Marbella Spain 48 C2 ....36.31N 4.52W
Marburg S. Africa 86 C1 ....30.43S 30.26E
Marburg an der Lahn Germany 54 C4 ...50.48N 8.46E
March England 11 F3 ....52.33N 0.05E
Marche-en-Famenne Belgium 42 E3 ...50.14N 5.21E
Mar Chiquita, Laguna l. Argentina 77 H1 ...30.43S 62.38W
Marchtrenk Austria 54 F3 ....48.12N 14.07E
Mardan Pakistan 95 L6 ....34.14N 72.04E
Mar del Plata Argentina 73 D3 ....37.59S 57.35W
Mardin Turkey 94 F7 ....37.18N 40.46E
Maree, Loch l. Scotland 18 D2 ....57.38N 5.23W
Maresfield England 11 F1 ....50.59N 0.05E
Margarita, Isla de i. Venezuela 72 C8 ...11.06N 63.53W
Margate England 15 F2 ....51.23N 1.23E
Margery Hill England 15 F2 ....53.27N 1.44W
Margherita Peak Dem. Rep. Congo/Uganda 86 B5 ...0.25N 29.56E
Mārgōw, Dasht-e des. Afgh. 95 J6 ...30.27N 62.22E
Marhanets' Ukraine 55 P2 ....47.40N 34.37E
Mariana Ridge f. N. Pacific Oc. 108 F7 ...20.44N 144.30E
Mariana Trench f. N. Pacific Oc. 108 F6 ...10.35N 141.08E
Marías, Islas is Mexico 70 C5 ....21.25N 106.33W
Maria Van Diemen, Cape New Zealand 111 G3 ...34.29S 172.38E
Ma'rib Yemen 95 G3 ....15.32N 45.26E
Maribor Slovenia 54 F2 ....46.32N 15.40E

Marie-Galante i. Guadeloupe 71 L4 ....15.56N 61.14W
Mariehamn Finland 40 D3 ....60.06N 19.57E
Mariental Namibia 86 A2 ....24.39S 17.58E
Mariestad Sweden 40 C2 ....58.43N 13.50E
Marijampolė Lithuania 46 F5 ....54.33N 23.22E
Marília Brazil 77 K3 ....22.13S 49.57W
Mar''ina Horka Belarus 55 M5 ....53.31N 28.08E
Maringá Brazil 77 J3 ....23.27S 51.59W
Maritime Alps mts France/Italy 44 G4 ....44.16N 6.56E
Maritsa r. Bulgaria 56 G5 ....41.43N 26.20E
Mariupol' Ukraine 53 K6 ....47.06N 37.33E
Marka Somalia 85 I2 ....1.43N 44.44E
Markermeer I. Neth. 42 E5 ....52.34N 5.14E
Market Deeping England 11 E3 ....52.41N 0.19W
Market Drayton England 10 C3 ....52.54N 2.29W
Market Harborough England 10 E3 ....52.29N 0.55W
Markethill Northern Ireland 16 C2 ....54.17N 6.31W
Market Rasen England 15 G2 ....53.23N 0.20W
Market Warsop England 15 F2 ....53.13N 1.09W
Market Weighton England 15 G2 ....53.52N 0.40W
Markha r. Rus. Fed. 59 M4 ....63.29N 118.52E
Marlborough England 10 D2 ....51.25N 1.44W
Marlborough Downs hills England 10 D2 ....51.29N 1.48W
Marlow England 10 E2 ....51.34N 0.46W
Marmande France 44 D4 ....44.31N 0.10E
Marmara, Sea of g. Turkey 57 H5 ....40.43N 28.26E
Marmaris Turkey 57 H3 ....36.50N 28.15E
Marmolada mt. Italy 50 D7 ....46.26N 11.51E
Marne r. France 44 E6 ....48.49N 2.25E
Marne-la-Vallée France 44 E6 ....48.51N 2.36E
Maromokotro mt. Madagascar 86 D3 ....14.01S 48.58E
Marondera Zimbabwe 86 C3 ....18.13S 31.34E
Maroni r. French Guiana 72 D7 ....5.44N 54.01W
Maroua Cameroon 84 F3 ....10.37N 14.19E
Marple England 15 E2 ....53.24N 2.04W
Marquesas Islands French Polynesia 109 K5 ....8.39S 139.15W
Marquette U.S.A. 65 I6 ....46.32N 87.25W
Marra, Jebel mt. Sudan 85 G3 ....12.54N 24.11E
Marrakesh Morocco 84 D5 ....31.39N 7.58W
Marra Plateau f. Sudan 85 G3 ....13.24N 24.25E
Marsá ál 'Alam Egypt 53 J2 ....25.04N 34.50E
Marsa al Burayqah Libya 85 F5 ....30.22N 19.35E
Marsabit Kenya 87 B3 ....2.20N 37.59E
Marsabit National Reserve Kenya 87 B3 ....2.11N 37.58E
Marsala Italy 50 E2 ....37.48N 12.26E
Marsá Maṭrūḥ Egypt 85 G5 ....31.20N 27.16E
Marseille France 44 F3 ....43.18N 5.23E
Marsfjället mt. Sweden 40 C4 ....65.06N 15.23E
Marshall Islands N. Pacific Oc. 108 H6 ....13.59N 164.53E
Märsta Sweden 40 D2 ....59.37N 17.53E
Martaban Myanmar 97 I4 ....16.34N 97.34E
Martaban, Gulf of Myanmar 97 I4 ....16.20N 96.57E
Martapura Indonesia 104 C3 ....4.20S 104.21E
Martin Slovakia 54 H3 ....49.04N 18.55E
Martinique i. Central America 71 L3 ....14.36N 60.56W
Martock England 10 C1 ....50.58N 2.46W
Mary Turkmenistan 95 J7 ....37.34N 61.52E
Maryborough Australia 110 E4 ....25.32S 152.41E
Maryland d. U.S.A. 65 K4 ....38.39N 76.30W
Maryport England 14 D3 ....54.43N 3.30W
Masai Mara National Reserve Kenya 87 A2 ....1.20S 35.04E
Masai Steppe f. Tanzania 87 B1 ....4.47S 36.53E
Masan S. Korea 103 N5 ....35.14N 128.36E
Masbate Phil. 105 G6 ....12.20N 123.37E
Masbate i. Phil. 105 G6 ....12.20N 123.36E
Mascara Algeria 52 D4 ....35.23N 0.08E
Maseno Kenya 87 A3 ....0.01N 34.36E
Maseru Lesotho 86 B2 ....29.19S 27.29E
Mashhad Iran 95 I7 ....36.18N 59.35E
Mashkel, Hamun-i- f. Pakistan 96 B6 ....28.15N 63.02E
Masinga Reservoir Kenya 87 B2 ....0.54S 37.34E
Maṣīrah, Jazīrat i. Oman 95 I4 ....20.16N 58.58E
Maṣīrah, Khalīj b. Oman 95 I4 ....19.47N 58.22E
Masjed Soleymān Iran 95 G6 ....31.57N 49.17E
Mask, Lough l. Rep. of Ireland 41 B3 ....53.37N 9.21W
Mason City U.S.A. 65 H5 ....43.09N 93.12W
Massachusetts d. U.S.A. 65 L5 ....42.23N 72.18W
Massachusetts Bay U.S.A. 65 L5 ....42.25N 70.51W
Massakory Chad 84 F3 ....12.59N 15.43E
Massawa Eritrea 85 H3 ....15.36N 39.27E
Massif Central mts France 44 E4 ....45.16N 3.25E
Mastung Pakistan 95 K5 ....29.45N 66.56E
Masty Belarus 46 G4 ....53.25N 24.31E
Masuda Japan 106 B2 ....34.40N 131.50E
Masvingo Zimbabwe 86 C2 ....20.04S 30.48E
Matadi Dem. Rep. Congo 86 A4 ....5.49S 13.29E
Matagami Canada 65 K6 ....49.46N 77.38W
Matam Senegal 84 C3 ....15.40N 13.16W
Matamoros Mexico 70 E6 ....25.53N 97.34W
Matanzas Cuba 71 H5 ....23.04N 81.34W
Matara Sri Lanka 96 F2 ....5.58N 80.29E
Mataram Indonesia 104 F2 ....8.35S 116.10E
Mataró Spain 48 F4 ....41.33N 2.26E
Matā'utu Wallis and Futuna Is 108 I5 ....13.17S 176.07W
Matehuala Mexico 64 F1 ....23.40N 100.38W
Matera Italy 50 G4 ....40.40N 16.37E
Mathura India 96 E6 ....27.26N 77.43E
Matlock England 15 F2 ....53.08N 1.33W
Mato Grosso d. Brazil 77 J5 ....12.17S 54.47W
Mato Grosso, Planalto do f. Brazil 77 J4 ....15.05S 54.12W
Mato Grosso do Sul d. Brazil 77 J3 ....20.42S 53.59W
Maṭraḥ Oman 95 I4 ....23.37N 58.32E
Matsue Japan 106 B3 ....35.28N 133.03E
Matsumoto Japan 106 C3 ....36.15N 137.58E
Matsusaka Japan 106 C2 ....34.34N 136.33E
Matsu Tao i. Taiwan 103 M3 ....26.13N 120.03E
Matsuyama Japan 106 B2 ....33.49N 132.46E
Matterhorn mt. Italy/Switz. 50 B6 ....45.59N 7.40E
Maturín Venezuela 72 C7 ....9.44N 63.09W
Mau r. Kenya 87 A2 ....0.29S 35.52E
Maubeuge France 42 C3 ....50.17N 3.58E
Mauchline Scotland 16 E3 ....55.31N 4.23W
Maughold Head Isle of Man 14 C3 ....54.18N 4.18W
Maug Islands N. Mariana Is 105 L8 ....20.01N 145.16E
Maui i. U.S.A. 109 J7 ....20.48N 156.00W
Mauke i. Cook Is 109 J4 ....20.11S 157.18W
Maumere Indonesia 105 G2 ....8.40S 122.13E
Maun Botswana 86 B3 ....19.57S 23.25E
Mauritania Africa 84 C3 ....19.51N 11.35W
Mauritius country Indian Oc. 115 L4 ....20.10S 58.00E
May, Isle of i. Scotland 17 G4 ....56.11N 2.33W
Maya r. Rus. Fed. 59 O4 ....60.26N 134.33E
Mayaguana i. Bahamas 71 J5 ....22.23N 72.56W
Mayagüez Puerto Rico 71 K4 ....18.12N 67.08W
Mayamey Iran 95 I7 ....36.27N 55.40E
Mayar hill Scotland 19 F1 ....56.51N 3.15W
Maybole Scotland 16 E3 ....55.21N 4.41W
Mayen Germany 42 G3 ....50.19N 7.13E
Mayenne France 44 C5 ....47.30N 0.32W
Maykop Rus. Fed. 57 N7 ....44.36N 40.07E
Mayo Canada 62 E4 ....63.37N 135.54W
Mayo d. Rep. of Ireland 41 B3 ....53.46N 9.13W
Mayotte i. Africa 86 D3 ....12.59S 45.09E
Mazār-e Sharīf Afgh. 95 K7 ....36.43N 67.07E

Mazatlán Mexico 70 C5 ....23.14N 106.27W
Mažeikiai Lithuania 40 E2 ....56.18N 22.22E
Mazyr Belarus 55 M5 ....52.03N 29.15E
Mbabane Swaziland 86 C2 ....26.20S 31.09E
Mbandaka Dem. Rep. Congo 86 A4 ....0.00S 18.17E
M'banza Congo Angola 86 A4 ....6.14S 14.15E
Mbarara Uganda 87 A3 ....0.35S 30.37E
Mbeya Tanzania 86 C4 ....8.53S 33.26E
Mbuji-Mayi Dem. Rep. Congo 86 B4 ....6.06S 23.36E
Mbulu Tanzania 87 A2 ....3.50S 35.31E
McClintock Channel Canada 62 H5 ....71.10N 101.39W
McClure Strait Canada 62 G5 ....74.09N 114.57W
McCook U.S.A. 64 F5 ....40.14N 100.39W
McGrath U.S.A. 62 C4 ....62.52N 155.37W
McKinley, Mount U.S.A. 62 C4 ....63.05N 150.20W
Mdantsane S. Africa 86 B1 ....32.58S 27.48E
Mead, Lake resr U.S.A. 64 D4 ....36.12N 114.24W
Mealasta Island Scotland 18 B3 ....58.05N 7.10W
Meall a' Bhuiridh mt. Scotland 18 E1 ....56.37N 4.51W
Meath d. Rep. of Ireland 41 E3 ....53.41N 6.35W
Meaux France 44 E6 ....48.58N 2.53E
Mecca Saudi Arabia 94 E4 ....21.25N 39.47E
Mechelen Belgium 42 D4 ....51.01N 4.29E
Mecheria Algeria 52 C3 ....33.33N 0.19W
Meckenheim Germany 42 G3 ....50.37N 7.02E
Medan Indonesia 104 B4 ....3.38N 98.40E
Medellín Colombia 72 B7 ....6.13N 75.35W
Meden r. England 15 G2 ....53.25N 0.59W
Medenine Tunisia 52 F3 ....33.21N 10.31E
Medetsiz Tepe mt. Turkey 57 K3 ....37.24N 34.37E
Mediaş Romania 56 F8 ....46.10N 24.22E
Medicine Hat Canada 62 G3 ....50.03N 110.41W
Medina Saudi Arabia 94 E4 ....24.31N 39.32E
Medina del Campo Spain 48 C4 ....41.19N 4.54W
Medvezh'yegorsk Rus. Fed. 58 E4 ....62.55N 34.29E
Medway d. England 9 F2 ....51.22N 0.34E
Medway r. England 11 F2 ....51.21N 0.27E
Meerut India 96 E6 ....29.02N 77.45E
Měga Ethiopia 87 B4 ....4.01N 38.20E
Mega Escarpment f. Ethiopia/Kenya 87 B4 ....4.01N 38.05E
Megara Greece 56 E3 ....38.00N 23.21E
Meghalaya d. India 97 H6 ....25.36N 91.22E
Meiktila Myanmar 97 I5 ....20.50N 95.53E
Meiningen Germany 54 D4 ....50.34N 10.25E
Meißen Germany 54 F4 ....51.10N 13.28E
Meizhou China 103 L2 ....24.17N 116.09E
Mejicana mt. Argentina 76 G2 ....29.01S 67.50W
Mek'elē Ethiopia 94 E2 ....13.31N 39.28E
Meknès Morocco 84 D5 ....33.53N 5.30W
Mekong r. Asia 97 K3 ....10.53N 105.14E
Mekong, Mouths of the Vietnam 104 D5 ....9.03N 106.31E
Melaka Malaysia 104 C4 ....2.09N 102.17E
Melanesia is Pacific Oc. 108 G5 ....10.00S 165.00E
Melanesian Basin f. Pacific Oc. 108 G6 ....0.19N 164.50E
Melbourn England 11 F3 ....52.05N 0.02E
Melbourne Australia 110 D3 ....37.49S 144.58E
Melbourne U.S.A. 65 J2 ....28.01N 80.43W
Melby England 11 F3 ....60.18N 1.40W
Melilla N. Africa 52 C4 ....35.18N 2.57W
Melitopol' Ukraine 55 P2 ....46.51N 35.22E
Melka Guba Ethiopia 87 B4 ....4.41N 39.13E
Melksham England 10 C2 ....51.22N 2.08W
Melo Uruguay 77 J1 ....32.22S 54.10W
Melrhir, Chott l. Algeria 84 E5 ....34.15N 6.23E
Melrose Scotland 17 G3 ....55.36N 2.43W
Meltham England 15 F2 ....53.36N 1.51W
Melton Mowbray England 10 E3 ....52.46N 0.53W
Melun France 44 E6 ....48.32N 2.39E
Melvich Scotland 19 F3 ....58.33N 3.55W
Melville Canada 62 H3 ....50.56N 102.49W
Melville Bay Greenland 63 L4 ....76.00N 64.00W
Melville Island Australia 110 C5 ....11.37S 130.55E
Melville Island Canada 62 H5 ....75.14N 109.26W
Melville Peninsula Canada 63 J4 ....68.09N 84.12W
Melvin, Lough l. Rep. of Ireland/U.K. 41 C4 ....54.25N 8.09W
Memberamo r. Indonesia 105 J3 ....1.32S 137.52E
Memmingen Germany 54 D2 ....47.59N 10.11E
Memphis U.S.A. 65 H4 ....35.09N 90.04W
Mena Ukraine 55 O4 ....51.31N 32.14E
Menai Bridge Wales 12 C5 ....53.13N 4.10W
Menai Strait Wales 12 C5 ....53.09N 4.17W
Mende France 44 E4 ....44.31N 3.30E
Mendebo mts Ethiopia 87 B4 ....5.50N 38.39E
Mendí Ethiopia 85 H2 ....9.49N 35.03E
Mendip Hills England 10 C2 ....51.19N 2.64W
Mendoza Argentina 73 C3 ....32.53S 68.50W
Menongue Angola 86 A3 ....14.38S 17.41E
Mentawai, Kepulauan is Indonesia 104 B3 ....3.17S 99.55E
Mentok Indonesia 104 C3 ....2.01S 105.12E
Menzel Bourguiba Tunisia 52 E4 ....37.09N 9.46E
Meppel Neth. 42 F5 ....52.41N 7.18E
Meppen Germany 42 G5 ....52.41N 7.18E
Merano Italy 50 D7 ....46.41N 11.10E
Merauke Indonesia 105 K2 ....8.31S 140.25E
Mercedes Uruguay 77 I1 ....33.16S 58.01W
Mere England 10 C2 ....51.05N 2.16W
Merefa Ukraine 55 Q3 ....49.49N 36.04E
Mergui Myanmar 97 I3 ....12.29N 98.37E
Mergui Archipelago is Myanmar 97 I3 ....11.38N 97.41E
Mérida Mexico 70 G5 ....20.59N 89.37W
Mérida Spain 48 B3 ....38.56N 6.20W
Mérida Venezuela 72 B7 ....8.36N 71.07W
Mérida, Cordillera de mts Venezuela 71 J2 ....7.59N 71.35W
Meridian U.S.A. 65 I3 ....32.23N 88.40W
Merkys r. Lithuania 46 G5 ....54.08N 24.12E
Merowe Sudan 85 H3 ....18.27N 31.51E
Merrick hill Scotland 16 E3 ....55.08N 4.28W
Mersch Lux. 42 F2 ....49.45N 6.07E
Mersey est. England 14 E2 ....53.21N 2.56W
Merseyside d. England 9 D3 ....53.32N 3.06W
Mersin Turkey 57 K3 ....36.49N 34.37E
Merthyr Tydfil Wales 12 D3 ....51.45N 3.23W
Merthyr Tydfil d. Wales 9 D2 ....51.44N 3.20W
Merti Kenya 87 B3 ....1.02N 38.39E
Mértola Portugal 48 B2 ....37.38N 7.39W
Méru France 42 A2 ....49.14N 2.08E
Meru Kenya 87 B3 ....0.05N 37.38E
Meru vol. Tanzania 87 B2 ....3.15S 36.44E
Merzifon Turkey 57 K5 ....40.52N 35.27E
Merzig Germany 42 F2 ....49.27N 6.39E
Mesolongi Greece 56 D4 ....38.22N 21.26E
Mesopotamia f. Iraq 85 I5 ....35.42N 42.19E
Messina Italy 50 F3 ....38.11N 15.33E
Messina, Strait of str. Italy 50 F3 ....38.11N 15.34E
Mesta r. Bulgaria 56 F5 ....41.26N 24.02E
Meta r. Col./Venez. 72 C7 ....6.10N 67.24W
Metheringham England 15 G2 ....53.08N 0.24W
Methwold England 11 F3 ....52.31N 0.33E
Metković Croatia 56 B6 ....43.03N 17.40E
Metlika Slovenia 54 F1 ....45.39N 15.19E
Metz France 44 G6 ....49.07N 6.11E
Meuse r. Belgium/France 42 E4 ....51.08N 5.51E

Mevagissey England 13 C2 ....50.16N 4.47W
Mexborough England 15 F2 ....53.30N 1.17W
Mexicali Mexico 70 A7 ....32.39N 115.28W
Mexico Central America 70 C5 ....31.47N 114.01W
México d. Mexico 70 E4 ....19.38N 99.46W
Mexico, Gulf of Mexico/U.S.A. 70 F5 ....25.29N 95.51W
Mexico City Mexico 70 E4 ....19.24N 99.12W
Meymaneh Afgh. 95 J7 ....35.56N 64.45E
Mezen' Rus. Fed. 35 I4 ....65.50N 44.18E
Mezha r. Rus. Fed. 55 N6 ....55.43N 31.30E
Mezőtúr Hungary 46 I1 ....46.59N 20.39E
Mezquital r. Mexico 70 C5 ....21.52N 105.29W
Mfangano Island Uganda 87 A2 ....0.27S 34.00E
Miami U.S.A. 65 J2 ....25.41N 80.18W
Miandowāb Iran 95 G7 ....36.58N 46.07E
Miandrivazo Madagascar 86 D3 ....19.30S 45.29E
Mīāneh Iran 95 G7 ....37.24N 47.40E
Mianwali Pakistan 95 L6 ....32.32N 71.34E
Miass Rus. Fed. 58 H3 ....54.58N 60.05E
Michalovce Slovakia 46 E2 ....48.45N 21.55E
Michigan d. U.S.A. 65 I6 ....46.12N 88.00W
Michigan, Lake U.S.A. 65 I5 ....43.02N 87.18W
Michipicoten Island Canada 65 I6 ....47.41N 85.48W
Michipicoten River town Canada 65 J6 ....47.57N 84.50W
Michoacán d. Mexico 70 D4 ....18.21N 102.59W
Michurinsk Rus. Fed. 58 F3 ....52.55N 40.30E
Micronesia is Pacific Oc. 108 F6 ....11.40N 147.31E
Micronesia, Federated States of N. Pacific Oc. 105 K5
..........3.37N 153.49E
Mid-Atlantic Ridge f. Atlantic Ocean 109 Q7 ....16.18N 49.57W
Middlesbrough England 15 F3 ....54.34N 1.14W
Middlesbrough d. England 9 E4 ....54.33N 1.14W
Middleton England 15 E2 ....53.33N 2.12W
Middleton St George England 15 F3 ....54.31N 1.28W
Middlewich England 15 E2 ....53.12N 2.27W
Midhurst England 10 E1 ....50.59N 0.44W
Mid-Indian Basin f. Indian Oc. 108 B5 ....8.48S 79.56E
Midland U.S.A. 64 F3 ....32.01N 101.58W
Midleton Rep. of Ireland 41 C1 ....51.55N 8.10W
Midlothian d. Scotland 8 D4 ....55.49N 3.12W
Mid-Pacific Mountains f. N. Pacific Oc. 108 G7 ....23.27N 150.34E
Midway Islands N. Pacific Oc. 108 I7 ....28.18N 177.17W
Miekojärvi l. Finland 40 F4 ....66.34N 24.25E
Mielec Poland 46 E3 ....50.17N 21.26E
Miercurea-Ciuc Romania 56 F8 ....46.22N 25.48E
Mikhaylovskiy Rus. Fed. 102 D8 ....51.40N 79.45E
Mikkeli Finland 40 F3 ....61.41N 27.17E
Milan Italy 50 C6 ....45.28N 9.11E
Milas Turkey 57 G3 ....37.18N 27.46E
Milborne Port England 10 C1 ....50.58N 2.28W
Mildenhall England 11 F3 ....52.20N 0.30E
Mildura Australia 110 D3 ....34.12S 142.11E
Miles City U.S.A. 64 E6 ....46.24N 105.47W
Milford Haven Wales 12 B3 ....51.43N 5.02W
Milk r. U.S.A. 64 E6 ....48.03N 106.19W
Millárs r. Spain 48 E3 ....39.57N 0.04W
Millau France 44 E4 ....44.06N 3.05E
Mille Lacs lakes U.S.A. 65 H6 ....46.14N 93.39W
Milleur Point Scotland 16 D3 ....55.01N 5.07W
Millom England 14 D3 ....54.13N 3.16W
Millport Scotland 16 E3 ....55.45N 4.56W
Milnthorpe England 14 E3 ....54.14N 2.46W
Milos i. Greece 56 F3 ....36.39N 24.25E
Milton Keynes England 10 E3 ....52.01N 0.44W
Milton Keynes d. England 9 E3 ....52.01N 0.44W
Milwaukee U.S.A. 65 I5 ....43.01N 87.55W
Mimizan France 44 C4 ....44.12N 1.14W
Mīnāb Iran 95 I5 ....27.09N 57.04E
Minas Indonesia 104 B3 ....0.52N 101.30E
Minas Gerais d. Brazil 77 L4 ....18.31S 44.00W
Minatitlán Mexico 70 F4 ....18.01N 94.33W
Mindanao i. Phil. 105 H5 ....7.48N 125.06E
Mindelo Cape Verde 84 B3 ....16.52N 24.59W
Mindoro i. Phil. 105 G6 ....13.05N 120.52E
Mindoro Strait Phil. 104 F6 ....12.47N 119.59E
Minehead England 13 D3 ....51.12N 3.29W
Mingulay i. Scotland 18 B1 ....56.49N 7.37W
Minna Nigeria 84 E2 ....9.38N 6.32E
Minneapolis U.S.A. 65 H5 ....44.59N 93.18W
Minnesota d. U.S.A. 65 H6 ....47.08N 92.44W
Minnesota r. U.S.A. 65 H5 ....44.55N 93.11W
Miño r. Portugal/Spain 48 A4 ....41.56N 8.45W
Minorca i. Spain 48 G4 ....40.06N 3.51E
Minot U.S.A. 64 F6 ....48.13N 101.18W
Minsk Belarus 55 L5 ....53.53N 27.34E
Mińsk Mazowiecki Poland 46 E4 ....52.11N 21.34E
Minsterley England 10 C3 ....52.38N 2.55W
Mintlaw Scotland 19 H2 ....57.31N 1.59W
Miraj Brazil 77 I3 ....20.11S 56.21W
Miranda r. Brazil 77 I4 ....19.27S 57.17W
Miranda de Ebro Spain 48 D5 ....42.42N 2.56W
Mirandela Portugal 48 B4 ....41.29N 7.10W
Mirbāṭ Oman 95 H3 ....17.02N 54.43E
Miri Malaysia 104 E4 ....4.27N 114.01E
Mirim, Lagoa l. Brazil/Uruguay 77 J1 ....32.40S 52.55W
Mirnyy Rus. Fed. 59 M4 ....62.25N 114.10E
Mirpur Khas Pakistan 96 C6 ....25.32N 69.04E
Mirzapur India 96 F6 ....25.06N 82.39E
Miskitos, Cayos is Nicaragua 71 H3 ....14.24N 82.44W
Miskolc Hungary 54 I3 ....48.06N 20.48E
Misoöl i. Indonesia 105 I3 ....1.53S 130.06E
Miṣrātah Libya 84 F5 ....32.21N 15.04E
Missinaibi r. Canada 63 J3 ....50.45N 81.31W
Mississippi d. U.S.A. 65 I3 ....32.33N 89.45W
Mississippi r. U.S.A. 65 H2 ....29.09N 89.17W
Mississippi Delta U.S.A. 65 I2 ....29.05N 89.06W
Missoula U.S.A. 64 D6 ....46.53N 113.58W
Missouri d. U.S.A. 65 H4 ....38.27N 92.10W
Missouri r. U.S.A. 65 H4 ....38.50N 90.09W
Mistassini, Lac l. Canada 63 K3 ....51.01N 73.34W
Mistissini Canada 63 K3 ....50.13N 73.48W
Mitchell r. Australia 110 D5 ....15.16S 141.37E
Mitchell U.S.A. 64 G5 ....43.42N 98.02W
Mitchelstown Rep. of Ireland 41 C2 ....52.16N 8.16W
Mito Japan 106 D3 ....36.23N 140.28E
Mitchell r. Australia ....
Mittimatalik Canada 63 K5 ....72.35N 77.46W
Mitumba, Chaîne des mts Dem. Rep. Congo 86 B3
..........11.46S 26.06E
Miyako Japan 106 D3 ....39.38N 141.57E
Miyazaki Japan 106 B2 ....31.54N 131.25E
Mizdah Libya 52 F3 ....31.25N 12.59E
Mizen Head Cork Rep. of Ireland 41 B1 ....51.26N 9.49W
Mizen Head Wick. Rep. of Ireland 41 E2 ....52.51N 6.03W
Mizhhir''ya Ukraine 46 F2 ....48.31N 23.31E
Mizoram d. India 97 H5 ....23.27N 92.50E
Mjölby Sweden 40 C2 ....58.20N 15.08E
Mkoani Tanzania 87 B1 ....5.23S 39.39E
Mkomazi Tanzania 87 B1 ....4.40S 38.06E
Mkomazi Game Reserve Tanzania 87 B2 ....3.53S 38.06E
Mladá Boleslav Czech Rep. 54 F4 ....50.25N 14.55E
Mława Poland 46 E4 ....53.07N 20.23E

Mljet i. Croatia 56 B6 ....42.44N 17.27E
Mmabatho S. Africa 86 B2 ....25.47S 25.37E
Mobile U.S.A. 65 I3 ....30.40N 88.04W
Mobile Bay U.S.A. 65 I3 ....30.25N 88.00W
Mobridge U.S.A. 64 F6 ....45.32N 100.25W
Moçambique Mozambique 86 D3 ....15.05S 40.41E
Mocha Yemen 95 F1 ....13.20N 43.12E
Mochudi Botswana 86 B2 ....24.25S 26.08E
Mocuba Mozambique 86 C3 ....16.53S 36.58E
Modbury England 13 D2 ....50.21N 3.53W
Modena Italy 50 D6 ....44.39N 10.56E
Moelfre Wales 12 C5 ....53.21N 4.14W
Moel Sych hill Wales 12 D4 ....52.53N 3.23W
Moffat Scotland 17 F3 ....55.20N 3.26W
Mogadishu Somalia 85 I2 ....2.04N 45.20E
Mohawk r. U.S.A. 65 L5 ....42.46N 73.44W
Mohyliv Podil's'kyy Ukraine 55 L3 ....48.27N 27.48E
Mo i Rana Norway 40 C4 ....66.19N 14.10E
Moji das Cruzes Brazil 77 K3 ....23.32S 46.10W
Mojos, Llanos de f. Bolivia 76 G5 ....14.42S 66.08W
Mold Wales 12 D5 ....53.10N 3.08W
Molde Norway 40 A3 ....62.44N 7.10E
Moldova Europe 53 I6 ....46.59N 28.55E
Moldoveanu, Vârful mt. Romania 56 F7 ....45.36N 24.45E
Molétai Lithuania 46 G5 ....55.14N 25.25E
Molfetta Italy 50 G4 ....41.12N 16.36E
Molopo watercourse Botswana/S. Africa 86 B2 ....28.32S 20.13E
Moluccas is Indonesia 108 E5 ....0.30S 127.26E
Molucca Sea Indonesia 105 H3 ....1.08S 125.11E
Mombasa Kenya 87 B2 ....3.59S 39.40E
Møn i. Denmark 46 C5 ....55.00N 12.22E
Mona, Isla i. Puerto Rico 71 K4 ....18.04N 67.52W
Monach, Sound of str. Scotland 18 B2 ....57.33N 7.39W
Monaco Europe 44 G3 ....43.44N 7.26E
Monadhliath Mountains Scotland 19 E2 ....57.04N 4.31W
Monaghan Rep. of Ireland 41 E4 ....54.15N 6.57W
Monaghan d. Rep. of Ireland 41 E4 ....54.10N 6.59W
Mona Passage str. Dom. Rep./Puerto Rico 71 K4 ....18.01N 68.06W
Monar, Loch l. Scotland 18 D2 ....57.25N 5.08W
Monbetsu Japan 106 D4 ....44.21N 143.21E
Monchegorsk Rus. Fed. 40 H4 ....67.57N 32.56E
Mönchengladbach Germany 42 F4 ....51.12N 6.25E
Monclova Mexico 70 D6 ....26.53N 101.30W
Moncton Canada 63 L2 ....46.04N 64.47W
Mondego r. Portugal 48 A4 ....40.10N 8.39W
Mondovì Italy 50 B6 ....44.23N 7.49E
Moneymore Northern Ireland 16 C2 ....54.41N 6.40W
Monforte de Lemos Spain 48 B5 ....42.32N 7.30W
Monga Dem. Rep. Congo 86 B5 ....4.11N 22.50E
Mongolia Asia 103 I7 ....46.59N 103.48E
Mongora Pakistan 95 L6 ....34.46N 72.30E
Mongu Zambia 86 B3 ....15.15S 23.08E
Moniaive Scotland 17 F3 ....55.12N 3.55W
Monmouth Wales 12 E3 ....51.49N 2.43W
Monmouthshire d. Wales 9 D2 ....51.47N 2.58W
Monnow r. U.K. 10 C2 ....51.49N 2.43W
Monroe U.S.A. 65 H3 ....32.30N 92.06W
Monrovia Liberia 84 C2 ....6.20N 10.46W
Mons Belgium 42 C3 ....50.27N 3.57E
Montana Bulgaria 56 E6 ....43.25N 23.13E
Montana d. U.S.A. 64 E6 ....46.44N 109.17W
Montargis France 44 E5 ....47.59N 2.44E
Montauban France 44 D4 ....44.01N 1.21E
Montbéliard France 44 G5 ....47.30N 6.49E
Mont-de-Marsan France 44 C3 ....43.53N 0.30W
Montdidier France 42 B2 ....49.39N 2.35E
Monte Alegre Brazil 77 J7 ....1.58S 54.04W
Monte-Carlo Monaco 44 G3 ....43.44N 7.25E
Montecristo, Isola di i. Italy 50 D5 ....42.19N 10.18E
Montego Bay town Jamaica 71 I4 ....18.28N 77.54W
Montélimar France 44 F4 ....44.33N 4.45E
Monte Lindo r. Paraguay 77 I3 ....23.57S 57.16W
Montemorelos Mexico 70 E6 ....25.11N 99.49W
Monterey U.S.A. 64 C4 ....25.42N 100.18W
Monte Santu, Capo di c. Italy 50 C4 ....40.04N 9.44E
Montes Claros Brazil 77 L4 ....16.42S 43.49W
Montevideo Uruguay 77 D3 ....34.52S 56.13W
Monte Vista U.S.A. 64 E4 ....37.36N 106.09W
Montgomery U.S.A. 65 I3 ....32.23N 86.19W
Montgomery Wales 12 D4 ....52.34N 3.09W
Mont-Joli Canada 65 M6 ....48.35N 68.12W
Montluçon France 44 E5 ....46.21N 2.36E
Montmagny Canada 65 L6 ....46.59N 70.34W
Montpelier U.S.A. 65 L5 ....44.16N 72.35W
Montpellier France 44 E3 ....43.37N 3.53E
Montréal Canada 63 K2 ....45.32N 73.35W
Montreuil France 11 G1 ....50.28N 1.46E
Montrose Scotland 19 G1 ....56.42N 2.28W
Montserrat i. Central America 71 L4 ....16.44N 62.12W
Monywa Myanmar 97 I5 ....22.05N 95.13E
Monza Italy 50 C6 ....45.35N 9.17E
Monzón Spain 48 F4 ....41.55N 0.11E
Moore, Lake Australia 110 A4 ....29.43S 117.28E
Moose r. Canada 63 J3 ....51.20N 80.31W
Moose Jaw Canada 62 H3 ....50.26N 105.33W
Moosomin Canada 64 F7 ....50.09N 101.41W
Moosonee Canada 63 J3 ....51.16N 80.40W
Mopti Mali 84 D3 ....14.30N 4.10W
Moquegua Peru 76 F4 ....17.09S 70.55W
Mora Sweden 40 C3 ....61.00N 14.32E
Morar, Loch l. Scotland 18 D1 ....56.57N 5.43W
Moray d. Scotland 8 D5 ....57.30N 3.16W
Moray Firth b. Scotland 19 E2 ....57.31N 4.11W
Morbach Germany 42 G2 ....49.48N 7.06E
Morden Canada 62 I2 ....49.12N 98.07W
More, Loch l. Scotland 18 E3 ....58.18N 4.53W
Morecambe England 14 D3 ....54.04N 2.52W
Morecambe Bay England 14 D3 ....54.07N 3.04W
Moree Australia 110 D4 ....29.28S 149.52E
Morehead P.N.G. 105 K2 ....8.44S 141.39E
Morelia Mexico 70 D4 ....19.39N 101.12W
Morelos d. Mexico 70 E4 ....18.47N 98.59W
Morena, Sierra mts Spain 48 B2 ....37.57N 6.06W
Moretonhampstead England 13 D2 ....50.40N 3.46W
Morgan City U.S.A. 65 H2 ....29.43N 91.25W
Mori Japan 106 D4 ....42.06N 140.34E
Morioka Japan 106 D3 ....39.42N 141.08E
Moriston r. Scotland 18 E2 ....57.13N 4.36W
Morlaix France 44 B6 ....48.35N 3.50W
Morley England 15 F2 ....53.45N 1.36W
Mornington Abyssal Plain f. S. Atlantic Oc. 109 O2
..........50.59S 89.12W
Morocco Africa 84 D5 ....31.57N 5.40W
Morogoro Tanzania 86 C4 ....6.47S 37.40E
Moro Gulf Phil. 105 G5 ....6.59N 123.21E
Morombe Madagascar 86 D2 ....21.46S 43.21E
Mörön Mongolia 103 I7 ....49.28N 100.08E
Morondava Madagascar 86 D2 ....20.18S 44.17E
Morón de la Frontera Spain 48 C2 ....37.08N 5.27W
Moroni Comoros 86 D3 ....11.39S 43.14E
Morotai i. Indonesia 105 H4 ....2.23N 128.27E
Moroto Uganda 87 A3 ....2.31N 34.40E

Moroto, Mount Uganda 87 A3 ....2.30N 34.47E
Morpeth England 15 F4 ....55.10N 1.41W
Morriston Wales 12 D3 ....51.40N 3.56W
Morro, Punta pt Chile 73 B4 ....27.07S 70.59W
Morrosquillo, Golfo de b. Colombia 71 I2 ..9.33N 75.39W
Morte Bay England 13 C3 ....51.10N 4.14W
Mortehoe England 13 C3 ....51.11N 4.12W
Mortes, Rio das r. Brazil 77 J5 ....11.49S 50.37W
Mortlock Islands Micronesia 108 G6 ....5.07N 153.51E
Morungole mt. Uganda 87 A3 ....3.48N 34.02E
Moruroa atoll French Polynesia 109 K4 ..21.50S 138.44W
Morvern f. Scotland 18 D1 ....56.36N 5.53W
Mosborough England 15 F2 ....53.20N 1.22W
Moscow Rus. Fed. 58 E3 ....55.45N 37.38E
Moscow U.S.A. 64 C6 ....46.44N 116.58W
Mosel r. Germany 42 G3 ....50.22N 7.36E
Moselle r. France 44 G6 ....49.27N 6.22E
Moshi Tanzania 86 C4 ....3.23S 37.20E
Mosina Poland 46 C4 ....52.14N 16.51E
Mosjøen Norway 40 C4 ....65.51N 13.22E
Mosquitos, Golfo de los b. Panama 71 H2 ..8.56N 81.17W
Moss Norway 40 B2 ....59.26N 10.39E
Mossel Bay town S. Africa 86 B1 ....34.11S 22.08E
Mossoró Brazil 77 M6 ....5.08S 37.15W
Mostaganem Algeria 52 D4 ....35.55N 0.06E
Mostar Bos.-Herz. 56 B6 ....43.20N 17.49E
Mosul Iraq 94 F7 ....36.18N 43.05E
Møsvatnet l. Norway 40 B2 ....59.51N 8.06E
Motala Sweden 40 C2 ....58.32N 15.02E
Motherwell Scotland 17 F3 ....55.48N 3.59W
Motril Spain 48 D2 ....36.45N 3.31W
Moulins France 44 E5 ....46.34N 3.20E
Moulmein Myanmar 97 I4 ....16.30N 97.40E
Moundou Chad 84 F2 ....8.36N 16.05E
Mount Gambier town Australia 110 D3 ..37.52S 140.48E
Mount Isa town Australia 110 C4 ....20.45S 139.29E
Mountmellick Rep. of Ireland 41 D3 ....53.07N 7.20W
Mountrath Rep. of Ireland 41 D3 ....53.00N 7.28W
Mount's Bay England 13 B2 ....50.05S 5.29W
Mountsorrel England 10 D3 ....52.44N 1.08W
Mourdi, Dépression du f. Chad 84 F3 ..18.01N 21.06E
Mourne r. Northern Ireland 16 B2 ......54.50N 7.28W
Mourne Mountains Northern Ireland 16 C2 ..54.06N 6.11W
Mousa i. Scotland 19 H5 ....60.00N 1.11W
Mouscron Belgium 42 C3 ....50.44N 3.13E
Mouzon France 42 E2 ....49.37N 5.05E
Moyale Ethiopia 85 H2 ....3.32N 39.03E
Moyen Atlas mts Morocco 52 B3 ....32.25N 5.37W
Moyle d. Northern Ireland 8 B4 ....54.09N 6.06W
Mozambique Africa 86 C3 ....20.09S 34.14E
Mozambique Channel Africa 86 D2 ....20.15S 40.16E
M'Saken Tunisia 52 F4 ....35.43N 10.35E
Msambweni Kenya 87 B1 ....4.25S 39.31E
Mtelo Kenya 87 A3 ....1.41N 35.22E
Mtsensk Rus. Fed. 55 Q5 ....53.17N 36.36E
Mtwara Tanzania 86 D3 ....10.19S 40.09E
Muar Malaysia 104 C4 ....2.02N 102.34E
Muarabungo Indonesia 104 C3 ....1.27S 102.08E
Muchinga Mountains Zambia 82 G3 ..12.00S 31.00E
Much Wenlock England 10 C3 ....52.36N 2.33W
Muck i. Scotland 18 C1 ....56.50N 6.14W
Muckish Mountain hill Rep. of Ireland 16 A3 ..55.06N 8.00W
Muckle Roe i. Scotland 19 H5 ....60.21N 1.25W
Mudan r. China 106 A5 ....46.15N 129.31E
Mudanjiang China 103 N6 ....44.32N 129.34E
Mudukani Tanzania 87 A2 ....3.54S 35.48E
Mudurnu Turkey 57 I5 ....40.27N 31.13E
Mueda Mozambique 86 C3 ....11.38S 39.34E
Muğla Turkey 57 H3 ....37.12N 28.21E
Muhammad Qol Sudan 94 E4 ....20.54N 37.07E
Mühlhausen Germany 54 D4 ....51.13N 10.27E
Muhos Finland 40 F4 ....64.48N 25.58E
Mui Ethiopia 87 A4 ....5.59N 35.33E
Muine Bheag Rep. of Ireland 41 E2 ....52.42N 6.58W
Muirkirk Scotland 17 F3 ....55.31N 4.04W
Muirneag hill Scotland 18 C3 ....58.22N 6.18W
Mukacheve Ukraine 55 J3 ....48.27N 22.43E
Mukalla Yemen 95 H2 ....14.34N 49.06E
Mukono Uganda 87 A3 ....0.21S 32.45E
Mulanje, Mount Malawi 86 C3 ....15.54S 35.35E
Mulde r. Germany 54 E4 ....51.52N 12.15E
Mulhacén mt. Spain 48 D2 ....37.02N 3.18W
Mulhouse France 44 G5 ....47.45N 7.20E
Muling r. China 106 B5 ....45.51N 133.26E
Mull i. Scotland 16 D4 ....56.27N 5.58W
Mull, Sound of str. Scotland 16 C4 ....56.37N 6.01W
Mullaghareirk Mountains Rep. of Ireland 41 B2 ..52.22N 9.17W
Mullaghcleevaun hill Rep. of Ireland 12 A5 ..53.06N 6.24W
Mull Head Scotland 19 G4 ....59.23N 2.53W
Mullingar Rep. of Ireland 41 D3 ......53.31N 7.20W
Mull of Galloway c. Scotland 16 E2 ....54.38N 4.52W
Mull of Kintyre hd Scotland 16 D3 ....55.17N 5.50W
Mull of Oa hd Scotland 16 C3 ....55.35N 6.20W
Multan Pakistan 96 D7 ....30.12N 71.35E
Mumbai India 96 E4 ....18.56N 72.51E
Muna i. Indonesia 105 G2 ....5.02S 122.30E
Muna r. Rus. Fed. 59 N4 ....67.51N 123.04E
Mundesley England 11 G3 ....52.53N 1.26E
Mundford England 11 F3 ....52.31N 0.39E
Munger India 96 G6 ....25.22N 86.28E
Munich Germany 54 D3 ....48.08N 11.35E
Munim r. Brazil 77 L7 ....2.49S 44.04W
Münster Germany 54 B4 ....51.57N 7.38E
Muojärvi l. Finland 40 G4 ....65.55N 29.38E
Muonio Finland 40 E4 ....67.57N 23.40E
Muonioälven r. Finland/Sweden 40 E4 ..67.10N 23.33E
Murallón, Cerro mt. Chile 73 B2 ....49.50S 73.27W
Muranga Kenya 87 B2 ....0.43S 37.09E
Murchison watercourse Australia 110 A4 ..27.39S 114.09E
Murcia Spain 48 E2 ....37.59N 1.06W
Mureşul r. Romania 56 D8 ....46.11N 20.29E
Muret France 44 D3 ....43.28N 1.20E
Muriaé Brazil 77 L3 ....21.08S 42.23W
Müritz l. Germany 54 E5 ....53.25N 12.43E
Murmansk Rus. Fed. 58 E4 ....68.57N 33.07E
Muroran Japan 106 D4 ....42.19N 140.58E
Murray r. Australia 110 C3 ....35.22S 139.18E
Murray Bridge Australia 110 C3 ......35.07S 139.17E
Murrumbidgee r. Australia 110 D3 ....34.42S 143.13E
Murwara India 96 F5 ....23.50N 80.23E
Murzuq Libya 84 F4 ....25.54N 13.55E
Mürzzuschlag Austria 54 F2 ....47.37N 15.41E
Musala mt. Bulgaria 56 E6 ....42.11N 23.35E
Muscat Oman 95 I4 ....23.36N 58.35E
Musgrave Ranges mts Australia 110 C4 ..26.17S 131.01E
Muskogee U.S.A. 65 G4 ....35.47N 95.23W
Musmar Sudan 94 E4 ....18.13N 35.40E
Musoma Tanzania 86 C4 ....1.32S 33.47E
Musselburgh Scotland 17 F3 ....55.57N 3.03W
Mustafakemalpaşa Turkey 57 H5 ....40.02N 28.23E
Mūţ Egypt 85 G4 ....25.28N 28.58E
Mut Turkey 57 J3 ....36.39N 33.26E

Mutare Zimbabwe 86 C3 ....18.58S 32.39E
Mutis, Gunung mt. Indonesia 105 G2 ..9.35S 124.14E
Mutsu Japan 106 D4 ....41.17N 141.10E
Mutuali Mozambique 86 C3 ....14.52S 37.01E
Muzaffargarh Pakistan 95 L6 ....30.03N 71.14E
Muzaffarpur India 96 G6 ....26.05N 85.28E
Mwanza Tanzania 86 C4 ....2.30S 32.56E
Mwene-Ditu Dem. Rep. Congo 86 B4 ..7.01S 23.27E
Mweru, Lake Dem. Rep. Congo/Zambia 86 B4 ..8.57S 28.46E
Myanmar Asia 97 I5 ....22.37N 95.02E
Mykolayiv Ukraine 53 J6 ....46.57N 32.02E
Myronivka Ukraine 55 N3 ....49.39N 30.59E
Myrtle Beach town U.S.A. 65 K3 ......33.43N 78.54W
Myślibórz Poland 46 B4 ....52.55N 14.52E
Mysore India 96 E3 ....12.16N 76.36E
My Tho Vietnam 104 D6 ....10.20N 106.23E
Mytilini Greece 56 G4 ....39.07N 26.33E
Mytishchi Rus. Fed. 55 O3 ....55.54N 37.45E
Mzuzu Malawi 86 C3 ....11.27S 34.00E

N

Naas Rep. of Ireland 41 E3 ....53.13N 6.40W
Naberera Tanzania 87 B1 ....4.12S 36.55E
Naberezhnyye Chelny Rus. Fed. 58 G3 ..55.42N 52.21E
Nabeul Tunisia 52 F4 ....36.29N 10.45E
Nacala Mozambique 86 D3 ....14.34S 40.40E
Nador Morocco 52 C4 ....35.11N 2.56W
Nadvirna Ukraine 46 G2 ....48.38N 24.35E
Nadym Rus. Fed. 58 I4 ....65.29N 72.34E
Næstved Denmark 40 B1 ....55.14N 11.46E
Nafplio Greece 56 E3 ....37.34N 22.49E
Naga Phil. 105 G6 ....13.35N 123.11E
Nagaland d. India 97 H6 ....26.03N 94.37E
Nagano Japan 106 C3 ....36.38N 138.11E
Nagaoka Japan 106 C3 ....37.26N 138.51E
Nagaon India 97 H6 ....26.19N 92.42E
Nagasaki Japan 106 A2 ....32.46N 129.52E
Nagercoil India 96 E2 ....8.10N 77.28E
Nagha Kalat Pakistan 95 K5 ....27.23N 65.13E
Nagichot Sudan 87 A4 ....4.14N 33.37E
Nagoya Japan 106 C3 ....35.10N 136.53E
Nagpur India 96 E5 ....21.09N 79.05E
Nagurskoye Rus. Fed. 58 F6 ....80.31N 47.57E
Nagykanizsa Hungary 54 G2 ....46.28N 16.59E
Naha Japan 103 N3 ....26.12N 127.39E
Nahāvand Iran 95 G6 ....34.12N 48.22E
Nailsworth England 10 C2 ....51.42N 2.13W
Nain Canada 63 L3 ....56.31N 61.31W
Na'īn Iran 95 H6 ....32.50N 53.03E
Nairn Scotland 19 F2 ....57.35N 3.52W
Nairn r. Scotland 19 F2 ....57.35N 3.52W
Nairobi Kenya 87 B2 ....1.17S 36.48E
Naivasha Kenya 87 B2 ....0.44S 36.27E
Naivasha, Lake Kenya 87 B2 ....0.46S 36.19E
Najafābād Iran 95 H6 ....32.37N 51.20E
Najd f. Saudi Arabia 94 F5 ....26.14N 40.21E
Najin N. Korea 106 B4 ....42.15N 130.18E
Najrān Saudi Arabia 94 F4 ....17.34N 44.17E
Nakhodka Rus. Fed. 59 O2 ....42.48N 132.54E
Nakhon Ratchasima Thailand 104 C6 ..14.57N 102.08E
Nakhon Sawan Thailand 104 C7 ....15.40N 100.06E
Nakhon Si Thammarat Thailand 104 B5 ..8.25N 99.58E
Nakina Canada 65 I7 ....50.10N 86.43W
Nakonde Zambia 86 C4 ....9.21S 32.42E
Nakskov Denmark 40 B1 ....54.49N 11.09E
Nakuru Kenya 87 B2 ....0.16S 36.05E
Nālūt Libya 84 F5 ....31.49N 10.57E
Namak, Kavīr-e f. Iran 95 I6 ....34.26N 57.32E
Namakzar-e Shadad f. Iran 95 I6 ....30.44N 58.01E
Namanga Kenya 87 B2 ....2.31S 36.49E
Namangan Uzbekistan 102 C6 ......40.59N 71.38E
Nam Co l. China 102 G4 ....30.42N 90.35E
Nam Đinh Vietnam 104 D8 ....20.22N 106.11E
Namib Desert Namibia 86 A2 ....25.21S 15.06E
Namibe Angola 86 A3 ....15.11S 12.10E
Namibia Africa 86 A2 ....23.22S 15.55E
Namlea Indonesia 105 H3 ....3.14S 127.05E
Namp'o N. Korea 103 N5 ....38.43N 125.23E
Nampula Mozambique 86 C3 ....15.10S 39.13E
Namsos Norway 40 B4 ....64.28N 11.31E
Namur Belgium 42 D3 ....50.28N 4.52E
Namur d. Belgium 42 D3 ....50.16N 4.53E
Nan Thailand 104 C7 ....18.47N 100.47E
Nanaimo Canada 64 B6 ....49.10N 123.56W
Nanao Japan 106 C3 ....37.03N 136.58E
Nanchang China 103 L3 ....28.42N 115.58E
Nanchong China 103 J4 ....30.46N 106.04E
Nancy France 44 G6 ....48.42N 6.11E
Nanjing China 103 L4 ....32.04N 118.50E
Nan Ling mts China 103 K2 ....24.59N 111.08E
Nanning China 103 J2 ....22.49N 108.24E
Nanortalik Greenland 63 N4 ....60.09N 45.15W
Nanping China 103 L3 ....26.41N 118.09E
Nansio Tanzania 87 A2 ....2.06S 33.03E
Nantes France 44 C5 ....47.13N 1.33W
Nantes à Brest, Canal de France 44 B5 ..47.42N 2.07W
Nantong China 103 M4 ....31.59N 120.56E
Nantucket Island U.S.A. 65 M5 ....41.17N 69.59W
Nantwich England 15 E2 ....53.04N 2.31W
Nant-y-moch Reservoir Wales 12 D4 ..52.28N 3.54W
Nanumea atoll Tuvalu 108 H5 ......5.38S 176.08E
Nanyang China 103 K4 ....33.01N 112.35E
Nanyuki Kenya 87 B2 ....0.00S 37.04E
Nao, Cabo de la c. Spain 48 F3 ....38.44N 0.15E
Napaimiut U.S.A. 62 C4 ....61.38N 158.24W
Napier New Zealand 111 G3 ....39.30S 176.53E
Naples Italy 50 F4 ....40.51N 14.15E
Napo r. Ecuador 76 F7 ....3.18S 72.37W
Narberth Wales 12 C3 ....51.48N 4.45W
Narbonne France 44 E3 ....43.11N 3.01E
Narborough Leics. England 10 D3 ..52.34N 1.13W
Narborough Norf. England 11 F3 ....52.41N 0.35E
Nares Strait Canada/Greenland 63 K5 ..79.12N 71.28W
Narmada r. India 96 D5 ....21.43N 73.06E
Naro-Fominsk Rus. Fed. 55 Q6 ....55.22N 36.45E
Narok Kenya 87 A2 ....1.06S 35.51E
Närpes Finland 40 E3 ....62.29N 21.21E
Narva Estonia 40 G2 ....59.22N 28.11E
Narvik Norway 40 D5 ....68.26N 17.25E
Nar'yan-Mar Rus. Fed. 58 G4 ......67.40N 53.10E
Naryn Kyrgyzstan 102 D6 ....41.19N 75.56E
Nashik India 96 D5 ....20.00N 73.52E
Nashville U.S.A. 65 I4 ....36.11N 86.46W
Näsijärvi l. Finland 40 E3 ....61.35N 23.44E
Nassau Bahamas 71 I6 ....25.05N 77.23W
Nassau i. Cook Is 108 I5 ....11.32S 165.22W
Nasser, Lake resr Egypt 85 H4 ......23.09N 33.02E
Nässjö Sweden 40 C2 ....57.39N 14.43E
Nata Botswana 86 B2 ....20.12S 26.10E
Nata r. Botswana 87 A2 ....2.01S 34.22E
Natal Brazil 77 M6 ....5.44S 35.10W
Natchez U.S.A. 65 H3 ....31.35N 91.24W

Natron, Lake Tanzania 86 C4 ....2.18S 36.02E
Natuna, Kepulauan is Indonesia 104 D4 ..4.12N 107.23E
Natuna Besar i. Indonesia 104 D4 ..4.04N 108.28E
Naturaliste Plateau f. Indian Oc. 108 D3 ..34.04S 111.21E
Nauru S. Pacific Oc. 108 H5 ....0.30S 166.56E
Navahrudak Belarus 46 G4 ....53.36N 25.50E
Navalmoral de la Mata Spain 48 C3 ..39.53N 5.32W
Navan Rep. of Ireland 41 E3 ....53.39N 6.41W
Navapolatsk Belarus 55 M6 ....55.32N 28.40E
Naver r. Scotland 19 E3 ....58.31N 4.13W
Naver, Loch l. Scotland 19 E3 ......58.17N 4.24W
Navlya Rus. Fed. 55 P5 ....52.49N 34.31E
Navojoa Mexico 70 C6 ....27.04N 109.32W
Nawabshah Pakistan 96 C6 ....26.13N 68.25E
Naxçıvan Azerbaijan 95 G7 ....39.13N 45.24E
Naxos i. Greece 56 F3 ....37.02N 25.35E
Nayarit d. Mexico 70 D5 ....22.07N 104.45W
Nazareth Israel 53 K3 ....32.40N 35.18E
Nazas r. Mexico 70 D6 ....25.34N 104.55W
Nazca Peru 76 F5 ....14.51S 74.54W
Nazca Ridge f. S. Pacific Oc. 109 O4 ..22.54S 83.41W
Nazilli Turkey 57 H3 ....37.55N 28.19E
Nazrēt Ethiopia 85 H2 ....8.32N 39.15E
Nazwá Oman 95 I4 ....22.56N 57.31E
N'dalatando Angola 86 A4 ....9.18S 14.56E
Ndélé C.A.R. 85 G2 ....8.24N 20.38E
Ndjamena Chad 84 F3 ....12.08N 15.03E
Ndola Zambia 86 B3 ....12.57S 28.39E
Ndoto mt. Kenya 87 B3 ....1.46N 37.09E
Neagh, Lough l. Northern Ireland 16 C2 ..54.40N 6.24W
Nea Liosia Greece 56 E4 ....38.04N 23.42E
Neapoli Greece 56 E3 ....36.31N 23.04E
Neath Wales 12 D3 ....51.39N 3.48W
Neath r. Wales 12 D3 ....51.39N 3.49W
Neath Port Talbot d. Wales 9 D2 ....51.43N 3.49W
Nebitdag Turkmenistan 95 H7 ......39.27N 54.17E
Neblina, Pico da mt. Brazil 76 G8 ..0.49N 66.13W
Nebraska d. U.S.A. 64 F5 ....41.30N 100.06W
Nebrodi, Monti mts Italy 50 F2 ....37.43N 14.02E
Nechisar National Park Ethiopia 87 B4 ..5.58N 37.45E
Neckar r. Germany 44 H6 ....49.31N 8.27E
Necker Island U.S.A. 108 J7 ....23.34N 164.42W
Needham Market England 11 G3 ..52.09N 1.03E
Needles U.S.A. 64 D3 ....34.50N 114.36W
Nefyn Wales 12 C4 ....52.56N 4.31W
Negēlē Ethiopia 87 B4 ....5.20N 39.34E
Negotin S.M. 56 E7 ....44.13N 22.33E
Negra, Cordillera mts Peru 76 E6 ..9.19S 78.15W
Negra, Punta pt Peru 76 D6 ....6.05S 81.21W
Negro r. Argentina 73 C2 ....41.01S 62.48W
Negro r. Brazil 77 I4 ....19.17S 57.15W
Negro r. S. America 77 H7 ....3.08S 59.57W
Negro r. Uruguay 77 I1 ....33.24S 58.21W
Negro, Cabo c. Morocco 48 C1 ......35.41N 5.17W
Negros i. Phil. 105 G5 ....9.43N 122.50E
Neijiang China 103 J3 ....29.35N 105.04E
Nei Mongol Zizhiqu d. China 103 I6 ..40.12N 103.26E
Neiße r. Germany/Poland 54 F5 ....52.04N 14.46E
Neiva Colombia 71 J2 ....2.55N 75.15W
Nek'emtē Ethiopia 85 H2 ....9.06N 36.32E
Neksø Denmark 54 F6 ....55.03N 15.08E
Nelidovo Rus. Fed. 55 O7 ....56.14N 32.47E
Nellore India 96 E3 ....14.29N 79.59E
Nelson Canada 62 G2 ....49.29N 117.17W
Nelson r. Canada 63 I3 ....56.58N 92.45W
Nelson England 15 E2 ....53.50N 2.13W
Nelson New Zealand 111 G2 ......41.17S 173.15E
Nelspruit S. Africa 86 C2 ....25.28S 30.59E
Neman Rus. Fed. 46 F5 ....55.02N 22.02E
Neman r. Rus. Fed. 55 J6 ....55.03N 22.14E
Nementcha, Monts des mts Algeria 52 E3 ..34.48N 6.23E
Nemuro Japan 106 E4 ....43.17N 145.30E
Nenagh Rep. of Ireland 41 C2 ......52.52N 8.12W
Nene r. England 11 F3 ....52.49N 0.13E
Nenjiang China 103 N7 ....49.04N 125.12E
Nephin hill Rep. of Ireland 41 B4 ..54.01N 9.22W
Neris r. Lithuania 40 F1 ....54.55N 23.53E
Ness r. Scotland 19 E2 ....57.29N 4.14W
Ness, Loch l. Scotland 19 E2 ......57.10N 4.37W
Neston England 14 D2 ....53.17N 3.04W
Nestos r. Greece 56 F5 ....40.51N 24.48E
Netherlands Europe 42 E5 ....52.35N 5.33E
Netherlands Antilles is Central America 71 K3 ..12.30N 68.43W
Netley England 10 D1 ....50.52N 1.19W
Nettilling Lake Canada 63 K4 ......66.30N 70.39W
Neubari r. Sudan 87 A4 ....7.05N 33.14E
Neubrandenburg Germany 54 E5 ..53.33N 13.15E
Neuchâtel Switz. 50 B7 ....46.59N 6.56E
Neuchâtel, Lac de l. Switz. 50 B7 ..46.51N 6.48E
Neufchâteau Belgium 42 E2 ....49.51N 5.27E
Neumünster Germany 54 C6 ......54.05N 9.59E
Neunkirchen Germany 42 G2 ......49.21N 7.10E
Neuquén Argentina 73 C3 ....38.57S 68.03W
Neuruppin Germany 54 E5 ....52.56N 12.48E
Neustrelitz Germany 54 E5 ....53.22N 13.04E
Neuwied Germany 54 B4 ....50.25N 7.28E
Nevada d. U.S.A. 64 C4 ....39.03N 117.06W
Nevada, Sierra mts Spain 48 D2 ....37.04N 3.20W
Nevada, Sierra mts U.S.A. 64 B5 ....40.07N 121.00W
Nevel' Rus. Fed. 55 M7 ....56.01N 29.55E
Nevers France 44 E5 ....47.00N 3.09E
Nevinnomyssk Rus. Fed. 53 L5 ....44.38N 41.56E
Nevis, Loch inlet Scotland 18 D2 ..57.00N 5.42W
Nevşehir Turkey 57 K4 ....38.37N 34.43E
New Addington England 11 E2 ....51.21N 0.01W
New Alresford England 10 D2 ......51.05N 1.10W
Newark U.S.A. 65 L5 ....40.44N 74.24W
Newark-on-Trent England 15 G2 ..53.04N 0.48W
New Bern U.S.A. 65 K4 ....35.05N 77.03W
Newbiggin-by-the-Sea England 15 F4 ..55.11N 1.31W
Newbridge Rep. of Ireland 41 E3 ..53.11N 6.48W
Newbridge Wales 12 D3 ....51.40N 3.09W
New Britain i. P.N.G. 110 D6 ....5.42S 148.56E
New Britain Trench f. S. Pacific Oc. 108 G5 ..6.43S 150.51E
New Brunswick d. Canada 63 L2 ..46.41N 66.28W
Newburgh Scotland 17 F4 ....56.21N 3.14W
Newbury England 10 D2 ....51.24N 1.19W
New Caledonia is S. Pacific Oc. 111 F4 ..21.41S 164.17E
New Caledonia Trough f. Tasman Sea 108 G4 ..32.56S 164.17E
Newcastle Australia 110 E3 ....32.56S 151.44E
Newcastle Northern Ireland 16 D2 ..54.04S 111.53E
Newcastle Emlyn Wales 12 C4 ....52.02N 4.28W
Newcastle Scotland 17 F3 ....53.51N 0.56W
Newcastle upon Tyne England 15 F3 ..54.59N 1.37W
Newcastle-under-Lyme England 15 E2 ..53.01N 2.13W
Newcastle West Rep. of Ireland 41 B2 ..52.27N 9.03W
New Cumnock Scotland 16 E3 ......55.23N 4.11W
New Delhi India 96 E6 ....28.36N 77.17E
Newent England 10 C2 ....51.56N 2.24W
New Forest nature res. England 10 D1 ..50.52N 1.35W
Newfoundland i. Canada 63 M2 ....48.30N 56.04W
Newfoundland and Labrador d. Canada 63 M3 ..55.44N 66.53W

New Galloway Scotland 16 E3 ......55.05N 4.08W
New Georgia Sound str. Solomon Is 110 E6 ..7.21S 156.36E
New Glasgow Canada 65 N6 ......45.35N 62.35W
New Guinea i. Indonesia/P.N.G. 105 K2 ..5.26S 140.49E
New Hampshire d. U.S.A. 65 L5 ....44.02N 71.34W
Newhaven England 11 F1 ....50.48N 0.03E
New Haven U.S.A. 65 L5 ....41.18N 72.56W
New Hebrides Trench f. S. Pacific Oc. 108 H4 ..22.43S 170.39E
New Ireland i. P.N.G. 110 E6 ......3.33S 152.14E
New Jersey d. U.S.A. 65 L4 ....39.57N 74.26W
New Liskeard Canada 65 K6 ......47.31N 79.41W
Newmarket England 11 F3 ....52.15N 0.25E
Newmarket-on-Fergus Rep. of Ireland 41 C2 ..52.46N 8.53W
New Mexico d. U.S.A. 64 E3 ......34.32N 105.55W
New Milton England 10 D1 ....50.45N 1.40W
Newnham England 10 C2 ....51.48N 2.27W
New Orleans U.S.A. 65 H2 ....29.58N 90.03W
New Pitsligo Scotland 19 G2 ......57.36N 2.12W
Newport Ess. England 11 F2 ......51.59N 0.13E
Newport I. o. W. England 10 D1 ..50.42N 1.17W
Newport Tel. Wre. England 10 C3 ..52.46N 2.22W
Newport New. Wales 12 E3 ....51.35N 2.59W
Newport Pem. Wales 12 C4 ....52.01N 4.50W
Newport d. Wales 9 D2 ....51.35N 2.59W
Newport Bay Wales 12 C4 ....52.02N 4.53W
Newport News U.S.A. 65 K4 ....37.00N 76.26W
Newport Pagnell England 10 E3 ....52.05N 0.43W
New Providence i. Bahamas 71 I6 ..25.03N 77.25W
Newquay England 13 B2 ....50.25N 5.04W
New Romney England 11 F1 ....50.59N 0.56E
New Ross Rep. of Ireland 41 E2 ....52.23N 6.57W
Newry Northern Ireland 16 C2 ......54.10N 6.18W
Newry and Mourne d. Northern Ireland 9 B4 ..54.10N 6.18W
Newry Canal Northern Ireland 16 C2 ..54.16N 6.21W
New Siberia Islands Rus. Fed. 59 P5 ..76.08N 149.21E
New South Wales d. Australia 110 D3 ..32.42S 146.24E
Newton Abbot England 13 D2 ......50.32N 3.37W
Newton Aycliffe England 15 F3 ....54.37N 1.34W
Newtonhill Scotland 19 G2 ....57.02N 2.09W
Newton-le-Willows England 14 E2 ..53.27N 2.38W
Newton Mearns Scotland 16 E3 ....55.46N 4.20W
Newtonmore Scotland 19 E2 ......57.04N 4.07W
Newton St Cyres England 13 D2 ..50.46N 3.35W
Newton Stewart Scotland 16 E2 ....54.58N 4.29W
Newtown Wales 12 D4 ....52.31N 3.19W
Newtownabbey Northern Ireland 16 D2 ..54.39N 5.54W
Newtownabbey d. Northern Ireland 9 C4 ..54.44N 5.59W
Newtownards Northern Ireland 16 D2 ..54.35N 5.41W
Newtown St Boswells Scotland 17 G3 ..55.35N 2.40W
Newtownstewart Northern Ireland 16 B2 ..54.43N 7.22W
New York U.S.A. 65 L5 ....40.41N 73.59W
New York d. U.S.A. 65 K5 ....42.43N 75.14W
New Zealand Oceania 111 G2 ......42.54S 174.10E
Neyrīz Iran 95 H5 ....29.12N 54.19E
Neyshābūr Iran 95 I7 ....36.12N 58.46E
Ngaoundéré Cameroon 84 F2 ......7.19N 13.34E
Ngorongoro Conservation Area Tanzania 87 A2 ..3.06S 35.20E
Nguigmi Niger 84 F3 ....14.14N 13.05E
Ngulu atoll Micronesia 105 J5 ......8.28N 137.37E
Nha Trang Vietnam 104 D6 ....12.11N 109.11E
Niamey Niger 84 E3 ....13.31N 2.07E
Niangara Dem. Rep. Congo 86 B5 ..3.40N 27.52E
Nias i. Indonesia 104 B4 ....1.11N 97.04E
Nīca Latvia 46 E6 ....56.21N 21.04E
Nicaragua Central America 71 G3 ..13.13N 85.57W
Nicaragua, Lake Nicaragua 71 G3 ..11.31N 85.17W
Nice France 44 G3 ....43.42N 7.17E
Nicobar Islands India 97 H2 ....8.00N 93.59E
Nicosia Cyprus 57 J2 ....35.10N 33.22E
Nicoya, Golfo de b. Costa Rica 71 H2 ..9.42N 84.48W
Nidd r. England 15 F3 ....54.01N 1.13W
Nidzica Poland 46 E4 ....53.22N 20.26E
Niedersachsen d. Germany 42 G5 ..52.43N 8.53E
Nienburg Germany 54 C5 ....52.38N 9.13E
Niers r. Germany 54 E5 ....51.42N 5.57E
Nieuwpoort Belgium 42 B4 ....51.08N 2.45E
Nieves, Pico de las mt. Canary Islands 48 Y1 ..27.57S 15.34W
Niğde Turkey 57 K3 ....37.59N 34.41E
Niger Africa 84 E3 ....17.03N 10.05E
Niger r. Africa 84 E2 ....4.17N 6.05E
Nigeria Africa 84 E2 ....9.09N 7.54E
Nigg Bay Scotland 19 E2 ....57.43N 4.05W
Niigata Japan 106 C3 ....37.55N 139.03E
Nijmegen Neth. 42 E4 ....51.50N 5.52E
Nikel' Rus. Fed. 40 G5 ....69.24N 30.13E
Nikopol' Ukraine 55 P2 ....47.34N 34.24E
Niksar Turkey 57 L5 ....40.35N 36.57E
Nikšić S.M. 56 C6 ....42.46N 18.56E
Nikumaroro atoll Kiribati 108 I5 ....4.43S 174.31W
Nile r. Africa 85 H5 ....30.11N 31.06E
Nilgiri Hills India 96 E3 ....11.08N 76.28E
Nîmes France 44 F3 ....43.51N 4.22E
Ninetyeast Ridge f. Indian Oc. 108 B3 ..34.14S 86.15E
Ningbo China 103 M3 ....29.54N 121.34E
Ningxia Huizu Zizhiqu d. China 103 J5 ..37.11N 105.28E
Niobrara r. U.S.A. 64 G5 ....42.46N 98.02W
Nioro Mali 84 D3 ....15.14N 9.36W
Niort France 44 C5 ....46.20N 0.28W
Nipigon Canada 63 J2 ....49.00N 88.17W
Nipigon, Lake Canada 63 J2 ......49.43N 88.33W
Nipissing, Lake Canada 65 K6 ....46.15N 79.39W
Niš S.M. 56 D6 ....43.19N 21.54E
Niterói Brazil 77 L3 ....22.54S 43.06W
Nith r. Scotland 17 F3 ....55.00N 3.36W
Nitra Slovakia 54 H3 ....48.19N 18.05E
Niue i. S. Pacific Oc. 108 I4 ......19.03S 169.45W
Nivelles Belgium 42 D3 ....50.36N 4.20E
Nizamabad India 96 E4 ....18.40N 78.07E
Nizhneudinsk Rus. Fed. 59 K3 ....54.55N 98.58E
Nizhnevartovsk Rus. Fed. 58 I4 ..60.56N 76.38E
Nizhniy Novgorod Rus. Fed. 58 F3 ..56.17N 43.54E
Nizhnyaya Tunguska r. Rus. Fed. 59 J4 ..65.47N 87.59E
Nizhyn Ukraine 55 N4 ....51.02N 31.53E
Nizip Turkey 57 L3 ....36.59N 37.48E
Nkongsamba Cameroon 84 E2 ....4.49N 9.57E
Nobeoka Japan 106 B2 ....32.34N 131.41E
Nogales Mexico 70 B7 ....31.19N 110.57W
Nogent-le-Rotrou France 44 D6 ..48.19N 0.49E
Nogent-sur-Oise France 42 B2 ....49.17N 2.28E
Nohfelden Germany 42 G2 ....49.35N 7.08E
Noirmoutier, Île de i. France 44 B5 ..46.58N 2.16W
Nok Kundi Pakistan 95 J5 ....28.49N 62.50E
Nome U.S.A. 62 B4 ....64.32N 165.28W
Nonthaburi Thailand 104 C6 ......13.51N 100.32E
Noord-Brabant d. Neth. 42 E4 ....51.32N 5.01E
Noord-Holland d. Neth. 42 D5 ....52.33N 4.55E
Nordaustlandet i. Arctic Oc. 58 D5 ..79.36N 22.37E
Norden Germany 42 G6 ....53.36N 7.12E
Norderney i. Germany 42 G6 ......53.44N 7.19E
Norderstedt Germany 54 D5 ......53.44N 10.00E
Nordhausen Germany 54 D4 ......51.30N 10.47E
Nordhorn Germany 42 G5 ....52.26N 7.05E
Nord-Pas-de-Calais d. France 42 B3 ..50.14N 2.43E

160 Index

Nordrhein-Westfalen d. Germany 42 G4 . . . . .51.04N 7.25E
Nordvik Rus. Fed. 59 M5 . . . . .74.01N 111.20E
Nore r. Rep. of Ireland 41 E2 . . . . .52.25N 6.58W
Norfolk d. England 9 F3 . . . . .52.44N 0.59E
Norfolk U.S.A. 65 K4 . . . . .36.53N 76.16W
Norfolk Broads f. England 11 G3 . . . . .52.43N 1.28E
Norfolk Island S. Pacific Oc. 111 F4 . . . . .28.59S 167.59E
Norfolk Island Ridge f. Tasman Sea 108 H4 . .23.53S 167.20E
Noril'sk Rus. Fed. 59 J4 . . . . .69.19N 88.08E
Normandy f. France 44 C6 . . . . .48.53N 0.32W
Normanton Australia 110 D5 . . . . .17.41S 141.05E
Norra Storfjället mts Sweden 40 C4 . . . . . .65.53N 15.07E
Norrköping Sweden 40 D2 . . . . .58.36N 16.12E
Norrtälje Sweden 40 D2 . . . . .59.45N 18.41E
Norseman Australia 110 B3 . . . . .32.14S 121.47E
Norte, Cabo c. Brazil 77 K8 . . . . .1.40N 49.59W
Northallerton England 15 F3 . . . . .54.20N 1.26W
North America 60
North American Basin f. Atlantic Oc. 116 G7 . . .30.00N 60.00W
Northampton England 10 E3 . . . . .52.14N 0.54W
Northamptonshire d. England 9 E3 . . . . . .52.12N 0.57W
North Australian Basin f. Indian Oc. 108 D5 . .14.09S 114.44E
North Ayrshire d. Scotland 8 C4 . . . . .55.44N 4.44W
North Battleford Canada 62 H3 . . . . .52.46N 108.17W
North Bay town Canada 63 K2 . . . . .46.19N 79.28W
North Berwick Scotland 17 G4 . . . . .56.04N 2.43W
North Cape New Zealand 111 G3 . . . . . . .34.25S 173.03E
North Cape Norway 40 F5 . . . . .71.10N 25.47E
North Carolina d. U.S.A. 65 K4 . . . . .36.13N 79.52W
North Cave England 15 G2 . . . . .53.47N 0.39W
North Channel U.K. 16 C3 . . . . .55.23N 6.13W
North China Plain f. China 90 I4 . . . . .34.30N 117.00E
North Dakota d. U.S.A. 64 F6 . . . . .47.19N 100.24W
North Dorset Downs hills England 10 C1 . . . .50.46N 2.32W
North Down d. Northern Ireland 9 C4 . . . . .54.39N 5.43W
North Downs hills England 11 E2 . . . . .51.14N 0.58W
North Eastern d. Kenya 87 C3 . . . . .1.16N 40.00E
North East Lincolnshire d. England 9 E3 . . . .53.37N 0.13W
Northern Dvina r. Rus. Fed. 58 F4 . . . . . . .64.31N 40.33E
Northern Ireland d. U.K. 9 B4 . . . . .54.38N 6.49W
Northern Mariana Islands N. Pacific Oc. 105 K7 . .17.15N 143.32E
Northern Territory d. Australia 110 C5 . . . . .17.40S 133.30E
North Esk r. Scotland 19 G1 . . . . .56.45N 2.26W
North European Plain f. Europe 34 G3 . . . . .56.00N 27.00E
North Foreland c. England 11 G2 . . . . .51.23N 1.27E
North Frisian Islands Germany 54 C6 . . . . . .54.52N 8.02E
North Harris f. Scotland 18 C2 . . . . .57.59N 6.48W
North Hykeham England 15 G2 . . . . .53.11N 0.35W
North Island New Zealand 111 G3 . . . . . . .38.11S 173.23E
North Korea Asia 103 N6 . . . . .40.01N 126.39E
North Lanarkshire d. Scotland 8 D4 . . . . . .55.53N 3.57W
North Lincolnshire d. England 9 E3 . . . . . .53.39N 0.15W
North Platte U.S.A. 64 F5 . . . . .41.09N 100.46W
North Platte r. U.S.A. 64 F5 . . . . .41.10N 100.48W
North Ronaldsay i. Scotland 19 G4 . . . . . .59.24N 2.26W
North Ronaldsay Firth str. Scotland 19 G4 . . .59.20N 2.29W
North Saskatchewan r. Canada 62 H3 . . . . .53.13N 105.11W
North Sea Europe 34 E3 . . . . .56.00N 4.00E
North Shields England 15 F4 . . . . .55.01N 1.27W
North Somercotes England 15 H2 . . . . . . .53.27N 0.09E
North Somerset d. England 9 D2 . . . . .51.24N 2.48W
North Sunderland England 15 F4 . . . . .55.35N 1.39W
North Tidworth England 10 D2 . . . . .51.14N 1.40W
North Tyne r. England 15 E3 . . . . .54.59N 2.08W
North Ugie r. England 19 H2 . . . . .57.32N 1.55W
North Uist i. Scotland 18 B2 . . . . .57.37N 7.26W
Northumberland d. England 8 D4 . . . . .55.09N 2.35W
Northumberland Strait Canada 65 N6 . . . . . .46.50N 64.43W
North Walsham England 11 G3 . . . . .52.49N 1.23E
North West Cape Australia 110 A4 . . . . . . .21.49S 114.12E
Northwest Pacific Basin f. N. Pacific Oc. 108 G8 .35.59N 154.41E
Northwest Territories d. Canada 62 H4 . . . . .63.48N 105.17W
Northwich England 15 E2 . . . . .53.16N 2.31W
North York Moors f. England 15 G3 . . . . . .54.23N 0.50W
North Yorkshire d. England 9 E4 . . . . .54.12N 1.59W
Norton England 15 G3 . . . . .54.08N 0.47W
Norton Fitzwarren England 13 D3 . . . . . . .51.02N 3.08W
Norton Sound str. U.S.A. 62 B4 . . . . .63.58N 163.01W
Norway Europe 40 B3 . . . . .62.46N 10.30E
Norway House Canada 62 I3 . . . . .53.56N 97.52W
Norwegian Sea N. Atlantic Oc. 34 D4 . . . . .66.00N 2.00E
Norwich England 11 G3 . . . . .52.38N 1.18E
Noshiro Japan 106 D4 . . . . .40.12N 140.01E
Noss, Isle of i. Scotland 19 H5 . . . . .60.09N 1.00W
Noteć r. Poland 46 B4 . . . . .52.43N 15.26E
Nottingham England 10 D3 . . . . .52.57N 1.09W
Nottingham d. England 9 E3 . . . . .52.58N 1.10W
Nottinghamshire d. England 9 E3 . . . . .53.03N 0.59W
Nouâdhibou Mauritania 84 C4 . . . . .21.04N 17.00W
Nouâdhibou, Râs c. Mauritania 84 C4 . . . . .20.51N 17.04W
Nouakchott Mauritania 84 C3 . . . . .18.06N 15.58W
Nouméa New Caledonia 111 F4 . . . . .22.18S 166.26E
Noup Head Scotland 19 F4 . . . . .59.20N 3.04W
Nova Friburgo Brazil 77 L3 . . . . .22.18S 42.32W
Nova Gradiška Croatia 56 B7 . . . . .45.16N 17.23E
Nova Iguaçu Brazil 77 L3 . . . . .22.44S 43.29W
Novara Italy 50 C6 . . . . .45.27N 8.37E
Nova Scotia d. Canada 63 L2 . . . . .43.53N 65.45W
Novaya Sibir', Ostrov i. Rus. Fed. 59 P5 . . . .75.04N 148.22E
Novaya Zemlya i. Rus. Fed. 58 G5 . . . . . . .71.41N 55.45E
Nové Zámky Slovakia 54 H2 . . . . .47.59N 18.09E
Novi Pazar S.M. 56 D6 . . . . .43.08N 20.30E
Novi Sad S.M. 56 C7 . . . . .45.16N 19.51E
Novo Aripuanã Brazil 77 H6 . . . . .5.07S 60.20W
Novodvinsk Rus. Fed. 58 F4 . . . . .64.25N 40.50E
Novo Hamburgo Brazil 77 J2 . . . . .29.40S 51.09W
Novohrad-Volyns'kyy Ukraine 55 L4 . . . . . .50.36N 27.37E
Novokuznetsk Rus. Fed. 58 J3 . . . . .53.45N 87.09E
Novo Mesto Slovenia 54 F1 . . . . .45.48N 15.10E
Novomoskovsk Rus. Fed. 58 E3 . . . . .54.01N 38.19E
Novomoskovs'k Ukraine 55 P3 . . . . .48.38N 35.14E
Novooleksiyivka Ukraine 55 K8 . . . . .46.14N 34.39E
Novorossiysk Rus. Fed. 58 E2 . . . . .44.43N 37.47E
Novosibirsk Rus. Fed. 58 J3 . . . . .55.03N 83.02E
Novovolyns'k Ukraine 55 K4 . . . . .50.43N 24.11E
Nový Jičín Czech Rep. 54 G2 . . . . .49.36N 17.59E
Novyy Port Rus. Fed. 58 I4 . . . . .68.13N 73.02E
Nowogard Poland 46 B4 . . . . .53.40N 15.07E
Nowshera Pakistan 95 L6 . . . . .34.00N 72.01E
Nowy Sącz Poland 46 E2 . . . . .49.38N 20.42E
Nowy Targ Poland 46 E2 . . . . .49.29N 20.03E
Noyabr'sk Rus. Fed. 58 I4 . . . . .63.13N 75.32E
Noyon France 42 B2 . . . . .49.35N 2.59E
Npitamaiong mt. Kenya 87 A3 . . . . .3.08N 35.01E
Nu'aym f. Oman 95 I4 . . . . .23.14N 55.59E
Nuba Mountains Sudan 94 D2 . . . . .11.28N 30.33E
Nubian Desert Sudan 85 H4 . . . . .20.25N 34.58E
Nuevo Casas Grandes Mexico 70 C7 . . . . .30.23N 107.56W
Nuevo Laredo Mexico 70 E6 . . . . .27.29N 99.31W
Nuevo León d. Mexico 70 E6 . . . . .25.51N 99.56W
Nui atoll Tuvalu 111 G6 . . . . .7.12S 177.12E

Nuku'alofa Tonga 108 I4 . . . . .21.07S 175.12W
Nukufetau atoll Tuvalu 111 G6 . . . . .8.03S 178.25E
Nuku Hiva i. French Polynesia 109 K5 . . . . . .8.52S 140.06W
Nukunonu atoll Tokelau 108 I5 . . . . .9.05S 171.50W
Nukus Uzbekistan 58 G2 . . . . .42.27N 59.36E
Nullarbor Plain f. Australia 110 B3 . . . . . . .31.01S 129.03E
Numazu Japan 106 C3 . . . . .35.05N 138.52E
Nunavut d. Canada 63 I4 . . . . .66.30N 89.54W
Nunivak Island U.S.A. 62 B3 . . . . .59.58N 166.18W
Nuoro Italy 50 C4 . . . . .40.19N 9.20E
Nuqrah Saudi Arabia 94 F5 . . . . .25.36N 41.26E
Nuremberg Germany 54 D3 . . . . .49.27N 11.06E
Nurmes Finland 40 G3 . . . . .63.33N 29.07E
Nushki Pakistan 95 K5 . . . . .29.34N 66.02E
Nuuk Greenland 63 M4 . . . . .64.11N 51.45W
Nyahururu Kenya 87 B3 . . . . .0.04N 36.23E
Nyala Sudan 85 G3 . . . . .12.03N 24.55E
Nyambeni Hills Kenya 87 B3 . . . . .0.18N 37.54E
Nyanza d. Kenya 87 A2 . . . . .0.26S 34.29E
Nyasa, Lake Africa 86 C4 . . . . .9.59S 34.05E
Nyborg Denmark 40 B1 . . . . .55.19N 10.47E
Nybro Sweden 40 C2 . . . . .56.44N 15.55E
Nyeri Kenya 87 B2 . . . . .0.23S 36.57E
Nyíregyháza Hungary 55 I2 . . . . .47.57N 21.43E
Nyiru, Mount Kenya 87 B3 . . . . .2.09N 36.50E
Nykarleby Finland 40 E3 . . . . .63.31N 22.33E
Nykøbing Denmark 40 B1 . . . . .54.46N 11.53E
Nyköping Sweden 40 D2 . . . . .58.45N 17.01E
Nynäshamn Sweden 40 D2 . . . . .58.54N 17.57E
Nysa Poland 46 C3 . . . . .50.29N 17.20E
Nysa r. Germany/Poland 54 F3 . . . . .51.57N 14.45E
Nyurba Rus. Fed. 59 M4 . . . . .63.17N 118.17E
Nyzhn'ohirs'kyy Ukraine 57 K7 . . . . .45.27N 34.45E
Nzoia r. Kenya 87 A3 . . . . .0.05N 33.57E

O

Oadby England 10 D3 . . . . .52.36N 1.05W
Oahe, Lake U.S.A. 64 F5 . . . . .44.49N 100.32W
Oahu i. U.S.A. 109 J7 . . . . .21.34N 157.54W
Oakengates England 10 C3 . . . . .52.42N 2.26W
Oakham England 10 E3 . . . . .52.40N 0.44W
Oakland U.S.A. 64 B4 . . . . .37.50N 122.15W
Oaxaca Mexico 70 E4 . . . . .17.05N 96.40W
Oaxaca d. Mexico 70 E4 . . . . .17.22N 96.20W
Ob' r. Rus. Fed. 58 H4 . . . . .66.47N 69.08E
Oban Scotland 16 D4 . . . . .56.25N 5.28W
Obi i. Indonesia 105 H3 . . . . .1.33S 127.41E
Óbidos Brazil 77 I7 . . . . .1.50S 55.32W
Obihiro Japan 106 D4 . . . . .42.55N 143.11E
Obninsk Rus. Fed. 55 Q6 . . . . .55.04N 36.38E
Oborniki Poland 46 C4 . . . . .52.38N 16.49E
Oboyan' Rus. Fed. 55 Q4 . . . . .51.13N 36.16E
Obskaya Guba est. Rus. Fed. 58 I4 . . . . . . .67.13N 72.49E
Occidental, Cordillera mts Colombia 72 B7 . . .1.36N 77.47W
Occidental, Cordillera mts Peru 76 F4 . . . . .16.07S 71.41W
Ocean Falls town Canada 62 F3 . . . . .52.21N 127.41W
Oceania 117
Oceanside U.S.A. 64 C3 . . . . .33.12N 117.23W
Ochil Hills Scotland 17 F4 . . . . .56.12N 3.49W
Oda, Jebel mt. Sudan 85 H4 . . . . .20.20N 36.39E
Ódáðahraun f. Iceland 40 Y2 . . . . .64.48N 17.37W
Ōdate Japan 106 D4 . . . . .40.16N 140.34E
Ödemiş Turkey 57 G4 . . . . .38.13N 27.58E
Odense Denmark 40 B1 . . . . .55.24N 10.23E
Oder r. Germany 54 C4 . . . . .51.43N 9.56E
Odesa Ukraine 53 J6 . . . . .46.28N 30.39E
Odessa U.S.A. 64 F3 . . . . .31.50N 102.20W
Odintsovo Rus. Fed. 55 Q6 . . . . .55.40N 37.18E
Odra r. Germany/Poland 54 H3 . . . . .49.54N 18.19E
Ofanto r. Italy 50 G4 . . . . .41.21N 16.13E
Offaly d. Rep. of Ireland 41 D3 . . . . .53.15N 7.35W
Offenbach am Main Germany 54 C4 . . . . . .50.06N 8.46E
Offenburg Germany 54 C3 . . . . .48.29N 7.57E
Ogadēn f. Ethiopia 85 I2 . . . . .7.09N 45.27E
Ōgaki Japan 106 C3 . . . . .35.21N 136.37E
Ogbomosho Nigeria 84 E2 . . . . .8.08N 4.14E
Ogden U.S.A. 64 D5 . . . . .41.14N 111.57W
Ogilvie r. Canada 62 E4 . . . . .65.50N 137.13W
Oglio r. Italy 50 D6 . . . . .45.01N 10.40E
Ogoki r. Canada 65 I7 . . . . .51.40N 85.58W
Ogulin Croatia 56 A7 . . . . .45.16N 15.14E
Ohio d. U.S.A. 65 J5 . . . . .40.27N 82.28W
Ohio r. U.S.A. 65 I4 . . . . .37.05N 89.12W
Ohrid Macedonia 56 D5 . . . . .41.07N 20.49E
Ohrid, Lake Albania/Macedonia 56 D5 . . . . .41.02N 20.43E
Oich r. Scotland 18 E2 . . . . .57.09N 4.40W
Oich, Loch l. Scotland 18 E2 . . . . .57.04N 4.46W
Oise r. France 44 E6 . . . . .49.59N 2.04E
Ōita Japan 106 B2 . . . . .33.13N 131.37E
Oiti mt. Greece 56 E4 . . . . .38.48N 22.16E
Ojinaga Mexico 70 D6 . . . . .29.33N 104.25W
Ojos del Salado, Nevado mt. Argentina/Chile 73 C4
. . . . .27.06S 68.35W
Oka r. Rus. Fed. 55 Q5 . . . . .56.20N 43.59E
Okanogan r. U.S.A. 64 C6 . . . . .48.06N 119.44W
Okavango Delta f. Botswana 86 B3 . . . . . . .19.42S 23.02E
Okaya Japan 106 C3 . . . . .36.03N 138.04E
Okayama Japan 106 B2 . . . . .34.39N 133.55E
Okeechobee, Lake U.S.A. 65 J2 . . . . .26.56N 81.00W
Okehampton England 13 C2 . . . . .50.44N 4.00W
Okha India 96 C5 . . . . .22.26N 69.08E
Okha Rus. Fed. 59 P3 . . . . .53.33N 143.01E
Okhotsk Rus. Fed. 59 P3 . . . . .59.22N 143.22E
Okhotsk, Sea of Japan/Rus. Fed. 106 D4 . . .44.58N 146.04E
Okhtyrka Ukraine 55 P4 . . . . .50.19N 34.54E
Okinawa i. Japan 103 N3 . . . . .26.27N 127.58E
Oki-shotō is Japan 106 B3 . . . . .36.07N 133.26E
Oklahoma d. U.S.A. 64 G4 . . . . .35.41N 97.24W
Oklahoma City U.S.A. 64 G4 . . . . .35.31N 97.31W
Oksskolten mt. Norway 40 C4 . . . . .66.01N 14.20E
Oktyabr'skoy Revolyutsii, Ostrov i. Rus. Fed. 59 K5
. . . . .79.09N 96.42E
Öland i. Sweden 40 D2 . . . . .56.45N 16.48E
Oława Poland 46 C3 . . . . .50.56N 17.17E
Olbia Italy 50 C4 . . . . .40.55N 9.30E
Old Crow Canada 62 E4 . . . . .67.36N 139.54W
Oldenburg Germany 54 C5 . . . . .53.09N 8.14E
Oldenzaal Neth. 42 F5 . . . . .52.19N 6.56E
Oldham England 15 E2 . . . . .53.33N 2.07W
Old Head of Kinsale Rep. of Ireland 41 C1 . . .51.36N 8.31W
Old Leake England 15 H2 . . . . .53.02N 0.06E
Oldmeldrum Scotland 19 G2 . . . . .57.20N 2.19W
Olean U.S.A. 65 K5 . . . . .42.05N 78.26W
Olecko Poland 46 F5 . . . . .54.02N 22.31E
Olekma r. Rus. Fed. 59 N4 . . . . .60.05N 121.07E
Olekminsk Rus. Fed. 59 N4 . . . . .60.24N 120.21E
Oleksandriya Ukraine 55 O3 . . . . .48.41N 33.07E
Olenek r. Rus. Fed. 59 N4 . . . . .68.28N 112.26E
Olenek r. Rus. Fed. 59 M5 . . . . .72.58N 119.45E
Olenekskiy Zaliv b. Rus. Fed. 59 N5 . . . . . .73.22N 121.09E
Oléron, Île d' i. France 44 C4 . . . . .45.55N 1.20W

Olevs'k Ukraine 55 L4 . . . . .51.13N 27.39E
Olinda Brazil 77 N6 . . . . .7.58S 34.46W
Oliva, Cordillera de mts Argentina/Chile 76 G2 .29.56S 69.57W
Olmos Peru 76 E6 . . . . .5.59S 79.46W
Olney England 10 E3 . . . . .52.09N 0.42W
Olomouc Czech Rep. 54 G3 . . . . .49.35N 17.16E
Oloron-Ste-Marie France 44 C3 . . . . .43.12N 0.36W
Olsztyn Poland 46 E4 . . . . .53.47N 20.29E
Olteţ r. Romania 56 F7 . . . . .44.22N 24.07E
Olympia U.S.A. 64 B6 . . . . .47.02N 122.53W
Olympus, Mount Greece 56 E5 . . . . .40.05N 22.21E
Olympus, Mount U.S.A. 64 B6 . . . . .47.45N 123.47W
Olyutorskiy Zaliv b. Rus. Fed. 59 R3 . . . . . .59.51N 168.08E
Omagh Northern Ireland 16 B2 . . . . .54.36N 7.17W
Omagh d. Northern Ireland 9 B4 . . . . .54.35N 7.10W
Omaha U.S.A. 64 G5 . . . . .41.17N 95.58W
Oman Asia 95 H3 . . . . .18.15N 53.34E
Oman, Gulf of Asia 95 I5 . . . . .25.37N 56.49E
Ombersley England 10 C3 . . . . .52.16N 2.14W
Ombrone r. Italy 50 D5 . . . . .42.39N 11.01E
Omdurman Sudan 85 H3 . . . . .15.38N 32.28E
Ommen Neth. 42 F5 . . . . .52.32N 6.25E
Omolon r. Rus. Fed. 59 Q4 . . . . .68.44N 158.43E
Omo National Park Ethiopia 87 A4 . . . . .5.42N 35.47E
Omono r. Japan 106 D3 . . . . .39.41N 140.04E
Omo Wenz r. Ethiopia 87 B4 . . . . .4.36N 36.01E
Omsk Rus. Fed. 58 I3 . . . . .55.00N 73.22E
Omsukchan Rus. Fed. 59 Q4 . . . . .62.25N 155.43E
Omulew r. Poland 46 E4 . . . . .53.04N 21.33E
Ōmuta Japan 106 B2 . . . . .33.02N 130.28E
Onchan Isle of Man 14 C3 . . . . .54.11N 4.27W
Ondjiva Angola 86 A3 . . . . .17.04S 15.44E
Onega, Lake Rus. Fed. 58 E4 . . . . .62.05N 35.21E
Oneşti Romania 56 G8 . . . . .46.16N 26.46E
Ongole India 96 F4 . . . . .15.32N 80.02E
Onitsha Nigeria 84 E2 . . . . .6.08N 6.48E
Ono-i-Lau i. Fiji 108 I4 . . . . .20.39S 178.45W
Ontario d. Canada 63 I3 . . . . .51.51N 91.22W
Ontario, Lake Canada/U.S.A. 63 K2 . . . . . .43.31N 77.57W
Ontong Java Atoll Solomon Is 111 E6 . . . . . .5.24S 159.34E
Oosterschelde est. Neth. 42 C4 . . . . .51.38N 3.35E
Oost-Vlaanderen d. Belgium 42 C3 . . . . . . .50.56N 3.44E
Opala Dem. Rep. Congo 86 B4 . . . . .0.36S 24.22E
Opava Czech Rep. 54 G3 . . . . .49.56N 17.54E
Opochka Rus. Fed. 40 G2 . . . . .56.43N 28.41E
Opole Poland 46 C3 . . . . .50.40N 17.56E
Oporto Portugal 48 A4 . . . . .41.11N 8.36W
Oradea Romania 55 I2 . . . . .47.04N 21.57E
Oran Algeria 84 D5 . . . . .35.42N 0.38W
Orange France 44 F4 . . . . .44.09N 4.49E
Orange r. Namibia/S. Africa 86 A2 . . . . . . .28.36S 16.28E
Orange, Cabo c. Brazil 72 D7 . . . . .4.22N 51.17W
Oranmore Rep. of Ireland 41 C3 . . . . .53.16N 8.55W
Orchila, Isla i. Venezuela 71 K3 . . . . .11.45N 66.09W
Orchy r. Scotland 16 D4 . . . . .56.24N 5.01W
Ord, Mount hill Australia 110 B5 . . . . .17.19S 125.29E
Ordu Turkey 57 L5 . . . . .40.59N 37.53E
Örebro Sweden 40 D2 . . . . .59.16N 15.14E
Oregon d. U.S.A. 64 B5 . . . . .43.43N 120.32W
Orel Rus. Fed. 58 E3 . . . . .52.58N 36.05E
Orenburg Rus. Fed. 58 G3 . . . . .51.46N 55.05E
Orford Ness hd England 11 G3 . . . . .52.05N 1.35E
Oriental, Cordillera mts Bolivia 76 G4 . . . . .16.47S 66.35W
Oriental, Cordillera mts Colombia 72 B7 . . . .7.42N 72.45W
Oriental, Cordillera mts Peru 76 F5 . . . . . .10.29S 74.41W
Orillia Canada 65 K5 . . . . .44.36N 79.25W
Orinoco r. Col./Venez. 72 C7 . . . . .8.35N 61.50W
Orinoco Delta Venezuela 72 C7 . . . . .9.22N 60.40W
Orissa d. India 96 F5 . . . . .20.57N 84.15E
Oristano Italy 50 C3 . . . . .39.55N 8.35E
Oristano, Golfo di b. Italy 50 C3 . . . . .39.49N 8.30E
Orivesi l. Finland 40 G3 . . . . .62.14N 29.27E
Orizaba Mexico 70 E4 . . . . .18.53N 97.06W
Örkelljunga Sweden 54 E7 . . . . .56.17N 13.17E
Orkney d. Scotland 8 E6 . . . . .58.59N 3.04W
Orkney Islands Scotland 19 F4 . . . . .59.06N 3.20W
Orlando U.S.A. 65 J2 . . . . .28.33N 81.21W
Orléans France 44 D5 . . . . .47.55N 1.54E
Ormoc Phil. 105 G6 . . . . .11.00N 124.37E
Ormskirk England 14 E2 . . . . .53.34N 2.53W
Orne r. France 44 C6 . . . . .49.16N 0.14W
Örnsköldsvik Sweden 40 D3 . . . . .63.18N 18.43E
Oromīya d. Ethiopia 87 B5 . . . . .9.03N 37.33E
Oronsay i. Scotland 16 C4 . . . . .56.01N 6.16W
Orosei Italy 50 C4 . . . . .40.23N 9.42E
Orosei, Golfo di b. Italy 50 C4 . . . . .40.15N 9.44E
Orrin r. Scotland 19 E2 . . . . .57.33N 4.29W
Orrin Reservoir Scotland 18 E2 . . . . .57.33N 4.39W
Orsha Belarus 55 N6 . . . . .54.30N 30.26E
Orsk Rus. Fed. 58 G3 . . . . .51.07N 58.33E
Orşova Romania 56 E7 . . . . .44.42N 22.25E
Oruro Bolivia 76 G4 . . . . .17.59S 67.09W
Osa, Península de pen. Costa Rica 71 H2 . . . .8.34N 83.32W
Ōsaka Japan 106 C2 . . . . .34.42N 135.30E
Oshakati Namibia 86 A3 . . . . .17.45S 15.43E
Oshawa Canada 65 K2 . . . . .43.54N 78.51W
O-shima i. Japan 106 C2 . . . . .34.44N 139.28E
Osijek Croatia 56 C7 . . . . .45.35N 18.42E
Ösjön l. Sweden 40 D3 . . . . .63.54N 15.26E
Oskarshamn Sweden 40 D2 . . . . .57.16N 16.26E
Oslo Norway 40 B2 . . . . .59.55N 10.46E
Osmancık Turkey 57 K5 . . . . .40.58N 34.48E
Osmaniye Turkey 57 L3 . . . . .37.04N 36.15E
Osnabrück Germany 54 C5 . . . . .52.17N 8.04E
Osorno Chile 73 B2 . . . . .40.35S 73.09W
Osorno Spain 48 C5 . . . . .42.25N 4.22W
Oss Neth. 42 E4 . . . . .51.45N 5.32E
Ossa mt. Greece 56 E4 . . . . .39.48N 22.41E
Ossa, Mount Australia 110 D2 . . . . .41.56S 146.12E
Ostend Belgium 42 B4 . . . . .51.13N 2.55E
Österdalälven r. Sweden 40 C3 . . . . .61.40N 13.15E
Österdalen f. Norway 40 B3 . . . . .62.05N 10.36E
Östersund Sweden 40 C3 . . . . .63.11N 14.39E
Ostróda Poland 46 D4 . . . . .53.41N 19.59E
Ostrov Rus. Fed. 58 D3 . . . . .57.21N 28.21E
Ostrów Świętokrzyski Poland 46 E3 . . . . . .50.56N 21.24E
Ostrów Mazowiecka Poland 46 E4 . . . . . . .52.49N 21.54E
Ostrów Wielkopolski Poland 46 C3 . . . . . . .51.39N 17.49E
Ostrzeszów Poland 46 C3 . . . . .51.26N 17.56E
Osūm r. Bulgaria 56 F6 . . . . .43.42N 24.50E
Osumi-kaikyo str. Japan 106 B2 . . . . .30.50N 130.52E
Ōsumi-shotō is Japan 106 B2 . . . . .30.32N 130.36E
Osuna Spain 48 C2 . . . . .37.14N 5.06W
Oswego U.S.A. 65 K5 . . . . .43.12N 140.59E
Oswestry England 10 B3 . . . . .52.51N 3.03W
Otaru Japan 106 D4 . . . . .43.12N 140.59E
Otjiwarongo Namibia 86 A2 . . . . .20.29S 16.38E
Otley England 15 F2 . . . . .53.54N 1.41W
Otranto Italy 50 H4 . . . . .40.09N 18.28E
Otranto, Strait of Albania/Italy 56 C5 . . . . . .40.36N 18.42E
Otta Norway 40 B3 . . . . .61.46N 9.31E
Ottawa Canada 63 K2 . . . . .45.25N 75.40W
Ottawa r. Canada 63 K2 . . . . .45.28N 74.16W

Ottawa Islands Canada 63 J3 . . . . .59.57N 80.09W
Otter r. England 13 D2 . . . . .50.38N 3.18W
Otterburn England 15 E4 . . . . .55.14N 2.11W
Ottery r. England 13 C2 . . . . .50.39N 4.20W
Ottignies Belgium 42 D3 . . . . .50.39N 4.34E
Otukpo Nigeria 84 E2 . . . . .7.13N 8.05E
Ouachita r. U.S.A. 65 H3 . . . . .31.50N 91.49W
Ouagadougou Burkina 84 D3 . . . . .12.22N 1.31W
Ouargla Algeria 84 E5 . . . . .31.59N 5.22E
Ouarzazate Morocco 84 D5 . . . . .30.56N 6.54W
Oudenaarde Belgium 42 C3 . . . . .50.51N 3.36E
Ouessa Congo 84 F2 . . . . .1.36N 16.04E
Ouezzane Morocco 52 B3 . . . . .34.46N 5.32W
Oughter, Lough l. Rep. of Ireland 41 D4 . . . .54.01N 7.28W
Ouistreham France 44 C6 . . . . .49.17N 0.16W
Oujda Morocco 84 D5 . . . . .34.44N 1.54W
Oulainen Finland 40 F4 . . . . .64.16N 24.49E
Oulton England 11 G3 . . . . .52.30N 1.43E
Oulu Finland 40 F4 . . . . .65.01N 25.30E
Oulujärvi l. Finland 40 F4 . . . . .64.17N 27.15E
Oundle England 11 E3 . . . . .52.29N 0.28W
Oupeye Belgium 42 E3 . . . . .50.42N 5.39E
Ourense Spain 48 B5 . . . . .42.21N 7.51W
Ouse r. E. Sussex England 11 F1 . . . . .50.48N 0.03E
Ouse r. E. Yorks. England 15 G2 . . . . .53.44N 0.54W
Outer Hebrides is Scotland 18 B2 . . . . . . .57.53N 7.21W
Outokumpu Finland 40 G3 . . . . .62.43N 29.01E
Out Skerries is Scotland 19 I5 . . . . .60.26N 0.47W
Ovamboland f. Namibia 86 A3 . . . . .17.50S 15.41E
Overijssel d. Neth. 42 F5 . . . . .52.25N 6.32E
Overton Wales 12 E3 . . . . .52.58N 2.56W
Övertorneå Sweden 40 E4 . . . . .66.24N 23.37E
Oviedo Spain 48 C5 . . . . .43.22N 5.50W
Ovruch Ukraine 55 M4 . . . . .51.20N 28.49E
Owando Congo 84 F1 . . . . .0.29S 15.55E
Owen Falls Dam Uganda 87 A3 . . . . .0.29N 33.14E
Owen Stanley Range mts P.N.G. 110 D6 . . .8.59S 147.57E
Owyhee r. U.S.A. 64 C5 . . . . .43.48N 117.04W
Oxarfjörður b. Iceland 40 Y2 . . . . .66.12N 16.47W
Oxelösund Sweden 40 D2 . . . . .58.40N 17.05E
Oxford England 10 D2 . . . . .51.45N 1.15W
Oxfordshire d. England 9 E2 . . . . .51.54N 1.27W
Oxnard U.S.A. 64 C3 . . . . .34.12N 119.12W
Oxted England 11 F2 . . . . .51.16N 0.01E
Oyama Japan 106 C3 . . . . .36.18N 139.48E
Oykel r. Scotland 18 E2 . . . . .57.55N 4.24W
Oyonnax France 44 E5 . . . . .36.58N 93.31W
Ozark Plateau f. U.S.A. 65 H4 . . . . .36.58N 93.31W
Ozarks, Lake of the U.S.A. 65 H4 . . . . . . .38.14N 93.08W
Özd Hungary 54 I3 . . . . .48.13N 20.19E
Ozernovskiy Rus. Fed. 59 Q3 . . . . .51.30N 156.35E

P

Paamiut Greenland 63 N4 . . . . .62.01N 49.40W
Pabbay i. W. Isles Scotland 18 B1 . . . . . . .56.51N 7.34W
Pabbay i. W. Isles Scotland 18 B2 . . . . . . .57.46N 7.18W
Pabianice Poland 46 D3 . . . . .51.40N 19.22E
Pacasmayo Peru 76 E6 . . . . .7.26S 79.36W
Pachuca Mexico 70 E5 . . . . .20.09N 98.44W
Pacific Ocean 108
Paczków Poland 46 C3 . . . . .50.28N 17.00E
Padang Indonesia 104 C3 . . . . .0.58S 100.23E
Paderborn Germany 54 C4 . . . . .51.43N 8.45E
Padiham England 15 E2 . . . . .53.48N 2.19W
Padre Island U.S.A. 64 G2 . . . . .26.57N 97.22W
Padstow England 13 C2 . . . . .50.32N 4.56W
Padua Italy 50 D6 . . . . .45.24N 11.53E
Pag i. Croatia 56 A7 . . . . .44.31N 14.53E
Pagadian Phil. 105 G5 . . . . .7.50N 123.29E
Pagai Selatan i. Indonesia 104 C3 . . . . . . .2.58S 100.24E
Pagai Utara i. Indonesia 104 C3 . . . . .2.36S 100.04E
Page U.S.A. 64 D4 . . . . .36.55N 111.28W
Paget, Mount S. Atlantic Oc. 73 F1 . . . . . .54.23S 36.44W
Paignton England 13 D2 . . . . .50.26N 3.34W
Päijänne l. Finland 40 F3 . . . . .61.30N 25.26E
Painswick England 10 C2 . . . . .51.47N 2.12W
Paisley Scotland 16 E3 . . . . .55.51N 4.26W
Pakanbaru Indonesia 104 C4 . . . . .0.34N 101.30E
Pakaraima Mountains S. America 71 L1 . . . .3.47N 63.40W
Pakistan Asia 96 D6 . . . . .29.00N 64.37E
Pakokku Myanmar 97 I5 . . . . .21.21N 95.07E
Pakxé Laos 104 D7 . . . . .15.04N 105.50E
Palana Rus. Fed. 59 Q3 . . . . .59.05N 159.52E
Palangkaraya Indonesia 104 E3 . . . . .2.18S 113.55E
Palatka Rus. Fed. 59 Q4 . . . . .60.28N 150.56E
Palau N. Pacific Oc. 105 I5 . . . . .7.23N 134.07E
Palawan i. Phil. 104 F5 . . . . .8.50N 117.43E
Palawan Trough f. N. Pacific Oc. 108 D6 . . . .7.53N 116.15E
Palembang Indonesia 104 C3 . . . . .2.56S 104.46E
Palencia Spain 48 C5 . . . . .42.01N 4.31W
Palermo Italy 50 E3 . . . . .38.07N 13.21E
Pali India 96 D6 . . . . .25.46N 73.26E
Palikir Micronesia 108 G6 . . . . .6.55N 158.10E
Palk Strait India/Sri Lanka 96 E2 . . . . .9.36N 79.18E
Pallisa Uganda 87 A3 . . . . .1.10N 33.43E
Palma de Mallorca Spain 48 G3 . . . . .39.35N 2.40E
Palmas, Cape Liberia 84 D2 . . . . .4.22N 7.32W
Palmerston atoll Cook Is 108 I5 . . . . .18.01S 163.03W
Palmerston North New Zealand 111 G2 . . . .40.22S 175.37E
Palmi Italy 50 F3 . . . . .38.21N 15.51E
Palmira Colombia 72 B7 . . . . .3.31N 76.16W
Palmyra Atoll N. Pacific Oc. 108 J6 . . . . . . .5.51N 162.06W
Palopo Indonesia 104 G3 . . . . .3.01S 120.11E
Palos, Cabo de c. Spain 48 E2 . . . . .37.37N 0.41W
Palu Indonesia 104 F3 . . . . .0.54S 119.54E
Pamiers France 44 D3 . . . . .43.07N 1.37E
Pamir mts Asia 90 B4 . . . . .38.39N 72.48E
Pampas f. Argentina 73 C3 . . . . .36.23S 64.07W
Pamplona Spain 48 E5 . . . . .42.49N 1.39W
Panagyurishte Bulgaria 56 F6 . . . . .42.30N 24.10E
Panaji India 96 D4 . . . . .15.30N 73.50E
Panama Central America 71 H2 . . . . .8.22N 81.33W
Panamá, Gulf of Panama 71 I2 . . . . .7.38N 79.19W
Panama, Isthmus of f. C. America 60 K3 . . . .9.00N 80.00W
Panama Canal Panama 71 I2 . . . . .9.07N 79.45W
Panama City U.S.A. 65 I3 . . . . .30.10N 85.40W
Panay i. Phil. 104 G6 . . . . .11.10N 122.30E
Pančevo S.M. 56 D7 . . . . .44.52N 20.39E
Panevėžys Lithuania 40 F1 . . . . .55.44N 24.21E
Pangani Tanzania 87 B1 . . . . .5.29S 38.56E
Pangkalanbuun Indonesia 104 E3 . . . . . . .2.40S 111.38E
Pangkalpinang Indonesia 104 D3 . . . . . . .2.08S 106.06E
Pangnirtung Canada 63 L4 . . . . .66.03N 65.48W
Panjgur Pakistan 95 J5 . . . . .26.55N 64.07E
Pantanal f. Brazil 77 I4 . . . . .18.00S 57.00W
Pantelleria, Isola di i. Italy 50 E2 . . . . .36.46N 12.00E
Panzhihua China 103 I3 . . . . .26.35N 101.43E
Paola Italy 50 G3 . . . . .39.21N 16.03E
Papa Stour i. Scotland 19 H5 . . . . .60.21N 1.42W
Papa Westray i. Scotland 19 G4 . . . . .59.22N 2.52W

Papeete French Polynesia 109 K4 .....17.30S 149.31W
Papenburg Germany 42 G6 .....53.05N 7.24E
Paphos Cyprus 57 J2 .....34.47N 32.25E
Papua, Gulf of P.N.G. 110 D6 .....8.34S 144.45E
Papua New Guinea Oceania 110 D6 .....6.05S 146.34E
Par England 13 C2 .....50.21N 4.42W
Pará d. Brazil 77 J7 .....3.46S 51.57W
Paracel Islands S. China Sea 104 E7 .....16.46N 112.33E
Paragua r. Bolivia 77 H5 .....13.31S 61.50W
Paraguai r. Brazil 77 I3 .....22.06S 57.57W
Paraguay r. Argentina/Paraguay 73 D4 .....27.12S 58.39W
Paraguay S. America 77 I3 .....22.45S 58.44W
Paraíba d. Brazil 77 M6 .....7.06S 36.43W
Parakou Benin 84 E2 .....9.22N 2.36E
Paramaribo Suriname 72 D7 .....5.51N 55.17W
Paraná Argentina 73 C3 .....31.44S 60.31W
Paraná d. Brazil 77 J3 .....24.50S 51.01W
Paraná r. Brazil 77 K5 .....12.31S 48.12W
Paraná r. S. America 77 I1 .....33.52S 59.12W
Paranaguá r. Brazil 77 K2 .....25.35S 48.33W
Paranaíba r. Brazil 77 J3 .....20.04S 51.00W
Paranapanema r. Brazil 77 J3 .....22.36S 53.01W
Paranapiacaba, Serra mts Brazil 77 J3 .....24.58S 50.21W
Parângul, Vârful mt. Romania 56 E7 .....45.21N 23.33E
Pardo r. Bahia Brazil 77 M4 .....15.41S 38.59W
Pardo r. Mato Grosso do Sul Brazil 77 J3 .....21.39S 52.14W
Pardubice Czech Rep. 54 F4 .....50.03N 15.47E
Parecis, Serra dos hills Brazil 77 H5 .....11.28S 63.12W
Parepare Indonesia 104 F3 .....4.01S 119.40E
Paria, Península de pen. Venezuela 71 L3 .....10.43N 62.58W
Parima, Serra mts Brazil 71 L1 .....2.57N 64.15W
Parintins Brazil 77 I7 .....2.38S 56.46W
Paris France 44 E6 .....48.52N 2.21E
Parma Italy 50 D6 .....44.48N 10.19E
Parnaíba Brazil 77 L7 .....2.56S 41.45W
Parnaíba r. Brazil 77 L7 .....3.02S 41.51W
Parnassos mt. Greece 56 E4 .....38.32N 22.38E
Pärnu Estonia 40 F2 .....58.23N 24.30E
Paropamisus mts Afgh. 95 J7 .....35.06N 61.20E
Paros i. Greece 56 F3 .....37.06N 25.08E
Parrett r. England 13 D3 .....51.08N 3.00W
Parry, Cape Canada 62 F4 .....70.12N 124.31W
Parry Islands Canada 62 G5 .....76.50N 111.03W
Parsęta r. Poland 46 B5 .....54.11N 15.34E
Parthenay France 44 C5 .....46.39N 0.15W
Partry Mountains hills Rep. of Ireland 41 B3 .....53.36N 9.39W
Paru r. Brazil 77 J7 .....1.31S 52.41W
Pasadena U.S.A. 64 C3 .....34.11N 118.08W
Pasado, Cabo c. Ecuador 76 D7 .....0.22S 80.28W
Pașcani Romania 55 L2 .....47.15N 26.44E
Pasewalk Germany 46 B5 .....53.30N 14.00E
Pasłęka r. Poland 46 D5 .....54.26N 19.46E
Pasni Pakistan 95 J5 .....25.13N 63.31E
Passau Germany 54 E3 .....48.34N 13.25E
Passero, Capo c. Italy 50 F2 .....36.40N 15.08E
Passo Fundo Brazil 77 J2 .....28.18S 52.24W
Pastavy Belarus 55 L6 .....55.07N 26.50E
Pasto Colombia 72 B7 .....1.11N 77.17W
Pastaza r. Peru 76 E7 .....4.56S 76.24W
Pasvalys Lithuania 46 G6 .....56.03N 24.25E
Patagonia f. Argentina 73 B1 .....51.44S 71.19W
Patchway England 10 C2 .....51.32N 2.34W
Pate Island Kenya 87 C2 .....2.06S 41.08E
Paterson U.S.A. 65 L5 .....40.54N 74.09W
Patna India 96 G6 .....25.35N 85.16E
Patos Albania 56 C5 .....40.40N 19.39E
Patos, Lagoa dos f. Brazil 77 J1 .....30.39S 50.58W
Patos de Minas Brazil 77 K4 .....18.36S 46.30W
Patquía Argentina 76 G1 .....30.03S 66.53W
Patraïkos Kolpos b. Greece 56 D4 .....38.15N 21.26E
Patras Greece 56 D4 .....38.14N 21.45E
Patrington England 15 G2 .....53.41N 0.01W
Pau France 44 C3 .....43.18N 0.22W
Paulo Afonso Brazil 77 M6 .....9.20S 38.13W
Pavia Italy 50 C6 .....45.11N 9.09E
Pavlodar Kazakhstan 58 I3 .....52.18N 77.02E
Pavlohrad Ukraine 55 P3 .....48.31N 35.53E
Pavlovskaya Rus. Fed. 53 K6 .....46.09N 39.47E
Payapon Myanmar 97 I4 .....16.16N 95.41E
Paysandú Uruguay 73 D3 .....32.19S 58.05W
Pazardzhik Bulgaria 56 F6 .....42.12N 24.20E
Peace r. Canada 62 G3 .....58.54N 111.50W
Peacehaven England 11 E1 .....50.48N 0.00W
Peace River town Canada 62 G3 .....56.15N 117.17W
Peale, Mount U.S.A. 64 E4 .....38.26N 109.13W
Pearl r. U.S.A. 65 I3 .....30.10N 89.37W
Peć S.M. 56 D6 .....42.39N 20.17E
Pechora r. Rus. Fed. 58 G4 .....68.13N 53.54E
Pecos U.S.A. 64 F3 .....31.23N 103.30W
Pecos r. U.S.A. 64 F2 .....29.50N 101.28W
Pécs Hungary 54 H2 .....46.05N 18.13E
Pedro Juan Caballero Paraguay 77 I3 .....22.29S 55.44W
Peebles Scotland 17 F3 .....55.39N 3.12W
Peel r. Canada 62 E4 .....68.03N 134.26W
Peel Isle of Man 14 C3 .....54.13N 4.41W
Pegasus Bay New Zealand 111 G2 .....43.17S 172.49E
Pegu Myanmar 97 I4 .....17.18N 96.28E
Pegwell Bay England 11 G2 .....51.19N 1.21E
Peipus, Lake Estonia/Rus. Fed. 40 F2 .....58.38N 27.28E
Pekalongan Indonesia 104 D2 .....6.54S 109.38E
Pelat, Mont mt. France 44 G4 .....44.16N 6.43E
Peleng i. Indonesia 105 G3 .....1.15S 123.29E
Pello Finland 40 E4 .....66.47N 23.59E
Pelotas Brazil 77 J1 .....31.46S 52.19W
Pelotas, Rio das r. Brazil 73 D4 .....27.35S 51.24W
Pemba Mozambique 86 D3 .....12.59S 40.32E
Pemba Zambia 86 B3 .....16.33S 27.22E
Pemba Channel Tanzania 87 B1 .....5.33S 39.19E
Pemba Island Tanzania 86 C4 .....5.25S 39.46E
Pembrey Wales 12 C3 .....51.41N 4.17W
Pembroke Canada 65 K6 .....45.49N 77.06W
Pembroke Wales 12 C3 .....51.40N 4.55W
Pembroke Dock Wales 12 C3 .....51.41N 4.57W
Pembrokeshire d. Wales 9 C2 .....51.55N 4.48W
Pembury England 11 F2 .....51.09N 0.19E
Peñalara mt. Spain 48 D4 .....40.51N 3.56W
Peña Nevada, Cerro mt. Mexico 70 E5 .....23.46N 99.50W
Peñaranda de Bracamonte Spain 48 C4 .....40.55N 5.11W
Penarth Wales 13 D3 .....51.26N 3.10W
Peñas, Golfo de g. Chile 73 B2 .....47.18S 75.35W
Pendine Wales 12 C3 .....51.45N 4.34W
Pendlebury England 15 E2 .....53.30N 2.19W
Pendle Hill England 15 E2 .....53.52N 2.18W
Pendleton U.S.A. 64 C6 .....45.39N 118.48W
Penicuik Scotland 17 F3 .....55.50N 3.13W
Peninsular Malaysia Malaysia 104 C4 .....3.59N 102.43E
Penitente, Serra do hills Brazil 77 K6 .....9.20S 46.41W
Penkridge England 10 C3 .....52.43N 2.07W
Pennines hills England 15 E3 .....54.23N 2.18W
Pennsylvania d. U.S.A. 65 K5 .....41.18N 78.00W
Penny Icecap Canada 63 L4 .....67.10N 66.02W
Penrhyn atoll Cook Is 109 J5 .....8.58S 157.53W
Penrhyn Basin f. S. Pacific Oc. 109 J5 .....7.12S 157.13W
Penrhyn Mawr pt Wales 12 C4 .....52.51N 4.43W

Penrith England 14 E3 .....54.40N 2.45W
Penryn England 13 B2 .....50.10N 5.06W
Pensacola U.S.A. 65 I3 .....30.27N 87.13W
Penticton Canada 64 C6 .....49.30N 119.35W
Pentire Point England 13 B2 .....50.35N 5.00W
Pentland Firth str. Scotland 19 F3 .....58.43N 3.16W
Pentland Hills Scotland 17 F3 .....55.43N 3.30W
Pentland Skerries is Scotland 19 G3 .....58.41N 2.54W
Penygadair hill Wales 12 D4 .....52.42N 3.55W
Pen-y-Ghent hill England 15 E3 .....54.10N 2.15W
Penza Rus. Fed. 58 F3 .....53.12N 45.01E
Penzance England 13 B2 .....50.07N 5.32W
Penzhinskaya Guba b. Rus. Fed. 59 R4 .....62.05N 163.30E
Peoria U.S.A. 65 I5 .....40.41N 89.37W
Pereira Colombia 72 B7 .....4.45N 75.41W
Peremyshlyany Ukraine 46 G2 .....49.40N 24.34E
Périgueux France 44 D4 .....45.11N 0.43E
Perija, Sierra de mts Venezuela 71 J2 .....9.09N 73.12W
Perito Moreno Argentina 73 B2 .....46.36S 71.02W
Perlas, Punta de pt Nicaragua 71 H3 .....12.24N 83.31W
Perm' Rus. Fed. 58 G3 .....58.01N 56.14E
Pernambuco d. Brazil 77 M6 .....8.23S 37.51W
Pernik Bulgaria 56 E6 .....42.36N 23.02E
Péronne France 42 B2 .....49.56N 2.56E
Perpignan France 44 E3 .....42.42N 2.54E
Perranporth England 13 B2 .....50.21N 5.09W
Pershore England 10 C3 .....52.07N 2.04W
Perth Australia 110 A3 .....31.56S 115.47E
Perth Scotland 17 F4 .....56.24N 3.26W
Perth and Kinross d. Scotland 8 C5 .....56.37N 4.07W
Perth Basin f. Indian Oc. 108 D4 .....29.52S 109.00E
Peru S. America 76 E5 .....5.50S 77.14W
Peru-Chile Trench f. S. Pacific Oc. 109 O5 .....9.16S 81.56W
Perugia Italy 50 E5 .....43.07N 12.23E
Pervomays'k Ukraine 55 N3 .....48.03N 30.51E
Pesaro Italy 50 E5 .....43.55N 12.53E
Pescara Italy 50 F5 .....42.27N 14.12E
Pescara r. Italy 50 F5 .....42.28N 14.13E
Pesebre, Punta pt Canary Islands 48 Y2 .....28.07N 14.29W
Peshawar Pakistan 96 D7 .....34.01N 71.40E
Peshkopi Albania 56 D5 .....41.41N 20.26E
Peterborough Canada 63 K2 .....44.18N 78.20W
Peterborough England 11 E3 .....52.34N 0.14W
Peterborough d. England 9 E3 .....52.36N 0.16W
Peterhead Scotland 19 H2 .....57.31N 1.47W
Peterlee England 15 F3 .....54.46N 1.20W
Petersfield England 10 E2 .....51.00N 0.56W
Petersville U.S.A. 62 C4 .....62.33N 150.50W
Petit Mécatina r. Canada 63 M3 .....50.40N 59.30W
Petra Velikogo, Zaliv b. Rus. Fed. 106 B4 .....42.41N 131.50E
Petrich Bulgaria 56 E5 .....41.24N 23.12E
Petrolina Brazil 77 L6 .....9.22S 40.25W
Petropavlovsk Kazakhstan 58 H3 .....54.51N 69.06E
Petropavlovsk-Kamchatskiy Rus. Fed. 59 Q3 .....53.01N 158.44E
Petroşani Romania 56 E7 .....45.25N 23.23E
Petrozavodsk Rus. Fed. 58 E4 .....61.48N 34.19E
Petworth England 11 E1 .....50.59N 0.36W
Pevensey England 11 F1 .....50.49N 0.21E
Pewsey England 10 D2 .....51.20N 1.46W
Pforzheim Germany 54 C3 .....48.53N 8.42E
Phan Thiết Vietnam 104 D6 .....10.55N 108.06E
Phatthalung Thailand 104 C5 .....7.39N 100.06E
Phayao Thailand 104 B7 .....19.10N 99.57E
Phet Buri Thailand 104 B6 .....13.06N 99.56E
Philadelphia U.S.A. 65 K4 .....39.57N 75.10W
Philippeville Belgium 42 D3 .....50.12N 4.33E
Philippine Basin f. N. Pacific Oc. 108 E7 .....16.41N 126.12E
Philippines Asia 105 G6 .....15.36N 122.55E
Philippine Trench f. N. Pacific Oc. 108 E6 .....15.40N 123.45E
Phitsanulok Thailand 104 C7 .....16.50N 100.18E
Phnom Penh Cambodia 104 C6 .....11.33N 104.57E
Phoenix U.S.A. 64 D3 .....33.31N 112.07W
Phoenix Islands Kiribati 108 I5 .....2.43S 173.22W
Phöngsali Laos 104 C8 .....21.41N 102.08E
Phrae Thailand 104 C7 .....18.07N 100.12E
Phuket Thailand 104 B5 .....7.53N 98.23E
Piacenza Italy 50 C6 .....45.03N 9.42E
Pianosa, Isola i. Italy 50 D5 .....42.34N 10.06E
Piatra Neamţ Romania 55 L2 .....46.56N 26.22E
Piauí d. Brazil 77 L6 .....7.39S 42.52W
Piave r. Italy 50 E6 .....45.32N 12.44E
Picardie f. France 42 B2 .....49.42N 2.54E
Picardy f. France 44 D6 .....49.47N 1.35E
Pichanal Argentina 76 H3 .....23.18S 64.11W
Pickering England 15 G3 .....54.15N 0.47W
Pickering, Vale of f. England 15 G3 .....54.13N 0.45W
Piedras Negras Mexico 70 D6 .....28.40N 100.34W
Pieksämäki Finland 40 F3 .....62.18N 27.10E
Pielinen i. Finland 40 G3 .....63.14N 29.41E
Pierre U.S.A. 64 F5 .....44.23N 100.23W
Pietermaritzburg S. Africa 86 C2 .....29.36S 30.23E
Pietrosa mt. Romania 55 K2 .....47.34N 24.41E
Pihlajavesi l. Finland 40 G3 .....61.45N 28.46E
Pijijiapan Mexico 70 F4 .....15.46N 93.14W
Piła Poland 46 C4 .....53.09N 16.45E
Pilar Paraguay 77 I2 .....26.49S 58.19W
Pilcomayo r. Bolivia/Paraguay 77 I2 .....25.18S 57.43W
Pilica r. Poland 46 E3 .....51.52N 21.17E
Pimperne England 10 C1 .....50.53N 2.08W
Pinang i. Malaysia 104 C5 .....5.21N 100.11E
Pınarbaşı Turkey 57 L4 .....38.44N 36.25E
Pinar del Río Cuba 71 H5 .....22.25N 83.43W
Pindaré r. Brazil 77 L7 .....3.17S 44.50W
Pindus Mountains Greece 56 D4 .....39.52N 20.56E
Pine Bluff U.S.A. 65 H3 .....34.16N 92.02W
Pinega Rus. Fed. 58 F4 .....64.41N 43.24E
Pineios r. Greece 56 E4 .....39.53N 22.43E
Pinerolo Italy 50 B6 .....44.53N 7.20E
Pingdingshan China 103 K4 .....33.45N 113.18E
Pingxiang Guangxi China 103 J2 .....22.03N 106.50E
Pingxiang Jiangxi China 103 K3 .....27.42N 113.52E
Pinsk Belarus 55 L5 .....52.08N 26.06E
Piombino Italy 50 D5 .....42.56N 10.32E
Piotrków Trybunalski Poland 46 D3 .....51.25N 19.41E
Pipmuacan, Réservoir Canada 65 L6 .....49.37N 70.33W
Piracicaba Brazil 77 K3 .....22.44S 47.38W
Piraeus Greece 56 E3 .....37.56N 23.38E
Pirot S.M. 56 E6 .....43.09N 22.34E
Pisa Italy 50 D5 .....43.42N 10.24E
Pisco Peru 76 E5 .....13.43S 76.12W
Pisuerga r. Spain 48 C4 .....41.34N 4.50W
Pisz Poland 46 E4 .....53.38N 21.48E
Pitcairn Islands S. Pacific Oc. 109 M4 .....25.03S 130.06W
Pitcairn Islands S. Pacific Oc. 109 L4 .....23.35S 126.31W
Piteå Sweden 40 E4 .....65.19N 21.30E
Pitești Romania 56 F7 .....44.52N 24.53E
Pitlochry Scotland 19 F1 .....56.42N 3.44W
Pittsburgh U.S.A. 65 K5 .....40.26N 79.59W
Piz Bernina mt. Italy/Switz. 50 C7 .....46.23N 9.54E
Platinum U.S.A. 62 B3 .....58.59N 161.48W
Platte r. U.S.A. 64 G5 .....41.04N 95.53W

Plauen Germany 54 E4 .....50.30N 12.08E
Plavsk Rus. Fed. 55 Q5 .....53.42N 37.18E
Playa Blanca Canary Islands 48 Z2 .....28.52N 13.50W
Plenty, Bay of g. New Zealand 111 G3 .....37.37S 176.59E
Pleven Bulgaria 56 F6 .....43.25N 24.37E
Płock Poland 46 D4 .....52.33N 19.43E
Pločno mt. Bos.-Herz. 56 B6 .....43.36N 17.35E
Ploiești Romania 56 G7 .....44.56N 26.02E
Plomb du Cantal mt. France 44 E4 .....45.03N 2.46E
Płoty Poland 46 B4 .....53.49N 15.16E
Plovdiv Bulgaria 56 F6 .....42.10N 24.44E
Plunge Lithuania 46 E5 .....55.55N 21.51E
Plymouth England 13 C2 .....50.22N 4.08W
Plymouth d. England 9 C2 .....50.24N 4.08W
Plympton England 13 C2 .....50.23N 4.03W
Plymstock England 13 C2 .....50.21N 4.06W
Plynlimon hill Wales 12 D4 .....52.28N 3.47W
Plzeň Czech Rep. 54 E3 .....49.45N 13.23E
Po r. Italy 50 E6 .....44.52N 12.11E
Pobeda, Gora mt. Rus. Fed. 59 P4 .....65.12N 145.54E
Pocatello U.S.A. 64 D5 .....42.54N 112.25W
Pochep Rus. Fed. 55 O5 .....52.56N 33.27E
Pocklington England 15 G2 .....53.56N 0.47W
Poços de Caldas Brazil 77 K3 .....21.48S 46.31W
Podgorica S.M. 56 C6 .....42.27N 19.17E
Podkamennaya Tunguska r. Rus. Fed. 59 K4 .....61.36N 90.08E
Podol'sk Rus. Fed. 55 Q6 .....55.25N 37.34E
P'ohang S. Korea 106 A3 .....36.01N 129.22E
Pohnpei atoll Micronesia 108 G6 .....6.53N 158.22E
Pointe-à-Pitre Guadeloupe 72 C8 .....16.15N 61.32W
Pointe-Noire Congo 84 F1 .....4.44S 11.53E
Poitiers France 44 D5 .....46.35N 0.20E
Pokaran India 96 D6 .....26.53N 71.57E
Poland Europe 46 D4 .....52.07N 19.27E
Polatlı Turkey 57 J4 .....39.35N 32.08E
Polatsk Belarus 55 M6 .....55.29N 28.47E
Polegate England 11 F1 .....50.49N 0.15E
Pol-e Khomrī Afgh. 95 K7 .....35.56N 68.46E
Policastro, Golfo di b. Italy 50 F3 .....39.57N 15.33E
Police Poland 46 B4 .....53.33N 14.35E
Polis Cyprus 57 J2 .....35.01N 32.25E
Polkowice Poland 46 C3 .....51.30N 16.04E
Pollaphuca Reservoir Rep. of Ireland 41 E3 .....53.08N 6.30W
Pollino, Monte mt. Italy 50 G3 .....39.54N 16.12E
Polokwane S. Africa 86 B2 .....23.54S 29.27E
Polperro England 13 C2 .....50.20N 4.31W
Poltava Ukraine 55 P3 .....49.36N 34.34E
Polygyros Greece 56 E5 .....40.23N 23.27E
Polykastro Greece 56 E5 .....40.59N 22.34E
Polynesia is Pacific Oc. 108 I6 .....8.00S 170.00E
Pombal Portugal 48 A3 .....39.55N 8.37W
Ponce Puerto Rico 71 K4 .....18.00N 66.37W
Pondicherry India 96 E3 .....11.57N 79.48E
Ponferrada Spain 48 B5 .....42.33N 6.36W
Ponta do Sol Cape Verde 84 B3 .....17.10N 25.05W
Ponta Grossa Brazil 77 J2 .....25.03S 50.07W
Pont-à-Mousson France 42 F1 .....48.54N 6.03E
Pontardawe Wales 12 D3 .....51.43N 3.51W
Pontefract England 15 F2 .....53.41N 1.18W
Ponteland England 15 F4 .....55.03N 1.44W
Pontevedra Spain 48 A5 .....42.27N 8.37W
Pontianak Indonesia 104 D3 .....0.03S 109.18E
Pontine Islands Italy 50 E4 .....40.59N 12.59E
Pontoise France 44 E6 .....49.03N 2.06E
Pont-Ste-Maxence France 42 B2 .....49.18N 2.37E
Pontycymer Wales 12 D3 .....51.37N 3.35W
Pontypool Wales 12 D3 .....51.42N 3.02W
Pontypridd Wales 12 D3 .....51.36N 3.20W
Poole England 10 D1 .....50.43N 1.59W
Poole d. England 9 E2 .....50.44N 1.57W
Poole Bay England 10 D1 .....50.40N 1.55W
Pooley Bridge England 14 E3 .....54.37N 2.49W
Poopó, Lago de l. Bolivia 76 G4 .....18.50S 67.05W
Popayán Colombia 76 E8 .....2.24N 76.37W
Popigay r. Rus. Fed. 59 M5 .....72.56N 106.10E
Poplar Bluff U.S.A. 65 H4 .....36.47N 90.23W
Popocatépetl, Volcán vol. Mexico 70 E4 .....19.02N 98.38W
Poprad Slovakia 46 E2 .....49.04N 20.18E
Porbandar India 96 C5 .....21.39N 69.40E
Pori Finland 40 E3 .....61.29N 21.48E
Porlock England 13 D3 .....51.13N 3.36W
Poronaysk Rus. Fed. 59 P2 .....49.16N 143.03E
Porsangerfjorden str. Norway 40 F5 .....70.19N 25.18E
Porsangerhalvøya pen. Norway 40 F5 .....70.45N 25.01E
Porsgrunn Norway 40 B2 .....59.08N 9.39E
Porsuk r. Turkey 57 I4 .....39.41N 31.58E
Portadown Northern Ireland 16 C2 .....54.25N 6.26W
Portaferry Northern Ireland 16 D2 .....54.23N 5.32W
Portage la Prairie Canada 62 I2 .....49.58N 98.19W
Portalegre Portugal 48 B3 .....39.18N 7.25W
Port Angeles U.S.A. 64 B6 .....48.06N 123.25W
Port Arthur U.S.A. 65 H2 .....29.51N 93.58W
Port Askaig Scotland 16 C3 .....55.51N 6.06W
Port Augusta Australia 110 C3 .....32.29S 137.45E
Port-au-Prince Haiti 71 J4 .....18.33N 72.19W
Portavogie Northern Ireland 16 D2 .....54.27N 5.26W
Port Blair India 97 H3 .....11.41N 92.42E
Port-de-Paix Haiti 71 J4 .....19.57N 72.50W
Port Elizabeth S. Africa 86 B1 .....33.57S 25.37E
Port Ellen Scotland 16 C3 .....55.38N 6.11W
Port Erin Isle of Man 14 C3 .....54.05N 4.45W
Port-Gentil Gabon 84 E1 .....0.46S 8.49E
Port Glasgow Scotland 16 E3 .....55.56N 4.41W
Port Harcourt Nigeria 84 E2 .....4.46N 7.01E
Port Hedland Australia 110 A4 .....20.23S 118.37E
Porthcawl Wales 13 D3 .....51.29N 3.42W
Porthleven England 13 B2 .....50.05N 5.19W
Porthmadog Wales 12 C4 .....52.56N 4.08W
Port Hope Simpson Canada 63 M3 .....52.31N 55.47W
Portimão Portugal 48 A2 .....37.08N 8.32W
Port Isaac Bay England 13 C2 .....50.36N 4.49W
Portishead England 10 C2 .....51.29N 2.46W
Portknockie Scotland 19 G2 .....57.42N 2.51W
Portland Australia 110 D3 .....38.21S 141.34E
Portland Me. U.S.A. 65 L5 .....43.40N 70.17W
Portland Oreg. U.S.A. 64 B6 .....45.29N 122.38W
Portland, Isle of pen. England 10 C1 .....50.33N 2.25W
Portlaoise Rep. of Ireland 41 D3 .....53.02N 7.17W
Portlethen Scotland 19 G2 .....57.04N 2.08W
Port Lincoln Australia 110 C3 .....34.43S 135.49E
Port Macquarie Australia 110 E3 .....31.25S 152.53E
Port Moresby P.N.G. 110 D6 .....9.29S 147.13E
Portnahaven Scotland 16 C3 .....55.41N 6.30W
Port Ness Scotland 18 C3 .....58.30N 6.14E
Porto Alegre Brazil 77 J1 .....30.03S 51.11W
Porto Esperidião Brazil 77 I4 .....15.50S 58.32W
Port of Spain Trinidad and Tobago 71 L3 .....10.37N 61.30W
Portogruaro Italy 50 E6 .....45.46N 12.50E
Porto-Novo Benin 84 E2 .....6.30N 2.40E
Porto Primavera, Represa resr Brazil 77 J3 .....21.27S 52.03W
Porto Santana Brazil 77 J7 .....0.01S 51.09W
Porto Torres Italy 50 C4 .....40.50N 8.25E
Porto-Vecchio France 44 H2 .....41.35N 9.16E

Porto Velho Brazil 76 H6 .....8.47S 63.54W
Portoviejo Ecuador 76 D7 .....1.06S 80.28W
Portpatrick Scotland 16 D2 .....54.51N 5.07W
Port Pirie Australia 110 C3 .....33.10S 138.02E
Portree Scotland 18 C2 .....57.25N 6.12W
Portrush Northern Ireland 16 C3 .....55.12N 6.39W
Port Said Egypt 85 H5 .....31.16N 32.18E
Portsmouth England 10 D1 .....50.48N 1.06W
Portsmouth d. England 9 E2 .....50.50N 1.04W
Portsmouth U.S.A. 65 J4 .....38.44N 82.59W
Portsoy Scotland 19 G2 .....57.41N 2.41W
Portstewart Northern Ireland 16 C3 .....55.11N 6.43W
Port Sudan Sudan 85 H3 .....19.36N 37.12E
Port Talbot Wales 12 D3 .....51.36N 3.48W
Portugal Europe 48 B3 .....39.41N 7.57W
Portumna Rep. of Ireland 41 C3 .....53.06N 8.13W
Port Vila Vanuatu 108 H4 .....17.44S 168.17E
Port William Scotland 16 E2 .....54.46N 4.35W
Posadas Argentina 73 D4 .....27.23S 55.52W
Poso Indonesia 105 G3 .....1.24S 120.47E
Posse Brazil 77 K5 .....14.06S 46.22W
Potenza Italy 50 F4 .....40.38N 15.48E
P'ot'i Georgia 53 L5 .....42.09N 41.40E
Potiskum Nigeria 84 F3 .....11.42N 11.04E
Potosí Bolivia 76 G4 .....19.36S 65.47W
Potsdam Germany 54 E5 .....52.24N 13.04E
Poulton-le-Fylde England 14 E2 .....53.51N 2.59W
Poŭthĭsăt Cambodia 104 C6 .....12.32N 103.57E
Považská Bystrica Slovakia 46 D2 .....49.07N 18.27E
Powell, Lake resr U.S.A. 64 D4 .....37.34N 110.37W
Powick England 10 C3 .....52.10N 2.15W
Powys d. Wales 9 D3 .....52.23N 3.25W
Poyang Hu l. China 103 L3 .....29.05N 116.22E
Požarevac S.M. 56 E6 .....44.37N 21.11E
Poza Rica Mexico 70 E5 .....20.35N 97.26W
Poznań Poland 46 C4 .....52.25N 16.56E
Pozoblanco Spain 48 C3 .....38.23N 4.50W
Prabumulih Indonesia 104 C3 .....3.26S 104.13E
Prachatice Czech Rep. 46 B2 .....49.01N 14.00E
Prachuap Khiri Khan Thailand 104 B6 .....11.49N 99.48E
Prague Czech Rep. 54 F4 .....50.04N 14.26E
Praia Cape Verde 84 B3 .....14.55S 23.29W
Prapat Indonesia 104 B4 .....2.41N 98.57E
Prato Italy 50 D5 .....43.52N 11.06E
Pravdinsk Rus. Fed. 46 E5 .....54.27N 21.01E
Prawle Point England 13 D2 .....50.12N 3.44W
Pregolya r. Rus. Fed. 46 E5 .....54.41N 20.22E
Prenzlau Germany 46 A4 .....53.19N 13.52E
Preparis Island Cocos Is 97 H3 .....14.51N 93.39E
Přerov Czech Rep. 54 G3 .....49.27N 17.27E
Presidencia Roque Sáenz Peña Argentina 77 H2 .....26.44S 60.27W
Presidente Prudente Brazil 77 J3 .....22.10S 51.23W
Prešov Slovakia 54 I3 .....48.59N 21.16E
Prespa, Lake Europe 56 D5 .....40.52N 21.03E
Presque Isle town U.S.A. 65 M6 .....46.41N 68.01W
Prestatyn Wales 12 D5 .....53.20N 3.24W
Presteigne Wales 12 D4 .....52.16N 3.00W
Preston Dor. England 10 C1 .....50.39N 2.25W
Preston Lancs. England 14 E2 .....53.46N 2.42W
Prestonpans Scotland 17 G3 .....55.58N 2.59W
Prestwick Scotland 16 E3 .....55.30N 4.37W
Pretoria S. Africa 86 B2 .....25.44S 28.13E
Preveza Greece 56 D4 .....38.57N 20.45E
Prienai Lithuania 46 F5 .....54.38N 23.57E
Prievidza Slovakia 54 H3 .....48.47N 18.38E
Prijedor Bos.-Herz. 56 B7 .....44.59N 16.43E
Prijepolje S.M. 56 C6 .....43.23N 19.39E
Prilep Macedonia 56 D5 .....41.21N 21.33E
Primorsko-Akhtarsk Rus. Fed. 57 M8 .....46.03N 38.10E
Prince Albert Canada 62 H3 .....53.12N 105.44W
Prince Alfred, Cape Canada 62 F5 .....74.20N 124.47W
Prince Charles Island Canada 63 K4 .....67.48N 76.12W
Prince Edward Island d. Canada 63 L2 .....46.41N 63.09W
Prince Edward Islands Indian Oc. 117 K3 .....47.00S 37.00E
Prince George Canada 62 F3 .....53.55N 122.46W
Prince of Wales Island Australia 110 D5 .....10.43S 142.09E
Prince of Wales Island Canada 63 I5 .....72.27N 99.08W
Prince of Wales Island U.S.A. 62 E3 .....55.38N 132.45W
Prince Patrick Island Canada 62 G5 .....76.57N 118.47W
Prince Rupert Canada 62 E3 .....54.19N 130.19W
Princes Risborough England 10 E2 .....51.43N 0.50W
Príncipe i. São Tomé and Príncipe 84 E2 .....1.39N 7.22E
Pripet r. Ukraine 55 N4 .....51.16N 30.16E
Pripet Marshes Belarus/Ukraine 55 K4 .....51.39N 24.34E
Priština S.M. 56 D6 .....42.40N 21.10E
Privas France 44 F4 .....44.44N 4.36E
Prizren S.M. 56 D6 .....42.13N 20.43E
Probolinggo Indonesia 104 E2 .....7.47S 113.13E
Probus England 13 C2 .....50.18N 4.57W
Providence U.S.A. 65 L5 .....41.50N 71.25W
Providence, Cape New Zealand 111 F2 .....46.01S 166.28E
Providencia, Isla de i. Caribbean Sea 71 H3 .....13.21N 81.00W
Provins France 44 E6 .....48.34N 3.18E
Provo U.S.A. 64 D5 .....40.17N 111.41W
Prudhoe Bay town U.S.A. 62 D5 .....70.18N 148.10W
Prüm Germany 42 F3 .....50.13N 6.25E
Pruszków Poland 46 E4 .....52.10N 20.49E
Prut r. Europe 55 M1 .....45.28N 28.12E
Pryluky Ukraine 55 O4 .....50.35N 32.24E
Przemyśl Poland 46 F2 .....49.47N 22.46E
Psara i. Greece 56 F4 .....38.37N 25.35E
Psebay Rus. Fed. 57 N7 .....44.07N 40.47E
Psel r. Rus. Fed./Ukraine 55 P4 .....51.05N 35.15E
Pskov Rus. Fed. 40 G2 .....57.49N 28.19E
Pskov, Lake Estonia/Rus. Fed. 40 F2 .....58.02N 27.56E
Pucallpa Peru 76 F6 .....8.22S 74.35W
Pudsey England 15 F2 .....53.48N 1.40W
Puebla Mexico 70 E4 .....19.02N 98.12W
Puebla d. Mexico 70 E4 .....18.04N 98.39W
Pueblo U.S.A. 64 F4 .....38.17N 104.38W
Puente-Genil Spain 48 C2 .....37.23N 4.46W
Puerto Ángel Mexico 70 E4 .....15.42N 96.31W
Puerto de la Estaca Canary Islands 48 X1 .....27.47N 17.54W
Puerto del Rosario Canary Islands 48 Z2 .....28.30N 13.52W
Puertollano Spain 48 C3 .....38.41N 4.06W
Puerto Maldonado Peru 76 G5 .....12.39S 69.14W
Puerto Montt Chile 73 B2 .....41.27S 72.58W
Puerto Natales Chile 73 B1 .....51.35S 72.24W
Puerto Peñasco Mexico 70 B7 .....31.19N 113.32W
Puerto Princesa Phil. 104 F5 .....9.45N 118.45E
Puerto Rico i. Central America 71 K4 .....17.45N 66.34W
Puerto Vallarta Mexico 70 C5 .....20.40N 105.14W
Pukch'ŏng N. Korea 106 A4 .....40.14N 128.21E
Puksubaek-san mt. N. Korea 106 A4 .....40.38N 127.47E
Pula Croatia 54 E1 .....44.53N 13.51E
Pulborough England 11 E1 .....50.57N 0.30W
Pułtusk Poland 54 I5 .....52.42N 21.05E
Pune India 96 D4 .....18.32N 73.57E
Punjab d. India 96 E7 .....30.17N 75.18E
Punta Arenas Chile 73 B1 .....53.09S 70.57W
Punto Fijo Venezuela 71 J3 .....11.39N 70.11W
Pur r. Rus. Fed. 58 I4 .....67.37N 77.53E
Purari r. P.N.G. 110 D6 .....7.46S 144.54E
Purbeck, Isle of pen. England 10 C1 .....50.39N 2.01W

Puri India 96 G4 ....19.48N 85.55E
Purmerend Neth. 42 D5 ....52.31N 4.57E
Purus r. Brazil/Peru 77 H7 ....3.42S 61.28W
Pusan S. Korea 103 N5 ....35.09N 129.03E
Pustoshka Rus. Fed. 55 M7 ....56.20N 29.22E
Puting, Tanjung pt Indonesia 104 E3 ......3.35S 111.50E
Putrajaya Malaysia 104 C5 ....2.55N 101.39E
Puttalam Sri Lanka 96 E2 ....8.01N 79.50E
Putumayo r. Colombia 72 B6 ....2.43S 70.03W
Puvurnituq Canada 63 K4 ....60.02N 77.17W
Puy de Dôme mt. France 44 E4 ....45.46N 2.58E
Puy de Sancy mt. France 44 E4 ....45.31N 2.49E
Pwllheli Wales 12 C4 ....52.53N 4.25W
Pyaozero, Ozero l. Rus. Fed. 40 G4 ....66.11N 30.47E
Pyasina r. Rus. Fed. 59 J5 ....73.35N 86.19E
Pyè Myanmar 97 I4 ....18.48N 95.13E
Pyhäjoki r. Finland 40 F4 ....64.28N 24.15E
Pyhäselkä l. Finland 40 G3 ....62.31N 29.41E
Pyinmana Myanmar 97 I4 ....19.44N 96.13E
Pyle Wales 13 D3 ....51.32N 3.42W
Pylos Greece 56 D3 ....36.55N 21.42E
P'yŏngyang N. Korea 103 N5 ....39.01N 125.44E
Pyramid Lake U.S.A. 64 C5 ....40.09N 119.37W
Pyrenees mts Europe 48 G5 ....42.30N 2.00E
Pyrgos Greece 56 D3 ....37.40N 21.27E
Pyryatyn Ukraine 55 O4 ....50.14N 32.30E
Pyrzyce Poland 46 B4 ....53.08N 14.54E

Q

Qamanittuaq Canada 63 I4 ....64.17N 95.43W
Qamdo China 102 H4 ....31.13N 97.08E
Qarshi Uzbekistan 95 K7 ....38.52N 65.48E
Qasigiannguit Greenland 63 M4 ....68.48N 51.11W
Qatar Asia 95 H5 ....25.25N 51.57E
Qattara Depression f. Egypt 85 G4 ......29.48N 27.06E
Qāyen Iran 95 I6 ....33.42N 59.05E
Qazvin Iran 95 G7 ....36.17N 49.58E
Qeshm Iran 95 I5 ....26.57N 56.15E
Qiemo China 102 F5 ....38.05N 85.33E
Qijiaojing China 102 G6 ....43.25N 91.38E
Qilian Shan mts China 102 H5 ....39.21N 97.06E
Qinā Egypt 85 H4 ....26.08N 32.45E
Qingdao China 103 M5 ....36.05N 120.24E
Qinghai d. China 102 H4 ....36.07N 96.31E
Qinghai Hu l. China 103 I5 ....36.49N 100.06E
Qinhuangdao China 103 L5 ....39.56N 119.38E
Qinzhou China 103 J2 ....21.57N 108.31E
Qionghai China 103 K1 ....19.13N 110.29E
Qiqihar China 103 M7 ....47.13N 123.58E
Qitaihe China 106 B5 ....45.41N 130.46E
Qom Iran 95 H6 ....34.38N 50.51E
Qornet es Saouda mt. Lebanon 57 L2 .....34.18N 36.06E
Quang Ngai Vietnam 104 D7 ....15.04N 108.50E
Quantock Hills England 13 D3 ....51.10N 3.15W
Quanzhou China 103 K3 ....25.57N 111.05E
Quchan Iran 95 I7 ....36.59N 58.29E
Québec d. Canada 63 K2 ....46.48N 71.15W
Québec d. Canada 63 K3 ....54.45N 74.31W
Queenborough England 11 F2 ....51.25N 0.45E
Queen Charlotte Islands Canada 62 E3 ...53.59N 133.20W
Queen Charlotte Sound str. Canada 62 F3 .51.24N 129.09W
Queen Elizabeth Islands Canada 63 I4 ...76.31N 107.31W
Queen Maud Gulf Canada 62 H4 ....68.13N 102.08W
Queensland d. Australia 110 D4 ....22.37S 144.17E
Quelimane Mozambique 86 C3 ....17.53S 36.53E
Querétaro Mexico 70 D5 ....20.37N 100.22W
Querétaro d. Mexico 70 E5 ....20.51N 99.50W
Quetta Pakistan 96 C7 ....30.14N 67.03E
Quetzaltenango Guatemala 70 F3 ....14.50N 91.30W
Quezon City Phil. 105 G6 ....14.36N 121.01E
Quibala Angola 86 A3 ....10.44S 14.59E
Quibdó Colombia 72 B7 ....5.39N 76.38W
Quilon India 96 E2 ....8.53N 76.36E
Quimper France 44 A5 ....47.59N 4.06W
Quintana Roo d. Mexico 70 G4 ....18.44N 88.47W
Quito Ecuador 76 E7 ....0.14S 78.30W
Quixadá Brazil 77 M7 ....4.55S 38.59W
Quoich, Loch l. Scotland 18 D2 ....57.03N 5.18W
Quoile r. Northern Ireland 16 D2 ......54.21N 5.42W
Quy Nhon Vietnam 104 D6 ....13.44N 109.13E
Quzhou China 103 L3 ....28.57N 118.52E

R

Raahe Finland 40 F4 ....64.41N 24.29E
Raalte Neth. 42 F5 ....52.23N 6.17E
Raasay i. Scotland 18 C2 ....57.23N 6.02W
Raasay, Sound of str. Scotland 18 C2 ...57.26N 6.06W
Raba Indonesia 104 F2 ....8.32S 118.46E
Rabat Morocco 84 D5 ....34.01N 6.47W
Rābigh Saudi Arabia 94 E4 ....22.50N 39.00E
Race, Cape Canada 63 M2 ....46.38N 53.09W
Rach Gia Vietnam 104 D5 ....9.59N 105.06E
Racibórz Poland 46 D3 ....50.06N 18.13E
Radom Poland 46 E3 ....51.24N 21.09E
Radomsko Poland 46 D3 ....51.04N 19.27E
Radstock England 10 C2 ....51.17N 2.27W
Radun' Belarus 46 G5 ....54.03N 24.59E
Radviliškis Lithuania 46 F5 ....55.49N 23.32E
Radyyyliv Ukraine 55 J3 ....50.08N 25.15E
Rafḩā' Saudi Arabia 94 F5 ....29.33N 43.25E
Rafsanjān Iran 95 I6 ....30.24N 55.59E
Raglan Wales 12 E3 ....51.46N 2.51W
Ragusa Italy 50 F2 ....36.55N 14.44E
Rahachow Belarus 55 N5 ....53.05N 30.03E
Rahimyar Khan Pakistan 96 D6 ....28.22N 70.19E
Raichur India 96 E4 ....16.13N 77.18E
Rainier, Mount vol. U.S.A. 64 B6 ......46.54N 121.44W
Raipur India 96 F5 ....21.14N 81.39E
Raivavae i. French Polynesia 109 K4 ...23.51S 147.39W
Rajahmundry India 96 F4 ....17.00N 81.52E
Rajanpur Pakistan 95 L5 ....29.05N 70.24E
Rajasthan d. India 96 D6 ....26.40N 73.31E
Rajkot India 96 D5 ....22.14N 70.53E
Rakhiv Ukraine 55 K3 ....48.03N 24.12E
Rakitnoye Rus. Fed. 55 P4 ....50.50N 35.50E
Rakvere Estonia 40 F2 ....59.21N 26.22E
Raleigh U.S.A. 65 K4 ....35.47N 78.37W
Ramapo Deep f. N. Pacific Oc. 108 F8 ...30.59N 142.13E
Rame Head England 13 C2 ....50.19N 4.15W
Rāmhormoz Iran 95 G6 ....31.10N 49.55E
Râmnicu Vâlcea Romania 56 F7 ....45.07N 24.22E
Ramsbottom England 15 E2 ....53.39N 2.19W
Ramsey England 11 E3 ....52.27N 0.06W
Ramsey Isle of Man 14 C3 ....54.19N 4.23E
Ramsey Bay Isle of Man 14 C3 ....54.20N 4.22W
Ramsey Island Wales 12 B3 ....51.51N 5.22W
Ramsgate England 11 G2 ....51.20N 1.25E
Ramu r. Kenya 87 C3 ....3.53N 41.14E

Rancagua Chile 73 B3 ....34.11S 70.44W
Ranchi India 96 G5 ....23.22N 85.20E
Randers Denmark 40 B2 ....56.27N 10.03E
Rangiroa atoll French Polynesia 109 K5 .14.59S 147.42W
Rangoon Myanmar 97 I4 ....16.49N 96.08E
Rangpur Bangl. 97 G6 ....25.46N 89.16E
Rankin Inlet Canada 63 I4 ....62.52N 92.03W
Rannoch, Loch l. Scotland 19 E1 ....56.41N 4.23W
Rannoch Moor f. Scotland 18 E1 ....56.38N 4.46W
Ranong Thailand 104 B5 ....9.57N 98.38E
Rantauprapat Indonesia 104 B4 ....2.06N 99.47E
Raoul Island Indian Oc. 111 H4 ....29.16S 177.57W
Rapa i. French Polynesia 109 K4 ....27.35S 144.21W
Rapallo Italy 50 C6 ....44.21N 9.14E
Raphoe Rep. of Ireland 16 B2 ....54.52N 7.35W
Rapid City U.S.A. 64 F5 ....44.04N 103.14W
Raroia atoll French Polynesia 109 K4 ..16.05S 142.23W
Rarotonga i. Cook Is 109 J4 ....21.12S 159.46W
Ras Dejen mt. Ethiopia 85 H3 ....13.12N 38.23E
Rasht Iran 95 G7 ....37.16N 49.34E
Raskoh mts Pakistan 95 K5 ....28.54N 65.26E
Ras Tannūrah Saudi Arabia 95 H5 ....26.38N 50.10E
Rat Buri Thailand 104 B6 ....13.31N 99.50E
Rathdrum Rep. of Ireland 41 E2 ....52.56N 6.14W
Rathenow Germany 54 E5 ....52.37N 12.20E
Rathfriland Northern Ireland 16 C2 ....54.14N 6.09W
Rathkeale Rep. of Ireland 41 C2 ....52.32N 8.56W
Rathlin Island Northern Ireland 16 C3 .55.17N 6.10W
Rathluirc Rep. of Ireland 41 C2 ....52.21N 8.41W
Ratne Ukraine 55 K4 ....51.40N 24.32E
Rattray Head Scotland 19 H2 ....57.37N 1.49W
Rättvik Sweden 40 C3 ....60.53N 15.08E
Rauma Finland 40 E3 ....61.08N 21.31E
Raunds England 11 E3 ....52.20N 0.32W
Ravenna Italy 50 E6 ....44.25N 12.13E
Ravensthorpe Australia 110 B3 ....33.34S 120.01E
Rawaki i. Kiribati 108 I5 ....3.42S 170.40W
Rawalpindi Pakistan 96 D7 ....33.38N 73.08E
Rawicz Poland 46 C3 ....51.37N 16.51E
Rawlins U.S.A. 64 E5 ....41.48N 107.13W
Rawson Argentina 73 C2 ....43.15S 65.06W
Rawtenstall England 15 E2 ....53.42N 2.17W
Rayleigh England 11 F2 ....51.35N 0.36E
Razgrad Bulgaria 56 G6 ....43.32N 26.30E
Ré, Ile de i. France 44 C5 ....46.10N 1.22W
Reading England 10 E2 ....51.27N 0.58W
Reading d. England 9 E2 ....51.27N 0.59W
Rebiana Sand Sea des. Libya 94 B4 .....24.42N 21.18E
Reboly Rus. Fed. 40 G3 ....63.50N 30.48E
Rechytsa Belarus 55 N5 ....52.22N 30.26E
Recife Brazil 77 N6 ....8.02S 34.48W
Reconquista Argentina 77 I2 ....29.09S 59.38W
Red r. U.S.A. 65 H3 ....31.05N 91.40W
Red Bluff U.S.A. 64 B5 ....40.11N 122.14W
Redcar England 15 F3 ....54.37N 1.03W
Redcar and Cleveland d. England 9 E4 ..54.33N 1.02W
Red Deer Canada 62 G3 ....52.16N 113.49W
Redding U.S.A. 64 B5 ....40.36N 122.29W
Redditch England 10 D3 ....52.19N 1.56W
Redhill England 11 E2 ....51.14N 0.10W
Red Lake town Canada 63 I3 ....51.01N 93.50W
Red Lakes U.S.A. 65 H6 ....37.56N 91.46W
Redruth England 13 B2 ....50.14N 5.14W
Red Sea Africa/Asia 94 E4 ....26.30N 34.42E
Red Wharf Bay Wales 12 C5 ....53.19N 4.11W
Ree, Lough l. Rep. of Ireland 41 D3 ...53.32N 7.59W
Regensburg Germany 54 E3 ....49.01N 12.06E
Reggane Algeria 84 E4 ....26.46N 0.09E
Reggio di Calabria Italy 50 F3 ....38.06N 15.39E
Reggio nell'Emilia Italy 50 D6 ....44.41N 10.38E
Regina Canada 62 H3 ....50.27N 104.37W
Reidh, Rubha pt Scotland 18 D2 ....57.52N 5.51W
Reigate England 11 E2 ....51.14N 0.12W
Reims France 44 F6 ....49.15N 4.03E
Reindeer Lake Canada 62 H3 ....57.24N 102.23W
Reinosa Spain 48 C5 ....42.59N 4.07W
Reiphólsfjöll hill Iceland 40 X2 ......65.41N 22.20W
Reliance Canada 62 H4 ....62.43N 109.06W
Relizane Algeria 52 D4 ....35.44N 0.40E
Rena Norway 40 B3 ....61.08N 11.22E
Renfrewshire d. Scotland 8 C4 ....55.52N 4.31W
Reni Ukraine 57 H7 ....45.27N 28.18E
Rennell i. Solomon Is 111 F5 ....11.40S 160.18E
Rennes France 44 C6 ....48.07N 1.41W
Reno r. Italy 50 E6 ....44.35N 12.17E
Reno U.S.A. 64 C4 ....39.32N 119.48W
Republican r. U.S.A. 64 G4 ....39.06N 96.52W
Repulse Bay town Canada 63 J4 ....66.32N 86.08W
Resistencia Argentina 73 D4 ....27.24S 58.59W
Reşiţa Romania 56 D7 ....45.18N 21.53E
Resolute Canada 63 I5 ....74.41N 94.46W
Resolution Island Canada 63 L4 ....61.34N 64.52W
Retford England 15 G2 ....53.19N 0.57W
Rethel France 42 D2 ....49.31N 4.23E
Rethymno Greece 56 F2 ....35.21N 24.28E
Réunion i. Indian Oc. 117 L4 ....20.00S 55.00E
Reus Spain 48 F4 ....41.09N 1.06E
Reutlingen Germany 54 C3 ....48.30N 9.12E
Revillagigedo, Islas is Mexico 70 B4 ..18.34N 112.24W
Rewa India 96 F5 ....24.32N 81.18E
Reykjavík Iceland 40 X2 ....64.08N 21.55W
Reynosa Mexico 70 E6 ....26.04N 98.17W
Rēzekne Latvia 40 F2 ....56.31N 27.20E
Rhayader Wales 12 D4 ....52.18N 3.31W
Rheine Germany 42 G5 ....52.17N 7.28E
Rheinland-Pfalz d. Germany 42 G2 ......49.46N 7.27E
Rhine r. Germany 34 E3 ....51.59N 6.03E
Rhode Island d. U.S.A. 65 L5 ....41.40N 71.35W
Rhodes Greece 57 H3 ....36.26N 28.13E
Rhodes i. Greece 57 H3 ....36.15N 28.10E
Rhodope Mountains Bulgaria/Greece 56 E5 .41.52N 23.41E
Rhondda Cynon Taff d. Wales 9 D2 ......51.36N 3.23W
Rhône r. France/Switz. 44 F3 ....43.20N 4.40E
Rhyl Wales 12 D5 ....53.19N 3.29W
Riau, Kepulauan is Indonesia 104 C4 ...0.34N 104.11E
Ribble r. England 15 E2 ....53.45N 2.45W
Ribe Denmark 40 B1 ....55.20N 8.46E
Ribeira r. Brazil 77 K3 ....24.39S 47.25W
Ribeirão Preto Brazil 77 K3 ....21.12S 47.48W
Riberalta Bolivia 76 G5 ....11.01S 66.05W
Ribniţa Moldova 55 M2 ....47.46N 29.00E
Říčany Czech Rep. 46 B2 ....49.59N 14.40E
Richfield U.S.A. 64 D4 ....38.47N 112.05W
Richland U.S.A. 64 C6 ....46.19N 119.17W
Richmond Rep. of Ireland 41 D2 ....54.24N 4.44W
Richmond England 15 F3 ....54.24N 1.44W
Richmond U.S.A. 65 K4 ....37.34N 77.28W
Riesa Germany 54 E4 ....51.18N 13.17E
Rietavas Lithuania 46 E5 ....55.43N 21.56E
Rifstangi pt Iceland 40 Y2 ....66.33N 16.13W
Rift Valley f. Kenya 87 A3 ....0.50N 35.34E
Rīga Latvia 40 F2 ....56.57N 24.07E
Riga, Gulf of Estonia/Latvia 40 E2 ....57.24N 23.45E
Rigside Scotland 17 F3 ....55.36N 3.47W

Riihimäki Finland 40 F3 ....60.44N 24.47E
Rijeka Croatia 56 A7 ....45.20N 14.26E
Rimini Italy 50 E6 ....44.04N 12.34E
Rimouski Canada 63 L2 ....48.27N 68.32W
Rimsdale, Loch l. Scotland 19 E3 ......58.17N 4.10W
Ringkøbing Denmark 40 B2 ....56.05N 8.15E
Ringvassøya i. Norway 40 D5 ....69.55N 18.56E
Ringwood England 10 D1 ....50.51N 1.47W
Riobamba Ecuador 76 E7 ....1.41S 78.42W
Rio Branco Brazil 76 G5 ....10.01S 67.48W
Río Cuarto Argentina 73 C3 ....33.08S 64.21W
Rio de Janeiro Brazil 77 L3 ....22.55S 43.17W
Rio de Janeiro d. Brazil 77 L3 ....22.00S 42.30W
Río Gallegos Argentina 73 C1 ....51.39S 69.15W
Rio Grande r. Mexico/U.S.A. 71 E6 .....25.57N 97.10W
Rio Grande Brazil 77 J1 ....32.04S 52.08W
Rio Grande do Norte d. Brazil 77 M6 ...5.49S 36.21W
Rio Grande do Sul d. Brazil 77 J1 .....30.39S 54.07W
Ríohacha Colombia 72 B8 ....11.32N 72.58W
Rio Verde Brazil 77 J4 ....17.48S 50.55W
Ripley England 15 F2 ....53.03N 1.24W
Ripon England 15 F3 ....54.08N 1.32W
Risca Wales 12 D3 ....51.37N 3.06W
Rishton England 15 E2 ....53.46N 2.25W
Riva del Garda Italy 50 D6 ....45.53N 10.50E
Rivera Uruguay 77 I1 ....31.00S 55.33W
Riverside U.S.A. 64 C3 ....33.57N 117.24W
Rivière-du-Loup Canada 63 L2 ....47.50N 69.32W
Rivne Ukraine 55 L4 ....50.37N 26.14E
Riyadh Saudi Arabia 95 G4 ....24.43N 46.41E
Rize Turkey 57 N5 ....41.02N 40.30E
Rjuvbrokkene mt. Norway 40 A2 ....59.11N 7.10E
Roadford Reservoir England 13 C2 ......50.42N 4.13W
Roanne France 44 F5 ....46.03N 4.05E
Roanoke U.S.A. 65 K4 ....37.16N 79.58W
Roanoke r. U.S.A. 65 K4 ....36.02N 76.22W
Robertsfors Sweden 40 E4 ....64.12N 20.52E
Roberval Canada 63 K2 ....48.31N 72.14W
Robson, Mount Canada 62 G3 ....53.07N 119.06W
Roca, Cabo da c. Portugal 48 A3 ....38.47N 9.29W
Rocca Busambra mt. Italy 50 E2 ....37.51N 13.24E
Rocha Uruguay 73 D3 ....34.30S 54.19W
Rochdale England 15 E2 ....53.37N 2.10W
Rochefort Belgium 42 E3 ....50.10N 5.13E
Rochefort France 44 C4 ....45.57N 0.58W
Rochester England 11 F2 ....51.23N 0.30E
Rochester Minn. U.S.A. 65 H5 ....44.02N 92.27W
Rochester N. Y. U.S.A. 65 K5 ....43.09N 77.38W
Rockford U.S.A. 65 I5 ....42.17N 89.04W
Rockhampton Australia 110 E4 ....23.25S 150.34E
Rockingham Forest England 11 E3 ....52.31N 0.32W
Rocky Mountains Canada/U.S.A. 62 F3 ...40.57N 107.58W
Rodel Scotland 18 C2 ....57.45N 6.58W
Rodez France 44 E4 ....44.22N 2.34E
Rodrigues Island Mauritius 108 A4 .....19.37S 63.40E
Roe r. Northern Ireland 16 C3 ....55.06N 6.58W
Roermond Neth. 42 E4 ....51.12N 5.59E
Roeselare Belgium 42 C3 ....50.56N 3.08E
Rogaguna, Laguna l. Bolivia 76 G5 .....14.03S 67.05W
Roggeveen Basin f. S. Pacific Oc. 109 O3 .32.50S 89.54W
Rokiškis Lithuania 40 F1 ....55.57N 25.35E
Rolla U.S.A. 65 H4 ....37.56N 91.46W
Rom mt. Uganda 87 A3 ....3.23N 33.37E
Roma i. Indonesia 105 H2 ....7.31S 127.25E
Roma Romania 55 L2 ....46.56N 26.55E
Roman Romania 55 L2 ....46.56N 26.55E
Romania Europe 53 H6 ....46.07N 24.36E
Romanzof, Cape U.S.A. 62 B4 ....61.49N 166.06W
Rombas France 42 F2 ....49.15N 6.05E
Rome Italy 50 E4 ....41.54N 12.30E
Romford England 11 F2 ....51.35N 0.11E
Romney Marsh f. England 11 F2 ....51.03N 0.54E
Romny Ukraine 55 O4 ....50.45N 33.28E
Romsey England 10 D1 ....50.59N 1.30W
Ronaldsway town England 14 C2 ....54.04N 4.38W
Ronas Hill Scotland 19 H5 ....60.32N 1.27W
Ronda Spain 48 C2 ....36.45N 5.10W
Rondônia d. Brazil 76 H5 ....11.18S 62.19W
Rondonópolis Brazil 77 J4 ....16.29S 54.38W
Rønne Denmark 40 C1 ....55.06N 14.43E
Ronse Belgium 42 C3 ....50.45N 3.36E
Roosendaal Neth. 42 D4 ....51.31N 4.28E
Roque de los Muchachos vol. Canary Islands 48 X2
....28.45N 17.51W
Roquefort France 44 C4 ....44.02N 0.19W
Roraima d. Brazil 77 H8 ....1.27N 60.48W
Roraima, Mount Guyana 72 C7 ....5.15N 60.44W
Røros Norway 40 B3 ....62.34N 11.23E
Rosario Argentina 73 C3 ....32.56S 60.41W
Roscoff France 44 B6 ....48.43N 3.59W
Roscommon Rep. of Ireland 41 C3 ......53.38N 8.11W
Roscommon d. Rep. of Ireland 41 C3 ...53.49N 8.16W
Roscrea Rep. of Ireland 41 D2 ....52.57N 7.48W
Roseau Dominica 71 L4 ....15.17N 61.23W
Roseburg U.S.A. 64 B5 ....43.13N 123.21W
Roseires Reservoir Sudan 94 D2 ....11.33N 34.31E
Rosenheim Germany 54 E2 ....47.51N 12.08E
Rosiori de Vede Romania 56 F7 ....44.07N 25.00E
Roslavl' Rus. Fed. 55 O5 ....53.57N 32.51E
Rossan Point Rep. of Ireland 41 C4 ...54.41N 8.48W
Rossel Island P.N.G. 110 E5 ....11.24S 154.10E
Rossington England 15 F2 ....53.29N 1.03W
Rosslare Harbour Rep. of Ireland 41 E2 .52.15N 6.20W
Rosso Mauritania 84 C3 ....16.29N 15.47W
Ross of Mull pen. Scotland 16 C4 .....56.18N 6.19W
Ross-on-Wye England 10 C2 ....51.55N 2.35W
Rossvatnet l. Norway 40 C4 ....65.46N 14.19E
Rostock Germany 54 E6 ....54.05N 12.07E
Rostov-na-Donu Rus. Fed. 58 E2 ....47.13N 39.44E
Roswell U.S.A. 64 F3 ....33.21N 104.30W
Rota i. N. Mariana Is 105 L6 ....14.09N 145.12E
Rote i. Indonesia 105 G1 ....10.29S 123.24E
Rothbury England 15 F4 ....55.19N 1.54W
Rother r. England 10 E1 ....50.57N 0.32W
Rotherham England 15 F2 ....53.26N 1.21W
Rothes Scotland 19 F2 ....57.32N 3.12E
Rothesay Scotland 16 D3 ....55.50N 5.03W
Rothwell England 15 F2 ....52.25N 0.48W
Rotorua New Zealand 111 G3 ....38.08S 176.16E
Rotterdam Neth. 42 D4 ....51.55N 4.30E
Rotuma i. Fiji 111 G5 ....12.29S 177.05E
Roubaix France 44 E7 ....50.42N 3.10E
Rouen France 44 D6 ....49.26N 1.06E
Round Hill England 15 F3 ....54.24N 1.05W
Round Mountain Australia 110 E3 ......30.24S 152.15E
Rousay i. Scotland 19 F4 ....59.10N 3.02W
Rouyn-Noranda Canada 65 K6 ....48.14N 79.02W
Rovaniemi Finland 40 F4 ....66.29N 25.42E
Rovigo Italy 50 D6 ....45.04N 11.47E
Roxas City Phil. 105 G6 ....11.33N 122.45E
Royal Leamington Spa England 10 D3 ...52.17N 1.32W
Royal Tunbridge Wells England 11 F2 ..51.08N 0.16E
Royan France 44 C4 ....45.38N 1.01W

Roye France 42 B2 ....49.42N 2.48E
Royston England 11 E3 ....52.03N 0.01W
Royton England 15 E2 ....53.34N 2.07W
Ruabon Wales 12 D4 ....52.59N 3.02W
Rub' al Khālī des. Saudi Arabia 95 G3 .19.01N 46.30E
Rubtsovsk Rus. Fed. 58 J3 ....51.33N 81.07E
Rudnaya Pristan' Rus. Fed. 106 C4 ....43.43N 135.20E
Rudnya Rus. Fed. 55 N6 ....54.57N 31.06E
Rudnyy Kazakhstan 58 H3 ....52.57N 63.07E
Rufiji r. Tanzania 86 C4 ....8.02S 39.17E
Rugby England 10 D3 ....52.22N 1.16W
Rugby U.S.A. 64 F6 ....48.20N 100.01W
Rugeley England 10 D3 ....52.46N 1.56W
Rügen i. Germany 54 E6 ....54.23N 13.27E
Ruhr r. Germany 42 F4 ....51.26N 6.43E
Rukwa, Lake Tanzania 86 C4 ....8.09S 32.25E
Rum i. Scotland 18 C1 ....56.59N 6.22W
Ruma S.M. 56 C7 ....45.01N 19.50E
Rum Cay i. Bahamas 71 J5 ....23.42N 74.48W
Runcorn England 14 E2 ....53.20N 2.42W
Rundu Namibia 86 A3 ....17.54S 19.47E
Ruoqiang China 102 F5 ....38.58N 88.08E
Rururtu i. French Polynesia 109 J4 ...22.28S 151.21W
Ruse Bulgaria 50 F6 ....43.49N 25.57E
Rushden England 11 E3 ....52.17N 0.36W
Russian Federation Asia/Europe 58 I4 .57.12N 40.44E
Ruteng Indonesia 104 G2 ....8.33S 120.25E
Ruthin Wales 12 D5 ....53.07N 3.19W
Rutland d. England 9 E3 ....52.42N 0.38W
Rutland Water resr England 10 E3 .....52.39N 0.40W
Ruza Rus. Fed. 55 O6 ....55.42N 36.13E
Ružomberok Slovakia 54 H3 ....49.05N 19.17E
Rwanda Africa 85 G1 ....2.16S 29.58E
Ryan, Loch b. Scotland 16 D3 ....55.01N 5.05W
Ryazan' Rus. Fed. 58 E3 ....54.37N 39.44E
Rybinsk Rus. Fed. 58 E3 ....58.03N 38.51E
Rybinskoye Vodokhranilishche resr Rus. Fed. 58 E3
....58.21N 38.27E
Rybnik Poland 46 D3 ....50.06N 18.33E
Ryde England 10 D1 ....50.44N 1.10W
Rye England 11 F1 ....50.57N 0.44E
Rye r. England 15 G3 ....54.10N 0.44W
Rye Bay England 11 F1 ....50.55N 0.47E
Ryōtsu Japan 106 C3 ....38.04N 138.25E
Ryukyu Islands Japan 103 M2 ....24.13N 124.52E
Rzeszów Poland 46 F3 ....50.02N 22.01E
Rzhev Rus. Fed. 55 P7 ....56.16N 34.20E

S

Saale r. Germany 54 D4 ....51.57N 11.56E
Saarbrücken Germany 54 B3 ....49.15N 6.58E
Saaremaa i. Estonia 40 E2 ....58.14N 22.46E
Saarland d. Germany 42 F2 ....49.28N 6.53E
Saarlouis Germany 42 F2 ....49.20N 6.46E
Sab' Ābār Syria 57 L1 ....33.42N 37.47E
Šabac S.M. 56 C7 ....44.46N 19.42E
Sabadell Spain 48 G4 ....41.33N 2.05E
Sabah d. Malaysia 104 F5 ....5.27N 116.59E
Sabana, Archipiélago de is Cuba 71 H5 .23.18N 80.46W
Sabha Libya 84 F4 ....27.02N 14.28E
Sabinas Mexico 70 D6 ....27.52N 101.07W
Sable, Cape Canada 63 L2 ....43.25N 65.39W
Sable, Cape U.S.A. 65 J2 ....25.08N 81.10W
Sable Island Canada 63 M2 ....43.57N 59.55W
Şabyā Saudi Arabia 94 F3 ....17.07N 42.35E
Sabzevār Iran 95 I7 ....36.12N 57.37E
Sacramento U.S.A. 64 B4 ....38.34N 121.25W
Sacramento Mountains U.S.A. 64 E3 ....34.23N 106.04W
Sado r. Portugal 48 A3 ....38.25N 8.36W
Sadoga-shima i. Japan 106 C3 ....37.56N 138.33E
Säffle Sweden 40 C2 ....59.08N 12.56E
Saffron Walden England 11 F3 ....52.01N 0.15E
Safi Morocco 84 D5 ....32.22N 9.15W
Safonovo Rus. Fed. 55 O6 ....55.07N 33.14E
Sagar India 96 E5 ....23.50N 78.45E
Sagres Portugal 48 A2 ....37.01N 8.57W
Sahand, Kūh-e mt. Iran 95 G7 ....37.38N 46.28E
Sahara des. Africa 84 E4 ....19.01N 4.03E
Saidpur Bangl. 96 G6 ....25.46N 88.58E
Saimaa l. Finland 40 G3 ....61.15N 28.21E
St Abb's Head Scotland 17 G3 ....55.55N 2.09W
St Agnes England 13 B2 ....50.19N 5.12W
St Agnes i. England 13 A1 ....49.53N 6.21W
St Albans England 11 E2 ....51.45N 0.20W
St Alban's Head England 10 C1 ....50.35N 2.03W
St-Amand-les-Eaux France 42 C3 ....50.26N 3.25E
St-Amand-Montrond France 44 E5 ....46.44N 2.30E
St Andrews Scotland 17 G4 ....56.20N 2.48W
St Anne Channel Is 13 Z9 ....49.43N 2.12W
St Ann's Head Wales 12 B3 ....51.41N 5.12W
St Anthony Canada 63 M3 ....51.20N 55.23W
St Asaph Wales 12 D5 ....53.15N 3.27W
St Austell England 13 C2 ....50.20N 4.47W
St Austell Bay England 13 C2 ....50.19N 4.45W
St-Barthélemy i. Central America 71 L4 .17.54N 62.49W
St Bees England 14 D3 ....54.30N 3.35W
St Bees Head England 14 D3 ....54.31N 3.38W
St Brelade Channel Is 13 Z8 ....49.11N 2.12W
St Bride's Bay Wales 12 B3 ....51.48N 5.18W
St-Brieuc France 44 B6 ....48.31N 2.45W
St Catherine's Point England 10 D1 ...50.34N 1.17W
St Clears Wales 12 C3 ....51.49N 4.30W
St Cloud U.S.A. 65 H6 ....45.34N 94.10W
St Columb Major England 13 C2 ....50.26N 4.56W
St David's Wales 12 B3 ....51.53N 5.16W
St David's Head Wales 12 B3 ....51.54N 5.20W
St-Denis France 42 B1 ....48.57N 2.22E
St-Dié France 44 G6 ....48.17N 6.57E
St-Dizier France 44 F6 ....48.38N 4.57E
Saintes France 44 C4 ....45.45N 0.37W
St-Étienne France 44 F4 ....45.26N 4.24E
Saintfield Northern Ireland 16 D2 ....54.27N 5.49W
St Gallen Switz. 50 C7 ....47.26N 9.23E
St-Gaudens France 44 D3 ....43.07N 0.44E
St George's Grenada 71 L3 ....12.04N 61.45W
St George's Channel Rep. of Ireland/U.K. 41 E1 .51.58N 6.08W
St Germans England 13 C2 ....50.24N 4.19W
St Govan's Head Wales 12 C3 ....51.36N 4.55W
St Helena i. Atlantic Oc. 116 I5 .....16.00S 6.00W
St Helena Bay S. Africa 86 A1 ....32.43S 18.07E
St Helens England 14 E2 ....53.27N 2.44W
St Helens, Mount vol. U.S.A. 64 B6 ...46.08N 122.13W
St Helier Channel Is 13 Z8 ....49.11N 2.06W
St Ives Cambs. England 11 E3 ....52.20N 0.04W
St Ives Corn. England 13 B2 ....50.13N 5.29W
St Ives Bay England 13 B2 ....50.13N 5.28W
St-Jean, Lac l. Canada 65 L6 ....48.36N 72.00W
St Joe r. U.S.A. 64 C6 ....47.25N 116.45W
Saint John Canada 63 L2 ....45.16N 66.04W
St John Channel Is 13 Z8 ....49.15N 2.08W
St John r. U.S.A. 65 M6 ....45.46N 66.12W

t John's Antigua 71 L4 ....17.05N 61.51W
t John's Canada 63 M2 ....47.28N 52.18W
t John's Point Northern Ireland 16 D2 ....54.13N 5.39W
t John's Town of Dalry Scotland 16 E3 ....55.06N 4.10W
t Joseph U.S.A. 65 H4 ....39.48N 94.51W
t Joseph, Lake Canada 65 H7 ....50.59N 90.57W
t Just England 13 B2 ....50.08N 5.41W
t Keverne England 13 B2 ....50.03N 5.05W
t Kilda i. Scotland 18 A2 ....57.49N 8.33W
t Kitts and Nevis Central America 71 L4 ....17.17N 62.35W
t Lawrence inlet Canada 63 L2 ....48.18N 69.06W
t Lawrence, Gulf of Canada 63 L2 ....48.20N 61.29W
t Lawrence Island U.S.A. 62 B4 ....63.05N 169.50W
t-Lô France 44 C6 ....49.07N 1.05W
t-Louis Senegal 84 C3 ....16.00N 16.29W
t Louis U.S.A. 65 H4 ....38.43N 90.14W
t Lucia Central America 71 L3 ....13.57N 60.53W
t Magnus Bay Scotland 19 H5 ....60.24N 1.37W
t-Malo France 44 B6 ....48.39N 2.00W
t-Malo, Golfe de g. France 44 B6 ....48.48N 2.16W
t Margaret's Hope Scotland 19 G3 ....58.49N 2.57W
t Martin Channel Is 13 Z8 ....49.26N 2.33W
t Martin Channel Is 13 Z8 ....49.13N 2.03W
t-Martin i. Central America 71 L4 ....18.08N 62.59W
t Martin's i. England 13 A1 ....49.58N 6.17W
t Mary's England 13 A1 ....49.56N 6.16W
t Matthew Island U.S.A. 62 A4 ....60.27N 172.49W
t-Maurice r. Canada 65 L6 ....46.22N 72.32W
t Mawes England 13 B2 ....50.09N 5.01W
t Moritz Switz. 50 C7 ....46.30N 9.50E
t-Nazaire France 44 B5 ....47.17N 2.13W
t Neots England 11 E3 ....52.14N 0.16W
t-Niklaas Belgium 42 D4 ....51.10N 4.10E
t-Omer France 42 B3 ....50.45N 2.16E
t Ouen Channel Is 13 Z8 ....49.14N 2.12W
t Paul U.S.A. 65 H5 ....44.57N 93.05W
t Peter Port Channel Is 13 Y9 ....49.28N 2.32W
t Petersburg U.S.A. 65 J2 ....27.45N 82.42W
t Petersburg Rus. Fed. 58 E3 ....59.56N 30.18E
t Pierre and Miquelon is N. America 63 M2 ....46.42N 56.29W
t-Pol-sur-Ternoise France 11 H1 ....50.23N 2.20E
t Pölten Austria 54 F3 ....48.12N 15.38E
t-Quentin France 44 E6 ....49.51N 3.17E
t Sampson Channel Is 13 Y9 ....49.29N 2.31W
t Vincent and the Grenadines Central America 71 L3 ....12.50N 60.52W
t-Vith Belgium 42 F3 ....50.17N 6.07E
t Wendel Germany 42 G2 ....49.28N 7.09E
aipan i. N. Mariana Is 108 F7 ....15.15N 145.49E
aittanulkki hill Finland 40 F4 ....66.57N 25.48E
ajama, Nevado mt. Bolivia 76 G4 ....18.09S 68.52W
aka Morocco 48 D1 ....34.37N 3.23W
akai Japan 106 C2 ....34.34N 135.29E
akakah Saudi Arabia 94 F5 ....29.56N 40.05E
akakawea, Lake U.S.A. 64 F6 ....47.45N 102.15W
akarya r. Turkey 57 I5 ....41.07N 30.38E
akata Japan 106 D3 ....38.54N 139.49E
akhalin i. Rus. Fed. 59 P2 ....48.10N 142.40E
akura Japan 106 D3 ....35.44N 140.13E
al i. Cape Verde 84 B3 ....16.49N 22.59W
ala Sweden 40 D2 ....59.55N 16.36E
alado r. Argentina 73 C3 ....32.27S 60.49W
alado r. Mexico 70 E6 ....26.45N 99.26W
alalah Oman 95 H3 ....17.02N 54.10E
ale England 15 E2 ....53.26N 2.19W
alehurst England 11 F2 ....50.59N 0.30E
alekhard Rus. Fed. 58 H4 ....66.31N 66.43E
alem India 96 E3 ....11.37N 78.08E
alem U.S.A. 64 B5 ....44.54N 122.58W
alerno Italy 50 F4 ....40.40N 14.47E
alerno, Golfo di g. Italy 50 F4 ....40.25N 14.43E
alford England 15 E2 ....53.29N 2.18W
algado r. Brazil 77 M7 ....4.27S 37.46W
alihli Turkey 57 H4 ....38.29N 28.08E
alihorsk Belarus 55 L5 ....52.47N 27.32E
alinas Brazil 77 L4 ....16.10S 42.17W
alinas U.S.A. 64 B4 ....36.41N 121.39W
alisbury England 10 D2 ....51.04N 1.48W
alisbury U.S.A. 65 K4 ....38.22N 75.36W
alisbury Plain f. England 10 C2 ....51.15N 2.03W
alitre r. Brazil 77 L6 ....9.30S 40.33W
alluit Canada 63 K4 ....62.11N 75.42W
almon r. Canada 64 C6 ....45.52N 116.45W
almon Arm Canada 64 C7 ....50.42N 119.17W
almon River Mountains U.S.A. 64 C5 ....44.46N 115.01W
alo Finland 40 E3 ....60.23N 23.08E
al'sk Rus. Fed. 53 L6 ....46.28N 41.33E
alt U.S.A. 64 D3 ....33.22N 112.17W
alta Argentina 73 C4 ....24.45S 65.29W
altash England 13 C2 ....50.24N 4.13W
altcoats Scotland 16 E3 ....55.38N 4.47W
altee Islands Rep. of Ireland 41 E2 ....52.07N 6.36W
altillo Mexico 70 D6 ....25.25N 101.01W
alto Uruguay 77 I1 ....31.23S 57.57W
alton Sea i. U.S.A. 64 C3 ....33.28N 115.58W
alvador Brazil 77 M5 ....12.57S 38.25W
alween r. China/Myanmar 97 I5 ....24.06N 98.35E
alyan Azerbaijan 95 G7 ....39.35N 48.58E
alzburg Austria 54 F2 ....47.48N 13.03E
alzgitter Germany 54 D5 ....52.10N 10.24E
amandağı Turkey 57 K3 ....36.04N 35.58E
amani Japan 106 D2 ....42.08N 142.54E
amar i. Phil. 105 H6 ....11.54N 125.43E
amara Rus. Fed. 58 G3 ....53.11N 50.09E
amarinda Indonesia 104 F3 ....0.29S 117.11E
amarra'i Iraq 94 F6 ....34.12N 43.54E
amba Dem. Rep. Congo 86 B4 ....4.38S 26.20E
ambalpur India 96 F5 ....21.27N 83.59E
ambas Indonesia 104 D4 ....1.22N 109.19E
ambir Ukraine 55 J3 ....49.31N 23.12E
ambre r. Belgium/France 42 D3 ....50.17N 4.06E
ame Tanzania 87 B1 ....4.05S 37.45E
amer France 11 G1 ....50.38N 1.45E
amoa S. Pacific Oc. 108 I5 ....13.58S 173.23W
amoa Basin f. S. Pacific Oc. 108 I4 ....15.26S 165.38W
amos i. Greece 56 G3 ....37.49N 26.44E
amothraki i. Greece 56 F5 ....40.24N 25.34E
ampit Indonesia 104 E3 ....2.34S 112.55E
amsun Turkey 57 L5 ....41.17N 36.19E
an Mali 84 D3 ....13.18N 4.54W
an'a' Yemen 94 F3 ....15.23N 44.11E
an Andrés, Isla de i. Caribbean Sea 71 H3 ....12.33N 81.41W
an Angelo U.S.A. 64 F3 ....31.28N 100.23W

San Antonio U.S.A. 64 G2 ....29.22N 98.27W
San Antonio, Cabo c. Cuba 71 H5 ....21.51N 84.55W
San Benedicto, Isla i. Mexico 70 B4 ....19.19N 110.47W
San Bernardo Chile 76 F1 ....33.36S 70.41W
San Borja Bolivia 76 G5 ....14.49S 66.54W
San Cristóbal i. Solomon Is 111 F5 ....10.38S 161.38E
San Cristóbal Venezuela 72 B7 ....7.45N 72.15W
San Cristóbal, Isla i. Ecuador 76 C7 ....0.48S 89.20W
San Cristóbal de la Laguna Canary Islands 48 X2 ....28.28N 16.19W
Sancti Spíritus Cuba 71 I5 ....21.56N 79.26W
Sanda Island Scotland 16 D3 ....55.16N 5.35W
Sandakan Malaysia 104 F5 ....5.51N 118.05E
Sandane Norway 40 A3 ....61.47N 6.14E
Sandanski Bulgaria 56 E5 ....41.34N 23.16E
Sanday i. Scotland 19 G4 ....59.15N 2.29W
Sanday Sound str. Scotland 19 G4 ....59.12N 2.34W
Sandbach England 15 E2 ....53.09N 2.22W
Sandhurst England 10 E2 ....51.21N 0.48W
San Diego U.S.A. 64 C3 ....32.43N 117.05W
Sandıklı Turkey 57 I4 ....38.28N 30.16E
Sandnes Norway 40 A2 ....58.51N 5.44E
Sandnessjøen Norway 40 C4 ....66.01N 12.39E
Sandomierz Poland 46 I3 ....50.41N 21.45E
Sandoway Myanmar 97 H4 ....18.27N 94.22E
Sandown England 10 D1 ....50.40N 1.09W
Sandpoint U.S.A. 64 C6 ....48.16N 116.33W
Sandray i. Scotland 18 B1 ....56.54N 7.30W
Sandviken Sweden 40 D3 ....60.37N 16.46E
Sandwich England 11 G2 ....51.16N 1.20E
Sandy England 11 E3 ....52.08N 0.18W
Sandy Cape Australia 110 E4 ....24.42S 153.15E
Sandy Lake town Canada 63 I3 ....53.03N 93.18W
San Felipe Mexico 70 B7 ....31.02N 114.50W
San Félix Chile 76 E1 ....28.54S 70.30W
San Fernando Argentina 77 I1 ....34.28S 58.31W
San Fernando Phil. 104 G2 ....16.38N 120.18E
San Fernando Spain 48 B2 ....36.28N 6.11W
San Fernando de Apure Venezuela 72 C7 ....7.49N 67.28W
San Francisco U.S.A. 64 B4 ....37.45N 122.25W
San Francisco, Cabo de c. Ecuador 76 D8 ....0.40N 80.03W
San Francisco de Paula, Cabo c. Argentina 73 C2 ....49.42S 67.40W
Sangha r. Congo 82 E4 ....1.10S 16.47E
Sangir, Kepulauan is Indonesia 105 G4 ....2.15N 124.57E
Sangkulirang Indonesia 104 F4 ....0.55N 117.58E
Sangli India 96 D4 ....16.53N 74.38E
Sangre de Cristo Range mts U.S.A. 64 E4 ....38.19N 106.01W
Sangue r. Brazil 77 I5 ....11.02S 58.32W
San Jorge, Golfo de g. Argentina 73 C2 ....45.57S 65.55W
San José Costa Rica 71 H2 ....9.57N 84.02W
San José U.S.A. 64 B4 ....37.18N 121.57W
San José, Isla i. Mexico 70 B5 ....24.54N 110.33W
San José del Cabo Mexico 70 C5 ....23.04N 109.44W
San Juan Argentina 73 C3 ....31.33S 68.31W
San Juan r. Costa Rica/Nicaragua 71 H3 ....10.47N 83.44W
San Juan Puerto Rico 71 K4 ....18.26N 66.04W
San Juan Bautista Paraguay 77 I2 ....26.34S 57.06W
San Juan Mountains U.S.A. 64 E4 ....37.35N 107.17W
Şanlıurfa Turkey 57 M3 ....37.09N 38.49E
San Lorenzo mt. Spain 48 D5 ....42.14N 2.58W
Sanlúcar de Barrameda Spain 48 B2 ....36.46N 6.21W
San Luis Argentina 76 G1 ....33.19S 66.21W
San Luis, Lago de f. Bolivia 76 H5 ....13.40S 64.00W
San Luis Obispo U.S.A. 64 B4 ....35.18N 120.40W
San Luis Potosí Mexico 70 D5 ....22.10N 100.57W
San Luis Potosí Mexico 70 D5 ....22.51N 100.48W
San Marcos U.S.A. 64 G2 ....29.51N 97.56W
San Marino San Marino 50 E5 ....43.58N 12.27E
San Marino San Marino 50 E5 ....43.57N 12.27E
San Martín Bolivia 77 H5 ....13.05S 63.48W
San Matías, Golfo g. Argentina 73 C2 ....41.20S 64.35W
San Miguel r. Bolivia 77 H5 ....13.05S 63.48W
San Miguel El Salvador 70 G3 ....13.32N 88.08W
San Miguel de Tucumán Argentina 73 C4 ....26.48S 65.16W
Sanming China 103 L3 ....26.11N 117.39E
San Nicolás de los Arroyos Argentina 77 H1 ....33.20S 60.14W
Sanok Poland 46 F2 ....49.34N 22.11E
San Pablo Phil. 105 G6 ....14.04N 121.18E
San Pedro Paraguay 77 I3 ....24.08S 57.08W
San Pedro, Sierra de mts Spain 48 B3 ....39.31N 7.15W
San Pedro de Ycuamandyyú Paraguay 73 D4 ....24.07S 57.07W
San Pedro Sula Honduras 70 G4 ....15.28N 88.01W
San Pietro, Isola di i. Italy 50 C3 ....39.10N 8.14E
Sanquhar Scotland 17 F3 ....55.22N 3.56W
San Quintín, Cabo c. Mexico 64 C3 ....30.23N 116.01W
San Remo Italy 50 B5 ....43.49N 7.47E
San Salvador i. Bahamas 71 J5 ....24.07N 74.27W
San Salvador El Salvador 70 G3 ....13.43N 89.11W
San Salvador de Jujuy Argentina 73 C4 ....24.10S 65.20W
San Sebastián de la Gomera Canary Islands 48 X2 ....28.05N 17.06W
San Severo Italy 50 F4 ....41.41N 15.23E
Santa Ana El Salvador 70 G3 ....14.00N 89.31W
Santa Ana U.S.A. 64 C3 ....33.45N 117.56W
Santa Barbara U.S.A. 64 C3 ....34.27N 119.43W
Santa Catarina d. Brazil 77 J2 ....27.00S 50.57W
Santa Clara Cuba 71 I5 ....22.24N 79.56W
Santa Cruz Bolivia 76 H4 ....17.47S 63.12W
Santa Cruz, Isla i. Ecuador 76 D7 ....0.36S 90.10W
Santa Cruz de la Palma Canary Islands 48 X2 ....28.41N 17.46W
Santa Cruz de Tenerife Canary Islands 48 X2 ....28.27N 16.15W
Santa Cruz do Sul Brazil 77 J2 ....29.44S 52.25W
Santa Cruz Islands Solomon Is 111 F5 ....10.46S 167.21E
Santa Elena, Bahía de b. Ecuador 76 D7 ....2.07S 81.05W
Santa Fé Argentina 73 C3 ....31.37S 60.42W
Santa Fe U.S.A. 64 E4 ....35.42N 105.57W
Santa Isabel i. Solomon Is 111 E6 ....7.54S 159.11E
Santa Margarita, Isla i. Mexico 70 B5 ....24.25N 111.50W
Santa María Brazil 77 J2 ....29.41S 53.48W
Santa Maria U.S.A. 64 B3 ....34.58N 120.26W
Santa Maria di Leuca, Capo c. Italy 50 H3 ....39.47N 18.21E
Santa Marta Colombia 72 B8 ....11.16N 74.12W
Santander Spain 48 D5 ....43.28N 3.48W
Santarém Brazil 77 J7 ....2.27S 54.43W
Santarém Portugal 48 A3 ....39.15N 8.41W
Santa Rosa Argentina 73 C3 ....36.37S 64.17W
Santa Rosalía Mexico 70 B6 ....27.21N 112.18W
Santiago i. Cape Verde 84 B3 ....15.19N 23.45W
Santiago Chile 73 B3 ....33.28S 70.39W
Santiago Dom. Rep. 71 J4 ....19.31N 70.39W
Santiago de Compostela Spain 48 A5 ....42.53N 8.32W
Santiago de Cuba Cuba 71 I5 ....20.00N 75.49W
Sant Jordi, Golf de g. Spain 48 F4 ....40.49N 0.56E
Santo André Brazil 77 K3 ....23.40S 46.31W
Santo Antão i. Cape Verde 84 B3 ....17.01N 25.21W
Santo Domingo Dom. Rep. 71 K4 ....18.31N 69.57W
Santoña Spain 48 D5 ....43.27N 3.27W
Santos Brazil 77 K3 ....23.58S 46.20W
Santos Plateau f. S. Atlantic Oc. 109 Q4 ....27.20S 45.43W
Santo Tomé Argentina 77 I2 ....28.32S 56.05W
San Valentín, Cerro mt. Chile 73 B2 ....46.36S 73.21W
San Vincenzo Italy 50 D5 ....43.05N 10.32E
São Carlos Brazil 77 K3 ....22.02S 47.53W

São Francisco r. Brazil 77 M5 ....10.19S 36.31W
São José do Rio Preto Brazil 77 K3 ....20.49S 49.22W
São Luís Brazil 77 L7 ....2.35S 44.18W
São Marcos, Baía de b. Brazil 77 L7 ....2.31S 44.19W
São Mateus Brazil 77 M4 ....18.42S 39.51W
Saône r. France 44 F4 ....45.44N 4.49E
São Paulo Brazil 77 K3 ....23.35S 46.43W
São Paulo d. Brazil 77 K3 ....22.19S 48.23W
São Raimundo Nonato Brazil 77 L6 ....9.01S 42.37W
São Sebastião, Ilha do i. Brazil 77 K3 ....23.51S 45.17W
São Tomé São Tomé and Príncipe 84 E2 ....0.19N 6.44E
São Tomé i. São Tomé and Príncipe 84 E2 ....0.21N 6.35E
São Tomé, Cabo de c. Brazil 77 L3 ....22.00S 40.59W
São Tomé and Príncipe Africa 84 E2 ....1.00N 7.04E
São Vicente, Cabo de c. Portugal 48 A2 ....37.01N 8.59W
Sapporo Japan 106 D4 ....43.04N 141.20E
Sapri Italy 50 F4 ....40.04N 15.38E
Saqqaq Greenland 63 M5 ....70.01N 51.56W
Saqqez Iran 95 G7 ....36.12N 46.15E
Sáráb Iran 95 G7 ....37.55N 47.31E
Sara Buri Thailand 104 C6 ....14.29N 100.57E
Sarandë Albania 56 D4 ....39.53N 20.01E
Saransk Rus. Fed. 58 F3 ....54.11N 45.12E
Sarasota U.S.A. 65 J2 ....27.19N 82.33W
Saratov Rus. Fed. 58 F3 ....51.34N 45.59E
Saravan Iran 95 J2 ....27.20N 62.25E
Sarawak d. Malaysia 104 E4 ....1.46N 111.55E
Saray Turkey 57 G5 ....41.26N 27.55E
Sardindida Plain f. Kenya 87 B3 ....2.41N 39.59E
Sardinia i. Italy 50 C4 ....40.16N 8.04E
Sarektjåkkå mt. Sweden 40 D4 ....67.27N 17.43E
Sar-e Pol Afgh. 95 K7 ....36.15N 65.57E
Sargodha Pakistan 96 D7 ....32.01N 72.41E
Sarh Chad 85 F2 ....9.07N 18.23E
Sārī Iran 95 H7 ....36.33N 53.03E
Sarigan i. N. Mariana Is 105 L7 ....16.42N 145.48E
Sanyer Turkey 57 H5 ....41.10N 29.03E
Sark i. Channel Is 13 Y9 ....49.26N 2.24W
Şarkışla Turkey 57 L4 ....39.21N 36.25E
Şarköy Turkey 56 G5 ....40.37N 27.06E
Särna Sweden 40 C3 ....61.42N 13.08E
Saros Körfezi b. Turkey 56 G5 ....40.34N 26.36E
Sarpsborg Norway 40 B2 ....59.17N 11.08E
Sarrebourg France 44 G6 ....48.44N 7.03E
Sarreguemines France 42 G2 ....49.07N 7.04E
Sarria Spain 48 B5 ....42.47N 7.24W
Sarthe r. France 44 C5 ....47.34N 0.31W
Sasebo Japan 106 A2 ....33.09N 129.44E
Saskatchewan d. Canada 62 H3 ....53.08N 106.03W
Saskatchewan r. Canada 62 H3 ....53.40N 100.27W
Saskatoon Canada 62 H3 ....52.08N 106.39W
Sassandra Côte d'Ivoire 84 D2 ....4.57N 6.05W
Sassari Italy 50 C4 ....40.43N 8.34E
Sassnitz Germany 54 E6 ....54.31N 13.38E
Satpura Range mts India 96 D5 ....21.47N 74.23E
Satu Mare Romania 55 J2 ....47.47N 22.53E
Saudárkrókur Iceland 40 Y2 ....65.45N 19.40W
Saudi Arabia Asia 94 F4 ....23.41N 44.13E
Sault Sainte Marie Canada 63 J2 ....46.31N 84.20W
Saumlakki Indonesia 105 I2 ....8.00S 131.20E
Saundersfoot Wales 12 C3 ....51.43N 4.42W
Saurimo Angola 86 B4 ....9.39S 20.25E
Sava r. Europe 56 D7 ....44.50N 20.28E
Savai'i i. Samoa 108 I5 ....13.25S 172.39W
Savannah U.S.A. 65 J3 ....32.04N 81.07W
Savannah r. U.S.A. 65 J3 ....32.02N 80.53W
Savannakhét Laos 104 C7 ....16.32N 104.46E
Save r. Mozambique/Zimbabwe 86 C2 ....20.56S 35.03E
Savona Italy 50 C6 ....44.19N 8.29E
Savu Sea Indonesia 105 G2 ....9.51S 121.22E
Sawel Mountain hill Northern Ireland 16 B2 ....54.49N 7.02W
Sawhaj Egypt 85 H3 ....26.31N 31.38E
Sawston England 11 F3 ....52.07N 0.10E
Sawtry England 11 E3 ....52.26N 0.17W
Sawu i. Indonesia 105 G1 ....10.32S 121.58E
Saxilby England 15 G2 ....53.16N 0.40W
Saxmundham England 11 G3 ....52.13N 1.29E
Sayhût Yemen 95 H3 ....15.15N 51.19E
Saylac Somalia 85 I3 ....11.17N 43.28E
Saynshand Mongolia 103 K6 ....44.46N 110.12E
Scafell Pike hill England 14 D3 ....54.27N 3.13W
Scalasaig Scotland 16 C4 ....56.04N 6.11W
Scalby England 15 G3 ....54.18N 0.27W
Scalloway Scotland 19 H5 ....60.08N 1.17W
Scalp hill Rep. of Ireland 41 C2 ....52.59N 8.29W
Scalpay i. High. Scotland 18 D2 ....57.18N 5.59W
Scalpay i. W. Isles Scotland 18 C2 ....57.52N 6.39W
Scalp Mountain hill Rep. of Ireland 16 B3 ....55.06N 7.22W
Scampton England 15 G2 ....53.18N 0.34W
Scandinavia f. Europe 34 F4 ....65.00N 18.00E
Scapa Flow inlet Scotland 19 F3 ....58.54N 3.08W
Scarba i. Scotland 16 D4 ....56.10N 5.45W
Scarborough England 15 G3 ....54.17N 0.24W
Scarp i. Scotland 18 B3 ....58.01N 7.11W
Schaffhausen Switz. 50 C7 ....47.42N 8.38E
Schagen Neth. 42 D5 ....52.47N 4.48E
Schefferville Canada 63 L3 ....54.47N 66.48W
Scheldt r. Belgium 42 D4 ....51.21N 4.15E
Schiehallion mt. Scotland 19 E1 ....56.40N 4.06W
Schiermonnikoog i. Neth. 42 F6 ....53.31N 6.17E
Schleswig Germany 54 C6 ....54.31N 9.33E
Schwäbische Alb mts Germany 54 C2 ....47.59N 8.43E
Schwaner, Pegunungan mts Indonesia 104 E3 ....0.46S 112.26E
Schwarzer Mann hill Germany 42 F3 ....50.15N 6.21E
Schwedt an der Oder Germany 54 F5 ....53.04N 14.18E
Schweinfurt Germany 54 D4 ....50.03N 10.13E
Schwerin Germany 54 D5 ....53.38N 11.25E
Scilly, Isles of England 13 A1 ....49.53N 6.17W
Scioto r. U.S.A. 65 J4 ....38.44N 82.59W
Scole England 11 G3 ....52.22N 1.09E
Scone Scotland 17 F4 ....56.25N 3.24W
Scotland U.K. 8 D5 ....57.01N 3.53W
Scottish Borders d. Scotland 8 D4 ....55.33N 2.55W
Scottsbluff U.S.A. 64 F5 ....41.54N 103.41W
Scourie Scotland 18 D3 ....58.21N 5.10W
Scranton U.S.A. 65 K5 ....41.25N 75.39W
Scridain, Loch inlet Scotland 16 C4 ....56.21N 6.11W
Scunthorpe England 15 G2 ....53.35N 0.39W
Scuol Switz. 50 D7 ....46.48N 10.18E
Scutari, Lake Albania/S.M. 56 C6 ....42.14N 19.12E
Seaford England 11 F1 ....50.46N 0.06E
Seaham England 15 F3 ....54.50N 1.20W
Seamer England 15 G3 ....54.14N 0.26W
Seascale England 14 D3 ....54.24N 3.29W
Seaton Cumb. England 14 D3 ....54.40N 3.31W
Seaton Dev. England 13 D2 ....50.42N 3.04W
Seaton Delaval England 15 F4 ....55.05N 1.31W
Seattle U.S.A. 64 B6 ....47.36N 122.20W
Sebastián Vizcaíno, Bahía b. Mexico 70 B6 ....28.08N 114.45W
Sebeş Romania 56 E7 ....45.58N 23.34E
Şebinkarahisar Turkey 57 M5 ....40.17N 38.25E

Sechura, Bahía de b. Peru 76 D6 ....5.42S 81.18W
Secunderabad India 96 E4 ....17.25N 78.27E
Sedan France 44 F6 ....49.42N 4.57E
Sedbergh England 15 E3 ....54.19N 2.31W
Sedlčany Czech Rep. 46 B2 ....49.39N 14.26E
Šeduva Lithuania 46 F5 ....55.46N 23.44E
Seefin hill Rep. of Ireland 41 D2 ....52.14N 7.36W
Segen Wenz watercourse Ethiopia 87 B4 ....4.58N 36.54E
Segera Tanzania 87 B1 ....5.20S 38.34E
Segorbe Spain 48 E3 ....39.51N 0.28W
Segovia Spain 48 C4 ....40.57N 4.06W
Segura r. Spain 48 E3 ....38.06N 0.38W
Segura, Sierra de mts Spain 48 D2 ....37.59N 2.46W
Seiland i. Norway 40 E5 ....70.28N 23.18E
Seinäjoki Finland 40 E3 ....62.47N 22.51E
Seine r. France 44 D6 ....49.26N 0.15E
Seine, Baie de la b. France 44 C6 ....49.29N 0.32W
Sejny Poland 46 F5 ....54.06N 23.21E
Sekondi Ghana 84 D2 ....4.58N 1.43W
Selaru i. Indonesia 105 I2 ....8.13S 130.55E
Selatan, Tanjung pt Indonesia 104 E3 ....4.09S 114.38E
Selattyn England 10 B3 ....52.54N 3.05W
Selawik U.S.A. 62 B4 ....66.36N 160.16W
Selby England 15 F2 ....53.47N 1.04W
Selkirk Canada 62 I3 ....50.09N 96.53W
Selkirk Scotland 17 G3 ....55.33N 2.50W
Sellindge England 11 F2 ....51.06N 0.59E
Selsey England 11 E1 ....50.44N 0.47W
Selsey Bill hd England 10 E1 ....50.43N 0.49W
Selvas f. Brazil 76 F6 ....6.29S 71.47W
Selwyn Mountains Canada 62 E4 ....64.16N 131.38W
Selwyn Range hills Australia 110 C4 ....21.14S 139.54E
Semarang Indonesia 104 E2 ....6.55S 110.29E
Semenivka Ukraine 55 O5 ....52.10N 32.35E
Seminoe Reservoir U.S.A. 64 E5 ....42.06N 106.51W
Semipalatinsk Kazakhstan 58 J3 ....50.25N 80.19E
Semnän Iran 95 H7 ....35.30N 53.21E
Semois r. Belgium/France 42 D2 ....49.53N 4.45E
Sena Madureira Brazil 76 G6 ....9.07S 68.42W
Sendai Japan 106 D3 ....38.15N 140.53E
Senegal Africa 84 C3 ....14.29N 14.41W
Sénégal r. Mauritania 84 C3 ....16.00N 16.31W
Senftenberg Germany 46 B3 ....51.31N 14.00E
Senja i. Norway 40 D5 ....69.20N 17.14E
Senlis France 42 B2 ....49.12N 2.36E
Sennar Sudan 85 H3 ....13.31N 33.36E
Sens France 44 E6 ....48.12N 3.17E
Seoul S. Korea 103 N5 ....37.32N 127.00E
Sepik r. P.N.G. 105 K3 ....3.53S 144.33E
Sept-Îles Canada 63 L3 ....50.13N 66.23W
Seram i. Indonesia 105 H3 ....3.03S 129.24E
Serang Indonesia 104 D2 ....6.04S 106.09E
Serbia and Montenegro Europe 56 D6 ....44.01N 20.53E
Şereflikoçhisar Turkey 57 J4 ....38.56N 33.33E
Seremban Malaysia 104 C4 ....2.41N 101.56E
Serengeti National Park Tanzania 87 A2 ....2.28S 34.46E
Serengeti Plains f. Kenya 87 B2 ....3.43S 38.05E
Serere Uganda 87 A3 ....1.31N 33.28E
Seret r. Ukraine 55 K3 ....48.36N 25.51E
Sergipe d. Brazil 77 M5 ....10.30S 37.14W
Serik Turkey 57 I3 ....36.57N 31.07E
Serov Rus. Fed. 58 H3 ....59.38N 60.34E
Serowe Botswana 86 B2 ....22.24S 26.42E
Serpukhov Rus. Fed. 55 R6 ....54.55N 37.25E
Serra da Mesa, Represa resr Brazil 77 K5 ....14.17S 48.30W
Serres Greece 56 E5 ....41.06N 23.33E
Serui Indonesia 105 J3 ....1.52S 136.17E
Sestroretsk Rus. Fed. 40 G3 ....60.05N 29.57E
Sète France 44 E3 ....43.24N 3.42E
Sete Lagoas Brazil 77 L4 ....19.28S 44.13W
Setesdal f. Norway 40 A2 ....59.15N 7.23E
Sétif Algeria 84 E5 ....36.11N 5.25E
Seto-naikai sea Japan 106 B2 ....33.38N 132.17E
Settat Morocco 84 D5 ....32.58N 7.36W
Settle England 15 E3 ....54.04N 2.17W
Setúbal Portugal 48 A3 ....38.32N 8.53W
Setúbal, Baía de b. Portugal 48 A3 ....38.20N 9.02W
Seul, Lac l. Canada 65 H7 ....50.21N 92.29W
Sevastopol' Ukraine 53 J5 ....44.36N 33.31E
Seven Heads Rep. of Ireland 41 C1 ....51.34N 8.42W
Sevenoaks England 11 F2 ....51.16N 0.12E
Severn r. Canada 63 J3 ....55.59N 87.36W
Severn r. U.K. 10 C2 ....51.51N 2.21W
Severnaya Zemlya is Rus. Fed. 59 L6 ....80.09N 103.23E
Severo-Kuril'sk Rus. Fed. 59 Q3 ....50.40N 156.06E
Sevier Lake U.S.A. 64 D4 ....38.56N 113.09W
Seville Spain 48 C2 ....37.24N 5.58W
Seward U.S.A. 62 D4 ....60.09N 149.24W
Seward Peninsula U.S.A. 62 B4 ....65.29N 164.05W
Seychelles Indian Oc. 85 J1 ....4.40S 55.43E
Seydişehir Turkey 57 I3 ....37.25N 31.52E
Seyðisfjörður Iceland 40 Z2 ....65.16N 14.02W
Seyhan r. Turkey 57 K3 ....36.44N 34.54E
Seym r. Rus. Fed./Ukraine 55 P4 ....51.16N 34.16E
Seymchan Rus. Fed. 59 Q4 ....62.50N 152.20E
Sfântu Gheorghe Romania 56 F7 ....45.52N 25.48E
Sfax Tunisia 52 F3 ....34.45N 10.45E
Sgurr Alasdair hill Scotland 18 C2 ....57.12N 6.13W
Sgurr Dhomhnuill hill Scotland 18 D1 ....56.45N 5.27W
Sgurr Mòr mt. Scotland 18 D2 ....57.42N 5.01W
Shaanxi d. China 103 J4 ....34.43N 108.13E
Shaftesbury England 10 C2 ....51.00N 2.12W
Shahr-e Kord Iran 95 H6 ....32.19N 50.49E
Shahrezā Iran 95 H6 ....32.00N 51.52E
Shakhovskaya Rus. Fed. 55 P7 ....56.02N 35.30E
Shakhty Rus. Fed. 53 L6 ....47.42N 40.12E
Shalkar Kazakhstan 58 G2 ....47.50N 59.37E
Shandong d. China 103 L5 ....36.22N 117.45E
Shandong Bandao pen. China 103 M5 ....37.05N 121.02E
Shanghai China 103 M4 ....31.15N 121.29E
Shangqiu China 103 L4 ....34.24N 115.38E
Shanklin England 10 D1 ....50.38N 1.10W
Shannon r. Rep. of Ireland 41 C2 ....52.40N 8.38W
Shannon, Mouth of the Rep. of Ireland 41 B2 ....52.31N 9.51W
Shantarskiye Ostrova is Rus. Fed. 59 O3 ....55.20N 137.22E
Shantou China 103 L2 ....23.24N 116.42E
Shanxi d. China 103 K5 ....38.03N 111.48E
Shaoguan China 103 K2 ....24.48N 113.37E
Shaoxing China 103 M4 ....30.01N 120.38E
Shaoyang China 103 K3 ....27.14N 111.30E
Shap England 14 E3 ....54.32N 2.41W
Shapinsay i. Scotland 19 G4 ....59.02N 2.48W
Shaqrā' Saudi Arabia 94 G5 ....25.15N 45.16E
Sharjah U.A.E. 95 I5 ....25.21N 55.23E
Shark Bay Australia 110 A4 ....25.17S 113.32E
Shashemenë Ethiopia 85 H2 ....7.12N 38.36E
Shasta, Mount vol. U.S.A. 64 B5 ....41.23N 122.10W
Shchigry Rus. Fed. 55 Q4 ....51.52N 36.56E
Shchuchyn Belarus 46 G4 ....53.37N 24.44E
Sheberghän Afgh. 95 K7 ....36.42N 65.45E
Sheboygan U.S.A. 65 I5 ....43.45N 87.43W
Sheelin, Lough l. Rep. of Ireland 41 D3 ....53.49N 7.21W
Sheep Haven b. Rep. of Ireland 16 B3 ....55.12N 7.55W
Sheerness England 11 F2 ....51.26N 0.46E

Sheffield England 15 F2 ....53.23N 1.28W
Shelby U.S.A. 64 D6 ....48.29N 111.48W
Shelikhova, Zaliv g. Rus. Fed. 59 Q4 ....60.40N 157.23E
Shelikof Strait U.S.A. 62 C3 ....57.27N 155.17W
Shengena mt. Tanzania 87 B1 ....4.16S 37.56E
Shenyang China 103 M6 ....41.46N 123.24E
Shenzhen China 103 K2 ....22.33N 114.09E
Shepetivka Ukraine 55 L4 ....50.11N 27.04E
Sheppey, Isle of i. England 11 F2 ....51.24N 0.46E
Shepshed England 10 D3 ....52.46N 1.18W
Shepton Mallet England 10 C2 ....51.11N 2.33W
Sherborne England 10 C1 ....50.57N 2.31W
Sherbrooke Canada 63 K2 ....45.24N 71.54W
Shereiq Sudan 94 D3 ....18.42N 33.40E
Sheridan U.S.A. 64 E5 ....44.48N 106.55W
Sheringham England 11 G3 ....52.57N 1.13E
's-Hertogenbosch Neth. 42 E4 ....51.41N 5.19E
Sherwood Forest England 15 F2 ....53.04N 1.07W
Shetland d. Scotland 8 E7 ....60.14N 0.57W
Shetland Islands Scotland 19 I5 ....60.36N 0.47W
Sheyenne r. U.S.A. 64 G6 ....47.03N 96.50W
Shiant Islands Scotland 18 C2 ....57.53N 6.25W
Shibām Yemen 95 G3 ....15.59N 48.57E
Shiel, Loch l. Scotland 18 D1 ....56.47N 5.35W
Shieldaig Scotland 18 D2 ....57.31N 5.39W
Shifnal England 10 C3 ....52.40N 2.22W
Shihezi China 102 F6 ....44.14N 86.03E
Shijiazhuang China 103 K5 ....38.00N 114.30E
Shikarpur India 96 E3 ....14.14N 75.18E
Shikarpur Pakistan 95 K5 ....27.56N 68.42E
Shikoku i. Japan 106 B2 ....33.08N 133.49E
Shikoku-sanchi mts Japan 106 B2 ....33.26N 132.53E
Shildon England 15 F3 ....54.38N 1.39W
Shillong India 97 H6 ....25.33N 91.53E
Shimoga India 96 E3 ....13.54N 75.31E
Shimoni Kenya 87 B1 ....4.39S 39.22E
Shimonoseki Japan 106 B2 ....33.57N 130.57E
Shin, Loch l. Scotland 19 E3 ....58.09N 4.38W
Shingū Japan 106 C2 ....33.43N 136.00E
Shining Tor hill England 15 E2 ....53.16N 2.00W
Shipley England 15 F2 ....53.50N 1.47W
Shipston on Stour England 10 D3 ....52.04N 1.37W
Shirane-san mt. Japan 106 C3 ....35.40N 138.13E
Shīrāz Iran 95 H5 ....29.37N 52.31E
Shire r. Malawi 86 C3 ....17.41S 35.19E
Shizuishan China 103 J5 ....38.58N 106.27E
Shizuoka Japan 106 C2 ....34.58N 138.23E
Shklow Belarus 55 N6 ....54.13N 30.17E
Shkodër Albania 56 C6 ....42.04N 19.31E
Shona, Eilean i. Scotland 18 D1 ....56.48N 5.53W
Sho'rchi Ukraine 55 O4 ....51.51N 33.29E
Shostka Ukraine 55 N3 ....49.01N 31.23E
Shpola Ukraine 55 N3 ....49.01N 31.23E
Shreveport U.S.A. 65 H3 ....32.29N 93.46W
Shrewsbury England 10 C3 ....52.42N 2.45W
Shropshire d. England 9 D3 ....52.45N 2.38W
Shuangjiang China 103 H2 ....23.28N 99.49E
Shumagin Islands U.S.A. 62 C3 ....55.09N 161.01W
Shumen Bulgaria 56 G6 ....43.16N 26.56E
Shuqrah Yemen 95 G2 ....13.24N 45.40E
Shushtar Iran 95 G6 ....32.01N 48.49E
Shwebo Myanmar 97 I5 ....22.34N 95.43E
Shwegyin Myanmar 97 I4 ....17.56N 96.52E
Shymkent Kazakhstan 58 H2 ....42.19N 69.38E
Siahan Range mts Pakistan 95 J5 ....27.13N 63.38E
Šiauliai Lithuania 40 E1 ....55.56N 23.19E
Siaya Kenya 87 A3 ....0.02N 34.15E
Šibenik Croatia 56 A6 ....43.44N 15.54E
Siberia r. Rus. Fed. 59 M4 ....65.18N 115.57E
Siberut i. Indonesia 104 B3 ....1.23S 98.41E
Sibi Pakistan 95 K5 ....29.30N 67.55E
Sibiloi National Park Kenya 87 B3 ....3.59N 36.24E
Sibiu Romania 56 F7 ....45.48N 24.10E
Sibolga Indonesia 104 B4 ....1.40N 98.48E
Sibsey England 15 H2 ....53.02N 0.01E
Sibu Malaysia 104 E4 ....2.17N 111.51E
Sibut C.A.R. 85 F2 ....5.44N 19.05E
Sichuan d. China 103 I4 ....30.05N 103.11E
Sicily i. Italy 50 F3 ....38.21N 14.09E
Sidi Bel Abbès Algeria 84 D5 ....35.12N 0.38W
Sidi Kacem Morocco 52 B3 ....34.12N 5.39W
Sidlaw Hills Scotland 17 F4 ....56.26N 3.21W
Sidmouth England 13 D2 ....50.41N 3.14W
Sidney U.S.A. 64 F5 ....41.12N 103.09W
Sidon Lebanon 53 K3 ....33.33N 35.23E
Siedlce Poland 46 F4 ....52.10N 22.17E
Siegen Germany 54 C4 ....50.52N 8.01E
Siena Italy 50 D5 ....43.19N 11.20E
Sieradz Poland 46 D3 ....51.36N 18.44E
Sierra Leone Africa 84 C2 ....8.35N 11.58W
Sighetu Marmaţiei Romania 55 J2 ....47.56N 23.54E
Sighișoara Romania 56 F8 ....46.14N 24.47E
Siglufjörður Iceland 40 Y2 ....66.08N 18.52W
Sigüenza Spain 48 D4 ....41.05N 2.37W
Siguiri Guinea 84 D3 ....11.28N 9.10W
Sihanoukville Cambodia 104 C6 ....10.38N 103.34E
Siilinjärvi Finland 40 F4 ....63.05N 27.40E
Siirt Turkey 94 F7 ....37.55N 41.58E
Sikar India 96 E6 ....27.31N 75.13E
Sikasso Mali 84 D3 ....11.19N 5.40W
Sikeston U.S.A. 65 I4 ....36.51N 89.34W
Sikhote-Alin' mts Rus. Fed. 59 O2 ....43.58N 133.53E
Sikkim d. India 96 G6 ....27.31N 88.27E
Sil r. Spain 48 B5 ....42.28N 7.42W
Šilalė Lithuania 46 E5 ....55.29N 22.11E
Silesia f. Europe 46 C3 ....50.45N 17.01E
Siletiteniz, Ozero l. Kazakhstan 102 C8 ...53.11N 72.53E
Silifke Turkey 57 J3 ....36.22N 33.56E
Siling Co l. China 102 F4 ....31.47N 88.41E
Silistra Bulgaria 56 H6 ....44.07N 27.16E
Silivri Turkey 57 H5 ....41.04N 28.16E
Siljan l. Sweden 40 C3 ....60.53N 14.46E
Šilutė Lithuania 46 E5 ....55.21N 21.28E
Silver City U.S.A. 64 E3 ....32.45N 108.19W
Silverstone England 10 D3 ....52.05N 1.02W
Silverton England 13 D2 ....50.49N 3.29W
Simav Turkey 57 H4 ....39.05N 28.58E
Simēn mts Ethiopia 94 E2 ....13.16N 37.50E
Simeulue i. Indonesia 104 B4 ....2.41N 96.08E
Simferopol' Ukraine 53 J5 ....44.57N 34.07E
Şimleu Silvaniei Romania 46 F1 ....47.14N 22.50E
Simplon Pass Switz. 50 C7 ....46.15N 8.02E
Simpson Desert Australia 110 C4 ....24.59S 136.50E
Simrishamn Sweden 54 F6 ....55.33N 14.21E
Sinai pen. Egypt 85 H4 ....29.13N 33.47E
Sinai, Mont hill France 42 D2 ....49.09N 4.08E
Sinaloa d. Mexico 70 C6 ....25.42N 108.11W
Sincelejo Colombia 72 B7 ....9.17N 75.24W
Sinclair's Bay Scotland 19 F3 ....58.30N 3.07W
Sines Portugal 48 A2 ....37.58N 8.52W
Singa Sudan 94 D2 ....13.09N 33.54E
Singapore Asia 104 C4 ....1.27N 104.32E
Singapore town Singapore 104 C4 ....1.19N 103.51E

Singaraja Indonesia 104 F2 ....8.06S 115.06E
Singida Tanzania 86 C4 ....4.50S 34.45E
Singkawang Indonesia 104 D4 ....0.57N 108.59E
Sinj Croatia 56 B6 ....43.42N 16.38E
Sinkat Sudan 94 E3 ....18.45N 36.49E
Sinop Turkey 57 K6 ....42.02N 35.08E
Sint Maarten i. Neth. Antilles 71 L4 ......18.02N 63.04W
Sion Mills Northern Ireland 16 B2 ....54.47N 7.28W
Sioux City U.S.A. 64 G5 ....42.32N 96.23W
Sioux Falls town U.S.A. 64 G5 ....43.32N 96.43W
Sioux Lookout Canada 63 I3 ....50.06N 91.56W
Sipacate Guatemala 70 F3 ....13.59N 91.08W
Siping China 103 M6 ....43.04N 124.24E
Sipura i. Indonesia 104 B3 ....2.12S 99.42E
Sira r. Norway 40 A2 ....58.16N 6.24E
Siret r. Romania 56 H7 ....45.25N 28.02E
Sīrjān Iran 95 I5 ....29.27N 55.40E
Sirrei Ethiopia 87 C4 ....6.43N 42.05E
Sirte Libya 85 F5 ....31.09N 16.40E
Sirte, Gulf of Libya 85 F5 ....31.11N 18.03E
Širvintos Lithuania 46 G5 ....55.02N 24.58E
Sisak Croatia 56 B7 ....45.29N 16.23E
Sisimiut Greenland 63 M4 ....66.56N 53.40W
Sisophon Cambodia 104 C6 ....13.34N 102.59E
Sistan, Daryācheh-ye marsh Afgh./Iran 95 J6 ...31.33N 61.10E
Sisteron France 44 F4 ....44.12N 5.57E
Siteia Greece 56 G2 ....35.12N 26.06E
Sitka U.S.A. 62 E3 ....57.03N 135.18W
Sittard Neth. 42 E3 ....50.59N 5.51E
Sittingbourne England 11 F2 ....51.20N 0.44E
Sittwe Myanmar 97 H5 ....20.08N 92.54E
Sivas Turkey 57 L4 ....39.43N 37.00E
Siverek Turkey 57 M3 ....37.44N 39.21E
Sivrihisar Turkey 57 I4 ....39.27N 31.32E
Siwah Egypt 85 G4 ....29.09N 25.30E
Skadovs'k Ukraine 57 J8 ....46.07N 32.54E
Skaftárós r. mouth Iceland 40 Y1 ....63.41N 17.47W
Skagen Denmark 40 B2 ....57.43N 10.35E
Skagerrak str. Denmark/Norway 40 B2 ....57.27N 8.13E
Skagway U.S.A. 62 E3 ....59.29N 135.18W
Skara Sweden 40 C2 ....58.23N 13.26E
Skarżysko-Kamienna Poland 46 E3 ....51.07N 20.53E
Skegness England 15 H2 ....53.09N 0.20E
Skellefteå Sweden 40 E4 ....64.45N 20.58E
Skellefteälven r. Sweden 40 E4 ....64.42N 21.07E
Skelmersdale England 14 E2 ....53.33N 2.46W
Skerries Rep. of Ireland 41 E3 ....53.35N 6.06W
Ski Norway 40 B2 ....59.43N 10.50E
Skibbereen Rep. of Ireland 41 B1 ....51.33N 9.16W
Skiddaw hill England 14 D3 ....54.39N 3.09W
Skien Norway 40 B2 ....59.12N 9.36E
Skierniewice Poland 46 E3 ....51.57N 20.09E
Skikda Algeria 84 E5 ....36.54N 6.57E
Skipton England 15 E2 ....53.58N 2.01W
Skive Denmark 40 B2 ....56.34N 9.02E
Skokholm Island Wales 12 B3 ....51.41N 5.16W
Skomer Island Wales 12 B3 ....51.44N 5.20W
Skopje Macedonia 56 D5 ....41.59N 21.27E
Skövde Sweden 40 C2 ....58.23N 13.51E
Skovorodino Rus. Fed. 59 N3 ....54.05N 123.52E
Skuodas Lithuania 46 E6 ....56.16N 21.32E
Skwierzyna Poland 46 B4 ....52.36N 15.30E
Skye i. Scotland 18 C2 ....57.21N 6.20W
Skyros i. Greece 56 F4 ....38.53N 24.35E
Slagelse Denmark 40 B1 ....55.24N 11.22E
Slamet vol. Indonesia 104 D2 ....7.14S 109.10E
Slaney r. Rep. of Ireland 41 E2 ....52.25N 6.34W
Slatina Romania 56 F7 ....44.26N 24.22E
Slave r. Canada 62 G4 ....61.17N 113.31W
Slavonski Brod Croatia 56 C7 ....45.10N 18.01E
Slavyansk-na-Kubani Rus. Fed. 57 M7 ....45.16N 38.08E
Slawharad Belarus 55 N5 ....53.27N 31.00E
Sławno Poland 46 C5 ....54.22N 16.41E
Sleaford England 11 E4 ....53.00N 0.24W
Sleat, Sound of str. Scotland 18 D2 .....57.02N 5.53W
Sleights England 15 G3 ....54.27N 0.40W
Slieve Anierin hill Rep. of Ireland 41 B2 ..54.05N 7.59W
Slieve Beagh hill Rep. of Ireland/U.K. 16 B2 ...54.20N 7.12W
Slievecallan hill Rep. of Ireland 41 B2 ...52.51N 9.16W
Slieve Car hill Rep. of Ireland 41 B4 .....54.03N 9.40W
Slieve Donard hill Northern Ireland 16 D2 ...54.11N 5.55W
Slievenamon hill Rep. of Ireland 41 D2 ...52.26N 7.34W
Slieve Snaght hill Rep. of Ireland 41 D5 ...55.12N 7.20W
Sligo Rep. of Ireland 41 C4 ....54.17N 8.28W
Sligo d. Rep. of Ireland 41 C4 ....54.07N 8.30W
Sligo Bay Rep. of Ireland 41 C4 ....54.19N 8.40W
Sliven Bulgaria 56 G6 ....42.41N 26.19E
Slobozia Romania 56 G7 ....44.34N 27.23E
Slonim Belarus 55 K5 ....53.05N 25.19E
Slough England 11 E2 ....51.31N 0.36W
Slough d. England 9 E2 ....51.30N 0.35W
Slovakia Europe 54 H3 ....48.45N 19.35E
Slovenia Europe 54 F1 ....46.09N 14.37E
Slovyechna r. Belarus 55 M4 ....51.39N 29.43E
Sluch r. Ukraine 55 L4 ....51.37N 26.39E
Słupsk Poland 46 C5 ....54.27N 17.02E
Slutsk Belarus 55 L5 ....53.01N 27.32E
Slyne Head Rep. of Ireland 41 A3 ......53.24N 10.14W
Slyudyanka Rus. Fed. 103 I8 ....51.28N 103.36E
Smallwood Reservoir Canada 63 L3 .....54.01N 64.50W
Smarhon' Belarus 55 L6 ....54.29N 26.25E
Smila Ukraine 55 N3 ....49.12N 31.54E
Smoky r. U.S.A. 62 G3 ....56.08N 117.20W
Smøla i. Norway 40 A3 ....63.23N 7.59E
Smolensk Rus. Fed. 55 N6 ....54.47N 32.04E
Smolikas mt. Greece 56 D5 ....40.06N 20.55E
Smolyan Bulgaria 56 F5 ....41.35N 24.41E
Snæfell mt. Iceland 40 Z2 ....64.48N 15.35W
Snaefell hill Isle of Man 14 C3 ....54.16N 4.28W
Snaith England 15 F2 ....53.41N 1.01W
Snake r. U.S.A. 64 C6 ....46.13N 118.59W
Snares Islands New Zealand 108 H2 ....48.02S 166.37E
Snåsa Norway 40 C4 ....64.15N 12.23E
Sneek Neth. 42 E6 ....53.02N 5.40E
Snettisham England 11 F3 ....52.53N 0.30E
Snežnik mt. Slovenia 54 F1 ....45.35N 14.26E
Śniardwy, Jezioro l. Poland 46 E4 ......53.46N 21.42E
Snizort, Loch b. Scotland 18 C2 ....57.33N 6.28W
Snøtinden mt. Norway 40 C4 ....66.38N 13.57E
Snov r. Ukraine 55 N4 ....51.32N 31.32E
Snowdon mt. Wales 12 C5 ....53.04N 4.04W
Soay i. Scotland 18 B2 ....57.08N 6.15W
Sobradinho, Barragem de resr Brazil 77 L5 ...10.14S 42.24W
Sobral Brazil 77 L7 ....3.43S 40.18W
Sochi Rus. Fed. 58 E2 ....43.36N 39.44E
Société, Archipel de la is French Polynesia 109 J4 ...17.22S 152.28W
Socorro, Isla i. Mexico 70 B4 ....18.51N 110.58W
Socotra i. Yemen 95 H2 ....12.34N 54.58E
Sodankylä Finland 40 F4 ....67.25N 26.34E
Söderhamn Sweden 40 D3 ....61.18N 17.04E
Södertälje Sweden 40 D2 ....59.12N 17.38E
Sodo Ethiopia 85 H2 ....6.49N 37.42E

Södra Kvarken str. Finland/Sweden 40 D3 ...60.19N 19.02E
Sofia Bulgaria 56 E6 ....42.41N 23.19E
Sognefjorden inlet Norway 40 A3 ....61.05N 5.33E
Soham England 11 F3 ....52.20N 0.20E
Soignies Belgium 42 C3 ....50.35N 4.04E
Soisson France 44 E6 ....49.23N 3.20E
Sokal' Ukraine 46 G3 ....50.29N 24.17E
Söke Turkey 56 G3 ....37.45N 27.23E
Sokhumi Georgia 58 F2 ....43.00N 41.02E
Sokółka Poland 46 F4 ....53.24N 23.31E
Sokoto Nigeria 84 E3 ....13.05N 5.15E
Sokoto r. Nigeria 84 E3 ....11.23N 4.09E
Solapur India 96 E4 ....17.41N 75.55E
Solihull England 10 D3 ....52.25N 1.47W
Solikamsk Rus. Fed. 58 G3 ....59.42N 56.44E
Solleftéa Sweden 40 D3 ....63.10N 17.17E
Solomon Islands S. Pacific Oc. 111 F6 ...7.13S 157.49E
Solomon Sea S. Pacific Oc. 110 E6 .....7.01S 152.18E
Solothurn Switz. ....
Solway Firth est. Scotland 17 F2 .....54.48N 3.33W
Solwezi Zambia 86 B3 ....12.10S 26.26E
Soma Turkey 56 G4 ....39.10N 27.36E
Somalia Africa 85 I2 ....3.56N 46.23E
Sombor S.M. 56 C7 ....45.47N 19.07E
Somerset d. England 9 D2 ....51.04N 2.56W
Somerset Island Canada 63 I5 ....73.19N 93.22W
Somerton England 10 C2 ....51.03N 2.44W
Sommen l. Sweden 40 C2 ....58.00N 15.17E
Sønderborg Denmark 54 C6 ....54.55N 9.48E
Sondrio Italy 50 D7 ....46.10N 9.52E
Songea Tanzania 86 C3 ....10.39S 35.38E
Songkhla Thailand 104 C5 ....7.10N 100.35E
Son La Vietnam 104 C8 ....21.20N 103.57E
Sono r. Brazil 77 K6 ....8.58S 48.07W
Sonora r. Mexico 70 B6 ....29.42N 110.36W
Sonora d. Mexico 70 B6 ....28.47N 111.54W
Soria Spain 48 D4 ....41.47N 2.26W
Soroca Moldova 53 I6 ....48.09N 28.17E
Sorocaba Brazil 77 K3 ....23.30S 47.30W
Sorol atoll Micronesia 105 K5 ......8.10N 140.22E
Sorong Indonesia 105 I3 ....0.54S 131.17E
Soroti Uganda 85 H2 ....1.42N 33.37E
Sørøya i. Norway 40 E5 ....70.34N 22.32E
Sorraia r. Portugal 48 A3 ....39.02N 8.50W
Sorsele Sweden 40 D4 ....65.31N 17.33E
Sortavala Rus. Fed. 40 G3 ....61.42N 30.41E
Soshanguve S. Africa 86 B2 ....25.31S 28.06E
Sosna r. Rus. Fed. 55 R5 ....52.41N 38.54E
Sosneado mt. Argentina 73 C3 .....34.44S 69.59W
Sosnowiec Poland 46 D3 ....50.17N 19.08E
Souk Ahras Algeria 52 E4 ....36.17N 7.59E
Souk el Arbaâ du Rharb Morocco 48 C1 ...34.40N 5.58W
Souris r. Canada 64 G6 ....49.41N 99.40W
Sousse Tunisia 52 F4 ....35.47N 10.39E
Soustons France 44 C3 ....43.45N 1.20W
South Africa, Republic of Africa 86 B1 ...30.06S 24.04E
Southam England 10 D3 ....52.15N 1.23W
Southampton d. England 9 E2 .....50.55N 1.24W
Southampton England 10 D1 ......50.56N 1.24W
Southampton Island Canada 63 J4 ...64.31N 85.04W
South Anston England 15 F2 ......53.21N 1.13W
South Australia d. Australia 110 C4 ...30.27S 132.43E
South Australian Basin f. Indian Oc. 108 D3 ...37.58S 119.18E
South Ayrshire d. Scotland 8 C4 ....55.09N 4.47W
South Bank England 15 F3 ....54.35N 1.10W
South Bend U.S.A. 65 I5 ....41.40N 86.13W
Southborough England 11 F2 ......51.09N 0.16E
South Carolina d. U.S.A. 65 J3 .....34.02N 80.47W
South Cave England 15 G2 ....53.46N 0.36W
South China Sea N. Pacific Oc. 104 F6 ...12.00N 117.49E
South Dakota d. U.S.A. 64 F5 ......44.27N 100.14W
South Dorset Downs hills England 10 C1 ...50.42N 2.37W
South Downs hills England 10 E1 ....50.53N 0.28W
South East Cape Australia 110 D2 ....43.38S 146.55E
Southeast Indian Ridge f. Indian Oc. 108 A4 ...31.15S 76.54E
Southeast Pacific Basin f. S. Pacific Oc. 116 D2 .63.41S 112.50W
Southend d. England 9 F2 ....51.33N 0.42E
Southend-on-Sea England 11 F2 ....51.32N 0.43E
Southern Alps mts New Zealand 111 G2 ...43.26S 170.28E
Southern Ocean 116 H2
Southern Uplands hills Scotland 16 E3 ...55.14N 4.32W
Southery England 11 F3 ....52.32N 0.24E
South Esk r. Scotland 19 G1 ......56.43N 2.33W
South Fiji Basin f. S. Pacific Oc. 108 H4 ...25.53S 175.02E
South Georgia i. S. Atlantic Oc. 73 F1 ...53.50S 36.30W
South Gloucestershire d. England 9 D2 ...51.33N 2.27W
South Harris pen. Scotland 18 B2 ...57.49N 7.03W
South Honshu Ridge f. N. Pacific Oc. 108 F8 ...31.09N 138.30E
South Horr Kenya 87 B3 ....2.10N 36.56E
South Island New Zealand 111 G2 ...44.24S 172.31E
South Kirkby England 15 F2 ....53.36N 1.19W
South Kitui National Reserve Kenya 87 B2 ...1.43S 38.50E
South Korea Asia 103 N5 ....35.32N 128.04E
South Lanarkshire d. Scotland 8 D4 ...55.38N 3.49W
South Molton England 13 D3 ......51.40N 0.50E
South Nahanni r. Canada 62 F4 ....61.03N 123.18W
South Ockendon England 11 F2 ....51.31N 0.18E
South Platte r. U.S.A. 64 F5 ....41.08N 100.47W
Southport Australia 110 E4 ....27.56S 153.23E
Southport England 14 D2 ....53.39N 3.00W
South Ronaldsay i. Scotland 19 G3 ...58.47N 2.54W
South Saskatchewan r. Canada 62 H3 ...53.09N 105.08W
South Shields England 15 F3 ....54.59N 1.26W
South Solomon Trench f. S. Pacific Oc. 108 G5 ...11.28S 162.19E
South Tasman Rise f. Southern Oc. 108 F2 ...45.34S 146.08E
South Tyne r. England 15 E3 ....54.59N 2.08W
South Uist i. Scotland 18 B2 ....57.17N 7.22W
Southwell England 15 G2 ....53.05N 0.58W
Southwest Pacific Basin f. S. Pacific Oc. 116 A4 ...36.11S 158.10W
Southwest Peru Ridge f. S. Pacific Oc. 109 O4 ...22.54S 83.41W
Southwold England 11 G3 ....52.19N 1.41E
South Woodham Ferrers England 11 F2 ...51.39N 0.37E
South Wootton England 11 F3 .....52.46N 0.26E
South Yorkshire d. England 9 E3 ...53.28N 1.16W
Sovetsk Rus. Fed. 46 E5 ....55.05N 21.53E
Soweto S. Africa 86 B2 ....26.15S 27.50E
Sozh r. Europe 55 N4 ....51.57N 30.49E
Spain Europe 48 D4 ....40.26N 3.48W
Spalding England 11 E3 ....52.47N 0.09W
Span Head hill England 13 D3 .....51.07N 3.49W
Sparks U.S.A. 64 C4 ....39.32N 119.46W
Sparti Greece 56 E3 ....37.04N 22.26E
Spartivento, Capo c. Italy 50 G2 ....37.56N 16.05E
Spas-Demensk Rus. Fed. 55 P6 .....54.25N 34.02E
Spassk-Dal'niy Rus. Fed. 106 B4 ....44.32N 132.48E
Spatha, Akra pt Greece 56 E2 ......35.41N 23.44E
Speke Gulf Tanzania 87 A2 ....2.19S 32.57E
Spencer Gulf est. Australia 110 C3 ...34.54S 136.27E
Spennymoor England 15 F3 ....54.42N 1.35W
Sperrin Mountains hills Northern Ireland 16 B2 ...54.47N 7.09W
Spey r. Scotland 19 F2 ....57.39N 3.06W
Speyer Germany 44 H6 ....49.19N 8.24E

Spijkenisse Neth. 42 D4 ....51.50N 4.19E
Spilsby England 15 H2 ....53.10N 0.06E
Split Croatia 56 B6 ....43.31N 16.27E
Spofforth England 15 F2 ....53.57N 1.27W
Spokane U.S.A. 64 C6 ....47.38N 117.22W
Spratly Islands S. China Sea 104 E6 ...10.01N 114.21E
Spree r. Germany 54 E5 ....52.32N 13.13E
Springfield Ill. U.S.A. 65 I4 ......39.48N 89.39W
Springfield Mass. U.S.A. 65 L5 ...42.05N 72.35W
Springfield Mo. U.S.A. 65 H4 .....37.16N 93.18W
Sprowston England 11 G3 ....52.39N 1.19E
Spurn Head England 15 H2 ....53.34N 0.05E
Srebrenica Bos.-Herz. 56 C7 .....44.07N 19.19E
Srednekolymsk Rus. Fed. 59 Q4 ...67.32N 153.38E
Sretensk Rus. Fed. 59 M3 ....52.08N 117.41E
Sri Aman Malaysia 104 E4 ....1.12N 111.30E
Sri Jayewardenepura Kotte Sri Lanka 96 E2 ...6.56N 79.54E
Sri Lanka Asia 96 F2 ....7.29N 80.42E
Srinagar India 96 D7 ....34.08N 74.51E
Stadskanaal Neth. 42 F5 ....52.59N 6.59E
Staffa i. Scotland 16 C4 ....56.26N 6.20W
Stafford England 10 C3 ....52.48N 2.07W
Staffordshire d. England 9 D3 ....52.52N 2.04W
Staines England 11 E2 ....51.26N 0.31W
Stalbridge England 10 C1 ....50.57N 2.23W
Stalham England 11 G3 ....52.46N 1.31E
Stalowa Wola Poland 46 F3 ....50.34N 22.03E
Stamford England 11 E3 ....52.39N 0.29W
Stamford Bridge England 15 G2 ...53.59N 0.55W
Standish England 14 E2 ....53.35N 2.40W
Stanley England 15 F3 ....54.52N 1.42W
Stanley Falkland Is. 73 D1 ....51.43S 57.52W
Stannington England 15 F4 ....55.06N 1.40W
Stanovoy Khrebet mts Rus. Fed. 59 N3 ...57.21N 120.44E
Stansted Mountfitchet England 11 F2 ...51.54N 0.12E
Stanton England 11 F3 ....52.19N 0.53E
Starachowice Poland 46 E3 ....51.02N 21.04E
Stara Zagora Bulgaria 56 F6 .....42.26N 25.38E
Starbuck Island Kiribati 109 J5 ...5.36S 155.51W
Stargard Szczeciński Poland 46 B4 ...53.20N 15.03E
Starogard Gdański Poland 46 D4 ...53.58N 18.31E
Starokostyantyniv Ukraine 55 L3 ...49.45N 27.13E
Start Bay England 13 D2 ....50.18N 3.37W
Start Point England 13 D2 ....50.13N 3.38W
Staryya Darohi Belarus 55 M5 ...53.02N 28.17E
Staryy Oskol Rus. Fed. 58 E3 .....51.18N 37.51E
Stavanger Norway 40 A2 ....58.58N 5.44E
Staveley England 15 F2 ....53.16N 1.21W
Stavropol' Rus. Fed. 53 L6 ....45.03N 41.59E
Stavropol'skaya Vozvyshennost' hills Rus. Fed. 58 F2 ...45.05N 42.35E
Steenwijk Neth. 42 F5 ....52.47N 6.07E
Steep Holm i. England 10 B2 .....51.20N 3.06W
Stefansson Island Canada 62 H5 ...73.21N 105.34W
Steinfurt Germany 42 G5 ....52.09N 7.21E
Steinkjer Norway 40 B4 ....64.01N 11.30E
Stenness, Loch of l. Scotland 19 F4 ...59.00N 3.16W
Sterling U.S.A. 64 F5 ....40.39N 103.09W
Sterlitamak Rus. Fed. 58 G3 .....53.36N 55.53E
Stevenage England 11 E2 ....51.54N 0.12W
Stewart Canada 62 F3 ....55.57N 129.59W
Stewart r. Canada 62 E4 ....63.18N 139.26W
Stewart Island New Zealand 111 F2 ...47.09S 167.55E
Stewarton Scotland 16 E3 ....55.41N 4.31W
Steyning England 11 E1 ....50.53N 0.20W
Steyr Austria 54 F3 ....48.02N 14.25E
Stikine r. Canada 62 E3 ....56.41N 132.19W
Stilton England 11 E3 ....52.29N 0.17W
Stinchar r. Scotland 16 D3 ....55.06N 5.01W
Stirling Scotland 17 F4 ....56.07N 3.56W
Stirling d. Scotland 8 C5 ....56.17N 4.23W
Stjørdalshalsen Norway 40 B3 ...63.28N 10.55E
Stob Choire Claurigh mt. Scotland 18 E1 ...56.50N 4.51W
Stockholm Sweden 40 D2 ....59.20N 18.04E
Stockport England 15 E2 ....53.24N 2.09W
Stockton U.S.A. 64 B4 ....37.57N 121.17W
Stockton-on-Tees England 15 F3 ...54.34N 1.19W
Stockton-on-Tees d. England 9 E4 ...54.34N 1.21W
Stœng Trêng Cambodia 104 D6 ...13.28N 105.59E
Stoer, Point of Scotland 18 D3 ...58.16N 5.23W
Stoke-on-Trent England 15 E2 ...53.00N 2.11W
Stoke-on-Trent d. England 9 D3 ...53.01N 2.10W
Stokesay England 10 C3 ....52.26N 2.50W
Stokesley England 15 F3 ....54.28N 1.11W
Stolin Belarus 55 L4 ....51.53N 26.50E
Stone England 10 C3 ....52.54N 2.09W
Stonehaven Scotland 19 G1 ......56.58N 2.12W
Stony Rapids town Canada 62 H3 ...59.15N 105.59W
Stora Lulevatten l. Sweden 40 D4 ...67.09N 19.28E
Storavan l. Sweden 40 D4 ....65.40N 18.16E
Støren Norway 40 B3 ....63.02N 10.17E
Stornoway Scotland 18 C3 ....58.13N 6.23W
Storrington England 11 E1 ......50.55N 0.27W
Storsjön l. Sweden 40 C3 ....63.13N 14.16E
Storskrymten mt. Norway 40 B3 ...62.22N 9.03E
Storuman Sweden 40 D4 ....65.05N 17.09E
Storuman l. Sweden 40 D4 ......65.11N 16.54E
Stotfold England 11 E3 ....52.01N 0.14W
Stour r. Dor. England 10 D1 .....50.44N 1.46W
Stour r. Kent England 11 G2 ....51.18N 1.21E
Stour r. Warwicks. England 10 D3 ...52.11N 1.44W
Stourbridge England 10 C3 .....52.27N 2.09W
Stourport-on-Severn England 10 C3 ...52.20N 2.17W
Stowbtsy Belarus 55 L5 ....53.28N 26.44E
Stowmarket England 11 F3 ......52.11N 0.59E
Stow-on-the-Wold England 10 D2 ...51.56N 1.43W
Strabane Northern Ireland 16 B2 ...54.50N 7.27W
Strabane d. Northern Ireland 9 B4 ...54.47N 7.21W
Stradbroke England 11 G3 ......52.19N 1.16E
Stranraer Scotland 16 D2 ....54.54N 5.02W
Strasbourg France 44 G6 ....48.35N 7.45E
Stratford-upon-Avon England 10 D3 ...52.11N 1.43W
Strathaven Scotland 17 E3 ....55.41N 4.04W
Strathbeg, Loch of l. Scotland 19 H2 ...57.37N 1.54W
Strathbogie f. Scotland 19 G2 ....57.26N 2.53W
Strathmore f. Scotland 19 F2 .....56.35N 4.39W
Strathspey f. Scotland 19 F2 .....57.11N 3.47W
Strathy Point Scotland 19 E3 .....58.36N 4.01W
Stratton England 13 C2 ....50.50N 4.31W
Stratton St Margaret England 10 D2 ...51.35N 1.45W
Straubing Germany 54 E3 ....48.54N 12.35E
Straumnes pt Iceland 40 X2 .....66.26N 23.10W
Streatley England 10 D2 ....51.32N 1.09W
Street England 10 C2 ....51.07N 2.44W
Strelka Rus. Fed. 59 Q4 ....61.52N 152.11E
Stretham England 11 F3 ....52.20N 0.13E
Strimonas r. Greece 56 E5 ....40.48N 23.51E
Stroma, Island of Scotland 19 F3 ...58.42N 3.08W
Stromboli, Isola i. Italy 50 F3 .....38.45N 15.14E

tromness Scotland 19 F3 ....58.58N 3.18W
trömsund Sweden 40 C3 ....63.52N 15.34E
tronsay i. Scotland 19 G4 ....59.08N 2.33W
tronsay Firth str. Scotland 19 G4 ....59.06N 2.50W
troud England 10 C2 ....51.45N 2.13W
truer Denmark 40 B2 ....56.29N 8.36E
trule r. Northern Ireland 16 B2 ....54.43N 7.21W
truma r. Bulgaria 56 E5 ....41.23N 23.20E
trumble Head Wales 12 B4 ....52.02N 5.08W
trumica Macedonia 56 E5 ....41.26N 22.38E
tryy Ukraine 55 J3 ....49.15N 23.51E
tryy r. Ukraine 46 G2 ....49.23N 24.13E
tudley England 10 D3 ....52.16N 1.54W
tupino Rus. Fed. 55 R6 ....54.54N 38.05E
turry England 11 G2 ....51.18N 1.07E
turt Stony Desert Australia 110 D4 ....28.20S 141.15E
tuttgart Germany 54 C3 ....48.47N 9.10E
tyr r. Belarus/Ukraine 55 L5 ....52.08N 26.35E
uakin Sudan 85 H3 ....19.06N 37.18E
ubotica S.M. 56 C8 ....46.06N 19.41E
uceava Romania 55 L2 ....47.40N 26.16E
uck r. Rep. of Ireland 41 C3 ....53.16N 8.03W
ucre Bolivia 76 G4 ....19.06S 65.18W
udak Ukraine 57 K7 ....44.51N 34.59E
udan Africa 85 G3 ....13.34N 30.02E
udbury Canada 63 J2 ....46.29N 80.59W
udbury England 11 F3 ....52.03N 0.44E
udety mts Czech Rep./Poland 54 F4 ....50.46N 15.50E
uez Egypt 85 H4 ....29.58N 32.33E
uez, Gulf of Egypt 85 H4 ....28.03N 33.33E
uez Canal Egypt 53 J3 ....30.47N 32.19E
uffolk d. England 9 F3 ....52.10N 0.52E
uguta r. Kenya 87 B3 ....2.01N 36.32E
uguti Bay Tanzania 87 A2 ....1.44S 33.33E
uhār Oman 95 I4 ....24.22N 56.44E
uhl Germany 54 D4 ....50.36N 10.42E
uifenhe China 106 B4 ....44.20N 131.11E
uir r. Rep. of Ireland 41 D2 ....52.20N 7.23W
uizhou China 103 K4 ....31.42N 113.20E
ukabumi Indonesia 104 D2 ....6.58S 106.53E
ukadana Indonesia 104 D3 ....1.12S 109.59E
ukhinichi Rus. Fed. 55 P6 ....54.07N 35.22E
ukkur Pakistan 96 C6 ....27.42N 68.55E
ula i. Norway 40 A3 ....61.09N 4.55E
ulabesi i. Indonesia 105 H3 ....2.12S 125.58E
ulaiman Range mts Pakistan 90 F5 ....30.00N 68.00E
ulina Romania 57 H7 ....45.09N 29.39E
ullana Peru 76 D7 ....4.56S 80.41W
ully Wales 13 D3 ....51.24N 3.13W
ulmona Italy 50 F5 ....42.02N 13.56E
ulu Archipelago is Phil. 105 G5 ....6.55N 123.10E
ulu Sea N. Pacific Oc. 104 F5 ....8.20N 119.46E
umatra i. Indonesia 104 B4 ....3.05N 98.12E
umba i. Indonesia 104 G2 ....9.49S 120.11E
umbawa i. Indonesia 104 F2 ....8.54S 118.45E
umburgh Scotland 19 H4 ....59.52N 1.17W
umburgh Head Scotland 19 H4 ....59.51N 1.16W
ummer Isles Scotland 18 D3 ....58.01N 5.30W
umy Ukraine 55 P4 ....50.55N 34.48E
unart, Loch inlet Scotland 18 D1 ....56.40N 5.51W
unda, Selat str. Indonesia 104 C2 ....6.32S 104.55E
unda Trench r. Indian Oc. 108 C5 ....8.48S 104.02E
underland England 15 F3 ....54.54N 1.23W
undsvall Sweden 40 D3 ....62.24N 17.17E
unga Tanzania 87 B1 ....4.27S 38.14E
ungurlu Turkey 57 K5 ....40.11N 34.22E
uolijärvet i. Finland 40 G4 ....66.14N 28.04E
uonenjoki Finland 40 F3 ....62.37N 27.07E
uperior U.S.A. 65 H6 ....46.41N 92.01W
uperior, Lake Canada/U.S.A. 63 J2 ....47.46N 87.14W
ūq ash Shuyūkh Iraq 95 G6 ....30.51N 46.20E
ūr Oman 95 I4 ....22.34N 59.31E
urab Pakistan 95 K5 ....28.29N 66.19E
urabaya Indonesia 104 E2 ....7.13S 112.45E
urakarta Indonesia 104 E2 ....7.31S 110.52E
urat India 96 D5 ....21.11N 72.53E
urgut Rus. Fed. 58 I4 ....61.13N 73.22E
urigao Phil. 105 H5 ....9.48N 125.29E
urin Thailand 104 C6 ....14.52N 103.32E
uriname S. America 72 D7 ....4.05N 56.22W
urrey d. England 9 E2 ....51.15N 0.29W
urtsey i. Iceland 40 X1 ....63.18N 20.36W
ūsangerd Iran 95 G6 ....31.37N 48.04E
uşehri Rus. Fed. 57 M5 ....40.10N 38.04E
usuman Rus. Fed. 59 P4 ....62.47N 148.02E
usurluk Turkey 57 H4 ....39.55N 28.09E
utak Jammu and Kashmir 96 E7 ....33.07N 77.34E
utherland f. Scotland 19 E3 ....58.16N 4.24W
utterton England 11 E3 ....52.54N 0.06W
utton England 11 F3 ....52.23N 0.07E
utton Bridge England 11 F3 ....52.46N 0.11E
utton Coldfield England 10 D3 ....52.34N 1.49W
utton in Ashfield England 15 F2 ....53.08N 1.16W
uva Fiji 111 G5 ....18.07S 178.28E
uvorov Rus. Fed. 55 Q6 ....54.07N 36.31E
uwałki Poland 46 F5 ....54.06N 22.56E
uwarrow atoll Cook Is 108 J5 ....13.11S 162.57W
uzhou Anhui China 103 L4 ....33.34N 116.59E
uzhou Jiangsu China 103 M4 ....31.18N 120.40E
uzu Japan 106 C3 ....37.26N 137.15E
uzuka Japan 106 C2 ....34.53N 136.35E
valbard is Arctic Oc. 58 C5 ....79.47N 16.13E
vapa r. Rus. Fed. 55 P4 ....51.44N 34.57E
veg Sweden 40 C3 ....62.02N 14.23E
vendborg Denmark 40 B1 ....55.04N 10.37E
vetlograd Rus. Fed. 53 L6 ....45.20N 42.51E
vetogorsk Rus. Fed. 40 G3 ....61.07N 28.51E
víáhnúkar vol. Iceland 40 Y2 ....64.25N 17.09W
vitava r. Czech Rep. 46 C2 ....48.54N 16.37E
vitavy Czech Rep. 46 D3 ....49.03N 33.15E
vitlovods'k Ukraine 55 O3 ....49.03N 33.15E
vobodnyy Rus. Fed. 59 N3 ....51.23N 128.04E
vyetlahorsk Belarus 55 M5 ....52.38N 29.46E
wadlincote England 10 D3 ....52.46N 1.33W
waffham England 11 F3 ....52.39N 0.41E
wains Island atoll American Samoa 108 I5 ...11.01S 171.03W
wakopmund Namibia 86 A2 ....22.41S 14.32E
wale r. England 15 F3 ....54.05N 1.21W
wanage England 10 D1 ....50.36N 1.58W
wanley England 11 F2 ....51.24N 0.11E
wan River town Canada 64 F7 ....52.06N 101.16W
wansea Wales 12 D3 ....51.37N 3.57W
wansea d. Wales 9 D2 ....51.37N 3.58W
wansea Bay Wales 12 D3 ....51.34N 3.54W
waziland Africa 86 C2 ....26.29S 31.30E
weden Europe 40 C3 ....61.48N 15.08E
weetwater r. U.S.A. 64 E5 ....42.27N 106.55W
widnica Poland 46 D3 ....50.51N 16.29E
widwin Poland 46 B4 ....53.47N 15.47E
wiebodzin Poland 46 B4 ....52.15N 15.32E

Świecie Poland 46 D4 ....53.25N 18.27E
Swift Current Canada 62 H3 ....50.17N 107.47W
Swilly, Lough inlet Rep. of Ireland 41 D5 ...55.15N 7.34W
Swindon England 10 D2 ....51.33N 1.47W
Swindon d. England 9 E2 ....51.35N 1.45W
Swineshead England 11 E3 ....52.57N 0.10W
Świnoujście Poland 46 B4 ....53.54N 14.15E
Switzerland Europe 50 B7 ....46.44N 8.18E
Swords Rep. of Ireland 41 E3 ....53.27N 6.13W
Sybil Point Rep. of Ireland 41 A2 ....52.11N 10.28W
Sychevka Rus. Fed. 55 P6 ....55.49N 34.17E
Sydney Australia 110 E3 ....33.54S 151.11E
Sydney Canada 63 L2 ....46.06N 60.08W
Syktyvkar Rus. Fed. 58 G4 ....61.41N 50.48E
Sylarna mt. Norway/Sweden 40 C3 ....63.01N 12.12E
Sylt i. Germany 40 B1 ....54.49N 8.15E
Syracuse Italy 50 F2 ....37.04N 15.17E
Syracuse U.S.A. 65 K5 ....43.04N 76.11W
Syr Darya r. Asia 102 A7 ....46.05N 60.55E
Syria Asia 94 E6 ....35.25N 39.17E
Syrian Desert Asia 94 E6 ....32.02N 39.22E
Syros i. Greece 56 F3 ....37.27N 24.53E
Syzran' Rus. Fed. 58 F3 ....53.10N 48.29E
Szczecin Poland 46 B4 ....53.26N 14.34E
Szczecinek Poland 46 C4 ....53.42N 16.42E
Szczytno Poland 46 E4 ....53.34N 20.59E
Szeged Hungary 54 I2 ....46.15N 20.09E
Székesfehérvár Hungary 54 H2 ....47.12N 18.25E
Szekszárd Hungary 54 H2 ....46.22N 18.42E
Szolnok Hungary 54 I2 ....47.10N 20.12E
Szombathely Hungary 54 G2 ....47.15N 16.38E

T

Ţabas Iran 95 I6 ....33.35N 56.52E
Tabasco d. Mexico 70 F4 ....18.03N 92.59W
Tabatinga, Serra da hills Brazil 77 L5 ....10.56S 44.37W
Tábor Czech Rep. 54 F3 ....49.24N 14.42E
Tabora Tanzania 86 C4 ....5.00S 32.47E
Tabriz Iran 95 F7 ....38.04N 46.17E
Tabuaeran atoll Kiribati 109 J6 ....3.49N 159.16W
Tabūk Saudi Arabia 94 E5 ....28.23N 36.38E
Täby Sweden 40 D2 ....59.27N 18.04E
Tacheng China 102 E7 ....46.43N 83.01E
Tacloban Phil. 105 H6 ....11.12N 125.01E
Tacna Peru 76 E4 ....18.01S 70.15W
Tacoma U.S.A. 64 B6 ....47.15N 122.27W
Tacuarembó Uruguay 73 D3 ....31.42S 55.59W
Tadcaster England 15 F2 ....53.53N 1.16W
Tadjoura Djibouti 94 F2 ....11.46N 42.48E
Tadmur Syria 94 E6 ....34.34N 38.17E
Taegu S. Korea 103 N5 ....35.52N 128.35E
Taejŏn S. Korea 103 N5 ....36.22N 127.24E
Taf r. Wales 12 C3 ....51.47N 4.27W
Taganrog Rus. Fed. 53 K6 ....47.14N 38.55E
Taganrog, Gulf of Rus. Fed./Ukraine 53 K6 ...47.00N 38.51E
Tagbilaran Phil. 105 G5 ....9.38N 123.53E
Tagula Island P.N.G. 110 E5 ....11.33S 153.23E
Tagus r. Portugal 48 A3 ....38.59N 8.56W
Tahat, Mont mt. Algeria 84 E4 ....23.18N 5.78E
Tahiti i. French Polynesia 109 K4 ....17.49S 149.15W
T'aichung Taiwan 103 M2 ....24.09N 120.42E
T'ainan Taiwan 103 M2 ....23.01N 120.13E
Tainaro, Akra pt Greece 56 E3 ....36.23N 22.29E
T'aipei Taiwan 103 M3 ....25.04N 121.33E
Taiping Malaysia 104 C4 ....4.55N 100.42E
Taita Hills Kenya 87 B2 ....3.26S 38.21E
Taiti mt. Kenya 87 B3 ....1.20N 35.57E
T'aitung Taiwan 103 M2 ....22.45N 121.08E
Taivalkoski Finland 40 G4 ....65.34N 28.14E
Taivaskero hill Finland 40 F5 ....68.04N 24.02E
Taiwan Asia 103 M2 ....23.30N 121.00E
Taiwan Strait China/Taiwan 103 L2 ....23.49N 119.16E
Taiyuan China 103 K5 ....37.48N 112.38E
Ta'izz Yemen 94 F2 ....13.35N 43.59E
Tajikistan Asia 115 M7 ....38.54N 71.08E
Tak Thailand 104 B7 ....16.51N 99.08E
Takabba Kenya 87 C3 ....3.21N 40.13E
Takamatsu Japan 106 B2 ....34.19N 134.03E
Takaoka Japan 106 C3 ....36.45N 137.01E
Takaungu Kenya 87 B2 ....3.41S 39.50E
Taklimakan Desert China 102 E5 ....38.25N 80.50E
Talagang Pakistan 95 L6 ....32.55N 72.29E
Talara Peru 76 D7 ....4.37S 81.18W
Talaud, Kepulauan is Indonesia 105 H4 .....4.05N 127.24E
Talavera de la Reina Spain 48 C3 ....39.58N 4.49W
Talca Chile 73 B3 ....35.26S 71.39W
Talcahuano Chile 73 B3 ....36.44S 73.07W
Taldykorgan Kazakhstan 58 I2 ....44.59N 78.22E
Talgarth Wales 12 D3 ....51.59N 3.14W
Taliabu i. Indonesia 105 G3 ....1.47S 124.43E
Tallahassee U.S.A. 65 J3 ....30.26N 84.17W
Tallinn Estonia 40 F2 ....59.27N 24.45E
Taloyoak Canada 63 I4 ....69.27N 93.22W
Talsi Latvia 40 E2 ....57.15N 22.35E
Taltal Chile 76 F2 ....25.24S 70.33W
Taltson r. Canada 62 G4 ....61.24N 112.43W
Tamale Ghana 84 D2 ....9.25N 0.51W
Tamanrasset Algeria 84 E4 ....22.48N 5.33E
Tamar r. England 13 C2 ....50.29N 4.13W
Tamaulipas d. Mexico 70 E5 ....22.41N 99.13W
Tama Wildlife Reserve Ethiopia 87 B4 ....6.02N 36.12E
Tambacounda Senegal 84 C3 ....13.47N 13.40W
Tambelan, Kepulauan is Indonesia 104 D4 ...1.03N 107.03E
Tambov Rus. Fed. 58 F3 ....52.43N 41.26E
Tambre r. Spain 48 A5 ....42.49N 8.51W
Tâmega r. Portugal 48 A4 ....41.05N 8.17W
Tamiahua, Laguna de lagoon Mexico 70 E5 ...21.39N 97.36W
Tamil Nadu d. India 96 E3 ....11.11N 78.08E
Tampa U.S.A. 65 J2 ....27.57N 82.29W
Tampere Finland 40 F3 ....61.30N 23.48E
Tampico Mexico 70 E5 ....22.16N 97.52W
Tamworth Australia 110 E3 ....31.06S 150.56E
Tamworth England 10 D3 ....52.38N 1.41W
Tana r. Kenya 87 C2 ....2.31S 40.30E
Tana, Lake Ethiopia 85 H3 ....11.59N 37.16E
Tanafjorden inlet Norway 40 G5 ....70.32N 28.13E
Tanami Desert Australia 110 C5 ....19.26S 131.26E
Tanana r. U.S.A. 62 C4 ....65.12N 152.04W
Tanaro r. Italy 50 C6 ....45.01N 8.47E
Tando Adam Pakistan 96 C6 ....25.43N 68.40E
Tandragee Northern Ireland 16 C2 ....54.21N 6.24W
Tanega-shima i. Japan 106 B2 ....30.28N 130.58E
Tanga Tanzania 87 B1 ....5.06S 39.05E
Tanga d. Tanzania 87 B1 ....5.59S 38.02E
Tanganyika, Lake Africa 86 B4 ....5.00S 29.50E
Tangier Morocco 84 D5 ....35.47N 5.49W
Tangshan China 103 L5 ....39.34N 118.13E

Tanimbar, Kepulauan is Indonesia 105 I2 ...7.29S 131.40E
Tanjay Phil. 105 G5 ....9.29N 123.09E
Tanjungpandan Indonesia 104 D3 ....2.46S 107.37E
Tanjungredeb Indonesia 104 F4 ....2.09N 117.27E
Tank Pakistan 95 L6 ....32.14N 70.29E
Tanna i. Vanuatu 111 F5 ....19.32S 169.14E
Tanout Niger 84 E3 ....14.56N 8.53E
Ţanţā Egypt 85 H5 ....30.47N 31.00E
Tanzania Africa 86 C4 ....6.14S 34.03E
Taonan China 103 M7 ....45.12N 122.48E
Taourirt Morocco 52 C3 ....34.25N 2.55W
Tapachula Mexico 70 F3 ....14.56N 92.15W
Tapajós r. Brazil 77 I7 ....2.23S 54.48W
Tapauá r. Brazil 76 H6 ....5.52S 64.27W
Tapi r. India 96 D5 ....21.13N 72.58E
Taquari r. Brazil 77 I4 ....19.05S 57.22W
Tar r. Rep. of Ireland 41 D2 ....52.17N 7.50W
Tara i. Bos.-Herz./S.M. 56 C6 ....43.20N 18.53E
Tarakan Indonesia 104 F4 ....3.20N 117.37E
Taran, Mys pt Rus. Fed. 46 D5 ....54.58N 19.59E
Taranaki, Mount vol. New Zealand 111 G3 ...39.18S 174.03E
Taransay i. Scotland 18 B2 ....57.55N 7.02W
Taranto Italy 50 G4 ....40.28N 17.14E
Taranto, Gulf of Italy 50 G4 ....40.07N 17.20E
Tarapoto Peru 76 E6 ....6.31S 76.24W
Tarauacá Brazil 76 F6 ....8.10S 70.43W
Tarbat Ness pt Scotland 19 F2 ....57.52N 3.46W
Tarbert A. and B. Scotland 16 D3 ....55.58N 5.50W
Tarbert W. Isles Scotland 18 C2 ....57.54N 6.48W
Tarbes France 44 D3 ....43.14N 0.05E
Târgovişte Romania 56 F7 ....44.56N 25.27E
Târgu Jiu Romania 56 E7 ....45.03N 23.17E
Târgu Mureş Romania 55 K2 ....46.32N 24.34E
Târgu Secuiesc Romania 56 G8 ....46.00N 26.08E
Tarija Bolivia 76 H3 ....21.36S 64.47W
Tarim Yemen 95 G3 ....16.08N 49.23E
Tarim Basin China 102 E5 ....39.41N 80.53E
Tarime Tanzania 87 A2 ....1.21S 34.20E
Tarleton England 14 E2 ....53.41N 2.50W
Tarn r. France 44 D4 ....44.05N 1.03E
Tarnica mt. Poland 46 F2 ....49.05N 22.46E
Tarnobrzeg Poland 46 E3 ....50.34N 21.40E
Tarnów Poland 46 E3 ....50.01N 20.59E
Tarnowskie Góry Poland 46 D3 ....50.27N 18.52E
Tarragona Spain 48 F4 ....41.07N 1.15E
Tarsus Turkey 57 K3 ....36.54N 34.53E
Tartu Estonia 40 F2 ....58.23N 26.43E
Tartūs Syria 57 K2 ....34.54N 35.53E
Tashk, Daryācheh-ye l. Iran 95 H5 ....29.42N 53.29E
Tashkent Uzbekistan 58 H2 ....41.16N 69.15E
Tasiilaq Greenland 63 O4 ....65.37N 37.42W
Tasikmalaya Indonesia 104 D2 ....7.19S 108.17E
Tasman Abyssal Plain f. Tasman Sea 108 G3 ...32.04S 154.38E
Tasman Basin f. Tasman Sea 108 G3 ....41.29S 158.18E
Tasmania d. Australia 110 D2 ....42.27S 145.20E
Tasman Sea S. Pacific Oc. 110 G2 ....40.31S 170.54E
Tatabánya Hungary 54 H2 ....47.34N 18.26E
Tatarbunary Ukraine 57 H7 ....45.50N 29.37E
Tatarsk Rus. Fed. 58 I3 ....55.13N 75.59E
Tatarskiy Proliv str. Rus. Fed. 59 P3 ....50.29N 141.05E
Tatvan Turkey 94 F7 ....38.29N 42.17E
Taua Brazil 77 L6 ....6.01S 40.23W
Taubaté Brazil 77 K3 ....22.59S 45.32W
Taung China 102 E5 ....20.49N 97.05E
Taunton England 13 D3 ....51.01N 3.06W
Taunus hills Germany 54 B4 ....50.10N 7.59E
Taupo, Lake New Zealand 111 G3 ....38.48S 175.55E
Tauragė Lithuania 46 F5 ....55.15N 22.17E
Taurus Mountains Turkey 57 J3 ....37.00N 32.09E
Taverham England 11 G3 ....52.41N 1.12E
Tavira Portugal 48 B2 ....37.08N 7.38W
Tavistock England 13 C2 ....50.33N 4.08W
Tavoy Myanmar 97 I3 ....14.06N 98.13E
Tavşanlı Turkey 57 H4 ....39.32N 29.28E
Taw r. England 13 C3 ....51.04N 4.03W
Tawau Malaysia 104 F4 ....4.16N 117.54E
Tawe r. Wales 12 D4 ....51.37N 3.55W
Tawitawi i. Phil. 104 F5 ....5.14N 119.57E
Tay r. Scotland 17 F4 ....56.23N 3.24W
Tay, Firth of est. Scotland 17 F4 ....56.25N 3.07W
Tay, Loch l. Scotland 16 E4 ....56.30N 4.11W
Taymā' Saudi Arabia 94 E5 ....27.39N 38.28E
Taymura r. Rus. Fed. 59 K4 ....63.43N 98.05E
Taymyr, Ozero l. Rus. Fed. 59 L5 ....74.20N 101.51E
Taymyr Peninsula Rus. Fed. 59 J5 ....73.54N 89.21E
Tây Ninh Vietnam 104 D6 ....11.17N 106.07E
Tayport Scotland 17 G4 ....56.27N 2.53W
Taytay Phil. 104 F6 ....10.49N 119.30E
Taz r. Rus. Fed. 58 I4 ....67.34N 78.36E
Taza Morocco 52 C3 ....34.16N 3.56W
T'bilisi Georgia 58 F2 ....41.42N 44.48E
Tczew Poland 46 D5 ....54.06N 18.48E
Te Anau, Lake New Zealand 111 F2 ....45.18S 167.48E
Tébessa Algeria 52 E4 ....35.23N 8.12E
Tebingtinggi Indonesia 104 B4 ....3.19N 99.08E
Tecuci Romania 56 G7 ....45.51N 27.26E
Tedzhen Turkmenistan 95 J7 ....37.22N 60.25E
Tees r. England 15 F3 ....54.35N 1.15W
Tees Bay England 15 F3 ....54.41N 1.09W
Tefé r. Brazil 76 H7 ....3.41S 64.52W
Tegucigalpa Honduras 70 G3 ....14.05N 87.12W
Tehrān Iran 95 H6 ....35.39N 51.23E
Tehuantepec, Gulf of Mexico 70 F4 ....15.47N 94.53W
Teide, Pico del vol. Canary Islands 48 X2 ...28.16N 16.37W
Teifi r. Wales 12 C3 ....52.05N 4.40W
Teign r. England 13 D2 ....50.32N 3.35W
Teignmouth England 13 D2 ....50.33N 3.30W
Teith r. Scotland 16 F4 ....56.09N 3.59W
Tekirdağ Turkey 56 G5 ....40.59N 27.30E
Tel Aviv-Yafo Israel 53 J3 ....32.04N 34.46E
Teles Pires r. Brazil 77 I6 ....7.20S 58.03W
Telford England 10 C3 ....52.41N 2.27W
Telford and Wrekin d. England 9 D3 ....52.43N 2.29W
Telšiai Lithuania 46 F5 ....55.59N 22.16E
Tembenchi r. Rus. Fed. 59 K4 ....64.35N 99.49E
Teme r. England 10 C3 ....52.10N 2.13W
Temirtau Kazakhstan 58 I3 ....50.03N 72.57E
Temple Ewell England 11 G2 ....51.09N 1.16E
Templemore Rep. of Ireland 41 D2 ....52.48N 7.50W
Temryuk Rus. Fed. 57 L7 ....45.17N 37.23E
Temuco Chile 73 B3 ....38.44S 72.35W
Tena Ecuador 76 E7 ....0.59S 77.49W
Tenasserim Myanmar 97 I3 ....12.02N 98.58E
Tenbury Wells England 10 C3 ....52.18N 2.36W
Tenby Wales 12 C3 ....51.40N 4.42W
Ten Degree Channel India 97 H2 ....9.57N 92.51E
Tendō Japan 106 D3 ....38.21N 140.22E
Tenerife i. Canary Islands 48 X2 ....28.16N 16.39W
Tennessee d. U.S.A. 65 I4 ....36.12N 85.01W
Tennessee r. U.S.A. 65 I4 ....37.08N 88.25W

Tenterden England 11 F2 ....51.04N 0.41E
Tentudia mt. Spain 48 B3 ....38.03N 6.19W
Teófilo Otôni Brazil 77 L4 ....17.52S 41.31W
Tepic Mexico 70 D5 ....21.31N 104.55W
Teplice Czech Rep. 54 E4 ....50.38N 13.50E
Teraina i. Kiribati 109 J6 ....4.42N 160.24W
Teramo Italy 50 E5 ....42.39N 13.42E
Terebovlya Ukraine 55 K3 ....49.18N 25.42E
Teresina Brazil 77 L6 ....5.07S 42.44W
Tergnier France 42 C2 ....49.40N 3.18E
Terme Turkey 57 L5 ....41.12N 36.59E
Terminillo, Monte mt. Italy 50 E5 ....42.29N 12.59E
Términos, Laguna de lagoon Mexico 70 F4 ...18.30N 91.37W
Termiz Uzbekistan 95 K7 ....37.15N 67.17E
Termoli Italy 50 F4 ....41.59N 14.59E
Tern r. England 10 C3 ....52.40N 2.40W
Ternate Indonesia 105 H4 ....0.49N 127.20E
Terneuzen Neth. 42 C4 ....51.19N 3.50E
Terni Italy 50 E5 ....42.34N 12.44E
Ternopil' Ukraine 55 K3 ....49.33N 25.36E
Terrace Canada 62 F3 ....54.32N 128.37W
Terrassa Spain 48 G4 ....41.34N 2.00E
Terre Haute U.S.A. 65 I4 ....39.28N 87.24W
Terrington Marsh England 11 F3 ....52.47N 0.16E
Terschelling i. Neth. 42 E6 ....53.27N 5.28E
Teseney Eritrea 94 E3 ....15.07N 36.39E
Teslin Canada 62 E4 ....60.12N 132.39W
Test r. England 10 D1 ....50.56N 1.29W
Tetas, Punta pt Chile 73 B4 ....23.28S 70.34W
Tetbury England 10 C2 ....51.38N 2.09W
Tete Mozambique 86 C3 ....16.10S 33.36E
Tetney England 15 G2 ....53.29N 0.01W
Tétouan Morocco 84 D5 ....35.34N 5.23W
Tetovo Macedonia 56 D6 ....42.00N 20.58E
Teuco r. Argentina 73 C4 ....25.39S 60.11W
Teviot r. Scotland 17 G3 ....55.36N 2.26W
Teviothead Scotland 17 G3 ....55.20N 2.56W
Tewkesbury England 10 C2 ....51.59N 2.09W
Texarkana U.S.A. 65 H3 ....33.25N 94.08W
Texas d. U.S.A. 64 F3 ....31.58N 99.13W
Texel i. Neth. 42 D6 ....53.09N 4.46E
Texoma, Lake U.S.A. 64 G3 ....33.59N 96.53W
Tezpur India 97 H6 ....26.36N 92.49E
Thabana-Ntlenyana mt. Lesotho 86 B2 .....29.29S 29.16E
Thai Binh Vietnam 104 D8 ....20.24N 106.19E
Thailand Asia 104 C7 ....16.14N 101.59E
Thailand, Gulf of Asia 104 C6 ....11.08N 101.16E
Thai Nguyên Vietnam 104 D8 ....21.31N 105.52E
Thal Desert Pakistan 95 L6 ....31.25N 71.33E
Thame England 10 E2 ....51.45N 0.58W
Thame r. England 10 D2 ....51.38N 1.10W
Thames est. England 11 F2 ....51.30N 0.31E
Thames r. England 11 F2 ....51.27N 0.21E
Thanet, Isle of pen. England 11 G2 ....51.22N 1.17E
Thanh Hoa Vietnam 104 D7 ....19.47N 105.49E
Thar Desert India/Pakistan 96 C6 ....25.48N 69.50E
Thasos i. Greece 56 F5 ....40.40N 24.31E
Thatcham England 10 D2 ....51.24N 1.16W
Thaton Myanmar 97 I4 ....16.54N 97.23E
Thaxted England 11 F2 ....51.57N 0.21E
The Bahamas Central America 71 I6 ....24.55N 77.44W
The Calf hill England 15 E3 ....54.22N 2.31W
The Cheviot hill England 15 E4 ....55.29N 2.09W
The Fens f. England 11 F3 ....52.42N 0.08E
The Gambia Africa 84 C3 ....13.22N 16.25W
The Great Oasis Egypt 94 D4 ....24.52N 30.42E
The Gulf Asia 95 H5 ....28.03N 50.06E
The Hague Neth. 42 D5 ....52.04N 4.18E
Thelon r. Canada 62 I4 ....64.17N 96.18W
The Marsh England 11 F3 ....52.50N 0.10E
The Minch str. Scotland 18 C3 ....58.02N 6.02W
The Mullet b. Rep. of Ireland 41 A4 ....54.10N 10.07W
The Mumbles Wales 12 D3 ....51.34N 4.00W
The Naze pt England 11 G2 ....51.52N 1.17E
The Needles f. England 10 D1 ....50.40N 1.37W
The North Sound str. Scotland 19 G4 ....59.17N 2.43W
Theodore Roosevelt r. Brazil 77 H6 ....7.35S 60.21W
The Old Man of Coniston hill England 14 D3 ...54.22N 3.07W
The Pas Canada 62 H3 ....53.49N 101.16W
The Rinns of Galloway pen. Scotland 16 D2 ...54.55N 5.07W
Thermaïkos Kolpos r. Greece 56 E5 ....40.11N 22.54E
The Solent str. England 10 D1 ....50.45N 1.23W
The Sound est. England 13 C2 ....50.21N 4.09W
Thessaloniki Greece 56 E5 ....40.38N 22.57E
The Storr hill Scotland 18 C2 ....57.31N 6.11W
Thet r. England 11 F3 ....52.25N 0.45E
Thetford England 11 F3 ....52.25N 0.45E
The Trossachs hills Scotland 16 E4 ....56.13N 4.26W
The Wash b. England 11 F3 ....52.54N 0.20E
The Weald f. England 11 F2 ....51.05N 0.18E
Thiers France 44 E4 ....45.51N 3.33E
Thiès Senegal 84 C3 ....14.48N 16.56W
Thika Kenya 87 B2 ....1.03S 37.05E
Thimbu Bhutan 97 G6 ....27.29N 89.42E
Thionville France 44 G6 ....49.22N 6.10E
Thira i. Greece 56 F3 ....36.27N 25.27E
Thirlmere resr England 14 D3 ....54.33N 3.04W
Thirsk England 15 F3 ....54.14N 1.20W
Thiruvananthapuram India 96 E2 ....8.30N 76.57E
Thisted Denmark 40 B2 ....56.57N 8.41E
Thomastown Rep. of Ireland 41 D2 ....52.31N 7.07W
Thompson Canada 62 I3 ....55.48N 97.55W
Thornaby-on-Tees England 15 F3 ....54.32N 1.17W
Thornbury England 10 C2 ....51.36N 2.31W
Thorne England 15 G2 ....53.37N 0.58W
Thornhill Scotland 17 F3 ....55.15N 3.46W
Thornton England 14 D2 ....53.53N 3.00W
Thrakiko Pelagos sea Greece 56 F5 ....40.22N 24.46E
Thrapston England 11 E3 ....52.24N 0.32W
Thuin Belgium 42 D3 ....50.20N 4.17E
Thule Greenland 63 L5 ....77.28N 69.11W
Thun Switz. 50 B7 ....46.45N 7.38E
Thunder Bay town Canada 63 J2 ....48.26N 89.15W
Thurles Rep. of Ireland 41 D2 ....52.41N 7.49W
Thurrock d. England 9 F2 ....51.31N 0.22E
Thursby England 14 D3 ....54.51N 3.03W
Thurso Scotland 19 F3 ....58.36N 3.31W
Thurso Bay Scotland 19 F3 ....58.38N 3.32W
Tianjin China 103 L5 ....39.04N 117.15E
Tianshui China 103 J4 ....34.30N 105.37E
Tiaret Algeria 52 D4 ....35.20N 1.19E
Tibagi r. Brazil 77 J3 ....23.07S 50.57W
Tibati Cameroon 84 F2 ....6.26N 12.35E
Tiber r. Italy 50 E4 ....41.44N 12.14E
Tibesti mts Chad 85 F4 ....20.53N 17.03E
Tibet, Plateau of f. China 102 E6 ....33.03N 84.00E
Tiburón, Isla i. Mexico 70 B6 ....29.08N 112.24W
Ticehurst England 11 F2 ....51.03N 0.25E
Tidjikja Mauritania 84 C3 ....18.31N 11.26W
Tiel Neth. 42 E4 ....51.52N 5.25E
Tielt Belgium 42 C3 ....50.59N 3.20E
Tienen Belgium 42 D3 ....50.48N 4.56E
Tien Shan mts China/Kyrgyzstan 102 D6 ...40.48N 76.25E

Tierra del Fuego, Isla Grande de *i.* Argentina/Chile 73 C1
54.11S 68.48W
Tiétar *r.* Spain 48 C3 ....39.56N 5.54W
Tighina Moldova 53 I6 ....46.49N 29.29E
Tigre *r.* Ecuador/Peru 76 F7 ....4.27S 74.06W
Tigre *r.* Venezuela 72 C7 ....9.26N 62.25E
Tigris *r.* Iraq/Syria 95 G6 ....30.59N 47.25E
Tihāmah *f.* Saudi Arabia 85 I3 ....17.18N 42.25E
Tijuana Mexico 70 A7 ....32.29N 117.02W
Tikhoretsk Rus. Fed. 57 N7 ....45.52N 40.06E
Tiki Basin *f.* S. Pacific Oc. 109 L4 ....18.48S 129.30W
Tikrīt Iraq 94 F6 ....34.33N 43.37E
Tiksi Rus. Fed. 59 N5 ....71.38N 128.36E
Tilburg Neth. 42 E4 ....51.33N 5.05E
Tilbury England 11 F2 ....51.28N 0.22E
Tilehurst England 10 D2 ....51.27N 1.02W
Tillabéri Niger 84 E3 ....14.13N 1.29E
Tillicoultry Scotland 17 F4 ....56.09N 3.44W
Ţimā Egypt 53 J2 ....26.53N 31.25E
Timashevsk Rus. Fed. 57 M7 ....45.37N 38.56E
Timbuktu Mali 84 D3 ....16.46N 2.59W
Timiş *r.* Romania 56 D7 ....45.46N 21.14E
Timişoara Romania 56 D7 ....45.46N 21.14E
Timmins Canada 63 J2 ....48.29N 81.21W
Timon Brazil 77 L6 ....5.08S 42.48W
Timor *i.* East Timor/Indonesia 105 H2 ....8.49S 126.62E
Timor Sea Australia/Indonesia 110 B5 ....11.23S 126.22E
Timrå Sweden 40 D3 ....62.30N 17.20E
Tindouf Algeria 84 C4 ....27.42N 8.07W
Tinian *i.* N. Mariana Is 108 F6 ....14.58N 145.41E
Tinos *i.* Greece 56 F3 ....37.40N 25.12E
Tintagel England 13 C2 ....50.40N 4.45W
Tinto *hill* Scotland 17 F3 ....55.36N 3.40W
Tipasa Algeria 48 G2 ....36.33N 2.28E
Tipperary Rep. of Ireland 41 C2 ....52.28N 8.10W
Tipperary *d.* Rep. of Ireland 41 D2 ....52.43N 7.54W
Tiptree England 11 F2 ....51.49N 0.45E
Tiracambu, Serra do *hills* Brazil 77 K7 ....3.15S 46.30W
Tirana Albania 56 C5 ....41.19N 19.49E
Tiraspol Moldova 53 I6 ....46.51N 29.37E
Tiree *i.* Scotland 16 C4 ....56.30N 6.57W
Tirga Mòr *hill* Scotland 18 C2 ....57.59N 6.59W
Tirso *r.* Italy 50 C3 ....39.53N 8.32E
Tiruchchirappalli India 96 E3 ....10.49N 78.41E
Tiruppur India 96 E3 ....11.06N 77.18E
Tisa *r.* S.M. 56 D7 ....45.08N 20.17E
Tisza *r.* Hungary 55 I2 ....46.09N 20.04E
Tiszafüred Hungary 46 E1 ....47.36N 20.46E
Titicaca, Lake Bolivia/Peru 76 G4 ....15.49S 69.40W
Tiverton England 13 D2 ....50.54N 3.29W
Tivoli Italy 50 E4 ....41.58N 12.48E
Tizi Ouzou Algeria 52 D4 ....36.41N 4.05E
Tiznit Morocco 84 D4 ....29.41N 9.43W
Tiztoutine Morocco 48 D1 ....34.58N 3.09W
Tlaxcala Mexico 70 E4 ....19.21N 98.13W
Tlaxcala *d.* Mexico 70 E4 ....19.35N 98.20W
Tlemcen Algeria 84 D5 ....34.54N 1.19W
Toamasina Madagascar 86 D3 ....18.09S 49.22E
Toba, Danau *l.* Indonesia 104 B4 ....2.32N 98.59E
Tobago *i.* Trinidad and Tobago 71 L3 ....11.17N 60.38W
Tobelo Indonesia 105 H4 ....1.44N 127.57E
Tobermory Scotland 18 C1 ....56.38N 6.04W
Toboali Indonesia 104 D3 ....2.59S 106.30E
Tobol *r.* Kazakhstan/Rus. Fed. 58 H3 ....58.10N 68.13E
Tobol'sk Rus. Fed. 58 H3 ....58.14N 68.16E
Tocantins *d.* Brazil 77 K5 ....11.15S 48.38W
Tocantins *r.* Brazil 77 K7 ....1.49S 49.13W
Tocopilla Chile 76 F3 ....22.04S 70.10W
Todmorden England 15 E2 ....53.43N 2.06W
Toft Scotland 19 H5 ....60.28N 1.13W
Togian, Kepulauan *is* Indonesia 105 G3 ....0.06S 121.53E
Togo Africa 84 E2 ....8.27N 1.11E
Tok U.S.A. 62 D4 ....63.21N 143.01W
Tokaj Hungary 46 E2 ....48.06N 21.25E
Tokara-rettō *is* Japan 106 A1 ....28.34N 129.00E
Tokat Turkey 57 L5 ....40.19N 36.32E
Tokelau *is* S. Pacific Oc. 108 I5 ....8.30S 171.28W
Tokushima Japan 106 B2 ....34.04N 134.34E
Tōkyō Japan 106 C3 ....35.40N 139.46E
Tōkyō *d.* Japan 106 C3 ....35.22N 139.03E
Tôlañaro Madagascar 86 D2 ....25.02S 46.58E
Toledo Spain 48 C3 ....39.52N 4.01W
Toledo U.S.A. 65 J5 ....41.39N 83.33W
Toledo, Montes de *mts* Spain 48 C3 ....39.39N 4.54W
Toledo Bend Reservoir U.S.A. 65 H3 ....31.38N 93.43W
Tolentino Italy 50 E5 ....43.13N 13.19E
Toliara Madagascar 86 D2 ....23.22S 43.39E
Tolitoli Indonesia 105 G4 ....1.05N 120.50E
Tollesbury England 11 F2 ....51.45N 0.50E
Tolsta Head Scotland 18 C3 ....58.21N 6.10W
Toluca Mexico 70 E4 ....19.18N 99.39W
Tol'yatti Rus. Fed. 58 F3 ....53.31N 49.26E
Tomakomai Japan 106 D4 ....42.38N 141.36E
Tomanivi *mt.* Fiji 111 G5 ....17.37S 178.00E
Tomaszów Lubelski Poland 46 F3 ....50.28N 23.25E
Tomaszów Mazowiecki Poland 46 E3 ....51.32N 20.01E
Tombigbee *r.* U.S.A. 65 I3 ....31.11N 87.57W
Tombua Angola 86 A3 ....15.50S 11.50E
Tomelloso Spain 48 D3 ....39.09N 3.00W
Tomini, Teluk *g.* Indonesia 104 G3 ....0.21S 120.54E
Tomsk Rus. Fed. 58 J3 ....56.30N 85.01E
Tomtabacken *hill* Sweden 40 C2 ....57.30N 14.29E
Tonbridge England 11 F2 ....51.12N 0.17E
Tondano Indonesia 105 G4 ....1.21N 124.56E
Tønder Denmark 54 C6 ....54.57N 8.52E
Tone *r.* England 10 C2 ....51.04N 2.56W
Tonelagee *hill* Rep. of Ireland 12 A5 ....53.03N 6.23W
Tonga S. Pacific Oc. 108 I4 ....20.05S 173.45W
Tongatapu Group *is* Tonga 108 I4 ....21.07S 174.45W
Tonga Trench *f.* S. Pacific Oc. 108 I4 ....21.47S 173.51W
Tongeren Belgium 42 E3 ....50.47N 5.28E
Tonghua China 103 N6 ....41.43N 125.57E
Tongking, Gulf of China/Vietnam 103 J2 ....20.29N 108.15E
Tongliao China 103 M6 ....43.31N 122.14E
Tongling China 103 L4 ....30.55N 117.52E
Tongshan China 103 L4 ....34.12N 117.14E
Tongue Scotland 19 E3 ....58.29N 4.25W
Tonle Sap *l.* Cambodia 104 C6 ....13.04N 103.51E
Tonopah U.S.A. 64 C4 ....38.04N 117.14W
Tønsberg Norway 40 B2 ....59.17N 10.23E
Toowoomba Australia 110 E4 ....27.33S 151.58E
Topeka U.S.A. 65 G4 ....39.04N 95.36W
Topozero, Ozero *l.* Rus. Fed. 40 H4 ....65.42N 32.00E
Topsham England 13 D2 ....50.41N 3.28W
Torbat-e Heydarīyeh Iran 95 I7 ....35.13N 59.06E
Torbat-e Jām Iran 95 J7 ....35.15N 60.34E
Torbay *d.* England 9 D2 ....50.26N 3.34W
Tor Bay England 13 D2 ....50.25N 3.32W
Tordesillas Spain 48 C4 ....41.31N 4.59W
Torenberg *hill* Neth. 42 E5 ....52.12N 5.49E
Torfaen *d.* Wales 9 D2 ....51.44N 3.05W
Tormes *r.* Spain 48 B4 ....41.18N 6.27W
Torneälven *r.* Sweden 40 F4 ....65.49N 24.09E
Torneträsk *l.* Sweden 40 D5 ....68.23N 18.56E

Tornio Finland 40 F4 ....65.50N 24.11E
Toronto Canada 63 K2 ....43.40N 79.23W
Toropets Rus. Fed. 55 N7 ....56.30N 31.38E
Tororo Uganda 87 A3 ....0.39N 34.10E
Torpoint England 13 C2 ....50.22N 4.12W
Torquay England 13 D2 ....50.28N 3.31W
Torre *mt.* Portugal 48 B4 ....40.20N 7.35W
Torrecerredo *mt.* Spain 48 C5 ....43.12N 4.49W
Torre del Greco Italy 50 F4 ....40.47N 14.23E
Torremolinos Spain 48 C2 ....36.36N 4.30W
Torreón Mexico 70 D6 ....25.31N 103.27W
Torres, Lake Australia 110 C3 ....30.32S 137.28E
Torres Islands Vanuatu 111 F5 ....13.08S 166.17E
Torres Strait Australia 110 D6 ....9.50S 142.11E
Torres Vedras Portugal 48 A3 ....39.06N 9.15W
Torrevieja Spain 48 E2 ....37.59N 0.40W
Torridge *r.* England 13 C2 ....50.59N 4.11W
Torridon Scotland 18 D2 ....57.33N 5.31W
Torridon, Loch *b.* Scotland 18 D2 ....57.37N 5.50W
Tortosa Spain 48 F4 ....40.50N 0.32E
Toruń Poland 46 D4 ....53.01N 18.37E
Tory Island Rep. of Ireland 41 C5 ....55.16N 8.13W
Tosno Rus. Fed. 40 G2 ....59.33N 30.54E
Tosya Turkey 57 K5 ....40.59N 34.04E
Totland England 10 D1 ....50.41N 1.32W
Totnes England 13 D2 ....50.26N 3.41W
Totton England 10 D1 ....50.55N 1.29W
Tottori Japan 106 B3 ....35.29N 134.14E
Toubkal, Jbel *mt.* Morocco 84 D5 ....31.03N 7.57W
Touggourt Algeria 84 E4 ....33.06N 6.04E
Toulon France 44 F3 ....43.08N 5.56E
Toulouse France 44 D3 ....43.37N 1.26E
Toungoo Myanmar 97 I4 ....18.55N 96.25E
Touraine *f.* France 44 D5 ....47.14N 0.21E
Tournai Belgium 42 C3 ....50.36N 3.24E
Tournon-sur-Rhône France 44 F4 ....45.04N 4.50E
Tours France 44 D5 ....47.23N 0.42E
Tove *r.* England 10 E3 ....52.05N 0.50W
Towada Japan 106 D4 ....40.36N 141.12E
Towcester England 10 E3 ....52.08N 0.59W
Towori, Teluk *b.* Indonesia 105 G3 ....2.02S 121.57E
Towot Sudan 87 A4 ....6.10N 34.23E
Toyama Japan 106 C3 ....36.41N 137.13E
Toyama-wan *b.* Japan 106 C3 ....36.54N 137.14E
Toyota Japan 106 C3 ....35.05N 137.10E
Tozeur Tunisia 52 E3 ....33.55N 8.07E
Trabzon Turkey 57 M5 ....40.59N 39.44E
Trafalgar, Cabo *c.* Spain 48 B2 ....36.11N 6.02W
Trakai Lithuania 46 G5 ....54.38N 24.56E
Tralee Rep. of Ireland 41 B2 ....52.16N 9.42W
Tralee Bay Rep. of Ireland 41 B2 ....52.18N 9.57W
Tramore Rep. of Ireland 41 D2 ....52.10N 7.09W
Tranås Sweden 40 C2 ....58.02N 14.59E
Trangan *i.* Indonesia 105 I2 ....6.35S 134.16E
Transylvanian Alps *mts* Romania 55 J1 ....45.35N 24.40E
Trapani Italy 50 E3 ....38.01N 12.31E
Trasimeno, Lago *l.* Italy 50 E5 ....43.08N 12.06E
Traunsee *l.* Austria 54 E2 ....47.54N 13.47E
Traverse City U.S.A. 65 I5 ....44.46N 85.37W
Travnik Bos.-Herz. 56 B7 ....44.14N 17.40E
Trawsfynydd, Llyn *resr* Wales 12 D4 ....52.55N 3.59W
Trebišov Slovakia 55 I3 ....48.39N 21.44E
Tredegar Wales 12 D3 ....51.46N 3.15W
Tregaron Wales 12 D4 ....52.13N 3.56W
Treig, Loch *l.* Scotland 18 E1 ....56.48N 4.44W
Trelleborg Sweden 40 C1 ....55.22N 13.10E
Tremadog Bay Wales 12 C4 ....52.52N 4.16W
Trenčín Slovakia 54 H3 ....48.53N 18.02E
Trent *r.* England 15 G2 ....53.38N 0.43W
Trento Italy 50 D7 ....46.04N 11.08E
Trenton U.S.A. 65 L5 ....40.13N 74.47W
Tresco *i.* England 13 A1 ....49.57N 6.19W
Tres Puntas, Cabo *c.* Argentina 73 C2 ....47.08S 65.53W
Treviso Italy 58 E6 ....45.40N 12.15E
Trevose Head England 13 B2 ....50.33N 5.06W
Trier Germany 54 C4 ....49.45N 6.38E
Trieste Italy 50 E6 ....45.39N 13.46E
Trikala Greece 56 D4 ....39.33N 21.46E
Trim Rep. of Ireland 41 E3 ....53.33N 6.47W
Trincomalee Sri Lanka 96 F2 ....8.37N 81.13E
Tring England 10 E2 ....51.48N 0.39W
Trinidad Bolivia 76 H5 ....14.44S 64.51W
Trinidad *i.* Trinidad and Tobago 71 L3 ....10.27N 61.13W
Trinidad U.S.A. 64 F4 ....37.11N 104.30W
Trinidad and Tobago Central America 71 L3 ......10.49N 61.00W
Tripoli Greece 56 E3 ....37.31N 22.23E
Tripoli Lebanon 53 K3 ....34.26N 35.52E
Tripoli Libya 84 F5 ....32.52N 13.08E
Tripolitania *f.* Libya 52 F3 ....30.39N 13.17E
Tripura *d.* India 97 H5 ....23.45N 91.35E
Tristan da Cunha *i.* Atlantic Oc. 116 I4 ....38.00S 12.00W
Trnava Slovakia 54 G3 ....48.22N 17.36E
Trobriand Islands P.N.G. 110 E6 ....8.33S 151.09E
Troisdorf Germany 42 G3 ....50.49N 7.09E
Trois-Rivières Canada 63 K2 ....46.21N 72.35W
Trollhättan Sweden 40 C2 ....58.16N 12.18E
Trombetas *r.* Brazil 77 I7 ....1.31S 56.06W
Tromsø Norway 40 D5 ....69.39N 18.57E
Trondheim Norway 40 B3 ....63.36N 10.23E
Troödos, Mount Cyprus 57 J2 ....34.56N 32.51E
Troon Scotland 16 E3 ....55.32N 4.40W
Trostan *hill* Northern Ireland 16 C3 ....55.03N 6.09W
Troup Head Scotland 19 G2 ....57.42N 2.18W
Trout Lake Canada 65 H7 ....51.15N 93.06W
Trowbridge England 10 C2 ....51.19N 2.12W
Troyes France 44 F5 ....48.18N 4.05E
Trubchevsk Rus. Fed. 55 O5 ....52.35N 33.47E
Trujillo Peru 76 E6 ....8.07S 79.02W
Truro Canada 63 L2 ....45.23N 63.13W
Truro England 13 B2 ....50.16N 5.03W
Trutnov Czech Rep. 46 C3 ....50.16N 15.55E
Trzebiatów Poland 46 B5 ....54.04N 15.16E
Tsaratanana, Massif du *mts* Madagascar 86 D3 ...13.44S 48.59E
Tsavo *r.* Kenya 87 B2 ....2.58S 38.31E
Tsavo East National Park Kenya 87 B2 ....2.43S 38.45E
Tsavo West National Park Kenya 87 B2 ....3.18S 37.58E
Tsetserleg Mongolia 103 I7 ....47.19N 101.29E
Tshchikskoye Vodokhranilishche *resr* Rus. Fed. 57 M7
45.07N 39.28E
Tshwane S. Africa 86 B2 ....25.44S 28.13E
Tsimlyanskoye Vodokhranilishche *resr* Russian Fed. 35 I2
48.00N 43.00E
Tsna *r.* Belarus 55 L5 ....52.09N 27.01E
Tsu Japan 106 C2 ....34.43N 136.31E
Tsuchiura Japan 106 D3 ....36.04N 140.12E
Tsugarū-kaikyō *str.* Japan 106 D4 ....41.16N 140.21E
Tsumeb Namibia 86 A3 ....19.14S 17.43E
Tsumis Park Namibia 86 A2 ....23.47S 17.31E
Tsuruga Japan 106 C3 ....35.38N 136.04E
Tsushima *is* Japan 106 A2 ....34.24N 129.23E
Tuam Rep. of Ireland 41 C3 ....53.31N 8.51W
Tuamotu, Archipel des *is* French Polynesia 109 K5
14.29S 142.50W

Tuapse Rus. Fed. 57 M7 ....44.06N 39.04E
Tuban Indonesia 104 E2 ....6.55S 112.02E
Tubbercurry Rep. of Ireland 41 C4 ....54.03N 8.43W
Tübingen Germany 54 C3 ....48.31N 9.04E
Tubruq Libya 85 G5 ....32.04N 23.57E
Tubuai *i.* French Polynesia 109 K4 ....23.21S 149.30W
Tubuai Islands French Polynesia 109 J4 ....23.34S 153.12W
Tucavaca Bolivia 77 I4 ....18.37S 58.56W
Tucson U.S.A. 64 D3 ....32.14N 110.54W
Tucumcari U.S.A. 64 F4 ....35.12N 103.44W
Tucuruí Brazil 77 K7 ....3.42S 49.44W
Tucuruí, Represa *resr* Brazil 77 K7 ....4.26S 49.07W
Tudela Spain 48 E5 ....42.04N 1.36W
Tuela *r.* Portugal 48 B4 ....41.38N 7.08W
Tufts Abyssal Plain *f.* N. Pacific Oc. 109 K9 ....49.37N 146.59W
Tuguegarao Phil. 105 G7 ....17.37N 121.43E
Tui Spain 48 A5 ....42.03N 8.38W
Tukangbesi, Kepulauan *is* Indonesia 105 G2 ....5.40S 123.55E
Tukums Latvia 40 E2 ....56.58N 23.10E
Tula *watercourse* Kenya 87 B2 ....0.50S 39.48E
Tula Rus. Fed. 58 E3 ....54.12N 37.37E
Tulcea Romania 57 H7 ....45.10N 28.48E
Tul'chyn Ukraine 55 M3 ....48.41N 28.50E
Tuli'a Uganda 62 F4 ....64.55N 125.31W
Tullamore Rep. of Ireland 41 D3 ....53.17N 7.30W
Tulle France 44 D4 ....45.16N 1.46E
Tullow Rep. of Ireland 41 E2 ....52.48N 6.44W
Tullybrack *hill* Northern Ireland 16 B2 ....54.23N 7.52W
Tulsa U.S.A. 64 G4 ....36.09N 95.58W
Tumaco Colombia 72 B7 ....1.48N 78.49W
Tumba, Lac *l.* Dem. Rep. Congo 86 A4 ....0.52S 18.05E
Tumbes Peru 76 D7 ....3.35S 80.27W
Tumen *r.* Asia 106 A4 ....42.18N 130.41E
Tumen China 106 A4 ....42.59N 129.51E
Tumkur India 96 E3 ....13.19N 77.06E
Tummel *r.* Scotland 19 F1 ....56.39N 3.40W
Tummel, Loch *l.* Scotland 19 F1 ....56.42N 3.58W
Tump Pakistan 95 J5 ....26.06N 62.26E
Tumucumaque, Serra *hills* Brazil 77 I8 ....1.59N 56.09W
Tunceli Turkey 57 M4 ....39.06N 39.33E
Tundzha *r.* Bulgaria 56 G5 ....41.39N 26.33E
Tunis Tunisia 52 F4 ....36.46N 10.16E
Tunis, Golfe de *g.* Tunisia 50 D2 ....37.08N 10.31E
Tunisia Africa 52 E3 ....34.52N 9.24E
Tunja Colombia 72 B7 ....5.30N 73.22W
Tunnsjøen *l.* Norway 40 C4 ....64.42N 13.24E
Tuolumne *r.* U.S.A. 64 B4 ....37.36N 121.10W
Tupinambarama, Ilha *i.* Brazil 77 I7 ....3.50S 58.55W
Tupiza Bolivia 76 G3 ....21.27S 65.45W
Tura Rus. Fed. 59 L4 ....64.16N 100.15E
Turabah Saudi Arabia 94 F4 ....21.14N 41.37E
Turbat Pakistan 96 B6 ....26.01N 63.07E
Turbo Colombia 72 I2 ....8.05N 76.43W
Turda Romania 55 J2 ....46.34N 23.47E
Turgutlu Turkey 56 G4 ....38.29N 27.42E
Turhal Turkey 57 L5 ....40.23N 36.04E
Turia *r.* Spain 48 E3 ....39.26N 0.18W
Turin Italy 50 B6 ....45.04N 7.41E
Turiys'k Ukraine 46 G3 ....51.05N 24.32E
Turkana, Lake Ethiopia/Kenya 85 H2 ....3.59N 35.57E
Turkey Asia/Europe 57 I4 ....39.19N 34.21E
Turkmenabat Turkmenistan 58 H1 ....39.05N 63.34E
Turkmenbashi Turkmenistan 58 G2 ....40.02N 52.59E
Turkmenistan Asia 115 L7 ....40.00N 60.00E
Turks and Caicos Islands Central America 71 J5 ..21.59N 71.36W
Turks Islands Turks and Caicos Is 71 J5 ....21.25N 71.09W
Turku Finland 40 E3 ....60.27N 22.15E
Turkwel *watercourse* Kenya 87 B3 ....3.03N 36.08E
Turnhout Belgium 42 D3 ....51.19N 4.57E
Turnu Măgurele Romania 56 F6 ....43.45N 24.51E
Turpan China 102 F6 ....42.52N 89.12E
Turquino, Pico *mt.* Cuba 71 I5 ....20.02N 76.51W
Turriff Scotland 19 G2 ....57.32N 2.28W
Tuscaloosa U.S.A. 65 I3 ....33.11N 87.30W
Tutbury England 10 D3 ....52.51N 1.41W
Tuticorin India 96 E2 ....8.48N 78.08E
Tuttlingen Germany 54 C2 ....47.59N 8.49E
Tutuila *i.* American Samoa 108 I5 ....14.16S 170.33W
Tuvalu S. Pacific Oc. 111 G6 ....7.24S 178.20E
Tuxford England 11 E1 ....53.14N 0.54W
Tuxpan Mexico 70 E5 ....20.58N 97.22W
Tuxtla Gutiérrez Mexico 70 F4 ....16.46N 93.08W
Tuz, Lake Turkey 57 J4 ....38.42N 33.24E
Tuzla Bos.-Herz. 56 C7 ....44.33N 18.42E
Tver' Rus. Fed. 58 E3 ....56.50N 35.54E
Tweed *r.* U.K. 15 E4 ....55.45N 2.06W
Twin Falls *town* U.S.A. 64 D5 ....42.35N 114.27W
Twyford England 10 E2 ....51.29N 0.52W
Tyler U.S.A. 65 G3 ....32.22N 95.18W
Tynda Rus. Fed. 59 N3 ....55.07N 124.44E
Tyne *r.* Scotland 17 G4 ....56.00N 2.36W
Tyne and Wear *d.* England 8 E4 ....54.56N 1.16W
Tynemouth England 15 F4 ....55.01N 1.25W
Tynset Norway 40 B3 ....62.16N 10.47E
Tyre Lebanon 53 K3 ....33.15N 35.14E
Tyrrhenian Sea France/Italy 50 D4 ....40.13N 10.15E
Tyumen' Rus. Fed. 58 H3 ....57.09N 65.28E
Tywi *r.* Wales 12 C3 ....51.48N 4.20W

U

Uaupés Brazil 76 G7 ....0.06S 67.02W
Ubangi *r.* C.A.R./Dem. Rep. Congo 85 F1 ......0.25S 17.44E
Úbeda Spain 48 D3 ....38.01N 3.22W
Uberaba Brazil 77 K4 ....19.46S 47.53W
Uberlândia Brazil 77 K4 ....18.56S 48.14W
Ubon Ratchathani Thailand 104 C7 ....15.14N 104.53E
Ucayali *r.* Peru 76 F7 ....4.40S 73.30W
Uchur *r.* Rus. Fed. 59 O3 ....57.19N 131.17E
Uckfield England 11 F1 ....50.58N 0.06E
Uda *r.* Rus. Fed. 59 O3 ....54.41N 135.18E
Udaipur India 96 D5 ....24.35N 73.47E
Uddevalla Sweden 40 B2 ....58.21N 11.57E
Uddjaure *l.* Sweden 40 D4 ....65.56N 17.52E
Udine Italy 50 E7 ....46.04N 13.14E
Udon Thani Thailand 104 C7 ....17.22N 102.50E
Udupi India 96 D3 ....13.20N 74.45E
Uele *r.* Dem. Rep. Congo 86 B5 ....3.32N 25.16E
Uelzen Germany 54 D5 ....52.58N 10.34E
Ufa Rus. Fed. 58 G3 ....54.44N 55.58E
Uganda Africa 85 H2 ....2.34N 32.37E
Uglegorsk Rus. Fed. 59 P2 ....49.02N 142.02E
Uherské Hradiště Czech Rep. 46 C2 ....49.04N 17.28E
Uig Scotland 18 C2 ....57.35N 6.21W
Uíge Angola 86 A4 ....7.37S 15.02E
Uinta Mountains U.S.A. 64 D5 ....40.36N 110.59W
Ukerewe Island Tanzania 87 A2 ....1.57S 32.53E
Ukhta Rus. Fed. 58 G4 ....63.33N 53.46E
Ukiah U.S.A. 64 B4 ....39.20N 123.13W
Ukmergė Lithuania 46 G5 ....55.15N 24.46E
Ukraine Europe 55 N3 ....49.23N 31.18E

Ulaangom Mongolia 102 G7 ....49.57N 92.09E
Ulan Bator Mongolia 103 J7 ....47.48N 106.58E
Ulanhot China 103 M7 ....46.04N 122.03E
Ulan-Ude Rus. Fed. 59 L3 ....51.49N 107.38E
Ulchin S. Korea 106 A3 ....36.59N 129.23E
Uliastay Mongolia 102 H7 ....47.36N 96.48E
Ulithi *atoll* Micronesia 105 J6 ....10.07N 139.40E
Ullapool Scotland 18 D2 ....57.54N 5.10W
Ullswater *l.* England 14 E3 ....54.34N 2.54W
Ullŭng-do *i.* S. Korea 106 B3 ....37.30N 130.55E
Ulm Germany 54 C3 ....48.25N 9.59E
Ulster Canal Rep. of Ireland/U.K. 16 B2 ....54.14N 7.01W
Uludağ *mt.* Turkey 57 H5 ....40.06N 29.17E
Ulundi S. Africa 86 C2 ....28.19S 31.25E
Uluru *hill* Australia 110 C4 ....25.20S 131.05E
Ulva *i.* Scotland 16 C4 ....56.28N 6.13W
Ulverston England 14 D3 ....54.12N 3.05W
Ul'yanovsk Rus. Fed. 58 F3 ....54.18N 48.23E
Uman' Ukraine 55 N3 ....48.45N 30.14E
Umboi *i.* P.N.G. 110 D6 ....5.42S 147.50E
Umeå Sweden 40 E3 ....63.50N 20.17E
Umeälven *r.* Sweden 40 D4 ....63.46N 20.19E
Umm Keddada Sudan 94 C2 ....13.35N 26.42E
Umm Ruwaba Sudan 94 D2 ....12.52N 31.10E
Umm Sa'ad Libya 85 G5 ....31.34N 25.03E
Umtata S. Africa 86 B1 ....31.35S 28.47E
Umuarama Brazil 77 J3 ....23.46S 53.19W
Una *r.* Bos.-Herz./Croatia 56 B7 ....45.16N 16.56E
'Unayzah Saudi Arabia 94 F5 ....26.05N 43.57E
Unecha Rus. Fed. 55 O5 ....52.51N 32.41E
Ungava, Péninsule d' *pen.* Canada 63 K4 ......60.46N 74.25W
Ungava Bay Canada 63 L3 ....59.16N 67.29W
Unggi N. Korea 106 B4 ....42.21N 130.24E
Ungwana Bay Kenya 87 C2 ....2.47S 40.28E
Unimak Island U.S.A. 62 B3 ....54.58N 164.62W
Unini *r.* Brazil 76 H7 ....1.41S 61.43W
United Arab Emirates Asia 95 H4 ....23.30N 52.20E
United Kingdom Europe 8-9 ....54.35N 1.53W
United States of America N. America 64 G4 .....38.59N 99.57W
Unst *i.* Scotland 19 I5 ....60.46N 0.53W
Upa *r.* Rus. Fed. 55 Q6 ....54.01N 36.20E
Upavon England 10 D2 ....51.18N 1.48W
Upemba, Lac *l.* Dem. Rep. Congo 86 B4 ....8.39S 26.29E
Upernavik Greenland 63 M5 ....72.48N 56.09W
Upington S. Africa 86 B2 ....28.28S 21.15E
Upolu *i.* Samoa 108 I5 ....14.04S 171.39W
Upper Klamath Lake U.S.A. 64 B5 ....42.22N 121.53W
Upper Lough Erne *l.* Northern Ireland 16 B2 ....54.15N 7.34W
Upper Tean England 10 D3 ....52.57N 1.59W
Uppingham England 10 E3 ....52.35N 0.43W
Uppsala Sweden 40 D2 ....59.51N 17.38E
Upton upon Severn England 10 C3 ....52.04N 2.13W
Ural *r.* Kazakhstan/Rus. Fed. 58 G2 ....46.55N 51.46E
Ural Mountains Rus. Fed. 58 H4 ....66.50N 63.48E
Ural'sk Kazakhstan 58 G3 ....51.11N 51.24E
Uranium City Canada 62 H3 ....59.31N 108.43W
Urawa Japan 106 C3 ....35.51N 139.39E
Ure *r.* England 15 F3 ....54.05N 1.20W
Urengoy Rus. Fed. 58 I4 ....65.55N 78.13E
Urganch Uzbekistan 58 H2 ....41.32N 60.39E
Urie *r.* Scotland 19 G2 ....57.16N 2.22W
Urla Turkey 56 G4 ....38.17N 26.46E
Urmia, Lake Iran 94 G7 ....37.57N 45.17E
Uruaçu Brazil 77 K5 ....14.31S 49.10W
Uruapan Mexico 70 D4 ....19.25N 102.04W
Urubamba *r.* Peru 76 F5 ....10.46S 73.47W
Urucara Brazil 77 I7 ....2.31S 57.45W
Uruguaiana Brazil 77 I2 ....29.45S 57.03W
Uruguay *r.* Argentina/Brazil/Uruguay 77 I1 ....33.52S 58.25W
Uruguay S. America 73 D3 ....32.45S 55.56W
Ürümqi China 102 F6 ....43.44N 87.34E
Urziceni Romania 56 G7 ....44.43N 26.37E
Uşak Turkey 57 H4 ....38.40N 29.24E
Ushuaia Argentina 73 C1 ....54.46S 68.19W
Usk Wales 12 E3 ....51.42N 2.54W
Usk *r.* Wales 12 E3 ....51.34N 2.59W
Usk Reservoir Wales 12 D3 ....51.56N 3.44W
Usol'ye-Sibirskoye Rus. Fed. 59 L3 ....52.40N 103.30E
Ussuri *r.* China/Rus. Fed. 106 C5 ....48.24N 135.01E
Ussuriysk Rus. Fed. 59 O2 ....43.48N 131.57E
Ustica, Isola di *i.* Italy 50 E3 ....38.41N 13.10E
Ust'-Ilimsk Rus. Fed. 59 L3 ....58.02N 102.42E
Ústí nad Labem Czech Rep. 54 F4 ....50.40N 14.03E
Ustka Poland 46 C5 ....54.35N 16.52E
Ust'-Kamchatsk Rus. Fed. 59 R3 ....56.15N 162.32E
Ust'-Kamenogorsk Kazakhstan 58 J2 ....49.52N 82.46E
Ust'-Kut Rus. Fed. 59 L3 ....56.45N 105.42E
Ust'-Maya Rus. Fed. 59 O4 ....60.27N 134.31E
Ust'-Olenek Rus. Fed. 59 M5 ....72.55N 119.44E
Ustyurt Plateau *f.* Kazakhstan/Uzbekistan 58 G2 .43.29N 56.11E
Utah *d.* U.S.A. 64 D4 ....39.34N 111.34W
Utena Lithuania 46 G5 ....55.30N 25.36E
Utica U.S.A. 65 K5 ....43.06N 75.15W
Utiel Spain 48 E3 ....39.34N 1.11W
Utrecht Neth. 42 E5 ....52.05N 5.07E
Utrecht *d.* Neth. 42 E5 ....52.07N 5.12E
Utrera Spain 48 C2 ....37.11N 5.46W
Utsunomiya Japan 106 C3 ....36.34N 139.54E
Uttaradit Thailand 104 C7 ....17.37N 100.04E
Uttaranchal *d.* India 96 E7 ....30.11N 79.08E
Uttar Pradesh *d.* India 96 E6 ....27.37N 79.17E
Uttoxeter England 10 D3 ....52.54N 1.52W
Uusikaupunki Finland 40 E3 ....60.48N 21.25E
Uvs Nuur *l.* Mongolia 102 G8 ....50.20N 92.39E
Uwajima Japan 106 B2 ....33.13N 132.34E
Uxbridge England 11 E2 ....51.33N 0.29W
Uyuni Bolivia 76 G3 ....20.30S 66.51W
Uyuni, Salar de *f.* Bolivia 76 G3 ....20.13S 67.36W
Uzbekistan Asia 115 M8 ....41.37N 62.17E
Uzhhorod Ukraine 55 J3 ....48.37N 22.17E
Užice S.M. 56 C6 ....43.51N 19.51E
Uzunköprü Turkey 56 G5 ....41.15N 26.41E

V

Vaal *r.* S. Africa 86 B2 ....29.05S 23.39E
Vaasa Finland 40 E3 ....63.06N 21.38E
Vác Hungary 54 H2 ....47.47N 19.09E
Vadodara India 96 D5 ....22.16N 73.14E
Vadsø Norway 40 G5 ....70.05N 29.44E
Vaduz Liechtenstein 54 D2 ....47.08N 9.32E
Værøy *i.* Norway 40 C4 ....67.39N 12.36E
Vaganski Vrh *mt.* Croatia 56 A7 ....44.22N 15.30E
Váh *r.* Slovakia 54 H3 ....47.46N 18.08E
Vaiaku Tuvalu 108 H5 ....8.28S 179.10E
Vaitupu *i.* Tuvalu 108 H5 ....7.27S 178.43E
Valdai Hills Russian Fed. 34 H3 ....57.10N 33.00E
Valdepeñas Spain 48 D3 ....38.46N 3.22W
Valdés, Península *pen.* Argentina 73 C2 ....42.31S 63.25W
Valdez U.S.A. 62 D4 ....61.07N 146.16W
Valdivia Chile 73 B3 ....39.50S 73.13W
Val-d'Or Canada 63 K2 ....48.06N 77.47W

ildosta U.S.A. 65 J3 ...30.51N 83.18W
ldres f. Norway 40 B3 ...60.56N 9.13E
lea lui Mihai Romania 46 F1 ...47.30N 22.09E
lence France 44 E2 ...44.56N 4.54E
lencia Spain 48 E3 ...39.29N 0.21W
lencia Venezuela 72 C8 ...10.10N 67.59W
lencia, Golfo de g. Spain 48 F3 ...39.28N 0.02E
le of Glamorgan d. Wales 9 D2 ...51.26N 3.21W
lenciennes France 44 E7 ...50.21N 3.32E
lera Venezuela 72 B7 ...9.14N 70.35W
ller, Mont mt. France 44 D3 ...42.48N 1.05E
linco, Golfe de b. France 50 C4 ...41.40N 8.52E
linco, Gulf of Italy 44 H2 ...41.40N 8.50E
ljevo S.M. 56 C7 ...44.17N 19.55E
lka Latvia 40 F2 ...57.46N 26.00E
lkeakoski Finland 40 F3 ...61.15N 24.03E
lkenswaard Neth. 42 E4 ...51.21N 5.27E
lladolid Spain 48 D4 ...41.39N 4.43W
lledupar Colombia 72 B8 ...10.30N 73.16W
lle de la Pascua Venezuela 71 K2 ...9.10N 65.57W
lley Wales 12 C5 ...53.17N 4.34W
lparaíso Chile 73 B3 ...33.03S 71.36W
ls, Tanjung c. Indonesia 105 J2 ...8.26S 137.40E
mmala Finland 40 E3 ...61.20N 22.56E
n Turkey 94 F7 ...38.30N 43.22E
n, Lake Turkey 94 F7 ...38.37N 42.47E
ncouver Canada 62 F2 ...49.16N 123.08W
ncouver Island Canada 62 F2 ...49.28N 125.39W
n Diemen Gulf Australia 105 I1 ...11.54S 132.00E
nern l. Sweden 40 C2 ...59.05N 13.36E
nersborg Sweden 40 C2 ...58.23N 12.20E
ngaindrano Madagascar 86 D2 ...23.22S 47.34E
nimo U.S. 105 K3 ...2.42S 141.20E
nnäs Sweden 40 D3 ...63.55N 19.46E
nnes France 44 B5 ...47.39N 2.45W
ntaa Finland 40 F3 ...60.18N 24.57E
nua Levu l. Fiji 111 G5 ...16.10S 179.40E
nuatu S. Pacific Oc. 111 F5 ...16.05S 167.04E
ranasi India 96 F6 ...25.20N 83.04E
rangerfjorden str. Norway 40 G5 ...70.04N 29.07E
raždin Croatia 54 G2 ...46.19N 16.22E
rberg Sweden 40 C2 ...57.07N 12.16E
rdar r. Macedonia 56 E5 ...41.07N 22.32E
rèna Lithuania 46 G5 ...54.13N 24.35E
rese Italy 50 C6 ...45.49N 8.50E
rkaus Finland 40 F3 ...62.19N 27.54E
rna Bulgaria 57 G6 ...43.12N 27.54E
rnamo Sweden 40 C2 ...57.11N 14.03E
rpalota Hungary 54 H2 ...47.12N 18.08E
rasa Barris r. Brazil 77 M5 ...11.02S 37.11W
rsterås Sweden 40 D2 ...59.37N 16.33E
rsterdälälven r. Sweden 40 C3 ...60.32N 15.07E
rstervik Sweden 40 D2 ...57.45N 16.39E
rsyl'kiv Ukraine 55 N4 ...50.11N 30.19E
rtersay i. Scotland 18 B1 ...56.56N 7.38W
rtnajökull ice cap Iceland 40 Y2 ...64.28N 16.37W
rttern l. Sweden 40 C2 ...58.05N 14.21E
rva'u Group is Tonga 108 I4 ...18.24S 174.21W
rwkavysk Belarus 55 K5 ...53.09N 24.27E
rxjö Sweden 40 C2 ...56.53N 14.49E
rechte r. Germany 42 F5 ...52.37N 6.43E
reendam Neth. 42 F6 ...53.06N 6.53E
reenendaal Neth. 42 E5 ...52.01N 5.33E
rega i. Norway 40 B4 ...65.39N 11.53E
rjle Denmark 40 B1 ...55.43N 9.32E
rlen Germany 42 F4 ...51.53N 6.59E
rles Macedonia 56 D5 ...41.42N 21.47E
rléz-Málaga Spain 48 C2 ...36.47N 4.06W
relhas r. Brazil 72 E5 ...17.13S 44.49W
relika Morava canal S.M. 56 D7 ...44.43N 21.03E
relikaya r. Rus. Fed. 55 M7 ...57.50N 28.15E
relikaya r. Rus. Fed. 59 S4 ...64.32N 176.06E
relikiye Luki Rus. Fed. 58 E3 ...56.20N 30.31E
relikiy Novgorod Rus. Fed. 58 E3 ...58.33N 31.16E
reliko Türnovo Bulgaria 56 F6 ...43.05N 25.39E
relino, Monte mt. Italy 50 E5 ...42.09N 13.23E
relizh Rus. Fed. 55 N6 ...55.36N 31.12E
rellore India 96 E3 ...12.56N 79.07E
rel'sk Rus. Fed. 58 F4 ...61.03N 42.05E
relten Germany 46 A4 ...52.41N 13.11E
rendôme France 44 D5 ...47.48N 1.04E
renezuela S. America 71 K2 ...7.35N 66.30W
renezuela, Golfo de g. Venezuela 72 B8 ...11.32N 71.03W
renezuelan Basin f. Caribbean Sea 109 P7 ...15.44N 70.59W
renice Italy 50 E6 ...45.26N 12.20E
renice, Gulf of Europe 50 E6 ...45.19N 12.43E
renray Neth. 42 E4 ...51.31N 5.58E
renta r. Latvia/Lithuania 40 E2 ...56.24N 22.14E
rentnor England 10 D1 ...50.36N 1.12W
rentspils Latvia 40 E2 ...57.23N 21.36E
rera Spain 48 E2 ...37.15N 1.52W
reracruz Mexico 70 E4 ...19.11N 96.09W
reracruz d. Mexico 70 E5 ...20.54N 97.46W
rercelli Italy 50 C6 ...45.19N 8.26E
rerdalsøra Norway 40 B3 ...63.47N 11.29E
rerde r. Brazil 77 J3 ...21.05S 51.58W
rerde r. Paraguay 77 I3 ...23.01S 57.46W
rerde r. Cabo 84 D3 ...33.33N 111.39W
rerdun France 44 F6 ...49.10N 5.24E
rerín Spain 48 B4 ...41.56N 7.25W
rerkhnevilyuysk Rus. Fed. 59 N4 ...63.26N 120.12E
rerkhoyansk Rus. Fed. 59 O4 ...67.32N 133.27E
rerkhoyanskiy Khrebet mts Rus. Fed. 59 N5 ...67.00N 129.00E
rermont d. U.S.A. 65 L5 ...44.03N 72.42W
reroia Greece 56 E5 ...40.32N 22.13E
rerona Italy 50 D6 ...45.26N 10.59E
rersailles France 44 E6 ...48.48N 2.08E
rert, Cap c. Senegal 84 C3 ...14.44N 17.31W
rerviers Belgium 42 E3 ...50.35N 5.52E
rervins France 42 C2 ...49.50N 3.54E
rerwood England 10 D1 ...50.53N 1.52W
resoul France 44 G5 ...47.38N 6.09E
resterålen is Norway 40 C5 ...68.43N 13.59E
restfjorden str. Norway 40 C4 ...67.60N 13.54E
restmannaeyjar is Iceland 40 X1 ...63.24N 20.13W
resturhorn hd Iceland 40 Z2 ...64.15N 14.32W
resuvius vol. Italy 50 F4 ...40.50N 14.26E
reszprém Hungary 46 G4 ...47.06N 17.54E
rettore, Monte mt. Italy 50 E5 ...42.49N 13.17E
reurne Belgium 42 B4 ...51.04N 2.40E
rézère r. France 44 D4 ...44.53N 0.53E
rezirköprü Turkey 57 K5 ...41.09N 35.28E
riana do Castelo Portugal 48 A4 ...41.42N 8.49W
riborg Denmark 40 B2 ...56.27N 9.24E
ribo Valentia Italy 50 G3 ...38.40N 16.06E
ric Spain 48 G4 ...41.56N 2.15E
ricenza Italy 50 D6 ...45.33N 11.33E
rictoria d. Australia 110 D3 ...36.56S 144.52E
rictoria Canada 62 F2 ...48.25N 123.22W
rictoria U.S.A. 64 G2 ...28.49N 96.59W

Victoria, Lake Africa 86 C4 ...0.59S 32.51E
Victoria, Mount Myanmar 97 H5 ...21.11N 93.56E
Victoria, Mount P.N.G. 110 D6 ...8.49S 147.30E
Victoria Falls Zambia/Zimbabwe 86 B3 ...17.49S 25.42E
Victoria Island Canada 62 H5 ...70.42N 106.38W
Victoria Nile r. Uganda 87 A3 ...2.15N 31.21E
Viedma Argentina 73 C2 ...40.50S 63.00W
Viedma, Lago l. Argentina 73 B2 ...49.35S 72.49W
Vienna Austria 54 G3 ...48.12N 16.23E
Vienne France 44 F4 ...45.31N 4.53E
Vienne r. France 44 D5 ...47.13N 0.05E
Vientiane Laos 104 C7 ...17.58N 102.37E
Vierzon France 44 E5 ...47.14N 2.04E
Vieste Italy 50 G4 ...41.53N 16.11E
Vietnam Asia 104 D7 ...19.20N 104.48E
Vignemale mt. France 44 C3 ...42.46N 0.09W
Vigo Spain 48 A5 ...42.14N 8.43W
Vijayawada India 96 F4 ...16.33N 80.39E
Vík Iceland 40 Y1 ...63.26N 19.02W
Vikna i. Norway 40 B4 ...64.53N 10.50E
Vilagarcía de Arousa Spain 48 A5 ...42.36N 8.45W
Vilaine r. France 44 B5 ...47.35N 2.16W
Vila Real Portugal 48 B4 ...41.18N 7.44W
Vila Velha Brazil 77 L3 ...20.22S 40.20W
Vilcabamba, Cordillera mts Peru 76 F5 ...12.30S 73.27W
Vilhelmina Sweden 40 D4 ...64.37N 16.41E
Vilhena Brazil 77 H5 ...12.42S 60.07W
Viljandi Estonia 40 F2 ...58.22N 25.35E
Vilkaviškis Lithuania 46 F5 ...54.39N 23.03E
Vilkija Lithuania 46 F5 ...55.03N 23.35E
Vil'kitskogo, Proliv str. Rus. Fed. 59 K5 ...77.30N 98.42E
Villach Austria 54 E2 ...46.37N 13.50E
Villahermosa Mexico 70 F4 ...18.00N 92.53W
Villa Insurgentes Mexico 70 B6 ...25.16N 111.47W
Villa Montes Bolivia 76 H3 ...21.14S 63.30W
Villaputzu Italy 50 C3 ...39.26N 9.35E
Villarrica Paraguay 77 I2 ...25.43S 56.25W
Villarrobledo Spain 48 D3 ...39.16N 2.36W
Villavicencio Colombia 72 B7 ...4.07N 73.36W
Villefranche-sur-Saône France 44 F4 ...45.59N 4.44E
Villena Spain 48 E3 ...38.38N 0.51W
Villeneuve-sur-Lot France 44 D4 ...44.25N 0.42E
Villers-Cotterêts France 42 C2 ...49.15N 3.06E
Villeurbanne France 44 F4 ...45.46N 4.54E
Vilnius Lithuania 40 F1 ...54.40N 25.16E
Vilvoorde Belgium 42 D3 ...50.55N 4.27E
Vilyuy r. Rus. Fed. 59 N4 ...64.24N 126.28E
Viña del Mar Chile 76 F1 ...33.02S 71.34W
Vindelälven r. Sweden 40 D3 ...63.56N 19.51E
Vinh Vietnam 104 D7 ...18.38N 105.42E
Vinkovci Croatia 56 C7 ...45.17N 18.49E
Vinnytsya Ukraine 55 M3 ...49.14N 28.30E
Viranşehir Turkey 57 M3 ...37.13N 39.47E
Virden Canada 64 F6 ...49.51N 100.56W
Vire France 44 C6 ...48.50N 0.53W
Virginia d. U.S.A. 65 K4 ...37.47N 78.19W
Virgin Islands (U.K.) Central America 71 L4 ...18.37N 64.37W
Virgin Islands (U.S.A.) Central America 71 L4 ...18.14N 64.53W
Virovitica Croatia 56 B7 ...45.50N 17.23E
Virton Belgium 42 E2 ...49.34N 5.33E
Vis i. Croatia 56 B6 ...43.05N 16.06E
Visaginas Lithuania 55 L6 ...55.36N 26.26E
Visby Sweden 40 D2 ...57.38N 18.18E
Viscount Melville Sound str. Canada 62 G5 ...73.50N 112.57W
Viseu Portugal 48 B4 ...40.40N 7.55W
Vishakhapatnam India 96 F4 ...17.42N 83.22E
Viso, Monte mt. Italy 50 B6 ...44.40N 7.06E
Viterbo Italy 50 E4 ...42.24N 12.07E
Viti Levu i. Fiji 111 G5 ...18.05S 177.19E
Vitim r. Rus. Fed. 59 M3 ...59.26N 112.35E
Vitória Brazil 77 L3 ...20.19S 40.21W
Vitória da Conquista Brazil 77 L5 ...14.50S 40.47W
Vitoria-Gasteiz Spain 48 D5 ...42.51N 2.39W
Vitsyebsk Belarus 55 N6 ...55.12N 30.10E
Vittel France 44 F6 ...48.12N 5.57E
Vizianagaram India 96 F4 ...18.08N 83.31E
Vlaams-Brabant d. Belgium 42 D3 ...50.56N 4.36E
Vlaardingen Neth. 42 D4 ...51.54N 4.21E
Vlădeasa, Vârful mt. Romania 55 J2 ...46.45N 22.50E
Vladimir Rus. Fed. 58 F3 ...56.08N 40.24E
Vladivostok Rus. Fed. 59 O2 ...43.07N 131.56E
Vlieland i. Neth. 42 D6 ...53.16N 4.57E
Vlissingen Neth. 42 C3 ...51.27N 3.34E
Vlorë Albania 56 C5 ...40.28N 19.30E
Vltava r. Czech Rep. 54 F4 ...50.19N 14.29E
Voe Scotland 19 H5 ...60.21N 1.16W
Vohimena, Tanjona c. Madagascar 86 D2 ...25.36S 45.12E
Voi Kenya 87 B2 ...3.24S 38.35E
Volcano Islands Japan 108 F7 ...24.53N 140.34E
Volda Norway 40 A3 ...62.08N 6.05E
Volga r. Rus. Fed. 58 F2 ...45.47N 47.34E
Volga Uplands hills Rus. Fed. 35 I3 ...53.15N 45.45E
Volgograd Rus. Fed. 58 F2 ...48.44N 44.30E
Völklingen Germany 42 F2 ...49.15N 6.51E
Volodymyr-Volyns'kyy Ukraine 55 K4 ...50.51N 24.20E
Vologda Rus. Fed. 58 F3 ...59.13N 39.54E
Volos Greece 56 E4 ...39.22N 22.57E
Volta, Lake resr Ghana 84 E2 ...6.23N 0.05E
Volta Redonda Brazil 77 L3 ...22.30S 44.07W
Volzhskiy Rus. Fed. 58 G3 ...53.24N 50.08E
Voreioi Sporades is Greece 56 E4 ...39.15N 23.27E
Vorkuta Rus. Fed. 58 I4 ...67.29N 64.05E
Voronezh Rus. Fed. 58 E3 ...51.38N 39.12E
Vorskla r. Rus. Fed. 55 P3 ...48.55N 34.08E
Vosges mts France 44 G5 ...47.46N 6.41E
Voss Norway 40 A3 ...60.38N 6.27E
Vostochnyy Sayan mts Rus. Fed. 59 K3 ...54.43N 94.48E
Vostok Island Kiribati 109 J5 ...10.04S 152.25W
Vouziers France 42 D2 ...49.24N 4.42E
Voznesens'k Ukraine 55 N2 ...47.33N 31.21E
Vranje S.M. 56 D6 ...42.33N 21.54E
Vratsa Bulgaria 56 E6 ...43.12N 23.33E
Vrbas r. Bos.-Herz. 56 B7 ...45.07N 17.31E
Vršac S.M. 56 D7 ...45.07N 21.17E
Vung Tau Vietnam 104 D6 ...10.22N 107.05E
Vuollerim Sweden 40 E4 ...66.26N 20.37E
Vyatka r. Rus. Fed. 58 G3 ...58.36N 49.41E
Vyaz'ma Rus. Fed. 55 P6 ...55.13N 34.18E
Vyborg Rus. Fed. 40 G3 ...60.42N 28.46E
Vychegda r. Russian Fed. 35 I4 ...61.15N 46.28E
Vyrnwy, Lake Wales 12 D4 ...52.46N 3.29W
Vyškov Czech Rep. 46 C2 ...49.16N 17.00E
Vyžuona r. Lithuania 46 G5 ...55.34N 25.31E

W

Wa Ghana 84 D3 ...10.04N 2.30W
Wabasca r. Canada 62 G3 ...58.18N 115.23W
Wabash r. U.S.A. 65 I4 ...37.50N 88.01W
Wabē Gestro r. Ethiopia 87 C4 ...4.19N 42.03E
Wabē Mena r. Ethiopia 87 C4 ...5.32N 41.12E

Wabush Canada 63 L3 ...52.51N 66.49W
Waco U.S.A. 64 G3 ...31.34N 97.08W
Wad Pakistan 96 C6 ...27.20N 66.30E
Waddān Libya 84 F4 ...29.09N 16.09E
Waddenzee str. Neth. 42 D5 ...52.51N 4.51E
Waddington England 15 G2 ...53.11N 0.32W
Waddington, Mount Canada 62 F3 ...51.21N 125.18W
Wadebridge England 13 C2 ...50.31N 4.50W
Wadhurst England 11 F2 ...51.04N 0.20E
Wadi Halfa Sudan 85 H4 ...21.48N 31.20E
Wad Medani Sudan 85 H3 ...14.22N 33.30E
Wagga Wagga Australia 110 D3 ...35.08S 147.23E
Wahât Jālū Libya 53 H2 ...29.14N 21.04E
Wahpeton U.S.A. 64 G6 ...46.15N 96.50W
Waigeo i. Indonesia 105 I3 ...0.11S 130.59E
Wainfleet All Saints England 15 H2 ...53.06N 0.14E
Waingapu Indonesia 104 G2 ...9.38S 120.15E
Waini Point Guyana 72 D7 ...8.22N 59.44W
Wainwright U.S.A. 62 C5 ...70.39N 159.51W
Wajir Kenya 87 C3 ...1.44N 40.03E
Wakasa-wan b. Japan 106 C3 ...35.45N 135.36E
Wakayama Japan 106 C3 ...34.13N 135.10E
Wakefield England 15 F2 ...53.41N 1.30W
Wake Island N. Pacific Oc. 108 H7 ...19.18N 166.39E
Wakkanai Japan 106 D5 ...45.24N 141.40E
Wafbrzych Poland 46 C3 ...50.46N 16.18E
Wałcz Poland 46 C4 ...53.17N 16.29E
Wales d. U.K. 9 D3 ...52.04N 3.41W
Wallasey England 14 D2 ...53.26N 3.04W
Wallingford England 10 D2 ...51.36N 1.08W
Wallis and Futuna Islands S. Pacific Oc. 108 I5 ...13.24S 177.57W
Walls Scotland 19 H5 ...60.14N 1.33W
Walney, Isle of i. England 14 D3 ...54.04N 3.16W
Walsall England 10 D3 ...52.35N 1.59W
Waltham on the Wolds England 10 E3 ...52.49N 0.49W
Walton-on-Thames England 11 E2 ...51.23N 0.25W
Walvis Bay town Namibia 86 A2 ...22.58S 14.30E
Wandsworth England 11 E2 ...51.27N 0.12W
Wangqing China 106 A4 ...43.19N 129.44E
Wantage England 10 D2 ...51.35N 1.25W
Warangal India 96 E4 ...17.59N 79.35E
Warboys England 11 E3 ...52.24N 0.05W
Warburton watercourse Australia 110 C4 ...27.54S 137.19E
Ward Hill Scotland 19 F3 ...58.54N 3.22W
Ward's Stone hill England 14 E3 ...54.02N 2.38W
Wareham England 10 C1 ...50.41N 2.07W
Waremme Belgium 42 E3 ...50.42N 5.15E
Warka Poland 46 E3 ...51.47N 21.11E
Warlingham England 11 E2 ...51.19N 0.03W
Warminster England 10 C2 ...51.12N 2.11W
Warrego r. Australia 110 D3 ...30.24S 145.21E
Warrenpoint Northern Ireland 16 C2 ...54.06N 6.15W
Warrington England 14 E2 ...53.23N 2.36W
Warrington d. England 9 D3 ...53.24N 2.33W
Warsaw Poland 46 E4 ...52.15N 21.01E
Warta r. Poland 46 C4 ...52.35N 14.37E
Warwick England 10 D3 ...52.17N 1.35W
Warwickshire d. England 9 E3 ...52.19N 1.32W
Washington England 15 F3 ...54.54N 1.30W
Washington U.S.A. 65 K4 ...38.54N 77.01W
Washington d. U.S.A. 64 B6 ...47.36N 120.19W
Washington, Mount U.S.A. 65 L5 ...44.18N 71.18W
Waskaganish Canada 63 K3 ...51.28N 78.46W
Wast Water l. England 14 D3 ...54.26N 3.18W
Watampone Indonesia 104 G3 ...4.31S 120.21E
Watchet England 13 D3 ...51.11N 3.20W
Waterford Rep. of Ireland 41 D2 ...52.15N 7.07W
Waterford d. Rep. of Ireland 41 D2 ...52.10N 7.53W
Watergate Bay England 13 B2 ...50.27N 5.05W
Waterlooville England 10 D1 ...50.53N 1.02W
Water of Saughs r. Scotland 19 G1 ...56.47N 2.37W
Watertown U.S.A. 64 G5 ...44.53N 97.07W
Watford England 11 E2 ...51.39N 0.23W
Watlington England 10 D2 ...51.38N 1.00W
Watson Lake town Canada 62 F4 ...60.05N 128.42W
Watten, Loch l. Scotland 19 F3 ...58.29N 3.21W
Watton England 11 F3 ...52.34N 0.50E
Wau Sudan 85 G2 ...7.40N 27.59E
Wausau U.S.A. 65 I5 ...44.58N 89.37W
Waveney r. England 11 G3 ...52.29N 1.41E
Wear r. England 15 F3 ...54.54N 1.27W
Weber Basin f. Indonesia 108 E5 ...5.42S 130.54E
Webi Shabeelle r. Somalia 85 I2 ...0.10N 42.46E
Webuye Kenya 87 A3 ...0.37N 34.44E
Wedmore England 10 C2 ...51.14N 2.49W
Weener Germany 42 G6 ...53.10N 7.21E
Weert Neth. 42 E4 ...51.15N 5.43E
Wegorzewo Poland 46 E5 ...54.13N 21.45E
Weifang China 103 L5 ...36.42N 119.03E
Weihai China 103 M5 ...37.30N 122.07E
Weinan China 103 J4 ...34.27N 109.33E
Weipa Australia 105 K1 ...12.37S 141.55E
Wejherowo Poland 46 D5 ...54.36N 18.14E
Weldiya Ethiopia 85 H3 ...11.49N 39.36E
Welkom S. Africa 86 B2 ...27.59S 26.44E
Welland r. England 11 E3 ...52.52N 0.03W
Wellesley Islands Australia 110 C5 ...16.18S 139.33E
Wellingborough England 10 E3 ...52.18N 0.42W
Wellington Som. England 13 D2 ...50.59N 3.13W
Wellington Tel. Wre. England 10 C3 ...52.42N 2.31W
Wellington New Zealand 111 G2 ...41.18S 174.46E
Wells England 10 C2 ...51.13N 2.39W
Wells, Lake Australia 110 B4 ...26.40S 123.16E
Wells-next-the-Sea England 11 F3 ...52.57N 0.51E
Wels Austria 54 F3 ...48.10N 14.01E
Welshpool Wales 12 D4 ...52.40N 3.09W
Welwyn Garden City England 11 E2 ...51.48N 0.12W
Wem England 10 C3 ...52.51N 2.44W
Wembley England 11 E2 ...51.33N 0.18W
Wemel Shet' r. Ethiopia 87 C4 ...5.41N 40.58E
Wemyss Bay town Scotland 16 E3 ...55.53N 4.53W
Wenchi Ghana 84 D2 ...7.45N 2.07W
Wendo Ethiopia 85 H2 ...6.35N 38.25E
Wendover England 10 E2 ...51.46N 0.44W
Wenlock Edge f. England 10 C3 ...52.27N 2.49W
Wensleydale f. England 15 E3 ...54.09N 2.02W
Wensum r. England 11 G3 ...52.37N 1.20E
Wenzhou China 103 M3 ...27.59N 120.41E
Wesel Germany 42 F4 ...51.40N 6.38E
Weser r. Germany 54 C5 ...53.15N 8.29E
Wessel, Cape Australia 105 C5 ...11.03S 136.46E
Wessel Islands Australia 110 C5 ...11.19S 136.26E
West Australian Basin f. Indian Oc. 117 O5 ...17.42S 102.36E
West Bank Asia 53 N3 ...31.52N 35.19E
West Bengal d. India 96 G5 ...22.34N 87.20E
West Berkshire d. England 9 E2 ...51.28N 1.20W
West Bridgford England 10 D3 ...52.56N 1.08W
West Bromwich England 10 D3 ...52.31N 1.59W
Westbury England 10 C2 ...51.15N 2.11W
West Calder Scotland 17 F3 ...55.51N 3.34W
West Caroline Basin f. N. Pacific Oc. 108 F6 ...2.42N 136.26E
West Dunbartonshire d. Scotland 8 C4 ...55.59N 4.31W
Western d. Kenya 87 A3 ...0.22N 34.35E

Western Australia d. Australia 110 B4 ...24.24S 121.53E
Western Desert Egypt 53 I2 ...26.42N 29.45E
Western Dvina r. Europe 55 N6 ...55.28N 30.54E
Western Ghats mts India 96 D3 ...14.19N 74.54E
Western Isles d. Scotland 8 B6 ...58.15N 6.33W
Western Sahara Africa 84 C4 ...22.14N 15.05W
Wester Ross f. Scotland 18 D2 ...57.39N 5.20W
Westerschelde est. Neth. 42 C4 ...51.27N 3.27E
West Falkland i. Falkland Is 73 C1 ...51.16S 61.32W
West Fen f. Cambs. England 11 F3 ...52.32N 0.00E
West Fen f. Lincs. England 15 G3 ...53.04N 0.05W
West Frisian Islands Neth. 42 D6 ...53.11N 4.37E
Westhill Scotland 19 G2 ...57.09N 2.17W
West Kirby England 14 D2 ...53.22N 3.11W
West Lavington England 10 D2 ...51.17N 1.59W
West Linton Scotland 17 F3 ...55.45N 3.21W
West Loch Roag b. Scotland 18 C3 ...58.15N 6.57W
West Lothian d. Scotland 8 D4 ...55.54N 3.31W
West Malling England 11 F2 ...51.18N 0.25E
West Mariana Basin f. N. Pacific Oc. 108 F7 ...17.32N 140.09E
Westmeath d. Rep. of Ireland 41 D3 ...53.34N 7.24W
West Mersea England 11 F2 ...51.47N 0.56E
West Midlands d. England 9 E3 ...52.28N 1.49W
Weston-super-Mare England 10 C2 ...51.21N 2.59W
West Palm Beach town U.S.A. 65 J2 ...26.40N 80.09W
Westport Rep. of Ireland 41 B3 ...53.48N 9.31W
Westray i. Scotland 19 F4 ...59.18N 3.02W
Westray Firth str. Scotland 19 F4 ...59.16N 3.07W
West Siberian Plain f. Rus. Fed. 58 J4 ...62.39N 80.21E
West Sussex d. England 9 E2 ...51.00N 0.18W
West-Terschelling Neth. 42 E6 ...53.22N 5.13E
West Virginia d. U.S.A. 65 J4 ...38.45N 80.27W
West-Vlaanderen d. Belgium 42 B3 ...50.59N 2.56E
Westward Ho! England 13 C3 ...51.02N 4.14W
West Yorkshire d. England 9 D3 ...53.46N 2.04W
Wetar i. Indonesia 105 H2 ...7.49S 126.13E
Wete Tanzania 87 B1 ...5.04S 39.43E
Wetherby England 15 F2 ...53.56N 1.23W
Wetzlar Germany 44 H7 ...50.34N 8.30E
Wexford Rep. of Ireland 41 E2 ...52.20N 6.28W
Wexford d. Rep. of Ireland 41 E2 ...52.37N 6.32W
Wexford Bay Rep. of Ireland 41 E2 ...52.25N 6.19W
Weybridge England 11 E2 ...51.22N 0.27W
Weyburn Canada 64 F6 ...49.40N 103.52W
Weymouth England 10 C1 ...50.37N 2.27W
Whalsay i. Scotland 19 I5 ...60.21N 0.57W
Whangarei New Zealand 111 G3 ...35.43S 174.19E
Wharfe r. England 15 F2 ...53.50N 1.08W
Wheeler Peak N. M. U.S.A. 64 E4 ...36.33N 105.24W
Wheeler Peak Nev. U.S.A. 64 D4 ...38.57N 114.17W
Whernside hill England 15 E3 ...54.14N 2.24W
Whitburn England 17 F3 ...55.52N 3.41W
Whitby England 15 G3 ...54.29N 0.37W
Whitchurch England 10 C3 ...52.58N 2.41W
Whitchurch Wales 13 D3 ...51.31N 3.13W
White r. U.S.A. 65 H3 ...33.59N 91.09W
White, Lake Australia 110 B4 ...21.03S 129.07E
Whitecourt Canada 62 G3 ...54.08N 115.43W
Whitehaven England 14 D3 ...54.33N 3.35W
Whitehead Northern Ireland 16 D2 ...54.45N 5.42W
Whitehill England 10 E2 ...51.06N 0.52W
Whitehorse Canada 62 E4 ...60.44N 135.06W
White Nile r. Sudan/Uganda 85 H3 ...15.38N 32.30E
White Sea Rus. Fed. 58 E4 ...65.51N 36.58E
White Volta r. Burkina/Ghana 84 D2 ...9.07N 1.10W
Whitfield England 11 G2 ...51.09N 1.17E
Whithorn Scotland 16 E2 ...54.44N 4.25W
Whitland Wales 12 C3 ...51.49N 4.37W
Whitley Bay town England 15 F4 ...55.03N 1.27W
Whitney, Mount U.S.A. 64 C4 ...36.35N 118.16W
Whitsand Bay England 13 C2 ...50.20N 4.20W
Whitstable England 11 G2 ...51.22N 1.01E
Whittlesey England 11 E3 ...52.34N 0.08W
Whyalla Australia 110 C3 ...33.03S 137.31E
Wichita U.S.A. 64 G4 ...37.42N 97.20W
Wichita Falls town U.S.A. 64 G3 ...33.55N 98.29W
Wick Scotland 19 F3 ...58.26N 3.06W
Wick r. Scotland 19 F3 ...58.26N 3.05W
Wickford England 11 F2 ...51.37N 0.31E
Wickham England 10 D1 ...50.54N 1.11W
Wickham Market England 11 G3 ...52.09N 1.22E
Wicklow Rep. of Ireland 41 E2 ...52.59N 6.02W
Wicklow d. Rep. of Ireland 41 E3 ...53.02N 6.27W
Wicklow Head Rep. of Ireland 41 E2 ...52.58N 5.59W
Wicklow Mountains Rep. of Ireland 41 E2 ...52.53N 6.34W
Widecombe in the Moor England 13 D2 ...50.34N 3.49W
Wide Firth str. Scotland 19 F4 ...59.01N 3.02W
Widnes England 14 E2 ...53.21N 2.44W
Wielka Sowa mt. Poland 46 C3 ...50.40N 16.29E
Wieluń Poland 46 D3 ...51.13N 18.34E
Wiener Neustadt Austria 54 G2 ...47.49N 16.15E
Wieprz r. Poland 46 E3 ...51.32N 21.50E
Wiesbaden Germany 54 C4 ...50.05N 8.14E
Wiesmoor Germany 42 G6 ...53.25N 7.45E
Wieżyca hill Poland 46 D5 ...54.14N 18.08E
Wigan England 14 E2 ...53.33N 2.38W
Wight, Isle of i. England 10 D1 ...50.39N 1.07W
Wigston England 10 D3 ...52.35N 1.06W
Wigton England 14 D3 ...54.50N 3.10W
Wigtown Scotland 16 E2 ...54.52N 4.27W
Wigtown Bay Scotland 16 E2 ...54.48N 4.19W
Wijchen Neth. 42 E4 ...51.48N 5.43E
Wildhorn mt. Switz. 50 B7 ...46.22N 7.22E
Wilhelm, Mount P.N.G. 110 D6 ...5.46S 144.52E
Wilhelmshaven Germany 54 C5 ...53.32N 8.08E
Willebroek Belgium 42 D4 ...51.03N 4.22E
William, Mount Australia 110 D3 ...37.19S 142.35E
Williams Lake town Canada 62 F3 ...52.08N 122.09W
Willingdon England 11 F1 ...50.48N 0.15E
Williston U.S.A. 64 F6 ...48.10N 103.37W
Williston Lake Canada 62 F3 ...55.51N 123.43W
Williton England 13 D3 ...51.10N 3.19W
Wills, Lake Australia 110 B4 ...21.20S 128.37E
Wilmington Del. U.S.A. 65 K4 ...39.43N 75.38W
Wilmington N. C. U.S.A. 65 K3 ...34.13N 77.58W
Wilmslow England 15 E2 ...53.20N 2.14W
Wilson's Promontory pen. Australia 110 D3 ...38.55S 146.27E
Wilton England 10 D2 ...51.05N 1.52W
Wiltshire d. England 9 E2 ...51.24N 1.53W
Wiltz Lux. 42 E2 ...49.58N 5.56E
Wimblington England 11 F3 ...52.31N 0.05E
Wimborne Minster England 10 D1 ...50.48N 1.59W
Wimereux France 11 G1 ...50.46N 1.37E
Winam Gulf Kenya 87 A2 ...0.20S 34.24E
Wincanton England 10 C2 ...51.03N 2.25W
Winchester England 10 D2 ...51.04N 1.19W
Windermere England 14 E3 ...54.23N 2.54W
Windermere l. England 14 E3 ...54.18N 2.57W
Windhoek Namibia 86 A2 ...22.34S 17.04E
Windrush r. England 10 D2 ...51.43N 1.25W
Windsor Canada 65 J5 ...42.18N 83.01W
Windsor England 11 E2 ...51.29N 0.37W
Windsor and Maidenhead d. England 9 E2 ...51.28N 0.40W
Windward Islands Caribbean Sea 71 L4 ...15.42N 60.03W

Windward Passage *str.* Cuba/Haiti 71 J4 ....19.40N 74.11W
Wingate England 15 F3 ....54.44N 1.23W
Winisk *r.* Canada 63 J3 ....55.01N 85.22W
Winkleigh England 13 D2 ....50.51N 3.57W
Winnebago, Lake U.S.A. 65 I5 ....44.00N 88.28W
Winnemucca U.S.A. 64 C5 ....40.59N 117.44W
Winnipeg Canada 62 I2 ....49.53N 97.10W
Winnipeg, Lake Canada 62 I3 ....51.31N 96.40W
Winnipegosis, Lake Canada 62 H3 ....53.05N 100.40W
Winsford England 15 E2 ....53.12N 2.31W
Winslow England 10 E2 ....51.57N 0.53W
Winslow U.S.A. 64 D4 ....35.02N 110.42W
Winston-Salem U.S.A. 65 J4 ....36.07N 80.17W
Winterswijk Neth. 42 F4 ....51.58N 6.42E
Winterthur Switz. 50 C7 ....47.30N 8.43E
Winterton England 15 G2 ....53.39N 0.36W
Wirksworth England 15 F2 ....53.05N 1.34W
Wirral *pen.* England 14 D2 ....53.22N 3.07W
Wisbech England 11 F3 ....52.40N 0.10E
Wisconsin *d.* U.S.A. 65 I5 ....44.30N 89.32W
Wishaw Scotland 17 F3 ....55.46N 3.55W
Wismar Germany 54 D5 ....53.53N 11.28E
Witham England 11 F2 ....51.48N 0.38E
Witham *r.* England 11 F3 ....52.56N 0.05E
Witheridge England 13 D2 ....50.55N 3.42W
Withernsea England 15 H2 ....53.44N 0.02E
Witney England 10 D2 ....51.47N 1.29W
Wittenberge Germany 54 D5 ....52.59N 11.45E
Wittlich Germany 42 F2 ....49.59N 6.53E
Wittmund Germany 42 G6 ....53.35N 7.47E
Witu Kenya 87 C2 ....2.23S 40.27E
Wiveliscombe England 13 D3 ....51.03N 3.19W
Wivenhoe England 11 F2 ....51.51N 0.58E
Wkra *r.* Poland 46 E4 ....52.27N 20.45E
Władysławowo Poland 46 D5 ....54.47N 18.25E
Włocławek Poland 46 D4 ....52.39N 19.05E
Włodawa Poland 46 F3 ....51.33N 23.33E
Wokam *i.* Indonesia 105 I2 ....5.45S 134.31E
Woking England 11 E2 ....51.19N 0.34W
Wokingham England 10 E2 ....51.25N 0.50W
Wokingham *d.* England 9 E2 ....51.24N 0.53W
Wolfsberg Austria 54 F2 ....46.50N 14.51E
Wolfsburg Germany 54 D5 ....52.25N 10.48E
Wolgast Germany 46 A5 ....54.03N 13.47E
Wolin Poland 46 B4 ....53.51N 14.36E
Wollaston Lake Canada 62 H3 ....58.16N 103.22W
Wollongong Australia 110 E3 ....34.25S 150.51E
Wolsingham England 15 F3 ....54.44N 1.53W
Wolvega Neth. 42 F5 ....52.53N 6.00E
Wolverhampton England 10 C3 ....52.35N 2.08W
Wombwell England 15 F2 ....53.31N 1.24W
Wŏnsan N. Korea 103 N5 ....39.09N 127.27E
Woodbridge England 11 G3 ....52.06N 1.19E
Woodcote England 10 D2 ....51.32N 1.04W
Woodhall Spa England 15 G2 ....53.09N 0.13W
Woodlark Island P.N.G. 110 E6 ....8.58S 152.47E
Woods, Lake of the Canada/U.S.A. 63 I2 ....49.22N 94.50W
Woodstock England 10 D2 ....51.51N 1.21W
Wooler England 15 E4 ....55.33N 2.01W
Wootton Bassett England 10 D2 ....51.32N 1.54W
Worcester S. Africa 86 A1 ....33.38S 19.27E
Worcester England 10 C3 ....52.12N 2.13W
Worcester U.S.A. 65 L5 ....42.16N 71.48W
Worcestershire *d.* England 9 D3 ....52.12N 2.12W
Wörgl Austria 54 E2 ....47.29N 12.05E
Workington England 14 D3 ....54.39N 3.32W
Worksop England 15 F2 ....53.19N 1.07W
Worms Germany 44 H6 ....49.38N 8.21E
Worms Head Wales 12 C3 ....51.34N 4.21W
Worth England 11 E2 ....51.07N 0.09W
Worthing England 11 E1 ....50.49N 0.22W
Wowoni *i.* Indonesia 105 G3 ....4.09S 123.13E
Wragby England 15 G2 ....53.17N 0.18W
Wrangel Island Rus. Fed. 59 T5 ....71.07N 178.56W
Wrangell U.S.A. 62 E3 ....56.28N 132.22W
Wrangle England 15 H2 ....53.02N 0.07E
Wreake *r.* England 10 D3 ....52.42N 1.06W
Wrexham Wales 12 E5 ....53.03N 2.59W
Wrexham *d.* Wales 9 D3 ....53.01N 2.59W
Wrigley Canada 62 F4 ....63.12N 123.24W
Wrocław Poland 46 C3 ....51.06N 17.02E
Września Poland 46 C4 ....52.19N 17.34E
Wuhai China 103 J5 ....39.36N 106.53E
Wuhan China 103 K4 ....30.37N 114.18E
Wuhu China 103 L4 ....31.21N 118.25E
Wuppertal Germany 42 G4 ....51.16N 7.09E
Würzburg Germany 54 C3 ....49.48N 9.55E
Wuvulu Island P.N.G. 105 K3 ....1.43S 142.50E
Wuwei China 103 I5 ....37.52N 102.38E
Wuxi China 103 M4 ....31.31N 120.18E
Wuzhou China 103 K2 ....23.28N 111.22E

Wye England 11 F2 ....51.11N 0.56E
Wye *r.* Wales 12 E3 ....51.37N 2.40W
Wylye *r.* England 10 D2 ....51.04N 1.48W
Wymondham England 11 G3 ....52.34N 1.07E
Wyndham Australia 110 B5 ....15.29S 128.05E
Wynyard Canada 64 F7 ....51.46N 104.12W
Wyoming *d.* U.S.A. 64 E5 ....42.57N 107.30W
Wyszków Poland 46 E4 ....52.36N 21.28E
Wythall England 10 D3 ....52.23N 1.53W

X

Xai-Xai Mozambique 86 C2 ....25.02S 33.41E
Xankändi Azerbaijan 95 G7 ....39.49N 46.46E
Xanthi Greece 56 F5 ....41.09N 24.53E
Xavantes, Serra dos *hills* Brazil 77 K5 ....12.34S 49.14W
Xiamen China 103 L2 ....24.29N 118.11E
Xi'an China 103 J4 ....34.12N 108.59E
Xiangfan China 103 K4 ....32.03N 112.07E
Xiangkhoang Laos 104 C7 ....19.21N 103.23E
Xiangtan China 103 K3 ....27.52N 112.47E
Xichang China 103 I3 ....27.55N 102.11E
Xigazê China 102 F3 ....29.17N 88.45E
Xi Jiang *r.* China 90 I4 ....22.23N 113.28E
Xilinhot China 103 L6 ....43.54N 116.08E
Xingtai China 103 K5 ....37.01N 114.33E
Xingu *r.* Brazil 77 J7 ....1.37S 52.12W
Xining China 103 I5 ....36.35N 101.40E
Xinjiang Uygur Zizhiqu *d.* China 102 D6 ....40.15N 78.50E
Xintai China 103 L5 ....35.55N 117.45E
Xinxiang China 103 K5 ....35.14N 113.54E
Xizang Zizhiqu *d.* China 102 F4 ....31.26N 88.12E
Xun Jiang *r.* China 103 K2 ....23.27N 111.25E
Xuwen China 104 E8 ....20.18N 110.09E

Y

Yabēlo Ethiopia 87 B4 ....4.51N 38.08E
Yabēlo Wildlife Sanctuary *nature res.* Ethiopia 87 B4
Yablonovyy Khrebet *mts* Rus. Fed. 59 L3 ....50.48N 108.47E
Yacuma *r.* Bolivia 76 G5 ....13.39S 65.25W
Yakima U.S.A. 64 B6 ....46.36N 120.29W
Yakumo Japan 106 D4 ....42.15N 140.15E
Yaku-shima *i.* Japan 106 B2 ....30.15N 130.36E
Yakutsk Rus. Fed. 59 N4 ....61.59N 129.40E
Yala Thailand 104 C5 ....6.32N 101.17E
Yalova Turkey 57 H5 ....40.39N 29.17E
Yalta Ukraine 55 K7 ....44.30N 34.11E
Yamagata Japan 106 D3 ....38.15N 140.20E
Yamal Peninsula Rus. Fed. 58 H5 ....70.40N 69.23E
Yambol Bulgaria 56 G6 ....42.29N 26.30E
Yamoussoukro Côte d'Ivoire 84 D2 ....6.48N 5.15W
Yamuna *r.* India 96 F6 ....25.26N 81.57E
Yana *r.* Rus. Fed. 59 O5 ....71.09N 135.57E
Yanbu' al Baḥr Saudi Arabia 94 E4 ....24.05N 38.06E
Yangôn Myanmar 97 I4 ....16.49N 96.08E
Yangquan China 103 K5 ....37.52N 113.33E
Yanji China 103 N6 ....42.54N 129.31E
Yanskiy Zaliv *g.* Rus. Fed. 59 O5 ....71.55N 135.13E
Yantai China 103 M5 ....37.30N 121.21E
Yaoundé Cameroon 84 F2 ....3.51N 11.30E
Yap *i.* Micronesia 105 J5 ....9.30N 138.12E
Yapen *i.* Indonesia 105 J3 ....1.46S 136.12E
Yap Trench *f.* N. Pacific Oc. 108 F6 ....7.14N 136.38E
Yaqui *r.* Mexico 70 B6 ....27.36N 110.36W
Yare *r.* England 11 G3 ....52.35N 1.38E
Yaren Nauru 108 H5 ....0.33S 166.55E
Yarm England 15 F3 ....54.30N 1.21W
Yarmouth Canada 63 L2 ....43.50N 66.07W
Yarmouth England 10 D1 ....50.42N 1.30W
Yaroslavl' Rus. Fed. 58 E3 ....57.37N 39.53E
Yartsevo Rus. Fed. 55 O6 ....55.04N 32.41E
Yasawa Group *is* Fiji 111 G5 ....16.56S 177.18E
Yasyel'da *r.* Belarus 55 L5 ....52.08N 26.27E
Yatağan Turkey 57 H3 ....37.20N 28.09E
Yata Plateau *f.* Kenya 87 B2 ....1.20S 37.42E
Yate England 10 C2 ....51.32N 2.25W
Yatton England 10 C2 ....51.23N 2.49W
Yavari *r.* Brazil/Peru 76 G7 ....4.18S 69.59W
Yaví, Cerro *mt.* Venezuela 72 C7 ....5.32N 65.58W
Yavoriv Ukraine 46 F2 ....49.57N 23.25E
Yawatahama Japan 106 B2 ....33.27N 132.24E
Yazd Iran 95 H6 ....31.53N 54.21E
Yealmpton England 13 D2 ....50.21N 3.59W
YeDebub Bihēroch Bihēreseboch na Hizboch *d.* Ethiopia 87 B4
                                                6.14N 36.32E
Yekaterinburg Rus. Fed. 58 H3 ....56.53N 60.35E

Yell *i.* Scotland 19 H5 ....60.35N 1.06W
Yellowknife Canada 62 G4 ....62.29N 114.19W
Yellow Sea N. Pacific Oc. 103 N5 ....35.28N 125.29E
Yellowstone *r.* U.S.A. 64 F6 ....47.59N 103.59W
Yell Sound *str.* Scotland 19 H5 ....60.37N 1.15W
Yemen Asia 95 G3 ....14.48N 45.46E
Yenisey *r.* Rus. Fed. 59 J5 ....70.22N 82.59E
Yeniseysk Rus. Fed. 59 K3 ....58.27N 92.13E
Yeovil England 10 C1 ....50.56N 2.38W
Yerevan Armenia 58 F2 ....40.11N 44.32E
Yereymentau Kazakhstan 102 C8 ....51.36N 73.08E
Yeşilırmak *r.* Turkey 57 L5 ....41.27N 36.36E
Yevpatoriya Ukraine 53 J6 ....45.12N 33.22E
Yeysk Rus. Fed. 53 K6 ....46.43N 38.17E
Yibin China 103 I3 ....28.46N 104.36E
Yichang China 103 K4 ....30.41N 111.19E
Yichun China 103 N7 ....47.37N 128.52E
Yıldızeli Turkey 57 L4 ....39.53N 36.35E
Yinchuan China 103 J5 ....38.26N 106.18E
Yingkou China 103 M6 ....40.40N 122.15E
Yining China 102 E6 ....43.54N 81.22E
Yirga Alem Ethiopia 87 B4 ....6.47N 38.22E
Yirga Ch'efē Ethiopia 87 B4 ....6.06N 38.11E
Yli-Kitka *l.* Finland 40 G4 ....66.10N 28.46E
Ylitornio Finland 40 E4 ....66.20N 23.41E
Ylöjärvi Finland 40 E3 ....61.34N 23.36E
Yogyakarta Indonesia 104 E2 ....7.47S 110.23E
Yokohama Japan 106 C3 ....35.26N 139.37E
Yonne *r.* France 44 E6 ....48.23N 2.58E
York England 15 F2 ....53.58N 1.05W
York *d.* England 9 E3 ....53.57N 1.04W
York, Cape Australia 110 D5 ....10.41S 142.36E
York, Cape Canada 63 J5 ....73.47N 87.15W
York, Vale of *f.* England 15 F3 ....54.13N 1.32W
Yorkshire Wolds *hills* England 15 G2 ....53.53N 0.35W
Yorkton Canada 62 H3 ....51.12N 102.27W
Youghal Rep. of Ireland 41 D1 ....51.58N 7.51W
Yozgat Turkey 57 K4 ....39.49N 34.47E
Yser *r.* France 11 H1 ....50.54N 2.37E
Ystad Sweden 40 C1 ....55.26N 13.49E
Ystalyfera Wales 12 D3 ....51.46N 3.47W
Ystwyth *r.* Wales 12 C4 ....52.24N 4.05W
Ysyk-Köl *l.* Kyrgyzstan 102 D6 ....42.25N 77.12E
Ythan *r.* Scotland 19 G2 ....57.22N 2.01W
Yūbari Japan 106 D4 ....43.04N 141.59E
Yucatán *d.* Mexico 70 G5 ....20.35N 89.05W
Yucatán *pen.* Mexico 70 F4 ....19.17N 90.15W
Yucatan Channel Cuba/Mexico 71 G5 ....22.16N 86.46W
Yueyang China 103 K3 ....29.23N 113.07E
Yukon *r.* Canada/U.S.A. 62 B4 ....62.44N 164.41W
Yukon Territory *d.* Canada 62 E4 ....63.23N 135.52W
Yulin China 103 K2 ....22.37N 110.12E
Yuma U.S.A. 64 D3 ....32.43N 114.38W
Yumen China 102 H5 ....39.46N 97.33E
Yunak Turkey 57 I4 ....38.48N 31.44E
Yungas *f.* Bolivia 76 G4 ....16.51S 65.20W
Yunnan *d.* China 103 I2 ....24.45N 101.07E
Yushu China 102 H4 ....32.59N 96.59E
Yuxi China 103 I2 ....24.20N 102.33E
Yuzhno-Kuril'sk Rus. Fed. 106 E4 ....44.04N 145.49E
Yuzhno-Sakhalinsk Rus. Fed. 59 P2 ....46.57N 142.39E
Yuzhnoukrayinsk Ukraine 55 N2 ....47.50N 31.11E

Z

Zaandam Neth. 42 D5 ....52.26N 4.51E
Zabīd Yemen 94 F2 ....14.11N 43.15E
Zābol Iran 95 J6 ....30.59N 61.31E
Zacatecas Mexico 70 D5 ....22.46N 102.38W
Zacatecas *d.* Mexico 70 D5 ....23.56N 102.42W
Zadar Croatia 56 A7 ....44.07N 15.14E
Zafra Spain 48 B3 ....38.26N 6.25W
Zagreb Croatia 56 A7 ....45.48N 15.58E
Zagros Mountains Iran 95 G6 ....34.02N 47.10E
Zāhedān Iran 95 J5 ....29.30N 60.52E
Zahlé Lebanon 53 K3 ....33.50N 35.55E
Zaječar S.M. 56 E6 ....43.54N 22.16E
Zākhō Iraq 94 F7 ....37.08N 42.42E
Zakynthos Greece 56 D3 ....37.47N 20.54E
Zakynthos *i.* Greece 56 D3 ....37.45N 20.42E
Zalaegerszeg Hungary 54 G2 ....46.51N 16.53E
Zalău Romania 55 J2 ....47.11N 23.04E
Zambezi *r.* Africa 86 C3 ....15.41S 30.25E
Zambia Africa 86 B3 ....14.13S 27.30E
Zamboanga Phil. 105 G5 ....6.56N 122.05E
Zamora Spain 48 C4 ....41.31N 5.44W
Zamość Poland 46 F3 ....50.43N 23.16E
Zanjān Iran 95 G7 ....36.40N 48.27E

Zanzibar Tanzania 86 C4 ....6.08S 39.14E
Zanzibar Island Tanzania 86 C4 ....6.17S 39.12E
Zaozhuang China 103 L4 ....34.52N 117.34E
Zapadnaya Dvina Rus. Fed. 55 O7 ....56.16N 32.16E
Zapadnyy Sayan *f.* Rus. Fed. 59 J3 ....51.41N 88.08E
Zapolyarnyy Rus. Fed. 40 G5 ....69.26N 30.50E
Zaporizhzhya Ukraine 55 P2 ....47.50N 35.10E
Zara Turkey 57 L4 ....39.54N 37.45E
Zaragoza Spain 48 E4 ....41.40N 0.51E
Zarand Iran 95 I6 ....30.49N 56.34E
Zarasai Lithuania 55 L5 ....55.44N 26.15E
Zaraza Venezuela 71 K2 ....9.21N 65.18W
Zaria Nigeria 84 E3 ....11.07N 7.43E
Zarubino Rus. Fed. 106 B4 ....42.39N 131.04E
Żary Poland 46 B3 ....51.38N 15.08E
Zarzis Tunisia 52 F3 ....33.30N 11.05E
Zawiercie Poland 46 D3 ....50.29N 19.25E
Zawilah Libya 52 G2 ....26.08N 15.08E
Zaysan Kazakhstan 102 E7 ....47.27N 84.55E
Zaysan, Lake Kazakhstan 58 J2 ....48.05N 83.84E
Zealand *i.* Denmark 40 B1 ....55.23N 11.46E
Zeebrugge Belgium 42 C4 ....51.20N 3.16E
Zeeland *d.* Neth. 42 C4 ....51.31N 3.49E
Zeil, Mount Australia 110 C4 ....23.24S 132.24E
Zelenograd Rus. Fed. 55 Q7 ....56.00N 37.12E
Zelenogradsk Rus. Fed. 46 E5 ....54.58N 20.29E
Zémio C.A.R. 85 G2 ....5.00N 25.05E
Zenica Bos.-Herz. 56 B7 ....44.11N 17.55E
Zereh, Gowd-e *f.* Afgh. 95 J5 ....29.50N 62.27E
Zeya Rus. Fed. 59 N3 ....53.47N 126.54E
Zêzere *r.* Portugal 48 A3 ....39.28N 8.20W
Zgierz Poland 46 D3 ....51.51N 19.24E
Zhabinka Belarus 46 G4 ....52.11N 24.00E
Zhambyl Kazakhstan 102 C6 ....42.50N 71.25E
Zhangjiakou China 103 K6 ....40.41N 114.55E
Zhangping China 103 L3 ....25.21N 117.28E
Zhangshu China 103 L3 ....28.04N 115.30E
Zhanjiang China 103 K2 ....21.10N 110.22E
Zhaotong China 103 I3 ....27.22N 103.41E
Zhashkiv Ukraine 55 N3 ....49.15N 30.08E
Zhejiang *d.* China 103 M3 ....29.21N 120.06E
Zheleznogorsk Rus. Fed. 55 P5 ....52.19N 35.23E
Zhengzhou China 103 K4 ....34.41N 113.43E
Zhezkazgan Kazakhstan 58 H2 ....47.45N 67.44E
Zhlobin Belarus 55 N5 ....52.54N 30.02E
Zhmerynka Ukraine 55 M3 ....49.03N 28.06E
Zhob Pakistan 95 K6 ....31.21N 69.32E
Zhovti Vody Ukraine 55 O3 ....48.21N 33.30E
Zhukovskiy Rus. Fed. 55 R6 ....55.35N 38.08E
Zhuzhou China 103 K3 ....27.49N 113.07E
Zhydachiv Ukraine 46 G2 ....49.23N 24.09E
Zhytkavichy Belarus 55 L5 ....52.13N 27.52E
Zhytomyr Ukraine 55 M4 ....50.15N 28.40E
Zibo China 103 L5 ....36.47N 118.06E
Zielona Góra Poland 46 B3 ....51.57N 15.30E
Zĩghan Libya 53 H2 ....25.27N 22.07E
Zigong China 103 I3 ....29.24N 104.49E
Žilina Slovakia 54 H3 ....49.14N 18.44E
Zillah Libya 53 G2 ....28.32N 17.33E
Zima Rus. Fed. 103 L8 ....53.54N 101.59E
Zimbabwe Africa 86 B3 ....22.06S 30.59E
Zimmi Sierra Leone 84 C2 ....7.16N 11.17W
Zimnicea Romania 56 F6 ....43.40N 25.22E
Zinder Niger 84 E3 ....13.48N 8.59E
Zlín Czech Rep. 54 G3 ....49.13N 17.41E
Złotów Poland 46 C4 ....53.22N 17.04E
Zmiyevka Rus. Fed. 55 Q5 ....52.40N 36.23E
Znam"yanka Ukraine 55 O3 ....48.43N 32.41E
Znojmo Czech Rep. 54 G3 ....48.51N 16.04E
Zolochiv Ukraine 55 K3 ....49.48N 24.54E
Zolotonosha Ukraine 55 O3 ....49.42N 32.02E
Zonguldak Turkey 57 I5 ....41.27N 31.46E
Żory Poland 46 D3 ....50.03N 18.42E
Zouar Chad 85 F4 ....20.27N 16.35E
Zouérat Mauritania 84 C4 ....22.46N 12.29W
Zrenjanin S.M. 56 D7 ....45.23N 20.25E
Zugdidi Georgia 53 L5 ....42.30N 41.52E
Zugspitze *mt.* Austria/Germany 54 D2 ....47.26N 10.59E
Zuid-Holland *d.* Neth. 42 D4 ....51.57N 4.28E
Zújar *r.* Spain 48 C3 ....39.01N 5.46W
Zülpich Germany 42 F3 ....50.41N 6.40E
Zunyi China 103 J3 ....27.40N 106.54E
Zürich Switz. 50 C7 ....47.23N 8.32E
Zutphen Neth. 42 F5 ....52.09N 6.12E
Zuwärah Libya 52 F3 ....32.56N 12.05E
Zvolen Slovakia 54 H3 ....48.35N 19.08E
Zvornik Bos.-Herz. 56 C7 ....44.24N 19.07E
Zwickau Germany 54 E4 ....50.43N 12.30E
Zwolle Neth. 42 F5 ....52.30N 6.06E
Zyryanovsk Kazakhstan 102 E7 ....49.46N 84.21E

References

BP Statistical Review of World Energy
British Geological Survey
Census 2001
Dartmouth Flood Observatory
Department of Trade and Industry, UK
Department of Transport, UK
Met Office, UK
UK National Statistics
UN Commodity Trade Statistics

UNESCO World Heritage Sites
United Nations Population Information Network
US Census Bureau
USGS Earthquake Hazards Program
USGS Minerals Yearbook
World Bank Group
World Resources Institute
World Tourism Organization

Photo credits

MODIS Rapid Response Team, NASA/GSFC
p73 Argentina and Paraguay, p80 Rondônia, p118 Hurricane Isabel
NASA/GSFC/MITI/ERSDAC/JAROS, and U.S./Japan ASTER Science Team
p51 Vesuvius
Science Photo Library
p32 Manchester, p43 Europoort CNES 1999 Distribution Spot Image, p68 San Francisco, p101 and front cover thumbnail Bangladesh
USGS Land Processes Data Center
p97 Kolkata

Acknowledgements

General Bathymetric Chart of the Oceans (GEBCO)
Ministry of Planning and National Development, Nairobi, Kenya
Rotterdam Municipal Port Management, Rotterdam, Netherlands
Instituto Geográfico e Cartográfico, São Paulo, Brazil
International Hydrographic Organisation, Monaco
National Atlas and Thematic Mapping Organisation, Kolkata, India

Maps on the pages listed below are derived in part from material originally published in the **Collins Longman Student Atlas**.
Pp20-21, p23, p24 (part), p27 (part), p28 (part), p29, p30, p32-33, p36, p38, p39, p61, p67 (part), pp68-69, p74, p76 (inset), p78 (part), p79 (part),
p83, p88 (part), p89 (part), p92-93, p94 (inset), p97 (inset), p99 (part), p107 (part), p111 (part), p113, p114-115, p116-117, p118-119 (part)